An Abyss of Dreams

Also by Giacomo Donis

The Empty Shield

An Abyss of Dreams

tails of the night of the world

meta-memoir

Giacomo Donis

Shearsman Books

First published in the United Kingdom in 2022 by
Shearsman Books
P O Box 4239
Swindon
SN3 9FN

Shearsman Books Ltd Registered Office
30–31 St. James Place, Mangotsfield, Bristol BS16 9JB
(this address not for correspondence)

www.shearsman.com

ISBN 978-1-84861-846-6

CONTENTS

APPENDIX

PART THREE

IN MEMORY OF GIANFRANCO DI GIUSEPPE
25 January 1945–29 November 2010
SEI SEMPRE CON NOI

All my thanks to Anthony Rudolf, great friend!
— mon semblable, — mon frère!

When you asked me how I was doing, was that some kind of joke
—Bob Dylan, 'Desolation Row'

it's the abyss that keeps us all alive, only the abyss,
—Thomas Bernhard

A decision. Thinking. Imagining. An idea just pops into my head.
Fine. No problem. The problem is that then I start to chase it. Like
a cat chasing her tail. OK. But, then, this idea I'm chasing leads me
to another idea. And I chase it. From one idea, another. Another.
Another again. Free association. How free? What association.
—*The Empty Shield*

PART ONE

I. Marmari Nights
an abyss of dreams

I.
Returning around midnight to my large room, with the ping-pong table, I noticed the lights were on, which was a very bad sign. The door was unlocked. I opened it, went inside, and a burly intruder rushed upon me and thrust his long knife straight into my stomach, twisting it all the way to the left, then all the way to the right.

II.
Returning around midnight to my room with the ping-pong table, I was surprised and concerned to see that the lights were on. The door was unlocked, I went inside, and an old friend came forward and embraced me. He had come with his mother to pay me a visit. They had found the key in its usual place, under a rock, and let themselves in.

III.
Returning around midnight to my room, darkness and silence hung over it like a shroud. I took the key from under the rock, opened the door, went inside and turned on the light. A huge black fly—I had never seen a fly anywhere near this big before—took off from the ping-pong table and flew right into my face. It took all my strength and ability to fend off the attacks of this atrocious fly.

IV.
I left the lights on and the door wide open—there's a screen door to keep out the dogs—in my room, in case someone wished to play ping-pong while I was out. Returning around midnight, I found everything exactly as I had left it.

V.
Returning to my room around midnight, I was met by a gaping hole instead of a door. It looked as if the iron door had been mangled by some incredible powerful alien life form. I stepped through the hole and turned on the light. Looking around the room, I discovered that all the ping-pong balls had been stolen.

VI.
The oleanders were bathed in moonlight when I returned to my room, with the ping-pong table, around midnight. What peace! What quiet! I opened the door with the key under the rock, stepped inside, turned on the light, and discovered a gray cat curled up asleep at the foot of my bed.

July 2006, Marmari, Greece

II. Parroty: a parody of origin

for the people of a shattered Yugoslavia

The winter rain was falling in big slow drops. By some quirk of fate I found myself, barely on the wrong side of forty, subtracted three times a week from my adopted hearth in Venice, somehow fallen prey to a poorly paid lecturer's job at the University of Padua. I had been engaged to lecture on 'The Puritan Spirit in North American Literature,' and almost at once I made myself perfectly at home in my new position, much like a goldfish in the Sahara desert. Perhaps, thanks to this aura of alienation that I emitted from every pore, three students flocked to my lectures. Faithful, unflagging in their presence, albeit somewhat sleepy, since my lessons were just after lunch, and the Latin digestion, compared to the Anglo-Saxon, is rightfully reputed to be rather slow. I droned on, lucidly, brilliantly, and in the full originality of my exalted bewilderment, about 'Sinners in the Hands of an Angry God,' the poetics of Edgar Allan Poe, Emersonian obscurity, Thoreau's 'different drummer,' Melville's relation to Hegel's first triad, and the intimate vivacity of Emily Dickinson. Oddly enough, my 'class' followed me enthusiastically and without fear in my not infrequent forays into the realm of philosophy (a place where in fact I did feel quite at home), but they manifested with great disdain—drooping eyelids or frozen stares—their utter aversion to poetry. To poetry! O tempora! O mores! Out of Whitman's relentless, unhaltingly endless verses I offered them pieces of true genius like this, 'Reconciliation,' written at the end of the Civil War:

> Word over all, beautiful as the sky!
> Beautiful that war and all its deeds of carnage must in time be utterly lost,
> That the hands of the sisters Death and Night incessantly softly wash
>   again, and ever again, this soil'd world;
> For my enemy is dead, a man divine as myself is dead,
> I look where he lies white-faced and still in the coffin—I draw near,
> Bend down and touch lightly with my lips the white face in the coffin.

I even tried to batter them with Dickinsonian masterpieces:

> There is a solitude of space
> A solitude of sea
> A solitude of death, but these
> Society shall be
> Compared with that profounder site
> That polar privacy
> A soul admitted to itself—
> Finite Infinity.

Finally, Allen Ginsberg's 'A Supermarket in California' did seem to disturb their slumber somewhat, making the poetry pill less bitter—but that was in late spring, at term's end. As usual I've gotten carried away, racing far ahead of my story.

The winter rain was falling in big slow drops. As was the case every Wednesday from noon till 1 p.m. I was sitting at the corner table of a rather charming bar near the University—one of the least frequented bars in all Padua, the devil knows why!—drinking mineral water, eating a small sandwich, and keenly observing a middle-sized mangy parrot immobile on its perch in the far corner of the room. I say 'middle sized' because its dimensions were somewhere between tiny parrots *de poche* of my acquaintance and certain enormous creatures big as buzzards. Wednesday from noon till one was my hour for receiving students, and given the madding throng that sat before me three times a week, and given my life-long sympathy (I could nearly say empathy) for parrots, who share with mankind the divine gift of speech (in some cases), I figured I might as well kill two birds with one stone and hold my reception hour not in my office, as one usually does, but in this bar, where for an hour I could count on gazing at the speechless creature. The color of the bird was splendid, despite its manginess. A vivid soft green that more than made up for its silence. And as for my class, my flock, my throng of students—in the seven months I taught, from November to May, never, not once did one appear! So I had plenty of time to contemplate 'my' parrot (I say 'my' because no one else ever seemed to notice it), and think: Oh divine gift of speech, Language, the House of Being, do we humans pronounce one phrase out of ten thousand that shows us to be *truly* more intelligent (or closer to God or to Being) than my cat? This, just to explain my personal empathy for parrots, whose iterations are, on the whole, not much more senseless than my own.

Gray, gray, the winter rain was falling, but the ineffable softness of the green of those mangy feathers took me far away, transported me far from Padua in winter and from the gray light of Venice, to a place without students or salaries, taxes or telephones, fax machines or TV, a place where they don't even have computers! To endless soft green rolling hills, to an overpowering swirl of forest green. To a life of unremittingly requited passion. The huge gray drops, the parrot, the absent throng of students.

Some years ago—it doesn't matter how long anymore—on a broiling hot Manhattan morning in July I was sauntering down Hudson Street arm in arm with my new friend Tina. We were talking about sculpture, and I was thinking about the shortness of life, thinking about crossing Pound's 'infernal ripples.' I noticed a lot of people drinking beer. We had actually gone out to do some shopping—yogurt, bread, cat food, the usual things—when, just across the street, an astounding swirl of green captured my attention. That brilliant, shimmering, overpowering soft green that always makes me dream of places I've never seen and most likely never will. Naxos perhaps, or the *dolce* Umbria. The Amazon. I grabbed Tina by the hand, leaped off the curb—and by a sheer quirk of fate (and about three inches) was not utterly obliterated by an onrushing taxi. (Too many years in Venice, I forget about such things. Where I live about the worst that can happen is you get blind drunk and fall into a filthy canal.) Regaining my aplomb and calming my excitement, Tina and I carefully crossed the street and found ourselves before a pet store with an enormous, extremely exotic parrot in an even more enormous cage. The door to the shop was open and a well-dressed young man, his eye on the magnificent bird, was conversing with the owner. 'Fifteen thousand' we heard the owner reply—such was the price of this prize—and 'fifteen thousand' screeched the parrot, stoically. 'Fifteen thousand' said the young man. Some years ago, I can't remember how many. So much water has flowed through the canals since then. My mind wanders.

I was nearly lost in deep, dark thought as I crossed the Rialto bridge late one spring afternoon on my way home after visiting my psychiatrist. Once, when I was especially depressed, Tina talked to me on the phone from New York for more than an hour about 'the darkness and the dazzle.' (Made me think of Heraclitus, the way up is the way down.) My psychiatrist— who was also my friend—had just been talking about 'great depressions,' depressions that last a lifetime (cheerful thought), while I kept peering in my mind's eye at those infernal ripples—'whether there be any patch left of us/ after we cross the infernal ripples'—and just hoping that a lifetime would be long enough. Darkness, I mused, was darkness of the mind. And dazzle, the blindness of the spirit.

Walking slowly, very pensively, along the Riva del Vin, the twilight glimmering on the Grand Canal, I got to thinking about a line I'd read in a book review somewhere, that stuck in my mind: 'It affirms the absurd, passionate attachment of the dying to life—like the exile's to the roots.' On TV I'd seen a man crying, repeatedly—an Istrian—because the war, the wars had cut him off from his home, his village, his patch of land, his native speech, his history—in other words, his roots. Tears of terrifying pain, deeper, perhaps, than for the death of a loved one, because less ephemeral. But if you ask me where I come from, what can I say? I come from the land of the Puritans, from the shadows of Hiroshima and Cuba and Vietnam, from New York in the late '60s—these are my 'roots.' I've never set foot in the lands of my grandparents, wherever they were they don't exist anymore. I've lived these past twenty years—practically my entire adult life—here in Venice, a dying city absurdly attached to life. A labyrinth without monsters, just a web of twisting paths leading nowhere, and a slow swirl of images. An exile, but from what? From my own passions? from joy? from splendor? From my own mind, or from Zen mind? 'When you give up, when you no longer want something, or when you do not try to do anything special, then you do something.' Exiled from the dazzle of a homeland? rather, like a small ship on a sea without shores. The absurd, passionate attachment of the dying to life—just then a strange thing happened.

Lost in thought on the Riva del Vin, I was walking under the enormous scaffolding of an ancient *palazzo* that was in the process of having its face lifted when, all of a sudden, a splendid small green parrot dropped from the scaffolding and landed at my feet. The waters of the Grand Canal were silently streaking with orange. I looked down at the unmoving bird. It looked bewildered. This was no place for a parrot. A couple of Germans stopped and took some photographs. A passerby asked me 'È il tuo?'—'Is it yours?' There were already two or three stray cats shifting from paw to paw, maliciously. 'No,' I replied, 'e che facciamo?' I bent down and at once the parrot hopped onto my forearm, digging in gently with its claws. Not a mangy Paduan bar parrot, definitely not a fifteen-thousand-dollar New Yorker, it was a marvelous smallish bird with clean, unruffled feathers of that soft splendid green which makes me dream. 'What to do?' By now a small group of people had gathered round, there was a certain amount of Venetian chatter. One woman claimed to know the provenance of the parrot and rang two or three doorbells of a house nearby, but no one answered. The canal was flaming into night. At last the headwaiter of a restaurant near the Rialto came rushing towards me. 'Signora Gallo has lost her parrot!' he exclaimed as the bird hopped from my arm to his. And hot on his heels came Signora Gallo herself, a small skinny white-haired lady whose eyes lit up like twin suns when she saw the beloved creature. 'Tesoro mio! Il mio cattivello piccolo tesoro!' she cried as the parrot fluttered immediately onto her shoulder. 'My naughty little darling! Since they put up this scaffolding what an adventurer you have become!'

The cats had vanished by this time and the sun had set. The mind goes dark at the coming of night. I gazed for a while at the black waters, trying to make out the ripples. 'The waters of Styx poured over the wound.' An endless expanse of tender green filled my eyes and instantly absorbed my tears. My thoughts fled swiftly, escaping me. The splendor of those soft green wings. 'Oh, fatality! Oh, nature! Everyone on earth is alone. That is the tragedy!' The mourners carried chains at Dostoyevsky's funeral, to remind the living that Dostoyevsky too had been a prisoner and an exile. I cry out to humanity, but no one is listening. If only I had the soft, wondrous green feathers of the parrot, some skinny old lady would surely seek me out, I'd hop onto her shoulder and thank her with my parroty of speech. But alas, it was only an instant, without beginning, without end, already lost in the labyrinth of time. In death at last I shall go *swiftly*. Propelled by these huge black wings I am already a white speck on the horizon.

January 1992

references

whether there be any patch left of us/ after we cross the infernal ripples
    Ezra Pound, *Homage to Sextus Propertius*, XII

When you give up, when you no longer want something,
    Shunryu Suzuki, *Zen Mind, Beginner's Mind*, p. 47

The waters of Styx
    Ezra Pound, *Homage to Sextus Propertius*, XII

'Oh, fatality! Oh, nature!
    Fyodor Dostoyevsky, *A Gentle Creature*

'Parroty' was originally published in *Fine Madness*, Seattle, summer/fall 1993.

PART TWO

III. Why Dream?

a therapeutic ramble

Behold, this dreamer cometh. Come now therefore and let us slay him, and cast him into some pit, and we will say, Some evil beast hath devoured him: and we shall see what will become of his dreams.
Genesis, 37:19-20

To sleep! perchance to dream:
Hamlet, Act III Scene I

Logic is doubtless unshakable, but it cannot withstand a man who wants to go on living.
Franz Kafka, *The Trial*

'early to bed'

I had a good dream this morning, between 10:30 and 11:15. All my life my 'nights' have been out of sync with the world. Even as a kid I couldn't sleep at night. Nightmares, all the time. Bad dreams that really scared me. Long ones, and often. I got up early, for school, totally exhausted. I still remember what those dreams were like. Absolutely non-figurative, just huge bursts of color. Red, orange, FIERY, like sunsets in hell gruesomely blotting the horizon. Very frightening. Finally I went away to college, in New York. I lived by myself on the Lower East Side, and it was there that I found my rhythm. Studying until dawn, listening to records of Bach and Monk, a brisk jog to Brooklyn and back on the Williamsburg Bridge, and then to bed. And up at 11, fresh as a daisy, ready to set out for Washington Square. Great to be free and young. Some weekends and some summers I drove a taxi to support myself. Again nights, until dawn. Then, as always, 'early to bed.' The great thing was that for those four years (from 1968 to 1972), for the only time in my life, I had practically no dreams. Why no dreams? (But—Why Dream?! *That* is our question.) Perhaps because what I saw all around me every day was nightmare enough. My neighborhood (my block on Rivington Street was one of the most dangerous in New York at that time, but the rent was very low), Nixon on TV, the outrageous things I saw from my taxi. Then, there was my own *no-dream* question about the Vietnam war. It was a time of extreme isolation and solitude. And intense study. And practically no dreams.

When I moved to Europe—I was 21, I'm 61 now—I maintained my 'natural' rhythm, for a dozen years or so. Sun up, and 'early to bed.' (No more running, my knees swelled up if I jogged.) But the dreams were back, and they were not good. Some of them—some extremely powerful ones—left an indelible mark on my entire life. Still, after a period of near starvation there were some real good times. Lots of new friends. A little money—my Sardinian companions in Denmark taught me how to make necklaces to sell on the street and, thanks to them both (the Sardinians and the necklaces), I survived. But then I made my move. A big one. Back home here in Venice (I still live in this same house on this courtyard after all these years) I took a quantum leap, from Scandinavian street necklaces to *earrings* for boutiques. Italian boutiques for a year. Then Switzerland. Then Germany. A one-man show. A quantum leap. It was the proverbial *rags to riches*. Making earrings until dawn, listening to cassettes of Bach and Monk, drinking excellent vodka, enjoying night-visits from friends of all sorts, who loved to watch me work with my alpaca wire and splendid Venetian glass beads. But the dreams came back. The nightmares returned. Graphic this time, not the old terrible 'sunsets in hell.' Figures, characters, situations, even a few voices. (I *regressed* from abstract to figurative art.) Such good nights, splendid—all night till dawn—then those terrible dream-drenched mornings. Not sleeping till 11, then *up!* fresh as a daisy, but tossing tormented till noon, till 1 o'clock, till... whenever. Tired again. Why those dreams? Why Dream? I think about them now, those 'early to bed' years. Right up to 1984, when I quit making earrings and started translating books by Italian philosophers and, alas, Italian *art critics*. Lovers, travels, friends. Alas, *no cats*. But nightmares aplenty, and sleeplessness. Then a Paris fiancée *with cats*. Worse nightmares. (About her, not the cats.) Worse insomnia. Since then just a few cosmically exciting women (only extremes—love or passion, mutually exclusive) and two cats of my 'own.' (My partners. Nobody 'owns' cats. Gina for almost 17 years, now Gilda, she's 8.) But nightmares! *Dreams*, of every size, shape and description. *Why? Why Dream?* My mother says that even when I was an infant I had infant bad dreams, sputtering, making noises and little jerks. Well—now, at last, I have decided to *tackle* the question. Gently. But seriously. All my life, tormented, hounded, *pounded* with dreams. Dreams? Almost all of them bad. Nightmares, and day-mares—morning-mares, actually. Long heavy poundings. Why? Why Dream?

the blood gets into your dreams

OK, I'm over 60 now, I've had a bunch of ailments—disorders, let's say—and I need more 'sleeping time.' Right now, from 2 or 3 a.m. (or even 1:30) until 11, 11:30. Even 10:30. I can't sleep in the morning like before. Why not? Certainly not because I'm more in sync with the world. Quite the contrary,

I'm totally out of it. But then—why? Why can't I sleep in the morning like before? Just tired? Tired of nights? Absolutely. More 'tired of nights' than 'just tired.' But in permanent exile from mornings. Like the dying Goethe, I want 'more light.' But not in the morning. But—between night and morning, what is there? Noon light, afternoon light, evening light, is good light, like a good dream. But morning light—I treat this slab of the day like a burning coal, like embers up my ass. This is not simply an anti-morning prejudice. The fact is, every day I need time to recover from my dreams.

For forty years now, this storm of killing dreams, one, two, three, four a 'night,' each lasting an hour, two hours, each followed by an hour's torment of sleeplessness. Or, sometimes, by just a short quivering 'break,' a few minutes, then the next one, then the next, and the next. Probably. Or, sometimes, short dreams, lasting five, ten, fifteen minutes. But a slew of them. Too many to count. Serial dreams, like serial killers, with short interruptions. Like endless TV programs, with commercials. How have I survived a lifetime of these dreams? Why Dream? Why do I dream? I have a suspicion but no idea. It's not self-hatred. Why can't I sleep—ever—even for five blessed minutes—without a dream? Even if I take an afternoon nap after a 'bad night' and *finally*, after a couple of hours, fall asleep—BANG, I wake up dreaming. Badly. I often cry after my dreams, because almost all of them are bad. Four, five in the morning, my cat snuggled up so peacefully, the peaceful silent town, and me, crying after a dream. A good dream? Yes, it's possible, but once in a blue moon. A blue *full* moon. Do I always dream because I always—always—*think?* Monkey mind, the Zen master calls it. That's my suspicion, but it's not an idea, not an explanation. 'The mind as Ixion, unstill, ever turning.' Even when I have nothing to think about, I think anyway. Why? *Why* do I always think? I have done Zen meditation most of my life, all alone, without a master or companions. (Though Gilda, my second cat, is a Zen master in disguise.) In some periods I've *really* done it. Forty minutes in which the mind waves die away, almost to nothing. I've even known first hand what satori is. But—all the same—all day, all night, I constantly talk to myself, in my head (no, not out loud), about things I hope will happen and things I hope won't happen. (But is talking thinking, exactly? Are talking and thinking the same?) Big things, medium-sized things, very small things. I admit it, I daydream. A lot. But this is completely different from my night-dreams. (Many of them in the morning, as I said.) At 'night' you have no control, but when you daydream you are conscious. You can 'consciously' give some direction to things when you daydream. It's something completely different. Of course I have both recurrent day-dreams and recurrent night-dreams. For example, during the day I often 'see' (in my mind) the broken pieces of my beloved black ceramic teapot that C. brought me from Tokyo twenty years ago. It's horrible! A horrible sight. But, immediately—simultaneously, perhaps—I know it's not true, fortunately. Not now anyway, but some day it could be true. (Will be true? Won't be true?) Wish fulfillment—forget it. Death wish—well, could be, but what in the world does that mean? But, above all, what does it mean to be 'conscious'? Now *this*, for me, is a *big* question. I've thought about it all my life. That was *my* question. *The* question. This question right now—Why Dream?—even if it has *been there* all along, is actually a new question, I never posed it before like this. Why pose it now? Basically, out of desperation, out of *too many dreams*, and too few dreamless 'nights.' Almost *none*. I shall definitely get back to that question—What is consciousness?—later. And the dream I had this morning. Later. I am trying to ramble in an orderly fashion, and not to rant too much. (Hopefully.) (And if I do—gently.) And what about this talking to myself all day. (And night?) Even when I work, translating books of philosophy, if possible (instead of art critics)—well, it's a little better. I feel less alone, more focused, not thinking about a million useless things. But, come to think of it, all this translation business is basically a 'talking to myself.' It's a self-conversation about a tangle of someone else's dreams. A strange business. OK, let me tell you about a very strange sort of dream (night-dream) I often have. In the dream I'm working on a translation that I did maybe years, decades ago, or perhaps am doing now. So far it's not all that strange, translating 'gets into your blood' and the blood gets into your dreams. (It's like taxi driving. The old-timers in New York used to tell me, Don't let hacking get into your blood. Fat chance! I had other fish to fry.) Or, I'm working on the translation of a book I never translated. (Slightly stranger.) Or, on the translation of a book that doesn't exist. Pretty damn strange. But the really strange part comes now. In these dreams, which go on for hours and hours, and even if the dream-book is a book that actually exists and that I'm actually translating, the actual text itself *actually doesn't exist*. I mean, I never dream some phrase or term that I actually translated—badly perhaps, with difficulty, at least *that* would make sense. No, I dream—or the dream dreams—actual phrases, texts, that don't exist. That are actual dream-texts. I can actually see the dream making up the text I have to translate as we (the dream and I) go along. The 'dream work,' as Freud put it. Then, in the dream, I actually do translate the nonexistent text. I don't know if I've made this clear enough for you. Words tend to fail. You have to be there yourself to get a grip on it. What's more, in the dream the text itself I'm translating sort of flickers, it comes and goes, exists and slips into nothingness. It's something well-defined and then, gradually, *I'm translating nothing*. Finally, I wake up. How do I feel? It depends. On what? On the text itself? How tough to translate it was? Or on how much it flickered? I'm not sure. After these *extremely long* dreams sometimes I feel refreshed and happy but most of the time I feel totally exhausted, as if I'd been translating for a hundred hours straight. For the record, I have a frequent variant on these dreams, where instead of translating I'm writing a story, novel, philosophy essay or some such, that I'm actually writing now, or actually wrote perhaps long ago. Or—most of the time—that I actually never wrote, am not writing, or will never write, on some subject that I've never even thought about in the least. But the 'dream work' is the same. Freud's term. In this case *le mot juste*.

'I have a dream'

I'll get back to the subject of 'dream work' later. I should tell you about a couple of dreams I've had this past month, this warm November. I warn you, not cheerful stuff. Some of the sad, bad, disturbing dreams that have induced me, finally, to tackle this question—why? Why Dream? Especially if they're almost always bad. By the way—have you noticed how incredibly often everyone talks about dreams these days, but in a stupid sense that obviously has nothing to do with my question, or even with dreams in the *proper* sense at all. It seems that everyone, everywhere, *always*, 'has a dream.' (You say I'm 'out of it' because I have dreams—nightmares, actually—in the morning. But 'always' means morning, noon, afternoon, evening, and night.) If you ask any soccer, football, baseball, basketball, hockey, cricket, chess, ping-pong, or stamp-collecting coach, or whatever, about the team, or whatever, How's it going?, they all answer 'We have a dream.' All of them. I kid you not. *All of them*. All the time. 'We have a dream.' Winning the championship, winning the next match, not losing the next match since we've already lost five in a row. A dream! To say nothing of *miracles*. Sports has become the world of miracles. Lourdes is a speck of dust besides it. If the worst team in the league beats the best, *miracle*. If a goaltender blocks a tricky shot, the guy on Italian TV screams—screams!—*MIRACOLO! MIRACOLO!* Isn't it ridiculous. Just think, with all the matches, all around the world, every week, every day—thousands, *millions* of miracles. ('Which way to the miracle?' as Fellini put it, a long time ago, in the first scene of *La dolce vita*.) Let me tell you about a guy I knew, a Greek, L., many years ago on a Greek island. L. had a small taverna on the beach and rented out a few rooms. If ever anyone happened to say, 'Hi L. How's it going?' he said, 'Exo ena oneiro.' 'I have a dream.' (He wanted to demolish the taverna and build a small hotel, big deal.) He drove everyone crazy with that 'exo ena oneiro' of his. I mean, he said it *all the time* (all the time!), I can still remember his voice forty years later. Low, grave, determined, almost reverent. But actually it was very funny. Downright ridiculous. But he drove us crazy. We wanted to kill him and throw him in some pit like Joseph in the Bible, just to shut him up. I mean, just how many times did we have to listen to this constant 'exo ena oneiro' of his? A few years later he did get that hotel built (big deal), and then he didn't know what to say anymore. If you asked him How's it going? he just grunted. Ridiculously. In fact, after all these years, I still have this funny dream from time to time about L. and his hotel. Most of the dream is a good one. (For once.) Entertaining. Right there on the beach L. had built a real *DREAM hotel.* A skyscraper, one hundred stories high. And a small taverna on the top, on the roof. On this little island that had more donkeys than people. Nothing else around, some normal little tavernas a couple of miles away, and this giant tower right there on the beach. But the plot thickens. L., in fact, was a religious person like many Greeks (Orthodox), but strictly in the sense of crossing himself hundreds of times a day and being extremely superstitious. Especially about numbers, so, OK, no room 13, no 13th floor. It's called triskaidekaphobia. But he was deeply concerned about a lot of other numbers too. Worried. The solution: in this *DREAM* hotel, he decided not to number anything at all. I mean, no room numbers and no floor numbers at all. In the dream hordes of people show up, get their keys from L. at the reception, and head up to their rooms—*and I wake up screaming.* It turns out to be a horror dream! Total chaos. Violent. Destructive. Totally bewildered people, totally lost, totally frightened, violent, people hiding, running for their lives through the numberless unnumbered floors. Wake up! Wake up! It's only a dream. 'Exo ena oneiro,' L. always said. What a stupid way of putting it. All he had to say was, I'd like to build a hotel, I'd *really* like to build a hotel, I *hope* to build a hotel. *Voilà*, the proper expression. It's not Faith, *Dream*, and Charity—forget it. *Hope.* Why doesn't the coach say, quite simply, I *hope* we win the championship. I *hope* we don't lose the next game, we've already lost ten in a row. Believe me, he has dreams *about* losing the eleventh game in a row. It's called a *nightmare* and it is, indeed, in the true and proper sense, a dream.

But I was trying to make a point here if I can just remember what it was. Freud. 'Dream work.' (A cure for unemployment.) Wish fulfillment! I'll get back to this later. But, for the moment, I need to confront this 'I have a dream' *army of occupation.* It's clear, I think, that this daytime daydream mundane and extraordinarily banal 'I have a dream' (Martin Luther King excepted) is indeed an expression of wish fulfillment, or of a wish for wish fulfillment. But my point is, if the dream in 'I have a dream' is always something positive, something wished-for (no coach on earth says 'I have a dream that we'll lose the eleventh game in a row'!), then—I mean, what about all my bad dreams? This flood, this mayhem of dreams that makes me ask, finally, Why Dream? I mean, when you dream about building a hotel or winning the championship, you never ask yourself, Why Dream? You just do it. You dream. But—this is my point—if *practically everyone on earth* goes around saying 'I have a dream' all the time in a totally positive sense—well, I have a question. I raise my hand. Let's limit ourselves to their *real* dreams, the so-called night-time ones (but I have lots in the morning) they have when they're (theoretically) unconscious (but what does *that* mean?), or, more simply, when they're *asleep.* Are all *these* such marvels of happiness and satisfaction that during the 'daytime' (when they are, so to speak, 'conscious') they say 'I have a dream' to express happiness and satisfaction? Or, at the very least, to hope for it. And—my point—if their dreams are such paradigms of happiness 'by day' (so to speak) then, I figure, logically speaking, they must be pretty damn happy 'by night' too. I mean, happy in their 'real' dreams. Their *DREAM* dreams, so to speak. But then, how come mine are so miserable and frightening? Sure, I could say, if I wanted, 'I have a dream' (say, to get this ramble finished and be done with it), but I'd never say it, considering the miserable dreams I actually have. But everyone else's dreams? Are they really all so great? So happy? Their *DREAM* dreams I mean. The ones they have when they're asleep.

My grandfather, whom I adored, was a wonderful man and an uncomplicated one. He never learned to read or write in any language, neither of the 'old country' nor of the new one either. He put an X (and even that was pretty illegible, as I recall) when he had to sign his name. He was close to a hundred years old when he died. I can't imagine him having nightmares. Maybe I'm wrong. It's way too late to ask him about it now, but I can't imagine it. Once he told me—with such supreme calm and ease, that was it, he was at ease with himself—about how when he was about fifteen, in Lithuania (it was either Poland or Russia then, or possibly both), his parents died and, with his younger sister, they had to walk for days from their village through the countryside to get to Vilnius to find their uncle. 'Without even an egg to eat,' he told me. But so serenely. A sack of onions and dry bread. ('Be strong as an onion' he always said, all his life.) He told me about a flat gray misty land with small trees and many lakes. The way he described it did sound like a dream. (I saw land that looked just like it in a scene from Tarkovsky's *Andrey Rublyov*.) But certainly not a nightmare. Just a land. Just a journey. My grandfather was truly not a philosopher. He did things, simply, with intelligence. When he had something to do (and he did lots of things in his long life) he didn't chew the fat about it, he did it. But then, the last time I saw him, in 1972, he was over 90, he told me something that stunned me, it seemed so totally out of character. So philosophical. I can remember his voice exactly, now, forty years later, he said: 'Life is a dream. Only when you die you wake up and find out if it was a good dream or a nightmare.' I quote him exactly, word for word. I bet in all his life my grandfather never said 'I have a dream.' He just did it. Worked, slept. Woke up.

some miserable dreams

On the other hand, I've had some *miserable* dreams this past month. This warm November. Let me tell you about three of them, real short versions. Good examples of my typical dreams. To let you know—finally—something about the sort of dream I have and that bothers me so much and has finally made me ask this question: Why Dream? Just the gist, for now. I'll give you much better accounts of some dreams later on.

For example—I live in a beautiful little house in Venice, on a beautiful ancient courtyard, on a beautiful canal, with a back garden where I can't go but 'my' cats go, through their flap. (First Gina, now Gilda.) A kitchen and guest-room downstairs, and up here a nice big open space with lots of light. I've lived here since I was 26. Lucky me! First I rented it, then I bought the house when I was 35 with the 'riches' I made making and selling *earrings*. So, the dream. (Let's try to find some wish fulfillment in *this*.) I dreamed I was moving out of this house—leaving my cats behind!—and moving into a 'castle.' Good news. Good news my ass! When I got to the 'castle' it turned out to be an enormous rectangular one-story structure with incredibly *thick walls*, dozens of windowless window-openings along the endless walls on both sides, and *really* damp, dark, and full of huge rats. And bats. And no cats. And I had left my beautiful cats and home for *this*, I said to myself, and woke up.

Another example, a couple of days later. (Just the gist.) I was moving away— to start another life—it had to do with redemption, rebirth, regeneration, that's all I can say about it. Something like Raskolnikov at the end of *Crime and Punishment*. So far so good. This one wasn't so bad, you say? No, in fact it was one of the worst. Practically the whole dream was about leaving my (second) cat all alone here in the house, saying goodbye to Gilda and leaving her totally completely and utterly *all alone in this house*—I woke up. Believe you me, a terrible dream. I wish I could forget all about it.

One more for now. (This is a pretty good bad one.) Every day, day after day, I had to go to some sort of law office holding a tiny piece of paper with a row of very tiny square boxes printed on it. (Like in a multiple-choice test, except that the boxes were in a horizontal row, and there were no questions. Just boxes.) I needed the lawyer's signature—or just his initials maybe, the squares were so small—in one of the squares. Or in all the squares. Or the signature (or initials—or perhaps one initial?) of a different lawyer in each square. I kept going back to this office, 2, 3, 4, 5 times, getting absolutely nowhere. Not even close to getting a single initial. Finally—at the end of the dream—completely exhausted I went home to bed. I started taking off my pants to get into bed—but I couldn't figure out how to do it! My hands were stiff, I fumbled, I didn't know what to do, I got my pants off part way but my legs and my pants were getting tangled up. I started getting painful cramps in my feet, then in my legs, tangled, fumbling—and then, suddenly, my legs were completely *paralyzed*. And I woke up.

what is sleep?

Let me raise a few questions. Apart, of course, from the question *here*—Why Dream? And apart from *the* question, which we'll get back to later—What is consciousness? Though it's very hard to get around this question, ever. And apart from Freud's questions—wish fulfillment and death wish. We'll see about them too. Soon, maybe. But for now I want to ask this (a *big* one): Do I ever sleep? Stupid question? You say, if I have all these heaps of dreams, it's obvious that I must sleep. And plenty too. But the question is not so stupid at all, I'm afraid. Try to follow my logic here. As I said earlier, it's my impression that, all my life, I've never managed to *sleep* for five blessed minutes in a row without dreaming. Maybe not for three minutes. Maybe not even *one* minute. But then, if for me sleeping *does not exist* without dreaming—if sleeping and dreaming are absolutely inseparable—well, that's why I ask: Do I ever sleep? This is not about splitting hairs, my friend, it is a *major* question, inseparable from this one: What is sleep? Not to be confused with: Why sleep? Now *that* is a stupid question. It *may* possibly be true, as some 'experts' claim, that whales, bats, and mosquitoes never sleep. (Personally I don't believe that mosquitoes never sleep, they're tricky, that's all.) (Or was it only Moby Dick that never slept?) But humans—animals, animals of all sorts need to sleep. Must sleep. Why? No, come on, please, let's not ask this one. A tree, a plant doesn't sleep. (Perhaps! who knows?) (Just because grass doesn't scream when we mow it doesn't mean—what?) But if we animals don't sleep *we get tired*. You can't deny it. *Unshakable* logic. As an insomniac from birth, take it from me—damn it all, we *have* to sleep. SLEEP, sometime, sooner or later, or die. Cease to exist. There is absolutely—but completely, totally, and absolutely—no getting around it. You might not follow my logic in this ramble or accept any of my other conclusions, but you have to grant me this one. Try not sleeping for three days. (It's happened so many times to me and millions of other insomniacs in this world.) I rest my case. Why sleep? is a totally stupid question, which we shall not ask here. But there is—not so far away—another, *much trickier* and not so stupid question: *What* is sleep? (Believe me, this is not just a 'stuff happens' question.) And is sleep inseparable from dreams? Or does it just happen to appear to be so in my case? If, in my case, it is really so.

The first thing I have to say here is that there's a major problem with this major question, What is sleep? Namely, it's inseparable from that other major question, What is consciousness? Which, as I said, in my humble opinion is *the* question and also *the most difficult* question. I'll get back to it, somehow or other, later. Meanwhile, let me tell you about something Aristotle once said, about the sleeping Sardinians. (No, not the ones in Denmark who taught me to make necklaces out of silver-coated copper wire.) It's about time I said something serious here, or at least quoted someone serious. Let's hope the Stagirite helps us untangle some of all these threads, or else tangles them up completely so that I can give the whole thing up. Aristotle! In the *Physics*, Book IV, Section 11: 'Time as Dependent on Events.' He is actually concerned about time here, which, ye gods! we shall not go into, but he says, indirectly, something quite interesting about sleep. The gist: in sleep time does not pass, because, as I would put it, when we sleep we are not conscious. Aristotle says:

> Time is not independent of change. In fact when we do not change in our consciousness, or, even if changed, the change is concealed from us, it does not seem that time has passed. In this respect we are like the people in the legend who slept near [in] the tombs of the heroes in Sardinia who, awakening out of their long sleep, link the earlier with the later time into a unified present, disregarding the interval, *of which they were not conscious.*

An interesting story. In ancient times, to cure themselves of 'visions' and 'obsessions' (a.k.a. *dreams*) the Sardinians used to sleep near (or possibly in) the tombs of the revered ancient Sardinian heroes for days on end, without interruption. To sleep 'deeply' and 'without consciousness,' which is, presumably, a way of saying *without dreams*. While in Greece people were visiting oracles and sleeping there precisely *to dream*, over in Sardinia they were sleeping near (with) (on top of) the heroes precisely *not to dream*. It seems. But—and this is what I find problematic—dreams—'visions,' 'obsessions'—were precisely their problem to begin with or, to put it differently: Over in Sardinia sleep, and the lack of it, and dreams, was the problem, and sleep, apparently without dreams, was the solution. What powerful dead heroes they had in Sardinia, to make sleepless dreamers sleep like the dead! A strange story, if you think about it. Aristotle's point was that when you sleep you're not conscious, and when you're not conscious time does not pass. (For you, of course.) (Or, *if we all slept together,* time would stop!?) But my problem is: Who sleeps and who doesn't? And *how* do they or don't they do it? Is Aristotle *really* saying that when we sleep we're not conscious? Or that we're not conscious *only* when we sleep in the tombs of dead Sardinian heroes where, for some unexplained reason, we don't dream? And everywhere else we dream like hell, like I do. And if he's *really* saying that when we sleep we're not conscious, then my question is: *If we're not conscious how in the world do we dream?!*

So, I'm afraid, thanks to Aristotle we're back where we were a while ago. I mean, to that formidable question: What is sleep? Now, why did I ask 'What is sleep?'? Let me remind you—of what? I just forgot—yes! of this so-called *existential* question of mine: If, for someone, for example, sleeping does not exist without dreaming (and I bet this was true for the Sardinians who went to sleep in/near the tombs of the heroes, I bet this was exactly *why* they went to sleep in/near those tombs), does this not-sleeping-without-dreaming actually qualify as sleep? Or is this not-sleeping-without-dreaming actually not 'sleep' at all? And then, *if* it's not sleep, what is it? Does it matter? Did I just beg the question? (Sorry, my head is spinning.) Wait! Of course it matters. It sure as hell matters. For me—existentially speaking, so to speak—it's actually a life-and-death question. Like master-and-slave in Hegel. *If* it is true that for me it is not possible to sleep—*at all*, not even for one fraction of one nanosecond—like this new faster-than-light neutrino they came up with in Switzerland, those tricky Swiss—without dreaming—well! existentially, it means that for me *sleeping and dreaming are the same*. A bad fucking rap. Bad news, if true, to say the least. Terrible. I remember when I was a little kid, four or five years old, three maybe, what do I know. My mother used to read me bedtime stories (*Winnie the Pooh* was my favorite), great, then, Time to sleep! Sweet dreams! The kiss of death. Those terrible nightmares. I hated to go to sleep. My mother used to ask: Darling, why don't you want to go to sleep? And I used to answer: Because sleep is like death. No! she said. It's life! It's *rest!* It refreshes and restores you, body and mind. I don't actually know it for a fact, but I am convinced that all lifelong insomniacs feel, at some level, that sleep is death. But I also think we need to put the horse before the cart here. I don't think insomniacs can't sleep because they feel that sleep is death, I think they feel that sleep is death because they can't sleep. A serious distinction. And why can't we insomniacs sleep? Again, I don't actually know, it's not that I've ever gone around and interviewed ten thousand insomniacs, I'm just a translator trying to eke out a living. But I have a vague sensation that there may be two broad classes of insomniacs. The ones in the second class can't sleep because—they can't, period. That may seem like a pretty dumb answer (to the question: Why can't insomniacs sleep?), but actually it might not be so dumb. I don't believe there is a reason for everything. I think you have to distinguish between what there's a reason for and what there isn't. Remember, we're talking about lifelong insomniacs here, not once-in-a-while insomniacs. And the ones in the first class—my class—can't sleep because they can't sleep one nanosecond without dreaming. ('First class' because we at least have some sort of reason—explanation—tall tale—for/about why we can't sleep, while the poor 'second class' insomniacs don't even have that.) The 'second-class' insomniacs have practically nothing to say about all the questions we're posing here, they just can't sleep, period. But we first-class insomniacs—at least we can talk about it, as I'm doing here. Rant, rave, and ramble, presumably without ever getting anywhere. Still, we have some idea of what it's all about, and it's about sleeping and dreaming being the same. That's why it makes *a lot* of sense to ask: What is sleep? Do I ever sleep? (What is consciousness? *I hope*—'I have a dream!'—that you'll see, later, *that it's all connected.*) If it's true that I never sleep without dreaming (but, practically speaking, I have to admit that this is more relatively than absolutely true, perhaps), then it may also be true that, technically speaking, I never sleep. Why? you ask. Why can't I do both together, sleep and dream? Isn't it like walking and chewing gum? Only a real jerk is incapable of doing both together. But you have to have been there yourself to see what I mean. A dream from time to time, an unbelievably terrifying nightmare from time to time, that's quite another matter. (Most people put it down to acute indigestion—some outrageously huge, heavy dinner.) No, sleep—as my mother so rightly put it—is *rest*. It refreshes and restores you. Oh refreshing sleep! It's like a glass of clear water. And a dream from time to time is like a little sand in the glass, a little silt at the bottom. But the problem here is *never* sleeping without dreaming. *That* is the problem. There is no rest, no refreshment, no restoration in that. No, devoted reader, believe me, it is deep shit. Not just a little sand in the glass, but the glass silted right up to the rim. Dream work? No, my friend, this is forced labor. It's a Marx-Dickens nineteenth-century halls-of-hell factory. A sweatshop as big as Yankee Stadium.

But—may I ask?—what about you? Do you ever sleep without dreaming? You do! All the time! you say. You *never* dream, you say. (Watch out! Freud doesn't believe you.) Except, of course, when you say 'I have a dream.' (Not every five minutes, I hope, like L. in Greece used to do.) Or you just have dreams for your birthday, or on Christmas. About having sex with ye gods know who, with the Madonna, with Marilyn Monroe, with your sister, with Brad Pitt, Clark Gable, Lady Gaga. With your uncle. But if what you say is true, why oh why can't I ever sleep without dreaming? *WHY DREAM?* If what you say is true, of course. And now you want to claim that—*in fact*—I've slept a zillion hours in my 61 years without dreaming. Gilda, 'my' second cat, dreams—to my knowledge—once a week on average, but it seems like a lot. But *what do I know*, I'm not Gilda's encephalogram. I must say, though, I've rarely seen her dreaming in the afternoon—and most afternoons she sleeps all afternoon, she's very lazy—where 'dream' means making gurgling sounds, twitching, and bouncing around. At 'night' we 'sleep' together but I'm busy dreaming-sleeping myself, what do I know about what Gilda is doing all that time? But when *I* dream I wake *her* up. But when *she* dreams—OK, forget it, who knows. My head is spinning. Is it true that—contrary to my own *impression*—I sleep *plenty* without dreaming, but don't *remember* my dreamless sleep? That I only remember my dreamful dream-drenched torment of 'dream-sleep'? It doesn't seem like that to me. Even when I take an afternoon nap, I can't remember any dreamless sleep. No, as *soon* as I finally fall asleep, a dream wakes me up. Somewhat refreshed, I must say, just for that borderline moment between waking and sleeping. That moment of actual—'instant'—sleep. But, you insist, I don't *know* that I never sleep without dreaming. How could I? 'Know thyself' said the Delphic oracle. Bullshit, replied Socrates, What do I know? Philosophy to this point my grandfather would have liked. Shit, what do I know, I just do it, I try to sleep, I wish I didn't dream so much, and so badly. 'I have a dream' that one 'night' I won't have a DREAM. I ask questions—a good practice—such as Why Dream? et cetera. If anyone answers them, so much the worse. This, as I said at the beginning, is a therapeutic ramble. It's a public self-psychotherapy. It's what we call 'trying to cope.' It's an attempt to not take things lying down (so to speak), after all these years of torment from dreams. To not play the victim. To talk about it. To fight back. To react. To stop keeping it pent up inside.

what, me dream?

> The classification of the constituents of a chaos, nothing less is here essayed.
>> *Moby Dick*, Chapter 32

Before I tell you about my latest reading of Freud, at this point it might be a good idea to report a few of my very recent, warm-November serial dreams. A few real killers. Some 'dream highlights,' so to speak. I write them down when I get up. Here's a few of the more 'entertaining' ones (from between November 12th and 15th), faithfully reported. Unvarnished. No bullshitting.

Just a few days ago, one 'night' I had a perfectly outrageous series of dreams. Perhaps because it was the first pretty cold night of the year. (It's November.) I had plenty of blankets on me but my cat was quite agitated and probably squeezed me a lot and snuggled quite aggressively, since she keeps warm not from what's above (blankets) but from what's below (me). (An old friend of mine in Geneva—a rug expert—once told me that a truly tip-top quality Persian carpet, with its zillions of knots, is worth a heated and air-conditioned apartment all by itself. You can live on it, eat on it, and sleep on it. From below, it will keep you warm when it's cold and cool when it's hot. But is it true?) (I also know myself that if you have to sleep outside on the ground on a cold night and, apart from your sleeping bag, you have one narrow—hopefully wool—blanket, you'll be warmer—relatively—if you put it under rather than over you.) (And don't forget to dig a hip-hole.) So be it, but I'm ashamed to say that these dreams were just wild and stupid. As usual, the worst was between 8 and 10 in the morning. I feel ridiculous writing this down—such a senseless jumble—and I'll be brief. I won't do it again. I promise. I'm just making a damn fool of myself. A jackass. Anyway, there were a series of episodes, with brief interludes. Waking up more or less, 'coming up for air' so to speak, then back into this abyss of dreams. My mother and sister were here in the house (this, in itself, is absurd—they live in America, my sister's been to Venice once in forty years), because I was leaving for a long trip. In fact I was going away to college. How about that! I finished college forty years ago. Freudian 'compulsion to repeat'? It was all very vague and confusing. Then suddenly I went into a huge totally empty building. A college? Then someone appeared and ushered me into a fairly small room where two or three people were lounging around. It was all plush red, like a cocktail lounge. Then the usher reappeared and pushed us out into a huge corridor with *thousands* of people, young people—students I guess—and me with my 1968 beard heavily flecked with white. *Thousands* of people. Then, the usher said something like (this, Doktor Freud, is just an impression, it is not a direct dream-quote): Go on, go on, they're all yours. Then I woke up somewhat, feeling upset and—drunk. My head was spinning and my stomach churning threateningly. Then, almost immediately, here in the house again. My friend P. was here and a few other people. We were all busy planting—actually transplanting—plants, which were *all over the place*, and especially in every possible kind of container. Tin cans, bottles, pots—pans—plastic cups, small plastic trash cans, bigger metal trash cans, dishes, glasses, colanders. One plant was in a big rubber boot, like the ones we wear in Venice for *acqua alta*. It was incredible, a total chaos. To say nothing of the plants themselves, a chaos in their own right. Plants of every kind imaginable. (In fact most were probably imaginary.) Then, all over the house there was a chaos of pots, of all shapes and sizes, all absolutely terra cotta, many of them broken. And piles of soil *all over*—DIRT, I mean—upstairs and downstairs, tiny piles and big piles. P. was saying something like 'We've got to get them all into the pots.' I was (dream) working with quite a pretty girl (for once!), we had a *very* strange plant growing on a plastic tray (like in school cafeterias), she said it was a 'pumpkin-seed plant.' In fact the tray was full of orange plant-like things and we were trying to transplant them into a rather small pot. Suddenly these plants—as if infuriated—started smoking, and groaning, and stinking, and bursting slowly into ugly dull orange flames—I woke up. Feeling rotten to the core. 'Asleep' again—perhaps? Immediately heard the low buzz buzz buzzzzz of a mosquito, our great tormentor. Mid-November, and these miserable motherfucking bloodsuckers coming out buzz buzz as soon as I turn off the light, the fucking cowards! How we hate them, my second cat and I. Up half the night, October, now November, with my recently-purchased electric mosquito-killer tennis racquet, which my cat hates. (In the hardware store I'd just asked for a fly swatter. Doesn't exist anymore, he told me. Out of style.) But I have killed a lot of the buggers with it. Electrocuted! Fucking fried. Sing Sing prison blues. And now in a dream? Just after the (potentially) explosive rebellious pumpkin-seed plant. Why a dream? (Why Dream?) A *dream* because when I grabbed the electric tennis racquet in the dark something incomprehensible was going on. It was swelling up into something HUGE, some sort of big irregularly round (oval?) ball made of aluminum screen, like the cat-proof screens I have in the windows downstairs, to keep the cats in, or out, as the case may be. (And the mosquitoes OUT.) Shit, I thought, never mind the mosquito, with this one I'm going to electrocute the whole fucking world. Buzz buzzz, the mosquito. (The cat had already taken off like a shot.) Then GRZZILLL—BAM—the 'racquet' (more like a big lopsided cage than a racquet) exploded. Then silence. I turned on the lamp next to my bed, and there it was, a sort of crumpled ball of mosquito-screen with a gaping hole in it. Shit, I thought, *now I need a new mosquito-killing racquet!!* I wonder if they still sell them in November—and I woke up. I turned on the lamp by my bed and examined my racquet. Unscathed. Same as ever. (Cat, sound asleep, purring.) A relief, on the one hand. On the other, these dreams that convince you, to an extent—sometimes (almost) completely—that they're *reality* are the very worst dreams possible, in my experience. The very worst. They mangle your mind. I call them 'reality' dreams.

By the way, I'm not making anything up about this racquet, it actually exists. (Believe me, I'm not making *any* of all this up.) A recent Chinese invention that has made the old fly swatter obsolete. Doesn't smear the paint on your walls with dead mosquitoes and their (your) blood. It's called 'Family Helper' and is truly in the form of a tennis racquet with 'electric shockproof net.' To be exact—and *I quote* the translation by the Chinese from the Chinese:

'New Very Powerful Rechargeable Mosquito-hitting Swatter'

Main Character:
It can kill mosquito which is sucking blood in human bodies but it is harmless to human when touching the net on flat surface without any feeling of electric shock.

Warning:
Please shake swatter for cleaning off insect carcasses which remain in net.

Be sure don't wash it with water so as to avoid shortcircuit.

Children must instruce under adult when use it.

End of quote. 'Instruce'? Well, so be it. I hope the children will do so. Anyway, the racquet works, if you manage to hit the mosquito. My cat hates the sound of the serial mini-electrocutions.

But that dream went on! You see what I mean when I say that these dreams are terribly exhausting. After the 'college,' the transplanting, and then the mosquito, I needed some rest, badly. Asleep again. Next dream. The house was extremely dirty and full of very bizarrely potted plants all over the place. P. was still there and seemed pretty much satisfied. My poor little house was an incredible mess. OK, so be it. But then we heard a lot of noise—yelling, screaming—from the other side of the canal. There's a long garden there and then a four-story apartment building (in Italy we say *palazzo*, even my little house is a small *palazzo*), with a kind of small hut or shed (not even a proper mansard) on top of the fourth story—and it had burst into flame! A beautiful but hellish sight. P. said 'Here come my two friends with the crane.' And sure enough out of nowhere this huge crane appeared. With one of those big wrecking balls dangling from the top (a veritable ball and crane) and P.'s two friends dangling with the ball, holding on for dear life, and the people in the burning hut screaming. Now, *this* was definitely a dream. (But WHY dream?) In this heroic rescue attempt—a scene straight out of Hieronymus Bosch—P. and I watched as the ball (and P.'s two friends) smashed right into the blazing hut on the roof, totally demolishing … everything. I woke up. And Freud calls it wish fulfillment.

After all this spectacle, the next night I had an endless, dull, tedious, and very disturbing dream. I believe I woke up four times during this one, and each time the dream picked up again more or less from where it had left off. There was absolutely no avoiding it. I won't even tell you the details, it was so dull. But so disturbing. At the beginning there was P. again. (It's true I've been seeing a lot of him lately. Translation projects.) And somehow or other we were in London, I think for some sort of convention (which never made its way into the dreams). We were in a hotel in London. We met the manager, who was very friendly. He showed me my room and gave me the key. Strange, just a plain small metal key, a normal door key, not a hotel-type key. Nice room. Not too small. A little dark. P. was never seen again in these dreams. But the manager, yes. Then it turned out that I owned a huge mansion—thirty rooms—in the countryside just outside London. It was possible to get there on the Underground. Underground all the way, it seems, right out into the countryside. Most of the dreams took place in the Underground. Very frightening somehow. I couldn't tell whether it was very crowded or completely empty. More an Afterworld than an Underground. Endless anxious trips. In more than one dream I did make it to the mansion. Thirty rooms, and completely empty. Bare floors full of dust, endless dust, heavy like sawdust. In fact I think it *was* sawdust. There were just a few people sweeping here and there. Endlessly sweeping. So that's what I did too. Sweep sawdust. The four dreams were quite similar. Perhaps Freud would say a 'compulsion to repeat' compulsively repeated. The last was a little different. I was in the hotel again, and finally noticed that I'd come to London with absolutely nothing. Not a stitch of luggage, no money, *nothing*. The friendly manager said 'Let's take the train together, I'm going home.'

(No, he didn't actually *say* it. As I said, or will say, or might forget to say, only on *extremely* rare occasions are any actual *words spoken* in my dreams. No words! No wish fulfillment! What would Freud say about *this!*) Then we were in the Underground and on the train. Definitely crowded, but also empty. (*Contradiction*, which is something Freud did like, he said.) I was upset about the fact that I had no money or anything else (but it didn't seem to be a problem). By this time I absolutely couldn't remember how and why I'd come to London. Anyway, I chatted with the friendly hotel manager. (Actually, he chatted with me, I think.) Also, we changed trains a number of times in this last dream. The Underground had become extremely complex and very confusing. Then he said (not really 'said') 'Here's my stop' and got off. It was a terribly long journey but I did get to the house (again), and was sweeping the sawdust (again). That's all, but I was frightened, bewildered, upset. A whimper, not a bang as in the previous night's dream. I woke up totally exhausted. Wiped out. 'Dream work'? WHY dream?

'reality'

Let me tell you about two 'reality' dreams I had many years ago. I have had many, but these are the two I can never forget. But—do you see exactly what I mean by 'reality' dream? I don't just mean 'realistic' dreams (though they are that too), I mean dreams that while you're dreaming them you think they're real. Wait, put like that does it make any sense? Maybe, maybe not. (It's not that in your normal run-of-the-mill dream you see the word 'DREAM' flashing on your screen—along with, say, 'Parental Guidance Suggested' or some such—to let you know for sure that it's a dream and not reality.) It's also true—and much easier to understand—if I put it like this: When you wake up from this sort of dream you think ('think'?) the content of the dream is/ was real. In short, that it actually happened. You know you've been sleeping (how?). You also *do* have the impression that you've been dreaming (why?). But for a few minutes you 'think'—you confuse?—what you dreamed with everyday waking reality. (Whatever in the world *that* is.) For a few minutes, or hours, or days, or for the rest of your life. I'm going to tell you now about two dreams that I've had 'doubts' about (on some level I can't quite name) my whole life, and always will. 'Doubts.' 'Thoughts.'

The second of the two took place here in this house in Venice in November, 1976. It was a cold and rainy late-afternoon. (Not at all clear and balmy like today.) I had been living in this house (I've already described it to you) for just under a year. But not like now, alone with my first and second cat, in this house I later bought with the *riches* from my beautiful *earrings*. Those were still the lean years, but right on the *edge* of the earrings. (Just between necklaces and earrings, lets say. Rags and riches.) I was renting the house together with about 4 young students, about 6 or 7 years younger than I was. I was 26. I say 'about 4' because it depends on whether you count the various girl- and boyfriends—*fidanzate* and *fidanzati*, we say in Italian, with considerable, and rather grotesque, exaggeration—as actual residents or just permanent visitors. So, let's say between 3 and 5, depending. One of the 3 to 5—named C.—originally moved in because she was my *fidanzata*. Frankly, she was the first girl/woman I was ever really in love with. But I screwed it up. Too many travels, to Scandinavia, to sell necklaces, to survive, and then there was R., the Norwegian girl/woman, 16 years old, I fell in love with her *big time*. Differently from C. *Extremely* big. I love R. to this day. She got into my marrow, and stayed there. — Anyway, I screwed up my life pretty badly for quite a while. Possibly forever. A long story. Meanwhile, when I got back from Scandinavia C. was seriously pissed off and made a concerted effort (with great success, initially) to make me pay—dearly—for my (so to speak) travels. Her gelid blood cried *vendetta*. And she had allies inside the house. (I had allies too, but outside the house. Everyone *inside* the house was *her* ally.) In this bitter struggle, that cold November, there is not doubt that she was winning. Big. I was coming apart at the seams. Badly. It was a cold rainy late-afternoon (as I said) and C. was downstairs in the kitchen with one of the other students, M. Out of nervous exhaustion, and for lack of anything better to do, I was upstairs, sleeping (presumably). Sleeping? In my opinion I slept. And dreamed. But—no, no buts. I heard the doorbell ring downstairs. (We had a very loud electric doorbell back then, it smashed my nerves every time it rang. A few years later I smashed *it*. Now I have a brass knocker in the shape of a hand.) C. or and/or M. (sorry, I mean one or the other or both together, how should I know) presumably opened the house door since I distinctly heard loud talking downstairs. A strange, loud, very shrill voice I'd never heard before. (Did all this wake me up? Well, judge for yourselves.) The talking went on for quite some time. The rain was beating hard on the leaky roof. (I have a new roof now.) Then I heard people coming up the stairs. The upstairs was divided into two rooms back then—it's one open space now, as I might have said earlier. I had the small room (alas, minus the *fidanzata*) right at the top of the stairs. The door opened, and I clearly—terribly clearly—saw the shriveled face of a very old woman. Very old but with very black hair. I'd recognize her today if I saw her. (That's ridiculous! Let's say, I'd recognize her portrait from back then, 35 years ago.) She looked in, stared at me for what seemed like a long time, then the door closed. She went back downstairs. I heard them talking again. The heavy house door opening, then closing with its inherent violent thump. (I have a new door now too.) Then silence. The rain. Then I woke up. Then I woke up? That's the story. Woke up [?] and got up. Got up, for sure. (Here I am!) Went downstairs, cautiously. C. and M. were in the kitchen drinking tea.

Talking. Looking normal. I said/asked, 'There was/Was there? an old woman who came to the house a little while ago. Who is she?' They stared at me for a moment. Fuck you, C. said, succinctly. *Vaffanculo*. What old woman? *Che cazzo dici*. What the fuck are you talking about. To this day I don't know. A 'reality' dream? What else could it have been?

But the dream I had in 1975 shook me up even more than that one, which I call the 'old woman'—dream—. I call this one the 'tent'—dream—. This one was *extremely* realistic. (More realistic than reality itself in a sense, maybe that was/ is the problem.) It made a huge impression on me, but I can't report it in detail, graphically, as I can the 'old woman'—dream—. I can't tell you why I can't. What happened had such a clear outline but it immediately became a blur. No, not immediately, but in just a few minutes. I never wrote it down. I've never actually told anyone about it. Well, for what it's worth. Maybe it will have gained a grain of sense, at last, after 36 years, in the context of this therapeutic ramble. I don't know. I write this down with sincerity, as best I can. It's hard to do it, after all these years. But no harder than it would have been that very day. Summer, 1975. Late June actually. I was in Denmark selling necklaces with my Sardinian companions. (No! They didn't sleep in/near the tombs of the heroes, those were Aristotle's friends.) That weekend we all went to one of the biggest necklace-selling occasions of the entire summer in Denmark, a gigantic horse market in the north of Jutland, where, of course, we went every year, for a number of years, until we stopped selling necklaces, and many but not all of us left Denmark. (But, obviously, even my companions who remained in Denmark, since they stopped making and selling necklaces, also stopped going to this or other markets.) (The other major occasion was a huge sheep market in the south of Jutland at the end of August, intriguingly named the 'Ho' sheep market. They even had T-shirts of all colors with 'Ho' written on them along with a sheep. A Danish sheep market named after Ho Chi Minh! No. A reference to hos *tout court*? I doubt it.) Anyway, this horse market was a real Happening, over a hundred thousand people. This was the Danes' idea of a real good time. (Especially in Jutland.) Gigantic horse market. The horses were just an excuse. The most important thing—as usual—was *drinking lots of beer*. We, for example, didn't even see a horse, except on one occasion that I vividly recall. My friend L. and I were selling our necklaces near a wooden rail that had surreptitiously been put up just behind us to hitch horses to (like in the Wild West). In fact, in the morning someone had hitched three or four new-bought horses, and then left them there for practically the whole day. (I would guess the new owner was off drinking beer, getting pissed out of his mind.) The horses, very calmly, started chewing on the rail, they chewed and chewed all day, quite calmly. In the end, they were just standing there, calmly, hitched to nothing. The rail had been chewed out of existence. Anyway—the point—we didn't give a damn about the horses or the sheep, these markets were the best possible place to sell necklaces, which is what we were doing. For two or three days, as I recall. The market was in a huge empty field, which, for the occasion, was very full. Full of beer tents especially. Horse sellers and buyers. Horses (presumably). A hundred thousand horse lovers (or whatever), including thousands of young girls. (Ho Ho Merry Christmas.) Then, there was a large and motley crew of people (like us)—Italians, Turks, Greeks, Arabs, Armenians, Gypsies, even a few Danes and other Scandinavians—selling merchandise of all sorts (sometimes handmade), a disproportionate quantity of leather belts, as I recall. Also wooden shoes, a.k.a. clogs. A certain section of this field was occupied by the tents of this crew, a whole lot of tents, some small, many medium-sized, some big. It was a genuine 'tent city,' all for two or three days. Self-organized. (Anarchic, if you will.) Quite an orderly chaos of tents. Like an instant city. Actually it was pretty nice. A very careful disorder, just as Melville suggested: 'There are some enterprises in which a careful disorderliness is the true method.' Nice people, good energy, and very little beer. Arabs, Turks, excellent mint tea. We—there were eight or nine of us— had two medium-sized tents. One for the 'baby' Sardinians (*always* chasing 'baby' Danish girls, in fact the 'baby' Sardinians didn't spend a whole lot of time selling necklaces), and the calmer tent for the 'senior' Sardinians and me. Well, OK, it's taken a while but I've set the scene. On Sunday afternoon (last day of the market) we were all pretty tired, selling necklaces from morning to night to a hundred thousand Danes—most of them drunk—is no picnic. We 'seniors' (by then the 'babies' had pretty much disappeared, along with their *fidanzate*) took turns taking naps. The tent city was remarkably quiet. It was far from the center of the market, off in a corner so to speak, which was a very good thing. (In some markets—in Sweden especially—the space for our tents, and for our tables too, was right in the center, along with ten thousand policemen, many on horses. A garrison and a fortress. Swedes get *very violent* when they're drunk, and they get drunk *very easily.* Danes just piss and fall asleep.) I went to the tent, S. was sleeping, I woke him up, he was pissed off, but S. slept more than the rest of us put together. 'Fuck you, you third-rate poet' he said (I translate freely, from the Sardinian), and went back to the market. We were well equipped, with quite decent mattresses on tarps on the ground. Dead tired, I threw myself down and fell asleep immediately. And believe me, I fell *asleep.* But then what happened? No one will ever really know. Just a bad case of nerves perhaps? Three strange 'characters' came into the tent. Super strange. Even for the inhabitants of that tent city—strange. I had never seen 'people' like this before. I do not remember what they looked like, but even if I did I couldn't describe them. They were some sort of extremely vivid blurs. The weather was extremely good that afternoon. (In Scandinavia in that season the 'afternoon' went on till 'round midnight,' as Monk put it). Denmark glowed with its best June light. That was the only thing I liked about Denmark, a gray light that was so clear, sharp, but also soft. The opposite of beer. It was this graphic gray light that illuminated the interior of the tent. They spoke to me in low, soft voices. (Like the light.) Very distinctly. They *must* have had their logic. We conversed. Normal, but strange, visitors. I have absolutely no recollection of what we talked about. None at all. But we did talk. What I remember so well is the graphic (it's the right word) gray light inside the tent. Nothing special. Strange visitors are legion, if you're young, and a traveler, and a stranger. I woke up. I remember it still. Exactly. Now. I opened my eyes. I looked around the empty tent. The sharp gray light that cut such a sharp outline, even here where there was nothing. Empty space. The inside of the tent. I got up. Opened the flap of the tent. Went outside. The sea of tents. A magnificent gray light. No one around. The roar of the market—the crowd, and the beer—strangely muffled by the short distance. I had had a dream. I had had a dream? It did not feel like a dream, at all. There was—is—no great meaning in this, except this: It did not feel like a dream, at all. No message. No future. Just this.

I wrote a short poem later that summer. In Norway.

Travelers

Voyages, and nothing remains in their shadows,
material that does not exist anymore — or not yet —
a perfume, smoke, voyages, and nothing remains.

A scent, a shade, smoke, power, ash, and nothing remains,
travelers, an outline, emptiness, and the future.

sociality

Well, as I'm sure you recall, a while ago I was asking the question: Why do I always think? Philosophically speaking, perhaps *I am therefore I think*. Sum ergo cogito, as Descartes didn't put it. Ergo, my problem is precisely the 'ergo.' The consequence. The connection. Why can't I *be* without *thinking*. I can't? Ergo, I can't sleep! No being without thinking. Ergo the 'ergo': Just because when I'm sleeping *I am*, ergo *cogito*. I think. (Sorry, this Latin is a little tricky.) Ergo, I was also asking: Do I always dream because I always—always—think? Well, I've been thinking about this. (As usual.) Why Dream? Because I always think? Why always think? It's a chain sort of. Something like these sequences, these serial (killer) dreams I always have. No apparent logic, yet there must be a logic, there *is* a logic, and, what's more, it must be unshakable. As I said before, this is not a 'stuff happens' sort of story. Freud definitely agrees with me on this, as we shall soon see. (And we shall ask 'What is consciousness?' too.) So let me try a different approach. Sociality. A little more down to earth, perhaps. I always *think*, because I'm practically always *alone*. Alone in this house with my cat(s). (One 'dead'—Gina—and one 'alive'—Gilda. Both here with me.) (And I had a *big dream* just this morning about my dead neighbor Veniero, how I miss him! I found him dead in his apartment next-door four years ago, heart attack, a broiling hot 25th of May, a tricky heart, fourth floor mansard, broiling hot, which he decided to repaint, in that broiling hot weather. He was 69. First, move all the furniture around, second, have a heart attack and die.) If I had things to do, people to talk with, I'm sure I'd think a lot less. (I *used to* think less.) But—night or day—here I am, thinking the same half-dozen stupid banal boring thoughts. (I'm exaggerating here, I also have my good days, lofty politico-philosophical thoughts, poetic, plenty of them.) And then I dream unexpected unbelievable staggering scenes—dark and confusing worlds—and practically all of them horrors. Roofs bursting into flame and wrecking balls in the night! Outrageous 'pumpkin-seed plants' rioting against their transplantation! Why? Why Dream? I think therefore I dream—no, that's a stupid answer, which just takes us back to where we were before, and where we got nowhere, practically. I think too much. If I'm not translating I'm reading, or else thinking, period. Look, my cat! What is she thinking about? I have no idea. When she was smaller we used to play a lot together but now she sits there thinking. I sit here thinking. She goes out into the courtyard or into the back garden, thinking. I take a walk every day if possible, thinking. I stroll for half an hour, an hour, or a little more, or a little less, it depends, with luck I say 'ciao' once or twice, at least that's not thinking. Do I have this riot of dreams simply because I practically never talk to anyone anymore? Are dreams simply the negative sign of sociality? The sign of a suffering and a solitude I have somehow *learned to accept?* A deprivation of the public and overload of the private that has 'gotten into my blood,' as they say? Sure, what is more 'private' than a dream. You can sleep with three lovers and five cats all at once, in the same bed, and each member of this happy throng dreams *alone*. It's extraordinary. A dream is the direct reverse of a conversation, there is *nothing more private*. Even a daydream. Even in a crowd of a million in Tahrir Square you can 'daydream' about being in Los Angeles, on Sunset Boulevard, having your handprint cast in cement on the sidewalk. No problem. Now, I do *not* mean, of course, any of that 'I have a dream' business. *That* is a public affair if ever there was one. A crowd-pleaser (perhaps). A mass phenomenon (for sure). No, not that. I mean the DREAM dream. The one you have when you're asleep. (But—What is sleep?) When you are *not* conscious. (Unconscious? Watch out for *this one*.) Or *are* you conscious? (*The* question—What is consciousness?) No! When it comes to the DREAM dream every single one of us dreams alone. But, now, just for the hell of it—no, not out of desperation, just for the hell of it—I tried this different approach: Does a 'suffering from overdreaming' depend on a question of sociality? Namely, a paucity thereof. With an added artistic touch, namely, on an *acceptance* of this paucity. Well, maybe this is the key to the whole question. To my whole tangle of questions. Could be. But I have a bunch of problems with this key to the whole question. For example. Those prisoners/'non'-prisoners who spend weeks, months, years in solitary confinement (with just a few breaks to be tortured) in the Guantánamo Prison/'Non'-Prison—do they dream? A lot? About a suffering and solitude they [have been forced to] accept? I have no idea. Maybe so. Maybe they never dream. Maybe one dream a month. Bad (about torture, say) or, perhaps, good (about the incredible Yemenite desert, or a little village in Afghanistan). Or, then again, maybe they never sleep.

But what's this story about bats? About the possible fact that bats (like Moby Dick, possibly, and mosquitoes, I doubt it) never sleep. All their lives. This is a tricky question. No, honestly, I swear, it's not just because bats rhyme with cats, rats, and gnats. (And mats for that matter, as in the poetic phrase: The cat shat on the mat.) No, it's not a question of poetry. Poetry! (Later.) But the question is not all that clear. In Venice, here around the house, in the courtyard or in the back garden, I haven't noticed many bats. Mosquitoes for sure, but bats not many. Yet both my cats—my first and my second cat—both *by day* and *by night*—have *captured* live bats and brought them into the house, *SHRIEKING*. (The bat, not the cat.) You can't imagine the sound of a bat shrieking inside the house. Not from the courtyard, come to think of it, but from the back garden, through their cat flap. Both Gina the killer and Gilda the Buddha. *Live* bats in the house. (If just a little—or a little more than a little—*chewed on*.) Shrieking. By day. By night. (I, personally, saw a zillion bats in Zurich, on Limmatstrasse, when I was there in the late '70s and early '80s making earrings. At dusk and after dark, under the streetlamps, but there was also an honest-to-goodness *belfry* on the far corner.) But the question here is—getting back to Venice, to this house, where I saw—where I rescued! held in the palm of my hand, or gingerly between two fingers—live chewed-on bats with their incredibly *angelic* faces. (Barely, and inadvertently, chewed on.) (But then that sonar SHRIEK downstairs in the kitchen was absolutely hellish.) Giovanni Bellini could not have portrayed his lover (as the Madonna) as a whit more angelic, more beautiful, what extraordinary, unearthly beauty, the face of a bat. Screeching! Angelically beautiful. No, but, excuse me, the point—bats don't sleep? Well, this is truly an open question. It's possible. A contemporary philosopher of 'mind'—named Thomas Nagel—wrote a famous essay (but is it convincing?), about consciousness, with the title 'What is it like to be a bat?' What interests me here, however, is his claim that 'a bat spends the day hanging upside-down by [its] feet in an attic.' Well, not in the attic with small rooms for Zurich University students on Limmatstrasse. And I haven't seen any hanging-upside-down bats in the back garden either. But the real point is this: Hanging there (wherever), were they asleep or awake? *That* is the question. We—my cats and I—don't think they were just *hanging*. We think they were *hiding*. Can you hide when you're asleep? We have grave doubts about this. (This line of reasoning, by the way, leads us straight to the question of mosquitoes. We know very well that these horrible miniscule tormentors don't sleep at night, because, as we all know, at dusk they appear out of nowhere and buzz buzzz et cetera, as we have seen. But all day? Well, now, do you think they have tiny beds with tiny cushions where they lie down, sleep, and dream about all the blood they sucked during the night? Come on now! It's clear that during the day they *hide*. And not nowhere but somewhere. So we're back to the same question: Can you hide when you're asleep?) (And please note that bears—those supersleepers—do not hide, they hibernate, which is a whole other thing.) OK, no cat wants to admit she caught a *sleeping* bat. It would be unfair and cats are extremely fair. *More* than fair. Ergo a hiding bat is not a sleeping bat. So be it. That settles it. Let me just conclude by mentioning a very short news item I just read in the *Guardian Weekly* (actually it's from the *Washington Post* but I read it in the *Guardian Weekly*):

Fungus kills bats

A fungus is at fault for the deaths of 1 million North American bats from 'white-nose-syndrome,' according to a study that's the first to find the cause for the phenomenon. The next question was how to attack it, said researchers at the US Geological Survey, who identified the *Geomyces destructans* fungus in a report in the journal *Nature*. The flying mammals eat as much as two-thirds of their own weight in bugs nightly, including mosquitoes [!], grasshoppers, and locusts that can spread disease and devastate crops. Their loss could cost \$3.7bn a year.

Geomyces destructans! Ye gods, this is heavy stuff. No, no, sorry, I apologize and beg your pardon, carrying on about bats like this. I got carried *far* away. This is what can happen when a heavy dreamer like me gets 'down to earth.' 'Let's kill him and *cast* him into some *pit*. Deep shit for his dreams.' (Sorry, some day we'll get back to this more seriously, after all, it's in the Bible.) I was just saying—what?—yes, dreams the negative sign of sociality. In short—all these dreams because my cat(s) and I rarely get out of the house. But is this a convincing explanation? We saw the human beings in Guantánamo, wearing those orange, Hare-Krishna-color jumpsuits. Heavy dreamers? Sure, another question, not an answer. For myself, I do have something to say. Up to about ten years ago I knew and *frequented* dozens of people in Venice (and some were fantastically good friends, many of them dead now, alas!), I had crazed and—alas!—more, or less, demented lovers (women) who, if nothing else, lent a strong—*extremely strong*—sociality to my existence. But I was also flooded by dreams. Riots of dreams. Night, morning, afternoon if I had time (which I rarely did, given all that sociality)—dreams. No, *not* 'I have a dream' goddamit. Real DREAM dreams. Plenty of sociality, and more than plenty of dreams. And thinking? You bet your ass. Plenty of that too. And 'we shall see what will become of his dreams.' From the bottom of the pit, I ask you: WHAT? What will become of me and of my dreams? To paraphrase the immortal Alfred E. Neuman: What, me dream? A good question. My question. Why Dream?

Let me just say this. If some Really Big Entity existed in the universe—some Enormously Big Mind—*and* was available to answer questions, there's no question about what I'd ask: Why do I dream? Why can't I sleep for a nanosecond without dreaming? And why bad dreams?—no, that isn't quite the point. Some of my 'bad' dreams—as we saw—are, actually, more spectacular than they are bad. Entertaining! No, the real point is: Why Dream? OK then, since I don't have a Really-Big-Question-Answering Entity at my fingertips, let's do the next best thing. (Arguably. We might well do better if we could make it to the outback to ask some Aborigines.) Let's do the traditional bourgeois 'Western' thing. (I don't mean Wild or Spaghetti Western. No John Wayne or Clint Eastwood.) I mean Vienna. Siggy at last! Let's ask Freud.

Freud

So, finally—I know you've been waiting for this—our number one dream expert. Sigismund Schlomo Freud. In person. In flesh and blood books. A genuine authoritative answer to my question Why Dream? Why have I waited so long before giving you Freud's—authoritative—opinion. Well, we'll see. All I can say for the moment is, the buck does not stop here. In any event, I have to confess that I am not ignorant of Freud's work, I studied it—plenty—when I was a student in New York, I possess most of his books, and I have continued to read them from time to time, as the spirit—or some necessity—has moved me. (I once translated a very fine book on Freud, written by a wide-awake Sardinian, titled *Logics of Delusion*.) Still, I've never been a Freud fan. He's never wormed his way into my heart. But, since I asked this question Why Dream? it's obvious he has been on my mind. So, cheer up, I have some good and some bad news. The good news is that I've just reread two of Freud's *shortest* books. Namely, *On Dreams*, published in 1901, and my favorite, *Beyond the Pleasure Principle*, published in 1920. Now, for my present purposes—this therapeutic ramble, this public self-psychotherapy—I said to myself, to hell with it, let's not read that real long one again, *The Interpretation of Dreams*. (Published in the previous century,

1899.) ('Not vacation reading,' as his editor put it, not that we're on vacation.) We'd just get bogged down, the short one is good enough, after all, it's not from the Reader's Digest, no, Freud wrote it himself precisely because only his closest friends managed to wade through the long one, I mean, make heads or tails of it. So, the short one it is. That's the good news. The bad news is that I've read both (short) books twice in the past two weeks so, ready or not, here comes a blow-by-blow description, a.k.a. 'detailed analysis.' Free association with a million twists. Trust me, if you love Groucho Marx, well, Freud's not so bad—this Good Doktor who boasted he had 'agitated the sleep of mankind.' *On Dreams*. Have no fear, the book is not dull. Hell no. And it gets off to a flying start. Freud, in person, writes down for us, in startling detail, in 1901, in Vienna, pen on paper, in his study, by his own hand, his very own dream, 'which I actually had last night':

> Company at table or table d'hôte … spinach was being eaten … Frau E. L. was sitting beside me; she was turning her whole attention to me and laid her hand on my knee in an intimate manner. I removed her hand unresponsively. She then said: 'But you've always had such beautiful eyes.' … I then had an indistinct picture of two eyes, as though it were a drawing or like the outline of a pair of spectacles...
> (Standard Edition in paperback, p. 10)

Wow! Now *that's* a dream for you. My own modest 'nocturnal' visions pale beside this one. What's more, it's world famous. (It's in Freud's long dream book too, of course.) As famous as the men who shot Abraham Lincoln or the Archduke Franz Ferdinand. What's more, Freud devotes a hefty slice of the book to interpreting it. A genuine *tour de force*. (As we shall see.) (More or less.) But, in all fairness, let's first take half a step backwards and look for some essential background. (In the book it's forwards. He begins with the dream he 'actually had.' An instance of the 'reality principle,' I guess.) Two vitally important things, for now. First, Freud became—and is—famous for the theory (discovery, invention) (in his long and short dream books) that 'all dreams are distorted *wish fulfillments*.' Ye gods, it's one of his major claims to fame. It's true that twenty years later, in the other book *we shall examine*, which, indeed, I've also read twice in the past two weeks, with the 'discovery' of, first, the 'compulsion to repeat' and then—*no less!*—of *der Todestrieb*, the death instinct (or drive) (or *wish*, as Charles Bronson put it), Freud's waters get muddied. Somewhat. In some sense. Sigmund Freud was an eel. He was, arguably, the greatest expert of all time on muddy water. His genius was that he had an answer to everything *and* to nothing. Something like my penchant for a question about everything *and* about nothing. This is what *On Dreams* (and, obviously, *The Interpretation of Dreams*) is about: dreams as wish fulfillment. As we shall see in great detail. If I have the stomach for it. (Considering my own dreams, more than slightly different in 'tone' from Freud's and, indeed, the impetus for this ramble.) And if not, in less than great detail. We'll see. Wish fulfillment. But the other Big Discovery (Theory—Invention—Idea— let's not get bogged down in semantics) is what Freud called, in *On Dreams* (and in the long one), 'the dream work.' I *do* have the stomach for this one. Even more than I'd like to admit. Quite frankly, these 'discoveries' are entrancing, muddy waters or not. Captivating. Not only for Freud's dream, which I shall call the 'table d'hôte' dream, but, perchance, also for my own chaos of dreams. (Perchance. But it may be more than chance. Who knows.) (By the way, a 'table d'hôte' is a restaurant meal at a fixed price and with few if any choices.) Now, what does Freud mean by 'the dream work'? It's very simple and very complicated. In the first place you have to have someone who *has* a dream (simple enough), then someone—an analyst or PSYCHOanalyst—who *analyzes* it (less simple). In the case of the 'table d'hôte' dream—as, for that matter, in the case of all *my* dreams that I report in this ramble—the dreamer and the 'analyst' are the same person. Two birds as rare as they come, and with just one stone. (But—you object—what analysis have I done of my dreams? Well, just be patient. You'll see. Later.) However, for Freud the fun part of all this is the analysis. Maybe because his dream itself is so incredibly dull while many of mine are so spectacular that I think only a Cecil B. de Mille could get a grip on them. So be it. At this point Freud gives us one of his more memorable pages, regarding the—I quote—'newly discovered [i.e., in the previous six pages] *latent dream content*' (p. 16, my italics).

> In order to contrast the dream as it is retained in my memory with the relevant material discovered by analyzing it, I shall speak of the former as the '*manifest* content of the dream' and the latter— without, in the first instance, making any further distinction—as the '*latent* content of the dream.' I am now faced by two new problems which have not hitherto been formulated. (1) What is the psychical process which has transformed the latent content of the dream into the manifest one which is known to me from memory? (2) What are the motive or motives which have necessitated this transformation? I shall describe the process which transforms the latent into the manifest content of dreams as the 'dream work.' The counterpart to this activity—one which brings about a transformation in the opposite direction—is already known to us as the work of analysis.

Is that perfectly clear? Well, now we have to go back to the previous six pages, namely, Freud's analysis of the 'table d'hôte' dream he 'actually had last night.' But watch out! I told you, the Good Doktor is an eel, he twists and meanders his analysis of that boring little dream *all the way through the book*, it's amazing, almost an Agatha Christie. But, meanwhile, let me put it this way: The 'manifest content' is *the dream itself,* and the 'latent content'—as Freud himself patiently puts it—is the *meaning* of the dream as discovered through psychoanalysis. But the trick here is that, first, in the dreamer, you have some quite simple, often banal (as well shall see) meaning, which gets transformed into a very complicated and tricky dream. By the dream work. How—technically speaking—does the dream work go about this 'process of transforming the dream thoughts into the dream content'? (p. 50). (*Why* it goes about it is an entirely different question. A *mystery,* which, more or less convincingly—I'd say far more *less* than more—Freud pretends to solve.) Basically, through 'condensation and displacement of the material and its modification into pictorial form, to which must be added as a variable factor the final bit of interpretative revision.' (p. 50). Now, 'condensation' basically means, simply, that the dream makes the *long story* of its meaning *short.* Vice versa, analysis makes the short little dream long. (In just a moment we shall see an amazing example of this, in Freud's analysis of the stupendously condensed *spinach* in his 'table d'hôte' dream.) In short, Freud has/likes short dreams with long meanings. (Vice versa, it seems that I prefer long dreams with short meanings. But *why?* And, *Why Dream?*) 'Displacement' is quite a bit trickier. I'm afraid I'll have to ask Freud to explain it to us. Luckily, he's awfully good at it:

> We may put it in this way: in the course of the dream work the psychical intensity passes over from the thoughts and ideas to which it properly belongs on to others which in our judgment have no claim to any such emphasis. No other process contributes so much to concealing the meaning of a dream and to making the connection between the dream content and the dream thoughts unrecognizable. In the course of this process, which I shall describe as 'dream displacement,' the psychical intensity, significance or affective potentiality of the thoughts is ..... transformed into sensory vividness. We assume as a matter of course that the most distinct element in the manifest content of a dream is the most important one; but in fact [owing to the displacement that has occurred] it is often an *indistinct* element which turns out to be the most direct derivative of the essential dream thought. (p. 34).

This is awfully tricky. See why I spoke of Agatha Christie. Freud says here something like: In the dream you've got a giant with a bloody butcher knife in his hand and a corpse at his feet and—nevertheless—the butler did it. Somehow. (How?) We'll get back to this—again, in the 'table d'hôte' dream. Finally, as for 'the final bit of interpretative revision,' Freud himself says, mercifully, 'I shall not deal exhaustively with this part.' Anyway, he means, basically, that, as a finishing touch, the dream work itself somehow or other 'arranges the constituents of the dream in such a way that they form an approximately connected whole, a dream composition. In this way the dream is given a kind of façade … and thus receives a first preliminary interpretation.' (p. 48). It's possible that in my serial-killer dreams this part of the dream work is on strike. But, then, Freud says something quite nice about chaotic dreams. Lucky me! They save the analyst time and trouble. 'From the point of view of analysis, a dream that resembles *a disordered heap of disconnected fragments* is just as valuable as one that has been beautifully polished and provided with a surface. In the former case, indeed, we are saved the trouble of demolishing what has been superimposed upon the dream content.' (p. 49, my italics).

Great. Now we can get back to the 'table d'hôte' dream and—possibly—see what all this is about. Let me try to be orderly, for once. I shall follow Freud's associations. Frau E. L. is a very casual acquaintance. Spinach—Freud figures that one out too! A little later. The *company* at the 'table d'hôte'—the first serious clue to the dream work—reminds Freud that the previous evening he left a small party in the *company* of a friend who 'offered to take a cab and drive me home in it.' In short, to *pay* for the cab, thus putting Freud in his *debt*. Then, indeed, the 'taximeter' reminded the indebted Freud of a table d'hôte, where he always feels he's 'getting the worst of the bargain.' As with the taximeter, his 'debt seems to be growing too fast.' But, a second association to 'table d'hôte.' A few weeks earlier, at a hotel in the Tyrol, it seemed to poor Freud that his wife was paying more attention to 'some people sitting near us' than to him. Again, *'the worst of the bargain at the table d'hôte'* (p. 12). Unlike the casual acquaintance Frau E. L. (in the dream), 'who turned her whole attention to me.' *But*—and here Doktor Freud doesn't miss a clue—Frau E. L. is, indeed, 'the daughter of a man to whom I was once *in debt*' (p. 12). Indeed, he exclaims, *with pleasure* (he's not beyond the pleasure principle just yet), 'My associations to the dream were bringing to light connections which were not visible in the dream itself.' (p. 13). And then he luckily recalls the 'scornful' proverbial question: 'Do you suppose I'm going to do this or that for the sake of your *beaux yeux* [beautiful eyes]'—i.e., *for free* (my italics). *Voilà!* The mystery of the mysterious *direct dream quote*, 'You've always had such beautiful eyes,' is solved. This direct dream quote— Freud tells us—'can only have meant: People have always done everything for you for love; you have always had everything *without paying for it*.' (p. 13). Wait! The plot thickens: 'The truth is, of course, just the contrary: I have always paid dearly for whatever advantage I have had from other people. The fact that my friend took me home yesterday in a cab *without my paying for it* must, after all, have made an impression on me.' Wow! A blow to the stomach. And there's more. 'Incidentally, the friend whose guests we were yesterday has often put me in his debt.' *Eyes … spectacles* (not like the 'spectacles' in *my* dreams)—*and*, but of course! the man is an *eye surgeon* (p. 13). No, seriously now, despite my profound respect for Samuel Beckett (but it's Thomas Bernhard *I adore*), *unnamably*, 'I can't go on, I won't go on.' OK, I'll go on—just a little. After all, we already know about condensation and displacement. Now, Freud has the courage to ask: 'Why *spinach*, of all things?' But fear thee not! Dream work is *hard* work. I've gone this far, 'you must go on' (sez Beckett). I'm going on:

> The answer was that spinach reminded me of an episode which occurred not long ago at our family table, when one of our children—and precisely the one who really deserves to be admired for his beautiful eyes—refused to eat any spinach. I myself behaved in just the same way when I was a child; for a long time I detested spinach, till eventually my taste changed and promoted that vegetable into one of my favorite foods. My own early life and my child's were thus brought together by the mention of this dish. 'You ought to be glad to have spinach,' the little gourmet's mother exclaimed; 'there are children who would be only too pleased to have spinach.' Thus I was reminded of the duties of parents to their children. Goethe's words
>
> *Ihr führt ins Leben uns hinein,*
> *Ihr lasst den Armen schuldig werden*
>
> gained a fresh meaning in this connection.

Ye gods, from *spinach* in the dream we've ended up with Goethe. Help! *Luckily*, Freud decides to 'pause here to survey the results I had so far reached in my dream analysis.' (p. 14). Well, listen. To anyone who is still there, alive, and listening to this long rant of mine—about my dreams, and about the question Why Dream?—I am immensely grateful. You are a patient person. And if you're still there, following the Immense Siggy's analysis of his 'table d'hôte' dream—well, 'I have a dream' about such patient people as you. Maybe it would have been better if you'd just read Freud's book on dreams for yourselves. A lot more fun. More freedom. After all, we're not in Guantánamo here. It's a beautiful balmy November afternoon in Venice, Italy. (No, not California, not Florida.) Freud—well, it all depends on what grain of *what* salt you take him with. Anyway, perhaps you see now why I dreaded rambling *directly* into Freud, into his flesh and blood books. Let's try to recoup our strength, we still have a lot to cope with here, we're not even finished with the 'table d'hôte' dream yet! So, first, didn't we say that one of Freud's major claims to fame is his invention/discovery/theory that 'all dreams are distorted *wish fulfillments*'? You can bet your ass we said it. Now, do you—speaking honestly—see 'wish fulfillment' in the 'table d'hôte' dream? You don't! Well, that's just because you haven't read this dream book twice in the past two weeks like I have. It may be clear as mud to a non-Freud-reader, but to Freud it's crystal clear:

> The analysis showed that my wife had concerned herself with some other people at the table, and that I found this disagreeable; the dream contained precisely the opposite of this—the person who took the place of my wife was turning her whole attention to me. But a disagreeable experience can give rise to no more suitable wish than that its opposite might have occurred—which was what the dream represented as fulfilled. There was an exactly similar relation between the bitter thought revealed in the analysis that I had never had anything free of cost and the remark made by the woman in the dream—'You've always had such beautiful eyes.' Some part of the opposition between the manifest and the latent content of dreams is thus attributable to wish fulfillment. (p. 26).

If things are clear as mud, Freud—Supreme Master of Muddy Waters—tells us that 'the heart of the problem lies in *displacement*.' (p. 56, my italics). So he thickens the soup with perhaps the most famous of all the ingredients he discovered/invented. Namely, *repression*. At last! This explains a hell of a lot. (If you buy it, of course.) Speaking—again—about the 'table d'hôte' dream, Freud says that

> these thoughts really were present in my mind … but they were in a peculiar psychological situation, as a consequence of which they *could not become conscious* to me. (I describe this particular condition as one of 'repression.') We cannot help concluding, then, that there is a causal connection between the obscurity of the dream content and the state of repression (inadmissibility to consciousness) of certain of the dream thoughts, and that the dream had to be obscure so as not to betray the proscribed dream thoughts. Thus we are led to the concept of a 'dream distortion'… (pp. 56-57).

At this point (but *What is consciousness?*) the 'table d'hôte' dream has become as clear as those days we have in Venice a few times a year with that very special light that reveals the always-invisible Alps. Suddenly, out of nowhere, there they are, in their vivid majesty. Rising just the other side of the lagoon. For Freud, at last, repression makes everything clear:

> I recall that my free cab drive reminded me of my recent expensive drive with a member of my family, that the interpretation of the dream was 'I wish I might for once experience love that cost me

nothing,' and that a short time before the dream I had been obliged to spend a considerable sum of money on this same person's account. Bearing this context in mind, I cannot escape the conclusion that *I regret having made this expenditure.* Not until I have recognized this impulse does my wish in the dream for the love which would call for *no* expenditure acquire a meaning. Yet I can honestly say that when I decided to spend this sum of money I did not hesitate for a moment. My regret at having to do so—the contrary current of feeling—did not become conscious to me. (p. 57).

Earthshaking stuff. Hold on, just one very last quote. A short one, and then we can try to forget this 'table d'hôte' dream forever. Remember the *spinach?*

Our specimen dream [the 'table d'hôte' dream, in case you've forgotten] exhibits displacement to this extent at least, that its content seems to have a different *center* from its dream thoughts. In the foreground of the dream content a prominent place is taken by a situation in which a woman seems to be making advances to me; while in the dream thoughts the chief emphasis is laid on a wish for once to enjoy unselfish love, love which 'costs nothing'— an idea concealed behind the phrase about 'beautiful eyes' and the far-fetched allusion to 'spinach.' (p. 35).

Amen. OK, now that we have finally freed ourselves forever from the 'table d'hôte' dream I have to say that there are a bunch of other things in this book that could be of help to me in my analysis (if I ever do any) of my own dreams. (But my question, *Why Dream?* Hold on for a second. Freud's answer—his opinion/discovery/invention—is in the offing.) But I'll mention just a few of them. Just three examples. First, 'All dreams produced during a single night ['night'] will be found on analysis to be derived from the same circle of thoughts.' (p. 42). Cf. my 'serial-killer' dreams. Second, dreams love *contradiction*: 'The alternative *either—or* is never expressed in dreams, both of the alternatives being inserted in the text of the dream as though they were equally valid.' (Cf. Kierkegaard's—ludicrous—critique of Hegel, with Kierkegaard the heroic 'either—or' and Hegel the villainous 'both—and.') Therefore: 'The sensation of *inhibition of movement* which is so common in dreams also serves to express a contradiction between two impulses, a *conflict of will.*' (p. 42). Cf. my 'paralysis' dreams. The third is a big one—a really long story (for me). I like this one (and the others). The Good Doktor says: 'If, however, a dream strikes one as *obviously* absurd, if its content includes a piece of palpable nonsense, this is intentionally so; its apparent disregard of all the requirements of logic is expressing a piece of the intellectual content of the dream thoughts. Absurdity in a dream signifies the presence in the dream thoughts of *contradiction, ridicule, and derision.*' (p. 43). 'Palpable nonsense.' Truly a comforting thought. But now, alas, we have to stop playing around. I'm skipping some good stuff but, at last, on page 65 (the whole book is only 76 pages long), Freud finally speaks to us about the *function* of dreams: 'We shall no longer have any difficulty in discovering the *function* of dreams.' (We're not so far here from my question: Why Dream?!) 'It is commonly said that sleep is disturbed by dreams; strangely enough, we are led to a contrary view and must regard dreams as *the guardians of sleep.*' (p. 65). 'Strangely enough.' Well, as far as I am concerned, he shot himself in the foot this time—no, *he blew his fucking leg off.* Dreams the guardians of sleep. Like a tiger watching over a lamb, as far as I'm concerned. OK, calm down. But where in the world did he come up with this shit! This deep shit. Wait! I am only thinking about my own extremely modest lifetime 61-year-long experience. Siggy is thinking of humanity itself in its long history. (I hope he's also thinking of animals. Cats, for example.) He specifically mentions children: 'In the case of children's dreams there should be no difficulty in accepting this statement.' Well, shit, this riles me a bit. 'Let us observe a mother putting her child to sleep.' (p. 65). No, spare me this, Freud. This unadulterated wish fulfillment, this 'I want the rhino!' crap. (p. 66). OK, on the next page (p. 67), he does say that 'this guard may sometimes [sometimes!!] consider waking more advisable than a continuation of sleep.' (Thank you *beaucoup*.) But—*voilà* the *gran finale*—'The dream provides a kind of psychical consummation for the wish that has been suppressed (or formed with the help of repressed material) by representing it as fulfilled; but it also satisfies the other agency by allowing sleep to continue.' Well, good for you, Herr Doktor. Sleep well and sweet dreams. I have other problems. WHY DREAM? I ask, and this is your answer! OK, I have rambled long (and hard) over you, in this book of yours. Your other book that I shall ramble over is more interesting. The ramble shall be a lot shorter, and more incisive. Possibly. We'll see. 'Compulsion to repeat'—*Todestrieb*—no, *this* is serious business. Amen. Amen. 'Blessed be … only to … with your … Lord Lord Lord' (Allen Ginsberg, *Kaddish*). But, fuck you Freud. (No, sorry, really sorry, I take it back.) You open the last chapter of this book—no, it's the next-to-last, but the last is only a page and a half—all of a sudden all of a sudden (pardon my compulsive repetition)—suddenly—with this: 'Most of the dreams of adults are traced back by analysis to *erotic wishes.*' (p. 70). Ye gods, 'revealed by the work of interpretation as sexual wish fulfillments.' Well, Siggy, this is one reason why many people (many of us??) have considered you an asshole. With your great project 'to unravel what the dream work has woven.' Well, we'll see. Rest in peace. I'll be getting back to you. *TO* you, not *AT* you. *Auf wiedersehen.*

wish fulfillment: a recent dream

Wonderful news! In our dreams our wishes come true. Sez Siggy Freud. The 'form' may be a tiny bit distorted, but no matter. Just make a wish, blow out the candle, and dream! What a marvel. It's the human (and animal?) mind. But let's go back for a second to our poor football (i.e. soccer) coach. After losing ten in a row, of course he *hopes*—'he has a dream'—that he won't lose the next one too. (Poetic license of course. In Italy coaches are disposable. Lose three in a row and they'll have your head on a platter.) After all, there are limits to everything. Even great patience has a limit. He's making a *wish*. I mean, what crazy coach hopes he can make it eleven straight (losses!). Now, the night before the match, naturally, he dreams. Let's say he dreams he wins the next match. Well that's perfectly all right then. (At least as far as dreams are concerned.) But if he dreams he loses it! And gets fired! Freud would be horrified!! There must be a monkey wrench in the dream work! And how about the coach who actually did lose eleven in a row, got fired, and is now sitting around the house in his underwear drinking wine. He dreams too, of course. (Real *NIGHT DREAM* dreams I mean.) According to the Freudian logic of *Wunscherfüllung*, clearly he should dream he *won* the eleventh game and didn't get fired. Well, he just might. But I, personally, don't buy it. I'm not a betting man, but I'd bet you a dime he keeps dreaming about *losing* that eleventh game in a row. In short, wish fulfillment my ass.

In a moment I shall report a bitter and painful dream I had three nights ago. Actually between 9 and 10 in the morning, November 16th. I hate to write such bitter and painful things but I need to make a point. (It seems that, alas, all my rereading of Freud has done me no good at all.) I swear, I'll keep it as short as possible this time. But first, to lighten things up just for a second, here comes a short interlude. Not that the 'table d'hôte' dream wasn't light, it was Freud's dessert that was pretty damn heavy. Lighten things up! Henry Miller (hooray! now you're happier) and Lawrence Durrell were close friends for forty-five years, and they sure lived it up, as we know. Up, and also down. Sure, they had their problems, their pain, their defeats, but all in all they had one hell of a good time. In other words, in one way or another they fulfilled a hell of a lot of wishes. (And they *had* a hell of a lot of wishes. Especially Miller, of course. Zillions.) And I do not mean that 'I have a dream' stuff, like L. in Greece with his goddam hotel. Not at all. These guys were genuine realistic realists. Salt of the earth. I'm sure you agree. So be it. Now—what was my point? Yes! They did suffer a lot of *defeats*, and wrote thousands of pages about them. But, somehow, they were like the coach who *did* lose eleven in a row and got fired, but every night dreams he won the Italian championship. And the Champions League. And—why not!—the Davis Cup. I mean, *these* are people Freud would like. I bet he'd give them a triple-A rating in 'latent dream content,' and in 'dream work' too. No doubt about it, they were genuine dyed-in-the-wool Freudians. You've got to hand it to these guys, one way or another their entire—outrageously tormented—lives were wish fulfillments. No matter what. Defeats? Zillions. Durrell wrote this marvelous line on defeats (in *Justine*, I read it forty years ago and can never forget it):

> For us artists there waits the joyous compromise through art with all that wounded or defeated us in daily life; in this way, not to evade destiny, as the ordinary people try to do, but to fulfill it in its true potential—the imagination.

Awesome. I'm sure he had *great* dreams. Defeat, pain, the more the merrier. In art—in dreams—he comes out on top every time. But his friend Miller was merrier still. (And suffered a lot more.) Remember that fantastic thing he wrote in *Tropic of Cancer*, all that 'people are like lice' business? Fantastic. The worse the merrier.

> Everywhere I go people are making a mess of their lives. Everyone has his private tragedy. It's in the blood now—misfortune, ennui, grief, suicide. The atmosphere is saturated with disaster, frustration, futility. Scratch and scratch, until there's no skin left. However, the effect upon me is exhilarating. Instead of being discouraged or depressed, I enjoy it. I am crying for more and more disasters, for bigger calamities, grander failures. I want the whole world to be out of whack, I want everyone to scratch himself to death.

Fucking awesome. You can't beat Henry Miller. It's just like the 'table d'hôte' dream. Things look bad, the kids absolutely refuse to eat their spinach—your favorite vegetable!—but, after all, some Frau you barely know touches you under the table and compliments you on your *beaux yeux*. It's exhilarating! It's Henry Miller! It's dream work!

Now, unfortunately, the dream I had three nights ago, between 9 and 10 in the morning. Briefly. (The 'manifest' content. We all speak Freudian now.) (Alas.) (This time, a bit of analysis follows. That's what you get for rereading Freud.) Freud-style (if joyless):

> I was going to a French class on Tuesday nights. I was almost the only student in the class. (No, I think I was the *only* student in the class.) The teacher was a thirtyish-to-fortyish-year-old woman with lovely broad hips and fine full breasts, but, at the same time, the sense was of a *bona fide* mummy. Something long dead about her. Her French was atrocious. (No virtue for a French teacher.) It was so

terrible that by the end of the hour she was actually making senseless sounds, gentle grunts, and I was sitting there like a complete idiot, knowing full well that I was taking part in a farce, while all my friends (whom I dearly missed) were at the 'real' French lesson.

Well, in one sense Freud would fully approve of this dream. He'd appreciate the brevity, the bone-dry style, the strong sexual innuendo in a 'manifest dream content' that is even duller than his renowned world famous 'table d'hôte' dream. But, in a deeper sense, for the Freud of *The Interpretation of Dreams* and of *On Dreams* (1899 and 1901), this—sincerely—as we shall see—is deep shit. Because the 'latent' content here is PAIN, pure pain. Profound suffering and total defeat. Why Dream? Or, more precisely, Why Dream *this?*

Allow me to say, in all modesty, that my French is not so bad, even if I haven't had that much occasion to speak it since I broke up with my Parisian fiancée in 1984. (Sure, 30 years ago it was a lot better.) (That's when I suddenly became a translator, propelled, after the *rags*, by the *riches* from my *earrings*. That's when I bought this house, cash, in Venice, as you know.) (Back in 2001—A Space Odyssey—I translated a book by Jacques Derrida that got fine reviews, so how bad can my French be?) No, sorry, this is just a distraction. It's not the point. The fact is that analysis of this dream is extremely easy. (It could drag on forever, but I want to avoid that. It would *really* be a distraction and I actually have a *big point* to make. Relatively big. Relative to what?) (Namely, Why Dream? And Why Dream *this?* Relative to *that*, I mean.) First level of analysis—but *all* of the analysis, *both* levels, *just like* in the 'table d'hôte' dream, stem from the 'latent dream content.' (You see, thanks to Freud I'm getting downright scientific.) The 'manifest content' (the strenuously-labored result of the dream work) of the dream I had three nights ago weighs about as much as Henry Miller's lice. This is a lice-weight dream as far as the *manifest* content is concerned, but the *latent* content is a super-heavyweight. Now, first level of analysis. *Briefly.* I had a terrible time in high school. Politics, Vietnam, teachers thicker than bricks. For me personally the worst teacher of the (rotten) lot (perhaps not actually the 'thickest' but the one who caused me the most problems) was Miss T., my French teacher. OK, it's 45 years ago. She (latently) hated all her male students because of her outrageous sexual frustrations. (Mummifying repression, I'd say.) All my friends thought she was a lesbian but I knew better. At one point she actually got married, to a moronic but very handsome history teacher in our high school. The marriage was annulled a short time later because *he* turned out to be gay. Yes, Miss T. had problems. She hated me *a lot.* (She'd never admit it! Not even after 3,000 years in a tomb in a Pyramid. It was probably definitely a Freud-be-praised 'love-hate' anyway.) Let's not worry about the reasons for her love-hate, enough said about Miss T., who isn't the main point here. (Actually she wasn't *at all* bad looking, as, in fact, the 'manifest dream content' suggests. She was the sexiest teacher I had, in her twisted, disconcerting, mummified way.) But let me press on to the second level of analysis, which is absolutely the one that really concerns us (concerns *me*) here. Yes, Siggy (I saw in an old film—the one with Montgomery Clift— where his wife called him Siggy, it may or may not be true), we have a serious case of displacement here. Straight as an arrow from a class in high school in the '60s to a class in Venice that I had frequented for ten years, up until about two years ago. No, in fact by Freud's definition I can't even call it displacement. There's nothing tricky here. Nothing. I don't know what to call it, Freudianly. It's too simple. I had a very painful experience in a 'class' in Venice two years ago, and dreamed about a bad time I had in my French class 45 years ago. There is some dream work involved, to get from one class to the other, but it's not hard dream work, not at all. Wait—brace yourself. *I have a theory.* It's about time! you say, after all this bullshitting. Here it is: For a 'subject' such as myself who has this *enormous quantity* of dreams—who, if it's true, cannot *sleep* for a single nanosecond without dreaming—it's impossible to do hard, serious, strenuous dream work. With *all these dreams all the time*, the dream mechanism would blow a fuse, so to speak, if it had to do extremely subtle, clever and, above all, *tricky* things, like in the 'table d'hôte' dream, with spinach and the like. No, I believe my dream work, as a rule, is a lot simpler than all that. Not to a 'what you see is what you get' extent, with things like pumpkin-seed plants groaning and bursting slowly into flame some work has obviously been done. Plenty of it, I suppose, come to think of it. If you ask me the 'latent content' (i.e. the meaning) of that one, I have to say, well, I give up, you tell me. But, I've gotten off the track. For a moment.

Meta-memoir. After memoir. The story is this. *Very* briefly, because I'm really only interested in the *point* of the story (Why Dream THIS?), not in the story itself, which is just a private matter I'm very sorry I have to bring up, but I have to do it in order to get to the *point*. About a dozen years ago I herniated a number of cervical vertebrae. It was bad. After a variety of doctors and (physical) therapists I discovered, right around the corner, an Instructor who practices the Feldenkrais Method. (A fantastic Method invented by a genius named Moshe Feldenkrais.) The therapist is referred to as a Feldenkrais Instructor, or F. I. Now, this F. I. and I immediately did not hit it off on, let's say, a personal level, I mean, he thought I was a ball-busting jerk (sure, I ask a lot of questions) and I thought he was an obnoxious jerk. I mean, not everyone can be *simpatico* to everyone. Funny, I just thought again about those pumpkin-seed plants—they remind me now of the color of his hair. Smoking, groaning, stinking, and bursting slowly into ugly dull orange flames (a fine portrait of my F. I.!). I dreamed them just a few days before this dream about the French class, which—*voilà!*—I immediately called *not* the 'French class' dream but, instead, the 'Feldenkrais' dream. In any event, I greatly respected his skill as an F. I., he helped me a lot. (I also read all of Feldenkrais' books.) In fact I subsequently frequented his group lessons—a.k.a 'classes'—on Tuesday nights for some ten years. (Apart from the private therapy with him for a herniated lumbar vertebra five years ago and, two years ago, a terrible shoulder issue.) In all these years I must say that no great feeling of warmth every sprouted between us, but I loved going to the Tuesday-night classes, it was very good for me, and a rare opportunity for *sociality*. Two years ago I couldn't go because of that terrible shoulder issue. But let me skip to the end of the story. (And then the *point*.) The F. I. phoned me one day, and SCREAMED insults in my face (over the phone) for a full half hour, I couldn't get a word in edgewise: Shoulder or not you should have come to class! You paid for the class! If you didn't come it's your own damn fault! [Do you think I'm Instructing you for your *beaux yeux!*] You're a JERK. You've busted my balls every year for ten years. More than all my other 'clients' [he always used the word *clienti*] put together. And—basically— FUCK YOU. Last contact I ever had with him. My shoulder improved on its own eventually. I continue to read the books and do the Feldenkrais exercises on my own, as best I can. But, obviously, this was the end of Feldenkrais classes, on Tuesday nights or any other nights. I took being told to fuck off in that manner *very badly*. I didn't deserve it. Although it's been a real pleasure not seeing the F. I. himself or being subjected to the ugly dull orange flames of his horrible laugh anymore, I dearly miss the classes. I miss some of the people I used to see there. I have taken this *expulsion* from the class *very badly*. (Miss T. did *expel* me once, for a week, and I was the best student in the entire school.) Sure, I felt a lot worse about this two years ago, and for at least six months afterward. Still, even now, from time to time and in general, it hurts, a painful experience that is still with me, as the dream shows. Something to 'try not to think about,' as the saying goes. The 'Feldenkrais' dream is *pure pain*. It made me think, immediately, of that great line from Durrell I quoted a moment ago, about 'the joyous compromise through art with all that wounded or defeated us in daily life.' OK, a dream is not art, but in some sense it *is* an art. And Freud's whole *big* point about *Wunscherfüllung* could, really, be seen as a 'joyous compromise through dreams' with our defeats, which, somehow, in our dream-lives become victories. In fact, in one dream analysis in *On Dreams* (p. 21) he says: 'He made up in his dreams for what the previous day had failed to give him.' But why, then, in *my* dreams do I seem to do exactly the opposite? In my dreams I seem just to *repeat* the defeats. Revive them. Relive them. Renew and heighten their pain. WHY are practically all my dreams about pain and defeat? Old—very old—defeat, more recent defeat, yesterday's defeat. And what is even *worse*, in my dreams I suspect that I even turn things that were *not* defeats into defeats. What kind of wish fulfillment is this!? Or am I exaggerating? Some of my dreams, as we have seen, are kind of fun. (But the big problem is always that there are *too many of them.*) (Well, maybe not *fun* exactly.) (Entertaining? Spectacular?) But I can't recall *ever dreaming* about winning eleven games in a row, and the Champions League to boot. I mean *dreaming* it, in DREAM dreams. Sure, *thinking* about it, *hoping* for it, *day*-dreaming it, *wishing* that I—my team— could win all those games. But why DREAM dream all these *defeats?* Why?

three recurrent dreams

Maybe I got a little carried away there, that dream still gets me down—my high school French teacher and jackass Feldenkrais Instructor rolled up together. I just hope I don't dream it again. If I should dream it again—and again— and again—SHIT, that would not be good. Now, I want to tell you about three recurrent dreams I had, basically in three different periods of my life. Then we'll get back to Freud, *Beyond the Pleasure Principle*, a really good one. Here again, I don't think we'll find any wish fulfillment to speak of in these recurrent dreams, not even if we put them under an electron microscope, or try to squeeze some out under a thousand (non-paperback) volumes of Freud. But let's try not to think about wish fulfillment for the moment, we'll get back to it later. At least—in fact—these dreams I'll tell you about now are not really about defeats. (But they're sure as hell not about *victories* either.) I think I got a little carried away there. But the 'Feldenkrais' dream *is* about defeat, and *pure* pain. I'm sorry to say that, alas, my recurrent dreams are in fact, *in themselves*, painful. Even if, at least, they are not *just* about pure pain. What's interesting is the unshakable logic in them. They are reasonable. Still, I have to ask— Why have them? Who needs it! There's no good in them that I can see. They always upset me. Every time. Anyway, I call them—for short—the 'unfinished' dream, the 'packing' dream, and the 'moving' dream.

Now, the 'unfinished' dream. But this is perhaps a misnomer. It doesn't mean, at all, that the dream itself is unfinished. (On the contrary.) It's true that I never seemed to finish having this dream, hundreds, thousands, of times, but that's not why I call it the 'unfinished' dream either. Wait! I also want to say about all three 'recurrent' dreams that I do not mean to say I had the very same dream again and again. No, just to be musical (I'm listening to a Thelonious Monk MP3), let's say the same dream *riff.* I had the 'unfinished' dream riff—*very* approximately speaking—between the ages of 30 and 50. (I'm 61 now. As I said.) Believe me, for a *long* time, and many times. (Once a week, once a month, less often, sometimes *much more* often.) But not always exactly (by any means) the same in all cases. By no means. I had it *in tutte le salse*, as we say in Italian. 57 Varieties. I have to say that, after a while, *I nearly got used to* the 'unfinished' dream. In any event, it was the least disturbing, least painful of the three recurrent dreams. Simply because I was younger, and stronger? No, I wouldn't say so. In any event, now (at last!) the riff: I dreamed (for approximately twenty years) (aged 30 to 50) (approximately) that I never finished college or, substantially less often, never finished high school. I mean, never got my NYU diploma, which I did most definitely get, in 1972. Or even that piece of filthy toilet paper from that grisly high school (which, very gruesomely, I did by all means actually get, in June 1968). (*Very* gruesomely.) Now, first, in all fairness to this recurrent dream riff itself, let me give you a little background. In high school I had a *terrible* time, the victim of extreme ruthlessness. (I didn't like elementary school either, *not at all*, those 'exhilarating' moronic super-egotistic teachers, I swear, genuine Henry Miller *lice*.) As I mentioned. 'Teachers thicker than bricks.' Absolutely. But Miss T. was much more, she was a crazed mummified brick. *A Maenad in drag*— exactly! It makes no sense, it's ill-logical, but—after 45 years—it's Miss T. to a tee. Rembrandt himself couldn't have given us a more faithful, and profound, and literary, and tragic, portrait. Amen. It's true that she got me expelled for a week. (*For what?* I swear, twist my arm, for the life of me I can't recall, what in the world did she cook up that time?) It's also true that she refused to give me an A in French, even though (just barely exaggerating) my French was as good—or bad—as hers, thus and thereby preventing me from delivering the valedictory at the solemn graduation ceremony, *which I desperately wanted to do*. (And everyone knew it.) Let me tell you about my high school *IN 1968*. A 'few' MILLION Vietnamese had already been slaughtered, murdered, and/ or burned to a crisp by our red-blooded troops, thanks to our napalm, B-52s, et cetera, with a 'few' million yet to come. (Nixon! Kissinger!) If you asked the students—and the teachers—who Ho Chi Minh was, I swear that 98% of the students and 93% of the teachers could come up with, at best, Ho Ho Merry Christmas. You do not believe me, but I am telling you the unvarnished truth. I am telling you the *unvarnished truth*. (Pardon this compulsive repetition of mine, it might be Freudian. We shall—or shall not—see, a little later.) Dreams are dreams, facts are facts. (Dream facts are dream facts, but that's another story.) And this high-class highfalutin avant-garde high school was—is—fifteen miles from the island of Manhattan, in an *upper-middle-class* New Jersey suburb, not in the north-west corner of Montana. (With all due respects to the north-west corner of Montana.) (Where, probably, they already had seventeen guns per inhabitant but, hopefully, were just shooting one another, not murdering Vietnamese.) In high school I protested the Vietnam war *all by myself*. I refused to celebrate the Great Israeli Victory of 1967 like *everybody else* in the school. I know that the Principal (an *old* mummy) and his cohorts considered me a commie creep and desperately wanted to fuck me. Behold poor Miss T.! with her grisly sexual frustrations, repressions, and displacements, to say nothing of condensations, and a 'final bit of interpretative revision.' The scumbags *put her up* to expelling me for a week *and* giving me a B (plus) in French. They *put her up to it* just to keep me from graduating first in my class and, therefore, *talking about the Vietnam War* at their solemn, lofty, and grotesque graduation ceremony. In June 1968! Their hero Nixon hadn't even been elected yet. Cover your fucking asses, you grisly bitches and gruesome bastards. Well, today I say Fuck You All. Amen. Sure, thanks to Miss T. I only finished second in the class. (The Feldenkrais Instructor, a dyed-in-the-wool fucking jackass, at least did help me quite a lot with my various herniated discs, despite our longstanding mutual antipathy and unhappy ending.) But, believe me, *I did finish* high school, in June 1968. A diploma. A filthy piece of toilet paper with my name on it. I was the only one in the graduating class who refused to participate in the solemn, lofty, uplifting, and gruesome graduation ceremony. A magnificent June evening. But 'boycotting' (all by myself!)—*picketing* the ceremony—would have been excessively laughable. Even for me.

College. For the whole story you'll have to wait for the *long* novel I tried to write in 1992, and again five years ago (blocked by a herniated lumbar disc and, simultaneously, by a life-threatening autoimmune disorder). But, my friend, Next year in Jerusalem! For the moment, let's behave. Let us continue to ask ourselves: Why Dream? OK? Anyway, college—NYU—was very different from high school. In the fall of 1968 quite a few students and many of the professors knew who Ho Chi Minh was. (At least by name.) (He died on 2 September 1969.) Some of the studious lads were riled up, worried sick about their deferments. Real hard times, McNamara and his Band, Best and Brightest, were drafting anyone they could get their hooks into, to beef up our armed forces, in the defense of freedom. Drafting *hordes* of poor blacks from the ghettos, but white students in universities—no! They held onto their deferments for dear life. Bit into them with all thirty-two teeth. Meanwhile, a few did get riled up 'politically,' so to speak. Screaming things like STOP THE WAR and HO HO HO CHI MINH. (It's true, of the throngs screaming BOMB HANOI BOMB HANOI BOMB HANOI not too many were actually students.) 550,000 troops, red-blooded American boys, the peak level, the vast majority of them stoned out of their minds worse than the students, or, at the very least, yelling FUCK THIS all the time. It's true, a slightly less small slice of students (the troops on the ground had other problems) had actually discovered who Ho Chi Minh actually was. What he'd been doing all his long life. But this is another story. Meanwhile, high school had been bad enough but at NYU I got myself into *deep shit* immediately. Deep *political* shit. We occupied the NYU Library *immediately.* (I'd only been there a week or two.) (Solidarity with the big Columbia occupation and subsequent bloodbath.) A neat idea. Alas, I had a major spat—a difference of opinion—with *all* my erstwhile companions. *All* of them. A heated nocturnal debate. *All* they *all* wanted to talk about were *deferments*—about armor-plating them. I wanted to talk about *the war* and about the *injustice of deferments*. No, we did not see eye to eye. A long story, which I won't go into right now. In this

DREAM book. This abyss of dreams. In high school they wanted to fuck me. In college, immediately, my 'fellow travelers' just wanted me dead. That would have sufficed. Or, at least, 'disappeared.' So, my new policy: better disappeared than dead. I decamped downtown to Rivington Street, heart and soul of the Puerto Rican Lower East Side, which, for a Washington Square student at that time, is about as 'disappeared' as it gets. Isolation. 'Notes from the Underground.' Meanwhile at NYU I studied Greek—Greek tragedy, Greek philosophy, Ancient Greece generally, finally Ancient Greek itself. I wrote a *variety* of papers—Kierkegaard, Hegel, Marx, The Pharisees, Guido Cavalcanti. I finished first in my class, in 1972, Phi Beta Kappa, I didn't go to this graduation ceremony either, I wasn't protesting, I just don't like crowds. But, believe you me, I absolutely did graduate. I do need to say one thing, however, which is, I think, perhaps relevant to the 'unfinished' recurrent dream. In my last semester I wrote a wildly ambitious 'little' paper on 'The Division of the Soul in Ancient Greek Religion and in the Ashanti Religion of West Africa.' (In a nutshell, in both cultures the 'soul' was divided into various parts or 'types' of soul. I was making some sort of comparison between them.) This little paper turned out to be a *big* job. What's more, it was an optional. An extra. I wasn't obliged to write it at all. I was already graduating *summa cum laude* with or without it. But—believe me—I *did* actually write that paper. In other words, actually *finished* the paper. And graduated. It's true, at one point it *did* seem as if that *little* paper had gotten too complicated, was slipping out of control, and might remain unfinished. But no, somehow or other *I did actually finish it.* The funny thing is that, later, the paper totally disappeared. A mystery. When I left the country my mother put all my papers in a cardboard box. (The 'Kierkegaard and Marx' paper for Sidney Hook, for example, which he hated!) Along with various pieces of sheer junk. My high school diploma, for example. Even my high school yearbook! But that paper—the one really interesting thing I wrote—vanished. But I *did* write it, I mean, *I finished it.* Vanished! How? Why? Who knows. Stuff happens. My mother. It's also true that *she threw out all my baseball cards.*

After this short introduction let me tell you about the 'unfinished' dream. By which I mean I never finished college. Or, on occasion, high school. (On occasion, I must say, it *did* involve that last paper, on Greek and Ashanti religion, which later disappeared.) It's at least ten years since I've had this dream, it petered out, to be replaced by worse, more disturbing recurrent dreams, in addition, of course, to the 'regular' nonrecurring dreams. So I can only give you a sketchy report. What I remember best is that it was *extremely long*, it went on for hours and hours. As did the 'packing' dream in fact. In fact the worst part of it all—the worst thing about these dreams—was that they just went on for so goddam long, practically forever, they totally wore me out. (These 'guardians of sleep.') Both the 'unfinished' and the 'packing' dreams, which I had so often, and they wore me out every time. Now, very basically, here I am, in the dream, thinking, holy shit, I'm 30—40—50 years old, and I never took that last exam in high school (Latin, or History, or French, or some such), so I never *quite* got that fucking diploma, missed it by a hair, just because of that one exam. (Maybe I was sick that day. Or totally fed up. Or I'd run away from home. Or I was protesting something. Or I'd taken the bus to Atlantic City to visit my grandfather.) That one ridiculous exam, which I could have passed with flying colors with both hands tied behind my back, just because of that one exam the bastards never gave me the high school diploma. (That piece of filthy toilet paper.) And now here I am, in Italy, 30—40—50 years old, and everyone keeps telling me—constantly!—What a JERK you are! You don't even have a high school diploma! You never *finished high school!* You are a total ZERO. When I went to see my good friend the butcher, he said, immediately, A total zero! A jerk! You don't even have a high school diploma! (Remember, all this is in the DREAM, in the 'unfinished' dream. Don't get confused and think it's a true story. I mean, it *is* a true story, but the story of a recurrent *dream*.) It was even worse when I went to the Venice Police Headquarters to renew my residence permit (every blessed year, from 1981 when they finally *gave* me a residence permit, after nine years of *clandestinità*, until 1998 when I got Italian citizenship). *Immediately* they whipped out a piece of paper (in the dream) with, in *huge* letters covering the entire page, HIGH SCHOOL DIPLOMA on it, with two boxes: *sí* or *no*. But, somehow, this dream managed to go on for hours and hours. Both in the 'high school' and, even more often, in the 'college' versions. Quite often—or from time to time—my mother and even my *little sister* turned up in the 'unfinished' dream to bust my balls even more. My mother, or my sister—or, just imagine! both together—said things like (but said them for hours, hours, over and over, *in tutte le salse*) I/WE told you you'd be in trouble one day because you never took that Latin—History—French exam and therefore *didn't finish* high school. Told you so! Told you so! Told you so! (For hours and hours.) But in the 'college' version it was all much worse. My *not finishing college*, well, that was grist for *everyone's* mill. In fact—in real life—when I was 35 I started doing translations for the Venice University Philosophy Department and—in fact—there was always a *lot* of paper work, I mean forms to fill out, bureaucracy. In fact, for the University I really did have to have a *University* diploma, which I *did*—I *do*—have, goddamit. (But why in the world did my *butcher*, my friend, give a shit about whether I had a diploma or not. High school or college or whatever.) But in my dream, the 'unfinished' recurrent dream, there was no goddam sign of that goddam diploma. Shit! Signor Donis, we need to see your NYU diploma et cetera, and then—DREAM ON, for hours and hours. Absolute torture. I wouldn't wish this dream on my worst enemy. Speaking of torture, I certainly wouldn't wish it on the guys in Guantánamo with the Hare-Krishna-color jumpsuits. They have more than enough problems without it. No! I'd wish it on the *guards* in Guantánamo, whatever in the world they may be wearing. I really am a jerk! I never did take that last Greek exam, what a JERK I am. It was all the fault of that paper. (On the Greeks and the Ashanti.) (This did come up *a lot* in the 'unfinished' dream, come to think of it. In the 'university' version, obviously.) I was so busy, so *caught up* in that paper, I totally forgot about that Greek exam. I'd already taken hundreds of Greek exams, and now, it's absolutely true, I'm a jerk, a zero, they won't let me translate for the Philosophy Department. And then—hooray!—my mother and/or my *sister* leap right into the fray. That *stupid* paper! We told you not to spend all your time on that paper. (But I hardly ever even *saw* my mother when I was in college. I lived on Rivington Street, beyond the frontier. And my *sister* was living in a cabin in the middle of a forest god-knows-where in Vermont.) (Remember, I had this dream until I was 50, then it finally petered out. I mean, until thirty years after that excellent paper that I *did* write and *did* finish, even though it later disappeared, and I *finished NYU too*, goddamit.) You never finished college because of that stupid paper *that you did not have to write*. You did it for god knows what reason. Basically, because you're a jerk, simply. You were about to graduate *summa cum laude* and instead you never took that Greek exam. (I *did* graduate *summa cum laude*, I swear. But not in this pitiless dream.) For that matter, you never finished that *stupid* paper either. On and on, on and on. Enough. And I had this dream *often*—the 'unfinished' dream—from the age of 30 to the age of 50, approximately.

What's next. Ye gods, the 'packing' dream. This one is worse than the 'unfinished' dream, which, while *exhausting*, actually did have something comic about it, a sort of gruesome comic relief, which made it a bit more bearable. But there's nothing funny about the 'packing' dream. Nothing tragic either, for that matter. And definitely *nothing* entertaining. An unbearably banal but, also, disturbing and exhausting dream I had from the age of 35 to the age of 55, *approximately*. And this means that for fifteen years (aged 35 to 50) I had the 'unfinished' and the 'packing' dreams together. Taking turns. Like Scylla and Charybdis, like Humpty and Dumpty, so be it. Just one background note on the 'packing' dream. Let me say this. The first twelve years I lived in Europe (1972–1984) I traveled *all the time*. First the necklaces. (Scandinavia, Sardinians, streets, markets.) Then the *earrings* plus the *new* necklaces. Both with Venetian glass beads. (Boutiques in Switzerland and Germany, four long trips a year, plus Sicily in the summer.) I've been living in this house in Venice since 1976, as you well know (rented for ten years, then bought), but one of those years I was on the road for 250 days! I traveled, at first, for years, by autostop, a.k.a hitchhiking, then, for a short time, by train, then, for five years with the only car I've ever owned, a beautiful Renault 4 mini-minivan. Ten years old when I bought her, she sure drove me *crazy* with her many serious ailments and disorders, a great car, great personality, like (later) my cats. The car was a 'little camel,' not a cat. Finally, after the car collapsed definitively, I traveled for a year or two by train. Then, suddenly (1984), I totally stopped making and selling earrings. I cut my traveling down to at most a couple of airplane flights a year. (Never mind my flights of fancy.) A vacation in Greece or Sardinia, every few years a trip to the U.S. to see my family. I stayed here at home and started translating … but you know about this already. I shall *not* go into the story of my infinite adventures making and selling necklaces and earrings, that's a whole other ramble, and not a short one. I have just one thing to say here. One point, which is important for the 'packing' dream. (I think.) Each trip I made, taking all those earrings and necklaces with me, was an extremely complicated enterprise, technically speaking. Before a trip I had to work like hell every night all night ('early to bed') trying to make around a thousand *earrings* and necklaces. What's more, I had to organize the materials (alpaca wire, bigger beads, smaller beads, miniscule beads, et cetera) to take with me so that I could continue working during the trip itself, in Zurich, Munich, Sicily, et cetera. (Believe me, 'the constituents of a chaos.') In short, 'packing' for each of these trips was a big, delicate, demanding, and vitally important job. Vitally important. Extremely complicated. And I was damn good at it, evidently, since I *packed* a quantum leap, from *rags* to *riches*. As I said earlier. Then, when I stopped traveling, the 'packing' dream started. A dull, banal, miserable, but also *violently disturbing* dream. I had it often, for twenty years. (Fifteen of them *together* with the 'unfinished' dream.) A miserably *gruesome* dream, which is not easy to describe. Meta-memoir. I mean, the facts are easy, but the atmosphere (of anxiety, terror, bewilderment, panic, confusion, and total discombobulation) is hard to put into words.

In this genuinely horrible dream I am getting ready for a trip. (*En bref*, 'packing.') The destination is never of any importance. In the dream, as far as I can remember the question of where in the world I might be going never comes up. There are *never* any earrings, necklaces, or any kind of complicated things whatsoever that I have to pack. On the contrary. All this packing consists of, say, a pair of pants, two pairs of socks and underwear, a T-shirt, a sweater, a toothbrush, I mean, super-minimal super-simple packing. I always have to catch either a plane or a train—at a certain time, *bien sûr!* (Pardon my French. I'm afraid Miss T. is still on my mind.) But it's this 'certain time' factor that dominates the dream. I *always* have *plenty* of time. Usually *more* than plenty. Sometimes two or three entire days totally reserved for packing these half a dozen miserable things or, more often, at least an entire day. Say, I get up around noon, well rested, and have to be packed in time for a midnight plane or train. And most of the time I don't even have to pack these few scraps all by myself, there's someone helping me, a great variety of

people. One of the 'packing' dream's favorites is, of all people, my father!—
heaven help us! Which, right off the bat, is not good news, because my father
never helped me all his life, may he rest in peace. On the contrary. But in this
dream he is very nice and really tries to help. Anyway, whoever's helping, or
even if there's no one else in the dream, wild and terrible things manage to
happen. I have 24 hours to pack, but I go out, just for a short walk, in Venice,
a miniscule city, and end up lost in an open field somewhere, in the middle
of nowhere, the plane has taken off three hours ago, and I'm still desperately
struggling to … pack. And I'm lost in an open field at the same time. In the
middle of nowhere. I believe this may sound comic to you, written down
like this, reported dryly like this. But in fact, in the dream, it is *terrible*. I
don't want even to attempt to describe (or even to think about) how terrible
I feel. There, in that field, or meadow, or swamp, or whatever. Terrible. One
variant. With all this time to pack, my 'helper' in the dream (my father, some
friend, my friend Gianfranco, some girlfriend, my mother, my sister, my
cousin in Miami, my neighbor, my butcher, Gigi my cat's vet—one by one
and sooner or later they all turn up, I've had this dream maybe a thousand
times) *suggests* we go out just for a little while. 'A breath of fresh air.' And
then—forget it, you get the picture. But in the more common 'packing'
dream scenario I don't go out. Helped or not, I just attempt to pack, for
hours, hours and hours. I have 12 hours, till midnight, to catch the plane,
so around 10 I have to leave for the airport, just twenty minutes by bus to
the Venice Airport. At 2, 3, 4 in the morning I'm still desperately trying
to pack the suitcase. Desperately! In a panic. Completely discombobulated
and bewildered. And the plane took off hours ago! I lose my sense of humor
reporting this dream. And *now* comes the *worst* part. The most common
ending of the 'packing' dream. *Paralysis.* Finally, at the end of a dream lasting
hours—hours and hours—I make the SUPREME EFFORT to get these six
shreds of pathetic clothing and my poor little toothbrush into my miserable
little suitcase, I endeavor, struggle, and strive with all my strength and ability,
with—obviously—my own two hands until—believe me, hundreds of times
in hundreds of this version of the 'packing' dream (no, obviously not in the
'lost in an open field' version)—my hands start to cramp up, to freeze. I'm
trying to put a pair of socks, a toothbrush, into the suitcase until, suddenly,
total paralysis, not only of my hands, but of my entire body. And soul? No.
Let's forget about soul for the moment, let's leave soul to Billie Holiday, 'sad
and lonely,' all for you … body and soul. A great song.

In any event, I am *luridly* conscious of this, the total paralysis of my entire
body, in the 'packing' dream. If you recall, we've seen paralysis before in this
ramble. Twice. In my recent 'miserable dream' about visiting the law office,
and in Freud where, for once, he said something quite interesting. (I'm
kidding, he was a great guy with *lots* to say, even if he does piss me off pretty

often.) 'The sensation of *inhibition of movement* which is so common in dreams also serves to express a contradiction between two impulses, a *conflict of will.*' (p. 42). He also considered 'contradiction' and 'nonsense' the very flesh and blood of dreams. (And I agree.) It's his goddam wish fulfillment (and 'guardians of sleep'!) that I have *BIG* problems with. Personal problems. Based on my own modest lifetime experience of dreaming. 'Behold, this dreamer cometh!' Well, I'm sure that Freud would find lots of interesting things in the 'packing' dream. But, Siggy, pray tell me where you see the wish fulfillment here. We'll be getting back to that quite soon, when we get to *Todestrieb*—i.e., the death instinct, or *wish.* I have just one thing to say about this horrible 'packing' dream, something kind of funny. As I said, in 1984 I practically stopped traveling, cutting down to a plane trip or two a year. But, believe me, after all my *complicated* traveling and packing with my necklaces and my *earrings* for all those years, I swear, at that time I was one of the world's best packers. A top-flight packer. An ace. And that's precisely when the 'packing' dream started. (Why???) And went on for twenty years straight. Until about five years ago. In that twenty-year period, as I said, I did take a plane trip or two a year, and continued packing beautifully and with ease. Finally, five years ago, I became seriously ill, so I cut my traveling down considerably more. (Just two trips in five years. One to Sardinia and one to Sicily.) But, in these past five years, any form of 'packing' has become a total horror, nearly as bad as in the 'packing' dream itself! (Which I no longer have, as I said.) A fury of anxiety, anguish, and panic. In fact I *very* nearly missed both those planes. I even got cramps in my hands. What's more, now, even if I just have to go to the doctor in Padua (half an hour by train)—even if I have to go to the Philosophy Department (a quarter hour on foot)—I become totally flustered, and spend hours, panicky, 'packing'—I mean, deciding what I have to take with me. To Padua (a magazine? a book?). What in the world might I need at the university, what cap to wear, what time I have to leave the house to get to … It's a riot! First the tragedy, then the farce, said Marx. My waking packing has imitated my dream packing. Rejoice, Siggy. A fine piece of dream work for you.

Let me confess that I never imagined my rambling on about my three (main) recurrent dreams could assume such epic proportions. There's something like an *Iliad* atmosphere here. All created by two truly dumb dreams. Isn't it pathetic. A pathetic epic. An epic of the pathetic. I ask for mercy, not *pietas.* 'you must go on, I can't go on' — I'm going on to the last of the three (main) recurrent dreams. (Believe me, we'll skip the lesser ones.) (After all, we are human beings, not battleships.) Next—the 'moving' dream. Now here's a misleading name if ever there was one. I mean, *all* dreams are 'moving' (like Billie Holiday's singing 'Body and Soul'). By definition, I'd say. Based not on my re-rereading of Freud but on my overwhelming lifetime experience.

In this case, however, my 'moving' dream is, specifically, *about* 'moving'—I mean, moving out of one house (or apartment, or hole in the wall) to another. 'Moving' as in the expression 'moving van' or whatever. (OK, moving can be *moving* but let us make an effort not even to *think* about that.) (Show me a dream that isn't *moving* and I'll show you a dreamer who richly deserves to be 'cast into some pit'—and slain. I'll show you an *abyss* of dreams.) So be it. Now, the 'moving' dream is about my moving out of this house, where I've lived since 1976 (nearly 36 years). A house at that time with one of the leakiest roofs in Venice, I purchased it with the *riches* of my *earrings* in 1986 and without ado violently tore off the entire venerable ancient Venetian roof and made a new one in larch and white ash. After which my first cat, Gina, arrived *immediately* and where—at this very moment—my second cat, Gilda, has just had dinner (half a can of Gourmet) and is now sitting right on this page I'm trying to write on. (Pen on paper.) Never fear! Cats are not stubborn like we people are, they change their minds easily, on some issues, and they have no 'obstinate illusions.' (About refusing to let me turn the sheet of paper over, for example.) As in Einstein's defamatory accusation regarding *time*. Are we conscious *of* time or conscious *in* time? An obstinate illusion? What we tick in? Or what makes us tick?

The 'moving' dream—unlike the first two—is an ongoing recurrent dream. It just started about five years ago, five years after the petering out of the 'unfinished' dream and precisely when the 'packing' dream had itself just about petered out. We actually saw an example of this dream—quite a sad and pitiful one—quite a while ago, under the heading of 'some miserable dreams.' My this-November dreams. A dream that piteously involved Gilda. In terms of dream-details this one is *much* more difficult to report than *any* of the others, because it profoundly and intimately involves intricate issues of contemporary Venetian architecture (and, possibly, geometry) (and geography, possibly). For once, *first* the 'manifest content.' (But, for once, the 'manifest content' is architecturally highly complex.) As you know, I have a beautiful little house on a beautiful courtyard (in front), back garden (in back, where the cats go, through the flap), and magnificent canal (on one side). And on the other side, empty space. No one to bust my balls. Upstairs, drenched in sunlight all day (unless it happens to be cloudy). The dream. The 'moving' dream. Some (anonymous) tricky Venetian, or, more often, my own idiotically tricky mind, tells me — Yes, a beautiful little house, great back garden for the cats, great canal, mystic courtyard. *But* [but what?] it is small. 'Limited.' (What does this mean?) *Just around the corner*—behold!—a palace. A royal palace, a real big one, and we're willing to swap it for your extremely small and 'limited' house, which is also subject to *acqua alta*, which means a certain number of inches of canal-shit water on your ground floor, which—we know you agree (and I do!)—is a *royal* pain in the ass. This part of the 'manifest dream content' goes on and on (these recurrent dreams are dreadfully *long*). Meanwhile, I'm thinking 'just around the corner.' What in the world does this refer to? It's totally unrealistic in terms of real geography, real geometry, or real architecture. Can it mean the back wall of my house? Or the rear façade? Or some extremely ill-defined, and ill-logical, side façade? I don't get it. A royal palace. Swap my house for it. The dream goes on and on. Endlessly. Until, suddenly, in the end, I say: Yes, this is a lovely little house, but it has its problems, its 'limits.' So, OK, I'm willing to swap. *Not* to pay anything, a straight swap. And, FUCK ME, in the dream, the 'moving' dream, I do it! Gilda, along with Gina, who lived 'before' Gilda and who *is always with us*, and I move into this royal *palazzo*, which is *right here*, somewhere *attached* to this house, edgewise, somehow. But a *different* house. We move in. But there is also a recent variation on the 'moving' dream—I gave you an example under the heading of 'some miserable dreams'—in which *I have to leave the cats behind*. Why? I absolutely most certainly do not know. WHY DREAM something like that?! Of all my hordes of dreams, this one is the saddest, the worst, the most awful, the most horrible, the most terrible I could possibly imagine. But—luckily—most of the time we all move in together, the cats and I. So, OK, we move in. *Huge.* Impossibly *huge* rooms *all over the place*. I mean, a *big palazzo* but the rooms are *enormous*, like barns. The entire ground floor is pure 'show' (as in all the genuine Venetian *big palazzi*), by which I mean there's nothing there at all, just empty space, a *huge* entrance hall with nothing in it. In case of *acqua alta* I could harvest a ton of fish down there. Then, the two *gigantic* upper floors. Geometrically, a *piano nobile* duplex. But—most of all—the *façade*. I think this is the only real clue we have to the 'latent dream content' here. My gut feeling about this dream is that I am bewitched—enchanted—by the façade. It's not the Taj Mahal exactly, after all, this is Venice. But there is something truly gorgeously magic, mystic, stunning, and intriguing about it. My cats had definitely never seen a façade like *this* before. But the house, the *palazzo?* Well—to save ourselves some time—let me refer you again to 'some miserable dreams.' *Thick* fucking walls, windowless window-openings *à go-go*, but darkness, gloom, murk, no direct sunlight (which the cats love so much!). Damp, dank, cold, dismal, forlorn, desolate, cut off from any form of human or animal life. No self-respecting mosquito would be caught dead buzzing around a place like this, no bat would ever hang out in its attic. But *I am here*. The dream—still going on and on— gives me *plenty* of time to think: What the fuck have you done! Swapped Arcadia for Hades! Great move. The cats—and you—you'll all catch pneumonia and die, soon, in this place. You JERK—and, eventually, I wake up. *Voilà* my current recurrent dream. Its 'manifest dream content.' I could *all too easily* write a page, or a dozen pages, or a dozen dozens, on the 'latent dream content' here. Namely, the 'meaning.' What the 'moving' dream means. After all, Freud was 64 when he wrote his best book (in my opinion), *Beyond the Pleasure Principle*, and I'm 61. We both have vast dream experience. But this is a ramble, not a treatise. Write the treatise for yourself, if the spirit moves you. Actually, I didn't have—I haven't had—the 'moving' dream too often. Luckily. It is indeed an intricate and intriguing dream, but I don't like it at all. I do see the 'mystic' façade (of the *palazzo*, in the dream), it saves me a trip to the Taj Mahal. But the 'moving' dream is horrible, there is something downright *sinister* about it. It worries me. Luckily I've had this dream far less frequently (knock on wood) than the 'unfinished' or the 'packing' recurrent dreams. As I see it, this dream is, quite simply, a threat: If you ever do anything *that* stupid, well, fuck you. Pay up. In this sense, it is not a 'bad' dream. There's a 'positive' spirit here. A touch of Freudian 'Eros.' But, as you may know, Kafka, not Freud, is my guiding spirit. 'Logic is doubtless unshakable, but it cannot withstand a man who wants to go on living.'

Freud redux: death wish

If you recall, after rereading *On Dreams* (twice) I was perplexed about a couple of things. Wish fulfillment, for example. Since, for the life of me, I can't seem to find any in my own outrageously many dreams. And that neat idea about 'dreams the guardians of sleep'—shit, I call them the *butchers of sleep*. (Despite my love for butchers.) Destroyers, killers, vandals, assassins, stranglers — terrorists, lynch mobs, drawers and quarterers — veritable *tarrers and featherers* of sleep. This, indeed, is why I asked my question in the first place: Why Dream? All things considered, the question is reasonable enough, and Freud's answers are entertaining but, up to now, what have they been worth? To me anyway. But *Beyond the Pleasure Principle*, written in 1920, some twenty years after the short and long dream books, is truly superior entertainment. What's more, it brings up two new things that give food for thought. We might call the first of the two things the 'smaller' thing, and the second the 'really big one.' But appearances can be deceiving. The second, of course, is the discovery/invention of what Freud calls, as you've noted, *Todestrieb*. The official translation of this is 'death instinct' or, sometimes, 'death drive.' On occasion, it's referred to as Thanatos, as opposed to Eros, the life instinct. Since I like to be fanciful from time to time, I also like to call it 'death wish,' as an homage to those Freudian Charles Bronson films. This seems to fit so well into the *big dream idea* (which we shall *never* get away from) of wish fulfillment, and wishing in general. Anyway, a quick Freudian example of *Todestrieb*. Our coach! He's already lost ten straight. He has a wife and four little kids who need a roof over their heads and spinach on their plates. And now he dreams he loses the eleventh. 9 to 1! Ergo, deploying our new Freudian terminology, we say he has a 'death wish.' Possibly. (We'll see. Perhaps.) But I want to begin with the first thing, the 'smaller' one, which Freud calls 'compulsion to repeat.' (Or 'compulsive repetition,' or 'repetition compulsion'—as you wish.) This time, strangely enough, the first thing will lead us straight to the second. Unshakable logic. (But tricky.) The flesh-and-blood book, *Beyond the Pleasure Principle* (standard edition in paperback), opens (p. 3) with this awesome sentence: 'In the theory of psycho-analysis we have no hesitation in assuming that the course taken by mental events is automatically regulated by the pleasure principle.' Beautiful. Crystal clear. Even the second sentence is not all that muddy: 'We believe, that is to say, that the course of those events is invariably set in motion by an unpleasurable tension, and that it takes a direction such that its final outcome coincides with a lowering of that tension—that is, with the avoidance of unpleasure or a production of pleasure.' Please ponder this carefully. *Might* it have something to do with Freud's peculiar notion of the *function* of dreams? 'Unpleasure' is a pretty strange word, it's a tribute to translational consistency: *Lust—Unlust*. Pleasure—unpleasure. As far as I can tell, what it really means is *pain*, in the broadest sense of the word. Freud, however, is very precise—and technical: 'unpleasure corresponds to an *increase* in the quantity of excitation and pleasure to a *diminution* … the mental apparatus endeavors to keep the quantity of excitation present in it as low as possible or at least to keep it constant.' (pp. 4 and 5).

This is a key point for Freud. This point about 'excitation.' He presents it *very* scientifically—but—what does it really *mean?* He bases his definition of *consciousness* on it! 'What consciousness yields consists essentially of *perceptions of excitations* coming from the external world and of feelings of pleasure and unpleasure which can only arise from within the mental apparatus' (p. 26, my italics). And, for Freud, from consciousness it is a small step—or, rather, *no* step at all—to the *unconscious*. 'The unconscious—that is to say, the "repressed"—' (p. 20). *Voilà!* The 'repressed.' Namely, the unconscious. Great! From 'excitations'—to—'consciousness'—to—the 'unconscious'/the 'repressed.' Perfect. But, as Freud tells us—and say what you will, goddamit, Freud is an HONEST MAN—*we know nothing of the nature of the excitatory process that takes place in the elements of the psychical systems.*' (p. 35, all my italics). Holy shit. Did you read that! Well, listen, we shall get back to my question that I have referred to, repeatedly, as *the* question—namely, What is consciousness?—a little later. We'll follow Freud for now. But let me just say this. For the moment. Siggy bases consciousness on 'excitation' and then says, openly, that he don't know what excitation *is*. Then, happy as a lark, he goes right on to the *UN*-conscious. Well, may I ask: Isn't this a little like—say—*inventing* an animal called—let's say—a 'zat' and then writing a treatise on what it is like *not* to be a zat? But Freud, as usual, muddies the waters even more. He refers to 'the type of process found in the unconscious as the "*primary*" psychical process, in contradistinction to the "*secondary*" process which is the one obtaining in our normal waking life.' [By which he means?? In consciousness? Or what? Or where?] (p. 41, my italics). So much the better. What we actually have, then, is a treatise on what it is like *not* to be a zat, *followed* by the invention of the 'zat' itself. Double wow. Believe me, we shall get back to this. Somehow. Definitely. But first, let's see how Freud attempted to wriggle out of his problems caused by the discovery/invention of the 'compulsion to repeat' by discovering/inventing the 'death wish' (i.e. instinct). But you'll see—someday—I hope—that maybe the real problem is that no one takes the question 'What is consciousness?' *seriously*. As I do! (For whatever good it'll do me.) From Aristotle, to Descartes, to Hegel, to Freud, to Thomas Nagel and the galloping hordes of Philosophers of Mind, everybody *talks* about consciousness but nobody *does* anything about it. That's why they can't figure out *why I dream what I dream* or, basically and fundamentally, answer my question: Why Dream? But this ramble (alas) is (pretty) far from over and, as Yogi Berra said, It ain't over till it's over. (One of our Italian coaches, Giovanni Trapattoni, famously said the same thing—but quite *Italianly*: 'Don't say cat till you've got it in the sack.')

Meanwhile, *Beyond the Pleasure Principle* is a great book. It's short, with great stuff on practically every page. I just love Chapter II, for example, which opens with still more extremely memorable lines:

> A condition has long been known and described which occurs after severe mechanical concussions, railway disasters and other accidents involving risk to life; it has been given the name of 'traumatic neurosis.' The terrible war which has just ended gave rise to a great number of illnesses of this kind, but it at least put an end to the temptation to attribute the cause of the disorder to organic lesions of the nervous system brought about by mechanical force. (p. 10).

No! Freud says, it is not 'organic lesions' that cause these 'traumatic neuroses.' Neither is it fear (*Furcht*) or even anxiety (*Angst*). No! The cause is *surprise* and *fright* (*Schreck*). And—what's more—listen to this—'a wound or injury inflicted simultaneously works as a rule *against* the development of a neurosis.' (p. 11). Fantastic. You really have to hand it to Freud, he worked hard his whole life, and discovered/invented a whale of a lot of things. This one means you'll be more traumatized by seeing the soldier next to you *suddenly* blown to smithereens by some Moby Dick of a land mine than by stepping on an itty-bitty land mine yourself. (On the condition, *bien sûr*, that you survive.) I love this page. Great thinking here, no bullshitting about football coaches like I do. Then, in the very next paragraph, the Good Doktor lobs a *really big one* right across our bow. Watch out!

Now *dreams* occurring in traumatic neuroses have the characteristic of repeatedly bringing the patient back into the situation of his accident, a situation from which he wakes up in another fright. *This astonishes people far too little.* (p. 11, my italics).

Now, why does it astonish people far too little? Because it would mean that the patient is 'fixated to his trauma,' which, as I see it, is a way of saying *obsessed* with it. Thinking about it *day* and *night*, awake and asleep. But *no*. Suddenly—what a *fright*—we find ourselves up to our necks in waters so muddy that—much later in Freud's book—only a *death wish* can save us.

I am not aware, however, that patients suffering from traumatic neurosis are much occupied in their waking lives with memories of their accident. Perhaps they are more concerned with *not* thinking about it. Anyone who accepts it as something self-evident that their dreams should put them back at night into the situation that caused them to fall ill has misunderstood the nature of dreams. It would be more in harmony with their nature if they showed the patient pictures from his healthy past or of the cure for which he hopes. If we are not to be shaken in our belief in the wish-fulfilling tenor of dreams by the dreams of traumatic neurotics, we still have one resource open to us: we may argue that the function of dreaming, like so much else, is upset in this condition and diverted from its purposes, or we may be driven to reflect on the mysterious masochistic trends of the ego. (p. 12).

Freud! *What a man!* What a paragraph! (And I am *not* referring to 'the mysterious masochistic trends of the ego.' That's Greek to me.) It's absolutely amazing. In other words—*at last*—it is Freud *himself*, in person, in flesh and blood *Freud*, who asks: *Why Dream?* Or, as I have put it, on occasion, Why Dream *THIS?* What ever became of *Wunscherfüllung?* And the guardians are upset! Somehow they've turned into wolves. Wow. I wish I could report this whole book to you in such detail, blow-by-blow, it's worth it. We're only on page 13 and Siggy has a question that, in the end, only a death wish can answer. Forget Charles Bronson, this is the real McCoy. What's more, as we shall see, he will tell us—'manifestly'—that he is not entirely convinced by his own answer! A major speech on [scientific/psycho-analytic] humility. (At the end of this book.) This is great stuff. Now, let me say one important thing. Some—superficial—readers have seen our second book as a partial, or more than partial, repudiation of the first. Twenty years later, with his children grown up and joyfully eating their spinach, Freud, there in his studio, at his desk, in Vienna, pen on paper again, plunged his dream theory—*Wunscherfüllung*, its very heart!—into the muddy waters of a black lagoon. And then, implausibly, rescued it. No, believe me, it's not that simple, not by a long shot. Neither the plunge nor the rescue is that simple. Not at all. Now—let's look a little more closely at the 'plunge,' and then go on to examine the 'rescue.'

The 'plunge' (Chapter III) is, of course, the discovery/invention of the 'compulsion to repeat,' which is, of course, a first cousin (if not, in fact, the Siamese twin) of the 'traumatic neurosis' we have just been through (so to speak). There's a story here, naturally. Freud tells us how psychoanalysis started out as an art of 'interpreting,' but:

> Since this did not solve the therapeutic problem, a further aim quickly came in view: to oblige the patient to confirm the analyst's construction from his own memory. In that endeavor the chief emphasis lay upon the patient's resistances: the art consisted now in uncovering these as quickly as possible, in pointing them out to the patient and in inducing him by human influence—this was where suggestion operating as 'transference' played its part—to abandon his resistances.
>
> But it became ever clearer that the aim which had been set up— the aim that what was unconscious should become conscious— is not completely attainable by that method. The patient cannot remember the whole of what is repressed in him, and what he cannot remember may be precisely the essential part of it. Thus he acquires no sense of conviction of the correctness of the construction that has been communicated to him. He is obliged to *repeat* the repressed material as a contemporary experience instead of … *remembering* it as something belonging to the past. These reproductions, which emerge with such unwished-for exactitude, always have as their subject some portion of infantile sexual life— (pp. 18-19).

Pardon the long quote. Anyway, so far so good. (Don't worry, we won't get into the parts about 'infantile sexual life,' which is beside my point, which is: Why Dream?) But then—again!—the plot thickens. With this major question: 'But how is the compulsion to repeat—the manifestation of the power of the repressed—related to the pleasure principle?' Followed by this fateful answer: 'We come now to a new and remarkable fact, namely that the compulsion to repeat also recalls from the past *experiences which include no possibility of pleasure*, and which can never, even long ago, have brought satisfaction even to instinctual impulses which have since been repressed.' (p. 21, my italics). Freud's tone is pretty calm but he knows he's in trouble. But what honesty! If we were only talking about *bona fide* Freudian neurotics here (and 'traumatic neurotics' especially), things might not be so bad. But no! The 'compulsion to repeat'—which, we recall, means to repeat 'unpleasurable' a.k.a. *atrocious* 'material'—'can also be observed in the lives of *some* normal people' (p. 23, my italics). *Some?* How about me? (Insofar as I flatter myself to be 'normal.') And my question, Why Dream? And my DREAMS? And this RAMBLE? How about my football coach, with his lovely spinach-eating family. (Four small children, and they all eat their spinach.) A fine, upstanding, 'normal' person, with his livelihood on the line, after ten losses in a row, and ye gods he dreams about losing the eleventh 9 to 1! And does! (4 to 1.) Finally, he gets fired. (Not fired up, which he already was. Just fired.) And then he keeps on dreaming about it. Compulsively, repetitively, 9 to 1 every time. A normal guy. A great and extremely *simpatico* person. What in the world ever became of his dreams! Showing him *pictures from his healthy past or of the cure for which he hopes.* Such as finally *winning* a fucking game. Did he buy a ticket for the wrong movie theater? What do I know. I like Freud. I like this coach. (Even if, it's true, he brought my team to total disaster.) (But it was the players, on the field, who seemed to be dreaming, not the coach. Behold, these dreamers cometh. Come now therefore and let us slay them! With their enormous salaries and ludicrous, grisly, and gruesome playing.) Sorry, carried away. Next year in Jerusalem. But—Freud. As I was saying, all this, alas, leads him to make—in his flesh-and-blood book, his, in my humble opinion, most marvelous book—this confession:

> If we take into account observations such as these, based upon behavior in the transference and upon the life-histories of men and women [such as myself, and my coach], we shall find courage to assume that there really does exist in the mind a compulsion to repeat which overrides the pleasure principle. Now too we shall be inclined to relate to this compulsion the dreams which occur in traumatic neuroses… (p. 24).

In the conclusion of this chapter (Chapter III), his tones are tinged with tragedy: 'Enough [*alas*] is left unexplained to justify the hypothesis of a compulsion to repeat—something that seems more primitive, more elementary, more instinctual than the pleasure principle which it overrides.' (p. 25).

High drama here. Really. Well, after *all* this, Chapter IV is itself a magnificent chapter. Alas, for the sake of brevity (if not of soul, or of wit) I shall skip directly to its *dramatic* conclusion. (A little long, but bear with me.) High drama.

> This would seem to be the place, then, at which to admit for the first time an exception to the proposition that dreams are fulfillments of wishes. Anxiety dreams, as I have shown repeatedly and in detail,

offer no such exception. Nor do 'punishment dreams,' for they merely replace the forbidden wish-fulfillment by the appropriate punishment for it; that is to say, they fulfill the wish of the sense of guilt which is the reaction to the repudiated impulse. But it is impossible to classify as wish-fulfillments the dreams we have been discussing which occur in traumatic neuroses, or the dreams during psychoanalysis which bring to memory the psychical traumas of childhood. [How about the dreams in 'the lives of *some* normal people'?] They arise, rather, in obedience to the compulsion to repeat, though it is true that in analysis that compulsion is supported by the *wish* (which is encouraged by suggestion) to conjure up what has been forgotten and repressed. Thus it would seem that *the function of dreams*, which consists in setting aside any motives that might interrupt sleep, by fulfilling the wishes of the disturbing impulses, is not their *original* function. It would not be possible for them to perform that function until the whole of mental life had accepted the dominance of the pleasure principle. If there is a 'beyond the pleasure principle,' it is only consistent to grant that there was also a time before the purpose of dreams was the fulfillment of wishes. (pp. 37-38).

If this isn't a mouthful, what is! Gentle reader, did you get the Really Big One, right there at the end? *A time before*—but Siggy, pray tell, *what time was that?!* Help! And—behold—then he 'rescues' us. Right in this dire strait. With a *stunning gambit* worthy of Bobby Fisher (at his best). *Instincts.* The 'time before' is *instinct time.* Wow.

Let's go on. Just think, we are just half-way through the book. Just made it to Chapter V, which we might call '*The Rescue* of Freud's General Theory of the Psyche including his Theory of Dreams.' But from now on I'm going to *race* right to the end, even if it's a damn shame, there are so many real pearls here. Just look at the beginning of Chapter V.

The most abundant sources of this internal excitation are what are described as the organism's 'instincts'—the representatives of all the forces originating in the interior of the body and transmitted to the mental apparatus—at once the most important and the most obscure element of psychological research. (p. 40).

The most important and the most obscure. Pardon, again, my compulsive repetition—again. But, you can say *that* again, Siggy. 'Excitation' again— when, *as we know*, 'we know nothing of the nature of the excitatory process that takes place in the elements of the psychical systems.' Great. But the point—as we already know—is this: Freud *SUDDENLY* (*Schreck!*) discovers/

invents the death instinct and saves the day. (And night, morning, afternoon, and evening.) Saves us (?), and—above all—saves his theory. Sort of. More or less. *Todestrieb.* Truly an ingenious idea. What's more, *I believe there's a grain of truth in it.* The problem is *what* grain? And *what* truth? (And *what* salt? No, sorry, the salt was on the table d'hôte.) Alas I shall say few words about this, just (barely) enough to give you a basic idea about this *truly ingenious idea,* which would richly deserve an *entire ramble of its own.* (Some other time, perhaps.) In any event, let me say that, in the shrink field, these chapters on *Todestrieb* are my second cat's favorite reading. Her great loves, of course, are Parmenides, Thomas Bernhard, Mozart operas, Bach, and especially Thelonious Monk. Gilda and Monk have the same birthday, October 10th. But my first cat— *alas!*—adores Lacan. Just imagine! Gina can't get enough of Lacan.

At this point, in just a few pages—just a few lines—Freud tells us about his *discovery* of the death instinct. (He is referring here to 'the facts of embryology' and he'll also get into germs and amoebas, but we know what he's thinking about.) (And it's not the sex life of amoebas, or their dreams either.) Let us follow Freud's words here. Listen! The rest is—no! not silence. It's controversy.

> *It seems, then, that an instinct is an urge inherent in organic life to restore an earlier state of things* which the living entity has been obliged to abandon under the pressure of external disturbing forces; that is, it is a kind of organic elasticity, or, to put it another way, the expression of the inertia inherent in organic life. This view of instincts strikes us as strange because we have become used to see in them a factor impelling towards change and development, whereas we are now asked to recognize in them the precise contrary—an expression of the *conservative* nature of living substance. (p. 43).

The elementary living entity would from its very beginning have had no wish to change; if conditions remained the same, it would do no more than constantly repeat the same course of life. [This is Gilda's favorite line!] … Every modification which is thus imposed upon the course of the organism's life is accepted by the conservative organic instincts and stored up for further repetition. These instincts are therefore bound to give a deceptive appearance of being forces tending towards change and progress, whilst in fact they are merely seeking to reach an ancient goal by paths alike old and new. Moreover it is possible to specify this final goal of all organic striving. It would be in contradiction to the conservative nature of the instincts if the goal of life were a state of things which had never yet been attained. On the contrary, it must be an *old* state of things, an initial state from which the living entity has at one time or another departed and to which it is striving to return by the circuitous paths along which the development leads. If we are to take it as a truth that everything living dies for *internal* reasons—becomes inorganic once again—then we shall be compelled to say that '*the aim of all life is death*' and, looking backwards, that '*inanimate things existed before living ones.*' (p. 46).

Did we follow that? It's heavy stuff. What it all boils down to is that the 'first instinct' was/is 'the instinct to return to the inanimate state.' In other words, *to die.* (To die—to sleep;— To sleep! perchance to dream... no!no!no! We already know that.) The 'first instinct' is/was the death instinct. We devise 'ever more complicated *detours* before reaching [our] aim of death. These circuitous paths to death, faithfully kept to by the conservative instincts, would thus present us to-day with the picture of the phenomena of life.' (p. 46). And with this the Excellent Doktor pretty much rests his case. *What* case? Damn good question. He has explained how 'compulsive repetition,' which contradicts dream *Wunscherfüllung*, can be accounted for by *Todestrieb*. (Somehow.) (He also pointedly remarks that 'the sexual instincts' are *highly conservative*, which fits excellently into his general theory.) It's a neat idea (as someone once said). No, it's a brilliant idea actually and—if you read the book—you'll see that it's presented quite scientifically. From the germ to the psyche! 'Protozoa too are mortal,' Freud discovers. We are introduced to 'a ciliate infusorian, the "slipper-animalcule," which reproduces by fission into two individuals, persisted until the 3029th generation (at which point [the biologist] broke off the experiment).' (pp. 56-57). Let us not forget that the basis of it all is 'chemical tensions' and, of course, 'excitations'. Freud, meanwhile, has so humbly told us that 'we know nothing of the nature of [this] excitatory process.' Strange science. You base everything on something you know nothing about. I hated Freud for forty years because I always considered him a myth-maker. (There are a number of his books that I still absolutely can't stand.) A teller of tall tales. Snake oil. But this second book, which I have reread twice in the past two weeks, as you know, is a fine tail. An awesome example of a cat chasing her tail. Beautifully told. Beautifully chased.

> This tallies well with the hypothesis that the life process of the individual leads for internal reasons to an abolition of chemical tensions, that is to say, to death, whereas union with the living substance of a different individual increases these tensions, introducing what may be described as fresh 'vital differences,' which must then be lived off. As regards this dissimilarity there must of course be one or more optima. The dominating tendency of mental life, and perhaps of nervous life in general, is the effort to reduce, to keep constant or to remove internal tension due to stimuli—a

tendency which finds expression in the pleasure principle; and our recognition of that fact is one of our strongest reasons for believing in the existence of death instincts. (p. 67).

An eel. Tricky reasoning and muddy waters. But I don't hate Freud anymore. I still may not love him but I do respect him. Plenty. Why Dream? Has he helped me answer my question? I wish I knew. I have to think about it. The ramble abides. The jury is out. Need more time to think. But look at how Doktor Freud concludes this book, with an attestation of humility (both scientific and personal) that, to my ear, has a ring of genuine and deep sincerity. So, here's our last quote from Freud. It's a damn good one.

It may be asked whether and how far I am myself convinced of the truth of the hypotheses that have been set out in these pages. My answer would be that I am not convinced myself and that I do not seek to persuade other people to believe in them. Or, more precisely, that I do not know how far I believe in them. There is no reason, as it seems to me, why the emotional factor of conviction should enter into this question at all. It is surely possible to throw oneself into a line of thought and follow it wherever it leads out of simple scientific curiosity, or, if the reader prefers, as an *advocatus diaboli*, who is not on that account himself sold to the devil. I do not dispute the fact that the third step in the theory of the instincts, which I have taken here, cannot lay claim to the same degree of certainty as the two earlier ones—the extension of the concept of sexuality and the hypothesis of narcissism. These two innovations were a direct translation of observation into theory and were no more open to sources of error than is inevitable in all such cases. It is true that my assertion of the regressive character of instincts also rests upon observed material— namely on the facts of the compulsion to repeat. *It may be, however, that I have overestimated their significance.* And in any case it is impossible to pursue an idea of this kind except by repeatedly combining factual material with what is purely speculative and thus diverging widely from empirical observation. The more frequently this is done in the course of constructing a theory, the more untrustworthy, as we know, must be the final result. (pp. 71-72, my italics).

I like this humility. It's not self-criticism, it's humility. It's important. Here is my conclusion. If what Freud has been trying to say, without quite knowing how to articulate it, in the language of psychoanalysis he himself invented, is that not only life and death instincts, drives, and wishes, but life and death themselves are separate but inseparable—then yes, in that sense I'll most certainly go for it. My absolute master, Hegel, has been trying to teach me what this means for over forty years now. The inseparability of life and death. Of freedom and necessity. This ramble is not over yet. I hope to say something about Hegel, later. Not much later. About consciousness, which in my most humble opinion was not his strongest suit. Logic was. But are they inseparable? (This is Kafka's question.) What is consciousness? Well, when I practice Zen meditation, if there are words in my mind at all, they are these two words: On the in-breath, life. On the out-breath, death. Where do we begin? No matter! Suzuki-roshi, my Zen master, says: We exhale completely. We follow the out-breath. In every moment we follow death and, following death, we live life, which are not two, and not one. Inseparable.

> an abyss of dreams
> my body a fragile flower
> my hands no hands
> until they pick up flowers
> and offer them to the Buddha

[My gloss on a verse by Hui-neng, the Sixth Patriarch of Zen in China.]

the 'fingers' dream

Two nights ago I had the strangest dream of this entire month. Again, the last in a series. But no connection with anything. With nothing in this series of dreams, of which this was the last. But, also, no connection with *anything*. Still, I have a feeling that there is something very important in this dream. Something I need to figure out. Let me report it. It was around 9 or 10 in the morning (in the dream and in fact) and the cat woke me up. She was making strange whimpering sounds and doing little hip-hops at the foot of the bed, looking down at the tan-carpeted floor. I've learned to take the visions of cats seriously. Strangely enough, if they *seem* to be looking at something they *are* looking at something, though it might be a miniscule speck of dust floating in the air. (Or, it's often been a scorpion.) So, I sat up, switched on the 'night lamp' next to my bed (a lamp with a weak bulb and deep-purple lampshade), and looked down at the floor. (My bed is very low, just a foot above floor-level.) Now what the FUCK is that! The cat leaped off the bed and dashed downstairs. On the carpet at the foot of the bed I saw a whole row of ...... fingers. *Fingers.* And well-manicured, it seemed, the nails shimmering in the purplish light. At least a dozen of them, more or less. Lined up in a row, Indian file. Even in the dim light I could clearly see they were fingers—or actually half-fingers. Just the part from above the knuckle to the tip. Not *lying* on the carpet but standing straight up. As if they'd sprouted there like mushrooms. I swear, this was too much. And they were moving slightly. As much as a *live* half-finger can move. So, with very considerable courage I bent over and actually picked one up. It was a perfectly normal half-finger. A very nice-looking half-finger, actually. Fine, white, with quite an exquisite fingernail. It was moving slowly as I held it up to the dim light. The bottom, where it had presumably been cut off, severed—detached somehow—from the rest of the original finger and from its original hand was simply flat. There was absolutely nothing gruesome about it. I put it back down on its spot on the carpet. I could see at a glance that all the half-fingers were slightly different. Especially the nails. I mean, I could tell they were not from the same hand. (Besides, there was at least a dozen of them.) But it was at this point that a tidal wave of anxiety hit me. And *this* was the point. What the fuck was I going to *do?!*

It was the loneliness and isolation that really hit me. I've been living in this house in this courtyard in Venice for some 35 years. I used to have wonderful neighbors in the courtyard and many friends all over the town. But my old friends have died, or moved away. I've tried, but have not been able to make real contact with the younger people living around me. Practically no contact at all. Neighbors? 'Ciao.' That's all. So what was I to do about these fingers on my carpet? Call the police, or the Carabinieri? I guess so, I thought. But—it's crazy. I got out of bed and, for a start, tried to put on my pants. I couldn't do it! I got my pants all twisted around, my legs all tangled up, I was *paralyzed!* The half-fingers glimmered at me in the dim light. Then—suddenly—my cat jumped on me screaming and woke me up. For the past few days, since it's turned colder and the house is cold in the morning, she gets up earlier and—in fact—jumps on me around 10 and screams for her breakfast. (Her mixture—just 20 grams—of 'Mature Adult 7+ Senior Active Longevity' and 'Light — 17% Calorie Reduction.' She's only 8 but very lazy, she used to get more exercise.) Ravenously hungry. So I got up and gave it to her and then went back to bed. Totally exhausted. Gripped by a terrible anxiety. It wasn't the fingers themselves. It was the solitude. The isolation. I'm sure that Freud would pounce on the fingers as phallic symbols, little penises swaying in the breeze. It wasn't that at all. This *very* strange dream. What shook me up so much afterwards was the solitude, the fact that I didn't have a friend anymore who would come right over and help me. Help me figure out what to *do about* these fingers. That was the point. I lay there for an hour. Even my friend who had the wine shop at the corner moved out last year. R. would have been a good enough person to look for (if only I could get my pants on). But even if R. had come, or the Carabinieri, or my greatly beloved dead neighbor Veniero, perhaps the fingers wouldn't be there. Maybe they were strictly dream-fingers. My-dream fingers. After all, we are talking about a dream. (But Why Dream?!) Then again, in the dream, the Carabinieri too would be dream-Carabinieri. My-dream Carabinieri. R. would have been my-dream R., not the real R. But

still, *IN* in-the-dream, the fingers, the dream-fingers, the my-dream fingers …
it was a philosophical impasse. An abyss. A shadow's shadow.

Lying there I actually figured out what that recurrent 'paralysis' means in my
dreams. At last, after all these years and decades. It was so simple. It is quite
simply my attempt to *get out* of the dream. To wake up. The great effort to
wake up. Suddenly!—Satori.

> Awake! For Morning in the Bowl of Night
> Has flung the Stone that puts the Stars to Flight:
>   And Lo! the Hunter of the East has caught
> The Sultán's Turret in a Noose of Light.

Anyway, I had been awake for an hour when I *got* up and opened the shutters.
No fog today. There was a pale sun. No half-fingers in a row on the carpet.
The cat happily digesting her breakfast at the foot of the bed. But what about
those fingers? Who can forget them now. Why? Why Dream?

I think this 'fingers' dream is one of the few *really* important dreams of
the millions I have had. Before the end of this ramble I intend to tell you
about a dream I had in Budapest in 1974 that I've always called 'the tiny
dream gymnasts.' It's a dream, basically, about making a supreme effort, but
without striving to achieve or to gain anything. A dream that overwhelmed
me at the time. In some sense it has been decisive for the entire course of
my life. More—qualitatively more—than any of my other dreams. But the
'fingers' dream, too, will be important to me for the rest of my life. Certainly
not because of the grotesqueness of these fingers—half-fingers—lined up
in a row at the foot of my bed. It's because of something I've learned from
this dream, thinking about it for these past two days. This dream isn't really
about fingers at all. Half-fingers, phalluses. I think it's about sociality and
solitude. About the fact that certain strange—radically inexplicable—
things *do happen* in the life of an individual. (As in the 'life' of a society or a
nation.) Such things—seemingly so private—are instead profoundly public.
If something *truly anomalous exists, it is public.* That's why the dream was
really about *looking for help.* Not just falling back on one's self, one's own
ego, however capable we may be of doing it, and saying, What the fuck!
A dozen half-fingers lined up on the carpet at the foot of my bed. How
about *that.* No! This is eminently—paradoxically—something that must,
by its very nature, *be shared.* This was the point of the dream. What it was
about. And about the fact that with all my strenuous effort to live *in this
world* (what other world is there?)—to live *with other people*—I have failed.
I *have learned* that the private and the public are inseparable, but I have not
put into practice what I have learned. Two dreams, almost forty years apart.

My life. From the extreme effort (to no *end*) of 'the tiny dream gymnasts' to this extreme loss of sociality ('The End'). These dreams have spoken to me. But have they answered my question, Why Dream? I, of all dreamers, am absolutely convinced that the world is not a dream. Life is not a dream. These dreams actually exist. So do my two cats (even if consecutively and not concurrently). So do I. Have I found a *reason* to dream? I don't know. I don't think so. Or have I? Only you can tell me. Tell me if you see what I mean about these my-dream half-fingers. If *you* see what I mean, then, eureka! we absolutely *must* dream. *All* of us. But, still, Why Dream? Can it be because the most *private* thing we do is also the most *public?* What do I mean? How should I know. I don't know.

When I was a kid I used to read *Hamlet* a lot. A whole lot. Right up to forty years ago. Then I stopped. Completely. What shameless seduction! As shameless as it was 'bootless.' What's *really* going on here. What's all this. (Act II Scene II.) A rant.

> Hamlet: O God, I could be bounded in a nutshell, and count myself a king of infinite space, were it not that I have bad dreams.
>
> Guildenstern: Which dreams, indeed, are ambition; for the very substance of the ambitious is merely the shadow of a dream.
>
> Hamlet: A dream itself is but a shadow.
>
> Rosencrantz: Truly, and I hold ambition of so airy and light a quality, that it is but a shadow's shadow.
>
> Hamlet: Then are our beggars bodies, and our monarchs and outstretch'd heroes the beggars' shadows. Shall we to th' court? for, by my fay, I cannot reason.

But the Prince has a real point there, when he says 'I cannot reason.' Like me just now, with my 'my-dream Carabinieri.' No question. If the 'fingers' dream itself 'is but a shadow,' if the fingers in my dream are a shadow's shadow, then what in the world could I ask of the Carabinieri if I called them *IN* the/my dream? To come and help me out with this shadow's shadows lined up on the floor and moving slightly!? But the Carabinieri—if they ever showed up—in the dream (because I call them and tell them, Help! I have a dozen half-fingers standing at the foot of my bed) would, most definitely, be, themselves, shadows. *Of what?* Perchance of a shadow's shadow. Shadows of a shadow's shadows. No, Hamlet is quite right, 'reason' gets us nowhere here. It gets all tangled up, like my legs in the dream. And if I called the

Carabinieri *after I woke up* from the dream? Well at least we can reason about *this* and say it would be *unreasonable* in a big way, and would probably get me carted off to a madhouse.

Hold your horses. Let's slow down for a moment. As we know, the word 'shadow' has many meanings. It's been used in a thousand ways, and their opposites. On the whole, I think it has been stuck with a bad rap. 'A dream itself is but a shadow.' Don't you find this demeaning? I do. Shadows, traditionally, have been seen as inferior, dark, and menacing. To be 'shadowed' by someone in some dark shadowy street, with its dark shadows, is not a pleasant experience. (For Freud, definitely a cause of 'unpleasure.') (Jung: the *shadow self.* Deep shit.) 'Shadow' is the part of the picture we cannot make out—something unsubstantial and, therefore, quite possibly illusory. 'A freedom more shadow than substance.' 'He lived in his father's shadow.' 'He's the shadow of his former self.' The dark shadows beneath the insomniac's eyes. Then, from bad to worse. A shadow on her lungs in the X-ray. The shadow of war. And, worse still, shadow as a source of indefinable, unidentifiable fear, dread, anxiety. Less terrible, but still not good, 'shadow' as a metaphor for something we desire but that escapes us. That we cannot catch, cannot get hold of. The 'fleeting.' In a bad sense. What a bad name 'shadow' has. Even when it's 110 degrees (Fahrenheit, hopefully), we go looking for shade, not shadow. Shade trees, not 'shadow trees.' (Sounds like something in the *Twilight Zone.*) What a *bad name.* For me it's a bad rap. I love shadows but, I have to admit, it's a question of personal preference. *Perhaps* my love for shadows even has to do, in some way, with my university experience with Ancient Greek—no! Forget it. *Leave that dream alone* That miserable '*unfinished*' dream. That *rotten shadow.* I *did* take *all* my Greek exams, I *did* write a pile of papers, *including finishing* that one on the Soul in Ancient Greece and in the Ashanti (even if it's disappeared), I *did* graduate from NYU, with a degree in Ancient Greek. So, listen, *don't mess with me!* Not about graduating and not about Ancient Greek either. No, sorry, it's late at night for a rant. Calmly and, if possible, philosophically, I wish to make a minor point. Let's do some philology. The ancient, and, strangely enough, also modern, Greek word for 'shadow' is *skiá*: shadow, shade, hence ghost, specter of the dead. Later coming to mean *shade,* meaning the *shade of a tree.* (It's always been *very hot* in Greece, especially in the summer.) But 'shade' is a famous word in Homer, and I don't mean the shade of a tree. (As we shall see, in just *one* minute.) This brings us to a first-cousin word, namely, *eidolon.* A *big complicated* word. (Especially because of Plato, with his variety of Big Ideas.) First of all, *eidolon* comes, simply, from *eido*: 'I see.' *See* what I mean! *See* that cat? It originally meant 'shape,' 'image' (*big* word), 'specter' (*big* again), phantom. *Shade.* No, not of the tree, but the famous 'shades' in Hades. *Eidolon* then came to signify an 'image in the mind.' A vision. (Plato had lots of them.) And, last if possibly not least, the image or portrait of a god, hence an *idol, a false god*, which is something that has riled up zillions of monotheists for thousands of years. But, shit! I wanted to make a point here (however insignificant), what in the world was it—yes! About *shadow* (and/or shade, as you like, they're only *words*) in *Homer*. At this time of night and at this point of this ramble I feel an almost desperate need for some poetry. Without it, perhaps, I can't go on. And Homer was a *great* poet. In my opinion, Homer and Ezra Pound were the two greatest poets of all time. What's more, in my opinion a poem is the first cousin of a dream. Ever think about *that!* Poetic work and dream work are *cousins*. This chance combination of circumstances—shadows, shades, dreams, poetry—made me think of one of *the* most moving scenes in the history of literature, thought, poetry, and entertainment. (No! Not 'moving' in the sense of the 'moving' dream. Moving vans. Moving from Jersey City to Kansas City.) I mean Book XI of the *Odyssey*. To which one translator, Robert Fitzgerald, gave the poetic title 'A Gathering of Shades.' Homer is speaking here about the shades of the dead in Erebos, which is the first stop after death before they reach the end of the line, the *pit* of Hades. The abyss. The very bottom. The first lines of the first *Canto* is Pound's truly extraordinary *rendition* (*no! not* in the sense it's been used lately, of kidnapping Muslims and flying them off to dungeons to be tortured) of the beginning of this Book XI:

> And then went down to the ship,
> Set keel to breakers, forth on the godly sea, and
> We set up mast and sail on that swart ship,
> Bore sheep aboard her, and our bodies also
> Heavy with weeping, and winds from sternward
> Bore us out onward with bellying canvas,
> Circe's this craft, the trim-coifed goddess.

Ye gods I needed that! A ramble without poetry is no ramble. What's more, this is a *therapeutic* ramble. We need more poetry! Meanwhile, the story here, very briefly, is that Odysseus and the few men he's got left decide to give up *la dolce vita* with Circe, that tricky sorceress, and continue their problematic odyssey in search of Ithaca. Circe tells Odysseus, Your best bet for the trip is to sail to Erebos to speak with the shade/shadow/soul/spirit of Tiresias the prophet, who will tell you how to get home. (In fact it turned out to be a hot tip.) So off they sail, all the way to the River of Ocean, where they pour libations and perform sacrifices and, by god! 'the blurred and breathless dead' (Fitzgerald)—the shades—did indeed gather to speak with Odysseus. Tiresias showed up, followed by Odysseus' mother, and Agamemnon. And then, in the most famous scene of all, Achilles, strongest of all the Greeks! who looks daggers at life in Erebos (and he hasn't even seen Hades yet). Odysseus quite foolishly shoots his mouth off, and says, in my ramble-style rendition: 'Hey, Achilles, you lucky man! You were number one when you were alive, and now you're King of all the shades!' (Or shadows, or whatever you want to call them.) Achilles is furious. Pissed off as all hell. From ramble to *rumble*. 'Don't bullshit me about death, Odysseus, you tricky dicky man. I'd rather be a slave on earth than lord of these exhausted souls. These pathetic breathless blurs. Shit! Being a shadow down here in Erebos is *the pits.*'

What in the world is the point of this ramble/rumble in the ramble? I told you it was a *minor* point. Half this tiny point is that I often dream about Achilles down there in that *pit* full of *shadows*. And *pits* remind me of *Joseph*, 'this dreamer,' in the Bible ('cast him into some pit'). (Watch out, I'm coming to him soon.) Hegel—we're coming to him *very* soon—wrote the greatest *pit* pages of all time. About a 'nightlike pit [shaft, mine, abyss] within which a world of infinitely many images is preserved without being in consciousness.' (This is in his 'mature' work, the *Encyclopaedia of the Philosophical Sciences*, § 453. There's an even more spectacular 'look' at the abyss—*the night of the world*—in a work of his youth, the *Jena Philosophy of Spirit*.) A half page later he refers to it as 'this unconscious abyss.' *Unconscious*. A century before Freud. This, indeed, is the abyss where breathless shadows swarm. It's also what I've called 'an abyss of dreams.' Why Dream? Hegel may have a better answer to this than anyone else. But Hegel's hard to follow. We'll see.

Meanwhile, the other half of my tiny minor point. I wanted to ask Achilles—a genuine plain speaker! a friend! a dream! a fellow dreamer!—what do *you* call all those guys down there in the pit, alas, with you? Do you call them shades? So, I asked him. And he answered me. Vigorously. 'Shades my ass! Shades are those fancy glasses you put on when there's too much sun. Down here we sunless dead don't have a single ray of light. Let me have a sip of that slaughtered sacrificial sheep, before old man Tiresias laps it all up like a dog!' And he strong with the blood, said then: 'Trust Ezra Pound, he always knows the right word.' Thank you swift-footed Achilles! Full of wrath. Strongest of the Greeks. A dream! Where are you now! And—'strong with blood'— Pound answers, immediately, generously, beautifully, and to the point.

> When, when, and whenever death closes our eyelids,
> Moving naked over Acheron
> Upon one raft, victor and conquered together,
> Marius and Jugurtha together,
> one tangle of shadows.

Nothing shady here. Great poetry. Shadows. The right word.

I must admit that this has been some sort of ramble in the ramble. But now we'll mosey on back in the direction of the ramble proper. The proper ramble.

I still have quite a lot to say about the word 'shadow' and how it's used, and especially about how I *myself* have used it, for some forty years. 'A dream itself is but a shadow.' Ye gods, an *insult* to the dream *and* to the shadow. Hamlet would have done well to keep his trap shut and, in fact, as I said, I stopped reading him forty years ago. 'I cannot reason'—said he—I'll grant him that. *Now*—no more bullshitting—*shadow*. Just think, my all-time favorite use of the word is *very strongly connected* with—of all things—*reason*. Connected by Hegel in person. (My *first* cat adores him. Her *pets,* Hegel and Lacan.) In his flesh-and-blood book—his greatest book—*The Science of Logic*, which, in my opinion, is the supreme expression of reason. (Poor Hamlet, by his fay, 'cannot reason.') The most 'strenuous effort' to express what 'reason' is. In the 'Introduction' Hegel writes: 'The system of logic is the realm of shadows, the world of simple essentialities freed from all sensuous concreteness. The study of this science, to dwell and labor in this shadowy realm, is the absolute culture and discipline of consciousness.' We'll worry about 'consciousness' a little later, when I attempt to tackle *the* question: *What* is consciousness? This 'shadowy realm' of logic is a marvelous realm of *freedom. IN* its inseparability from (Hegelian) logical *necessity*. It's Plato's cave turned upside down and inside out. When I first read this book, forty years ago exactly, I fell in love with this idea of shadow. Ever since, for me, shadow has been an expression of light, brightness, freedom—and of necessity. In Hegel 'shadows' are the terms—the 'categories'—of the logical movement of thinking as such, which some see as 'shaky' logic, but no! *This* logic is unshakable. Precisely because it, itself, *shakes*. In and for itself. Shakes, quivers, and quakes. No! Let us not let this ramble slip into philosophical polemics. What concerns us is the question: Why Dream? Help! Can shadow help? Can *Venice* help?

Meta-memoir. The year before I arrived in Venice I'd been reading Hegel *most of the time.* Shadow as 'simple essentiality.' In Venice, right off the bat, I started talking about shadow *all the time, fino alla noia,* we say in Italian. Ad nauseam. *All the time.* Yes, something like L. in Greece with his infamous 'exo ena oneiro.' But, unlike L., I myself had something quite interesting to say, I've never understood why no one quite got the point at the time. (Or later either.) (My poor *mother* least of all. My shadows *terrified* her.) Well, now's the time. Shadow, ombra, skiá, Schatten. I was referring to the images (*eidola*) you see—if you *look*—on the canals of the city, be they (the canals) 'grand' or small. You see the city's double. The *palazzi*, trees, birds, the moon, you see them all *again*, on the water, but more beautiful. Why? Perhaps because more free. Their substance, their very colors lose all weight, all rigidity, and appear in absolute lightness, mobility—'essentiality,' as Hegel put it. It is simply gorgeous. Breathtaking. To see a Venetian *palazzo* (but even my little house is a *palazzo*) mirrored on a canal, its soft colors quivering on the ripples—there's nothing like it! But you can see wonderful shadows all over, not only in Venice. Last week I went to Padua to see one of my doctors. Standing on an embankment near the Brenta River I saw the shadow of a huge tree (no, not the *shade*) (we don't have any trees that big in Venice) on the light-brown water. What splendor! *This* is shadow. The *image* of the tree on the water. Its sheer essentiality. Still, there is something special about Venetian shadows. It's because of the geography (or geometry) of the canals, like blood vessels branching throughout the body of the city. The entire city is doubled—and freed? No, I guess not actually freed. Definitely not. But, it is something like a dream. *Something* like one. If I see my mother, or P., or my cat, in a dream, they are shadows (or, alas, a shadow's shadows). I guess they are a lot freer than in real life. But I've never noticed any great expressions of freedom in my own dream shadows. They're usually pretty agitated. Upset abut my never finishing college, about wrecking balls, frightened by half-fingers. I think it's because the dream work is such hard labor. The 'strenuous effort' of thinking as such, as Hegel put it. No, but when I take my afternoon walks (if I'm not *too* busy rambling here at home) I always stop for quite a while on the gentle graceful bridge in Campo San Zandegolà (my favorite bridge) and look down at the glistening film of bright shadows on the canal. The *palazzi*, the trees, often the shadows of seagulls, and I see another world. A parallel world. (And at night it is even more beautiful.) A clear world— of consciousness?—with no unconscious, no pit, no abyss. No, not *l'altro mondo*, which is the next world—Erebos, Hades, *death*, call it what you will—but *this* world turned to shadow 'by a great deliverance' (*Genesis*, 45, 7). In the case of Venice this 'deliverance' is no truer than a dream. But, also, no less true. No, the shadows of Venice are no true deliverance. No true freedom. If the *palazzi* crumble, the trees fall, and the birds vanish, we shall see what will become of its shadows. Its dreams. In time. But the *palazzi* have been standing for a long time now. Standing, and crumbling. Freedom. Simple essentialities freed from all sensuous concreteness. Venice, in its shadows, has another world. But it is *this* world, there *is no 'other' world*. Plato was an extremely great philosopher, and a great expert on shadows (and dreams), but not on Venetian shadows, and—shadow for shadow—I prefer Hegel's to Plato's. At the end of Book IX of the *Republic*—his 'dream' of an Ideal City (and of how to construct it)—Plato came to a stunning conclusion. Truly, a high point in the history of thought. It reminds me of waking from a dream. First he says, yes, it's true, there's no spot on earth where this city exists. But then he says: 'But perhaps there is a pattern [a shadow, an image, an idea] set up in the heavens for him who desires to see it and, seeing it, to found a city in himself.' A stunning conclusion. At the end of such a—genuinely—political work. Which has nothing at all to do with the shadows of Venice? Or, perhaps, for me personally, it does. Somehow. Not 'the other world'—no. But, another world. A parallel world. A double. In myself? A city of dreams and shadows. Something that makes a little more sense. But my dreams, my *dream* dreams—as we have seen—certainly don't make much sense. I guess I'm not cut out for the placid wish fulfillment of Freud's table d'hôte. I'm still trying to come up with *some sort* of answer to my question, Why Dream? Have I gotten anywhere? I'll have to keep trying. But how about shadows, 'simple essentialities'? Where have they gotten me? Where do they end? Some people don't realize (some do, of course) that the life of Venice depends on the tides. The tides are everything for this city, its lifeblood. Without them, the city would be a bloodless—stinking—shade, instead of this realm of glimmering shadows. Every day the tide flows in from the Adriatic, strong, powerful, into the fragile city (which is a lot more resilient than it seems), and then ebbs. And then flows. And then ebbs again. Flows, ebbs, flows, ebbs—strongly—twice every single day. The in-breath and the out-breath, constant change, life, death, inseparable. This is what makes the shadows of Venice unique. It's not a question of not passing twice through the same stream. (A friend of mine says you can't even sit twice on the same bank.) No, it's that the water that is the shadow's home is unceasing, infinite, absolute change. A permanent ripple. It's a tricky point actually. Is the shadow always the same (the image)? Or always different (the waters)? Or both? And where do the shadows end? Where do we end? 'Life is a dream,' my grandfather once said.

Bright shadows
dear companions
tangled threads my guide
lead me at last
to the heart of your mystery
to the center of this maze
where love embraces passion
where shadows end
in endless shadow.

Do dreams have a point? A meaning? My major beef with Hamlet is that he says '*but* a shadow.' In light of his very serious problem with dreams he might have done well to take shadows a lot more seriously. To try to have a healthier relationship with them. But, meanwhile, I've been thinking about the 'fingers' dream again. The dream I had two nights ago. Admit it, at first it just gave you a sense of unadulterated *grotesqueness* and *gruesomeness*. But, little by little, I think it's actually proved to have quite a *major point* to make. Could we say that dreams are the most *private* experience of consciousness? Wow, this is a *big* question. Especially because of *the* question, *the unanswered question*: What is consciousness? (We'll have to take a stab at it. Otherwise I have no hope of answering *my* question: Why Dream?) But, then, the *stunning* message of the 'fingers' dream is that the most *private* thing we do (dream) is also the most *public*. Why? For some 'reason' that only the *effect* of the dream can explain. (Explain?) What did/do I mean by this? OK, I'm going to shoot one by you now. Watch out! Remember the Big Bang? (Sorry! I certainly don't mean to imply you're so old you can *remember* the Big Bang. Words are such pranksters.) It was, unquestionably, the most *private* event of all time, obviously, because *absolutely no one was around*. It was the singularity of all singularities. But it's also the most *public, obviously*, because everything we all live and breathe is, in a sense, the Big Bang. Now, I've been thinking—every dream is like a miniscule Big Bang. It's absolutely singular. Like the shadow on the canal, it's never even the same as itself. But to paraphrase what I said before, if something truly singular exists, it is public. This is unshakable?

Let me try to make this point in a completely different way. Let's take the case of Joseph in the Bible. Behold, this dreamer cometh! (Again.) Here, we've got it all. Dreams, shadows, pits, gruesomeness, intrigue, consciousness, and— what really interests us right now—the *private* and the *public*. I wonder if I'll manage to help you (to help *myself*) see this slippery point I've been driving at. Who knows? We'll see. Anyway, it's a great story. But, first, a real short preamble. Remember Aristotle's Sardinians who were sleeping near/with/on the dead heroes? Here's the point. Again. These Sardinians were troubled by an extremely private problem. Visions. Dreams. (Like Hamlet.) A sleep disorder. And what did they do? They went to sleep near/in an extremely public place—ye gods, the tombs of the heroes! (Presumably a major tourist attraction, like Delphi, or Disneyland.) You see. It's all connected.

Let me tell you the story of Joseph, as I see it. Keep this in mind: Joseph got himself *into* big trouble because of his *own* dreams, but got himself *out* of big trouble because of someone *else's* dreams. It's quite a twist. So be it. Now, Jacob (a.k.a. Israel) lived in Canaan, he had eleven sons and a daughter but he 'loved Joseph more' than the others because he was the 'son of his old age.' What's more, he 'made him a coat of *many* colors' (*Genesis*, 37, 3). Naturally Joseph's brothers were pissed off. Seriously riled up, because of their father's favoritism in general and the coat issue in particular. It might have been an excellent idea for Joseph to keep a low profile for a while. After all, he was only 17 years old and things were definitely going his way. Instead, what did he do? First, he dreamed a dream *and told it to his brothers*. Then he dreamed another dream *and told that one to his brothers too*. And what dreams! Absolutely no half-fingers lined up in a row on the carpet. No. First, he dreamed that he and his brothers 'were binding sheaves in the field' and— listen to this—all his brothers' sheaves stood round Joseph's and bowed down to it. The second dream, if possible, was even worse. The sun (his father), the moon (his mother), and eleven stars (his brothers and sister) all bowed down to Joseph himself. And what did Joseph do? He *told* them all about it. My point here is this. Let's say I dreamed (when I was 17, like Joseph) that I got hold of my French teacher and threw her into a pit. Fine. Great. Fantastic. Freud, of course, would simply adore these dreams. (Joseph's and mine.) If this isn't wish fulfillment, what is. But if, then, I went right up to Miss T. and told her—right to her mummified face—Guess what! I dreamed about throwing you into a pit ('casting you into some pit'). This would *not* have been a good idea, especially under the already-strained circumstances. In fact the brothers were not overly pleased about these dreams. No, this time they got *really* riled up. As far as they were concerned Joseph would have been a lot better off if he'd dreamed about half-fingers, with exquisite fingernails, lined up on the carpet at the foot of his bed. Help! Brothers! Behold these half-fingers! They would most certainly have rushed to his bedside and helped him in this extraordinarily grotesque moment. After all, what are families for. Absolutely no dream-Carabinieri were needed. Instead, what happens? Joseph rambles on about his brothers' sheaves bowing down to his sheaf. About his brothers themselves—his *older* brothers, by the way— bowing down to this 17-year-old kid. Does this seem like a good idea to you? Not to me! And in fact his brothers got extremely riled up and their first idea—as we know—was to 'slay him, and cast him into some pit.' The idea here was that a dead brother in a pit does not dream. And as for what he'd dreamed previously, well, 'we shall see what will become of his dreams.' But, I'm a little perplexed. May I ask you, isn't this a somewhat strange way of putting it? If the boy is dead, and at the bottom of a pit, it's clear as day that no one will be bowing down to him. *Absolutely nothing* 'will become of his dreams.' This logic is *doubtless* unshakable. Well, so be it, in any event they changed their minds. They didn't kill him, but they *did* 'cast him into some pit' anyway. Isn't this strange? It seems that they were 'fixated' on pits, they absolutely had to get him into some pit at all costs. Had they been reading Homer, Hegel, or Freud while grazing their sheep? What's more, I find it quite enigmatic (don't you?) that they 'cast him into this [second] pit that *is* in the wilderness' (*Genesis*, 37, 22) *to buy time* to figure out what to *do* about this dreamer and his dreams. Strange behavior. I think they were pit neurotics. Meanwhile, while his brothers were doing these strange, neurotic things, Joseph somehow or other got sold into *slavery* and carted off to Egypt. But at least he got out of the pit.

Enough! Let me make, at this point, my first serious point. About Joseph. Dreams, great. Wish fulfillment, fantastic. But these are *private* matters, on a *very touchy* subject (remember the 'coat of *many* colors'), and what did Joseph *do?* He practically had the dreams printed, with banner headlines, on the front page of the *New York Times* or *Jerusalem Post,* or whatever it was that people were reading at the time. Does this seem wise to you? What's more, as his long life attests, Joseph was an intelligent man. A genuine *Phi Beta Kappa* type. Well, all I can say is that he confused the private with the public. Or—*or*—he figured that something *that singular*, so *truly anomalous*—the sun, moon, and stars 'making obeisance' to a 17-year-old sheep-grazing boy wearing 'a coat of *many* colors'—was *by its very nature* public, and must therefore *be shared*. Perhaps he wasn't wrong. In any event, as I said, he got himself sold into slavery and carted off to Egypt. But, as the saying goes (!?), Dreams the Destroyers, Dreams the Healers. The flesh-and-blood Pharaoh of Egypt (no, not a mummy, like Miss T., my French teacher) had just recently had two *very tricky* dreams. About 7 skinny cows devouring 7 fat cows and 7 withered ears of grain devouring 7 fat ears of grain. No one could figure out what in the world it was all about! And we're talking now about the *Pharaoh of Egypt*, not some 17-year-old kid grazing sheep. *These* 'private' dreams were front-page news. And none of the official dream-experts (perhaps more accustomed to material like the 'table d'hôte' dream) could make head or tail of them. Didn't have a clue. Cows. Ears of grain. Devouring. And such a *public* matter. (In fact, what was really needed was a dream-expert also prepped in political economy. Supply and demand. Global food supplies.) But have no fear, Joseph—'this dreamer cometh'—figured them out in a jiffy, saved Egypt from the famine, got his own famished family moved from Canaan to Egypt to save their lives 'by a great deliverance' (*Genesis*, 45, 7), and lived—rich and famous—to be 110 years old. See what became of his dreams! *Despite the pits, or thanks to the pits?* Well, let me say this. I've survived famine, and I've been in the pits. And I'm 61, as you know, since I compulsively repeat it. And I'm following Joseph's Biblical example, making public my most private dreams in this *therapeutic ramble*. But I'm doing it because I'm trying to answer *my* question, Why Dream? A philosophical, so-called existential, and gruesomely down-to-earth question. A bunch of 'related' questions make me do it. I bet I can't even remember the half of them at this point in the ramble. Why do I always think? Why can't I sleep for one nanosecond without dreaming? Why do I have miserable dreams? What is sleep? Do I ever sleep? Why sleep? (No, this one's a red herring.) Why dream *this?* What, me worry? (Sorry, that's *Mad.*) And, at last, *the* 'related' question: What is consciousness?

As for Joseph, why did he *tell* his brothers about those dreams? *That* is the question here. Doesn't it seem like a crazy thing to do? I'm not entirely convinced by my answer to this question, Why did he *tell?* All that stuff about the private and the public, I mean. Even though my answer may, actually, not be the dumbest of all time. But I always have this thought about Joseph. This idea, that I can't get out of my mind. Maybe he, Joseph, 'this dreamer,' *actually knew the answer* to my question, Why Dream? But he's not talking. So be it. Let's go on.

what is consciousness?

Let me say, right off the bat, that I shall now ramble considerably through this question, which, as you well know, I have called *the* question. But I do not say this because the question—the science—of consciousness has, for some time now, been a hot, hip, in, fashionable, topical question in certain intellectual circles going, basically, under the name of Philosophy of Mind. A question that is outrageously, fiercely, gruesomely, ruthlessly, and grotesquely debated. Indeed, Nagel's 'What is it like to be a bat?' has been debated by bats all over the world. *By the way*, speaking of bats, I just this minute heard from a friend of mine, an age-old admirer of my *earrings*. Now it seems he has turned out to be a genuine *bat expert*. (He absolutely insists on remaining *anonymous*.) He just told me that a bat, on average, or, vice versa, an average bat (or both) sleeps 18 to 20 hours per day! (Per day *and night*, I presume.) While hanging upside-down, somewhere or other. I *do* trust this expert—an old friend—but, up to a certain point. Could he be pulling my leg? Who was it, then, who told me, years ago, that bats, possibly, *never sleep?* (Like Moby Dick.) Because they are so busy hiding. (Like mosquitoes.) So be it. Science marches on. Meanwhile, we still don't know whether these angelic creatures were sleeping or awake when my cats captured them. And, if sleeping, were they dreaming? *If* bats really sleep that much, and *if* they dream—wow! they must dream a hell of a lot. Maybe even more than I do. Meanwhile, another expert I know—whom I don't particularly trust—told me that of all living organisms *opossums* and *armadillos* are the most prolific *dreamers*. Let's take this one with a grain of salt. As I was saying—there are certain *hip* and *fiercely* debated intellectual circles that I intend, sooner or later, to circle round myself, just a little. As a matter of fact, back in the 1990s I studied what was in these circles *quite* a lot. But I'm also going to talk about Hegel, a little. As far as Freud (and, possibly, Aristotle?) is concerned, enough said, I'd say. But this is not the point I set out to make. No. This point is this. I shall now ramble—plenty—perhaps *more* than plenty—through *the* question— What is consciousness? Because I have an idea (*regrettably*, a reasonably *vague* idea), based exclusively on my own personal lifelong experience of (I believe) never sleeping without dreaming. Of dreaming practically *all the time* I am, so to speak, *asleep*, thereby *butchering* my sleep. Alas, or not, I have an idea that *what we call consciousness* is right at the bottom of this situation. (What bottom?) What situation? I mean my not-sleeping-a-single-nanosecond-without-dreaming situation. This situation in which I ask all these engaging and enthralling questions, Why do I always think? et cetera et cetera. Mercifully, this time I will not run through the whole list. But, as you can gather, this past month I've been thinking *harder* and *more deeply* than ever about these questions, as this ramble demonstrates. Now, Why Dream? My question. I am going to *try* to answer it by *trying* to answer *the* question,

What is consciousness? *Because I am convinced* there is a real and intimate connection between the two. Will I be able to individuate and describe this connection? Or will it all be a *blur?* Or *both.* We'll see.

Let me say, for now: I have two hands to play. First the first, and second the second. In that order this time. The first has to do with my own lifelong experience—since I was a little kid—of asking myself (if not always in so many words), What in the world is consciousness?! What a mystery. *The* mystery. Now, I'm not a religious man—not in the theistic sense. (I practice Zen Buddhism.) Sure, I like to leaf through *Genesis, Exodus,* the Gospels, the Koran, et cetera as much as the next fellow, it's great reading, I enjoy it. But I've always felt about consciousness the way genuinely religious theistic people think about God, namely, if you take it at all, you had better take it *seriously.* It's not a game, or a cruise, or a TV series. No. And now, this very afternoon, in the midst of this ramble, I cooked up a little story. It's a little like Plato's Cave, but simpler. A small and very simple story about what, for me, consciousness might be. (*Not* what it might be *like* to be conscious. There are no bats in this belfry.) I even came up with an original—and not very convincing—title for this story. Not very convincing, but the best I could manage this afternoon. Then, the second hand has to do with the *connection* between this story about consciousness I cooked up and *my* dreams. In a *last-ditch attempt* to answer my question, Why Dream? At this point, you're saying to yourself: He's kidding, he's pulling my leg, he's kidding himself and me, there's *no way* he's going to answer his question, Why Dream? He's not going *anywhere* any more, he'll never *answer* anything, he's dug himself into a hole, goddamit. Into a goddam *deep* hole. Basically, he's rambled right into a *pit,* an *abyss.* Well, gentle reader, you may be right. But, never forget, it ain't over till the fat lady sings. (What fat lady? Some say Brünnhilde singing Wagner's *Götterdämmerung,* others say Kate Smith singing Irving Berlin's *God Bless America.* Take your pick, they're both fat.)

But I object to this *goddam deep hole* business. I still have a lot of things to say here. Two hands to play, however weak. *Arguments* to raise. *Serious* things. I was not kidding you in the least just now when I said that even when I was a kid I used to lie in bed at night thinking, thinking, thinking, *What IS it?* My eyes—and something happens. My ears—something happens. My stomach—something happens. I'm tired—something happens. It's so hard to put it into words. It's not just that I see, hear, feel. It's *not* that I think about—or am aware of—seeing, hearing, feeling either. No, it's something more like, 'seeing, hearing, feeling—*they happen.*' Here the problem, *for once,* is not *why* do they happen? Why am I conscious? No, it's *what* happens? What is consciousness? It's not, 'How come when I open my eyes I see things? No, it's 'my eyes are (already) open and I see things. *What's happening?*' (And

I do not mean in a neurophysiological sense.) What's happening? Look, my cat! She's looking around, listening, grimacing—what's happening? Consciousness—a mystery, a genuine mystery. *What's happening?* Why? What? Is it a continuous flashing in the darkness? A continuous darkness in the flashing? *What!* The trembling of the veil? The veiling of the trembling? Is it happening! It's happening! I've been thinking about it all my life. What can I say about it? Sometimes, for a long but fleeting moment, I just watch my cat doing something—licking her fur, for example. She doesn't think *about* it at all. It's just happening. Does this have anything to do with what I mean by consciousness? You know, Plato—or Socrates, if you prefer—liked to define a thing—a notion—by taking *long* rambles through all the things the thing *is not*. The *Republic* is a perfect example. What is justice? Practically the whole ramble is about what justice is *not*, and, in the end, things worked out fine. At the end we have a pretty good idea of what justice *is*. For Socrates/Plato at any rate. But with consciousness this method gets you nowhere. I've tried it. It doesn't work. Consciousness is *right here*. It's always been here. It's *not*, I look out the window and see the *palazzi* and the sky. No, it's—something is happening between—with—me and the *palazzi* and the sky. It's *not*, I feel sad because my friend died. No, it's the happening of the feeling itself. It's a tangle of me, the feeling, my friend. But—*what* is happening? Heidegger—*have not fear* I will not get bogged down for a single minute in Heidegger—asked 'why are there beings rather than nothing?' He called it 'the fundamental question of metaphysics.' However, this ramble, I hope, is *not* metaphysics. Meta-memoir, not metaphysics. *After* memoir. A dream itself has no 'before' but only a 'present,' which in consciousness is already an 'after.' Nevertheless I have to admit that there is, possibly, some sort of connection between the *spirit* of Heidegger's question and my 'what's happening?' Why is it happening rather than not happening? Why is *consciousness* happening rather than not happening? I know, this is a question again, not an answer. But—*if there is no answer, then asking the question can be the answer itself.* The answer can be: It's a mystery. There's no answer. No one knows what's happening. But it's the *asking* of the question that creates the mystery. (And creates the answer?) I mean, if you don't ask the question (if it's never crossed your mind that such a question exists), then *there is no mystery*. What's more, in my experience, if you ask the question 'What is consciousness?' even *once* in your whole entire life, you've asked it forever. Every moment of your—conscious—life is an asking of this question. (And what other life is there? Your un-conscious life perhaps? Remember the 'zat'? Your unconscious life! Be my guest. Tell me, by all means, what it's like *not* to be a zat.) It was St. Augustine (in a gloss by my NYU professor, Dave Leahy who said: In order to search for God, one must have found Him already. This is exactly the point I'm trying to make about consciousness.

So, at this point, you might be thinking, he's going to play his first hand right now, *suddenly*. Without beating around the bush. Spring it right on us, out of the blue. But, of course, you're wrong, and you know it. By now you know perfectly well that I never take the shortest possible route. I ramble. I *flit* chaotically. Sturdy as a butterfly. This reminds me of a quasi-haiku of mine, inspired by my second cat:

> fragile as a dewdrop
> each life weaves its gossamer web
> sturdy as a butterfly

Yes, this is a *ramble*. What's more, it's a *therapeutic ramble*. Ergo, 'a careful disorderliness is the true method.' Play my first hand now, suddenly! And then, maybe right after that, my second hand. Dream on! We need some *background* here goddamit. Plenty of it. We can't just dive right into these two hands (the only ones I have) like a pig into a mud hole. You must be kidding. I'm staking my last dime—the whole ramble—on this. You may think that all my ranting and raving here has quite simply, ruthlessly, gruesomely, and grotesquely been my own up-dated version of Richard Nixon's 'madman strategy.' (An extremely important historical issue that I intend to discuss in detail elsewhere.) (Anyway, the idea is/was: Let's make them think we're madmen and that *at any moment*, for no reason, we might bomb them back into the stone age.) Hell no. This time it's *you* who are kidding *me*. I am trying, somehow, to deal with serious, and major, questions here. Questions of *public interest*. And you expect me to play *both* my hands, suddenly, all at once, without beating around the bush. Without *thrashing* the bush, defoliating, smashing, and damn near *disintegrating* the goddam bush. You must be kidding. This is a serious ramble. Play both my hands at once, suddenly! 'Like the two hands of a shadow cast on the desert, our paths will never meet.' Like a departure—a separation from my hands, forever. A 'lone sail blots the far sky.' It's Ezra Pound! A translation from the Chinese.

SEPARATION ON THE RIVER KIANG

> Ko-Jin goes west from Ko-karu-ro,
> The smoke-flowers are blurred over the river.
> His lone sail blots the far sky.
> And now I see only the river,
> The long Kiang, reaching heaven.

This says it all. Nevertheless, I still have a great deal to say. Rambling. So please continue to be patient. For starters—for *background*. Ye gods! we are not gods! Without a little *background* what *ground* can we possible stand (or stagger) on? Brace yourself. Now I need to circle a little (no, not too much, you'll see, this circle, luckily, doesn't enchant me) around this hot hip Philosophy of Mind circle. *Along* with its *sister* circle (which enchants me infinitely less, and I know practically nothing about it), arguably called *cognitive neuroscience.* But by this circle I really mean *neurophysiology.* (If I could I'd turn both these circles into straight lines.) Let's take the second circle first, for a change. Do you remember when Freud told us about 'chemical tensions' and, especially, 'excitations … in the mental apparatus'? Saying—with remarkable intellectual and scientific honesty—'we know nothing of the nature of the excitatory process that takes place in the elements of the psychical systems.' (Remember? The process on which he based his whole caboodle.) Well, the neurosciences have come one hell of a long way since Freud's day. Neurophysiology. Mapping the brain, and all that. Do you think Freud imagined that we have some *100 billion* neurons in our brains? (No, not all of us *together.* I mean in *every single* human brain.) And all *firing away* all the time. Talk about excitations! And not just firing any old where, like a 3-year-old with a Kalashnikov. Firing along fibers called axons (they take up most of the space in a brain), sending *signals* to other neurons by means of specialized junctions called synapses, and we have about *100 trillion of them* in every single brain. (No, this is not something some half-wit brain-and-bat-expert friend of mine happened to tell me. I actually read it in a book.) This is heavy stuff, and it's just for starters.

Does all this (for starters) make it easier or harder to answer the question, What is consciousness? As you might imagine, second-circle members say *easier.* But I take this not with a *grain* of salt. No, this time I need the *entire salt mine.* In any event, Francis Crick, for example, is a *big name.* I'm sure you remember him for his DNA double-helix invention/discovery back in the '50s, along with his friend Dr. Watson, I presume. (Sorry, I'm confusing Stanley and Livingstone with Sherlock Holmes.) Well, after DNA he jumped head-first right into the brain. Into consciousness. Coming up with what he called 'the astonishing hypothesis' that all our thoughts, sensations, pleasures, and pains consist entirely of *physiological activity of the tissues of the brain.* I'll bet you a lot *more* than a dime that Freud would say, again (compelled to repeat), 'this astonishes people far too little!' Just for starters. Francis Crick goes on to tell us that consciousness is the *activity of the brain,* and he's *extremely* precise about it. Crick and a friend of his named Dr. Koch (no, not Dr. Watson this time) wrote a flesh-and-blood paperback in 1990 telling us that, basically, mental states become conscious when large numbers of neurons fire in synchrony and all have oscillations within the 35-75 hertz range (that is, 35-75 cycles per second). What would Siggy say about *that!* Meanwhile, so-called 'cognitive neuroscientists' have—they say—practically more or less proved this 'astonishing hypothesis,' thanks to their state-of-the-art *functional MRI*. (Have you noticed how all these scientists love this word 'astonishing,' while I myself almost never use it?) Proved it, or at least 'shown' it with their scans. Lately they've actually been *mapping* 'brain activity'— effectively reading people's thoughts from the blood flow in their brains. I read this in *Time* magazine, so it must be … whatever it is. Just by looking at an MRI, 'cognitive neuroscientists' can tell whether a person is thinking about a face or a place or whether a picture the person is looking at is of a bottle or of a shoe. Ye gods, is this possible! Of a bottle or of a shoe! No, but really, believe me, it's not *that* easy. In this case, strangely enough, it may be far easier in practice than in theory. In any event, we have somehow stumbled, or staggered, into the domain of 'neural theories of consciousness.' The domain of *strong identity* between consciousness and neural activity. The very heart and soul of our 'second circle,' whose Super Goal is to *track down* the 'neural correlates of consciousness.' NCCs! Ye gods how scientific we have become. In order to show how one or more specific kinds of neuro-*chemical* activity can underlie and explain conscious mental activity.

Wait, let's calm down. We shall see, in just a moment, that the first circle itself is traditionally divided into two *semicircles*. Two *fiercely* (et cetera) *debating* theories of mind. The first is known as dualism, and the second as materialism (a.k.a. physicalism). (Or, of course, without prejudice, *vice versa*. First, second, there's no special order.) Now, our 'second circle' in this ramble (with, or without, prejudice) (no, I mean *circle*, not *semicircle*) is, we might say, physicalism pushed to such an extreme that it exits the debate entirely. Slamming the door behind it. ('Astonishing hypothesis'!) Or does it? Well, theoretically, it does. There's no more theoretical debate. But in practice—I mean, *what* do they intend to *do* with these NCCs? This might—quite well—be a different debate. In any event, I think, personally, that this extremely neurophysiological brain-mapping absolutely and most definitely 'astonishes us too little.' *Far* too little. A *quantum leap* too little. I mean, just think about what the (relatively) elementary discovery of these zillions of neuron firings, axons, and synapses and *how they work* has meant for the practice of what our friend Freud called—quaintly—psycho-analysis. (Or psychotherapy.) (Or psychiatry.) Excitation, chemical tension … *chemical imbalance*. Well, it is thanks to our 'second circle' that—in some circles—the whole practice of psychiatry has been *boiled* right down to a question of *psychiatric drugs*. You're depressed. Could be because you just lost your job, or your sister got run over by a truck, or your daughter got arrested for possession *again* (half a pound of marihuana!). Hell no, it's clinical depression! Depleted brain chemicals! Clogging of the axons! Synapses panting for serotonin! We can see it with our own eyes on our state-of-the-art MRI. *Possibly*, one day, a genuine NCC problem. *Quick!* A dash of lithium! A pound of Prozac! And your kid in the third grade keeps falling on the floor (laughing?) or falling asleep and smashing his head on his desk. Perchance his teachers are complete and total JERKS? Hell no! It's a clear case of attention-deficit hyperactivity disorder. Ye gods! (Disorder! What would Melville make of *this*.) Get this kid some Ritalin! Not a minute to lose! Great! It's great because it's *scientific reality*. Absolutely! As I see it, the reality of my old beloved *Mad* magazine. Shrink versus Shrink. Alfred E. Neuman lives! And I think we shall see him *again*, soon. What, me worry! *In any event*, so be it. With this—*at long last*—we close the second circle. If 'elementary' modern neurophysiology has meant all this, time will tell what the neural correlates of consciousness will come to mean. For the moment, Good Night and Good Luck.

Great, now, at last, back to the first circle, which I know a *whole* lot more about and which may or may not help me answer my own extremely well-known questions. That second circle—what do I know about neurophysiology!—got me into a mini-ramble in the ramble that, believe me, I certainly didn't expect. Anyway, it's like a headache, it'll go away on its own pretty soon, or else turn out to be a *brain tumor* and kill you. So much the worse. Let's forget about *brains*. We have the chance, for a moment, to dive straight into the profound pit of *mind*. *Philosophy* of Mind. It's like a springtime flood of wisteria, an enormous expanse of lilacs, after the frightening field we've just been traipsing through. Minds. No more brains. Never again. *Hopefully*.

Now, the first circle. For starters I really should say a few words about Thomas Nagel. It's true that I read his classic world-famous 'bat' essay to my second cat a few days ago, and her rebuttal may be forthcoming. (My first cat, as I said, loves Lacan.) But it's also true that I've been pulling your leg about him one helluva lot. I do not know Dr. Nagel personally but I bet—I hope—he's a man who can take a joke. In any event, I've meant no disrespect. I actually have three flesh-and-blood books of his in the house. And I've read them, more than once. I kid you not. And what truly outstanding titles he comes up with. (The best I could do myself was *Why Dream?*) *What Does It All Mean?* (great question). *The View From Nowhere* (great title). *Mortal Questions* (sobering thoughts). As I mentioned, back in the 1990s I went on a Philosophy of Mind binge. Just look at this, a stack of books four feet high, right here by my desk. I pulled them all down from the (top) shelves in honor of this ramble. My cat is quite upset about it, she hates these novelties. *Out of nowhere*, a stack of books in the middle of the floor! She's already knocked it over. Twice. Meanwhile—in the early '90s I abandoned Derrida (and vice versa) and moved on to chaos theory, astrophysics, and quantum mechanics. After that, I plunged into Philosophy of Mind, which was particularly hot, hip, and in at the time. But that wasn't the reason. No, I was hoping, obviously, for some sort of answer to my question, *the* question, What is consciousness? (The root, possibly, of another *the* question: Why Dream?) Looking through these books, I see that

most of them were actually written in that hip hot period: Nicholas Humphrey
(*A History of the Mind*), Colin McGinn (*The Problem of Consciousness*), three
big ones by Roger Penrose (on quantum approaches to consciousness—great
stuff), Daniel Dennett, David Chalmers. I even have *If a Lion Could Talk:
Animal intelligence and the evolution of consciousness* by Stephen Budiansky.
Plus John Searle, of course. I really enjoy his witty 'Chinese room argument.'
It goes like this: You program a computer to converse in Chinese, then give
the program to a person in a closed room (the 'Chinese room'), and what
do you discover? Both the computer and the person are able to converse in
Chinese—no, not with one another, but with some real Chinese speaker—but
without having the slightest idea of what they're saying. (I got to know Searle a
little when he was in Venice in the '80s. He had *no* sense of humor. And such
a witty argument. I hope Nagel isn't humorless like him.) Plus older classics,
like *The Mind's I* and Julian Jaynes intriguing (if not helpful) *The Origin of
Consciousness in the Breakdown of the Bicameral Mind*. Consciousness galore.
Where shall we start? Where shall we finish! Don't worry, I am absolutely *not*
going to give you a blow-by-blow description of all these (long) books. (Like I
did with Freud's two—short—books.) No, I'm just going to make a few *really*
short and strikingly vague remarks on two—extremely long—books in this
circle. One by Dennett and one by Chalmers. And just a flit at Nagel's bat.

A good place—perhaps—to enter this circle is through the two semicircles
I mentioned recently, dualism and materialism (or physicalism). There
are many versions of each. Generally speaking, dualists maintain that the
conscious mind or a conscious mental state is nonphysical in some sense.
Materialists claim that conscious mental activity is identical with neural
activity (or, to put it bluntly, 'the mind is the brain'). A cousin of all this is
the famous mind—body problem: Is the mind (or 'soul' perhaps) separate
from the body (and therefore, presumably, 'eternal')? Or is it basically dust,
like the body is? Meanwhile, I don't want you to think that the tremendous
'second circle' we've just been through gobbled up the entire physicalist
tidbit. Far from it. It simply took it to an utter and grotesque extreme. But
the fact is that various forms of physicalism have pretty much dominated
the Philosophy of Mind debate. Dualism these days is old hat, despite its
formidable history. The great dualist hero (now villain) was Descartes, he
of the famous *cogito ergo sum* (which I turned upside down a while back,
with my insomniac *sum ergo cogito*). For him not only is the mind eminently
nonphysical and totally distinct from the body but the *cogito*—thinking—
the 'I think'—encompasses every possible kind of mental state. *Ergo*,
consciousness is essential to thinking, and the *ego*—the I—the 'self'—is its
agent. Descartes, like Hamlet, was a great believer in introspection, to which
mental states are infallibly transparent. The 'self' as an inner observer is the
absolute monarch of consciousness. Now, Daniel Dennett, in his—*long*—

book, *Consciousness Explained* (great title?), is on Descartes' case in a big way. Dennett is an extremely witty, ferocious, and entertaining writer, and the target of his pen in this book is what he famously calls the 'myth of the Cartesian Theater,' i.e., the *myth* 'that somewhere, conveniently hidden in the obscure "center" of the mind/brain there is a Cartesian Theater, a place where "it all comes together" and consciousness happens.' (p. 39). For Dennett it is this goddam *theater* that famously 'prevents theorists' of our first circle from *explaining* what consciousness *is*. The horror! (As Mr. Kurtz put it.) But have no fear, in this book Dr. Dennett gives us a 511-page performance that, as sheer and outstanding entertainment, is unequalled in this entire circle. He gives us his flesh-and-blood Multiple Drafts Model (MDM) of consciousness, replete with 'Orwellian and Stalinesque Revisions.' I kid you not, if I had the time I'd reread this book. Wait! I have something to say here. If *Mad* magazine didn't already exist, Daniel Dennett would have invented it. Spy versus Spy. He's the *mind* of Alfred E. Neuman in flesh-and-blood books. Not 'conveniently hidden' in some 'obscure center' but right here on the cover, with his magnificent immortal grin. What's more, he has *explained consciousness*. (He sez.) What, him worry! I think you have detected a touch of sarcasm here. A tiny dash.

Nagel! What's all this about the bat? It's serious business. Nagel, and another friend of ours, a member of this circle, a young Australian with long hair (and *long* books) named David Chalmers, said that Dennett has totally *missed the point* about consciousness. All Dennett does is re-define consciousness as an *external property* (going to town in a big way!) while ignoring the *subjective aspect* completely. Ye gods! *Ignoring the subjective aspect—of consciousness—completely.* But it is precisely this *subjective aspect* that is the lifeblood of this circle. The other members of the circle are goddam right when they say that Dennett hasn't *explained* consciousness, he's *explained it away*. Nagel himself had, arguably, the most original thing of all time to say about the subjective aspect. It's brilliant actually, he wrote it back in 1974, 'What is it like to be a bat?' *What is it like?* Nagel's idea is that when I'm in a conscious mental state, there is *something it is like* for me to be in that state from the subjective or first-person point of view. It's perfectly true that in his essay Nagel talks about animal—in this case, bat—consciousness. But what he's really asking is: What is consciousness? Animal rights advocacy was not his principal concern, though I'm sure he's made a very positive contribution. People forget easily about animal consciousness. Descartes denied it completely! For him only humans have nonphysical minds. A great excuse for a lot of cruelty to animals. Nagel's point is that when I have a pain in my ass or see a *palazzo*, there is something it 'seems' or 'feels' like from my perspective. 'The *fact* that an organism *has* conscious experience *at all* means, basically, that there is something it is like to *be* that organism.' (In his book *Mortal*

Questions, p. 166.) I'm coming right back *here*, almost immediately, to *the FACT that an organism HAS conscious experience*. Meanwhile, Nagel, here, makes two points at once. No small feat. It really is like walking and chewing gum. One is about—for example—bats. (A good example, it even rhymes with cats.) His point is that no matter how much we know about an animal's brain or behavior, we can never put ourselves in the mind of the animal and experience its world the way it does itself. Never know what it's *like* to *be* that animal. Gilda agrees. She's a genuine Nagel fan. (Or is she?) She asks me 'What is it *like* to be *you?*' with all the outrageously bizarre things you do. Like going *out* of the house and not coming back for *two* hours (pizzeria), *three* hours (philosophy seminar), even *four* hours (doctor's appointment in Padua). Cat meta-memoir. But Nagel's main point—made simultaneously with the 'like to be a bat' point—I think is 'What is it like to be conscious?' For a desk, a pen, or a pebble, there is nothing it is like to be conscious *at all*. But for Gilda, or for possible bats in the back garden, or for me, there's something. What? Great! I've kidded Nagel so much not just because 'bat' rhymes with 'cat,' 'shat,' 'mat,' and 'zat' but because what he says really is important. However, what he doesn't *realize* he says is a zillion times *more* important. 'The *fact* that an organism *has* conscious experience' (never mind the *at all*). In these eight words the water for my spaghetti boils out and burns the pot. *Have no fear*, to this I shall return, and very soon. And my infinitely respected 'target' will be not Nagel but Hegel, my master! 'Have faith and wait.' (A minute.) (As Kafka put it, 'In the Penal Colony.')

But first, I have some interesting things to say about the *last* member of our 'first circle' whom I shall ramble on about. At last the last. Of this circle. Otherwise this little ramble would go on for a week. You'll see (in a minute), I'm going to *complain—a lot and seriously*—about this circle. And it's a good circle. (It's the 'second circle' that worries me.) It's a formidable 'What, me worry?' circle. Penrose. McGinn. Humphrey. Great. Never mind the fact that Dennett tried to occupy the *entire* circle with his *Mad* magazine spirit. This is a happy circle. A cheerful circle. A lively circle. (No 'table d'hôte' dreams in *this* circle.) Meanwhile, for me David Chalmers entered the circle at the very end. *After* the end, actually. His—long—book, *The Conscious Mind*, was published in 1996, and only came out in paperback in 1998 (when I bought it). By that time I was translating some excellent, intelligent, dedicated, and extremely sensitive and sincere marxists. In my spare time I was reading Marx. I was also reading Hegel, as always, but a bit more than usual. So, let's close our 'first circle' with Chalmers. I think that his framing of the 'hard problem' of consciousness (it's become nearly as famous as Nagel's bat), as distinguished from the 'easy problems,' has been important in putting a lot of things into perspective. His basic premise—which I heartily agree with—is that the many forms of physicalism that pervade our 'first circle' (never mind the *second*, which is nothing *but* grotesque and gruesome physicalism) fail to account for the actual existence of consciousness itself. This total critique of physicalism *ipso facto* makes Chalmers a dualist of some sort. No, not a Cartesian. He calls himself a 'naturalistic' dualist. His point is that the (relatively) 'easy problems' have to do with the *functions* of consciousness, but solving them does nothing for the 'hard problem' of the *phenomenon* of consciousness. (Two more semicircles! Functionalism and phenomenalism.) His 'easy' problems, then, are a mix of physicalism and functionalism. They are all cognitive problems, such as the ability to discriminate and categorize stimuli or to access internal states of mind (introspection), or the difference between wakefulness and sleep (big problem!), or between conscious and unconscious (functional) processes. (Consciousness doesn't control your heart rate, for example.) The 'hard' problem, by contrast, refers to the difficulty (or impossibility?!) of explaining how physical processes in the brain—neural computations— give rise to subjective conscious experiences. In one paper Chalmers asked, 'How can we explain why there is something it is like to entertain a mental image, or to experience an emotion?' In another, 'Why does the *feeling* which accompanies awareness of sensory information exist at all?' It's not at all easy to *pose* the hard problem. To state it in genuinely clear terms. It's not at all like Crick's 'astonishing hypothesis,' it's easy as pie to pose that one. But the 'hard problem' is a good problem, in my opinion. Sure, Dennett (among others) denies that it exists *at all*, because nothing could settle the issue one way or another. Consciousness is consciousness. It's a *fact*. An actual *fact*. And we have *a lot of fun* explaining it. Far more cleverly, Colin McGinn (here he is after all) suggests that our problem with the 'hard problem' is itself a quirk of our brains. The brain is a product of evolution, so just as, for example, it can't visual the 11-dimensional space (time included) the physicists talk about so much, maybe brains just haven't evolved (yet) to the point where they can tackle the hard problem. A tricky way of looking at it.

Let's close this circle. Gilda will be happy. I'm putting all these books back on the (top) shelves. I just want to say this. In my own modest, crude, rough, and possibly grotesque fashion, I personally pose the 'hard problem' this way: What is consciousness? And, alas, I also want to say that even though this circle is entertaining, it has disappointed me. So many books, so many pages, such heated debate, but no answer to *my* question. What's my problem! Perhaps there really is something wrong with the way I've always posed the question. My way of asking it. But my problem, as I see it, is that all these consciousness experts—not just in our 'first circle' but, I'd say, from the beginning of the history of philosophy—start out with the *fact* of consciousness and *then* they attempt to analyze it, describe it, define it, take a position on it, explain it, cuddle it, bite into it, and—at best—account for our *experience of it*. Take Kant, for example—that man could *analyze* you, your cat, and your bat right out of your hat. Right off the face of the earth. But I *know* he never answered *my* question. He approached it from the wrong direction. In the Big Circle of the history of philosophy I know that lots of people prefer Kant, but I don't. Neither does Melville! In an outrageous gloss of mine on his novel *Pierre or, the Ambiguities*, I have him claim that Kant, with his 'stretchable Philosophy,' is *pure cant*, and that Pierre's tragedy is that he just *Kant/can't* get around him/it. But that was an old ramble ('The Failure of Meaning'). Meanwhile, it's always our experience *OF* the *FACT OF* consciousness, already there (somewhere or nowhere) and functioning (somehow or other). Even a quantum approach *to* consciousness takes consciousness as a fact already given. To me this is putting the cart before the horse. It's what I called some time ago 'not taking consciousness seriously.' It totally begs my question. What question? The one I tried to pose just now. The one I've *been stuck with* since I was a kid. The question I just can't frame. Except by saying that consciousness is not a fact but—if anything—a mystery. I still think that 'What is consciousness?' is a legitimate question, even if it doesn't have an answer. But if you take consciousness as a *fact*—a 'given'—from the word go, you can rant and ramble all you like and never even *approach* the question. It's something like the peasant in Kafka's parable 'Before the Law.' You just sit there at the side of the open door all your life but never cross the threshold, never find the answer, even though the door was *your* door all along. This could be a perfect metaphor for my own personal experience of consciousness. The door is open. The threshold of consciousness—its radiance—is *RIGHT HERE, and I cross it at every moment.* But I am not admitted to the mystery. Even though it is *my mystery.* I believe that this is why I dream so much. Why I never sleep without dreaming. I believe it is, in some sense, the answer to my question, Why Dream? Believe me, I'm coming back to this. I still have my two hands to play. But, for now, I want to say something extremely interesting about something I know a lot more about. Namely, Hegel. I'll keep it *short.*

A little later on Hegel is going to give me a *crucially* and *decisively BIG HAND* (I hope) when I—finally—play my first hand. (After all this business about the two circles, I do hope you remember that it's all *background* to the playing of *my two hands.*) But he's going to do it with his *Logic*, which, I always insist, is his strong suit. But right now, for just a moment, I want to glance—fleetingly—at the first of his two major works that are explicitly concerned with consciousness. Namely, the *Phenomenology of Spirit.* A *gigantic* ramble. The wild culmination of Hegel's youth. Completed in 1806, when he was 36. The second work is the first half of the third volume of his *Encyclopaedia of the Philosophical Sciences*, translated (badly) as *Philosophy of Mind* or (much better) as *Philosophy of Spirit.* The third, and final, edition was published the year before his sudden, shocking, and outrageously untimely death (some say of cholera but it's not likely) in 1831, at the age of 61. My age (as you know). I've decided—regretfully—not to get tangled up in his *Philosophy of Spirit* because I might not be able to get untangled again. Just *one single page* (not even the *whole* page). I can't resist. On waking, sleeping, and dreaming. Ye gods, I rambled on and on about Freud's endlessly rambling over if not trampling on that crazy 'table d'hôte' dream, with the spinach and the *beaux yeux*. Allow me to quote three lines from Hegel! Let me just say, to avoid confusion, that in this book of Hegel's 'soul' has nothing to do with the 'immortal soul' of Christianity or the shades/shadows in Hades. No, 'soul' is the basis of sensibility or feeling. A stage—which Hegel calls 'Anthropology'—that precedes consciousness, which is the first stage of Phenomenology. He calls soul 'only the *sleep* of spirit,' 'the dull stirring, the inarticulate breathing, of the spirit.' Now, listen to this (from §398):

> As regards the mental or spiritual difference between waking and sleep … We have defined sleep as the state in which the soul distinguishes itself neither inwardly nor from the outer world. This definition which has its own necessity is confirmed by experience. For when our soul goes on feeling or imagining only one and the same thing, it becomes sleepy. Thus can the regular motion of a cradle, a monotonous singing, or the murmuring of a brook induce somnolence in us. The same effect is produced by rambling talk [!!!], by disconnected pointless narration. Our mind only feels fully awake when it is presented with something interesting, something both new and meaningful, something with a differentiated and coherent content; for in such an object it finds itself again. … We can, while awake, taking the word in its abstract meaning, be very bored; and, conversely, it is possible for us to have a lively interest in something in a dream. But in a dream it is only our picture-thinking, not our conceptual thinking, whose interest is aroused. … It is also inadequate to fix the distinction by saying vaguely that it is only in the waking state that man *thinks*. For thought *in general* is so much inherent in the nature of man that he is always thinking, even in sleep. [!!!]

Hegel was the Muhammad Ali of philosophers. *'Always thinking, even in sleep.'* For me, for my ramble, this is truly the Rumble in the Jungle. A little later (§405) he speaks about 'natural dreaming' … 'a moment of sleep, [which] from a superficial standpoint can be regarded as proof of the identical nature of sleep and waking.' … 'In the dreaming state the human soul is filled not merely with single, isolated feelings but, more than is usually the case in the distractions of the waking soul, attains to a profound, powerful feeling of its *entire individual* nature, of the *total compass* of its past, present, and future.' I bet you didn't know that Hegel wrote things like this. Well, he did.

Time for a fleeting glance at the *Phenomenology of Spirit.* But first I have to ask my not-at-all fleeting question: In this work, which, for Hegel, is '*the science of the experience of consciousness,*' (§36), does he take consciousness as *A FACT*—a 'given'—from the very beginning? As something *already there*, to be analyzed, described, explained? As everyone in our 'first circle' does. To say nothing of the members of the 'second circle,' who do it in spades. On the one hand, it seems that he does. His first approach to consciousness in the *Phenomenology* is strictly cognitive. He defines consciousness, in its first stage, as 'a knowledge of the immediate or of what simply *is*' (§90). But doesn't knowledge require a subject that knows? An 'I,' a subject, or even a 'self'? Hegel says 'the science of the *experience of* consciousness.' But doesn't 'experience of' demand an 'I'? However unobtrusive the 'I' may be (not like in *my* ramble, that's for sure), it must be there, from the very beginning. And doesn't this take me right back to my major problem with '*the fact* that an organism *has* conscious experience'? (*At all.*) On the other hand, in Hegel *things are not that simple.* He also says, right at the beginning of §36: 'The immediate existence of Spirit, *consciousness,* contains the two moments of *knowing* and the *objectivity* [which is] *negative to* knowing.' (I added some italics.) This is what's so difficult about Hegel. Here, he *defines consciousness* for us. He actually says 'What Consciousness Is'! It's the immediate existence of *Geist.* 'Spirit,' sometimes (badly) translated as 'mind.' Hegel would say, no, there is no 'I' that is the subject of experience here. The subject is *Geist* itself. An extraordinary conception that only a Hegel could have cooked up. The *Phenomenology of Spirit* is—believe me—a *wild ramble.* It follows the *self*-development of spirit (but *without a 'self'*), *moved by its own inherent negativity,* on the pathway from consciousness to self-consciousness, reason, spirit, religion, to—last but not in the least least—absolute knowing. (What Hegel means by 'negativity' is *extremely tricky.* Possibly the *trickiest.* It's the direct reverse—as Melville put it—of deathly positive. It's something that *self*-relates something. Like in the shadows of a Venetian canal.) Spirit is, *somehow,* its own subject and its own object. This is exactly what spirit is, for Hegel. Where this 'somehow' (of mine) is the 'strenuous effort of the concept' (§58), by which he means thinking through, or by means of, the concept. (We might call it 'the power of negative thinking' as Hegel understands it.) *Phenomenologically* speaking, spirit, in its first, simplest, least developed, most primitive, 'immediate,' *original* stage, is consciousness. In Hegel—but *only* in Hegel—consciousness is not a *fact* but a stage—a 'moment'—of spirit. '*The science of the experience of consciousness.*' This is Hegel, not Daniel Dennett. This is not an external observer explaining a fact. Again, as I keep saying, Hegel's heart is his *Science of Logic.* His heart tells us to take *nothing* as '*given*' *fact.* No! Follow the shadows—the shaking, quivering, quaking, the 'simple essentialities' in their self-development through all the 'categories' of the *Logic.* Literally from 'nothing' all the way to what is most concrete, 'life' itself. This, for Hegel, is 'the absolute culture and discipline of *consciousness.*' And with all this, has Hegel actually answered the question, What is consciousness? No! Not on your life. In terms of 'phenomenology,' which Hegel defines as 'the Science of Knowing *in the sphere of appearance*' (§808, my italics), he has given *one* hell of an answer. Unfortunately, my question is an *existential* question (much as I hate to use that word). Still, if *anyone* can help me answer it, Hegel can. For the right word, ask Ezra Pound. For an original idea, ask Hegel. He won't *give* it to you, but he'll help you *look* for it. We'll see. I'm going to play my two hands, for better or worse, in just a moment. We'll see. It's pretty late. All this rambling I've done today. All through the afternoon, evening, night. If I open the shutters I may discover that dawn has already broken, or is about to. It ain't over.

Let's back up a little and go further into the background of consciousness. Let's say, to the back of the background. Where, exactly, does this word 'consciousness' come from? What did it mean originally? I know, a 'normal narrator' would have said this at the beginning, but I'm a rambler, not a narrator. This is no 'grand narrative' à la Jean-François Lyotard. So—pardon my *cliché*—better late than never. The origin of the modern concept of *Bewußtsein—consciousness*— goes back to the British philosopher John Locke and his *Essay Concerning Human Understanding*, published in 1690. Locke defined consciousness as 'the perception of what passes in a man's mind.' (Pardon his sexism. *Bien sûr* also women 'have' minds. As do, among others, cats, mosquitoes, Moby Dick, and bats.) Not a bad definition, even if a strange one. Locke makes no mention of perception of the external world. Strange, and *doubly* strange, I'd say. Since nowadays consciousness is often referred *only* to the external world. Here's a definition from the 1989 *Macmillan Dictionary of Psychology* (taken from the Wikipedia entry 'Consciousness'; my italics):

> *Consciousness*— The having of perceptions, thoughts, and feelings; awareness. The term is impossible to define except in terms that are unintelligible without a grasp of what consciousness means. Many fall into the trap of equating consciousness with self-consciousness— *to be conscious it is only necessary to be aware of the external world.* Consciousness is a fascinating but elusive phenomenon: *it is impossible to specify what it is, what it does, or why it has evolved. Nothing worth reading has been written on it.*

Wow, what a torpedo! This isn't what Hegel meant by the power of negativity. In any event, it's perfectly true that consciousness must not be confused with self-consciousness. (Hegel explains this *in great detail.* Luckily we won't go into it.) (As with all *dreamers*, Hamlet's problem is introspection, not self-consciousness.) But, as I see it, there definitely are *two* worlds of consciousness. In fact, in current usage we say that through consciousness one can have knowledge of the external world *and* of one's own mental states. Freud, of course, was well aware of this. Yikes, shall I give Siggy one last quote, after all he's put us through? (I still can't believe that in this whole ramble I've given you approximately *one* page of Hegel's and a zillion of Freud's. Where's the logic?) Yes? No? What the hell.

> The property of being conscious or not is *in the last resort* our one beacon-light in the darkness of depth-psychology. ...
>
> We have said that consciousness is the *surface* of the mental apparatus; that is, we have ascribed it as a *function* to a system which is spatially the first one reached from the external world—and spatially not only in the functional sense but, on this occasion, also in the sense of anatomical dissection. Our investigation too must take the perceiving surface as a starting point.
>
> All perceptions which are received from without (sense perceptions) and from within—what we call sensations and feelings—are conscious from the start. But what about those internal processes which we may—roughly and inexactly—sum up under the name of thought-processes?

Then he goes on and on, roughly and inexactly, about 'thought-processes.' Don't worry, I won't follow him. It's much too late in the day and/or night, and/or both. Why did he say 'in the last resort'? Personally I have no idea. Anyway, this is from another short book, *The Ego and the Id*, usual edition, pp. 10-12.

Meanwhile, getting back for a second to Locke and his curious lacuna. Strange to say, even I often think of consciousness in terms of the external world. Even I, 'obsessed' with consciousness as I am. No, let's say 'concerned' about, 'interested' in consciousness, ever since I was a kid. The external world. Especially in terms of *seeing*. (In fact, 'I see' and 'I know'—'I understand'—are nearly synonymous in English.) Forgetting that this is only half the story. Now, watch out! The *external* world. When a *bambino* on a skateboard, right around the corner in Campo San Giacomo, is *coming right at me*, I am damn well *conscious* of it. Never mind 'mental states.' But when I look at my cats I clearly see them conscious of both worlds. Gilda more of the internal, Gina, the action-cat, more of the external, the world of bats and especially *rats*. Not just because they rhyme. (In fact, Gilda *once* saw a *mouse* and she thought she was *dreaming*.) Just look at Moby Dick (you can't miss him). A *whale* of a consciousness. *Vast* knowledge of the external world *and* of his mental states. More internal or external? It's hard to say. He certainly had *plenty* of time for introspection. But he was definitely an action-whale. Ahab, of course, accused him of 'unexampled, intelligent malignity.' Wait! The mosquito. Just think, some—possibly *many*—people maintain that mosquitoes have no consciousness. What ignorance we find traipsing through the world. As far as Gilda and I are concerned, the mosquito is a *chess master* of consciousness, a veritable Bobby Fisher (on his good days). External *and* internal worlds. Our house. Inside and out. Our bodies. Our movements. Our *blood. WHO* is more *conscious* than our tormentor, the mosquito! What knowledge! And 'mental states'! Just imagine the satisfaction, the good cheer, the *gloating* when the tiny beast takes a bite. The incredible escaping, hiding, possibly fooling us into believing it never sleeps. Or, possibly, it *actually* never sleeps? Have no fear, a mosquito knows what it's doing, knows where it's doing it, and, possibly, never its *why*. Strategy and knowledge of the terrain. Consciousness personified. 'Mosquitoized,' so to speak.

Let me go back, again, to the *very* back of the background. Just for a second. The word itself. A strange, curious word. The earliest English language uses of 'conscious' and 'consciousness' date back to the 1500s. A long time before Locke. It is originally derived from the Latin *conscius*. Composed of *con* ('with,' together) and *scire* ('to know'). I read, many years ago, that as a matter of fact the Latin word meant, precisely, *knowing with*. In the sense of having joint or common knowledge with another. 'Knowing with' or 'knowing together' is—evidently—not what 'consciousness' means today. But today, rambling, it's given me food for thought. Lots of it. A banquet. I've been thinking, thinking, thinking about this *knowing with*. Knowing with what? I'm going to tell you what I think. Suddenly! I'm playing my first hand.

1. *'first hand': original consciousness*

Imagine you are in a room, a closed space. Small or big doesn't matter (but not *real* small or *real* big), as long as it has windows, and the windows have shutters. (Preferably traditional wooden shutters, and not dilapidated.) I'm imagining my own room where I pass almost all my time, this 'dark cellar' where I write my 'notes from the underground,' which, instead, is a nice-sized first- (in the U.S. second-) floor mansard, as you know. (And I am not 'a sick man' … 'an angry man' … 'an unattractive man.') Full of light if it's sunny, with three fine windows, with wooden shutters. (Quite new. The old ones fell apart completely.)

Then imagine—and here you'll need a bit more imagination, but you can do it!—*the very same room* but inside your body. Much smaller of course, it has to fit. Let's not imagine it anywhere special inside the body. No, let's not think about where inside the body it is. It could be anywhere at all. (In your big toe for example. But let's not think about it.) Anywhere and nowhere, as long as it's a closed space, with windows and with wooden shutters.

Now—What is consciousness? Consciousness is the 'original' opening of these shutters. 'Original' in the sense of the moment of opening them 'for the first time.' (Though, as we shall see, the true sense of 'original' here is more complex, it's not really a question of 'time.') Simple! I told you this would be a simple story. Just imagine these two rooms, one inside and one outside. Dark, silent, nothing happening *that you are conscious of*—then, suddenly, wow! All this light coming in, *pouring* into the rooms. (Especially if it's a sunny day. But never mind that. This is a story.) All of a sudden, everything is happening at once. In the big room you see, hear, smell, taste, touch—that's what the light means in *this* story. And the small room, so dark, so empty a moment ago, is suddenly full of a zillion things—take your pick. Thoughts of all sorts, feelings of all sorts, it's sensational, so much is happening. *What* is happening? Well—this is the story, my 'first hand.' *Consciousness* is happening. Two whole worlds of consciousness—and they are inseparable. Perhaps I should say 'the same' instead of 'inseparable.' Don't forget, the two rooms are *the same*. In this story they aren't *two* rooms, they're 'the very same room.' The one that you're in and the one that's in you. The same room. What's different is what's *happening* in the room imagined as inside, and what's *happening* in the room imagined as outside. It seems that two different worlds are happening. In the big room, the shutters open and—there she is! I see my second cat, Gilda. Wow, who knew where in the world she was, she might have been downstairs, or in the back garden. In the small room, the shutters open and—my *darling* Gilda, how I adore you, the gentlest cat in the world! I've been wondering where in the world you might be. I think Gilda is an excellent example for this point in the story. When the shutters opened I could have said instead (for example): 'Ye gods, there's my shoe' (external world) and 'All of a sudden I feel hungry and angry' (internal world). If I said that I could easily have given you the impression that I'm talking about two *different* worlds. But it's not so at all. It's the very same room. If we absolutely have to talk about *two* worlds, at the very least we have to say that they are 'inseparable.' (Hegel's word. My Zen master would prefer 'not two and not one.')

Get ready for two points I have to make. First the easier one (I guess). Then the harder one. First, consciousness. Second, 'original' consciousness. First: The 'happening' here when the shutters open is—for the sake of argument and for the sake of the story—consciousness. Because not only do I see (hear, taste, touch, smell) something in the room, I *know* I see (et cetera) it. I don't just *see* a world in the room, I *know* I see a world. (The same goes, of course, for the 'small world' of the so-called 'mental states' and feelings.) This is very important. But here's something even more important: *opening* the shutters and *seeing* the world is an *experience*. It's not just a sheer, pure, transparent, intangible happening, it's an *experienced* happening. Now, you *know* what an experience is. You can read in a book, 'I stubbed my toe.' Great, it doesn't even hurt. I guess you *could* call it a 'reading experience,' but it's sure not the same as when you stub your toe for real. *This* is what I mean by an *experience*. An experience lets you know a lot of things all at once, in 'both worlds' (so to speak). You see your stubbed toe (possibly turning black and blue), *and* it hurts like hell. But my first point is a *big* point. (Just wait until you see my *second* point, a real whopper.) Hegel—remember?—spoke about 'the science of *the experience of consciousness*.' (And, speaking for myself, when Hegel speaks I listen.) Well, in this little story of mine what we have, I think, is actually the opposite. It's something like 'the story of *the consciousness of experience*.' Remember how that etymology tickled my fancy—'conscious,' from 'knowing with'? Knowing with *what?* we wondered. Well, here's my simple, but *big*, answer. Consciousness means 'knowing with' *the world*. Not just *knowing the world*. Not just 'I know my cat' or 'I know my hunger' or 'I know what a cat is' or 'I know what hunger is.' When the shutters open and— *voilà!* my cat—this happening is my knowing-*with* my cat. It's a relation. A connection. Absolutely! Consciousness is no small matter. I've been telling you all along, Why Dream? is *my* question but What is consciousness? is *the* question.

I want to make this a little clearer. The shutters open—wow! a world. (Or two, if you insist.) This moment of consciousness is an experience, like stubbing your toe. It's the happening of your knowing-with the world *actually experienced*. This is the goddam point that I've been thinking about since I was a kid. How can I explain it better? I really can't, but at least I've created a *context* that may, I hope, help you see the point. As a kid I used to think, My eyes are closed, I open my eyes, wow! wow! a world. My eyes should be *burning*. The world should be *pulling them out of their sockets*. Such an incredible happening. Such an unbelievable experience. (*Experience*, like stubbing my toe.) And that's it. I can't say I *feel* anything *special*. Anything I can put my *finger* on. I'm conscious and that's that. But what has really tormented me all these years is that no one else seems to notice that this *CONSCIOUSNESS of our experience* is the greatest mystery of all time.

That's the first point. I can imagine you out there saying, *What in the world* is this guy trying to *say?* What does he *mean?* Consciousness, stubbing your toe. I think he's rambled right out of his mind. He's rambled off the face of the earth. Well, what can I say? Thanks a bunch for this vote of confidence. Maybe *someone* has gotten my (first) point. I hope so. I don't know. And here comes the *second* point, and it's a whole lot trickier. But *maybe*—I hope—you'll find this point easier to follow. As I said earlier, when I play my first hand *Hegel* is going to give me a *big hand*. Well, hold on. *Hegel's hand* is almost here.

But first, why did I call this hand—this story—*original* consciousness? For a number of reasons. The more I think about it, they're not all that bad. But what counts isn't the word itself, it's the second *point*. In any event, you're in a closed, dark, silent room. Suddenly the shutters open *for the first time*. The original opening. Fine and dandy. I think we're OK so far. If you want, you can also picture the 'original closing' and call the first, birth, and the second, death. (I find this unconvincing—possibly an obstinate illusion—but let's say so for the sake of argument.) Wait! At this point—I mean, *before* this (second) point—let me add just a few things, which are not absolutely essential to the story, but interesting. I asked you to imagine *wooden* shutters, precisely because they never close the window opening *completely* like these postmodern rolling shutters do. Especially not in Venice, where the windows are fine but the window *openings* are all infernally crooked. I didn't want you to imagine yourself in a *vault*, with walls of lead five-feet thick and exactly-fitting lead shutters two-feet thick. No! I wanted you to imagine a normal everyday closed room, where from little cracks tiny shafts of light filter in here and there, chaotically. Where even in the dead of night, with the windows and shutters closed, you might still see a ray of light from the courtyard and hear the muffled sound of a boat going by on the canal. Frankly, I'm not sure why I wanted this image, it could be the subject of a whole other ramble. My Zen master, Suzuki-roshi, doesn't believe in reincarnation but he does believe in a *continuous* flow of life. Life that is individual and common at the same time. He says, before birth my life is a serenely flowing river (*without consciousness*, I'd say), then it's a turbulent waterfall (the turbulence is the *consciousness of experience*), then I pass on, and am a serenely flowing river once again. Wow, what a story. I wish I could have told it to my grandfather. Read it for yourselves by all means, in *Zen Mind, Beginner's Mind*. What can I say about Zen meditation. Well, for one thing, it does not mean *stopping* your mind, as if—originally—it were a *vault*. Not at all. It means 'following' your breath and, with your breath, the waves of your mind, until they enter, *more or less*, our 'original' room with the wooden shutters closed. More or less. And the room is no vault, not at all. For that matter, a true Zen master could meditate in the center of Tahrir Square on a 'hot' day (in all senses). Suzuki-roshi once said that when you are practicing Zen 'you realize that your mind is like a screen. If the screen is colorful … it will not serve its purpose. So … to have a pure, plain white screen is the most important point.' But it's *never* pure white, it *never* goes completely blank. 'My' room—my modest mansard of two worlds, inseparable—is never an 'empty cipher' (as Melville put it). The Roshi once said, 'having a firm conviction in the original emptiness of your mind is the most important thing in your practice.' This is why, with humility, I called my tiny story '*original* consciousness.' I'm convinced we are here to have *experience* of the 'original emptiness of the mind.' This conviction is why I've spent my entire life thinking about consciousness. It's why I dream what—and how—I dream.

An aside: for most of my lifetime abortion has been a heatedly debated question, a truly painful existential dilemma. To say nothing of—more recently—euthanasia. When does (individual) life begin, and when does (can/should) it end? As I said, I have a preference for wooden shutters. A log cabin would have been great for my story. Certainly not a vault. Actually, in the story I wasn't really thinking about that so much. No, I was thinking about this goddam What is consciousness? question. What's more, as you've gathered by now (if you've gathered anything at all, or at least picked it up, like a flower) I believe in the continuity—the *inseparability*—of living and dying. Is abortion murder? Watch out, Hegel is back! He'll be with us for a while. In his 'Anthropology' he has a paragraph (in §405)—right after the one titled 'Dreaming'—titled 'The child in the womb.' A long paragraph. Another ramble. His point—or my point—is that, at this point, 'in the womb' we are dealing with 'The Feeling Soul in its immediacy.' 'Soul' in Hegel's sense that I briefly explained a while ago. Soul as 'only the *sleep* of spirit.' 'The dull stirring, the *inarticulate breathing* of the spirit.' Does Zen meditation *strive* for 'articulate breathing.' Absolutely not goddamit. We follow the breath. We breathe in life, but we *follow* the out-breath, the breath of consciousness—of knowing-with—as it fades into emptiness. With each out-breath we die. We stop holding onto the world with ten hands. We let go. And, letting go of life, we live.

Well 'bless my soul' so to speak, I said 'let me add just a few things' and I've rambled right off into the bush again, just when I was about to make my second point, with Hegel's help, the most important point of my first hand, and there I go trampling the bush, trying your patience, and possibly weakening my hand. What have I done! I never play cards. When I was a kid my cousin used to *savage* me at gin rummy, and poker—forget it. Now, you see, I have a good hand to play here. A fine hand. *Possibly* even a *strong* hand. A cunning little story. But I've overplayed it, as usual. Possibly also underplayed it, as usual. But enough is enough. I'm going *play out* this hand *right now*, at last. With Hegel's *crucial* and *decisive* help. Take it and/ or leave it. As Joseph K. put it, 'Logic is doubtless unshakable, but it cannot withstand a man who wants to go on living.' The problem, alas, is that he is in the grip of a logic *to die by*. What we need—and what Hegel gives me, I hope—is a logic to live by. Not a logic that dissolves the mystery, but one that makes it possible to know-with it and to live with it.

In my story, 'original consciousness,' there is a sense of 'original' that is *much* more important than 'the original opening of the shutters.' You may not have noticed, or thought about it, but if we leave it at that—at that sense—the story falls apart completely. The point is this. Experience of 'the original opening of the shutters' sure won't be much to go on—to live on—for an entire lifetime.

I have no doubt that being born is *quite* an experience. You come out into the world crying, screaming, and all that. Though I can't say I remember the moment myself. The way my story goes—or stands—or stalls—right now, this 'original consciousness' that grips me so much is, basically, something like remembering stubbing my toe *so bad* when I was, let's say, four years old that I've never gotten over it. A mystery. (In a lot of senses.) That toe-stubbing when I was four *keeps happening. Every moment.* In all my knowing-with the world, there it is. Look, my cat!—inseparable from 'I stubbed my toe when I was four.' I have a pain in my ass—inseparable from 'I stubbed my toe when I was four.' No, I'd better have a second sense of 'original' in mind. Luckily, I sure as hell do. I've had it from the very beginning. From sometime earlier today (yesterday, by now) when I got the idea for the story. I could put it like this. The *moment* of opening the shutters is *permanent*, it is always with me, with us, is *always there.* This, for me, is basically what I want to say. But what in the world do I *mean?* Put this way it's nothing but wishy-washy mystification. Where's the 'unshakable logic' here? A 'permanent moment'—it's just empty words. Ye gods, I'm talking about the actual happening of the 'original' consciousness of experience. Ergo—ready or not—to say this *a lot better* I need Hegel's *Logic*. I'm going to limit myself to the first triad that opens the *Science of Logic*. In fact, we could call it the 'original triad.' It consists of three *moments*: being, nothing, becoming. Hegel's word is 'moment' (in German, with capital letters on nouns, *Moment*). *This* is what I want to focus on. What does 'moment' mean here? It means that being, nothing, and becoming are *not* three *things* (or *facts*) in time—in, say, chronological order. Such as: I have a dog. Then I get a cat. Then the dog kills the cat. Then I bury the cat. Then I get rid of the dog. No! That's not it.

Let's follow Hegel carefully: '*Being, pure being*, without any further determin-ation. In its indeterminate immediacy it is equal only to itself.' If we wish, we could imagine it as a sheer, pure, and total whiteness (like a traditional virgin bride) or—why not? (if a lot less traditional)—as a sheer, pure, and total blackness. Why not. Since it's totally indeterminate. Remember Suzuki-roshi's 'your mind is like a screen'? You do! Well, in the case of 'being' the screen is actually totally *blank. Being!* And it's *completely totally blank!* (This, my friend, is *Hegel's* logic. Shaking, quivering, quaking.) At this point calling it totally blindingly white or totally blindingly black *makes no difference. Being*, says Hegel, 'is pure indeterminateness and emptiness.' His conclusion: 'Being, the indeterminate immediate, is in fact *nothing*, and neither more nor less than *nothing.*' Did you catch that! It's goddam catchy. *Being is nothing.* The 'original' in Hegel's logic. Wait! Without ado, he goes right on to tell us what 'nothing' is: '*Nothing, pure nothing*: it is simply equality with itself, complete emptiness, absence of all determination and content—undifferentiatedness in itself.' Pure blackness if you like. (People, traditionally, do like to dress it in black.) Or

how about pure whiteness, why not! Why Dream? (What is consciousness?)
The point is *it's totally blank*. It seems as if we haven't gone anywhere at all.
Meanwhile, Hegel concludes: 'Nothing is, therefore, the same determination,
or rather absence of determination, and thus altogether the same as, pure
being.' But—hold your horses. If *this* were the end of the story it would be as
bad as my 'first-hand' story without the *hand* Hegel is giving me right here.
Shit! 'Original consciousness' means remembering the first time they opened
the shutters, all your life? Dammit, we're not in kindergarten here. Wait just a
moment. I need to give you this paragraph in full. The title is *Becoming: Unity
of being and nothing*.

> *Pure being and pure nothing are therefore the same.* The truth is neither
> being nor nothing, but rather that being has passed over into nothing
> and nothing into being—'has passed over,' not passes over. But it
> is equally true that they are not undistinguished from each other,
> that, on the contrary, *they are not the same*, that they are absolutely
> distinct, and yet that they are unseparated and inseparable and that
> *each* immediately *vanishes in its opposite*. Their truth is therefore this
> *movement* of the immediate vanishing of the one into the other:
> *becoming*, a movement in which the two are distinguished, but by a
> distinction that has just as immediately dissolved itself.

Now, to make my point, which is *the* point here, I have to jump ahead some 20
pages. I need to quote—briefly—from three more paragraphs. Brace yourself.
Hegel is no picnic. I know Freud is a helluva lot easier, and he's got that gentle
avuncular tone. But we can't keep playing around with the 'table d'hôte' dream
all our natural (or unnatural) lives. I have my *hands* to play, and my first *hand*
is already on the table. OK, read this *carefully* and note *especially* how Hegel
uses the word *moment*. (The German word for moment is *Moment*, as I said.
The capital 'M' is only the German grammar.) If you read this *carefully*, you'll
see how my story makes *perfect sense*. (More or less.) 'Original consciousness'
is not *one* (original) moment *in time*. Not something we (I!) always remember
as the original *event*—at a certain time and place—that 'gave rise to' our (my)
consciousness. Hell no, not at all. *'Original consciousness' is the MOMENT
of consciousness in its relation to the world, which is the [its] other moment.
KNOWING-WITH*—the relation between the moments 'consciousness' and
'world' *in their vanishing the one in the other*—is the *formal* equivalent of Hegel's
first triad. Whose vanishing moments are being and nothing, the absence(s) of
determination. But in terms of *content* 'knowing-with' is the first triad turned
upside-down. It is the *richest* possible relation, its 'content' is the world, inner
and outer. Hegel's 'being is nothing'—on the other hand—is the poorest. It's
the gasp that precedes (logically, not *chrono*logically) the opening of content
itself. The opening of what Hegel calls 'determinate being.'

Watch out. *The moments of becoming,* coming-to-be and ceasing-to-be:

> *Becoming* is the unseparatedness of being and nothing, not the unity
> that abstracts from being and nothing; but as the unity of *being*
> and *nothing* it is rather this *determinate* unity, in which being and
> nothing equally *are.* However, inasmuch as being and nothing are
> each unseparated from its other, *each is not.* In this unity, therefore,
> *they are,* but only as vanishing, superseded moments. They sink
> from their initially imagined *self-subsistence* to the status of *moments,*
> which are *still distinguished* but at the same time are superseded. ...
>
> Becoming is in this way doubly determined. In one determination,
> *nothing* is the immediate, that is, the determination begins with
> nothing, which relates itself to being; which is to say, passes over
> into it. In the other determination, *being* is the immediate, that
> is, the determination begins with being, which passes over into
> nothing—*coming-to-be* and *ceasing-to-be.* ...
>
> The equilibrium in which coming-to-be and ceasing-to-be are
> poised is in the first place *becoming* itself. But this becoming equally
> collects itself in *quiescent unity.* Being and nothing are in this unity
> only as vanishing moments; yet becoming as such *is* only by virtue of
> their being distinguished. Their vanishing is therefore the vanishing
> of becoming, or the vanishing of the vanishing itself. Becoming is a
> ceaseless unrest that collapses into a quiescent result.

I hope you're still here. Shaking, quivering, and quaking. As for me, I
absolutely must not lose the connection between Hegel's logic and my first
hand. (And heaven help me with the second.) The key point is this. I am
talking, in the story, about *original* consciousness. *This* is the *mystery* that
grips me. The one that makes me ask my now famous collection of questions.
(*And*—we'll see—makes me experience my serial-killer dreams.) But
'original' only makes sense if we take it in *both* its senses *together.* The 'original
opening of the shutters'—the opening, or onset, of consciousness—*and*
'original' in the sense of Hegel's *logical moment.* (Logical, not *chrono*logical.)
Original consciousness—the *opening* of the shutters—is happening 'at' every
moment *precisely because it is a moment itself.* If you've been able to follow
me on this point, then my story holds together. Don't forget, the story is
not about 'everyday' or 'normal' consciousness, which comes and goes in
time, in constant flux, flow, and stream, becoming reduced one moment
and heightened the next. I read somewhere that (normal) consciousness
is 'reduced or absent' in sleep. (I'll come back to this.) No! 'Original
consciousness' does not 'come' moment after moment, chronologically, in

time. The '(*original*) moment' of consciousness is there in all consciousness of experience and all experience of consciousness. The 'quiescent result' is what Hegel calls *Dasein*—'there-being' or, in better English, 'being-there.' By which he means *determinate being*, the barest minimum of 'permanence.' It is in this sense that 'original consciousness' is a 'permanent' moment. Just as the world is. There is absolutely no consciousness without a world (or two). (Or one.) Original consciousness 'is there' in every moment, but not in the sense of every moment of time, unless we mean *logical* and not *chronological* time. Original-consciousness-with-the-world (the knowing-with) is an *original* moment. This is the mystery. The shutters *open IN every moment*. But just try to hear the *sound* of them opening. The *effort* will drive you crazy. The shutters open *in* every moment. Ergo, knowing-with happens *in* every moment. *THIS is the mystery. Who* opens them and *why* and *why* knowing-with happens is *mysterious* but not *the* mystery. The *mystery* is that all this *happens*. I can't say it any better than this, stories or no stories. Don't forget, these moments are *permanent* exactly in the sense that Hegel's 'becoming' is permanent (and *original*)—namely, as the vanishing of vanishing. In the science of logic—*the realm of shadows*—this is just fine. In my story it's not too bad. I hope it works. Again, the key is that in the story I am talking about *original* consciousness. If you forget that, I'm done for, my simple story will lose its clear outline. What worries me just a little is that I've used a *logical* concept to tackle a so-called *existential* problem. Logic is unshakable. But that was Joseph K.'s *problem*, not his solution.

I think I'd better play my second hand soon and hope for the best. I feel a little shaken myself. Well, cheer up. As Jim Morrison's father said, you can't burn out if you're not on fire. Time to beat around the bush again, just a tiny bit. OK. First let me say that the expression 'original consciousness' has been used by others, quite a while before I first used it myself, about an hour ago. So, let's avoid confusion. I know of two contexts where it is an important term. (And I'm sure there are others.) One is the Bhagavad Gita, a Hindu scripture some two thousand years old. It's the source of the famous Krishna Consciousness that our Hare Krishna friends in their Hare-Krishna-color robes (not to be confused with our unfortunate friends in Guantánamo) love to chant about. Well, in the Bhagavad Gita 'Original Consciousness' means a whole lot more than just 'opening the shutters.' It's what we have to return to, revive, elevate our 'conditioned' souls to, because without it we melt into complete darkness. So, it's important. Another context is Pure Land Buddhism, whose followers seek to unlock the wisdom and abilities hidden within 'Original Consciousness' in order to enter the Pure Lands. I've also seen references to 'original consciousness' as *eternal*—as an *eternal consciousness*. Personally I don't buy this, but it reminded me of someone who does, in a big way. An old college friend named Kierkegaard. A famous *existentialist* philosopher. An exceptional old Dane who almost certainly didn't drink beer. A space-time singularity. Kierkegaard saw himself as defender of the *true* Christian faith. Faith in the Paradox. A faith that *absolutely* demanded of the individual a so-called *existential decision*: *either* faith *or* despair. Anyway, Kierkegaard was a really good writer. A bit theatrical for my own tastes, but good. Since you might still be angry with me for quoting—what! twenty lines!—from Hegel's *Logic*, let me quote you something well-written from Kierkegaard. From his book with the not-exactly-cheerful title *Fear and Trembling* (in the same volume as the even less cheerful *The Sickness Unto Death*). I thought of this because of his reference to '*eternal consciousness*,' which is even more important to Kierkegaard than it is to our Hare Krishna friends. In my opinion by 'eternal consciousness' Kierkegaard actually means (or *also* means—a nice 'both/and' for the 'either/or' man) 'consciousness of the eternal.' Of Christ, God, Eternity, or some such. Anyway, here he is, with his usual histrionics. I really loved this passage when I was in college.

> If there were no eternal consciousness in a man, if at the foundation of all there lay only a wildly seething power which writhing with obscure passions produced everything that is great and everything that is insignificant, if a bottomless void never satiated lay hidden beneath all—what then would life be but despair?

Great, but I'm sticking with 'the opening of the shutters.' Wooden. Not dilapidated.

Speaking of bottomless voids—one last thing. I feel that, after apologizing to Dr. Nagel, I also should apologize to the Unconscious. I have given it very short shrift in this ramble. To say nothing of my pulling its leg with that 'zat' business. Well, I apologize. My *fear*—my problem—was that if I'd rambled—*trembling*—into you, my dear Unconscious, I don't know how I'd have climbed out again. Of your *pit*. Your *abyss*. But I know you're down there! Hegel, my master, admired you greatly. But you are a tricky fellow. See you around. Have no fear, rambling abides. Suddenly! I'm playing my second hand.

2. 'second hand': Why Dream?

Watch out for my second hand! It's nearly a sleight of hand. No, not really, but, to an extent, in a sense, it's a change of tune. Or tone. After thinking about this so much, day and night, this balmy month of November with its serial-killer dreams—apart from the *good* dream I had this morning, I still have to tell you about it—I've come up with a new idea. A new way of looking at my entire 'dream' situation. This was supposed to be a *therapeutic* ramble, and I think it actually *has* been. For *me* anyway. I hope it hasn't been a *nightmare* ramble for you. But I don't think so. Making up this story about the shutters has helped me quite a lot. I think that—in some sense—thanks to this 'original consciousness' story I've already answered—for myself—my question, Why Dream? The point of this 'second hand' is to answer it *for you*. To make *explicit* what I've already figured out—at last—thanks to the playing of my 'first hand.' I've actually started to think that there may be periods in my 'nights' (in my naps I still doubt it) in which I do actually sleep without dreaming. A few hours a 'night' here and there. If there weren't, I figure I'd be dead, killed long ago by all my dream work, butchered by serial-killer dreams. But the *trick*, I think, and my problem, is that when I *dream* I don't actually *sleep*, or don't *exactly* sleep, because I'm not exactly awake either. *Something strange is happening.* So, here's my new idea. My 'second hand.' *I don't think it's a second-hand idea.* In fact it's so goddam original that I can barely make heads or tails of it myself. Here goes. My new idea is that *my* questions What is consciousness? and Why Dream? are *inseparable.* And they are much more than just *questions.* They are *actual experiences.* *My* so-called existential experiences or, more exactly, *together*, are *one actual existential experience of mine.* My experience of *dreaming/[not]sleeping* is the experience of a *fringe* between *consciousness* and *sleep.* An experience in which consciousness and sleep become a *blur* we call a *dream.*

I'm not a scientist, as you well know. I have talked to a number of experts—remember my bat-expert? He was also real big on dreams. I've read some books and articles on 'dreams' (apart from Freud) and on 'sleep.' REM sleep, and those lovely stages of non-REM sleep, with deep, slow brain waves. But these 'sleep' books haven't helped me in the least. Sleep, 'characterized by reduced or absent consciousness.' But, excuse me, *reduced* or *absent?* No one seems to be sure. Aristotle, with his Sardinians, doesn't seem all that sure of himself. He *wanted* to say that when we sleep we are not conscious, therefore time does not pass. But it's not true and he knew it. When we sleep we are *often all too conscious.* It's called dreaming. His dragging those poor Sardinians into his *Physics* was a *strange* way of making his point (that when we sleep we are not conscious). Dragging in a bunch of dreaming insomniacs who had to stay for days and nights and nights and days near/on/in those tombs *just to get some sleep.* (And I hope it wasn't winter, it gets cold in Sardinia in the winter, especially at night.) Well, *the* point I want to make now is that *there is a COMPLEX relation/ connection between consciousness* and *sleep.* Wait! I need to be more precise. I mean: between a [my] consciousness of *original* consciousness and sleep. *Complex.* Personally, I think it should be a question for chaos and complexity theory. Along with the question of *time*, as a 'strange attractor.' I love these 'chaos' scientists, what a shame that Prigogine died. Maybe one of *them* will take me *seriously.* I seriously doubt it. You never know.

Why Dream? My answer is that if someone, like me, *is conscious of original consciousness*—and *this*, I believe, is the root of all my dream-problems—*then the line between sleep and consciousness becomes blurred*. Remember, the point of this 'second hand' is to give *you* some (possibly incredibly vague) idea of why, or how, my making up the story in the 'first hand' about the *consciousness of consciousness* (so to speak)—about *original consciousness*, which has nothing whatsoever to do with *self*-consciousness—has helped me answer (sort of) my 'original question.' My unforgettable question. The title of this ramble. Why Dream? Well, let me say this, for starters. My consciousness of this 'original' and permanent moment of my existence, *this* consciousness of mine that I have *created myself* by my 60-odd years of *asking* myself What is consciousness? again and again and again, *living* this mystery, living *with* this mystery, *knowing* everything I know *with* this mystery — this 'original' experience of my *always* asking, always wanting to *know*, What is consciousness? (a mystery is no mystery if no one is 'obsessed' with it) — *this* is the *cause* of my (practically) never sleeping without dreaming. (A mouthful!) Remember! In this *therapeutic ramble* I do not ask my *reader* the question, Why Dream? No! It is *my* question that I ask *myself*. 'Why Do I Dream?' would be a more correct way of putting it. What's more, I also clearly mean 'Why do I dream *like this?'* Why is it that only two or three times *a year if all goes well* I sleep for 6, 7, 8 hours without being *butchered* by dreams? My answer: It's the price I pay for being 'conscious' of consciousness. 'Conscious' in the sense I attempted to illustrate in my 'first hand.' Everything I *know* I *know-with* the mystery of consciousness.

Now, let's calm down for a second, I don't want the ramble to overheat. This ramble is quite a bit like the only car I've ever had, the 'little camel' ('la cammellina' to be precise), my companion from 1978 to 1983. (Purchased, just 10 years old, in Mulhouse, in Alsace, in France, from her loving family, during the World Cup match Italy-Austria, which I therefore missed.) A wild but gentle animal, and a great singer. An engine like a Wagnerian opera. It all depended on her mood. Quite often, when we stopped at a traffic light she figured, now's the time for my Moby Dick imitation, let's let off some *steam*. I kept buying her new radiators (and pumps—pistons—engines). She was an impatient camel, she overheated easily, this ramble is *far less* overheated. My cats 'let off steam' once in a while too, it's the nature of the beast. Gina gave vent to her steam by killing rats twice her size (she had a physique like Venus Williams), several hundred rats in her 15-year career. When Gilda lets off steam it's so funny, because she's so incredibly gentle. As you know, her birthday is the same as Thelonious Monk's. When she was a kitten I had her listen to Monk day and night, along with a few Mozart operas, the most cheerful ones. But I was telling a camel story, my cats have their own tails. One day I was stopped at a light in the dead center of Geneva and I could feel the little camel thinking, Time for Moby Dick! Surfacing and *steaming*. (*Spouting* is the proper term.) But my mind was fast in those old days. I was only about 30. I said to myself, better do something *fast* to cheer the camel up. Let me set the scene properly. I kid you not, with my over-10-year-old Alsatian Renault mini-minivan camel there I was, dead center of Geneva, circa 1980. At a red light, with a Jaguar behind me, a Rolls-Royce in front of me, and another Rolls right next to me. It was springtime. We all had our windows wide open, enjoying the magnificent Geneva air, we weren't far from the lake. The little camel, a *permanent* singer, an 'original' singer. Right next to a Rolls-Royce renowned for being *silent as a tomb* (whose tomb?). She was quite possibly approaching the climax of her *Götterdämmerung!* With my quick thinking (back then!) I leaned out of the window and captured the attention of the young well-dressed person (man) driving the Rolls right next to us. (Not a chauffeur, a *bona fide* Rolls-Royce owner.) I remember *how quiet* the street was, in the dead center of Geneva, in spring, mid-afternoon, those super-silent cars, and mine singing like Brünnhilde. I leaned out and—with astonishing nonchalance and infinite aplomb, sticking my *ear* out the window—said: 'What a strange *noise* your car is making.' I did it for my camel, and for *myself*. Not a 'bluff' certainly, nothing was at stake. Well, yes, actually, the camel's latest Moby Dick imitation was 'at stake.' No, not a bluff but a *subtle* and quite sophisticated *chess move*. Not a 'gambit' certainly. (That's the only name of chess moves I know, what else is there? The dead pawn?) Some other even trickier move. The horror! This Genevan looked at me with *horror*. Mr. Kurtz is back! A strange *noise!* In his *Rolls-Royce!* Luckily, at that moment, the light changed, and we rambled on.

I hope you enjoyed this miniscule 'aside' (as theater buffs say). Why Dream? As I said a second ago, it's the price I pay for being conscious of consciousness since I was a kid. Obsessed with it, so to speak. Just a kid, and already saying: Wow! What's going on! What's happening! Look! A shoe! My beloved old shoe! Ye gods, I'm knowing-with the world! How come all this doesn't *pull my eyes right out of their sockets!* What *is* this consciousness? *What a mystery.* Ever since—all my life—this mystery of consciousness has been like a flame licking at the edges of my *sleep*. Relentlessly, tirelessly, like the water in the canal a few feet below my window lapping against the foundation of my little *palazzo*. The gentle licking of a *flame*. This complex relation between consciousness and sleep, which is why I dream how and what I dream.

In all honesty I have to say that there's another *quite* good question lurking here. I would be delighted *not* to bring it up at all. In fact I'm going to *beg it completely*. No, not even beg it, just bring it up and then *ignore it*. Let's make believe it doesn't exist. What *quite* good question? *This* quite good question: *Why in the world* have I been obsessed with consciousness ever since I was a kid? Well, I leave the question up to you. If you happen to have a lot of time on your hands, answer away. Write your own ramble. Personally, my own answer is that I don't have the slightest idea. Was I reading Hegel in my crib? Sure, laugh it up. I was playing cowboys and Indians, and Zorro, I had my Zorro mask, cape, hat, sword, cummerbund, and ye gods know what else. But—why does all this *happen* when I open my eyes?! Or, to be more precise, 'Wow, my eyes are [already] open and I see things. What's *happening?*' I don't know why I asked this back then and still do today. People are funny. Why is the sky blue? Wait! Remember that famous 'unfinished' paper on the Greeks and the Ashanti? Which I *did* finish and which later disappeared. The one in the 'unfinished' dream. Well, for that paper I read every book in existence (at that time) on Ashanti religion. I still remember one in particular, a book of Ashanti proverbs (with commentary). One of these proverbs is, for me, the greatest thing ever said by a non-Zen-Buddhist: 'No one shows a child the sky. (Commentary: Because he sees it for himself.)' Knows-with it. This is actually *quite* a good answer to my *quite* good question, and I'll leave it at that. Let me just make one comment, about 'taking things for granted' and about what 'most' people are 'most' conscious of these days. (If it's true, and whoever these 'most' may be.) In Europe and North America, and not only there. (Not by a long shot, for that matter.) (Really, all this is just for the sake of argument. To make a point, which is obscure, and—I'm sure—will remain obscure.) Many people these days, when they meet a person, are most conscious of/interested in: cool or designer clothes; hair styling; electronic devices in hands or ears; possible tattoos and piercings. Many other people (who, in some cases, are the same people) are concerned about the person's religion, income, the kind of car they drive. But I take all these things for granted, they don't interest me in the least, I just never think about them. If you've got purple hair, a George W. Bush tattoo on your forehead, and drive a Rolls-Royce minivan, What, me worry! Actually, I only think, possibly, about a person's politics, if he/she has any. Otherwise, I take it all for granted. Let's say so at any rate. For the sake of argument. For this little example I'm trying to give you. Vice versa, as you well know, I've never taken *consciousness* for granted. Now, if I ask all of these 'most' people, 'Do you ever think about *consciousness?* Do you ever think about: Wow, my eyes are open and I see things, what's happening? Everything is happening and I'm knowing-with it'—if I ask this, what will happen? I'll tell you what! They'll say, You're nuts! What madhouse did you escape from? But, just for the sake of argument, let's say—most improbably!—they say: 'Why, come to think of it, I've never even thought about it in my entire life. I've always taken it for granted that when my eyes are open everything is happening and I'm knowing-with it.' See my point? Some people take certain things for granted. Others—me, for example—take other things for granted. That's just how it is. 'No one shows a child the sky.'

At this point I shall ramble on just a little about two cousins of consciousness, 'loss of consciousness' and waking/sleeping. Have no fear, this is interesting. Do you think that fainting is sort of like falling asleep, but real fast? Well, if you do it's because you've never fainted. Or never fallen asleep. *Wait,* I'm only half joking. This isn't just an Alfred E. Neuman line. Another thing that really used to get to me when I was a kid—and not only then, it still does, even if less—was the impossibility of being *conscious* of the exact *moment* I fell asleep. I nearly wrote *remembering* the exact moment. After you wake up, I mean. But it's actually a question of *being consciousness* of it. Because if you're not *consciousness* of it you can't *remember* it. Anyway, this used to drive me WILD when I was a kid (and not only a little kid). I've always wondered whether it's the same with other people. Or maybe with *everybody,* or perhaps *somebody,* or *nobody.* Not the 'going wild' part but the *thinking about* the 'not remembering' part. *Thinking about* not being *conscious* of the moment of falling asleep. I've always wondered, but I've always been *ashamed to ask.* Never asked anyone in my whole life. Something, again, about that 'taking things for granted' issue, in some sense or other. But this is nothing to be taken for granted! Why can't I remember the exact moment of falling asleep? Just one more *unanswerable* (but *askable*) question, like What is consciousness? But also a question that is *in some sense answerable,* like Why Dream? I've answered it, in some sense, already. There's a *complex* relation between consciousness and sleep, and there's *something* in the complexity of the relation that makes it impossible to remember/*be conscious* of the moment of falling asleep. A scientist would say that this answer is pretty (damn) far from being scientific. But, as I've said, I'm no scientist. This is a *therapeutic ramble* and—*quite* modestly—I'd say it's answering one hell of a lot of (scientifically unanswerable) questions. Perhaps.

Fainting! I don't know if you've ever fainted or if you faint a lot, but in my lifetime I've fainted a *lot* of times. When I was a kid I was a major-league-fainter. Even a flu shot, or even the *sight* of the needle for the flu shot, and I fainted dead away. Many times, for years. Then, luckily, I had a series of herniated discs over the past dozen years or so and have had to have a zillion injections, or more. So I stopped fainting for injections. Blood tests, same deal. Luckily I've had all sorts of health problems in recent years, with blood tests *all* the time, I once had seven in one morning! So, I stopped fainting for blood tests. But I do have high blood pressure now—I take pills for it—and unfortunately sometimes it crashes and I faint. And this *incredible heat wave* that started on August 15th when things normally cool off and went on way into October, to the delight of our tormentors, the mosquitoes. Yes, I fainted twice in August on account of the heat. So—you see—not only am I one of the most experienced *dreamers* you could ever wish for—Behold, this dreamer cometh!—but I can more than hold my own as a *fainter.*

Nevertheless, I shall not write a ramble about fainting. Dreaming is quite enough. But—What is fainting? It's known as a 'loss of consciousness' but I'm a little perplexed about this. When you faint, I'd say it's something like falling off a cliff. Possibly more like being hit by a small meteorite. You can actually see it coming, but when it hits it's unexpected anyway. You just can't believe it. You *see* everything go *completely black*—no, not white! Black. (You 'black out' not 'white out.' No Hegelian logic here.) It's not *instantaneous*. It takes a few seconds. Then, later, after ten seconds, two minutes, an *hour*, you 'regain consciousness' (as they put it). You open your eyes. But you *don't* say Wow! I'm knowing with! Not at all. You just say: I'm still alive. I'm back. *How long* was I gone? You have *no idea* how long, but you remember *perfectly* the moment you fainted. Wait! This 'how long' reminds me of Aristotle's Sardinians sleeping in/near/on the tombs of the heroes, for whom 'it does not seem that time has passed.' Sleep? How long? Possibly, no time! I myself have a similar—the same?—'how long' problem when I sleep (if I do happen to sleep). I always keep a clock with glow-in-the-dark numbers near my bed, because if I *do ever happen to sleep deeply*, without being butchered by dreams, when I wake up (with my wooden shutters closed, obviously) I have *no idea* how long I've been asleep. *None at all*. I'm always tricked into imagining, wow, that was one helluva long sleep. It most be almost noon. Then I look at the clock—4:40 a.m., and I distinctly remember checking the numbers at 4:04. So, one helluva long sleep my ass. But it's *really strange* how tricky my sleeping *is*. And it's all because of my *consciousness* of original consciousness.

Fainting! It's nothing at all like falling asleep. *Falling* asleep. What a curious expression. Nothing like fainting, which actually does involve falling. Falling *asleep*. The struggle of a lifetime for many unfortunate people, known as *insomniacs*. And *so easy* for so many other people. I can't even fall asleep in my own bed, yet *many* times I've seen people sleeping on trains, or sitting on public benches, they nod, nod, head drops—body relaxes—and they're *sitting* right there in front of me, *sleeping*. Sometimes actually snoring. And without *falling*. It's one of the most incredible sights I've ever seen. The Taj Mahal can't hold a candle to this. Now—fainting. Is it like *dying?* Shit, now that's a pretty good question. Too bad Lazarus isn't around (he died again). I have absolutely no intention of getting anywhere *near* 'scientific' answers to *this* question. In many, or most, cases of 'natural death' ('death from *natural* causes'), it seems people 'die in their sleep.' It's the way we all want to die. (Some day.) (Sure, a direct hit by a meteorite would be very *fast* and pretty damn *spectacular*.) You're asleep, and you 'fall asleep' forever. Best way to go. It fits in, possibly, with my story, with the *wooden* shutters. Natural death is not like suddenly turning off a bunch of 1000 watt spotlights, no, it's quite a different image. But—who knows? At the *moment* you 'fall asleep forever' in your sleep, could there still be a last gasp, a spasm, when it all goes *completely black*, like in fainting? (Fainting in itself is *painless*, by the way. It's the *falling* that can be a problem.) (And what if at the *last gasp* everything went *completely white*. Hegel wouldn't be surprised.) What *is* this 'suddenly going completely black'? In fainting I mean. Enough about dying for the moment. (After all, that's loss of *life*, not loss of *consciousness*.) OK, the scientist—a doctor, even—can tell me, it's the blood suddenly rushing out of (or into? I'm not sure now) your brain. But this doesn't tell me a *thing* about the *experience* of fainting, which is what interests me. 'Loss of consciousness' may not be wrong, but it doesn't sound right to me either. For one thing I'd have to rewrite my story (no! I don't want to). Make it about two *vaults* and tons of 1000 watt spotlights and exactly-fitting lead shutters, not only two feet thick but with incredibly powerful *springs* so that thy open and close *instantly*. Forget Hegel. Forget the 'moment.' Forget the whole actual *experience* of consciousness. That can't be right! Consciousness is a *flame* that licks at the edges of my sleep. But, in itself, I feel it's a very gentle creature, like Gilda. It moves around the house, sometimes goes out into the courtyard, or the back garden. But softly, gently, gracefully, like a cat. (And Gilda is the gentlest of cats.) (And sometimes it *struts majestically*, with Gina's regal gait.) Sure, it's a *little nervous* at times. Maybe fainting is a fit of nerves on the part of consciousness itself. Could be, it's not a bad idea. Consciousness is a wild but gentle beast. And always there, *in* its moment. In death, no, even if—thanks to the *wooden* shutters—it may let a few traces seep through. In sleep, *mais oui*. There it is! But I'm coming to that.

With all this *fainting* I've neglected the other cousin, *waking and sleeping*. I have already mentioned my 'strenuous efforts' to capture *the very moment* of falling asleep. But—what do you think?—this is most probably not unconnected with my bigger problem, namely, *falling asleep period*. It's called 'insomnia.' It would richly deserve an entire ramble of its own, titled 'Why Can't I Sleep?' or, more wittily, 'What, Me Sleep?' I joke abut it, but insomnia is actually the worst thing in the entire world. The scourge of humanity. And *humanity* alone. Do you know any cats, dogs, or goldfish who suffer from it? I don't. It comes in a number of varieties, the two major ones being: 'I can't fall asleep period' (type 1 insomnia) and 'I fall asleep but wake up after an hour or two and can't fall asleep again' (type 2). I have *plenty* of experience with both. Believe me, the experience of type 1 insomniacs is one of the ultimate human tragedies, if not *the* definitive human tragedy. Luckily I've only been type 1 for certain (fairly short) periods. But I've known genuine *bona fide* type 1s. A terrible existential situation. You sit there at breakfast with your wife and children, crying because you didn't sleep at all, all night. I don't know if anything else could ever be as bad for a human being. There are many extremely terrible ways to die. But what about terrible ways to live? Sorry, not a cheerful subject. When I was in my twenties I was a type 1 myself now and again. Then for quite a while type

2. *Then* I had that terrible time and reverted to type 1. (The time when I got to know my great friend Gianfranco at the Venice Mental Health Center.) Then I got over type 1 (again) (thanks to Gianfranco—*not to pills*, but to Gianfranco). Since then, I've basically been sticking to type 2. It's clear, obviously, that in type 1 insomnia dreams are not an issue because you *never sleep*. For days and days, nights and nights. Then you do, a little, but you're so totally FUCKED by then that you don't even have the strength to dream. Meanwhile *this* ramble is Why Dream? which, in the variety of insomnia I've managed to maintain over the past twenty years or so, is *my* major issue. In type 2 insomnia dreams hold center stage more than Hamlet could ever dream of doing. A type 2 insomniac is the Prince of Dreamers. The loyal and enormous effort to *sleep*, despite the flames and butchery of dreams. Many—or most—insomniacs, to survive, turn to naps, which are not bad at all. Personally I don't manage to sleep much when I nap, but I do tend to dream somewhat less. By the way, it's absolutely not true that the Mexicans invented naps. No! Cats did. The Mexicans had a lot of cats and, to their credit, they learned to nap from them.

Now, let me say one thing, which is actually two things. OK, I'll say both things at once. Falling asleep is a 'normal' question of *consciousness*. 'Normal' in the sense of 'normal' people who have never been *conscious* of original consciousness. It's never even crossed their minds. Sleep is a form of 'reduced' (*not absent*) consciousness, and most human beings—to say nothing of *animals*, who have it down *pat*—have figured out how to reduce it. Easily. (But I haven't.) It *may* be a question of evolution—you know, survival of the fittest—and I'm a little *behind*. (Still, I've survived. And I'm rambling.) *But*, then, this means that cats are more evolved than humans? Show me an insomniac cat and I'll burn my copy of *On the Origin of Species!* As for my own retarded evolution, what can I say. I've done my best. I lie there, I wait for sleep, I try to sleep, and *what's happening?* I'll tell you. What's happening is that my 'original consciousness'— my *experience* but, far more, my *consciousness* of 'original consciousness'—has stood up in defense of its *complex connection with my sleep*. Stood up vigorously, with banners, waving flags. But this is serious business. It's a *general strike*, or worse. A regular Haymarket Riot, now observed as May Day all over the world, except in the United States, where it happened. An entire life of *trying to fall asleep*—but—my *consciousness* of original consciousness is there. And that spells *struggle*. I know, for you—perhaps—sleep is like a glass of clear water. For me it's the *silt of dreams* right up to the brim. All because of this *moment* of original consciousness that I am *conscious of.* Especially when I'm in bed, trying to *sleep*. Why just exactly *then?* This question *may* have an easy answer. For once. Let's say, at least a 'common sense' answer. Even if, traditionally, common sense is not my strong suit. A far more 'original' and less 'common sense' answer would be that my *WISH* (Freud's word) to *fall asleep* is right on the fault line of the complex relation between consciousness and sleep.

But I just promised you some common sense (not to be demeaned), so let's take a stab at it. Let's say: During the day I'm distracted. I'm too busy *being* conscious to just stand, or sit, there and *be conscious* of original consciousness. But when I go to bed and try to sleep, here we go again! Wait! Think about this! Consciousness, original consciousness, and, especially, *consciousness* of original consciousness *is not thinking*. Thinking is one thing (ask Hegel!) but consciousness is consciousness, period. Knowing-with, period. Original consciousness, the 'moment' of opening the shutters, period. Sure, it's perfectly true, when I lie there and can't fall asleep I can't because I'm *thinking*. About stupid banal things. Monkey mind. But *why* am I thinking instead of reducing my consciousness and falling asleep like a normal person? Or like my cats? It's because I'm *conscious* of original consciousness. Lying there, what I'm doing is not actually *thinking*. No! It's a lot more *like dreaming* or, generally, *blurring*. In dreaming the world is fluid, flowing, streaming (in *day*dreaming too), and follows an—unknown!—logic. A logic of *blurs*. (In Freud the logic was in the *analysis*, not in the dream.) In *dreaming* the world has a logic *of its own*, which, in some cases, such as mine, can be frightening, and terrifyingly *shakable*. All because of the *complex* relation between consciousness and sleep that I call *my* dreaming. *Provoked* by my *consciousness* of original consciousness. The logic of *my* dreaming is a *shakable* logic. A logic of complexity and nonlinear relation. A *chaotic* logic. And I, the dreamer, am the sacrificial lamb. The sacred victim of serial killers, lackeys of this logic. Of serial killing in reverse. Just one victim and many killers.

Why Dream? Guess what, I believe that 'most' people—so-called 'normal' people—really are Freudian dreamers. A *coup de théâtre!* The old eel! I didn't ramble on so long and gleefully about him just for the hell of it. I think people—other people—dream because it's a good way of letting off steam. Cheap, ecological, harmless. Often even entertaining. I once had a girlfriend (a *fidanzata*, but she was German) who was a fantastic sleeper and a perfect dreamer. Every morning she'd report her really fun dreams to me. It was great! 'Letting off steam.' Or, Freudianly speaking, releasing the 'repressed' from way *down* there in the unconscious and letting it come *up* and *out*. Personally I prefer to call it 'psychical letting-off-stream' but if you like Freud-speak, be my guest. Wish fulfillment, guardians of sleep—why the hell not. I actually believe that my friend Siggy knew what he was talking about, basically. I truly respect his sincerity and scientific *humility*. I ranted and raved about him—but it was fun, a fun part of the ramble—because with the whole kit and caboodle of his dream theory he (obviously) *wasn't talking about me*. Or many others like me either.

Far be it from *me*, with this humble ramble, to seek to 'agitate the sleep of mankind.' On the contrary. No! Not 'contrary' in the sense that I'm writing this ramble to *put* you to sleep. That's not what I meant. Ready or not, let me take the bull by the horns (gently). The question Why Dream?—as I did explain, possibly, at some point, a few moments ago—is addressed not to you, a 'normal' Freudian dreamer, but to *myself*, a *far* from Freudian dreamer. Why do I dream what I dream? Why do I dream *this?* Why do I always think? Do I ever sleep? Why can't I sleep a single nanosecond without dreaming? Why do I ask so many *questions!?* How many have I *asked* in this ramble! I've lost count. Anyway, I do remember *quite* well that the title of the ramble is Why Dream? The bull by the horns. In a *nutshell* my answer, for myself, is this. I dream because I have no choice. My dreams *happen*. My serial-killer dreams. Why? I've already told you! It's the price I pay for being *conscious* of consciousness. Let me just say, *en bref*, how the paying of this price works, as I've come to understand it in the course of this ramble. As I see it, instead of dreaming in a Freudianly 'bottom-up' fashion my dreaming is 'top-down.' The boss decides. 'Top-down' is a downright *undemocratic* form of management (as you know). And the 'boss' here—as I've already made as clear as I ever will—is my being *conscious* of consciousness. I lie there in bed, and I see, hear, taste, touch, smell, *feel* and *think* consciousness *happening*. I have no choice. It's happening. Ergo—with all this *happening*—what happens to me in my pitiful effort *to sleep* is that I 'suffer from an insufficient reduction of consciousness in its descent into sleep.' (I made this up and put it in quotes just to make it look scientific. What a joker I am.) For 'normal' sleepers consciousness sinks into sleep like a stone, goes right to the bottom (the unconscious), and a dream—perchance—floats back up to the surface. Not my consciousness. My consciousness spreads out like a lily pad on the surface of sleep, taking little dips from time to time. But these little dips are *dramatic* dips because they are *drenched* in dreams. As I said, I guess I *do* sleep, more or less, from time to time. The lily pad gets so drenched it does go under. But in *my* sleep there is *no clear line* between waking-consciousness and sleeping-consciousness. It's a blur. That's why I have a sense of dreaming even before I actually 'fall asleep.' Some 'nights' I'm obliged to 'fall asleep' 6, 8, 10 times! *Butchered!* That's why I have a sense of *not exactly being asleep* when I am, actually, so to speak, *asleep*. (Or *as asleep* as I'm able.) Consciousness. *It's happening*. What I call dreams are a blur on the border between consciousness and sleep. Sleep may be there, but so is consciousness. That's why I like the one about the *wooden* shutters and the *crooked* window openings. *Absolute* blackness? No way! The light sings eternal. I close the shutters to sleep. (In death I close the shutters *TO* sleep. Against sleep. Because in death *I sleep no more*.) But even the faintest trickle of consciousness *IS* consciousness. Is *original consciousness*. I know-with it day and night. It's happening.

After all this rambling, believe it or not (I believe it!) I have given some sort of answer to the question I started out with, Why Dream? It's been pretty tricky.

Pretty hard going at times. Still, strangely enough, at a certain point in this *therapeutic ramble* the Why Dream? question somehow turned out to be the easier of my questions. Concentrating, at last, on the famous *the* question— What is consciousness?—turned out to be a good idea. Since, as we now know, my incessant and tireless *asking* of this question has turned out to be the key to *answering* (in a manner of speaking) the question Why Dream? No, I have definitely *not* answered the question What is consciousness? But—after all this—it's no longer *the* question. Now it's simply (did I say 'simply'?) *the* mystery. It is a fundamental, original, and permanent part of my experience, which I have to live (and dream) with, and which, thanks to this ramble, I will be able to live with better. No more crying after dreams. Meanwhile, I *don't* believe this 'What is consciousness?' question *can* be answered. (And to the extent that it corresponds to the 'hard problem,' I don't believe the problem can be solved.) However, I *do* believe that it can be *asked*, that I *have* asked it, and that *asking* it has had consequences in my life. *Existential* consequences, so-called. For example, after all this, asking one unanswerable question has actually answered *my* question, Why Dream? My 'first hand,' that little story, wasn't all that bad. It made absolutely no claim to 'explain consciousness' *or* to answer my question, What is consciousness? In chess terms, it was a 'gambit.' At a certain cost (the cost of this whole ramble! which made the little story possible) it served a purpose. It got me somewhere. Somewhere important. Meanwhile, the mystery is still there, alive and well. Opening—and closing— the shutters (being born, and dying) neither scathed nor strengthened it. For me, the mystery of consciousness is the same as the mystery of birth and death. I don't believe that we are born, and *then* we die. I believe that life means dying our birth and giving birth to our death, *in every moment*, because birth and death are themselves 'moments' in the sense that only Hegel could ever have taught me. The wonderful Zen master Shunryu Suzuki, who died in 1971, a year before Ezra Pound (difficult years, for me, and for my masters), told me many of the most important things that I 'know.' That I 'know-with.' For example: 'There is no way set up for us. Moment after moment we have to find our own way. … Each one of us must make his own true way, and when we do, that way will express the universal way. *This is the mystery.*' It's called Buddha nature. Buddha mind. Also known as big mind. The inseparable companion of monkey mind.

This part of my ramble has been long, tricky, and strenuous. Hard going at times. But I feel invigorated. I've got my second wind. I don't know the time. Already dawn. Not yet dawn. Maybe it's only 4 in the morning. Anyway, I'm not opening the shutters right now. (What's the use. After the ramble I'm going straight to bed.) I still have to tell you about the most important dream I've ever had. In Budapest, in 1974. It, too, is an 'original' and 'permanent' moment in my life. But first I want to say one thing about

Joseph K. His 'unshakable logic' stands at the head of this ramble. Kafka was the most profound thinker ever to think of writing 'fiction' (so to speak). Melville for scope (and humanity), Dostoyevsky for sustained intensity (and genius), Kafka for depth. The depth of the surface. This ramble has also been my strenuous effort to give Joseph K. a *hand*. Every day, I take care of my first cat, Gina, who has not been here for about nine years now. Every day I express my care for my friend Gianfranco who has not been here for a year. To him I dedicate this whole collection of rambles that I *am writing*, because I have finally learned this Big Lesson: The dead cannot speak to us, but *we can speak to them*, and we *must* do it. And every day I take care of and care for Joseph K., my long-lost brother, whom I found again, in New York, in 1969. I believe—I hope—that this ramble will help and encourage him. There are no answers to the big questions. To the *the* questions. *If we leave it at that we will be put on trial and condemned.* But what we need to realize, Joseph K., my brother, is that *we have been asked to ask the questions.* Asked by the same 'hand' that is 'no hand' that opens (and closes) the shutters. 'Hands are no hands until they pick up flowers and offer them to the Buddha' is what Hui-neng said exactly. Not to *answer* them but to *ask* them. Dammit all Joseph K., at the beginning of your case you wanted to finish it, and at the end you wanted to begin it again. It's all right now. Rest easy. We'll take care of you, my cats and I. Kafka, do you remember the Buddha's 'Flower Sermon'? Perhaps you don't remember it, but you do know very well—you *know-with* very well—that the people *want answers*. The Flower Sermon. One day— pardon me, my second cat, the 'present' one, Gilda, just looked at me with her *incomparably* (because I make no comparison!) beautiful green eyes, and took my breath away. For a moment everything stopped. Time stopped, the world stopped, the original opening, and closing, of the shutters stopped— and *this too* is consciousness. In these eyes, of birth, I saw her and my own mortality. And originality. What a cheap thrill time is. It's everything, and nothing at all. Sorry, I was saying: One day the Buddha was confronted by the assembled throng of his disciples. *People who wanted answers.* Just before going up onto the dais, someone—some *hand*—had given the Buddha a flower. (A lotus, certainly.) The Buddha, on the dais, silently held up this flower and showed it to the throng. This was the famous 'Flower Sermon.' It's true, *one* of his disciples in the galloping throng passed the gateless gate and *subtly smiled.* The Mind of Buddha is not 'two' and not 'one.'

the tiny dream gymnasts

How few are the sights we see in a lifetime! The house, the neighborhood, the town, the moon, perhaps the sea, perhaps a mountain. My cats have never seen the sea or a mountain. This reminds me of the day I bought my car, 'the little camel,' in 1978, in France, in Alsace, an ad in the paper, from a family that loved her and hated to see her go. I swear, the wife and all the kids bawled their eyes out when I finally drove off. I remember the husband telling me, she's ten years old, we've taken good care of her. Once we took her all the way to Marseille to show her the sea. He cried too. A great memory.

How few are the sights! We might take a trip somewhere from time to time. To India, you say. You saw the Taj Mahal! Great, you say, I saw the Taj Mahal. And the Pyramids! And the Great Wall of China! Great travels. And I barely get out of the house. When I was twenty I desperately wanted to see the Pyramids, I still haven't seen them. Why not? Who knows. But in my dreams—in a lifetime—I've seen it all, a zillion times over. Mountains of images that reach the sky. Have you seen the Tower of Babel? No? Well I've seen ten of them, stacked one on top of the other. In my dreams, in a single night I can see an entire galaxy. Sometimes I visit it too, and find out what the inhabitants have to say for themselves and how they live. But, in dreams, also real short trips can be great. There was a time in my life when I dreamed—every night—that I popped out of bed and floated around the house, hovering, reclining on thin air. Then I went out for a walk, at night, sailing through the narrow streets of Venice six feet above the ground. Skimming over the canals with their glimmering shadows, effortlessly. Coasting through the air. A traveler in a dream. Happy, a stranger, and alone.

I've enjoyed this ramble so far, it's been therapeutic. But now I come to the hard part. I confess: I've done all this rambling because I want to tell you about a dream that I've never been able to tell anyone about. The dream I had in Budapest in November of 1974. It's so vivid, but whenever I try to put it into words it slips away. Yesterday I spent the whole afternoon sifting through my papers, my old notebooks, and—after making a huge mess— managed to find quite a few different versions, all from the 1970s and early '80s, all fragments, some in very rough draft. (A few actually *scribbled*.) All trying to get at this dream from different angles. Or from the same angles. Different approaches, different metaphors. My favorite has always been a fragment called 'The Gardens of Budapest'—actually, in three versions. Just look at them all now, sitting here on my desk, staring at me like Cheshire cats. Grinning! and saying, OK, come on now, it's now or never.

There are two big problems about reporting this dream. First, the dream itself is so simple. Very little happens (the 'table d'hôte' dream is a Spaghetti Western by comparison). What does happen (except at the very end) is so—nondescript—that it's almost impossible to describe. But the second problem is the *big* one: No other experience in my entire life has had such a great impact on me—on who I am. This—genuinely nondescript—little dream, with its very simple but supremely effective 'dream work.' I thank Freud, sincerely, for this part of his theory of dreams, which I consider a truly great discovery/invention, it has helped me a whole lot in these past two weeks, since I've reread the dream book (twice). We dream, and there is something in us—in our psyche, soul, mind, spirit, *not* in our firing neutrons—that transforms the meaning of our thoughts (so to speak) into images. And stories. *Maybe* I'd even say: something in our consciousness that does it unconsciously. But now it's time to write about this dream, and I have to do it *consciously*. Have no fear, I shall beat around the bush as much as I possibly can. I need to ramble my way into this dream. Cozy up to it.

'The Gardens of Budapest' (a fragment) (1974 ff.)

The gardens of Budapest remain in memory for their natural, unkempt vitality, for the wild variety within each of the many gardens (I actually mean public parks, but I like to call them gardens)— but, even more, because of their geographical arrangement in the city. They seem to follow an almost mystical geometry. The foreign traveler making his way day-after-day through the November rains unfailingly comes upon one unexpectedly. Go off in any direction, go on for a short or a long time and—suddenly!—you find yourself before the—open!—gate of a new world. But, again, the magic resides less in the marvel of each individual garden (which is marvel enough!) than in the geographical (or geometrical) relation between all the gardens. If you walk *randomly*, you are *certain* to find one. But if you go out *looking for one* they all vanish. Like in a dream. It's very hard to explain. It's something like Bach's Well-Tempered Clavier. If you could imagine a kind of random configuration on a spatial plane, at the same time not random, in the way that the passions of an individual are accidental—perhaps if you could imagine a temporal plane, like a plane of seasons—and, at the same time, not accidental. Imagine traces on a flat surface, which in some sense is not flat. Like a desert or a sea, under wind. 'Like the two hands of a shadow cast on the desert, our paths will never meet.'

That's the best reconstruction of the fragment I can make. It ends with a verse from an Arabic poem my Jordanian friend in Denmark had just sent me (Poste Restante — Budapest). Another time, he recited a verse from the Lebanese singer Fairuz—from memory now, almost 40 years later: 'Let me be a sail in your eyes, heading for a forgotten harbor.' Ye gods! The faithful dead.

To make matters worse, while thrashing around in all those old papers yesterday I also came across a *really* strange piece of writing, also from that

November in Budapest. It might be useful background material for the dream, 'the tiny dream gymnasts.' I still have grave doubts about this, but in keeping with the *free spirit* of this ramble, here it is.

HO XENOS (THE STRANGER)

I. Silence of the metaphors, a sea, nothing exists. A flute, night sounds, hands and the blind man without voice: nothing exists, the dull footsteps of shadows in the street below, the rain.

II. Venice. The stranger looked out from the boat at the amber flakes on the obsidian night flood. The air was perfectly still. Then I heard the sound of my feet running, pounding on the stones of the street below.

III. Autumn. Leaves rattling in the streets, the sound of feet on the streets, my own feet, yet I am here in the house, and besides that I did not hear anything.

So be it, that's the kind of thing I was writing (and thinking) at the time. In Budapest. Have you by any chance been wondering what in the world I was doing in Budapest in October and November of 1974? I doubt it! Never mind, I'll tell you anyway. It's simple. I'd always dreamed about visiting Budapest. No real reason, just a sort of image that had sprouted, somehow, from my unconscious. (So to speak.) No, jokes aside, I didn't have the money to get to Giza when I really wanted to, so when I had a moment of leisure time I went to Budapest. For two months. It was right between selling necklaces in Denmark that summer, with Sardinians, and selling them in Barbados that winter, with a Florentine. (Who fucked me!) Why Budapest? Basically I was crazy about the name. Sometimes a name enchants me, I have no idea why. Magic. 'Budapest.' 'Wu.' 'Magda.' Apart from the name I'd heard the city was beautiful and *dirt cheap*. Which it was. *Great food*, and *cheap*. This, you see, was the moment when—after over two years—my $1,200 were close to extinction. That is, the $1,200 in traveler's checks—fruit of my nights driving New York taxis—with which I left 'the old country' in June, 1972. I was down to a few bucks and a handful of Danish kroner. I was also down to 49 kilos, a weight I was burdened with until 1977. *Earrings!* My first earrings. Rags to riches, and, soon, 60 kilos. (70 now.) What's more, I was sleeping on the ground most of the time, with bronchitis, or, if I was lucky, on somebody's floor. I *did* graduate from NYU in June of 1972. I *did* have a 4-F from my Draft Board. (Another story.) But I had 'decided' to leave the country. Why? Vietnam—absolutely!—and not so simple. LOVE IT OR LEAVE IT. I left. A decision, I guess. Most everyone took me for a nut case. A Martian. A creature with two heads, five arms, and three legs. Color, unknown. Unimaginable. The one person who actually *asked* me why I decided to do this was my grandfather, Harry Donishevsky. He lived in Atlantic City, was 91 at the time, in fine health but nearly blind. (Born—in the 'old country'—one month before Dostoevsky died.) The only person I used to have real talks with. I told him I didn't like this 'new world,' didn't want to live there, and wanted to write a book about what I didn't like. He looked at me for quite a while. (His eyes milky, snowy, clouded, he was nearly blind). Then he said, with perfect serenity: I think it'll be a long book. He wasn't wrong. How I loved my grandfather!

So, having no chance to sell necklaces anywhere for at least two months I set off for Budapest. From Venice. Autostop. Bad trip, cold rain, slept outside, again. October. So be it. Budapest was *awesome. Beautiful.* The colored fog. The *huge* river, massive and delicate. A dream! On every block there were two cafeterias. Self-service restaurants to be precise, but I like to call them cafeterias. Something like Katz's Delicatessen on Houston Street on the Lower East Side. Just as good but a million times *cheaper. So cheap* and *great food* and *cheap good wine and vodka* and such *vivacious* people, even if I never managed to actually speak with any of them. But, first off, I went to 'Budapest-Tourist' to find lodging. I said I wanted a room by the month. Wow. Two phone calls, and they sent me right off to Karl Marx Ter. (Just imagine, a square named after Karl Marx. This definitely wasn't New York. Or Venice either.) What a great experience. The room—for a month—cost me about as much as a room in Venice for a day. What a great time I had! It's true that all I did for two months was walk around in the rain all day, see a million people on the streets (and some in the public gardens), and *EAT!* extremely well for the first time in over two years. At night I read philosophy and Ezra Pound in my beautiful monthly-rented room. But I have to tell you about the apartment where I stayed, about the family that lived there, and especially about my *landlady.* What a time I had. What memories.

Wait, let's go back to the beginning. 'Budapest-Tourist'—the State Tourist Information Office—the *only* Tourist Information Office in Communist Hungary at that time. A *beautiful* blond (it's true! I gave her two handmade necklaces) phoned a couple of places. She found one room available immediately, by the month. She told me the price. (*Great!*) Then, with great patience and care, she showed me on the Budapest map *exactly* where it was. What trams to take *exactly.* So, with my huge backpack, containing every single thing I owned, including *all* the books I had with me in Europe at that time—Hegel, Aristotle, Plato, a smattering of Marx (1844), and, alas, Kierkegaard's *Concluding Unscientific Postscript*—off I went. She also gave me their card, 'Budapest-Tourist' (accent on the *íst*, pronounced *eest*) with, on the back, one word: the name of the family I was staying with. (Monthly, paid in advance, and *cheap.*) She said (in Italian, by the way), when you get there you'll see *lots* of people in the building, just show them this card. Fantastic. I got to the building (it was mid-afternoon), the street door was open, not much going on, I went in. It was one of those buildings with a big central rectangular courtyard with ramps (not stairs) at one end leading up to three or four floors of apartments, with a catwalk (no, not for cats!) running *all* the way around each floor. I mean, if you started at a certain point, on a certain floor, you could keep going round forever. Come off the ramp, turn right or left on the short side of the rectangle, walk the length of the catwalk, turn left if at the beginning you turned right or right if at the beginning you turned left, walk the width of the catwalk, then turn right, or left, or whatever. Shit, I'm making something perfectly simple sound extremely complicated. It was just like in many motels you may have stayed at, more or less. A rectangular catwalk. So be it. In any event, as I was saying—downstairs, not much going on. But from the courtyard below I could see that there were *tons* of people on the catwalks. Walking, standing, chattering, sitting on chairs chattering. Just like the blond at 'Budapest-Tourist' had told me. I went up the ramps to the first floor and showed my 'Budapest-Tourist' card and name to the first people I met. What a reaction! As if I were a returning hero from the devil knows what war. What a reception. An uproar of helpfulness. And thirty seconds later, *voilà* my landlady! Frau P, the head of the household, in whose home I then stayed for two months. Awesome. Unique. I'll never forget her. (In fact I still haven't.) The only language we had in common was, so to speak, German. Hers pretty bad and mine a whole lot worse. But no matter. What talks I had with Frau P, she was great! She was probably in her sixties (what do I know, I was only 24) and her husband had died (tragically, somehow or other, I never did figure out how) some ten years earlier. What a man her husband was! Erudite, a professor (of some sort), spoke eleven languages. (In fact he left quite a library, which absolutely no one was allowed to touch.) What a shame! What a shame he's not here now to speak with you. In Greek, Italian, French, English! (Never mind German.) This was the great refrain for the two months I stayed there. But it was great. No problem. Then, the rest of the family. Frau P's son (possibly a civil servant of some sort), his wife, and two girls. One maybe 10 or 12, one maybe 4 or 6. (I'm very bad at guessing ages.) Not loquacious generally, plus, of course, they only spoke Hungarian. (What a great job 'Budapest-Tourist' did, finding me Frau P, the only person I actually *spoke* with for two months.) The little girl was really cute. Frau P had her call me *Onkel* [uncle], which, as it turned out, in Hungarian is 'baci' (more or less). When I told her 'baci' in Italian is 'kisses'—wow!—every time the little girl saw me Frau P said (screamed) *'BACI für den BACI'* (or some such) and the girl happily kissed me. I had a beard at the time—still do in fact, I've had it since 1968—and Frau P's husband had had a beard too. So, it was all extremely exciting. (For Frau P the beard was exciting. The little girl, of course, hadn't even been born when Frau P's husband died, tragically, somehow.) The older sister, however, was much more reserved. Shy, actually, and we had a little situation to work out. I had a very nice room in the apartment. Quite big—and with the piano in it. (Of course, alas, I've never learned to play the piano, to this day. But I guess they wouldn't have let me touch this one anyway, unless I happened to be a genuine *virtuoso*.) I'm sure you've heard what great music lovers the Hungarians are. It's absolutely true. Fantastic! Free concerts all over the city every night. I heard Gidon Kremer play the violin at the Franz Liszt Conservatory (for free!). What an experience! He wasn't much older than I was and already a world-famous violinist. And what an audience! I think they made him play encores for about two hours. Unforgettable. So, meanwhile—obviously the girl needed to practice. When she got home from school. I told Frau P—and everyone else in the family, waving my arms—that she could practice all she wanted even if I was in the room. I adore piano! (Bach! Thelonious Monk!) But she was shy. We were all worried that she wasn't practicing enough. I started going out in the late afternoon whether I wanted to or not. (I could sense the whole family hovering outside my door, waiting for me to emerge.) Luckily, after a few weeks I won her over (helped, I think, by all the 'baci' her little sister was giving me) and she practiced even when I was there.

But the best part of this little story is the beginning, the first evening. Frau P had a devilish sense of humor, believe you me. The apartment was on the second floor (third if you count the ground floor as first, which we don't). My first evening. When I was getting ready to go out to a terrific cafeteria for dinner Frau P gave me a key to the apartment. (The street door was always open, there was no crime at the time.) (Totally unlike today, I'm sure.) And then came her *big one*. With a twinkle in her eye, she told me—in our *mutual massacre* of the German language, may it rest in peace—Pass auf! You know we're on the second floor—Jawohl! Zweiter Stock. But, you see, none of the apartments have numbers. (Unvarnished unshakable truth. In Budapest they were incredibly strong on music but outrageously weak on numbers.) So, *Pass auf! Be careful!* When you get back after dinner, up the ramps, zweiter Stock—Jawohl—then turn right—rechts! Jawohl again—and just keep going until you come to the apartment with the paprika hanging in the window. Schau! Look! and we went out on the catwalk and admired her paprika. Perfect! Più chiaro di così si muore, we say in Italian. Clear as day. Can't go wrong. Second floor. Turn right. Paprika. I remember it as if it were yesterday. Clear as the incredible dream I had two nights ago. (The 'fingers' dream.) So, out I went, found a cafeteria near Karl Marx Ter, great dinner, some Tokai, some vodka, beautiful atmosphere. Working people, mostly young, men and women. *Cheap.* Came home. Went up those ramps (three ramps per story, quite practical actually), zweiter Stock, great! Turn right, great! Paprika—*fantastic*. The first apartment I came to had paprika hanging in the window. But I kept going. A coincidence. I knew this wasn't the one. The second apartment I came to had paprika hanging in the window. I'll go on. The third apartment I came to had paprika hanging in the window. Great. The fourth apartment I came to had paprika hanging in the window. Jawohl Frau P, I can take a joke. After all, I'm 24! I'm in Budapest and everything is going just great. I took the *full* 360-degree tour of the second floor and I did not see *a single apartment without paprika hanging in the window*. Be my guest. Tour *any* floor of *any* apartment building in the entire city of Budapest, you won't see *a single apartment without paprika hanging in the window*. Ye gods, they eat it every day, they have to dry it somewhere, where are they supposed to put it, under the rug! Meine liebe Frau P, you have had your laugh. What a great lady she was, believe me, and so *witty*. I'll never forget her. In any event, no matter, a mishap, it's not the end of the world. So be it. I placed myself squarely at the top of the ramps. There was *not a sound* in the entire building. Silent as Kafka's door 'Before the Law.' Second floor. I look *rechts*. To the right. I follow the catwalk to the corner. (There are no apartments on the short side of the rectangle where the ramps are.) I turn left, stand very still, and look straight down the long catwalk. I take in the entire scene. The *dead silence*. I ponder, I figure—the apartment is, unquestionably, 3 or 4 doors down. Great! 3? or 4? 3 doors—paprika. 4 doors—paprika. We already know this by now. I did have a moment of Angst. Not at all a 'the lady or the tiger' type of Angst. After all, I was young, and Budapest—and this apartment building—had truly embraced me with open arms. Welcomed me, sheltered me, fed me. Still, it would not be all that fantastic to rattle my key in the wrong door. In this *dead silence*. The third or the fourth paprika—quite frankly, I was stuck. You see, Siggy, it wasn't a dream. In a *dream* we have both/and. Contradiction. I mean, both doors are just fine. Unfortunately this wasn't a dream. No, this was Kierkegaard country: either/or and fuck you. But there was no 'fuck you'—no! But it wasn't exactly a 'what me worry' either. I mean, I wasn't really crazy about the idea of waking up some sleeping family in the dead of night by sticking my key into the wrong door. Me! A total stranger, just arrived this afternoon, 'a sail in your eyes, heading for a forgotten harbor.' But—Frau P, you wish me well! I know it! I would have adored your husband too, if he hadn't died (tragically, somehow or other). Probably/maybe he would have played this *witzig* trick on me himself. He might even have played a *super witty one*, you say he was your master of *Witz*. I have faith in you, Frau P. Your neighbors will not call the Hungarian Secret Political Police and Armed Forces of the Communist Republic of Hungary if they happen to hear a tiny rattle in their door lock. In the dead of night. It's true. In any event—the third or the fourth? I picked the right one—it was *my door* all along, as Kafka put it—and went to bed happy. Happy about Budapest. Happy about cafeterias. Happy about paprika. Happy about *baci*. Happy about the piano I had in my new room. Happy about not selling necklaces for two months.

Great sense of humor. The next morning, of course, the whole family was hovering outside my door, looking like cats who had swallowed canaries. Except for Frau P, who looked just right. Normal, relaxed, cheerful, brilliant. Gut geschlafen? Ja sehr gut danke schön, said I, a picture of good cheer. Never slept better. No trouble finding the apartment? Not at all, I said. I saw the paprika.

Perhaps it's time—high time, possibly—to tell you about the dream I had in that very room, with the piano, about six weeks later. Or perhaps it would be better to beat around the bush a little more. Or a lot more. To trample the damn bush, reduce it to rubble, to splinters, to elementary *quantum* particles, with quantum *effects*. Or shall I tell you the dream right now? Right off the bat. As best I can. In any event, first I have to tell you just one more thing, because it's important for the dream. For describing and, so to speak, 'interpreting' the dream. Two things, actually. One directly important, the other indirectly important. Both important.

The second thing concerns my grandfather. A sad thing. Even though he was nearly blind, as I said earlier, he was in quite good health, living on his own in his apartment in Atlantic City, taking slow but long walks on the Boardwalk. (I loved to walk with him on the Boardwalk. When I was at NYU every couple of months I took the bus down and spent a day with him.) Doing his own shopping, picking out the cut of *fat* meat he loved, and taught me to love too. (He had been a butcher in his youth, now you see why I always make friends with butchers.) The previous summer (of 1974) there was a bad heat wave in Atlantic City, my grandfather went out shopping, he fell in the street and hit his head on the curb. My mother wrote me about it. When I was in Budapest I was upset and worried about him. He had been my best friend in the U.S. He spent the rest of his life in a hospital. Fully conscious, with a great appetite, but very confused, mentally. He didn't recognize people, or mixed them up. I did make it to the hospital to see him once before he died. He looked good. But he didn't know who I was. Anyway, all this has something to do with the dream. Indirectly. Or directly.

The other thing unquestionably had a direct and strong influence on the dream. (I'm not being very Freudian here. Freud said first report the dream and then analyze it. So, OK, this is backwards. Never mind.) (And I'll analyze the dream—plenty—after I finally report it.) Back in Budapest now. Mid-November. One night I woke up real early and decided to go out to see how the Danube looks at dawn. It was a good idea. I wanted to experience the city completely. Actually, just to *see* it completely (experience implies interaction). In autumn since it was autumn. In the rain since it almost always rained. See it in every light it had to offer, which meant at all hours of the day and the night. And I did. And that morning, still before dawn, it wasn't raining! There was a chromatic dazzle of fog. Budapest had an amazing way of capturing light and turning the buildings, the streets, the river into color. It was poorly illuminated at night (like Venice), the sparsely distributed streetlamps gave off a feeble light, it was very early, in the sky I could barely make out the faintest glimmer, but there were already quite a few people in the streets. A few shops were beginning to open. I was approaching Karl Marx Ter, the large square a couple of blocks from my house, when I noticed an old man with a shock of white hair coming out of a shop. It was a small dairy. Very small, perhaps it only sold (fresh) milk. In Budapest I had noticed something I'd never seen before: milk sold in plastic bags. Small bags. A liter, I presume. In a plastic bag, a liter of liquid seems like a lot less. Check it out for yourself. It sounds strange even to say it, but it's accurate. It looked pretty much like a small white balloon of milk. Maybe it was even knotted like a balloon, I'm not sure. I always thought, that's pretty damn fragile. The old man was just a few feet away from me, we were quite close to one of the streetlamps. He stepped off the curb into the street and—suddenly—somehow dropped the bag of milk. I can't recall it making any sound. The milk immediately spread out into a pool on the grayish pavement, the colors somehow merging under the dim light into an eerie milky gray, richly textured and rippled like a calm sea caressed by a gust of wind. The old man and I—together—bent over this pool of milk-and-pavement. Stunned. How well I remember that moment, such an insignificant event, so many years ago. But who is to say what is significant in our short lives and what is not. The old man raised his head—and I saw *horror* in his eyes. This—*this*—is what I remember best. 'Instinct'—perhaps—Freud would say. I don't think that losing a liter of milk spelled the ruin of that man's life. But—what? I saw his *horror*. I've never forgotten it.

The following night—actually, I think it was two nights later—I had the dream I have always called 'the tiny dream gymnasts.' The gymnasts were young girls. Very young. As I said, I'm not good at judging ages. (Also, there was an ageless quality about them.) Very young girls. And they were very small—'tiny' I've always said. As you may know, for a long time now (since the 1970s actually) very young, small, thin gymnasts—girls—have competed in the Olympics and won many medals. But at least they were 13, 14, 15 years old, and small but not *tiny*. The dream gymnasts seemed much younger than the real ones, and definitely *much* smaller. In fact, I'd say about three feet tall. Maybe four, at the most. Tiny. There were 6, 7, 8 of them, I don't know how many exactly, the exact number is not important. Let's just say a *group* of tiny gymnasts.

They were doing floor exercises on a mat, all at the same time, each doing them on her own, with no concern for what the others were doing. Not as far as I could tell, anyhow. But were they in fact *competing* with one another? Or, perhaps, somehow acting in concert? It's hard to say, I don't know. It's clear that each was making an enormous effort but they didn't seem to be competing. Or acting in concert either. They didn't seem to be *striving* for anything at all. It is clear that they were making a supreme effort, but, just to perform the exercises, not to achieve or gain anything. But what incredible exercises they were performing! Unbelievable! You could never see anything like this in any Olympics. No! Only in a dream! The tiny dream gymnasts were executing the most extreme—violently acrobatic—turns, leaps, and pivots, forward and backward twisting flips and somersaults, front and back handsprings. And each gymnast did all this, somehow, in a very small area, each in her own small region of the mat. Even though the gymnasts as a group covered practically the entire surface, there was something strange about the way they were distributed. There was some sort of strange geometry at work here that I couldn't figure out. The gymnasts seemed to be very close to one another and very far apart at the same time. Were they acting as a group, or each entirely on her own? Did they form a distinct configuration, established by design? Or were their positions on the mat completely random? I couldn't figure this out. It seemed, somehow, to be a combination of the two. It was disconcerting, and heightened the feverish effect of the scene. The frantic pace and frightening intensity of the gymnasts was almost unbearable to watch. These tiny gymnasts, twisting and turning in the air, twisting their tiny bodies into contortions no yogi could possibly imagine, stretching their tiny limbs as far as they could possibly go, and even farther, much farther, to the extreme limit. It was a somehow beautiful but terrifying sight. To see this *complete* effort, this *supreme* effort, holding absolutely nothing back, giving it *all* they had, going *all* out, giving it their *all*, without a shadow of reserve. And where was I in the dream? I don't know! I was there, I wasn't there. I myself was one of the tiny gymnasts—at some moments that's exactly how I felt. And I was a spectator—but a spectator in their *midst*. Not simply a spectator, or even an 'interested' spectator. I, too, was making a *supreme* effort, a *complete* and *total* effort. To do what? I have no idea! I had nothing to achieve, nothing to gain. There was absolutely nothing to be achieved, or gained. We were just twisting and turning in the air with all our might and all our ability, holding nothing back. The tiny gymnasts, and I, *and the dream—because it was the dream itself that was making a supreme effort*, that was *going all out*—went on struggling for a very long time. Not for one or two minutes, like in the Olympics, but *for a very long time*. What's more, it was not a striving but a *struggling*. A *pure* struggling. Not a struggling *for*—no! *Pure* struggling, with all our strength and ability, for a very long time. It was the profoundest, most inspiring, and most excruciating experience of my entire life. In life—theoretically—there can be more than one great love, more than one great passion. But not more than one dream like this dream, 'the tiny dream gymnasts.' And the climax of the dream is yet to come. I believe it will surprise you—*plenty*—just as it surprised me.

There was someone else on the mat, besides the gymnasts and, I suppose, me. A burly man with a shock of white hair. So unobtrusive I had barely noticed him but, believe me, he had always been there. I presume he was the referee, or judge, or some such. Even if this is a contradiction in terms because—I'm convinced now—there was no competition. No contest. Beyond any shadow of a doubt, his presence was *absolutely necessary*. What happened at a certain point in the dream is—in some sense—unassailable proof of this. But I need to say a few words about the mat itself, because it was extraordinary, and its special quality played a decisive role in the dream. And because I've never stopped thinking about this mat—not just the tiny gymnasts themselves, and the 'referee,' but also the mat. It was of a milky gray color, a stunning color, a unique color, that I had seen once before in my life. The color of milk spilled on a gray pavement, when the milk and the pavement somehow *mingled*. What is more, the mat had *ripples*. Do you see what that *means?* The mats that (real) gymnasts use for their exercises are very specially prepared— slightly elastic, certainly not slippery, and absolutely flat. The tiny dream gymnasts were doing their floor exercises *on ripples*. And the ripples *moved*, wavered, quivered. Exactly like a liter of fresh milk spilled violently on a pavement. In complete silence. This is a dream. The tiny gymnasts made absolutely no sound. Their feet, their bodies—their mouths—their supreme effort, in total silence. On a mat that was like an ocean. Like the roaring ocean in *Solaris*, I've always thought. But perfectly silent.

Suddenly all the dream gymnasts crowded around one of these tiny girls who was lying on the floor! I joined them to see what had happened. The 'judge' with the shock of white hair did too. We all huddled together and looked down at the tiny gymnast. It was clear that she was writhing, terribly, in pain, her tiny mouth was twisted almost out of any recognizable shape, yet she made no sound. Not a scream. Not a whimper. It was horrible! I looked down at her and saw that her leg had been broken into two separate pieces!! The pieces were aligned—there on the milky rippled mat—like dinosaur bones in a museum. I had to speak! I spoke. In the dream. 'Look! Look! The tiny leg broken, divided in two.' At last that man, who all that time had seemed more like a blur or a great mask than a man, looked up from the tiny gymnast and turned his face toward me. I had not expected to see this. Ancient skin white and crumbling, deep wrinkles without human design, like the furrows in a field tilled by a madman. But it was the eyes! So huge that, at the same time, his entire face was nothing but these two eyes, and I was looking straight into them! From less than a foot away. In these eyes, what looked like random flakes of snow twisting and turning in the wind suddenly became *an infinite blizzard of snow*. Believe me, I saw it. An infinite blizzard of snow in these two huge eyes. Then the man spoke. His words are with me at this moment exactly as they were then. I have repeated them to myself thousands and thousands of times. 'I think'—he said—'that love is as terrible as time.' I woke up.

This dream speaks for itself. (Alas, it is 'real life' that never quite speaks for itself.) We don't need Freud. You don't even need me anymore. I hope you will remember the tiny gymnasts in the dream and respect them for their supreme effort, as I have done and always will. This little ramble of mine may look pretty easy to you. Almost effortless. Believe me, it isn't. It's been a hard ride all the way. It is difficult to dream, and more difficult still to live with the dreams you dream. Why Dream? Well, after all this, I could very well say: Who Knows? But I think I know a little more now. Sometimes I think that the ending of 'the tiny dream gymnasts' is almost ridiculous. The old man's suddenly saying what he said, and—please remember—*he* said it, in the dream. I make *nothing* up here and change not a word. Almost ridiculous. Trite, almost. Not worthy of the overwhelming impact—and meaning—of the dream. But, especially now, when after *all* these years I have *finally* faithfully reported this dream (it was *not* easy), it doesn't seem so ridiculous or trite anymore. Time brings us love— perhaps! if we're lucky—and then takes it away again. This is logic. Kafka's logic. Unshakable. I think about this often, I'm sure you do too. But we think a whole lot less often about this other, equally unshakable truth: namely, that love brings us time. Love, combined with effort—the complete, supreme, *pure* effort of the tiny dream gymnasts—brings us time. Brings it, and then takes it away. Time to live and time to die are the same time, and different. Not two, and not one. This is what I saw in the ancient man's enormous eyes, in the blizzard of snow I saw there. I saw the *inseparability* of absolute effort and its absolute absence of destination. Of the sail and the forgotten harbor. Of life and death. Our destiny of death. Who is that old man, who speaks to me today *exactly* as he did 37 Novembers ago, in Budapest? In my bed in my room, with the piano, in Frau P's home, with the paprika hanging in the window. He is my grandfather. He is the man I saw drop a bag of milk in the street at dawn. He is at least one man I've known since then, my friend Gianfranco, who died one year ago. (I told him a lot *about* 'the tiny dream gymnasts,' but was never able to tell him the dream itself. Until now.) He is the life I've lived and the supreme efforts I've made, and whatever life I still have to live, and the supreme efforts I still have to make.

After I left Budapest at the end of November I had some very difficult years. Fortunately I got through them. Do you remember my first *fidanzata* in Venice, C.? We met her in the 'old woman' dream. She was extremely unfair but also very young (20 or so), and, basically, I was the one who screwed things up. Though she sure made the most of it! I really was in love with her. (Especially that last year, 1977, when she didn't love me anymore, to say the least.) At that same time, my grandfather was in the hospital, getting ready to die. I was a wreck, an abyss, terribly worn out, hungry, still no money. I thought I might not make it through those years at all. 27 years old. In any event, I wrote two poems at the time that I'd like to share with you. The first is in Italian, and I wrote it to express my great sorrow after dreaming that C. had died. The original title was, simply, 'Per C.: un sogno' [For C.: a dream]. I changed it some time later to a sharp title, full of meaning: 'Una macchia sullo specchio' [A stain on the mirror].

Una macchia sullo specchio

Non sapevo mai che cosa la morte fosse:
poi, in un sogno, moristi tu;
ed io, quando le foglie brillavano sul mare,
diventai un uccello bianco e solo,
quasi immobile, in alto,
una macchia sul nerissimo vetro.

It was extremely difficult to translate this little poem into English (a literal translation was disastrous). But a few months later I had a moment of inspiration—a flash of artistic freedom. I decided, among other things, to include my grandfather in the 'translation.' Along, perhaps, with something of 'the tiny dream gymnasts.' I also gave it the title that has been my guiding spirit forever. My *daimon*. It came out like this.

Separation of the Inseparable

In a dream I saw that you had died
(my grandfather is still alive,
but he doesn't know anyone anymore,
he can't see the shadows anymore,
I'll never see him again),
you had died, it was completely silent.

I was watching the white leaves falling
(they are bright and swirl,
like snow in an old man's eyes),
the leaves were shining,
white shades drifting on a sea of very black glass.

In a dream I saw that you had died,
then I saw the slow leaves falling,
drifting, swirling, falling,
until I became a plain white bird,
high, nearly still,
in a dream,
high and alone and blind
above the sea you had left behind.

last dream

All this, and I still haven't told you about the dream I had this morning. The good dream. Gentle reader, you must have the patience of a saint. It's been a long night. You don't believe I wrote this entire therapeutic ramble in one night, until dawn? Like in the old days, making earrings. Neither do I. You're not wrong. But you're not right either. Anyway, I guess I'm coming to the end. I must say the ramble's turned out a lot longer than I expected. The funny thing is that everything in it is absolutely true. All facts, no bullshitting. I really did read those two books of Freud's *twice* in the past two weeks. And everything in the dreams is true. I hope nobody sues me. Can somebody sue you for dreaming about them? No, surely not. But, for writing it down, I'm not so sure. In any event, let's hope for the best. Now! This morning's dream— the good one—let's see if I can still remember it. I was standing right here, at the window, just to the left of my desk (where I am now), together with a personage I call 'The Wittgenstein Man.' My greatest tormentor of all over the past year, worse than the heat wave and all the mosquitoes put together and multiplied by a zillion. (I'm exaggerating.) It was a beautiful clear November afternoon, we were chatting quite amicably—about Wittgenstein, of course— and looking out over the canal at the long garden. (I mean, longer than it is wide.) (The same one that was the scene of the wreaking-ball disaster a few nights ago.) We were admiring the magnificent tree that dominates the garden. (Not to say that the other, smaller trees are not lovely too.) (And in the spring a sea, a veritable flood of wisteria! Everything else pales beside it.) It's the 19th of November and the tree is still lush with its red autumn leaves. But, at the top, we see a brilliant sprinkling of leaves that are fresh and green. Beautiful vivid bright green leaves. A chaos!

This summer here in Venice we had a heat wave that, after a very cool June, July, and half of August, *started* on the 15th of August (exactly when it usually starts to rain and things cool off) and went on way into October. (To the infinite delight of our devoted companions, the mosquitoes.) I just heard from a friend that in Croatia, near Split, people—human beings—were swimming in the Adriatic *last week.* It's insane. It makes no sense. The weather has turned chaotic. Or, much more precisely, *we*—we so-called 'human' beings, of which I am one—have turned our weather into a chaos. Turned the environment into a chaos. Turned the planet into a chaos. A big job! A *chaos.* It's true, I've never been a *fan* of Sigmund Freud's, but when I chanced on 'chaos theory' about twenty years ago I did become a big *chaos fan,* Ilya Prigogine suddenly became my great hero. Orderly disorder. We've seen it in Melville. In this very ramble. 'The classification of the constituents of a chaos.' 'Careful disorderliness.' Chaos theory. In a tiny nutshell, we could boil it down to two animals (metaphorically speaking), the butterfly and the flea. Also known, respectively, as 'sensitive dependence on initial conditions' (the famous 'butterfly effect') and *nonlinearity,* which is really the heart of the matter. Don't worry, they are inseparable. The 'butterfly effect'—a butterfly flapping its wings today, say, in Tokyo can transform storm systems next month, say, in London—tells us that it's impossible to forecast the weather because any prediction you make (however powerful your computer) deteriorates rapidly. Uncertainties multiply, exponentially, and not 'accidentally' but 'necessarily.' (Philosophically speaking.) Scientifically. But 'nonlinearity' is even better. One nice way of putting it is that 'the act of playing the game has a way of changing the rules.' It means that things don't add up, they multiply 'chaotically' and add *way up,* branching out in all sorts of unexpected directions. The beautiful vivid leaves I see today in the garden just across the canal are an example of this. Now, the flea! I made this one up myself. A (stripped down) first cousin of 'chaos theory' is called 'catastrophe theory.' (It's a *lot* more than just a theory.) Up to a point it's not exactly nonlinear, which makes it easier to understand. Let's take *one* flea. (In *theory* hopefully! And *not* on my cats.) One flea has the power of *one flea*—this is both remarkable and unshakable. Namely, let's say the power to *reproduce* itself. (Freud likes this sort of reasoning, as with his story about the 'ciliate infusorian,' a.k.a 'slipper-animalcule.') So 1 flea is actually 2 fleas, and 2 are actually 4, and 4, 8—16, 32, 64, 128, 256—believe me, in a jiffy you've got millions and zillions. (Any exterminator who dreams *this* has one *hell* of a death wish.) The power of *one flea.* Now let's imagine that all these fleas form a pyramid like, let's say, the pyramids in Egypt, which I've never seen. (Scientists usually explain 'catastrophe theory' with grains of sand but, as we well know, I'm not a scientist.) A first gigantic layer of fleas, then a second, a third, a zillionth, and so on up to the apex of the pyramid. But hold onto your hats, here comes the good part. 'Catastrophe theory' tells us that, with our magnificent pyramid of fleas, at a certain point (called a 'tipping point'—it's famous too) (and here things become nonlinear as all hell, the rules of the game change *in a big way*) add just *one more tiny flea* (mighty beasts!) and the entire pyramid collapses, crumbles, and effectively *disappears.* Extinction! I rest my case.

With this humble thought. Beautiful vivid green leaves on the 19th of November, in Venice, means that something is profoundly *rotten* in our world, and it's something we have done ourselves. *Something* we have achieved. *Something* we have gained. *Rottenness*. Perhaps what we need now is a *long sleep*—a *real* long one—a *long long long* one. In the hope, perchance, to dream about the beautiful rottenness we have created. To sleep, to dream, and to *awake*. Fling the Stone! The Bowl of Night! Now *here* is an answer to my question: Why Dream? Dreaming and *waking from a dream* are inseparable. You never thought of such a thing! Elusive, but obvious. Not two and not one. Satori. Wu. Sudden enlightenment. Zen mind. Somehow or other, yesterday, while *thrashing* around in my old papers and making a *big mess*, looking for old fragments of 'the tiny dream gymnasts,' I came across an old annotation of mine. I'm convinced it's from Kafka, probably the *Diaries*, I'm sure I never wrote anything this profound myself. (Certainly not in the 1970s.) It's a reference to *Genesis*, 41, where our old friend Joseph—Behold, this dreamer cometh!—managed to interpret Pharaoh's *very* complicated and tricky dream. No mean feat. It saved the lives of his people 'by a great deliverance.' You see, This Dreamer! What was to become of his dreams! What Kafka noted was absolutely right. Even if Pharaoh's dream was a maze of metaphor, a labyrinth of his mind, 'more important than the metaphor itself was that Joseph *was able to understand the dream.*'

Such is life. So be it. The Wittgenstein Man and I standing at the window, chatting about Wittgenstein, and slowly, gradually, the long garden on the other side of the canal is transformed into a vast Greek amphitheater. (Like the ones I've seen at Siracusa in Sicily and Epidauros in Greece.) We stand happily at the top of the vast theater looking out over the invisible throngs. Far below us, the empty stage and, beyond, the brilliant sea and sky. And at the same time we are home, in this house, in Venice. As we are watching all this so contentedly suddenly something appears in the sky, way out in the distance but rapidly approaching. Now we recognized it. A huge jet airplane, a jumbo passenger jet. Coming slowly but straight at us, right at eye level. Right in our faces! It sure seems to have our number. Never mind the wrecking ball I dreamed last week, this jumbo is getting closer and closer, slowly, huger and huger, and so distinct we can see every rivet in its great metal nose. We can practically see (or imagine we see) the face of the pilot. *Coming straight at us.* Help! Where's my friend! Where's my coach! Closer, closer, bigger, closer! Then, at the last moment (as if already right over the canal! but distances are not real in dreams) the great plane does a slow graceful flip-flop, like a giant dream gymnast doing a magnificent super-slow-motion backward somersault. We—not with relief, but with admiration, happiness, and joy— we watch it fly back again in the direction it had come from, illuminated by a soft, sharp light. Shit, I say, in Italian, 'ho visto l'altro mondo.' The next world. The end of my life. *Another* world. What other world? A brush with death. *What* brush? Why dream? A close shave, but this one is a good dream. We feel good as we watch the huge plane slowly vanish. A beautiful sight. It is already a glimmering speck on the horizon.

> Die Logik ist zwar unerschütterlich, aber einem Menschen der leben will, widersteht sie nicht.
> —Franz Kafka

> What we cannot reach flying we must reach limping...
> The Book tells us it is no sin to limp.
> —*Maqamat al-Hariri*
> (quoted by Freud at the end of *Beyond the Pleasure Principle*)

'19 November 2011'

references (in chaotic order of appearance)

Franz Kafka, *The Trial*, translated by Willa and Edwin Muir, Schocken Books, 1968.
'Logic is doubtless unshakable…': The quote is from the end of the next-to-last paragraph of the book, p. 228.
'Before the Law' is in Chapter 9, 'In the Cathedral.'
'at the beginning of your case,' see p. 226.

Ezra Pound
Drafts and Fragments of Cantos CX—CXVII, New Directions, 1968

Canto CXIII
And in thy mind beauty, O Artemis
Daphne afoot in vain speed.
When the Syrian onyx is broken.
Out of dark, thou, Father Helios, leadest,
but the mind as Ixion, unstill, ever turning.

Canto CXV
A blown husk that is finished
but the light sings eternal
a pale flare over marshes
where the salt hay whispers to tide's change

The Cantos (1–95), New Directions, 1956
And then went down to the ship: Canto I, p. 3.

Personae, New Directions, 1971
When, when, and whenever: from *Homage to Sextus Propertius* (1917), p. 218.
Separation on the River Kiang, from *Cathay*, p. 137.

Herman Melville, *Moby Dick*, Chapter 82
There are some enterprises in which a careful disorderliness is the true method.

Sigmund Freud, *On Dreams*, The Standard Edition, W. W. Norton, 1952.
—— *Beyond the Pleasure Principle*, The Standard Edition, W. W. Norton, 1961.
—— *The Ego and the Id*, The Standard Edition, W. W. Norton, 1960.

The Rubáiyát of Omar Khayyám, translated by Edward FitzGerald (any edition, first quatrain): Awake! for Morning…

Michel Serres, *The Birth of Physics*, Clinamen Press, 2000.
…the course erodes the banks, erodes the mountains, fills the valleys, the solid flees, is atomized in the alluvial cones, I can never sit twice on the same bank. The solid is less stable than has been said, liquid is more solid than was thought. Time atomizes more than it flows.— p. 153.

D. T. Suzuki, *The Zen Doctrine of No-Mind*, Samuel Weiser, 1972.
Hands are no hands, have no existence, until they pick up flowers and offer them to the Buddha.— p. 42.

Shunryu Suzuki
Zen Mind, Beginner's Mind, Weatherhill, 1970.
a serenely flowing river: 'Nirvana, the waterfall'— pp. 92-95.
'original emptiness of your mind'— p. 128.
'There is no way set up for us'— p. 111.
not always so, HarperCollins, 2002.
'your mind is like a screen'— pp. 50-51.

Hegel!
Hegel's Science of Logic, translated by A. V. Miller, George Allen & Unwin, 1969— p. 58, pp. 82-83, and pp. 105-106.
But in my 'rereading' (i.e. reading) of Why Dream? in August, 2017, I partly/ mostly replaced the traditional Miller quotes with the new quotes by Di Giovanni: *The Science of Logic*, translated by George Di Giovanni, Cambridge University Press, 2010— p. 37, pp. 59-60, and pp. 80-81.
Hegel's Phenomenology of Spirit, translated by A. V. Miller, Oxford University Press, 1977.
Philosophy of Mind, translated by William Wallace and A. V. Miller, Oxford University Press, 1971. Much better translated as *Hegel's Philosophy of Subjective Spirit*, edited by M. J. Petry, Reidel, 1978. (Unfortunately I don't have a copy.)

Thomas Nagel, *Mortal Questions*, Cambridge University Press, 1979.
Daniel C. Dennett, *Consciousness Explained*, Back Bay Book, 1991.
David Chalmers, *The Conscious Mind*, Oxford University Press, 1998.

Søren Kierkegaard, *Fear and Trembling* and *The Sickness Unto Death*, translated by Walter Lowrie, Doubleday, 1954— p. 30.

IV.

Gilda's Tail: What is it like to be a cat?

a gentle rant

'Thinking and being are the same.'
Parmenides

My name's Gilda.* My partner, the giant, named me after a fly he knew and loved right around the time I was born. They used to eat yogurt together, and after her lunch the fly would perch on his arm for a while, then buzz happily around the kitchen—buzzz, jizzzz, jillll... Gilda! That's how I got my name.

How do I know all this? How should I know! What does a cat know! About time past, present, or future—about *time*, about history, about 'whether there be any patch left of us/ After we cross the infernal ripples.' How should I know. And my subject here—what is it like to be a cat?—well, hold your horses. For starters, how do I know I *am* a cat? Just because the giants in the house and in the courtyard said 'kitty kitty pussy pussy' when I was little? No way, never trust these giants. The only one I trust—completely—is my partner, a special giant with fur on his face but none on his head, who is always here. (The others come and go.) I love him. He never called me 'kitty kitty pussy pussy,' he's always called me Gilda. So how do I know I'm a cat? If I do know it—and I might be wrong, I might not be a cat at all. I might be a giant dreaming I'm a cat. And, for starters, what *is* the cat that perhaps I am? I have applied a sort of process of elimination to the question. It goes like this. I love birds (and try to catch them), but I am not a bird. I love lizards (rarely see them anymore), flies, and especially butterflies, but I'm not them either. I love the little fish I see swimming in the canal from time to time, but I'm definitely not a fish. I'm afraid of big dogs, and I'm not one of them. I don't care at all about mice (too fast) or rats (disgusting), and I'm not one of them either. I hate mosquitoes and you'll never convince me I'm one myself—just think, a mosquito dreaming it's a cat! And, for sure, I'm not a giant (like my partner). What is more, quite a few times I've met animals very much like me—about the same size, with fur—and I've liked them, usually. (One did try to hurt me once, he must have been crazy.) When I was little I played with a black one in the courtyard—wrestling—and once one even came to stay in the house for a week, it was a lot of fun, and once two came for a week. And one came often, once a week. They were a lot like me—not at all like birds, butterflies, or giants—and... and...

---

* 'Gilda' in Italian with a soft 'g', as in Gina, gin, ginger.

they were cats. What's a cat? How should I know. It's not a bird or a giant, it's like me. It's whatever I am.

So, what's it like to *be* one? It's pretty nice. It's fun. I feel really loved. Loved a lot. I always have lots and lots of things to do, but I never have to do anything. If I sleep all day, especially when it's rainy, it's perfectly normal. My favorite thing of all is trying to catch birds—we have pigeons, blackbirds, and real small quick birds (sparrows), both in the courtyard in front and in the back garden where I go when my cat flap isn't closed. Birds are very very very smart—for me, the smartest animal in the world is the bird. Blackbirds are the smartest. I try to sneak up on one, it just stands there as calm as could be, I'm all tensed up to leap—and it flits away. Too smart. It mocks me, but it's fun anyway. I have caught very few birds in my life, in the back garden (never in the courtyard), and carried them through my cat flap into the house to play, but my partner, the giant, was *not* happy. I don't know why. In the courtyard I love to chase little lizards, but I practically never see one anymore. (And their tails come off so easily.) But the greatest playmates in the world are butterflies (possibly along with cats, if there are any). (Playing with giants is usually just ridiculous.) I have captured a few in the garden, it's not at all easy, they are so delicate. The trick is to get them very gently but firmly by the very tip of one wing, without hurting them—it's hard but not impossible, I've done it! One time I brought one into the house and right upstairs into the sunny room where my giant was, and the butterfly and I played for a real long time until we were both totally exhausted. Flat on our backs. Then my partner—I was exhausted but I saw him—approached the exhausted butterfly with one finger, very gently. The butterfly hopped on, my giant opened the window, and my sturdy little friend flitter–fluttered happily back out into the garden. Another really fantastic thing is sneaking into other houses. Jumping on top of a wall is good, but sneaking into a house is something special. The other house on the canal is very tall and has lots of different giants in it. If one of them leaves the door open a little (and they often do) I sneak in and run in a flash all the way up the many many stairs. I come back down pretty quick, meeting a giant or two. Sometimes I get closed in but that's fun too, some giant will open the door pretty soon. But the most fun of all is sneaking into the house next door, in the corner of the courtyard. It's a challenge, it's almost always closed. But sometimes a giant comes and yells 'Gilda no! Gilda no!' when she opens the door—it's great fun—but I try my very best to sneak in and sometimes I do, and dash through the house and hide under the bed. It's great!

Another great thing about being a cat is that you don't have to think too much—I'm joking! A cat is actually a furry form of pure thought—we are actually whatever's around us *in thought*. (Unless we're asleep, which we very often are. But, then, there are those dreams…) Whenever I'm completely awake I'm edgy, nervous, and usually afraid—just because reality is *right here*, right before my eyes, and there's no escape. Reality is hard to take in but a cat has no choice, like giants do. Giants can think *about* things, think them into or out of existence, but we cats—if we happen to be awake—are thought itself, pure thinking. When I move around the house it's not exact to say that I think *about* every millimeter of space, the tiniest movement of things or shadows—no, I *am* all that, in thought. You say I'm boasting, that this can't possibly be what it's like to be a cat. How do you know! Remember, I'm not a rat or a bat but a CAT. What's the difference, we're all *animals*, you say, you giants. (Meaning all of us who are not giants.) Well then, I say, what's really the difference between a giant and a flea? OK, the size, but I mean the *real* difference. A big one, you say. Well, same here. Being a cat is something really different. And remember—*you* asked me what it's like to be a cat.

Let's not rant. I love being a cat, even if my life is not as easy as some giants think. My partner knows it's not so easy. I love him. I pet him with my paws keeping my claws all the way in to keep from scratching him. I lick him on the fur on his face and on his furless head, this strange giant. I sleep on top of him, next to him, between his legs. He dreams a lot. He loves me. He makes me feel free. He almost never goes out of the house (or for short times only), so we're together almost all of the time. I also love our house. I love it so much. I like the courtyard, though I liked it more when I was little. There was that black cat (whatever a cat is!) to play with, and I also liked all the strange giants taking photos, and sometimes little giants—I let them pick me up and carry me around (gently). I didn't mind it, it was strange but fun. Now all the strange courtyard giants frighten me, I prefer the back garden, it's quiet, and sometimes there are butterflies. But it's the house I really love, every millimeter of it. So many places to go! My partner's desk, under the lamp while he works. Many tables, rugs, many many chairs with wonderful cushions, especially the bed with its furry blanket, other blankets I can also hide under, many places to hide, the cushion on the floor under my giant's desk (a favorite hiding-not-hiding place), the special wooden sculpture just for me where I do my claws—I love my house! If I feel like it I can dash up and down the stairs all I want. I know my giant loves the house too but he has so much to think *about* it—too much! He's always doing something *about* the house, thinking about it, doing about it. I can feel him thinking about things, lots of things, sometimes doing something about them, usually— and all the time—thinking about them. I just love the house. And him. Still, I like to hide in the house, or go under a blanket, or just go far away, downstairs, to feel alone. I don't know why. Sometimes my giant thinks about it and misses me and carries—or chases—me back upstairs. But I don't think about it—remember, I am a furry form of thinking itself. I never think *about* eating for example: no, suddenly I just eat. I never think about being hungry: no, suddenly I *am* hungry. I might check on my bowls—my crunchy–food bowl or my smooth–food bowl—or not. If I see food in a bowl I might eat it, or not. If I'm hungry. I never think *about* it. Same deal if I'm thirsty, with my magic water bowl. I drink from it often, but it's always full! I never think about it, I just drink. If I'm thirsty. If it's a sunny day I'm happy. If it rains I'm happy—*not* happy *about* the rain, just happy. I say, I can't go out so I won't go out. No problem. Just a thought. Happy.

But being a cat is also hard. Pure thinking is not at all hard. What's hard is that, when I'm awake, there's always so many things right in front of me, all around me—if I turn my head just a fraction, new things! If I go from the chair to the bed, *so many things*. And I, a cat, a furry form of pure thought, think them all. (Not *about* them, but still, I have so much *thinking* to do.) I love them, but they are so many. And not only things but sounds, and light, and dark, and heat, and cool, and cold. And always changing—all the same, but always *changing*. I don't think *about* this, but that's how it *is*. Things as it is. I feel very very safe in our house, but I also have a lot of fears. It's hard. The sudden sound of a seagull in the dead of night. The sudden sound of a mosquito killed with the electric tennis racket. Sudden sound. I have no filter, no barrier, no distance, no judgment. It's just a pure event. In thought. I think: I thought thought. And what about thunder and lightning! I know, when I was small they were fun and exciting, like a butterfly. And now I'm terrified. Why? Why? I have always loved the sun, and the clear, calm sky. But I used to love the thunder and the lightning too and now I'm terrified. Change—that's the fear. That things change, and I change. I don't think about it, but it happens. I don't think about death, but it happens. Sometimes my giant gets very sick, and that frightens me. Why is it very hot sometimes and very cold other times? Why is there the bright sun I love, and then the total darkness—and very often! *Why do things happen?* There's a long time when in the courtyard and in the back garden it's cold all the time, and even in the house it's not all that warm. (But, strangely enough, there's one place in the house near my favorite chair where it's *real* warm and I cuddle up there on the soft cushion.) And then sometimes, for a long time, it's very hot, in the house, in the courtyard, in the back garden. Why? Why is the house full of mosquitoes now and we can't sleep and my partner has to chase them with an electric tennis racket, and it's cold in the courtyard and I hear the rain pattering on the roof? It wasn't always like this! Why do things change? Why do they happen? Why am I awake? Even when I was small I had wild dreams—that hasn't changed. Sometimes my crunchy–food bowl is empty, so I don't eat crunchy food. Sometimes it's not empty, so I eat crunchy food. Sometimes my smooth–food bowl is empty, so I don't eat smooth food. Sometimes my smooth–food bowl is not empty, so I eat smooth food. If I'm hungry. There's no problem. I feel very very safe. Even when

another cat—whatever 'cat' may be, and whatever it may be like to be one—
came to the house and ate the crunchy or the smooth food in my bowls, I was
always very happy, I was never afraid. I never thought about it. (At least not
when I was awake.) My giant *always* gives me food—crunchy food at noon,
smooth food in the evening. And the next day: crunchy food at noon, smooth
food in the evening. And the next. Always. Even when he was very sick, like
the last time when it was very hot everywhere—in the house, the courtyard,
the back garden. I am a furry form of pure thinking. I don't know why things
happen. But I know death happens. Why? We cats, whatever we are, see an
event of death in whatever we see—in whatever we see happen, whatever we
see change. All the time. This is the price we pay for never thinking *about*
things: no filter, no barrier, no distance, no judgment. The *acqua alta* comes
into our house in Venice (I confess, I am a Venetian 'cat') from under the floor.
Period. Just do it!

My bowl is never empty. Life is my bowl and death is my bowl but it is
never empty. As a 'cat' I know what death is *not*: death is not no food in my
crunchy–food bowl and no food in my smooth–food bowl. Death is not the
thunder and the lightning that terrify me. Is it the sudden sound of a seagull
in the night? I fear it may be. A cry of shadow. A change.

We 'cats' (whatever we may be) have a big—and well-earned—reputation for
sleeping a whole lot. We can sleep for many hours at a time. We can take
incredibly short naps. But what about our trances? The time we pass neither
sleeping nor awake? Believe me, this is not Zen meditation, that endless effort
not to think *about* anything. That is a problem for giants. No, I've been telling
you, we 'cats' do not, ever, think *about* anything. We are 'the furry form of pure
thinking.' Thinking *about nothing*—forget it! We are cats, not philosophers.
And no cat has ever been a Zen master either. But we are, also, animals that
sleep. All animals sleep. (OK, there are some doubts about whales, mosquitoes,
and possibly bats.) Hamlet sleeps, for sure. And dreams—in life for sure, if
not—'perchance'—in death. I dream a lot. I think that when I was smaller my
dreams were wilder, and now—perchance—I do have long times of dreamless
sleep. (Which, alas, my giant never does.) Perhaps. When I was small I often
had those wild dreams, making all sorts of noises and little jerks. My partner
would shake me very gently and I'd wake up, completely bewildered for just
a little while. Then I'd forget all about it. I still have dreams like that, and my
partner still shakes me gently awake. But a lot less often.

If you have followed my gentle rant all this way, practically to the end, you
can figure for yourself that I remember *absolutely nothing* about these dreams.
We cats are the event itself, not the remembrance. *That* is what it's like to
be a cat. *You* can surmise—thinking *about* it—that I dreamed, I dream, of

butterflies and blackbirds, thunder and lightning, mosquitoes and other cats, giants and my giant. Think *about* it—that's your business. Still, for me a dream is a problem—a Big Problem? Why dream? Why do things change? Why do things happen? What *about* the furry form of pure thought I am? Why dream? All over again, because we 'cats' (whatever we are) have love but no sociality? 'Gilda' he cries, my giant. To sleep or to act—*totally*, one or the other. No way. Forget it. Sometimes I think my life is a dream, and that when my bowl is empty forever I'll wake up and discover what it is *really* like to be a cat.

26 October 2011

references

'whether there be any patch left of us'
Ezra Pound, *Homage to Sextus Propertius*, XII

'we are liable to use our selfish scale when we analyze, or when we have an idea about something. That selfish part should be empty. How we empty that part is to practice zazen and become more accustomed to accepting *things as it is* without any idea of big or small, good or bad.'
Shunryu Suzuki, *not always so*, HarperCollins, 2002, p. 37

To be, or not to be, … To die—to sleep;— To sleep! perchance to dream
Hamlet! We already know this one.

Don't bother to read our friend Thomas Nagel's 'What is it like to be a bat?' (in *Mortal Questions*, Cambridge University Press, 1979). Sure, Nagel does tell us that a 'bat spends the day hanging upside-down by [its] feet in an attic.' (Asleep or not he does not say.) But—come on now!—this certainly does not tell us what it is *really* like to be a bat.

V.

Two Tails to Why Dream?
a self-critique

When we speak the word 'life,' it must be understood we are not referring to life as we know it from its surface of fact, but to that fragile, fluctuating center that forms never reach. And if there is still one hellish, truly accursed thing in our time, it is our artistic dallying with forms, instead of being like victims burnt at the stake, signaling through the flames.
—Antonin Artaud, *The Theater and its Double*

a recipe for exciting dreams

If any of you desperately wish to have exciting, entertaining, gruesome, and grotesque serial-killer dreams to give your lives that verve you feel is missing and animate your boring nights, I'm afraid it won't be sufficient suddenly to become conscious of consciousness, or to ask yourselves, obsessively, day and night, relentlessly and tirelessly, great questions like What is consciousness? and Why dream? I'm sorry, it might work, but I'm afraid it's probably not sufficient. To be butchered, lynched, terrorized, tarred and feathered, or just generally tormented by dreams that you not only *remember* but that you *cannot possibly forget*, you need to have been through at least a couple of genuinely major crises in your lives. At least a couple. Three or four could also be good, but let's not say the more the merrier. Try not to overdo it. These crises that sizzle your nerves are what the Latins called a *sine qua non* for genuinely gruesome dreaming. But, now, I need to explain a little better what I mean by crises. And that's not so easy, because it's so subjective. Your girlfriend, wife, or lover left you? So much the worse for her, you say, I'll find a better one tomorrow. Your cat (or dog) (or canary) died? Well, she was old, there are lots of homeless kittens out there. You lost your job— you're a professional bat-expert—your wife died last year, and you have 9 kids to bring up, currently aged 1 to 11, on a bat-expert's salary that you've just lost. To make matters worse, you're ugly as sin, your wife was the only person in the world who could stand you, and the market is flooded with bat-experts imported from China by Thomas Nagel. All of them experts on the *Geomyces destructans* fungus, and you'd never even heard of it until last week. With 9 mouths to feed, to say nothing of your own. What, me worry? you say! Things will work out. Fantastic. There are—incredibly, and *luckily*—a whole bunch of people like you. But—you know—in the very same circumstances other people will be on suicide watch before you can say Jiminy Cricket. The end of the world. Apocalypse now. It's not the event but how you experience the event that makes for a genuine dream-producing crisis. Inner experience, plus how resilient your nervous system is. I think this is a key factor, and far more objective than a lot of famously objective facts or events. Some people are born with very strong nervous systems. I don't mean nerves of steel (superheroes have issues of their own). I'd say nerves like rubber balls: squeeze them real hard, and when you let go they return immediately to their original shape. Resilience. Vice versa, I picture my own nervous system as made of stringy, flammable material, which can be singed, scorched, burned—I think *fried* is a tasteless way of putting it— and which may eventually burn out (completely). (OK, you can't burn out if you're not on fire, but this is extremely small consolation when your nerves are sizzled forever.) All this has nothing to do with 'high strung' but with what the string is actually made of, or what shape it's in, currently. Sure, it's also possible to start off with a naturally quite resilient nervous system that—thanks to strenuous and concerted effort—you manage to fray, wear down, wear out, damage, devastate, and possibly reduce to tatters in the course of your life, or even in quite a short time. In this endeavor you'll need to bring a number of external—a.k.a. objective—factors into play. Stress, for example, is an extremely poor example of such factors. The Italian coach of my Italian football team explained this quite recently, in a stunning and startling interpretation of the English language made by someone who actually can't tell English from Outer Mongolian. He said—this morning— there are two kinds of stress, one good, called *stress*, which keeps us sharp and on the ball, and one bad, called *dis-stress* (so to speak), which is *bad*. A pretty keen observation. No, by external factors I mean things like hunger, sleep deprivation, or disease. (For example, an infection requiring strong antibiotics for a long period of time would be perfect. Just what the doctor ordered.) Things like this can burn a perfectly healthy nervous system right down to the ground. But the causes of *nervous exhaustion* (as I like to call it) are tangled and tricky as a labyrinth. The nervous system of a human being— never mind a cat, rat, or bat—is a mysterious thing. Complicated. Complex. More of a mystery than consciousness? Or less? Mystery knows no degree! It's a mystery or it's not. The mystery of God is not a whit greater than the mystery of Gilda's opening her eyes to look at me at this very moment. As you know, ever since I was a kid I have been obsessed (so to speak) with the mystery of consciousness. (And I always will be, therapeutic ramble or not.) A mystery that unexpectedly turned out to be the leading player in a ramble that was supposed to be about dreams. You can't trust anyone. But, have faith. These Two Tails aren't about mystery, they're about Antonin Artaud, about my friend Gianfranco, about psychiatry, about Artaud's detestation of psychiatry, about artmaking, and—my real point—about *silence*. No mystery here. Nothing like the mystery of consciousness. A nervous system may be a mystery, or not. All I know is that I can't live without one and that, ever since mine caught fire, its cinders have been doused with dreams.

Distress is in the eye of the beholder. For a lifetime of serious dreaming a distressed adolescence hits the spot. I, personally, went from adolescent distress to big time distress about the Vietnam war. Major distress. I decided to transform myself into a skeleton, and ate practically nothing at all for five months. Ye gods was I ever hungry! A hunger I've never been able to forget. I managed to reduce my nervous system—permanently—to the shadow of its former self. How was I supposed to know it was so stringy and flammable!? These are things you discover after the fact. One year later I left for Europe, permanently (in fact I'm still here), with a few books, very little money and, basically, not the slightest idea of what I might do to survive. Not a clue. An *ideal situation* if someone, for some insane reason, happened to be in pursuit of gruesome, grotesque, tarring and feathering, outrageous serial-killer dreams. Which I sure as hell wasn't. Pumpkin-seed plants groaning and bursting slowly into flame. Call it collateral damage, or call it a fringe benefit. As you wish. It's a free country. (What country? What's free?) In any event, in just a few years my nervous system was worn to a frazzle—and then, suddenly, *voilà! Là cendre*, as Derrida put it. Cinders. What was left of the fire. There and not there. Silence. Ashes and rooms.

> like a drum-tap
> at the edge of the universe
> a single drop of water
> in a secluded mountain pool
> so faint
> so distant
> is the voice of the world
> so enormous the silence
> like a cry of shadow

That's when I really got to know my own nervous system, intimately. If there's anything I've known intimately in my life, it's my cats and my nervous system. I could feel its electrical impulses (Freud called them 'excitations,' I call them 'you're still alive—barely') all over the system, but instead of slender flames they were cinders. They wanted to come out into the world—my world, the external world—but were much too tired to make it to the surface. I call this *nervous exhaustion* or, as I said earlier, *crisis*. Or, an even better word: silence. My silence. The world's silence. Often a roaring silence. It has nothing whatsoever to do with depression, compulsion, neurosis, or psychosis, but it's definitely the best possible medicine for serial-killer dreams—for *producing* them, I mean. The best. Thanks to that period of total nervous exhaustion in the mid-70s I've been guaranteed an inexhaustible lifetime supply. It's true, I did suggest that two or three such crises are advisable, just to be sure. Though three like that one would have been gilding the lily. In any event, in 1990 I did an encore that brought down the house. 'Extreme decided flux.'

estremo rossocenere	*extreme ash-red*
al confine	at the border
dell'estasi perenne	of permanent ecstasy
di	exiles
stanza	rooms
anni luce	distance
dal corpo	light-years
mia scintilla!	from the body
ignota ombra	my spark!
linea fina	unknown shadow
viva cenere	fine line
del fuoco mai	live ash
spento	of a fire never
dal diluvio	spent
di	by the flood
un gesto	of
estremo	an act
deciso	extreme
flusso	decided
al confine	flux
rossocenere	ash-red
della notte	at the border
del mondo	of the night
	of the world

But I'll come to that in the second part of this Tail. Meanwhile, in 1977 I came up with a therapy that in just a few years actually revived my dead nerves, without compromising the gruesomeness of my dreams. Lady Luck and Mighty Necessity. There it was, right in front of me. Right in my hands. Action! Pick up the ball and run like hell. EARRINGS. *Rags to riches.* I've already told you bits and pieces of the story in my therapeutic ramble. Food! Shelter! Friends! Girlfriends! Vodka! With earrings I broke my silence, and practically everything else. Marvelous nights until dawn, in this room, at my table covered with velvet, with my slender silvery wire and my Venetian glass beads, glittering, glimmering, under the lamp, *clean* as the piano of Bach and of Monk. — extreme/ decided/ flux — Action! At my peak I was making a thousand pair of earrings every three months. (And selling them too, which was a big part of the deal.) But I haven't told you the whole story. I didn't tell you that *making* these little jewels was a *therapeutic action* that transformed spent cinders into raging fire. And that *none of it would have happened without Antonin Artaud.* It is here that this (double) Tail really begins.

I've learned many things from Antonin Artaud. For example: *in many cases* madness is in the eye of the beholder. Artaud reveled in his madness for much of his life. It was a sort of *personal therapy. Action* therapy. *Artaud Action* therapy. Artaud didn't believe—classically—that everyone *else* was mad. He believed, quite rightly, that everyone else *got him wrong.* Especially his psychiatrists. We know that one of his many psychiatrists in one of his many stays in mental hospitals encouraged him to write poetry. And he did!

> I speak
>   from above
>   time
> as if time
> were not fried,
> were not this dry fry
> of all the crumbles
> at the beginning
> setting out once more in their coffins.

Artaud was an extraordinary poet, a great hater of psychiatrists, and a great writer. In his 'Van Gogh: Le suicidé de la société' (The Man Suicided by Society) it is as if—ecstatically—he transformed himself into the very paint on Van Gogh's brushes and directly experienced the ultimate sacrifice of artistic creation. 'Flooding a landscape with blood and wine, drenching the earth with a final emulsion, happy and gloomy at the same time, with a taste of sour wine and turned vinegar.'

> It is no ordinary thing to see a man, who has the bullet that felled him lodged in his belly, stuffing a canvas with black crows and beneath them a plain, livid perhaps, but empty at any rate, where the whiney color of the earth clashes wildly with the dirty yellow of the wheat. But no other painter except Van Gogh would know how to find, the way he did, the truffle-black he used to paint the crows, that 'rich banquet' black and, at the same time, the excrement-like black of the crows' wings caught by the dwindling light of the evening.

An extreme, and unique, way of writing about art. And as for psychiatry, well, he tells us:

I, myself, spent 9 years in an insane asylum and never had any suicidal tendencies, but I know that every conversation I had with a psychiatrist during the morning visit made me long to hang myself because I was aware I could not slit his throat.

Things are bad because the sick conscience now has a vital interest in not getting over its sickness.

So a sick society invented psychiatry to defend itself against the investigations of certain visionaries whose faculties of divination disturbed it.

His *complaint* goes beyond psychiatry to society itself, for its hatred of the extraordinary and of genius. But what is genius for Artaud? The genius is an individual who 'fearlessly makes himself master of what does not yet exist, and brings it into being. And everything that has not been born can still be brought to life if we are not satisfied to remain mere recording organisms.' *Mere recording organisms*: this, for Artaud, is our sickness unto death. Our *silence*. Which *must be broken*. Artaud wrote, 'break through language in order to touch life.' A theater of *cruelty* to break the dead dark crust that separates us from life. A crust of *cowardice*, which he execrates and denounces, often and violently.

For mankind does not want to take the trouble to live, to take part in the spiritual elbowing of the forces that make up reality, in order to pluck a body from them so that no tempest could ever again harm it.

It has always preferred mere existence.

As for life, it seeks the artist within its own genius.

Therefore Van Gogh, who cooked one of his own hands, was never afraid of a struggle in order to live, that is to say, to disassociate the reality of living from the idea of existing,

and naturally, everything can exist without taking the trouble to be, unlike Van Gogh the madman, everything can exist without taking the trouble to radiate and glow.

Without taking the trouble to radiate and glow. This is what Artaud railed against and what *drove him mad*. The silence of a world that lacks the courage to *live*. Worming, gnawing, eating into the live marrow of his furious bones, devouring, plaguing, ravaging — this dry fry/ of all the crumbles — this Silence that (as I wrote some 20 years ago) in our culture is not (yet) called God. In his late poem 'Je hais et abjecte en lâche' Artaud is livid with rage, he is *himself* a landscape flooded with blood and wine:

I hate and renounce as a coward every being who consents to having
been made and does not wish to be remade.
That is, who agrees with the idea of a creator god, at the origin of
his being as at the origin of his thought.

I knew practically nothing about Artaud when I was a student in New York,
though I did hear a lot about *Paradise Now* in 1968. I also knew that *the*
text for the Living Theater was *The Theater and its Double*. But I met Artaud
later, in Denmark (not personally, he died in 1948, at the age of 51) in 1973,
along with the Sardinian necklace-makers. *Two* major discoveries. Artaud
was first and foremost a Creator of Theater. A theorist, but in a Mao Tse-tung
sense. A theorist of practice, of action, of doing, making, steering, directing,
struggling. In short, a revolutionary—and a theorist—whose element was
theater. My own passion, as you know, is not theater but logic, but in Artaud
the connection between them is extreme, inescapable, and ecstatic. In
Artaud, as in Kafka, we have what—if we wish—we might call an 'existential
logic.' We also have it in a *the* book like Suzuki's *Zen Mind, Beginner's Mind*.
In this particular Tail—as you see—I'm focusing on Artaud. For a number
of reasons. And I'm *trying* not to ramble. But, am I succeeding? After my
travels in Why Dream? I fear I have rambling in my blood. Yesterday, just
for the hell of it, I bought a white rose from a street vendor (an Indian from
India) and put it here on my desk in a glass vase to concentrate on its *stillness*.
The antithesis of a rambling rose! I'm doing my best. Gilda called her Tail
a gentle rant—vastly overstating it, don't you think? Gentle definitely, but
a rant? Strange choice of words. And just yesterday I discovered that at the
end of this Two Tails we shall meet my first cat, Gina. Over nine years after
her death. It seems that, theatrically, Gina will be unfurling, for us, the full
length of her Tail of shadows. A meta-memoir if ever there was one.

A Creator of Theater. Let me tell you why Artaud's 1938 *theater book*—in the
superb Grove Press edition, translated in 1958 by Mary Caroline Richards—
has become *the* book, or one of the few *the* books, for so many people. (And
for me not only a *theory* book but a true *action* book.) It's because—for
Artaud—theater is a logic. A *science of logic*. Hegel's 'realm of shadows' is *not*
supposed to be an *existential* logic (even if it *may be* one for me). But ask any
real philosopher, a Hegelian *logic of practice* does not exist. But—I insist—
Artaud's *action* logic, *dramatic* logic, *theater* logic, definitely does exist. But
what in the world do I *mean* by 'logic'? And why does Artaud call his book
The Theater and its Double? Hold on! These are major questions. (Ye gods!
we're back to questions.) We have no choice. At this point we have to take a
shot at the Greek word *logos*. A pot shot perhaps? A blast with a bazooka or
a Kalashnikov? (How about a stab?) It's a tricky word. Always has been, from
the very beginning, but now that it's been smothered in the love of Western

philosophy for 2,500 years it's become practically impervious. Cuddled, excessively. It means too many things. The word comes, originally, from the verb *legein*, which, possibly, originally meant 'to gather, to gather together, to bind.' Just like Joseph—Behold, this dreamer cometh!—and his brothers, binding sheaves in the field. Then, I suppose, since people binding sheaves in the field naturally tend to chit-chat—and why the hell not! are they supposed to do their binding in silence?—*legein* came to mean *speak, talk, tell.* And so we have one of the two main meanings of *logos*: *speech as opposed to silence.* Conversation, discussion, discourse. To say nothing of words, sayings, maxims, proverbs, rumors, fables, stories, tales, histories, chronicles, speeches (made by Athenians, originally), and the more the merrier. But the plot thickened from the very beginning. The simple story lost its clear outline, as Joseph K. so dramatically put it. ('In the Cathedral,' during his *Trial.*) First the Jews—i.e., Christians. St. John right off the bat in his Gospel, with his cosmically-famous 'In the beginning was the *Word.*' *Logos* with a capital W. But it was the *Latins*—those Wild West Romans—who muddied the waters unto death. *Ratio*, the other main meaning of *logos*. Gather, gather together, get your *head* together. *Thought, reason, logic.* These goddam Old West Romans with their Spaghetti Westerns *ante litteram,* there's just no getting around them. Well, OK, so be it. From binding sheaves in the field to St. Augustine—to Hegel. To Heidegger, alas. It's OK. That's life. Let's live with it. But—do you, perchance, note a possible *contradiction* between these two main meanings? Thought, reason—logic—are *silent.* They may have uproar within them, but for all the world they *make no sound.* So *logos* is speech—real sound—as *opposed* to silence, *and* silence as opposed to speech, to real sound. For me personally—*existentially*, so to speak—this contradiction has spelled big trouble at certain times in my life. My silence, silence of the other. A cutting edge that can, easily, slit your throat. Deadly. Contradiction:

> There are souls who, on certain days, would kill themselves over a simple contradiction, and it isn't necessary to be insane for that, a registered and catalogued lunatic; on the contrary, it is enough to be in good health and to have reason on one's side.

Nothing is *simply* simple. Remember Hegel's being is nothing? If you missed the message, here it is again: in his logic, the most simple is the most complex. Because it is unbounded: totally indeterminate, and therefore *in relation with everything*, without distinction. Logic, however *unshakable*, is, first of all, primordially *double. Like logic like silence.* Same deal. Perhaps you didn't notice it—maybe you were sleeping near/on/in some ancient tomb somewhere—but Why Dream? is a (rambling) exercise in *logic*. Did you notice? Big Philosophers have defined logic—*logos*—as a gathering of reason. A gathering and binding it. A getting it all together *in thought.* But that's

only half the story. How come they didn't let Joseph K. stay peacefully in his
room *thinking*. No! Logic is unshakable! They arrested him (*for no reason*),
put him on trial, and condemned him to death. Like a dog! *Wie ein Hund!*
Action! Logic is also a logic of *action*. A logic of society, of war, of survival,
of theater, you name it. Each and every *art* has a logic. *Living* has many
logics. *Dreaming* has a wild bunch of logics. But are they really *many* or
actually just *one? Getting it all together*. Getting your *head* together means
getting your *act* together. Let's take stock. There is a logic of *speech*. Of *sound*.
And there is a logic of *silence*. *Whose* silence? Mine or yours?! Or both? (Or
neither!) One logic for both or one logic each—two logics? Mine and yours.
And of speech and silence—two logics or one? Four logics? My sound my
silence your sound your silence. But what about *thought* (theory) and *action*
(practice). Doubled again! Eight logics, or 16, or—hold your horses! We're
galloping into an inflationary blind alley. The stuff that exhausted nervous
systems are made of. And how about theory and practice 'versus' shadow and
substance? Two? One? One doubling as two, two doubling as one? Doubling
or doubled? Hey baby, get it together! Be cool! To say nothing of this: How
about my mother's logic in Tampa, and my sister's in Northampton, and
my cousin's in Miami, and then there's *your* mother, sisters and cousins, and
their mothers, aunts and uncles—each with their own logics. And each with
one of speech and one of silence, and one of thinking and one of acting, and
ye gods know what else. At this point the only image we have of logic is the
cosmic inflation one nanosecond after the Big Bang. Sorry! I've been pulling
your leg. Pulling your *toe. Our-toe*. Another little gambit of mine, titled 'risk
and toe.' I, myself, put it this way, 'dipping my toe in the icy stream of time':

>   in the beginning was the toe
>   AR-TAUD
>   beginning of beginning
>   or end of end
>
>   but things have to start somewhere?
>   in rupture or unity?
>   root or branch?

Logic—the Double—is a question not of arithmetic—unless it be the
calculus of 'not two and not one'—but of *one essential drama*, which *lives*,
and, living, *doubles* (and is doubled). Or, more precisely, as Hegel would
put it, *has already doubled*. Hegel called it *abstraction, separation* of the
inseparable. Being is nothing, and the truth of both is becoming. And so
forth! The vanishing of vanishing. *One* essential drama. What is *art* if not
doubling and the doubled. Abstraction. What is life! Just try *just* to inhale,
forget about exhaling. (Or vice versa, as you wish.) Just try it! Know what it's

called? It's called *death*. Hegel, a logic of being, of essence, of the concept, a realm of shadows—remember? Artaud, a logic of theater, of art, of silence, of action. Let him tell it in his own words. The Theater and its Double.

And this essential drama, we come to realize, exists, and in the image of something subtler than Creation itself, something which must be represented as the result of one Will alone—and *without conflict*. We must believe that the essential drama, the one at the root of the Great Mysteries, is associated with the second phase of Creation, that of difficulty and the Double, that of matter and the materialization of the idea.

It seems indeed that where simplicity and order reign, there can be no theater nor drama, and the true theater, like poetry as well, though by other means, is born out of a kind of organized anarchy after philosophical battles which are the passionate aspect of these primitive unifications.

How hard it is, when everything encourages us to sleep, though we may look about us with conscious, clinging eyes, to wake and yet look about us as in a dream, with eyes that no longer know their function and whose gaze is turned inward.

This is how our strange idea of disinterested action originated, though it is action nonetheless, and all the more violent for skirting the temptation of repose.

Every real effigy has a shadow which is its double; and art must falter and fail from the moment the sculptor believes he has liberated the kind of shadow whose very existence will destroy his repose.

Like all magic cultures expressed by appropriate hieroglyphs, the true theater has its shadows too, and, of all languages and all arts, the theater is the only one left whose shadows have shattered their limitations. From the beginning, one might say its shadows did not tolerate limitations.

Our petrified idea of the theater is connected with our petrified idea of a culture without shadows where, no matter which way it turns, our mind (*esprit*) encounters only emptiness, though space is full.
....

For the theater as for culture, it remains a question of naming and directing shadows: and the theater, not confined to a fixed language and form, not only destroys false shadows but prepares the way for a new generation of shadows, around which assembles the true spectacle of life.

Artaud! This is not Freud. This *madman*—this *Mômo*—speaks for himself. This is what I mean by *logic*—this *always new* generation of shadows. This, which is also an abyss of dreams.

Let me back up for just a moment. Not logically this time, but chronologically. Let's take a little trip. An Artaud trip. A theater trip! Back to the *rags* and then on to the *riches*. As I told you a little while ago, I met Artaud in Denmark, a year after my continent-change operation. (You'll *never* guess how I ended up in Aarhus, Jutland, and I'm not going to tell you. Just a hint—it involved neither girls nor Kierkegaard.) How lucky I was to meet those Sardinians! A year and a half after leaving New York I had nearly consumed the old fruit of my taxi-driving loom. (No, I didn't buy a Ferrari, or a house in the country.) Then—suddenly—necklaces! Christmas in Jutland. There I was, on a street corner every day for the two weeks, freezing my ass off, selling handmade necklaces. A *long slow* start, like a stagecoach in the space age, that lasted for four years, of *rags*. A hard ride, but an *Artaud trip* that carried me through my first stretch of *nervous exhaustion* and left me, *with a big hug*, on the threshold of riches. Those years of progressively dilapidating my nervous system were, to say the least, not easy. It's true, there were the *fidanzate*. First the Italian—remember C. in the 'old woman' reality dream? Then the very young but unimaginable Norwegian, then the (alas) imaginable Italian again, then the Norwegian again, who suddenly disappeared—for 27 years! and even then did not fully reappear—then the Italian again, who *yearned for my disappearance and therefore my destruction*. But I had logic—and Artaud—on my side. On the heaths and in the villages of Jutland, with my Sardinian companions we staged each and every form of The Theater and its Double. One by one, or sometimes all together. The Theater and the Plague (our favorite, based on 'an astonishing historical fact' that took place in 1720, in Cagliari, *in Sardinia*). The Alchemical Theater, The Balinese Theater, the No More Masterpieces Theater, and—*bien sûr*—The Theater of Cruelty. We didn't sell many necklaces but we made one hell of a lot of *theater*, and Artaud would have been proud of us. Naming and directing shadows. Off we went, 6 or 7 of us piled into an old Volkswagen van, to visit some hick town, preparing our mise-en-scène en route. 10 Million Years in the History of Sardinia—a No More Masterpieces production. What, me worry? Mise-en-scène à la Antonin Artaud. Some days the troupe spread its velvet carpets the full length of the pedestrian street in towns so hick and tiny that our necklaces outnumbered its inhabitants. Magic mini-carpets, each one an abyss of dreams. *This*, my friend, was Theater. *Action!* Logic. No mere recording organisms. Artaud carried me through the skin-and-bones summer of 1974, and the next few years as well, directing and naming a gruesome, grotesque, and spine-tingling tangle of Danish, Swedish, and Norwegian shadows. *A goddam tangle*, to be named and directed. I did my best, and it *paid off.*

But not in my unhappy Scandinavia, fortunately. The *riches* slowly began to manifest themselves—in *EARRINGS*—in 1977, in Sicily. In Taormina, and then thanks to my friend in the sublimely Artaudian town of Palma di Montechiaro, near Agrigento. But the flood, in Swiss francs, began with a vengeance thanks to my friend in Zurich, along the 'little camel' earring-caravan from Zurich to Geneva and, later, from Zurich to Munich. Here at home in Venice a glorious 6 to 8 weeks of *earring-making therapy*. Design and manu-facture! Radiate and glow! A thousand pair of little jewels. But then I had to sell them. Four trips a year, to the lands of the Swiss-Germans, the Suisse-Romands, and the burly Bavarians, none of whom in all their born days ever expected *me*, suddenly appearing in their boutiques. Out of nowhere, as if I'd just fallen off the moon. Or—as Artaud put it with his customary extreme precision, at the end of 'Van Gogh: Le suicidé de la société'—as if shot from a recent volcanic eruption of the volcano Popocatépetl. A thousand pair, *and I wouldn't have sold a single one without Artaud.* Right before each and every trip, four times a year for five years, I read *The Theater and its Double*, meditating on the new mise-en-scène. The key word—the *logic*—was, again, this:

Fearlessly makes himself master of what does not yet exist, and brings it into being. And everything that has not been born can still be brought to life if we are not satisfied to remain mere recording organisms.

These folks in their boutiques didn't expect me the first time, and then expected of me the *extremely unexpected* every single time. Not just new earrings, the earrings were always first-rate, no, they wanted more! They expected a new mise-en-scène. A new Theater, a new Logic, a new Me every time. Not *solid things* but—every single time—*a new generation of shadows.* And they got it. The Tails I told! The acts I put on! The tanglings of tongues and images! Named and directed. All thanks to Antonin Artaud. If you have great masters, a Long March can be a stroll. The longest road is a walk around the block. A goddam ferocious walk and a goddam furious block. But even cats have their days in court.

Then, suddenly, in 1984, I decided to become a translator—a mere recording organism of the first water. Shit, life is strange. I had changed continents to write a book, as I'd promised my grandfather, so I figured I'd better get back to writing *something*, even if it was *someone else's*. I made a last trip to Switzerland and Germany (by train, I'd already sold the 'little camel'), said goodbye to all my clients, sold everything I could, and so long. *Auf wiedersehen.* Have fun, even without me. Starting all over. As a translator I needed a whole new mise-en-scène, from scratch, it wasn't so easy, I had to work the logic out gradually, over the years. At first I only translated Italian philosophy, but then the *art critics* came out of nowhere. (Luckily, they went away again after a while.) I started translating for a contemporary art magazine, published in Sicily. (A long story.) I met a lot of new people, some very good artists. Wolfango! my friend! my brother! Master of a political art that *never failed* to take the trouble to radiate and glow! In 1985 I bought this house. In 1986 I renovated it and—magic!—my first cat, Gina, appeared, immediately. I had money, plenty of work, was neither thin nor fat, enjoyed my trips to Sicily. For the first time in my life I even took a few vacations. I was doing OK.

Then, very suddenly, in the summer of 1988 my life fell apart. Completely. I had to deal, somehow, with the most excruciating years of my life, and I didn't think I would survive. A moment of glorious sound, followed by a terrible, unbearable silence. A silence I thought would never break.

my silence, silence of the other: preamble

It's been a month since I finished rambling through Why Dream? and ever since I finished there's been a painful thought sticking in my mind, like a thorn. This—theoretically (in the sense of *hopefully*)—is what Two Tails is really about. Sure, not two and not one all over again—Zen, Hegel's Logic, Artaud's Double. But from the *painful* side this time. Two tails on one animal is no picnic. It's a painful experience. In the first part of Two Tails I've been my usual chipper what-me-worry self. But this is just one of two ways of expressing the world of pain in which I have always lived. Cheerfully, at times. But not always. At times, possibly, *painfully* cheerfully. But there have also been times of pure pain, and my usual name for such times has been *silence*. My major crises have not been cheerful times and the patina they left is still with me. My first cat, Gina, went through a major trauma when she was five months old, and in fact was a moody cat all her life—strong, very strong, but with powerful ups and downs. A great hunger. She was a lot like me. I try to learn from Gilda, the Parmenidean, the gentlest creature on the face of the earth. She's amazing. Even when she's unhappy she's happy about being unhappy. If it's a cold rainy day she screams for me to let her out into the courtyard, I open the door, and she stands there—stunned, overwhelmed by what she sees and feels. A horrible day. Gilda, unlike Gina, is a *big* talker with a vast vocabulary. Dozens of words. (They're both big *writers*, of course, and only in English, a language they don't happen to know.) She stands there for half a minute taking in the Horror and saying horrible things. Then she retreats into the house and is happy as a lark. And not happy *despite* the horrible day, but happy *about being unhappy* about the horrible day. An essential existential distinction.

I'm writing this on one of my outrageously rare good days (barely a handful a year), which I define as follows: The day after sleeping for seven or eight hours, awakened only two or three times by gentle dreams. On such days I am a *new* man. *Another* man entirely. On such days I know—I feel, to the marrow of my bones—that, as Conrad put it (in *Heart of Darkness*), 'The mind of man is capable of anything—because everything is in it, all the past as well as all the future.' Or—it's the same thing—as Plato put it at the end of the *Republic*: 'The soul is immortal and able to endure all evil and all good.' Ye gods! Why do I have these days only three, four, five times a year? I'll tell you why. Exactly why. Because when I was twenty years old I decided to transform myself into a skeleton. I ate practically nothing at all for five months, and very seriously *damaged* my immune system, my nervous system, and ye gods only know what other systems, *for the rest of my natural or unnatural life*. For as long as you both shall live. (Who? Me and who else?) That little performance—that theater of cruelty—that new generation of shadows—cut jagged edges into my systems and left me with the kind of shadow whose very existence has permanently destroyed my repose. Just because I was *riled up* about the obscene, ferociously petty, and outrageously criminal attempt by my country (at the time) to destroy Vietnam in order to save it. For some reason. Pardon my rage. I'm angrier about it now than I was forty years ago, *much* angrier, and angry at myself too. Angry not because I got so riled up that time that I destroyed my body (but who knew, who could ever have imagined that my systems were, in fact, so fragile), but angry for two other reasons. First, because, back then, I was absolutely right about Vietnam—politically and, so-called, *existentially*. Hearts and minds. The only war the U.S.A. ever lost (never mind Iraq and Afghanistan) instead of leading to a change of direction in U.S. criminal imperialism became the *seed of a global explosion* of that criminal imperialism. The root and the branch. That's what I said in 1970, that's why I didn't eat for five months. A hunger strike? No, a *political action strike*. An individual absolute protest. My country—mine no longer, but for many of you, yours. A country that has been furiously engaged in destroying the world in order to save it. The second reason: For forty years my *raison d'être* has been to change the political direction of *this* Empire *through art*. By writing a *political novel*. A work of *art* that would affect, move, *change* hearts and minds. This was my decision, forty years ago, and I've stuck to it. Like a layer of moldy glue. But stuck to it *hard*. And what have I made? I've made my silence, and silence of the other. I am not happy about it. I'm glad I've survived, and have never become a mere recording organism. But I look at what I've made and my pain is unbounded. And then, at last, I break my silence and what have I made? A political novel! Hell no!! Why Dream? A therapeutic ramble. What in the world will it mean for the future of *my* silence—and of *yours?* This is the thorn in my mind. A doubled thorn, actually.

But—for now, or perhaps forever—let's stick to the first 'moment' of the thorn: In breaking my silence, what have I *made*? The world of dreams is a world of *silence*—this is unshakable. For all the uproar within them, dreams make no sound in the (outer) world. (By the way, I have a theory that even the inner-world sound of dreams is actually soundless sound. Like one hand clapping? No, that's different.) Lie next to me one night (a pure thought experiment!) as I dream wrecking balls smashing blazing huts and people *screaming*, and what do *you* hear? Nothing! Unless, of course, I happen to wake up *screaming* myself, or crying, or laughing hysterically. (It's happened! And fairly often too.) Or asking you *out loud*: WHY? Why Dream? But I don't want you to think that silence is a purely acoustic phenomenon. I may experience the outrageous uproar of hell in my dreams, but this uproar will never be heard in the world. (Unless, of course, I happen to *chase* the Tail. *After*-ward. In *meta*-memoir.) But not just not heard with ears (or seen with eyes: blindness is a silence of the eyes). It doesn't *exist* in the world, has no *impact* on the world. *This* is silence. This wild and passionate uproar (as Conrad put it) will almost certainly remain forever my own *private* uproar. It may actually have great consequences—but only for myself. *My silence*. It may be a blank silence, a silent silence, or it may be a wild and passionate uproar. *My* silence. All mine. Then again, what if *my* silence—be it by its blankness or its uproar—eventually drives me out of *my* mind? Drives me into a rage. Drives me to pick up my Kalashnikov, go out into the street, and shoot a bunch of people. Now, here we have great consequences, and not only for *me*. This is the other face of dreams. The face of a silence that may break *into* the silence of others.

There are reasons why I still haven't written that political novel. (The title is *Neighbors*.) I took a little stab at it in 1992, originally as the second story in Gianfranco's Five Stories psychotherapeutic project, which we shall get to a little later. Then, five years ago it was *burning* in my mind and I tried to take a *big* stab at it, and it was going quite well. But I was already suffering from this miserable autoimmune disorder (it all started with a little virus, which then, somehow, overheated my *immune* system, and since then has nearly killed me from time to time) that still torments me, and that finally forced me—with brute force—to stop writing. Then, suddenly, last October I started again. Why? For one simple and, to my mind, pathetic reason: My doctor *du jour* (an immunologist) took his own stab and sharply reduced my medication and, after a few days, instead of getting deathly sick, I started feeling lively and well. For the first time in five years I didn't feel totally exhausted. *Physically* exhausted I mean, my nervous system has been hanging in there magnificently. (Relatively speaking.) As long as I feed it generous helpings of gruesome dreams it seems—in its merry way—to be reasonably happy. Ho ho ho.

So, last October I suddenly felt pretty *healthy*, and after a month's wandering around and wondering whether it would last, all of a sudden I started writing again. I broke my (artmaking) silence, and what did I write? The political novel? A political story? (For me, 'Parroty' was/is a political story.) Hell no. I wrote Why Dream?! I broke my silence to write about a world of silence. About *both* worlds of silence, the *two great worlds of silence*: dreams and *logic*. The Double Realm of Shadows. The doubled world of silence. Of *my* silence—but also of *yours*, if, perchance, you dream, or if you have ever dipped your toe, gingerly, into the rip-roaring science of *logic*. In any event, now, after Why Dream? you know one helluva lot about my utterly grotesque, exceedingly gruesome, tarring and feathering, et cetera, dream experience. Probably a helluva lot more than you ever wanted to know. Who gives a shit about my dreams? *This* is a damn good question! Do I even give a shit about them myself? Perchance, Hamletically, only in the sense that if someone puts an elephant, or a *wooly mammoth* (of all things), *in* your house, you sure as hell *do* give a shit. I mean, there must still be one person in a zillion in the U.S.A. who's still riled up about the Vietnam war, and two or three in a zillion *seriously* pissed off at their country, ensconced in its Shining City upon a Hill, reveling in its exceptionalism, furiously engaged in destroying *the world* in order to save it. But who gives a shit about my dreams?! With all the pain and devastation *out there in the world*, why in the world did I write Why Dream? OK, maybe I'm being *too* hard on myself. Why Dream?—*really*—is an *exercise in logic*, and *logic* and *love* are the two most important things in *life*. (Just ask my cats.) Alas, I know a *whole* lot more about *logic* (but watch out for what I *mean* by logic) than I do about love, and I think it's for the best that I write more about what I know more and less about what I know less. But love is such a vast subject! The poets have written a zillion poems about it. Zillions. I love my mother, my sister, lots of people, lots of things, I love the color of the sky, sunsets, I love a good laugh. I'd love to sleep if only I could. The list goes on and on, I'd better leave it to the poets. (I love my cats!) (I love the plants in the courtyard.) Logic—by contrast—is small, and tight as a clenched fist: 'In the beginning was the *Logos*.' BAM! In your face. Or just ask that great logician Joseph K. (more familiarly known as 'K.'): 'But the hands of one of the partners were already at K.'s throat, while the other thrust the knife deep into his heart and turned it there twice.' *Mais oui*. Turned it there twice! Excuse me, but *this* is logic! *This* is unshakable! Like a dog! And you thought logic was some kind of joke. A moldy pastime for musty professors. And remember, when I say logic I mean *logic itself*, not intention, or tactics, or strategy, or some such, which *have* a logic but *are not* logic. Logic! Read Hegel!!! Read Kafka! Read the Roshi! Read Artaud! Action! Shadow! Life-and-death struggle! What's going on! Have they closed Disneyland overnight? Boarded it up? Has this ramble become a scream?

I cut off my toe
and serve it on a plastic plate
for lunch

tasty toe
can you risk the crispness
of a toe-nail
or the savory delight
of a toe broiled just right?

Let me try to put just a pinch of order in this fresh outburst of chaos, even
at the high cost of being *schematic.* Which is the Dead Letter of logic, dead
logic, or logic sick unto death. What I once called the *ill-logical.* Still, from
time to time, a schema can be useful, perhaps even necessary. (But *am I
capable* of being schematic??) (Behold, this dreamer cometh!) OK, let me try
to make my point, schematically, about *what I mean* by logic. And, at the
same time, by shadow and by silence. *And by art and the making of art.* (Shit,
I could use a blackboard here.) The first and foremost point is this: Logic is
Double. Not at all like 'night follows day' but *right now.* Not at all like so-
and-so but, then again, so-and-something-else. (Try that one on Joseph K.,
or on Artaud for that matter.) Logic *doubles* in the sense that it *contradicts
itself,* and this self-contradiction is not the *death* but is the *life* of logic.
Not its sickness but its health. Schema: Logic is speech/sound and silence/
shadow *together.* Inseparably. We all (my cats included) spend our entire lives
separating these moments—we *do* separate them—but they *refuse (logically!)
to separate.* This (this is *not so easy* to follow) is what Artaud means by this
essential drama—*without conflict*—difficulty and the Double. *We* think that
we separate the inseparable. (Hegel, and modern art, call it *abstraction.*) But
actually it's the inseparable *itself* that separates—itself—*by its very logic.* We
can only *care for* this separating inseparable that we *are,* that life *is,* watch
over it, watch it carefully, and in this way *participate* in the separation and
live. I mean, if you care for a plant, take care of it, give it water, put it in
the sun when it needs it, is it *you* that makes it thrive and grow? Forget it!
(Which is exactly what you do.) Hell no! (Let's take an extreme position.) If,
in fact, with your care, the plant grows—wow! that's great. But if you think
that *you make it grow* you're out of your mind. You're pulling your own leg.
Badly. There is a Zen saying that says it all: On the withered tree a flower
blooms. Form is form, and emptiness is emptiness.

It seems I've stopped screaming and started rambling again, what an *impossible*
fellow I am. (But, watch out, I expect to scream again soon.) Never trust me.
And in spite of everything perhaps you're *still there.* Because life itself is even
more impossible than I am, and we live it anyway. And quite soon, in this

Tail, I'll get to the story of my super-when-things-fall-apart crisis, and how I met my great friend (and psychiatrist) Gianfranco, who managed to pull off a sort of death and transfiguration, followed by something sort of *terrible*, which was neither death nor transfiguration. In fact, to this day, I wonder what in the world it was. All I know is that it all had to do with silence, the breaking of silence, and then the breaking *broken*. Now—my pinch of order. Schematically! The first and foremost: Logic is Double. Or, more precisely, is doubled. Or, perhaps *more* precisely, is *doubling*. How about this: Logic is the Double doubled, or the Double doubling. Or the doubled doubling. Put differently: It's a tangle of shadows. Shadows are the matter, the instrument, and the *expression* of logic. But that's only half the story. Logic must be doubled because it *is* doubling. When Artaud says naming and directing shadows— let's try not to fall off the edge of the world here—he is actually and most definitely talking about (let's say) Hegel's realm of shadows, simple and *silent* essentialities. But he's *also* talking about that wild and passionate uproar which is the *happening* of theater. A cry, a *roar* of shadows. *My point* is this. He is not talking about *two different things* but about one thing doubling and doubled—*essentially*. This *essential drama* that is not two and not one. Why is logic unshakable? *Because it's always already shaken.* Shadows, we might say, are the foot soldiers of silence *and* the generals of uproar—and vice versa. Listen! This is not easy, not simple, it's extremely difficult and complex. What I am *not* saying is this: Guiding, steering, ruling our action, all action, the uproar of our lives, there is a silent underground, a silently flowing underground stream of shadow called *logic* (or *logos*). A logic *of* action, a silence *beneath* the uproar—no! This is what I am *not* saying. The logic 'is' the uproar, the silence 'is' the uproar, and here the problem is the 'is,' because 'is' fails to express *this*: The uproar and the silence are *inseparable*, not two and not one. Believe me, if I write (perhaps in a poem) about a cry of shadow or a raging silence I am not trying to be cute or to bullshit anyone. I'm *trying* to say something really important—I'm actually saying it. The only problem (ultimately, *for me*) is that no one takes me *seriously*. My unwritten political novel is not a *rehash* of the Vietnam war and Islamic terrorism, it's an *exercise in logic*. A big one. But what does this mean. It means that the logic is what is important, 'the rest is dross.' I'm universally accused of being excessively autobiographical in my writing (to say nothing of my rambling, a recent vice), but this time I plead guilty: My story of logic is the story of a life. A fine line, a split hair that is not only my life and my world but is *life* and *the* world. OUR-TOE! Let's sniff at the last lines of 'risk and toe,' from my 'scherzo' for Antonin Artaud.

the scream of a barque
worse than a byte
drifting far from passion's slave
from the angry shore
on a sea that is open forever

the milky shark
yearns for a whiff
of your exquisite
wandering
death-defying toe

will you risk a dry fry?
a dead fly?
far from the crystal plunge
where rupture founders
and shadows end
in endless shadow

I'd better back up a little, and try—again—to be schematic. (I failed gloriously
the first time around.) We saw—*ages* ago—that *logos* has a double sense. It
is speech *as opposed to* silence, but is also thought, reason, logic, which are
themselves *forms of silence.* Ye gods, not bad for starters. A dilemma. A fork in
the road. What shall we do? We have a number of possibilities. We could raze
the road to the ground. (So to speak.) (Maybe by bulldozing or bombing.)
Fine—*logos* is whatever we say, which, on this basis, is whatever we do, and
goodnight and good luck. (As in the world-famous expression 'a logic *of*
action'—fine. But only as long as you realize that it *is* a contradiction.) No,
this one is not my favorite. How about this one: 'Let's go to the discotheque.'
'It's too noisy in here.' 'OK, let's leave.' Silence, uproar, silence, and what
have we done? Zilch. Or, we could attempt to *skirt* the fork (in drag?), à la
Joseph K., by saying: What's all this goddam doubled-doubling business, go
away and leave me alone. (And lots of luck.) Or, my favorite: Face it. Take
it! *Take both roads at once.* This is what this little book of mine—this abyss of
dreams—is *about*, and *is.*

Back up again. The real problem here is not *which one* of two logics or *whose*
silence—mine, yours, or my aunt's. Going *way* back, all my life, or for forty
years anyway, I've spoken of a good silence and of a bad silence. This has
been a touchstone of my existence. It's true, silence here is—to an extent—
short for silence and solitude. OK! Even better, it makes my point better.
I've lived alone—in solitude—most of my life. At times this solitude (and
silence) has been very good for me—and *not* because I *chose* it or not, it

just was—and other times very bad. I've chosen solitude at times and it's been great, or horrible. I've desperately and successfully sought to avoid it, at times, and that's been great, or horrible. Or, at times, I've just taken what comes, and that too has been great or horrible. I'm not bullshitting you. (In any event, it's absolutely true that my *cats* have kept me alive the past 25 years—and vice versa, even if one did die 9 years ago.) Well, so far so good: good silence, bad silence. Just like pizza: you order a pizza, it might be good, it might be bad. No problem. Alas, it's not so, there is a problem, and a big one. Because *silence is who you are*—silence, shadow, logic are *who you are*. And pizza is not. (Even if you happen to live on it.) Schematic my ass. I said I'd be schematic, and instead I've scrambled the ramble. I'm incurable. I remind myself of my second cat chasing her tail. (My first cat wouldn't be caught dead in such a pointless endeavor, but, I suppose, it *can* be an exercise in logic.) Good silence, bad silence—what the hell, let's be blunt and, for what little it may be worth, take a stand. The fork in the road—remember? I said it less than three minutes ago! OK. You have, and *are*, bad silence when you behave as if the road actually forks and becomes two separate roads, which means that logic is separate from life, silence is separate from action, and shadow is separate from substance. You *have*, and *are*, good silence when you *take* both roads at once. But how can you do it? There are a million ways, it's just that practically nobody knows them. Vice versa, there are millions of people who actually do take both roads at once, *but don't know it.* Enlightenment is right now, not later. The great Zen master Hui-neng, the Sixth Patriarch, wasn't even a monk, he was working in the granary attached to the monastery (some say in the kitchen), then, suddenly, he wrote a four-line poem expressing his views on Zen, and became the Sixth Patriarch. Of course. He had long since taken both roads at once. He was master of many disciples. He was a good silence.

Some artists actually take both roads at once. I call them good artists. Some good artists have also been great artists, like Michelangelo or Dostoyevsky. Good *and* great silence. Others have been just as good, but on a small scale. There have also been a great many bad artists. Bad silence, which separates logic from life. Nice people, good people perhaps, but bad silence, which makes them bad artists. I myself, apart from scribbling a few pages from time to time, have thought a great deal about art. What it is, what it means to *make* art, what it is about art that makes it *happen,* or not. I think you can see (bad) works of art where you can actually feel the artist saying to himself: Now I'm going to *make* this up. I'm going to *make* it happen. After all, what is art if not *making?* Well, how about naming and directing shadows! For me, this is (good) art. Artaud was right in considering art a form of magic, and Kafka understood the essence of magic, which 'does not create but summons.' (*Diaries*, 18 October 1921). Aristotle wrote something very important, which I believe is true (especially regarding art): Nothing can come into being unless there is something there beforehand. If you look closely you can see the (bad) artist making it all up, creating *being* out of thin air. *But nothing happens.* Action, sex, intrigue, brutality, intellectuality—it's just fine, a good read, but it doesn't *happen.* Then you read a half-page story or a three-line poem ('my heart/ a black cloud/ in your hands') and—it's happening. All good art is a Great Mediator—this is very important. It mediates speech and silence, substance and shadow, freedom and necessity. Good artists take both roads at once—sometimes without knowing it. Sometimes precisely their knowing it is their art.

This week I've been rereading *Heart of Darkness.* If you want to know what I mean by the *happening* of a work of art, well, this is as happening as it gets. But—I must confess—this time I reread *Heart of Darkness* to watch the way Conrad handles the relationship between silence and uproar (a favorite word of his) and, have no fear, he takes both roads at once! And he *knows* it. All too well. He knows the pain, The Horror! of taking both roads at once. His story is great art. It's also only slightly fictionalized autobiography. Conrad himself, a master mariner, a seafarer, had—incomprehensibly—sought and obtained the command of a tiny steamer serving the upper Congo. He had to walk two hundred miles through the jungle to Kinshasa before reaching his ship, and from there up the river to an Inner Station. This time I won't ramble on about Mr. Kurtz, or about the Conrad racist/imperialist debate either. I shall focus on this voyage up the river. Maybe I'll make my point this time—namely, the doubleness of silence or, more precisely, that silence is *essentially* doubled. Let's follow Conrad, he's traveling.

> Going up that river was like traveling back to the earliest beginnings of the world, when vegetation rioted on the earth and the big trees were kings. An empty stream, a great silence, an impenetrable forest. ...
>   It was the stillness of an implacable force brooding over an inscrutable intention. ...
>   On we went again into the silence, along empty reaches, round the still bends, between the high walls of our winding way, reverberating in hollow claps and the ponderous beat of the stern-wheel. Trees, trees, millions of trees, massive, immense, running up high; and at their foot, hugging the bank against the stream, crept the little begrimed steamboat, like a sluggish beetle crawling on the floor of a lofty portico. ......
>   But suddenly, as we struggled round a bend, there would be a glimpse of rush walls, of peaked grass-roofs, a burst of yells, a whirl of black limbs, a mass of hands clapping, of feet stamping, of bodies

swaying, of eyes rolling, under the droop of heavy and motionless foliage. The steamer toiled along slowly on the edge of a black and incomprehensible frenzy. ...

This wild and passionate uproar. ...

While the wooded banks slipped past us slowly, the short noise was left behind, the interminable miles of silence—and we crept on, towards Kurtz. ...

The dusk came gliding into it long before the sun had set. The current ran smooth and swift, but a dumb immobility sat on the banks. The living trees, lashed together by the creepers and every living bush of the undergrowth, might have been changed into stone, even to the slenderest twig, to the lightest leaf. It was not sleep—it seemed unnaturally like a state of trance. Not the faintest sound of any kind could be heard. You looked on amazed, and began to suspect yourself of being deaf—then the night came suddenly, and struck you blind as well. About three in the morning some large fish leaped, and the loud splash made me jump as though a gun had been fired. When the sun rose there was a white fog, very warm and clammy, and more blinding than the night. It did not shift or drive; it was just there, standing all around you like something solid. At eight or nine, perhaps, it lifted as a shutter lifts. We had a glimpse of the towering multitude of trees, of the immense matted jungle, with the blazing little ball of the sun hanging over it—all perfectly still—and then the white shutter came down again, smoothly, as if sliding in greased grooves. I ordered the chain, which we had begun to heave in, to be paid out again. Before it stopped running with a muffled rattle, a cry, a very loud cry, as of infinite desolation, soared slowly in the opaque air. It ceased. A complaining clamor, modulated in savage discords, filled our ears. The sheer unexpectedness of it made my hair stir under my cap. I don't know how it struck the others: to me it seemed as though the mist itself had screamed, so suddenly, and apparently from all sides at once, did this tumultuous and mournful uproar arise. It culminated in a hurried outbreak of almost intolerable excessive shrieking, which stopped short, leaving us stiffened in a variety of silly attitudes, and obstinately listening to the nearly as appalling and excessive silence. 'Good God! What is the meaning—' stammered at my elbow one of the pilgrims...

I most certainly won't apologize for giving you such a long quote. If you haven't read *Heart of Darkness* recently—or if you've never read it—well, you've read just a little bit of it now. A long quote to make a short—but quite magnificent—point, and this time I won't belabor it. Conrad's journey may appear to be one of extreme ('excessive') silence that suddenly and violently *alternates* with extreme noise. But if you look more closely you'll see that it's not so at all. There is no *suspense* here. (This is not Hitchcock's *The Birds*, even if that film does contribute to the making of my point. Be they in full screech or dead silence, the birds are always there, and everyone knows it. Screech and silence are the *moments* of their being-there, in the perfectly Hegelian sense.) Do you remember when—in Why Dream?—we took a look at Hegel's first triad? Being is nothing, which is self-contradictory and is therefore already becoming and determinate being (*Dasein*). When we said that being and nothing were *logical moments*. Well, Conrad gives us the same logic, at a more advanced—more *material*—stage of development. But the logic is the same. His silence and noise are *moments*, which do not alternate chronologically but *double* logically. (And by *double* here I mean, precisely, separation of the inseparable.) The boat on the empty stream in the great silence, closed by high walls of rioting (!) vegetation. Millions of (screaming?) trees. But there is absolutely no suspense. Both the author and the reader know perfectly well that this is the heart of darkness. The silent riot of vegetation is but a pasteboard mask (as Ahab put it, in a radically different context) right on the face of the wild and passionate uproar that is always there. It's been there since the earliest beginnings of the world. (Since the night of the first ages.) *And we all know it.* This black and incomprehensible frenzy—which has also embraced Mr. Kurtz, and/or vice versa—is what the story is about. But it is also—equally—about the silence. The frenzy and the silence—and we may, or may not, have gone beyond bad and good silence here. The silence has gained necessity and, with necessity, freedom. Freedom and necessity are inseparable logical moments, and *Heart of Darkness* is an expression of the *logic* of this abstraction, this separation of the inseparable.

Now, hold onto your hats, I've got a big surprise for you. An incredible surprise. A marvelous surprise. A big BAT surprise! I'm going to make the same point *I just made*—again. But we're going to have some real fun for a change. (And this second part of Two Tails was supposed to be from the *painful* side ... *pure pain*. Never trust me.) Last week I was leafing through my *Guardian Weekly* (17 February 2012)—a paper, as we know, that pays almost fanatical attention to *bat issues*—when—suddenly—I couldn't believe my eyes! A two-page spread: 'Bat man: an animal arthouse movie'—actually, a pretty *creepy* title for a truly remarkable story. 'Patrick Barkham joins artist Jeremy Deller in Texas on the site of his latest idiosyncratic work—a cave with a very large gathering of mammals.' (By mammals here they mean BATS.) This Jeremy Deller (he's from London) made a great impression on me, I think he and I would really hit it off, he seems to know what I mean by good and bad artists. I hope I get to see a show of his some day. (I bet he'd enjoy Why Dream?) OK, here come some more quotes, but I think you'll enjoy them. (The reporter doesn't write like Joseph Conrad but, then again, who does?) The article begins like this:

A small figure in an oversized Flowered-Up T-shirt dances around the rim of a dark and very fetid cave. 'Shit!' says Jeremy Deller. 'Woah!' He ducks as the first bat rising from the crater crashes into him. In the silence of the Texan countryside, the stirring of millions of bats below ground is like the wind getting up. Then the occupants of the cave emerge in a spiraling column, rising into the sky like smoke. There is lightning on the horizon, a storm coming in, and the flitter of bat wings sounds like a gentle rain on leaves. The bat detector haphazardly taped to the top of one of Deller's three cameras makes a frantic squelching noise. 'It's sort of electronic music, isn't it?' says the Turner-prize-winning artist delightedly, filming the sunset emergence of one of the largest gatherings of mammals in the world. [...]

Why bats? One evening Deller was watching *School of Saatchi*—a reality TV show in which Charles Saatchi set out to discover the next big thing. 'There was some poor sod trying to cut a piece of wood and create a sculpture, and I turned over to BBC1 and it was David Attenborough and time-lapse photography of sea anemones under Arctic ice. The art in that photography was so much more amazing than someone trying to create a crappy sculpture.'

Deller filmed the bats here once before as an unpredictable end to *Memory Bucket*, his 2003 film about Texas that became part of his Turner-prize-winning exhibition, but was not happy with the results. He says he is 'interested in the way they can co-exist pretty peacefully with each other. It's incredible to live as close to other mammals. We can't do it.' He wonders how well this explains his desire to make a better bat movie. 'I do it because I can do it. I'm allowed to do it. A lot of art—or certainly what I do—is related to that; having an opportunity.'

[...]

Back in London, Deller sits in his flat editing the 3D bat film. From the first flashes of thousands of bats clinging to the cave roof, pink mouths opening like baby birds, it slowly builds into a visceral swarm in flight. The bats move so fast they look like an abstract pattern; even slowed down, their screams sound like Space Invaders. Towards the end of the seven-minute film, the emergence of bats slows, and a weird, restless tranquility returns, just like the experience of this miraculous gathering of mammals in the wild. Deller wanted his film to be almost more than people could bear but is now having second thoughts. 'You have to be very careful people aren't going to be running out screaming after two minutes,' he says. 'Kids will either really love it or it will traumatize them.'

I know what he means. When my cats somehow managed to *capture* bats in the back garden and bring them into the house (slightly gnawed), believe me, the supersonic Space Invader scream of *one single bat* was almost more than I, personally, could bear. A *huge* scream for such a small mammal. Now, *my point* here is exactly the same as with *Heart of Darkness*: essentially doubled silence. Moments. Just imagine the *immensity* of the silence of millions of bats huddled together so peacefully down there in the cave. (I remind myself a little of my 'original consciousness' story.) Now imagine the unimaginable spiral of millions of screaming bats rising into the sky. Shrieking! Screeching! Screaming! Now bring your thoughts together: don't separate them, take both roads at once. The silence of the bats and the screaming of the bats are *different* but *inseparable*. One good and one bad? Why? They are the very same bats. We are not concerned here with ethical issues, or with individual bat behavioral analysis (bat IQ tests, bat personality evaluation, et cetera), what interests us is the *logic* of these millions of bats. Never mind 'shrieking silence' or 'silent screams'—that, in itself, is just facile, mediocre poetry, while this is an exercise in logic. The bats huddled together in silence and the bats in the sky screaming are not two and not one. They are two *moments*—dare I say it!—of what it is like to be a bat.

Well, in these few pages (not quite so few, as it's turned out) that preamble the second part of Two Tails (actually one tail, painfully doubled) I wanted to say something simple, even blunt, about what's been bothering me since I wrote Why Dream? In short, tormented by silence, I finally broke my silence and wrote about *my dreams*—a whole *world* of silence, and of *my* silence to boot. Why did I do it? This was the point of the preamble. Have I answered this question? Not on your life. I wanted to be blunt—direct—and instead I rambled, then scrambled the ramble, and then—flying by the seat of my pants—I took off on a tangent that led me all the way to the Congo, and from there to a cave in Texas full of bats. I rambled more in this preamble than I did in the ramble itself. I practically *parodied* the ramble. *My* ramble. A simple post-ramble preamble, and it's turned out to be *bona fide* rambling self-parody. I perambulated the question of silence, trying to take two roads at once, but, possibly, I've done nothing but throw myself on the ground screaming, or groveling, or foaming at the mouth, or, perchance, purring. Or whatever. This dry fry. So be it. Let's beat a retreat. Let's get back to the sizzling story of my second crisis, the one that brought down the house.

my silence, silence of the other

I know, at the end of the first part of these Two Tails I left you hanging. (If you happen to have a bad back—disc issues—hanging may, possibly, be one of the best things you can do.) But now—guess what—I'm *not* going to tell you my story of Maria the Sicilian! It is private. A dream is public. The devastating failure of passionate requited love is private. It all actually happened, just as my serial-killer dreams happened. The whole story. But I won't tell it. I will have to give you some crumbs, but only because the trail leads to Gianfranco, and all this is *his* Tail. From Maria to Gianfranco, but as little of Maria as possible. Gentle reader, have you been yearning for fiery tales of passion, love, violence, reversal? Racy. Graphic. Am I disappointing you? If so, I'm truly sorry. I chase other Tails. But, who knows, maybe you are happy with rambles and serial-killer dreams. Soul doctors. The entire history of psychiatry. The abyss! Never forget, 'it's the abyss that keeps us all alive, only the abyss.'

June 1988. June with its endless days. As I said a while ago, I was doing OK. Actually, things were going really well, I was (pretty) relaxed and (pretty) happy with myself and everyone else (pretty much), my health was (pretty) good, all things considered. My first cat had appeared and she was here to stay! As things turned out it was the best time of my entire life. My moment at the top of my heap. And then, for a moment, I touched the sky. How short-lived it was. How terrible the fall. The stars. The abyss. A beautiful sunny day, I'd just gotten back from Sicily, a week in Siracusa working on the art magazine. (No, not Syracuse, New York. To avoid confusion I say *Siracusa,* Sicily, the one the democratic Athenians unsuccessfully attempted to savage during the Peloponnesian War.) After lunch I went out for coffee in a square around the corner. I had a little stack of articles to be edited or translated for the next issue of the magazine. Practically nobody around, a bar with a bunch of tables in the square, I sat down, ordered a coffee, and got to leafing dreamily through my papers. Feeling good. Doing OK. After a while, suddenly, out of nowhere, a young woman *splashed* down on one of the chairs at the next table. Right next to me. With a huge sigh punctuated by invisible beads of sweat she *plopped*—carefully—a *big* stack of papers down on her table. We sat there in the afternoon sun, side by side, elbow to elbow, like two statues, for a full half hour, probably longer. I pretended to look at my papers from time to time, she didn't even pretend to look at hers. She looked hassled and out of breath. I am not actually a shy person (perhaps), but I've always been very bad at *breaking silence*—my own and that of others. Better known, in a case like this, as breaking the ice. With a clock right in front of me in the square (at least I wasn't wearing a watch), the best line I could come up with was a monumentally pathetic: Excuse me, have you got the time? She was from Sicily, from a town not far from the sublimely Artaudian Palma di Montechiaro, but she lived in Palermo. She had been living in Palermo with a man (from Palermo) for five years. A very serious relationship, she told me. A very serious *Sicilian* relationship. She hoped to have lots of children (with him). But also a tangled relationship. Like Sicily itself: great, generous, beautiful, and tangled. Meanwhile, the previous autumn she had been offered an extremely well-paid job in Venice, which, alas, she couldn't refuse, especially since in Sicily she had no work at all. We started talking. All afternoon in the square. Here in the house. Dinner at Vittorio's, my favorite *trattoria*. Time passed like a crystal stream. It was love. I held her in my arms that night. She had never slept with anyone other than her fiancé (she told me, and I believe her). But it *was love*. The night after that we made love. We made love all the following nights, and many afternoons, for the next six weeks.

I just said I was *not* going to tell you this story, and I'm going to keep my word. I'm looking through the hundreds of pages from the years that followed those six weeks. Our letters, then my diary pages. I feel horrible. A very loud cry, as of infinite desolation! Mistah Kurtz—he dead. The cry of Kurtz's primordial lover in the very heart of darkness. Conrad, Kafka, Dostoyevsky, Melville. Thomas Bernhard. Great literature has made it possible for me to survive. Painters. Poets! I started reading Ezra Pound at night after my parents had gone to bed, I must have been around twelve years old: 'What thou lovest well remains, the rest is dross.' All these pages. I see, with some surprise, that they are dominated by the word—the *logos*—'silence': my silence, silence of the other. 'The silence of God.' ('In order to search for God, one must have found Him already.' This had been with me, constantly, since my years in New York.) All of a sudden, I'm thinking—maybe writing Why Dream? wasn't such a bad idea after all. Not only because it was *possible*, in the sense that *I actually did it*. Again, Kafka (who also wrote, on 21 July 1913, 'I cannot sleep. Only dreams, no sleep.'), in his *Diaries* (5 January 1914): 'All things possible do happen, but only what happens is possible.' Perhaps Why Dream? really was a *start*, a new beginning. And hopefully not an end. All these old papers. So much pure pain.

> This morning I had a dream, completely different from any other. The light, the color, above all the image itself was totally different, it just came to me out of nowhere, time didn't exist, there was no future and no past. I was at the top of a white hill, slowly descending the smooth steps carved in the stone. The slope is terribly steep and the steps too smooth, and there's nothing to hold onto. Yet I have to keep coming down, down, the slope always steeper and the steps always narrower, and I realize that a little further down there will be no more steps at all. A faithful image of my life now. I can see my silence, the love that is lost forever.

Logic? There is no logic of—in—*falling* in love—I guess. Or, I don't know. Perhaps this is the logic of 'two is two' or, perhaps, 'two is one' (or even 'one is two'), when my whole life has been dedicated to the logic of 'not two and not one.' I don't know. I do know that infatuation—or even less than infatuation—can, actually, be an exercise in logic. Perhaps. Or, not really, in the sense that a game of chess is absolutely not an exercise in logic. And passion? (I have some experience in this field.) Passion may be an intense, and highly particular, form of logic itself. But falling in *love?* I don't know. Falling in *love*—just *happens?* Like the 'happening' of art? I'm not sure. I think that falling in love means *making a connection.* This is the word I like: connection. It's the same in *genuine* friendship. As for *being* in love—which means *in connection*, in as many ways and on as many levels as there are in this world—say, for fifty years, or more, or less, I have no doubt that love develops its own logic, which is exercised in every moment. But—let's say you move into a brand-new house and after six weeks, for whatever reason (there must be *some reason*: a match, a fireplace, a short circuit, an arsonist, a bolt of lightning), it burns to the ground. Call it what you like, but not logic. Logic is a different exercise.

What *happened* with Maria? It's hard to say, since I've decided not to say it. Six weeks. Every two months her fiancé came from Palermo or she went to Palermo. We had the same birthday, July 21st. She went to Palermo. Her fiancé beat her to a pulp. Her face, her eyes, were still black and swollen when she came back ten days later. Her fiancé phoned me, repeatedly: *Ti sparo in bocca.* I'm going to blow your brains out you and blow up your house. I laughed in his face. Maria quit her job and left Venice. I never saw her again.

Just one more smidgeon. A real crumb. (Which, on a long trail, after a hard trial, led me to Gianfranco.) A venereal disease. (I bet you weren't expecting this!) 'This dry fry/ of all the crumbles/ at the beginning/ setting out once more in their coffins.' Maria. A parting gift. It seemed like a minor urinary infection. A supernatural series of incompetent doctors turned it into something *big.* How I wish I could slit their throats! All it needed, at the beginning, was a few shots of penicillin. Nothing doing. In the end—nine months later I couldn't urinate without SCREAMING. I finally found a *good* urologist. *Eight months of antibiotics.* Cycles. A few weeks on, a few weeks off. From weaker to stronger and stronger antibiotics. November, nearly 18 months after the fact. I wasn't screaming every time I took a piss anymore, but it wasn't much fun either. A decision. My *good* doctor (we also became friends, I often make friends with my *good* doctors) said: Either quit the antibiotics and hope for the best (but he was *not* hopeful), or take a shot at it (three shots, actually) with the strongest antibiotic that exists. The mother of all antibiotics. I think it will cure you, but it *will wipe out your nervous system.* (Great news!) Not right away, it'll take a while. So we took the shot, and on New Year's Eve I took my first painless piss in a year and a half. The following Easter, 1990, I collapsed, went into a coma, and when I came out, Wow, I said, where the hell am I! You're on the floor, I said. So, at least I knew where I was.

On with the meta-memoir. I've kept my word. I've told you practically nothing about loving Maria and what I suffered when I lost her. Apart from the slippery slope dream, but that's nothing, it was the least terrible of the things I wrote. Meanwhile, the previous autumn—the super-antibiotic autumn of 1989—I made the dumbest decision I've ever made in my entire life. By far! On an intelligence scale from 1 to 100 this was around 400 below zero. A friend of mine (a high school English teacher) kept telling me I needed *distraction*. 'Distract yourself from your sea of troubles,' she said, Hamletically. Shit, I already had more translations than I could handle. I was managing editor of the contemporary art magazine in Siracusa. I had plenty—plenty—to do. What's more, I *was doing it*. I have no idea how. Doing it, and coming apart at the seams at the same time. And with all that, and *at the very moment* when my nervous system was *officially on its last legs,* what did I do? I let this friend of mine *drag me* into taking a job as a Lecturer at the University of Padua! Exactly what I didn't want to do, even in the best of circumstances. The Dead Lecturer. Theater of Cruelty and Theater of the Absurd, together, shaken *and* stirred. 007 meets Apocalypse Now. Life is strange. Especially life at the end of the world. If you've been reading this Abyss of Dreams from the beginning and didn't just open it at random somewhere around the middle, 'Parroty' (a blast at mere recording organisms, though what really concerned me was the shattering war in Yugoslavia) gave you a vague and understated idea of my predicament. The fact is, after my Easter collapse (what's the opposite of Resurrection? Insurrection?), smack in the middle of my term at that goddam university, those daily trips to Padua—in the morning! early!—were kicking the shit out of me. I didn't have much left, and *I was losing it.*

But let's not dwell on all this. After all, I'm still here. Here I am! I lucked out. Artaud again. Theater. Double. Logic. Action. I talked—separately, not together—to three friends here in Venice, real Venetians who knew lots and lots of people and, in particular, knew *me*, my underground lifestyle—knew the story of Maria, and of the infection too. I told them, I'm *totally* dis-stressed, I've lost it completely, I have to keep going to Padua and I'm *wiped out*, I'm dying, I need help—a psychiatrist, at any cost, but *the right one for me*, not one who will make me long to hang myself because I'm aware I cannot slit his throat. Not some Freudian with that goddam 'table d'hôte' dream. (I'm kidding, I didn't really say that.) Fuck my 'infantile sexual life'! Well, after a couple of days all three friends came to me with exactly the same name, at the Venice Mental Health Center. (Free public health. Chairs, no couches.) It was my salvation. The month of May, 1990. Gianfranco Di Giuseppe, just five years older than I, long white hair tied up in the back in a sort of bun. (At least he *had* hair, I lost most of mine all at once in 1976, that *fidanzata*, she practically tore it out with her bare hands.) Gianfranco was pretty 'dis-stressed' himself, as my coach put it. He was recently divorced and *wildly* overworked. (*He* could have used a couch!) Commitment. Dedication. A singularity! What can I say? A wonderful person and a wonderful friend. As you know, An Abyss of Dreams is dedicated to his memory. How I miss him. Our twenty-year friendship, based not only on great affection but also on intense mutual intellectual respect and constant dialogue, was cut short by his death, a little over a year ago. He had had a serious heart problem all his life, in the mid-1990s they tried to correct it with a highly problematic operation that was only partially successful, a couple of years later he was forced to retire. He hated that, and hated having to struggle with his poor health. (Don't we all.) If I say friends like that don't grow on trees I can hear, again, his unique, indescribable laugh! As laughs go you could even call it a silly laugh, a funny laugh, but in all my life I've never heard another laugh that so directly expressed the *esprit*—the mind, the spirit—of the laugher. I could call it a Zen laugh, but I'll refrain. Once again Artaud—my friend who so desperately wanted to slit his psychiatrist's throat—gives me the perfectly *juste mot*, since laughter, too, has its *logos*, its logic: Gianfranco's was the laugh of a man who *always took the trouble to radiate and glow*. Exactly. Took the trouble to radiate and glow. *Always. Absolutely* always. Gianfranco laughed that laugh almost to the very end—until he slipped and fell on the steps of his apartment building and hit his head. His bad heart gave out, gradually but completely. Two months on life support in the Venice Hospital, on the borderline between the lower limit of consciousness and the 'other world,' and then he died.

Telling the story of my first 18 months of twice- if not thrice-weekly sessions with Gianfranco is almost as problematic as telling my story of Maria. Both he and I had a *very hard time*. I was going through a permanent near-death experience, and it was deep shit for both of us. Believe me, for a year and a half *all* we did was talk about Maria. After all that—I remember it very well—Gianfranco, with his already *many years* as a psychiatrist, told me one day that he'd never met anyone *so devastated—così devastato*—by a woman. It made him suffer too. A year and a half, three hours a week, *only* talking about Maria. It *bends my mind* to think that Gianfranco, *obviously*, never met Maria. Everyone else I knew in Venice met Maria during those six weeks, she was *sociable*. But, obviously, Gianfranco didn't. He was *after* Maria. In her *wake*. Over the years he did meet practically everyone else who was important in my life—my friends in Venice, my friend in Zurich, my Sardinian friend shipwrecked in Denmark. My cats of course, Gina and then Gilda. Later—*bien sûr*—my new *really terrifying* lovers. He even met my *mother* when she came to Venice. Sure, we talked about my dreams, which, at the time, were *going wild.* But the real subject was always Maria. Full-time, for a year and a half. A million words, 'lost in time, like tears in rain.' Just talk. Keep talking. Together. At that time, with Gianfranco, it was absolutely necessary. And how lucky I was! We *never* talked about *why* it all happened—no! This was Gianfranco's absolute genius. Never the why, just the happening. The reality *tout court.* Artaud said—in the Van Gogh essay—something so huge that, as a rule, I never quote it:

Because reality is terribly superior to all history, to all fable, to all divinity, to all surreality. All that is needed is the genius to interpret it.

This dry fry. 'You must go on.' We'll go on.

The real story I want to tell begins around the time things started to get better. Around January 1992 when, at Gianfranco's *request/suggestion,* I wrote 'Parroty.' (I wrote the whole story in a single 'night,' between 4 and 11 in the morning, in bed with my first cat.) It's true, Gianfranco and I really did hit it off right away. Gianfranco with his indescribable laugh. Not *infectious,* it was all his own. His sitting there listening. His sudden, unexpected, seemingly irrelevant questions. For twenty years I tried to get him interested in Zen Buddhism but *he didn't need it.* He was already pure Zen. (He adored Buddhist art and spent outrageous sums for Buddhas of all sizes.) Forget the 'table d'hôte' dream. Forget about slitting throats. I'd found a psychiatrist far more Zen than I ever was. A *iatros* of the *psyche*—a *soul doctor,* whatever that is. (*Soul* goddamit. If only I still had that *finished* paper, 'The Division of the Soul in Ancient Greek Religion and in the Ashanti Religion of West Africa'—which I absolutely *did* finish.) Speaking of forgetting, one thing that I, personally, would very much like to forget are sleeping pills and psychiatric drugs. But—when I said a permanent near-death experience I wasn't kidding, unfortunately. Maria was *everything,* but there was a raft of *other* things too: what the antibiotics had done to my nervous system—translations—editing the art magazine—plus the *goddam university.* May 1990: I had nearly finished my two classes (English I: False Beginners, and 'The Puritan Spirit in North American Literature'). I'd actually held my own *amazingly well* until Easter, when I collapsed. (In January I *even* broke a little bone in my foot playing in the courtyard with my first cat. At least it got me ten days sick leave.) So, until the following November 1st when my contract expired (just think, they even asked me to renew it!) I only had occasional exam sessions and six months (!) of my monthly salary. (Dead or alive, wanted or not, lecturing in Padua was the only salaried job I've had in my entire life.) So! Gianfranco's idea, and I didn't disagree: Maria absolutely, keep talking, but we've got to patch you up somehow, keep you alive (and kicking, if possible). Keep you *going* to Padua when you have to, until November. *Voilà,* the *idea.* But its *materialization?* The *second* phase of

Creation, difficulty and the Double, matter and the materialization of the idea. OK, fair enough: I couldn't sleep, I was depressed, Gianfranco gave me sleeping pills and antidepressants, *di tutti i colori*, 57 varieties. The result: I stopped sleeping *completely* and got *more* depressed. *L'effetto paradosso*—it's the paradox effect, said Gianfranco. The last of the series was Prozac—I nearly got myself suicided on that one! (Sorry, I know this isn't great publicity for Big Pharma.) You see! We did *not* get off to a good or easy start. I remember one day in Padua, possibly in the merry month of June. A bunch of students taking an exam, and me! their fearless leader. Gianfranco had tried a new pill on me. Something *really bland*. (He said afterwards.) (But they give this to 10-year-olds! said he.) I was having *hallucinations* and, eventually, couldn't figure out where in the world I was. After the exams I just sat there on a bench in Padua hallucinating all afternoon and into the evening, when I finally managed to get on a train for Venice. Poor me, and poor Gianfranco, we never quite got over that one. Call it a snag. The drugs, which were supposed to help so much, especially in getting over the first phase of the crisis, had done a lot more harm than good. This was a crisis in the crisis—for both of us. Gianfranco told me, years later, psychiatric drugs can *save lives*, but in some cases they can be *deadly*. He had been a leader all along in the—losing—battle for more psychotherapy and fewer psychiatric drugs. A losing battle, even back then, twenty years ago. And just look at the carnage we have today.

But I don't want to dwell on this, so be it, in any event Gianfranco *did keep me alive*—mostly, I'd say, by convincing me, in the end, that I was more resilient than I thought I was *at that moment*. But the first year and a half were very painful. The pain was so desperately intense that I forgot to remember the *really important things* I had learned in the course of my life. Forgot to remember them. Gianfranco talked, grimly, about great depressions that last a whole lifetime, and about how the goal of psychotherapy in some cases can be no more than 'making the suffering bearable.' But that was a detour, it wasn't the road. (Maria! Keep talking! *That* was the road.) It's true, we talked about depression—but just because I was too wiped out to express what I really felt. Which was silence. A terrible inhuman silence. This was the devastation: My silence, silence of the other. A silence I was too silent to express. But with Gianfranco's help I began to find my voice again. I managed, in various ways, to tell him what My Silence was. But most of all—at last!—I told him exactly how, in the course of my life, I'd gotten to know my own nervous system *intimately*. At last I remembered what I had forgotten to remember. With my own voice, one day I said: I'm not depressed, my nervous system is burned out. I'm still alive, I can still feel its electrical impulses—just barely!—but instead of slender flames they are cinders. *Ridotti in cenere.* Burnt to cinders. They want to come out into the world—my world, my external world—but are much too tired to make it to the surface. Ashes. *Rossocenere*. After almost a year and a half of saying Silence Silence I started telling Gianfranco what I meant, or was trying to mean. Little by little, week by week, I *did* tell him. I told him, my silence is nervous exhaustion. I told him I was naming and directing shadows. I told him about a logic of silence, connected with a logic of dreams. 'Behold, this dreamer cometh!'—Gianfranco *knew* how much I *knew* about *dreams*. I said, Listen, Gianfranco, to *my* silence. The most furious nightmare makes no *sound*, in nervous exhaustion the energy of the system cannot make it to the *surface*. Listen! This is *my* silence, but by a sort of acoustic illusion I experience it as a silence of the *other*. The more intensely I suffer *my* silence, the more I experience it as a silence of *the world*. As *my* silence of the *other*. I said: This logic is unshakable—just ask Joseph K.! (We sure talked a river about Joseph K.) And he listened and listened. And listened. (And laughed from time to time!) Ye gods! To him it made perfect sense. This was the road. This was the idea to be materialized. If the problem is nervous *exhaustion* you've got to find a way to give the nerves some *rest*. The root and the branch. On the withered tree a flower blooms.

One day, as I mentioned, I talked about cinders, and at our next session Gianfranco gave me a photocopy of one of the few books by Jacques Derrida I didn't already have. The bilingual Italian edition. The untranslatable original title is FEU LA CENDRE. In Italian, *Ciò che resta del fuoco* (What remains of the fire). In the English almost-untranslatable translation, published several years later, *Cinders*. (English is not Latin, as a few of us know.) Gianfranco was magic, unique. He knew what we needed. That short book is my favorite of Derrida's (outrageously many) books, and Gianfranco and I talked about it forever, for twenty years, with its

> Et près de la fin, au bas de la dernière page, c'est comme si tu signais de ces mots: 'Il y a là cendre.' Je lisais, relisais, c'était si simple et pourtant je comprenais que je n'y étais pas, la phrase se retirait sans m'attendre vers son secret.

There is ash. *Là cendre*. The phrase withdrawing, without waiting for me, towards it secret. Best thing Derrida ever wrote. A few years later it instigated an essay of mine, 'The Failure of Meaning'—basically, a critique of Derrida's critique of Hegel. It also inspired a *doubled poem*—a series of doubled poems, one in Italian, one in English—*Di-stanze e cenere/ Ashes and rooms*: 'beyond ecstasy/ at the edge of chaos/ far from equilibrium/ là cendre.'

I have just one more issue to take up with you, gentle reader, if, somehow, you're still there. *Alas the issue is not a small one.* Actually, it's what this little Tail was supposed to be about. A Tail about mystery, Antonin Artaud, my friend Gianfranco, psychiatry, Artaud's detestation of psychiatry, artmaking! and—my real point—*silence*. Let's see, I've already covered: Artaud pretty well, Gianfranco not as much as I want to, psychiatry somewhat, Artaud's detestation of psychiatry sufficiently (so to speak). Mystery? *If*—which I doubt—you recall, the mystery in question in this Tail was the mystery of the nervous system, and, I agree, I have not cut its guts out as I did with the mystery of consciousness, though I have taken some slight but interesting stabs at it. Now—the *one* that still looms large on the list is artmaking. It's true, I have touched on it—with both hands, actually: on *making* and on *happening*. But now I need to do it *right*, as I did it with Gianfranco. Alas, schematically. Again. Let's see: art—making—happening—silence. Or, why not: silence— making—happening—art. How about: silence—art—making—happening. Or: making—happening—art—silence. Or: silence—happening—making— art. Without even trying I didn't repeat myself. *MIRACOLO!* A great goalkeeper! It's all bullshit—not that *everything* schematic is bullshit: I wake up—I get up—I take my pills—I wash my face—I brush my teeth—I go out/I don't go out. Just fine. But never mind silence, *art is art*, and this *demands chaotic logic*.

So—let's give the nerves some rest—and *recreation*. This was Gianfranco's idea. Rest and recreation. R&R—*hell no not that*, that was when our boys in Vietnam went whoring in Bangkok, also to do even more dope than they were doing already. No, not that. By recreation—in *my* case—Gianfranco meant *writing*. (A strange idea, actually. Why not basket weaving? Stamp collecting? Bungee jumping?) Ever since the invention of the alphabet crises of the *nervous system* have led to the production of huge amounts of (creative) writing—*most of it bad*, I'd say. But never mind. (You see, I've always been *hounded* by this reputation for being a gifted writer. Who was it that started this ugly rumor?) As a matter of fact, thanks to the art magazine, I had already been writing, a little. Short essays on artmaking. A longer essay inspired by my course in Padua, my passion for abstract art, and, naturally, by Hegel: 'The Puzzle of Meaning: Abstraction and Herman Melville.' Pieces that got translated into Italian, Gianfranco was gobbling them up. (Fast. They were *short*.) But for some reason—Why?—Why Dream?—Gianfranco wanted *stories*. *Racconti*. Why? You need to write *racconti*, he said. I'd never seen him so categorical. Actually, it all had to do with my *problem* with silence: My silence, silence of the other. Though the *real* silence at that time was still *the silence of my nervous system*. First Maria and then my urologist had burnt it out. Its electrical impulses were too weak to reach the surface, to come out into the world, to break the silence. Silence. Maria. Absolutely, a doubled silence—doubled and doubling. The 'Silence of God' is bad news (I suppose, whatever in the world it is), but the silence *of the world* is a terrible silence. 'Like a drum-tap/ at the edge of the universe …' I had started writing. Poems. Actually, I've been writing poems, sporadically, more or less since I was born. After Gianfranco's *racconti* I actually wrote a heap of poems, long chains of poems. *Where Shadows End*, then *Ashes and Rooms*. Unfinished chains. Innovative poetry it had taken me a lifetime to learn from Ezra Pound. Make it new! In English, but also (the best of the lot) in Italian. My great friend Wolfango's favorite, *estremo rossocenere*. After all, Italian is my actual speaking language. For three decades I used most of my English to translate intricate Italian philosophers, or marxists. (At some point I did escape from the art critics.) Giacomo the Translator, the passionately creative mere recording organism. A slave. Anyway, I've translated—beautifully— quite a number of fine (and complicated) books, and no one's complaining. But, believe me, I've seen things you people wouldn't believe. Attack ships on fire off the shoulder of Orion. Time to die, says the slave, the time-sharing *Blade Runner* replicant. But, in the new remodeled *palazzo* that killed my first cat, the entire ground floor is inhabited exclusively by time sharers, all from the city of Bergamo, and they aren't dying, as far as I can see. And *watch out* for the *plague* of bed-and-breakfasters, *barbarians*, driving the Venetians out of the city! I've been derailed! What in the world was I saying. C-beams glittering in the dark near the Tannhäuser gate. Just a few years ago, in the first- (i.e. second-) floor apartment, with the beautiful terrace I see in front of me right now, *four generations* of a Venetian family (plus a dog) were living together in one apartment, aged over-90 to close-to-zero. And then came the 'restoration' (!) of the *palazzo, which killed my first cat*, and now that apartment is occupied—occasionally—by a couple of art historians (my age) from Des Moines (where I was born). Call it progress, if you dare. We slaves dream rivers of blood, when nothing is out there but computer chips. Ye gods I'm rambling, with a vengeance. Raving, possibly. Shit—pardon my French—*fuck me*—I've been crying like a lamb the past couple of days, writing this. Maria was Maria—and still is, somewhere, I hope—but, Gianfranco, *I miss you, my friend*. I have cried so much the past couple of days, and worked so hard. Look! My second cat, huddled in the far corner of our bed—*under the blanket*. (She *never* goes under the blanket.) Remember, Gianfranco, you came to see her when she was three months old? One year to the day after Gina died. Gilda loves to see me type away on the computer. Recently, she saw me write by hand, pen on paper. What fun! Trying to chew on the (plastic) pen as I wrote. But now she's upset. About this Tail. Cats do not cry (tears), my first cat was tough as a nail, but she suffered so much, at the end of her life. Tonight Gilda, the philosopher, the Parmenidean, the cat-writer, is suffering. She hates to see me cry. You may, or may not, have noticed, but this is a hard story.

The translator. Born to be a slave. A marathon runner for whom the finish line does not exist. When translating gets me down I like to meditate on the story of Marpa the Translator, the first great figure of the 'second spreading' of Buddhism in Tibet in the 11th century. An incredible figure! A man of action, holding nothing back, uninhibited, direct, stubborn. He made three famous trips to India and translated the fundamental texts of Indian Buddhism into Tibetan. But—what's more—he, personally, *translated* Buddhism to Tibet. Now *this* is translation! A wild man, a tame man, a man of action who went through decades of Silence and came out on the other side. An inspiration.

The nature of mind cannot be thought.
Rest in this natural state.
When you see this truth, you will be liberated.
Just as a child would, watch the behavior of barbarians.
Be carefree; eat flesh; be a madman.

Marpa the Translator. Madmen don't grow on trees. (I hear Gianfranco laughing!) I've taken your words seriously. When translating gets me down, I think of you and invent ancient proverbs. Listen! Just a few examples:

1. Never send a painter to mow the lawn.
2. Never wipe your hands on a slimy ape.
3. Never wipe your ass with slimy wisdom.

Not much, I admit, but these things cheer me up. It's not easy to invent ancient wisdom these days.

Let's calm down. As I was saying—Gianfranco wanted *stories*. I *told* him, Gianfranco, *stories are hard*, they're not rest and recreation. I don't have stories in me right now, I have the sense and the absence of Maria, and that is *no story*, it is silence. My nerves are burned out. Gianfranco was as stubborn as time, Einstein's illusion. He wanted stories. *Five stories*, no less! You need to write five stories. Why? *To break your silence*. But nobody will read them, I said. That's not the point, said Gianfranco. I said: The silence will get worse! Even if I break *my* silence, what about the silence of the world, the silence of the *other*, who no longer speaks to me and who will *never read what I write*. But Gianfranco *knew* what he *wanted*. What about the unshakable logic of silence! If you break *your* silence you break *all* the silence—that's what he said. Frankly, I wasn't convinced at the time, and I'm rather *less* convinced right now. Logic is not so simple. 'Acoustic illusion' possibly, but I think we missed something. I think he was probably wrong. *Nevertheless*, all this wasn't about debating (neither of us were master debaters), it was about Psychotherapy and its Double. Logic. So, I took his request seriously. He said, Don't write them for the other, write them for yourself. (Gruesomely famous last words.) So be it. I had complete faith in Gianfranco (he'd earned it!), and that was not wrong. Plus, I figured, what the hell, stories—they're not sleeping pills that kill my sleep or antidepressants that depress me out of my mind. So—stories. I remember it very well—it seemed impossible. Then again, the war in Yugoslavia was very much on my mind (to say the least). A travesty! Possibly the dirtiest war, for the most dishonest motives, in modern history. (If you can find a copy—which you can't, they refuse to reprint it—read Peter Handke's *A Journey to the Rivers. Justice for Serbia.*) So, OK, I started thinking about the story, thinking, making a few notes, thinking—this went on for a couple of months I think, it was winter— then, one night, I slept for a couple of hours, woke up in the freezing house, grabbed a big notebook, sat up in bed, under the covers, my first cat sitting on my lap, and wrote 'Parroty.' Gianfranco was pleased as punch. He couldn't read it in English of course, but that wasn't his point. Later on it actually got published. (In Seattle!) There was an Italian translation. Most people, I think, thought it was a melancholy story of Venice when in fact it was about the war in Yugoslavia, but, so be it. For Gianfranco that wasn't the point. He laughed! Four more *racconti* please!

Now, four to go. Well, ever since I finished NYU, in 1972, I'd had this *fantastic* idea for a story, called 'The Empty Shield.' It was about the sixth challenger in Aeschylus' tragedy *Seven Against Thebes*, and was inspired by a brilliant essay by one of my NYU professors. A fantastic idea! The fact is, I've been thinking about this story ever since—for forty years now. *Just* thinking. The idea is fantastic, but its *materialization* is another matter. This idea demands one of the *trickiest* materializations of all time—and in fact less than one month ago *for the first time* I finally got an *inkling* of how in the world to do it. Maybe. And I *hope* to do it, and make it the last story in An Abyss of Dreams. But back in 1992, working on Gianfranco's psychotherapeutic project I scribbled away at the Shield for a couple of months or more, but nothing doing. 'No tripe for cats,' as we say in Italian. (An intriguing expression with an interesting history. In Rome, from time immemorial, the cats responsible for protecting rat-threatened documents in the municipal archives had— at public expense—been fed tripe, which is delicious and expensive, and killed their appetite for killing rats. A contradiction! So around 1910 the Mayor ordered: No tripe for cats. Two birds with one stone: He saved the city money, and the cats were obliged to dine exclusively on the rats.) Four to go! I told Gianfranco, it's like cleaning a runway with a toothbrush. Well, that's fine, he said, and laughed. Pick another subject. The point is *to do it!* (That was his point.) Well, I came up with another excellent idea, which I called 'Neighbors.' The real story of my life as a student at NYU, but as told by my actually imaginary neighbors in my building on Rivington Street. A political story. (But 'Parroty' was a political story, and so was/is/will be 'The Empty Shield.') Vietnam. I actually wrote some very lively scenes with my neighbors, Frank and Stumpy. But—guess what—the story started to grow! (Did you know that Why Dream? was supposed to be a *short story*, and just

look at it now. And this Tail or Two Tails or whatever was supposed to be
real short. As short as Gilda's Tail. But—as the saying went—stuff happens.)
(Let's went! as the Cisco Kid's sidekick Pancho used to say.) Meanwhile I was
working *very* hard on the art magazine—my English-language edition was
doing extremely well in the U.S.A. (a year or so later it suddenly collapsed
and disappeared completely, but that's *another* story)—so I had very little
time for 'Neighbors.' Meanwhile, I had been rereading Artaud, and suddenly
the story *doubled* into *two doubling stories*: New York 1968–72 and Venice
1991 or thereabouts. A great idea. The art magazine went on total Italian
vacation (Italians are great vacationers—real pros) from 15 August to 1
September, and I *wrote like crazy*—some 150 computerized pages, which
still exist. But that wasn't even *half* the story. Far from it! And when the
editorial office re-opened I had no more time at all. I said, Hey, Gianfranco!
Look at all these pages. You wanted *making/doing*, well, *voilà*, I *made/did* to
your heart's content. You've made your point, I said. Four more stories—all
this ought to count for *at least* four. Gianfranco laughed! How I miss him!

He had made his point. But what *was* his point? His point wasn't, You
promised your grandfather a *big* book, so start off with *racconti*. No, and it
wasn't the point my cousin in Miami has been making since he read Gilda's
Tail: You have *talent*, so *write!* No. Gianfranco's point was about *silence*—a
good point. An excellent point. It's his logic that I question. My silence,
silence of the other. Gianfranco's thesis is *if* you break *your* silence you break
all the silence. This may be logic, but it lacks what Artaud meant by *raison
d'être*. Which, he said, 'n'est pas trouvée':

> We are not yet born,
> we are not yet in the world,
> there is not yet a world,
> things have not yet been made,
> the *raison d'être* has not been found.

This, in the context of a poem—'I Hate and Renounce as a Coward'—that is
a violent tirade against *God*: 'Get back down in your grave god you lowdown
corpse.' But Artaud also knew more than anyone about the *raison d'être* of
art—of *making* art. In the quote that opens Two Tails—the last paragraph of
the Preface to *The Theater and its Double*—he answered the question 'Why
make art?' *perfectly*. Makers of art *must be* like victims burnt at the stake,
signaling through the flames. In other words, they have to have something
goddam important to say, and they have to have the *art* to say it. *To make
it happen*. This is art's *raison d'être*. No small claim, and no small demand.
But Artaud—and I, and many others—believe that art itself *is not small*.
Nations are small, governments are small, politicians are *goddam* small. But

art is big. Real big. In many cases it may have something small to say, but whatever's said *must* be said with total dedication and not just from the surface of fact. Commitment, engagement, *sacrifice*. This has been my creed all along. Creed, and *practice*. The end—the aim—of art is to break *the other's silence*. This is what I believe, this is Artaud, this is *raison d'être*. A culture where artists make art to break their *own* silence is a *culture without shadows* and an art that *is not happening*. It is dreamless reality and dead form. Viewed *artistically*, the *Logos* is the Double of Silence, and Silence *doubles* into logic (the realm of shadows) and dream (the realm of shadows doubled) and *is doubled* in my silence, silence of the other. It's all 'one tangle of shadows,' as Ezra Pound put it. What mediates this 'doubles' and this 'doubled' is *art*, and its Double: art as *making* and art as *happening*. Remember—in Why Dream?—when I said, *paradoxically* (but whoever's afraid of the paradoxical, raise your hand and leave the room!), about dreaming, that the most *private* thing we do is also the most *public*? A tricky point, but a damn good one. One of the best I've made lately. Well, it's exactly the same with art—but also completely different. *This* is the thorn that made me write Two Tails. I mean, nobody *publishes* their dreams. (Not true, of course. But it means *writing a book* of and/or about them.) For me personally (as you've gathered, I hope), good art does not dally with forms but dives straight—or rambles—into the utmost depths of the *abyss*. (Again, the most private that is the most public.) And—like Ishmael, buoyed up by his tattooed friend's coffin, picked up by the devious-cruising Rachel—escapes alone to tell thee. To tell *thee!* See what I mean? Not mee but *thee! Voilà* a *theatrical* quotation just for Artaud:

> And, behold, there came a great wind from the wilderness, and smote the four corners of the house, and it fell upon the young men, and they are dead; and I only am escaped alone to tell thee. (*Job*, 1: 19).

Ye gods, how can you not go crazy about stuff like this, as Melville sure as hell did. There came a great wind from the wilderness!! *OUR-TOE*, unrambling rose! I, alas, for better or worse, am an incurable rambler. But—my point— what is writing *for the writer* if no one *reads* it? *What?* If not a transition from inner to outer *silence*. Suicide! The suicided! Mine, *yours*. Me, *you*. An *untimely* death, time and again. The suicided artist. What am I doing *now*, this very moment? Who will read this? Gianfranco! What am I doing! Am I simply pouring coals onto the fire of *my* silence, my sickness unto death? A heap of embers glowing fiercely. Victims burnt at the stake are *witnesses*— witnesses *to* something. Not simply to their *own* faith, but to what they have faith *in*. And yet the world is full of artists dallying with forms. Artists who simply *have nothing to say*.

Well, guess what? At this point, gentle reader, we ought to be very close to the end of these Two Tails. (I think! Never trust me.) If you've actually read these Tails (and, heaven help you, the other chapters of this book), you may think it's all nothing but idle ranting and raving fueled by silence and solitude. But, believe me, I've had something to say. All my life—for the past forty years anyway—I have had *something to say.* 'He raised his hands and spread out all his fingers,' said Kafka, of Joseph K. You may be quite right (*but are you there?*), perhaps I've said it badly, perhaps I haven't *made* my points. Perhaps I don't deserve you. Perhaps I *richly deserve* your condemnation, your *death sentence.* Go ahead, don't read me! Your hands are already at my throat! For me, *to be unread*—for An Abyss of Dreams, in memory of my friend Gianfranco, to be unread—is to be sentenced to death. To endless silence. Gilda is *staring* at me with awe and horror. The cat-writer, the Parmenidean, the gentlest creature on the face of the earth, and not only the face. But Gina knows exactly what I mean, for her it's perfectly normal. What a cat! An action cat. Wait—speaking of Gina, my first cat, first reader of my first story of—theoretically—five—let's get back, just for a *moment,* to Gianfranco's logic, his thesis: If you break *your* silence you break *all* the silence. Well, thanks to Gianfranco—more to Gianfranco *himself,* to his laugh, his humanity, his friendship, than to his five stories thesis—I did start writing, more than ever before, and furiously. I'd actually already started to start writing again, but those few years after two years of sessions with Gianfranco were certainly the most prolific of my writing life. (Until last October anyway.) As I said, I'd already started writing a lot of 'make it new' poetry, in English and, especially, in Italian. (Too new for my own good, I suppose.) Then I worked, *like crazy,* for a full year on that philosophy essay, 'The Failure of Meaning.' Worked so hard I hardly went out of the house, I practically stopped going to my sessions with Gianfranco. On his way home after work he used to stop by here, to see how I was *doing,* say ciao to my first cat, and—Gianfranco!—quite often brought me a shopping bag, with meat, bread, vegetables. Derrida's friends who commissioned the essay *really hated it,* so it never got published. But I didn't jump out of my window into the canal. Instead, I decided to study chaos theory, which I'd never heard of until then. Orderly disorder, in art, in logic, in life. I worked on one long poem, then on the really long *doubled* poem, which started off with *estremo rossocenere* but ended up with its throat slit by silence and solitude. My silence? Silence of the other? I had created a new form/content—genuine state-of-the-art burnt-at-the-stake poetry. Apart from Gianfranco here and Wolfango in Siracusa, nobody gave a shit. Go ahead, don't read! So, one day, I suddenly got *totally and absolutely* pissed off and stopped writing completely. Translations, period. Heaps of them. I didn't jump out of any windows, but I did fall into a deep—and bitter—silence. My silence, or silence of the other? I have always insisted it was silence *of the other.* Gianfranco didn't agree, but, he wasn't so sure either. My position was that I broke *my* silence—my *writing* silence—worked like hell, wrote like hell—and produced a *new my-silence* that was deeper and more enduring than the old one. (As you may recall, the old one was the manifestation of a burnt-out nervous system.) What's more, the new my-silence wasn't just a writing silence but *a total and entrenched my-silence*. And thanks to this new and entrenched *my*-silence *the other* fell totally silent too. That's how I see it. And now I'm writing again. Who knows, maybe this time things will be different. Even footballers work miracles these days.

So be it. Let me end Two Tails this way: Gianfranco and I, together, worked our way through my terrible time of nervous exhaustion. I came out the better for it, and I guess he did too, since he found a real friend, and real friends don't grow on trees. It's amazing how resilient a human being can be in the end. How resourceful. It reminds me of the great chorus of Sophocles' *Antigone* (332-372, I attempted to translate it forty years ago). Sophocles' word for human being—his *logos*, his logic—is *deinos*, translated in a hundred ways: strange, marvelous, uncanny, wondrous—and from wondrous to able, clever, skillful, but the original meaning was fearful, *terrible*, and then powerful, mighty. (Dinosaur—*deino-sauros*—actually means *terrible lizard*.) For Sophocles the human was the strangest of beings but, I'd say today, strange precisely in the sense of the most *resourceful* and *resilient*. (But, today, I'd also say the most *terrible*.) Crossing the sea in the winter's storm.

> Language and thought like the wind
> and the feelings that make the city
> he has taught himself, and to take shelter against
> the clear-cold and stormy shafts of hard frosts;
> he always finds a way, he faces no future helpless.
> There is only death that he cannot escape.

Only death. And one other thing. If you ever make a connection—*truly connect*—with another human being (with *any* sentient being—just ask your cats!), there is no escape. It is a life sentence—or worse! or better! It is a sentence that continues to be in force after life and after death. It is something that has a beginning but no end. Terrible as time. This is the mystery.

Years later Gianfranco told me how much he looked forward to our sessions. I told him the story of my life, and it wasn't dull! Extremely painful. Terrible devastation. But not dull. I told him my dreams—wow! *That* was worth the price of admission. Sure, my recurrent dreams were high quality entertainment—I was having the 'unfinished' and the 'packing' dreams simultaneously at the time. But, as I said at the very beginning of this Tail, for genuinely gruesome dreaming there's nothing like a *bona fide* crisis that *sizzles* your nerves. For dreams that you not only *remember* but that you *cannot possibly forget*. And I hit Gianfranco with a couple of *really wild ones* every single week! *Di tutti i colori, in tutte le salse,* 57 varieties and the more the merrier. Believe me, the dreams I had last November—reported in Why Dream?—were *kid stuff* compared to those. Gianfranco was having a pretty good time goddamit, despite all the pain. He told me so himself. (Years later.) With most of his patients he had to worm little dreams out of them—Come on, come on, you can remember *something* about it!—and here I was with a raging flood. With a roaring/silent *abyss* of dreams. A conscious, not an unconscious abyss. And I had a good time too, though I certainly enjoyed our friendship a lot more a few years later, when my problems were a lot less extreme. The problem was that Gianfranco's problems were getting worse. We had incredible conversations. I, too, love to laugh, and laugh we did. The day Gianfranco died—29 November 2010— was an incredibly warm sunny day, I sat in the little courtyard near the house where he lived in Venice in the 1990s and cried all afternoon. (After he retired he moved to Mestre, the mainland.) The day of his funeral, in Mestre, three days later, there was flooding in Venice and a shroud of bitter freezing fog. What an ugly day! How things change! I'd never been to the Mestre cemetery and it looked like the ugliest place on earth. Bitter freezing fog. As I watched them lowering the coffin and covering it with the ugliest slimiest clay I've ever seen—how ugly!—I was thinking about how many people Gianfranco had helped in his years as a psychiatrist, how many he had brought back to life or, more modestly, kept alive. How many were strolling around Mestre and Venice the sunny day he died, today bundled against the bitter freezing fog, and tomorrow who knows? All thanks to Gianfranco. I wish Artaud could have met him.

I returned to the cemetery for the first time one year later, last November 29th. I was working hard on Why Dream?—which ends with my 'last dream' of November 19th, but I actually finished it at the end of January. The Mestre cemetery. It was a *gorgeous* warm sunny day. I simply couldn't believe it was the same place I had been to one year earlier. How things change! I wanted to ask Gianfranco about it! His family—his sister, brother-in-law, Erica, his beloved niece—had provided him (and me, and us) with a vast but simple and tasteful slab covering the length of the grave, and a headstone with a photo of him laughing! What peace. The sun slanting through the tall cypresses, the silence. It was early afternoon, there was practically nobody around. That was the day I realized that the dead cannot speak to us but we can speak to them, and we *must* do it. I do it, often. I'm doing it now.

February 2012

references

Antonin Artaud, *The Theater and its Double*, translated by Mary Caroline
Richards, New York: Grove Press, 1958.
I quote from the 'Preface':
    When we speak — p. 13
    fearlessly makes himself master — p. 13
    How hard it is — pp. 11-12;
    and from 'The Alchemical Theater':
    And this essential drama — p. 51.

Antonin Artaud, *Artaud Anthology*, edited by Jack Hirschman, Second Edition,
San Francisco: City Lights Books, 1965.

I quote from: 'Van Gogh: The Man Suicided by Society,' translated by Mary
Beach + Lawrence Ferlinghetti:
    It is no ordinary thing — p. 141
    I, myself, spent — p. 148
    Things are bad — p. 135
    For mankind does not want — p. 157
    There are souls who — p. 162
    Because reality is terribly superior — p. 143;
    from 'I hate and renounce as a coward,' translated by David Rattray:
    I hate and renounce as a coward — p. 222
    We are not yet born — p. 226;
    and from 'Here Lies,' translated by F. Teri Wehn & Jack Hirschman:
    I speak from above time — p. 248.
Translations modified.

Joseph Conrad, *Heart of Darkness*, I quote from Part II.

'like a drum tap' and 'estremo rossocenere' are from my *Di-stanze e cenere/
Ashes and rooms*, Italian and English coupled poems, 1994, unfinished and
unpublished.

fragments of 'risk and toe,' from 'scherzo: ear, nose, toe/ for Antonin Artaud,'
from my *Where Shadows End*, 1992–94, unfinished and unpublished.

'my heart/ a black cloud/ in your hands,' from my Italian:
'mio cuore/ una nuvola nera/ nelle tue mani' (2002)—nearly a haiku (it's 17
syllables).

Tsang Nyön Heruka, *The Life of Marpa the Translator*, Boston & London: Shambhala, 1995, p. 46.

'lost in time, like tears in rain'—and the 'C-beams' and 'attack ships'—is from the last scene of *Blade Runner.*

'you must go on' is a fleeting reference to the last line of Samuel Beckett's *The Unnamable.*

Ezra Pound, from Canto VXXXI:
What thou lovest well remains,
the rest is dross
What thou lov'st well shall not be reft from thee
What thou lov'st well is thy true heritage

VI. Gina's Tail: End and Shadow
a connection

'it seemed as though the mist itself had screamed'
Joseph Conrad, *Heart of Darkness*

You can't imagine how bad I felt the first night I spent in that bar, not that the next two weeks were any better. It was all my brother's fault. Sebastiano—Seba for short, that's what I called him. (My full name is Regina, but Giacomo didn't like it and always called me Gina.) Seba was too cute and too clever for my own good. Possibly for his own good too, who knows where he ended up. But if there was ever a cat who knew how to land on his paws it was Seba. We were born on April 22nd, 1986, in an apartment in the neighborhood of the Venice Hospital, the other side of the Rialto. The head of the household was a musician, he had lots of crazy friends, they all smoked dope and had fun, his wife was nice and took good care of us, they all adored cats. I lived there for the first five months of my life, with my mother and an older brother (a half-brother, I presume). (Giacomo has some great pictures, I looked just like my mom.) For a while I played with the brothers and sisters I was born with, but pretty soon they all moved out. I don't know why I was allowed to stay, it's a mystery, I must have been someone's special pet. I was a gray tabby with four white paws like elegant white boots, an athletic physique, and a regal gait. Sebastiano was white and gray, so cute and so clever, he was my favorite—I think he was everybody's favorite. I've never understood why they gave him away instead of me. But they did. And where did they send him? Not to a house but to a bar—just think, Seba went to live in a bar, in Rio Marin, around the corner from where I lived almost all my life, with Giacomo. A brand-new bar, owned by a man named Lili—a funny name. A nice man, like a big teddy bear, a good friend of our musician. But a bar is a bar. You can't tell me it's a home. Seba, though, was so smart, and a born wanderer (the opposite of me, a homebody), and he took that bar for exactly what it was—a bar. He went there to have a drink when he was thirsty, a bite to eat when he was hungry, and—usually—to sleep at night when the bar closed. But his main activity was visiting all the people in all the *palazzi* right up and down both sides of Rio Marin, which happens to be a canal straight as an arrow and with lanes running along both sides. (And if you happen to pass through it by boat, half a minute after the bend you come right to my house, where I lived with Giacomo for over sixteen years. But on foot you have to turn every which way, it takes forever, five minutes at least. That's how Venice is.) Seba was as sociable a cat as ever came down the pike, he loved people and people adored him. I don't know if, at first, he was just making a virtue of necessity, with all his rambling and sociality. For a ten-week-old cat, living in a bar (closed all day—it didn't open until around 7 in the evening) was not an ideal situation. But he sure made the most of it. He loved all that attention, evenings in the bar, and all day from the people living along Rio Marin. To say nothing of tourists—Seba loved them too. He was sociality in fur and blood, an extreme form of sociality. A rare cat.

Giacomo and Lili became friends that summer. It was the summer when Giacomo did the gigantic remodeling of our house. He took the ancient roof right off and made a new one. He took all the plaster off almost all the walls in the entire house, and had them replastered or paneled. He worked like crazy all summer long. While I was so happily and so peacefully playing with my mother and older brother, and with Lili's friend the musician and his wife, and all their friends, poor Giacomo was sleeping in a borrowed room next door to his ruin and getting up at six in the morning (he usually gets up around noon) to join the men working on the house. It's hard for me to imagine it all, three, four months like that, day after day. So every evening Giacomo went to Lili's bar, to get five minutes away from the dust and the rubble for a few hours. But he was pretty strong back then, he'd just turned 36 that summer. (That's when he met my Zio Terri—zio means uncle in Italian—one of my favorite zii.) And that's how he got to know my brother Sebastiano. In fact, in the evening, when the bar was open and full of people, have no fear, Seba is here! The center of attention. He was a star. Who knows what life had in store later on for my brother Seba, I think of him often. Maybe someone carried him off to who knows where—Milan, or Munich, or Paris. Or Mestre. Or Campo San Polo, out of sight inside a house. All we know is that one day in September he disappeared from Rio Marin. It was Giacomo himself who'd told Lili, if you let this great cat wander around all day like this someone is going to carry him off. (At least he didn't wander at night. I think he usually had a late dinner in the bar and then slept peacefully until Lili came the next morning—around noon, another late sleeper—to clean up and let him out.) Not because he looks like a stray—he looked much too good to be a stray—but just because he's asking for it, and because he's so fantastic. That's what Giacomo said. Anyway, whatever happened wasn't Lili's fault, Lili loved Sebastiano and was very kind to me during those terrible two weeks. These days all the Venetians ever seem to think about are dogs—dogs dogs dogs, tiny, small, medium, large, gigantic—but the real Venetians, the old-time Venetians like Lili loved cats. Cats have always been part of Venice, dogs are strangers, barbarians. They don't even have earth to shit on in this town. Have you ever seen a dog kill a rat?

Well, times change. Venetian cats were born to kill rats. In Italian a gray tabby like I was is called a *soriano*, because some five hundred years ago the Venetians brought cats from Syria to kill the rats—in Venetian dialect, *pantegane*—that were, literally, killing the city, infecting it with plague. And we've done a great job, for hundreds of years. At the Rialto fish market (our great friend and neighbor Veniero talked about this all the time, I'm so sorry he's dead too, Giacomo really misses him) up to the 1960s there was an entire long row of stalls with nothing but fish for cats. Amazing but true. In the 1970s there were still thousands, or hundreds, of stray—I'd say wild—cats all over the city. Cats who didn't live in houses like I do, but the whole city was their home. The famous cat-mothers—old-time Venetian cat-loving women—left piles of food for them in certain places. Believe me, in those days a *pantegana* had a very short life in this town. Then, in the 1980s, came the campaign against stray cats. Best news the rats ever had, they could hardly believe their ears. And the Venetians started getting dogs. (And let me assure you, it wasn't only the wild cats that killed *pantegane*, we house cats took very good care of our own areas, believe you me.) So the stray cats became outlaws. Before I arrived, Veniero and Giacomo had a small outlaw community right in the courtyard, in one corner. They built a little house there, and Giacomo gave the cats names. Iskra was the first, a real wet-rag of a cat, and he named her, ironically, after Lenin's famous newspaper, The Spark. Then the others, named after his old friends (and my uncles) Lello, Ulrico, Thanassi, and a red one named Ruth (after my aunt with red hair). There was also a period of some months when these cats had a guest—Veniero noticed it right away—a very sick cat, probably blind, who died in the little house, despite all the efforts of the other cats to look after him. When this cat died the others put him in front of their house and they all cried out together, a long low moan, for hours. Veniero put his body into the canal, it's true, the current of the canal is very strong. Veniero—a real old-time Venetian—was not exactly a cat lover but he had really great respect for cats, and he kept telling everyone this story for years. A moving story. It gives you some idea of the wonderful character of that generation of Venetian cats. And then, just a few months before I was born, on February 1st, 1986 there was a terrible *acqua alta* in the town, the third highest flooding of all time (since I died I pay much more attention to these things, Giacomo is always worried about water coming into the house), the outlaw cat house was floating around the courtyard, and all the cats disappeared. Completely. Who knows what became of them.

I was one of the last members of the great family of Venetian cats whose great passion and virtue was killing rats. In my lifetime there were practically no more strays at all, no more outlaws, it was the beginning of a new era. Today, in Venice, if a home cat (I don't like to say house cat—besides, some home cats like me, or Gilda, don't just stay in the house, but we certainly do have homes) meets a *pantegana* it's more or less a Close Encounter of the Third Kind. Just look at Gilda, a great cat—a philosopher, gentle, tender, so loving with my beloved Giacomo—but the day she encountered that tiny mouse in the courtyard she made the chickens laugh, as we say in Italian. She just wanted to play with it, to pet it, she'd never have killed it in a million years. The few old-time Venetians we still have in the courtyard laughed at Gilda from the windows. (Very few old-timers are still in the courtyard, and in the space behind the house, now known as the back garden—once my own great kingdom, my *regno*—there are no old-time Venetians at all.) And if she happens to see an actual rat—a *pantegana*—she dashes back into the house as if her tail were on fire. (No, not her Tail 'What is it like to be a cat?') Gilda really is the gentlest of all, but I don't think the other cats of her generation would have done much better. Some may still have a pinch of killer instinct, but they spend their lives sleeping in their houses. And there's another important factor. Cat owners today don't want killer cats in their homes, they think it's disgusting, they'd rather have the streets full of rats. What a world we live in, so many contradictions. Things change, for the worse. Now the city is full of rat poison, and full to the brim with rats. Gilda is absolutely no killer, but at least she looks around, and goes out, and plays. Anyway, Giacomo loves her and, believe me, I love her too. A philosopher, a linguist, and so tender. We're really lucky to have a second cat like Gilda.

But you must be wondering, How do I know all this? It's very simple. Since the day I died (it was so terrible to leave Giacomo alone that it made me cry, but what could I do, they murdered me), on January 15th, 2003, I pass all my time watching everything Giacomo does and listening to everything he says (and thinks). He doesn't do much anymore, but he says a lot, a whole lot—most of it to himself, in his head or written down, or to Gilda. I've learned a lot more things since I died than I did when I was alive. Back then I was so busy all the time, I had so much to do, what a busy life. They say cats sleep a whole lot but I didn't, I had too much to do. I was truly an action cat, not a dreamer, or a philosopher either. Though I did meet a whole lot of philosophers, famous or not, from all over—Italy, Germany, France, England, the U.S.A.—they all came to the house, for dinner, or to stay for a day or two or for a week. We had exciting guests and I listened closely to all those philosophical conversations, often sitting on our guest-philosopher's lap. In my honor they often discussed Montaigne's famous 'When I am playing with my cat, how do I know she is not playing with me?' A strange question. I think they're playing together. I find it remarkable that Gilda is such a great philosopher, despite the fact that since my death practically no philosophers have come to the house. She's philosophic by nature. She's certainly not an action cat, but she does have her moments, like when she sneaks into houses. As for me, I have to say that since I died and no longer do anything at all, just watch and listen, I've learned lots of things about my own life that I didn't know when I was alive. Giacomo talks about me very often. The first year or two after I died *very* often, first with our friend Gianfranco (he went to Gianfranco's house in Mestre almost every week, just to talk about me) and, later, with Gilda, but not only then, he always thinks or talks about me. He likes to tell Seba's story, for example, which I never knew when I was alive. And, of course, he still tells the story of how I came to live with him—but that's a story I know myself. The connection between us is as strong as anything in the world can be. Thanks to Gilda it's even stronger. And thanks to this connection I know all this, and I'm able to tell this Tail. Thanks to this connection I am here, in this house, nine years after my death. Not alive, but here. As long as Giacomo is here, so am I. We have a connection. A strong one. Very strong.

So it was because of my brother Seba's disappearing that I ended up in Lili's bar. A strange and terrible story. It was one of the worst days of all time. I definitely had some real bad ones in the last year and a half of my life— real bad—when I got so sick and then died. It's still hard for me—and for Giacomo—to be philosophical about that, to come to terms with it without bitterness and anger, because of the circumstances. But the day I suddenly found myself in the bar was *terrible*. Things did work out in the end, and in a wonderful way, I had a great life with Giacomo, full of excitement and action. But that day! It was so totally unexpected. It was just after dinner, there I was with my mother and older brother, and then! My musician put on his jacket—it was around mid-October—and then picked *me* up and put me inside his jacket, with just my head sticking out. I was petrified. Frozen. And then we went out on the street and he was walking, fast, I was stunned and absolutely *terrified*. I'd never even been out of the house before. And now, at night, and a cold night too, freezing cold, and very windy. I realized that something big, and terrible, was happening. (I remember the night Gilda arrived, at four in the morning on New Year's night, she was so happy! She'd never been out of her house near the Ghetto before either, but she was ten-weeks old and all set for her new life, the circumstances were completely different.) He walked for a long time, without stopping, it seemed like forever, and in fact it was a long way to Rio Marin. Dark, cold, windy, my head barely sticking out of his jacket, how horrible it all was. Then, suddenly, he went into a bar, crammed full of people, and noise, went right up to Lili behind the counter, took me out of his jacket and put me right on the bar. Right on the bar! Then he said to Lili—so calm, like saying 'Hi, how are you?' or like the postman delivering a parcel, he said, 'Since you lost the brother here's the sister.' *Ecco la sorella.* That's all! And without another word he went out of the bar, and I never saw him again—not him, or my mother, or the house where I was born. I thought my mind was going to explode. I can never forget that moment, or the two weeks afterwards either. I think Lili was pretty stunned too, but not like I was. Plus, Lili was a teddy bear, he took things as they came, calm, easy. He sure wasn't expecting me, but he had seen me quite a few times at the musician's house. All sorts of people crowded around to see me—poor me—shaking with terror right there on the bar. I know Giacomo was there too.

Many hours later the bar was empty and it was perfectly quiet. I had been trying to hide in a corner at the far end of the long counter, at least it was a pretty hidden place, no people could get back there, apart from Lili of course. The first night, after he closed the bar he was really nice to me. He got out Seba's old yellow litter box and fixed it up for me. He didn't have any cat food so he made me a little omelet, but I couldn't eat. He always talked to me and even sang me funny songs. But that first endless night all alone in the bar—really, I thought my mind was going to explode. Why? Why has all this happened? What am I doing here? It was impossible to think. There I was, and I couldn't do anything about it. Nothing. Nothing at all. For the next two weeks I spent most of my time in that corner—in the evenings anyway. But most of the days too. Even though the bar was empty all day I was so frightened, I felt so confused and awful. From time to time I'd come out from my corner and wander around the bar just a little, but what was the point? It only made me feel worse. Lili came around noon, or even earlier, he was so nice, and really very worried about me. That stupid friend of his, that musician. Lili kept cooking for me every day. Funny omelets, fish, liver, all sorts of things, plus cat foods all over the place—and I didn't eat anything. At all. Nothing. For two weeks. I felt like I had a hard rubber ball in my stomach, it was awful. I was hungry, but I couldn't possibly eat. In the evening the bar was always full. But it wasn't really the noise and the people that frightened me so much, sometimes in the musician's house it was pretty much like that, but that was my house, with my mother, my older brother, the house where I was born. What did it mean that now I was in this bar? I understood—*very* vaguely—that it all had something to do with Sebastiano, I had no idea what. It all made no sense to me, at all, and day after day it made less and less sense. The days in the empty bar, the evenings with the noise and the people, the terrible endless nights all alone—why? Why had all this happened?

And it all went on for two endless weeks. I kept thinking, thinking, when will it end? How will it end? What will become of me? Will I just die here, miserably, in this bar, and soon too? (Like Gregor Samsa in Kafka's *Metamorphosis*, Giacomo used to say.) I absolutely could not eat—it was impossible—and I was feeling weak and dizzy. Me! Until *that* day, a healthy and happy five-month-old cat. After a few days instead of asking Why? I started asking—day and night, every instant—What? What will happen? What will happen to me, a cat of no fortune. Meanwhile, the evenings were actually getting to be a little less unbearable than the nights and days. Lili was so sweet, and at least there was some distraction. Also, there were a few regulars in the bar who paid a lot of attention to me, or tried to anyway, if I let them. Some women, and

Giacomo, with his shiny bald head and beard. He looked almost as funny as Lili. At first I just shrank even deeper into my corner, but after a while I started creeping along and peering out from behind the bar. Giacomo used to come over very softly and talk to me. He even started coming quite early in the evening, when there were fewer people. But the main subject of conversation was always the same. My not eating. *Mangia, Gina, mangia,* Lili said all the time, and Giacomo said it in the evening, but it was impossible. The rubber ball in my little stomach was getting harder and harder.

Then it happened. Almost 26 years ago now. That decisive moment I'll never forget as long as I have this mind, in life or in death. The other side of the moment that happened two weeks before. At that time, I could not even imagine it happening. It's almost indescribable. I can describe the facts, but not all those things that happened inside—inside Lili, inside Giacomo, especially inside me. These are not facts, they are something else. Giacomo had come early in the evening, I peered out around the corner of the bar, he came over, kneeling, and spoke to me for a long time (Lili was serving his customers a foot or two away), then he went and sat at his usual table, in the corner. (From there he could see me if I peered out.) The bar filled with people and noises as usual, the people now with heavy coats, it must have been really cold out. It was the beginning of November, just after the Day of the Dead—*I Morti* it's called in Venice. The real start of winter and of the miserable *acqua alta* season. (It also used to mark the time when the tourists stopped coming, from *I Morti* until Easter, but now they're here all the time, like mosquitoes, they never sleep.) So, everything seemed pretty normal in the bar, it must have been around 10 o'clock, when *suddenly* Lili started SCREAMING. Right across the room, at Giacomo, sitting in the corner. *Giacomo!* 'What?'—Giacomo said. *Non vedi che questa gatta non può stare qui.* — Don't you see this cat can't stay here! — *Sì, hai ragione,* said Giacomo—you're right. *Non vedi che questa gatta non mangia.* — Don't you see this cat doesn't eat! — *Sì, lo so*—I know, Giacomo said. *Non vedi che questa gatta sta male.* — Don't you see this cat feels awful! — Yes, you're right. *Giacomo!* — Sì, Lili. — *NON VEDI CHE QUESTA GATTA STA MORENDO!!!* — Don't you see this cat is dying!!! — No! No! Lili! *spero di no!*—I sure hope not! said Giacomo. And then Lili SCREAMED — *Signori il bar è chiuso! Tutti fuori! Subito subito!* — The bar is closed! Everyone out! Right away! — WHAT WHAT WHAT was happening? Lili—a bear-sized teddy bear—practically shoved everyone out of the bar. Then he went and threw out my (untouched) kitty litter, gave the little yellow litter box and a half-bag of litter to Giacomo, along with whatever cat food caught his eye. Giacomo—surprised, stunned—put on his coat. Lili put on his coat, picked me up, and, with one huge hand, held me inside his coat. It was cold and stormy outside, a lot worse than two weeks earlier. ANDIAMO! Lili said, and dashed out, with Giacomo trailing behind. He held me tight inside his coat. Lili knew where our house was and was in a big hurry to get here. We got here. APRI! APRI! Open up! Giacomo opened the door, Lili took me out from under his coat—and tossed me right into the house! Just like that! Inside, everything was pitch dark for a moment. There was a pretty strong smell of fresh wood, plaster, and paint—a wonderful clean, fresh, new smell—but even in those seconds of darkness I felt good. I felt it. I heard Lili yell in the courtyard—he was in a yelling mood—CIAO, VADO A RIAPRIRE IL BAR—I'm going back to open the bar. Giacomo came in, turned on the light in the empty house, closed the front door. There was a marvelous silence, a silence I'd never heard in my life. It was just beautiful. I've loved that moment of silence ever since, really loved and remembered it, to this day, 26 years after my birth and 9 years after my death. Cherished it. For a moment like this it was well worth being born.

So, here I was. I saw a flight of stairs right in front of me—a few steps, then a turn to the right and a lot more steps. Without even thinking I dashed right up. (I was always much better at dashing or leaping up rather than down, that's how it is with most cats, I think.) Upstairs I found myself in a quite big and practically empty space, and in the dark, but that's no problem for cats. My Zio Lali, our neighbor and carpenter (Lali, short for Ilario, no relation to Lili—no one knows what Lili is short for) was building furniture for our house out of the wood left over from the roof, but first of all he made the new windows—that was more important. A beautiful fresh smell, especially the wood—the ceiling and the beams. Then at the far end of the room I saw the big low bed in beautiful wood, Lali had just finished making it. The bed itself is just a foot off the ground (for many years Giacomo had slept on mattresses on the floor, this was a real bed—but he wanted it low) and the space to get under it only about four inches—just perfect for a cat. How I loved this bed, Gilda does too. In my lifetime Maria *la siciliana* was in it, she took up practically the whole bed. Some years later there were quite a few other women. Camille was really nice, with her there was always room for me. Alas poor Gilda! There hasn't been one single woman in this bed in all her life, not even a shadow. I bet she'd like it a lot, she's sure not jealous. But, these are just the thoughts of a dead cat. Anyway, I figured, I'll squeeze under the bed and calm myself down for a while, my head is spinning. I had an overwhelming feeling of having gone from horror straight to ecstasy, all at once. It felt good under the bed, so solid, real low, real safe. I heard Giacomo coming upstairs, softly, he turned on some lamps (he's always loved lamps, his friend, my Zio Antonio, made beautiful shades), then I could tell he was wandering around the big room looking for me, in the corners. (Upstairs is all one big room, a big L-shaped desk surface at one end, custom-made by Lali, the bed at the other end, with a very high wood ceiling that is also the roof, I love to hear the patter of the rain.) After a few minutes he came over by the bed, lay down on his belly on the floor, and shined a little flashlight. Giacomo is no dope. He saw me! Ciao Gina, he said, easy, gently. (It's possible that he was more nervous at this point than I was, he absolutely adored cats but had never even imagined a cat of his own. Never even imagined it, and here I was. But he was so happy!) Then he lay down on the bed—hard, all wood, a hard mattress—right above me. It felt good. Everything was *really* quiet. What peace! Quiet, but not abandoned, not alone. What a great moment. For an instant it seemed as if the past two weeks had never happened. I stayed under the bed a good long while, a half hour maybe. Then real slowly I crept out. Skinny as a rail, I hadn't eaten for two weeks, but I felt OK. I sat on the floor at the foot of the bed and looked at Giacomo. Ciao Gina, he said. It was great. Then, suddenly, I jumped up onto the bed. I let Giacomo pet me softly for a minute, then he picked me up and threw me on the floor! *Non sul letto, Gina!* Not on the bed! (I've heard him tell his own version of this story so many times. He was only too happy to have me on the bed, he'd started loving sleeping with cats ever since his visits to his sister in Massachusetts, to say nothing of his Paris fiancée's beautiful black cat.) He just wanted to play a little game with me, a game of Who's Boss? But I'd already learned this game from my mother, so it was I who was playing it with him. (Let's say we were playing it together.) Immediately I hopped right back on the bed. He threw me a little farther off. I hopped on again. We did this a bunch of times. He threw me off real far. It was fun! I took a long leap and landed right in the center of the bed. Game over. Giacomo petted me for a long time, I started to feel *real* tired. I fell asleep. During the night, cuddling together with Giacomo, the hard rubber ball in my stomach dissolved and disappeared. The next day I was hungry—very hungry. I started eating again. I was a very hungry cat for the rest of my life.

The story of my life with Giacomo, in this house, from November 1986 until my death in January 2003, is an incredibly long story. It rivals Tolstoy's *War and Peace*. (This Tail will be an extremely abbreviated version.) So many things happened, big and small, good and bad, very good and very bad. It was the same with Giacomo, a very intense time of his life. (For a change.) The second summer I was here was the summer of Maria *la siciliana*, an endless summer that lasted for years, a winter of fire and ice. It was unspeakably good for such a short time, then unspeakably horrible for such a long time. He felt so terrible. It was hard on me too. I was so terribly afraid he was going to kill himself. He wanted to pour gasoline on his head and set himself on fire—not a protest, like the Vietnamese monks in the sixties, but because he felt so bad. It was very hard on me. I think he didn't do it because he loved me too much. Ours was a great and intense love. A connection. We cared so much about each other that this connection has survived my death. He didn't want to leave me alone, and still doesn't. Our connection. He felt what I felt and I felt what he felt.

Strongly. It's possible that he felt what I felt even more than I did, and vice versa. After I died and then Gilda arrived, I've heard Giacomo say many times (of course, he always says my cats, my first cat and my second cat, because I'm here—not alive, but here) Gina was my wife, Gilda is my lover. I like that—a *good* wife, he means. We took good care of our home and of each other. So many things happened during our life together, and we shared everything, even if, of course, our lives were different. Giacomo's passions were women, Hegel, his friends. Mine were killing rats, our house—and just living. I always had so much to do, I was an action cat, life was too short. Much too short. I think those two weeks in Lili's bar did something to me forever. Left me with a terrible hunger *to live*. A great hunger in general. Giacomo has a great hunger too. Those five months not eating because of the Vietnam war—like my two weeks in Lili's bar, these are things you never get over in all your life, they're part of you forever. Giacomo has always had a great hunger to change the world, politically—somehow—even a little. He believes in writing, in art— political art—like I do in killing rats. A passion, and a way to change the world. What sort of world would it be, of rats and no cats? I remember the last time I saw our friend Gianfranco—not so long ago, but it gets long if you're dead. (Even longer if you're both dead.) He was a great man, a special man. Like my Zio Wolfango in Siracusa, a great artist. Magicians. A special way of laughing, and of living, I can't explain it, Giacomo is much better at explaining these things. (He says, In the past ten years every time I called Gianfranco or Wolfango they answered the phone with voices like corpses, dark as night, but when they heard it was me they lit up like million watt bulbs.) Gianfranco, Wolfango, quiet people, very gentle, but magic. Magic people. The last time we saw Gianfranco (I was dead, of course) was at a little birthday party of Giacomo's, he had managed to get a few other people to come. (For many years for his birthday Giacomo and Gianfranco went out to dinner, just the two of them.) Poor Gianfranco was already very sick, that weak heart of his, he could hardly walk, he came all the way from Mestre in the July heat. He was exhausted. I think he knew he didn't have a lot more time to live. But he was *so hungry*. Famished. Not for food, he was almost too weak to eat. He kept telling Giacomo, we have to go out to dinner in Mestre, I want to invite you to dinner, I want to cook, why don't we take that little trip together—famished. It was so painful, a painful hunger. Sometimes hunger can be good, it can make you do good things (like writing books or, in my case, killing rats). But when hunger is painful it's the most painful thing in the world. I knew it. Gianfranco knew it. Giacomo knows it. It's all connected.

What a world I was in. This is such a great house for a cat. It's impossible to feel lonely here. (Which I wasn't anyway, not with Giacomo! Sometimes I think it's strange how quickly I stopped thinking about my mother and my five months in the house where I was born. It was the two weeks in the bar that I couldn't forget.) There are so many things to do here. If worst comes to worst you can have a great time just running up and down the stairs at top speed, or, even better, running from the far end of the upstairs room straight through the bathroom (the real center of the house, with two doors, always open), then down the stairs and all the way into the far corner of the guest room downstairs. And back. And then do it again. As many times as you like. It's fun, and it's quite a show for Giacomo and for any guests who happen to be in the house. Gilda does it too, especially on rainy days or if she's nervous, but not more than one round trip, one and a half at most, then she's exhausted. (OK, when she was younger she did more.) But I was a real athlete, I could do it all day if I wanted, I never got tired. I had a strange, a curious body—exactly like the cats you see in the drawings from ancient Egypt. Very long thin legs, a slim body, and a small head. They say I had a regal gait. I was built for running and jumping. Jumping up more than jumping down. I once played a really incredible trick on Giacomo, I must have been about a year old. Halfway down the length of the upstairs room there's a big beam running straight across from one side to the other, it must be ten feet off the floor. (The ceiling is even higher.) I'd had my eye on this beam for quite some time. One afternoon when Giacomo went out I thought about it for quite a while. (I wasn't like Gilda, a furry form of pure thought, I was an action cat and I thought *about* the things I did, I needed to prepare.) I said to myself, I definitely can do it. I got on my mark just like Usain Bolt (Giacomo's favorite right now) (I like Venus Williams) at the very far end of the room, then took off like a shot and leaped right up onto the beam—and held on too! No mean feat, believe me. (As things turned out that sort of leap was similar to the one for killing rats, though for rats it's longer, and not nearly so high.) When Giacomo got home, WOW, he just couldn't believe it. There I was, so proud of myself, up there on the beam. He still thinks it was impossible, there must have been some trick, but what sort of trick does he have in mind. I can assure you there was no trick. Meanwhile he gave a shout out the little window on the courtyard and my Zio Lali came over to take my picture. Zio Lali—a genuine old-time Venetian—really admired me. (He was my only zio who actually called me his 'nipote'—his niece.) He always said, *Guarda mia nipote, questa è una vera gatta!* Look at my niece, this is a real cat! (I'm so sorry, Lali died soon after I did—he was younger than Giacomo—of lung cancer. What a shame, he was a great zio. And don't think for one moment that there is some sort of 'society' for us, the dead, humans or animals or whatever, where we get together, meet, chat, reminisce. That doesn't happen. I am here because Giacomo is here—*alive*. I don't know if you, personally, understand this—maybe so, maybe not. I am here because Giacomo is here, alive, and I am here for him and he is here for me. A connection.) Later, though, after the photos, they had to get a ladder to get me down. There was no way I was going to jump down from that beam. Totally out of the question. *La vita è bella!* I'm too young to die! Another time I played another jumping trick, there are photos of this one too—I think it was before the beam trick, I was really small. Upstairs there are three big windows—one on the canal and two on the garden in the back (my future *regno*)—and a very small one on the courtyard. This window is almost always closed, unless someone knocks on the door (then Giacomo opens the window and looks down to see who it is unless, of course, he happens to be downstairs), or when Giacomo is hanging clothes on the line (or taking them back in). From the sill of this window it is a reasonably short leap *upwards* onto the roof. (The layout of this house is pretty strange, don't worry about it.) I'd had my eye on it all along, and one day when Giacomo was hanging clothes—zoom, like a flash, I hopped up onto the sill and leaped onto the roof. Another great leap! I was on the roof of our house, me, a real small cat. Fantastic. The problem was I didn't trust the leap back—those downward leaps are tricky, that's all I can say. Later on I learned to do them quite well (if I asked Giacomo to let me leap onto the roof he usually said OK), but, that first time, it was out of the question. Zio Lali had to come over with a long wooden plank, they put it from the sill up to the roof, and after thinking about it for *quite a while* (again, for me it was a practical and not a philosophical question, I'm not Gilda), OK, I walked the plank. Giacomo and Zio Lali were just a little pissed off in fact, it did take me *quite a while* to make up my mind, but it was nothing serious. Anyway, what a house. There were so many things I could do in this house— really, no end of things.

But this is only half the story. From *Gilda's Tail* you already know about the courtyard and the back garden. (As it is now, with the rich people and the time-sharers and not an old-time Venetian in sight. Or a rat either, for that matter. And it's not even really a garden at all.) When she was little and for quite a few years after that Gilda preferred the courtyard, she liked playing with the tourists and also with other cats, or sitting in the sun with Giacomo. Gilda is a sun worshipper, it gives her the energy she needs to philosophize. You should see her, she follows patches of sun all around the house. Her passions are sunning, philosophizing, and Giacomo. Now she prefers the peace of the back garden to the hectic life of the courtyard. The tourists have increased ten times over just in her lifetime (they put our quiet little courtyard in the guidebooks), and the neighbors keep her cat friends inside their houses. As for me, I have to say that the courtyard never interested me that much, apart from the last year of my life. If Giacomo was there, or some zio or friend or guest, OK, otherwise no. (Of course if a rat came into the courtyard Giacomo sent me out immediately and I took good care of it.) I think it had to do with my experience in the bar—I didn't want to see strangers. Guests in the house, friends, relatives (zii et cetera), great, I loved that. But not strangers in the courtyard. What I loved was the space in back of the house. In fact a lot—quite a lot—of the rest of this Tail is going to be about the many things that happened back there, the changes, the violent, murderous upheavals. The last great upheaval, which cost me my life. An injustice. An infamy. That space is the razor's edge between this house and chaos. Unjustly, tragically, when throats were slit, they were mine, and Giacomo's. But you can't stop progress by shooting it with a Kalashnikov, Giacomo says (sometimes). I'm not so sure. Be patient, this is a long story. The Long Tail of an action cat. I don't want you to trip over it.

The very first day I was in our house, after having a light lunch in the kitchen with Giacomo (my stomach was still a little crunched up), I couldn't help but notice this incredible garden right behind the house. It was completely different from how it is now—and I mean totally completely different. Our kitchen has two windows on the back of the house and the guest room has one big one (plus one on the front, where Gilda and I—and Giacomo—can watch what happens in the courtyard without being disturbed). But the ground-floor windows have bars so Giacomo can't go back there. (But Gilda and I can. If our cat flap is open.) If he wants to get in there for some reason (once upon a time, to visit our neighbors and help with the garden, which he loved to do; or, later, to collect the corpses of the rats I'd killed and throw them into the canal; or, now, to do some work on the wall of our house, or check out some other form of destruction), he has to go out, go through the courtyard, go around two corners and then down a long lane to the big door of the *palazzo* that's right behind our house, a few feet away, and meet someone who lets him in.

Even though it was a cold gray almost stormy November afternoon I thought, hey! look at that. A garden. I'd never seen one before. (Or since, for that matter.) It wasn't very big but it was wild, it was beautiful, it was free, it was an ancient Venetian garden with ancient carved stones—big ones, like headstones—marking the rows of vegetables, lettuce, tomatoes, with a fig tree much higher than our house! Giacomo always told people how in springtime there were so many birds of all kinds back there it was like living out in the countryside. And I only saw that garden from that November until the following March, when it was murdered. (The agony of the fig tree went on for the next fifteen years, up to its own sudden—first degree— murder.) In March—extremely suddenly—the Venetian garden disappeared forever. Along with our friends who lived on the ground floor of that tall five-story *palazzo*, while the others were squeezed out slowly, over the years, like dust from a tube. Squeezed out and sent away to die, which they did. The extermination of 'Venice for the Venetians.' (A famous political slogan not so long ago, but ancient history now.) As I told you, even the outlaw cats were exterminated—was it perhaps the rat lobby? The lobby of the *pantegane!* In the end, I, too, was exterminated. Murdered. It was a small but very ancient garden, a *garden* garden, not a mini-pleasure-park like now, bounded on one side—along the canal, on the left (from our viewpoint)—by a brick wall, and on the right by another brick wall. On the far side of the garden very old stone steps led up to a terrace, under its trellis of wisteria, right over the intersection of two magnificent canals (one was the end of Rio Marin). The terrace was part of the apartment where our friends lived. There was Ada (a widow, her husband was famous, a famous roof-repairer called 'the cat'—he died pretty young I guess), her mother (Giacomo's favorite), her two sons (the older one exactly Giacomo's age), and Ricky the dog. Ricky and I were great pals, he was already quite old, very gentle, and friendly. Some years later the older son moved out, the younger son got married, his wife came to live there, and they had a baby. Four generations of a Venetian family, all together. They were all our friends, Giacomo really liked the old old lady, the great-grandmother. She died after a few years, and poor Ricky got real old and died too. But everybody in that big *palazzo* was really nice, I'll tell you more about them later. Real old-time Venetians, very lively and talkative, especially the women, they spent most of the day at their windows talking with their neighbors, and why not! What else are neighbors for, Giacomo used to say. (He called it the outdoor movie theater.) And they all loved to talk to Giacomo, he was the only foreigner—a rarity back then. They are not *nosy*, he used to say, they are *curious*. They are *interested*. He liked that. He used to cook with a lot of garlic, and whenever he got back from a trip and started cooking the women would shout to each other, Just smell that garlic, the foreigner is back! But I'll have more to say about these neighbors later—about the tricks I played on them, and about rats.

So of course I really wanted to visit this garden, why not? But I was in no hurry, after everything I'd been through I was just so happy to be in our house with Giacomo, to feel loved and safe. My appetite was coming back completely. I never ate dry food like Gilda or those little cans of Gourmet, I had big cans, and later on (I was burning so much energy) Giacomo mixed my cat food with chicken livers. But, for all my life, the greatest moment of the day was dinner time—Giacomo's and mine together. Wherever I was, even if I was on the top floor of the high *palazzo* (I went up there every day during the many years the whole building was empty), I could tell when Giacomo started cooking and in two seconds here I was! Even before he'd finished dicing a clove of garlic. I was fast. I never missed a dinner—unless, of course, I was on the trail of a *pantegana*, Venetian rats are the smartest in the world, sometimes I didn't come home for two full days but I always got them in the end. The other thing I never missed was Giacomo's taking a shower. Around noon, every day. I was almost always outside at that hour, but wherever I was I heard that water and—zoom! I loved the sound of the shower (I loved rain too, I often went outside in the rain), but it was also my way of saying *buon giorno* to Giacomo. It was part of our connection.

Gilda is so completely different. We look pretty much alike (not that much actually, though we're both gray tabbies), but we're so different. I know how much she adores Giacomo and he adores her too, but—she never even keeps him company when he has dinner. OK, she's not interested in showers, or rain either. But she sure says *buon giorno*. Gilda is a linguist or, more simply, a big talker. (I was a cat of few words, an action cat.) Every day she says *buon giorno* to Giacomo in so many different words it's like the Pope saying *Buona Pasqua* in all those languages on Easter, but Gilda does it with *wild enthusiasm*. Gilda is a *greeting cat*. Even if Giacomo goes out for an hour she goes wild when he gets back. But—just imagine—she hates football. When Italy played, or especially if our team, Juventus, was on TV, I sat on Giacomo's lap for every minute of the game, and we jumped around whenever we scored a goal. It was great. And Gilda couldn't care less. Italy won the World Cup and poor Giacomo watched all by himself. She and I are so different, it amazes me sometimes how much he loves us both. I think having cats is a lot like having children, they're yours and you love them. It's true, though, she has an incredible sense of humor. Giacomo and I had lots and lots of laughs together (and shared some terrible times), but Gilda is a genuine comedian—philosopher and comedian—and they do laugh like crazy. But the wildest laughs I had with Giacomo were when he read me Lacan—that was really too much! He used to go to seminars of Venetian Lacanians and came home with notes and charts and diagrams that he read and explained to me. No, really, I thought we would die laughing. Gilda is a very unusual cat, it's true she's incredibly gentle. She can spend an afternoon playing with a mote of dust another cat wouldn't even notice. She's amazing. OK, she only eats her own cat food, no other food at all, but I feel sad seeing Giacomo all alone in the kitchen every night.

How I loved to see him making dinner! We didn't have a counter in our kitchen (my Zio Neno built a small one a few years ago, he's a good zio, I slept at his house three times when I was very young but after that I refused to leave our house) so Giacomo prepared everything on the kitchen table. He's a great cook and likes to cut up all sorts of things on a board and then put spices on them. I used to sit on the kitchen table with my nose about one inch from the board and watch *very* closely, it was the greatest moment of the day. (If we had guests I sat on the far corner of the table and then, during dinner, on a chair.) Then we waited for everything to cook—what beautiful smells. When the food was ready Giacomo put it on his big plate, then the first thing he did was cut off pieces of everything and put them on my little plate. He ate slowly, but I ate pretty fast. And then I sat on the table until he finished. My favorite food was fish—jumbo shrimp actually—but I loved everything (no, vegetables no). When a zio came to stay in the house for a week or two—Zio Ulrico, Zio Lello—they went to the Rialto to buy fish almost every day, wow, what dinners! And they always bought jumbo shrimp, my favorite, at least once. (For my birthday Giacomo always made them for me.) But when Zio Wolfango came—well, that was unbelievable. He even made sandwiches for lunch—so did Zio Lello—I was crazy about sandwiches. But the dinners! Zio Wolfango—I told you, he's a magician—refused to let Giacomo cook at all, he had to do everything himself. I loved to watch him cooking fish, what a show he put on. He was *really* exciting—and still is. He's the only person who ever got Gilda interested in cooking, she couldn't resist. I don't know how he did it, but there was a perfume in the kitchen that was out of this world. And when he put the spaghetti on my plate and cut it into short pieces for me, covered with little shrimp and pieces of fish and sauce, my head started spinning and I thought I'd lose my mind. What a beautiful life I had. Sure, no life can last forever. But still—as I shall tell you in due time—it's not right that such a big piece of mine was so infamously stolen.

Let me tell you now about the ancient garden, and about how it was murdered just a few months after I arrived in this house. There's a lot to tell. (I told you, this Tail is a sort of miniature Russian novel.) First, I'd better complete my description of the space back there, because the garden was only half of it. As I said, the garden was bordered by a brick wall on the canal and a brick wall on the other side, which separated the garden from the small courtyard of the family that lived in the ground-floor apartment. Two grown children and two *wild* parents—Luciano, who kept geese in a big cage (he always killed one for Easter by smashing it with a bat, Giacomo often talked about this and Zio Ulrico too, who once saw him do it), and his wife, known in the entire neighborhood (not just in the *palazzo*) as 'the dirty-words lady.' *La signora delle parolacce.* She cursed at everyone—family, friends, neighbors, her cats—it was just her manner of speaking, she did it very affectionately and everyone liked her. Giacomo was crazy about her—Plain speaking, he said. Good stuff. What a shame I barely got to know her, she hardly had a chance to curse at me (*Va in mona, Gina!*). Now, this brick wall was attached to our house just a little below and a little to the right of our upstairs window nearer the bed. And who was often on top of this wall? Two Siamese cats! Kika and Figlio, mother and son. (The son's name was Son—Figlio. Not a very original name.) I saw them myself from the upstairs window. Very beautiful and very shy. Before I arrived, Giacomo had been inviting them for years to jump up and come see him. Beautiful but very shy, that's how Siamese are. I think Figlio did come a couple of times, not often. Meanwhile, I was getting more and more interested in visiting that space, getting together with Ricky, with Kika and Figlio. Finding out what it felt like to be in a garden, even if it was winter. Naturally, I started scratching on the kitchen window (there is a perfect little sideboard in the corner right under the window, Zio Lali made it), just a little, from time to time, when Giacomo was in the kitchen of course. Then quite

often. Finally, one sunny afternoon in January Giacomo opened the window
for me and, cautiously, I went out on the sill (Gilda loves this sill, she suns
herself there, what a peaceful being she is), looked all around, and then jumped
down into the garden. Wow! It was two different things looking at it from
inside the house and being in it looking back at the house. Fantastic. Kika and
Figlio were up on the wall but they barely looked at me, so shy. I wandered
all around the garden, there were so incredibly unbelievably many things to
see, my mind was speechless. All at once so many new things. I saw Ricky
up on the terrace, he looked surprised to see me. A few days later he came
down—cautiously himself—and we made friends. The Siamese actually never
came down all winter, but they definitely did look down curiously when I was
in the garden. We just needed more time. Funny, as it turned out that would
have been my only chance in all my life to get to know other cats. (Gilda has a
whole bunch of cat friends—good friends, too.) When Giacomo called—the
first day—I came right back in. But the next day I wanted to stay out longer.
He ended up leaving the window open just a crack, so I could push on it and
come back in—leaving it wide open behind me, obviously. (Now he always
jokes about Gilda—she's a master at opening the front door but closing it
again has never crossed her mind.) So the kitchen did get a little cold. Finally
Giacomo managed to get a real genuine cat flap, a historic moment. A friend
brought it all the way from England, in Venice they didn't have cat flaps yet.
Zio Lali installed it, a big job, he had to take the glass out of the window, cut
it, fit in a piece of wood with the flap in the center, but he sure knew how to do
these things. And it's still here, some 26 years later, even though Zio Lali and
I are both dead. Now Gilda uses it, but only when Giacomo takes the cover
off for her, otherwise he keeps it closed. It's a pleasure park back there now,
with time-sharers and rich people, there are rules that have to be followed. But
me—from the day the flap was installed it was never ever shut, until the last
months of my life when I was too sick to go out anymore. And my kitty litter
box disappeared, I didn't need it anymore (again, until the last, terrible period
of my life). The great outdoors was much better than a box. I was perfectly free
to come and go as I wished, in the house, in the back, in the house, in the back,
day, night, whenever. Almost all my life I got out of bed at dawn, went outside
just for a few minutes to see how the day was shaping up, check for any signs
of rats, and then came back to bed, without even waking Giacomo up. (Gilda's
not the only one who knows how to be gentle.) Apart from the summer, when
I didn't have to go out at dawn because I was already out. I always slept outside
in summer. A beautiful life. Absolutely beautiful.

Then, at the end of that first winter the first BIG BIG THING happened to
our house, to our life together, a horrible crisis. The garden was murdered,
and the *palazzo* itself practically left for dead. We could never never ever have
imagined such a thing. Giacomo had just bought this peaceful house with a

beautiful back garden a year and a half before, then I had arrived (thanks to Lili, and we sure do thank him), we were very happy, things were really good. And then!! Giacomo had gone to Sicily for a week to work on the art magazine and I was staying at Zio Neno's about five minutes from here, near Campo San Polo. But when we got home! It was like a dream world for a moment, but then it sank in. A nightmare. There was a whole crowd of people in the back, workers, and all screaming at each other! In one week, while we were gone, they had torn down part of the brick wall on the canal and put in a door or gate (so to speak) made of some old planks slapped together miserably—and it stayed there just like that for some fifteen years. (Zio Lali used to come over and curse at it, he just couldn't stand such a travesty of woodworking.) They needed it to unload their material from boats. Cement, beams, bricks. But what else had they done? *They had already poured concrete over the entire garden!* It didn't exist anymore. At all. This is unspeakable—I'm shaking now as I write it, even though it happened so long ago, and even though I'm dead. The garden had become one big slab of concrete. And the fig tree, taller than our house, at least a hundred years old—they poured their concrete right up around the tree. Choking it! Was it in their way at all? Not in the least. Did they leave one foot of earth—six inches maybe—around the tree so it could live and breathe? No, they didn't. They choked it. And these workers were Venetians. We couldn't understand it. They didn't give a damn about a famous hundred-year-old fig tree in the center of Venice. Half its branches hung out over the canal and when the figs were ripe—it had thousands—people in boats and gondolas stopped to pick them. And it survived anyway for fifteen years, until the Total Invasion (the one that murdered me), the Final Solution. The tree got smaller and smaller, and then real small, but it survived, it even had a dozen or so figs on it to the end. It survived thanks to Giacomo. The First Invasion lasted for two years—it was nothing (call it nothing!) compared to the Final Solution—and when it ended Giacomo went back there with a hammer and chisel and with great difficulty—I watched him closely, the concrete was so thick—managed to chisel some concrete away from around the fig, so at least some water could go down. In just two years the poor tree had already been reduced to less than half its size.

That terrible day, when we got home what were all these workers doing? Venetians! Traitors! They were busy pouring tons of concrete right into the apartment of Luciano and the dirty-words lady—just pouring it right in. There was a giant boat on the canal full of concrete and all these workers with wheelbarrows, screaming, pouring concrete right into our neighbors' apartment. Everyone was screaming (I wanted to scream myself), you can just image how much the dirty-words lady was cursing, I'm sure she screamed every single dirty word that's ever existed in the Venetian dialect. And not affectionately. The result? They had to move out. As soon as possible. The City of Venice had found them another low-rent apartment—all seven apartments on five floors were low-rent, most of the tenants had been born there, all were working people, some were elderly—way over on the other side of the town. And they had to go. The whole family, the cats, I don't know what happened to the geese. So that apartment was completely abandoned for fifteen years and, guess what else, the rats moved in. I don't know if the City of Venice had sent out engraved invitations or whether it was just by word of mouth, from here to the Rialto, from here to Piazzale Roma, from here to La Salute: Come one and all to the *Pantegana* Suite! All rats welcome! Bring your families and friends. And I was the only cat. A month shy of my first birthday. Destiny is a funny thing. My destiny was set for the next fifteen years. I had my work cut out for me.

You must be wondering what in the world was going on! The story goes like this. Once upon a time there was a *Geometra*—a so-called Land Surveyor, like in Kafka's *Castle*, we're big Kafka readers. Basically, a Geometra is a half-assed architect who flies by the seat of his pants. Giacomo called this one Geometra Nixon, a tribute to Tricky Dick. He was a crook, this is the crux of the matter. (Not a Venetian, by the way.) Alas, like many crooks he was endowed by nature with a stiff dose of imagination. He was always on the lookout for deals. *Affari*. Schemes. Scams. It's true that the *palazzo* behind our house had one *little crack* running up and down the side. A big deal for a tricky Geometra. Ada's son, who was 36 like Giacomo, said the crack had been there, exactly the same, since he was born (there, in that *palazzo*)—they had some photos to prove it. But Geometra Nixon had friends in high places (or low places, I'd say) and— in short—he got the *palazzo* CONDEMNED. PERICOLO DI MORTE! Danger. Death. Run for your lives. The *palazzo* is about to collapse. Believe it or not, this was the story. Defending the people against the PERICOLO. Destroying the *palazzo* in order to save it. March 1987—I wasn't even a year old. They worked back there for about two years, a whole bunch of men. Venetians. Not too young either. Actually, these workers were very nice. They were old-time Venetians and old-time Venetians really love cats, especially *soriani* like me, the true original Venetian cat. Every day (five days a week, at least weekends we had some peace and quiet, Giacomo was having a hard time because they started making lots of noise at 7:30 on the dot) they had sandwiches for lunch, right there in the ex-garden, and they always gave me some (plenty, actually). Salami, cheese, mortadella—baccalà—you name it. I wasn't shy. Come to think of it, I guess that's where my love of sandwiches comes from. After I got over the shock, that period wasn't terribly bad for me. I was so happy not to be in Lili's bar and so very happy with Giacomo, and in our house, that the First Invasion was just a kind of exciting adventure. (The Final Solution was the night of the world.) I was unhappy only because Giacomo was *extremely* unhappy. For him it was a tragedy. He had already been in that very peaceful house with that garden and those neighbors for over ten years, and he was not happy at all. It was very good for him that I wasn't unhappy too, I did a lot—really a lot—to cheer him up. And a little over a year later, right in the middle of all this mess, Maria *la siciliana* appeared. And then, above all, disappeared. If only she had stayed! Just think, we could have had *bambini* in the house! Wow, really fantastic. Giacomo and I were all for it. But it didn't happen, and we had some terribly hard years. Together.

Meanwhile, the chief worker (not the Chief, Geometra Nixon), Toni, was the nicest of them all—not just to me I mean, I'm not talking about sandwiches now. He used to talk with Giacomo at lot, so at least poor Giacomo managed to have some idea of what was going on. (Not like in the days of the Final Solution, when they told us a million lies and murdered me.) Toni, in fact, told us that the whole problem was Geometra Nixon who was a crook. (And a statesman. Or a finagler at any rate, more or less the same thing, Giacomo said. The Geometra had *connections*—no relation at all at all to the connection between Giacomo and me.) Toni was a straight talker, an old-time Venetian, an honest man. He told us *things as it is*, Giacomo said. (It's a Zen saying.) I'd say, the shadow behind the visible reality. The end and the shadow. After the Geometra finished gobbling up all the money on his plate and moved on to his next big deal the City had a technical report done, Giacomo saw it, Toni let him read it. It said, in a nutshell, that 'the foundations of the building are more solid than any *palazzo* they build today' and that the infamous 'crack' was 'insignificant' and 'not dangerous.' But the Geometra was long gone by then—no, not true, he was looking for new victims all over town. By that time, though, what had they done to this poor *palazzo* and, especially, to the poor people who lived there? The only ones who were truly long gone were our friends with the Siamese cats, and geese. Our other neighbors hung on for as long as they could. Every few years the City would come up with an apartment who knows where and some other family would move out. Ada was the very last to move, almost ten years later. Her mother had died, Ricky died, her sons had moved out (weeping—I myself saw their tears—for the murder of the garden and of the house where they were born), she was old and all alone in the whole *palazzo*, we were her only neighbors. We tried to look after her as much as we could.

Now, let's get down to the crux of the matter, strategically speaking, as Geometra Nixon saw it. (As a rat killer I've always been a strategy enthusiast—no, I mean tactics, not strategy.) Listen to this very carefully, because it's hard to believe. (Unfortunately, many of our greatest minds have been crooks.) One day, very early in the First Invasion, a gigantic boat arrived at the Nixon Gate stacked high high high with wooden beams as long as the boat. An entire forest. (When I say *gigantic* I don't say it just because I'm a cat and cats are small compared to people and to boats. People are small too, compared to *palazzi*, and to their fearless political leaders.) They worked all day, *many* people, unloading these beams and piling them up in the ex-garden—a mountain of beams almost as high as our house. Geometra Nixon—a little runt, with a green cap and a turkey feather in it—had an epic spirit about him, as if he'd been born on the wildness of the steppes rather than in Bassano or Montebelluna, or some such local berg. An epic spirit like the Mayas or the ancient Egyptians. Well, as you can imagine, personally I was enthusiastic about all this wood (my claws were never that short again until the day I died), I really enjoyed it, wow. But, commanded by their fearless Geometra, what did they *do* with it all? Giacomo said it was the Madman Strategy. (NIXON! NIXON! He's back! It was driving Giacomo crazy.) The strategy is this. If you can make people *think* the end of the world is near, it *is* near. This is the true foundation of terrorism. The poor workers, apart from their lunch hour with marvelous sandwiches, spent well over a year cutting the beams into pieces and stuffing all these pieces into all the apartments. Giacomo was right, Nixon lives! Mingled, viciously, with LBJ—bombs, and hearts and minds. An eternal embrace. They said, to keep the apartments from collapsing—ha ha ha. What a joke. What a *strategic* joke. I told you, the Geometra was endowed (by the Creator of Crooks) with imagination. The whole point was, first, to gobble up the City's money, and second, to *make* the *palazzo* uninhabitable. In the supreme hope of becoming Executor of the Final Solution. But, as things turned out, our Geometra was not equal to his own epic. Anyway, he had his strategy. In the apartments they didn't put this forest of beams straight up the walls and straight across the ceilings, not at all. They put them at crazy angles—I saw it for myself every day, and Giacomo saw it too—running *obliquely* right through the rooms, in all directions. What logic! It was incredible. Giacomo said our Nixon must have got the idea from some heist film he saw on TV, with those burglar alarms with laser lights running in all crazy directions. All this work took them a long time, until they finished off all the beams in the ex-garden.

But after all this, since the Geometra still had money to gobble, he came up with two more masterpieces. Enough wood, *basta*, it's time for bricks. Gobble gobble. Do you remember that wall attached to our house where Kika and Figlio used to sit? Well, they'd knocked that down right away. It was ancient, very beautiful, and came down immediately in a heap of brick and dust. (And the Commission of *Belle Arti* that protects every centimeter of genuine ancient Venice, where in the world was it? Probably busy *gobbling* somewhere.) Anyway, as Giacomo said, knocking down that wall was, perhaps, the only possibly reasonable thing they ever did. Horrible, but reasonable. Since the garden no longer existed, the geese-courtyard no longer existed, the ground-floor apartment no longer existed, the wall was senseless and useless and kept them from getting their beams into the *palazzo*. One big open space wasn't half bad at this point. (It's how Gilda's back garden is now, in fact.) But wait, because this wall is a long story, it's a veritable Wailing Wall. Its second destruction was the immediate cause of my death. Meanwhile, brace yourselves for Geometra Nixon's two final masterpieces. First, the Mayan Temple of the Sun, as Giacomo called it, poetically. (If, probably, not accurately, after all we're not archeologists.) You really had to see this construction to believe it. The giant boat returned, full full full of bricks this time. Top quality (gobble gobble). Now, I forgot to explain the geometry here. The *palazzo* is L-shaped. The long part is to our right, perpendicular to us, facing the street on the front and the ex-geese-courtyard on the back. Then it turns left right in front of us, along a canal that intersects the canal our house is on. (After the intersection our canal changes its name to Rio Marin.) This is the shorter part of the L. At the end there's Ada's terrace, like a ship's prow looking out over two perpendicular canals. A great sight to see! Anyway, they decided to build a 'free-standing supporting structure' to keep the wall on the ex-geese-courtyard from collapsing. Pure-grain thievery, 200 proof. A move like this takes courage, and imagination galore. Like Nixon visiting the Great Wall of China, Giacomo said. They constructed a low but dramatically entrenched base in concrete, with steel (or iron) bars inside it, about four feet wide and forty feet long perpendicular (straight, for once) to the wall of the *palazzo*—a construction so solid (and useless) it's still there to this day. (Covered, now, with decorative white marble.) It was supposed to be eliminated as the last act of the Final Solution, perhaps as a *gran finale*, with dynamite and fireworks. Which probably would have brought down the house, literally. Addio new rich-people *palazzo*. A *final* solution in the full sense of the word. But they couldn't do it, it was indestructible. (I, alas, had been destroyed by then.) If these guys had built Hitler's bunker he'd probably still be alive, Giacomo said. With enormous difficulty they did destroy the Mayan Temple in the end, but not the base. How did these Venetians build it? The idea was very simple. They covered the entire base with one layer of bricks four feet wide—I could really use a diagram here—laid not crossways but longways. The next layer was just one brick-length shorter, and so on for hundreds of layers right to the top, with the top layer just one brick long. (Just long enough for me to sit on.) About thirty feet high. Simple but amazing. Strangely beautiful, actually. They destroyed it a couple of years after my death. The Architect of the restored *palazzo* couldn't come up with any possible reason for its being there, and the new (rich) owners certainly didn't want it, right there in the middle of their pleasure park. But—have you guessed—I just loved it! No other cat in Venice, or probably all Italy, or maybe in the whole world, apart from Mexico (or Guatemala), had a thing like this to play on. I often wonder—Giacomo does too—whether Gilda would have played on it like I did. It's possible. If she had, she wouldn't have the belly she has now. For almost fifteen years, many times every day, every day of the year, I used to dash right up to the top of the Temple, in about two seconds flat. It was *fantastic!* Around sunset I practically always went up, there was something magical about it, Giacomo loved to see me there at the top, illuminated by the last rays of the day. If he missed seeing me dashing up, no problem, I dashed right down and then dashed up again just for him. *Fantastic!* When we still had some neighbors left in the building, survivors of the First Invasion, they all watched me dash up that Temple. *Fantastica! Brava Gina!*

But the second—and last—First Invasion masterpiece was another story. The wall. The one where Kika and Figlio used to sit, and which they'd knocked down right away. Well, they decided to rebuild it. Apparently there was still some money to be gobbled up. To build about thirty feet of wall less than ten feet high they worked for about three months. Giacomo had a saying of Marx's for these two masterpieces—the first was tragedy, the second is farce. (Again, his poetic license. The Mayan Temple was more comedy than tragedy. The wall was certainly farce but, as you'll see, *it* turned out to be the tragedy.) Now, there are two questions to be asked here. First, why in the world rebuild the wall at all? The garden no longer existed. The courtyard with the geese no longer existed. Our friends on the ground floor were long gone forever. At this point, what was wrong with just one empty space? What use was the wall? For the next fifteen years no one was back there except for me, and the rats. Second question. Why such a super-deluxe wall? Super thick, and with lots of steel (or iron) bars inside it, and even attached to our house with steel bars hidden inside the bricks. And with a very intricately constructed arch right in the middle—a big wide opening. It makes no sense, Giacomo kept saying. But it did make sense—red cents. The two questions have one answer for both: gobbling up money. Alas, fifteen years later this wall came back to haunt us. In the meantime I used to sit on it sometimes, it was so wide, very comfortable. In any event, after the completion of this masterpiece of a wall the First Invasion came to and end. We never saw Geometra Nixon again. We sincerely hope he came to a bad end.

After two years of this sound and fury suddenly there was peace and quiet. In fact things were much quieter than ever before. No garden, no neighbors working in the garden on the plants and vegetables, no Siamese cats, no geese, no dirty-words lady. Ricky practically never came down the steps, he wasn't interested in a slab of concrete. He missed the garden. At least all the other neighbors were still there, though only for a few years longer. It was time to take stock. I wasn't even three years old yet, I'd been through a lot, but the first and most important thing I had to think about was Giacomo. I was concerned, worried, frightened. He had been through the Invasion of course, which was hard enough, but also Maria *la siciliana*, and now he had the terrible infection. Doctors, doctors, very strong medications, pain, big worries. Maria appeared, disappeared. I was so sorry, he suffered so much, he cried a lot, he was depressed. But what a fighter! He and I were two real fighters. I kept fighting as long as I had a single breath in my body. Giacomo fought back, he worked, he did things. I did everything I could to cheer him up. I started bringing him dead rats, but I could tell that actually this didn't cheer him up much. I think it was because these years were so hard that our connection got so strong. (This, and the *tonglen* meditation he did for me after I died.) Or maybe not. Maybe a connection like ours (and his connection with Gilda) is like a plant, you care for it but you don't make it grow, it just does. It's a mystery. I do know that every time Giacomo thought about dying I told him, No! Life. Together. He and I are not simple beings. (Neither is Gilda.) You see, I've been dead for nine years now and I'm still not simple. Of course not. I'm only here because Giacomo is alive and here, and he is not simple, and our connection is not simple. It's straight as an arrow and, at the same time, a labyrinth. It's the shining surface of the water and the depth of the sea. He is an abyss of a man. I was an abyss of a cat. We had a lot to think about. And a lot to do. A lot of struggling.

It wasn't easy being just one cat all alone in a whole world of rats. It seems that up until the First Invasion there had never been rats in the back, but it was sure full of them now. Let me tell you a little story about how I won our neighbors' hearts. I must admit it, I was an adventurous cat (but also a serious one), and I loved food. Not just because I was hungry, I loved good food for its own sake. Thanks to the great cooking in our house. Gilda is adventurous too, in her own way (not about food), like with her sneaking into houses, which she loves to do. But Gilda also invents adventures out of thin air, she's a thinker, a philosopher, she dreams things up. She sees tiny things no one else can see, and plays with them. She chases her tail a lot. (OK, she did it more often when she was small, but she still does it.) For her it's an adventure. I lived for almost 17 years and I never chased my tail, not once, I never saw the point. I'd have sooner hopped onto a barge to the Moon. But Gilda—the few times she decides to keep Giacomo company when he eats (for a few minutes), she gets on top of the refrigerator and chases her tail. It's great dinner entertainment. Sometimes when he's working she chases her tail round and round the computer. Sometimes she runs all over the house chasing it. But the greatest thing she ever did—I really admired her for this one, she was young, she doesn't do it anymore—was chasing her tail on a very small flat corner of the wall on the canal. Round and round like crazy on such a small surface without falling into the canal. (Each of us did fall in once—just once—and I hope she doesn't fall in again.) She nearly gave poor Giacomo a heart attack, but it was quite a show, and for a year or so she did it often. I am fascinated by how serious she is when she does her chasing, as if she were acting out a philosophical problem. She doesn't think about it, she just does it. In any event it's not at all like chasing rats. For Gilda chasing her tail is not a game, it's either a science of logic or Zen meditation, or both at once, if that's possible. We cats are amazing. We don't ask for love, we inspire it. Let me tell you how I won our neighbors' hearts.

The fact is, with all those beams all over the place—not only oblique ones inside, there were plenty of (more or less) straight ones on the outside too (gobble gobble) *holding up the palazzo*—it was child's play for me to climb up and go in any window I wanted. Which I did. If, of course, the window was open. But since the women chatted all the time they almost never closed them, it would have been like leaving the phone off the hook. What a wild young cat I was. (Once the Temple of the Sun had been built it was even easier—I practically had my own elevator.) What's more, from time to time I got lucky and—I confess—made off with a little steak or a pork chop, or even (especially) a fish. And for a little thing like that our neighbors were getting on my case. But they had no idea how many rats I was already killing in the empty ground-floor apartment, the *Pantegana* Suite, which was flourishing despite the Invasion. Once they'd poured the concrete and put up a few— useless—beams (no people were living there to drive away) the workers practically never went in there. (Anyway, they all quit at 4:30 sharp.) In any event, Geometra Nixon was not interested in the ground floor. According to the Madman Strategy you don't hold up a *palazzo* from the bottom, you do it with slanty beams at the top. So, as I said, at first I brought these dead rats— and I don't mean mice, never mind all the mice I killed, I mean rats bigger than I was—into the house, through my flap. But Giacomo was not pleased. Not at all. So I started leaving them outside just under the window of the guest room, then I went to call Giacomo and he came and scooped them up and threw them into the canal (from where they'd come). You need to understand that over the years—from that spring until the Final Solution, which began in September of 2001—I killed hundreds of rats back there. Hundreds. Plus quite a few in the front courtyard. I was already giving the *Pantegana* Suite a bad name so some guests took a little swim down the canal and ventured into the courtyard. Suicide! *Pantegana*-suicide. When I got wind of this their seconds were numbered. In the courtyard there was no place to hide. Believe me, especially when the *palazzo* was empty it was quite a job, on all those floors, in all those rooms, there were millions of hiding places for rats. But I was smart, patient, and never gave up. With me there was no escape. I was a genuine old-time Venetian cat, heir to a five-hundred-year-old rat-killing tradition. But also a modern cat. I wasn't as gentle as Gilda (on that score she's unique) but I was more affectionate. She won't even sit on Giacomo's lap. She lies all over him as soon as he goes to bed, but won't sit on his lap, I can't understand it. If I didn't have urgent rat business I was always so happy to sit on his lap, talking with him, or talking with guests, or watching TV, or cleaning up my fur in the evening—it took me a whole hour. When Zio Terri came I sat on his lap too, and cleaned my fur. I was a super rat killer, but with Giacomo I was as sweet and affectionate as any cat could be. Have you noticed that I've been rambling a little, I'm afraid I'm starting to take after him. I was such a plain speaking, no bullshitting, straight-shooting action cat. Not a rambler. I always knew (almost always) where I was going and what I was after. Destiny. Destination. But this is my very first (and only) Tail, and I've been dead for nine years, and the Tail's getting pretty long, don't trip over it—but I warned you about that. *War and Peace. The Brothers Karamazov.* Now, getting back to dead rats. There was no sense in bringing them in to Giacomo, so at first I left them in a hiding place on the ground floor of the *palazzo* and later, when the whole building was empty, I had places on every floor where I left them. But let me get back to the story of the neighbors, complaining to Giacomo because I made off with a sardine or two. Well, guess what happened. One day he went off to Sicily again for the art magazine, for a week. These trips did him good, he stayed at Zio Wolfango's and they were—are—great friends. And I went to stay at Zio Neno's, for the third and last time, after that I always refused to leave the house. Flatly and totally refused. But I had my reasons. Sure, I wanted to stay in my own home, but I also had important things to do here. Responsibilities. In fact, what happened when I was away? The *pantegane* started racing around the ex-garden and ex-geese-courtyard having the time of their lives, scaring and disgusting our neighbors at their windows. (Actually, the women already knew I'd been killing rats, otherwise they'd have been really mad about the pork chops and sardines.) Then we got back, and suddenly all the women were at their windows crying out so sweetly, 'Giacomo! Giacomo! You're back!' 'Yes, my darlings,' my Giacomo replied. He figured something was up. He smelled a rat, and he was dead right. '*E la gatta! La gatta!* She's back too?' 'Why of course!' And here I was. Right here, in fur and blood, in what from then on, for a dozen years, was my *regno*, my realm. Under the adoring eyes of our neighbors, who were never disturbed again by a *pantegana* running loose under their windows. No, the rats were cowering in dark corners until I tracked them down. From that day forth, until so sadly all these old-time Venetians, our neighbors, were forced to move out, I ate fresh sardines out of the palms of their hands. More than I could eat. I was a good cat. It's true. We cats don't ask for love. We inspire it.

So, we passed the next twelve years in relative tranquility, even if Giacomo's life was always stormy. Thanks to our wonderful new friend Gianfranco—I'll never forget how he looked at me when I was sick and dying, with such strong feeling, he, too, was an abyss of a man— Giacomo recovered, more or less, from the terrible loss of Maria. He finally recovered from the infection. He started writing like crazy. After a few years he had some new *fidanzate*, always a great thing for a cat. As long as they're cat-lovers of course, but Giacomo could never have had a *fidanzata* who didn't love cats. (Maria loved me the least actually, but she was here for such a short time and, believe me, it was intense, there was *a lot* of loving going on.) What a shame for Gilda that Giacomo hasn't had a single *fidanzata* in all her life. But let me tell you now about one big thing that happened in our house. The English lessons. Can you believe it, when our Fearless Leader, Berlusconi, was elected the first time, within one week they took Giacomo's work permit away. Carabinieri came right to our door early in the morning, took him to Police Headquarters, and then took away his work permit, so he couldn't translate anymore. It's true! Some years later, as soon as the Fearless Leader was out of office, Giacomo fought one of the very hardest fights of his life to get Italian citizenship, and he did it. Believe me, Giacomo is tough. Just like me. He's never given up. Meanwhile, since he wasn't allowed to translate, what did he do, my resourceful companion? Well, for years and years all sorts of people had been begging him for private English lessons—which he didn't want to do at all. But—flexibility. Labor market reform. No permits, no taxes, and for several years we had the house full full full of English students. We had single students, matched pairs (people who knew or were married to each other), unmatched pairs (cooked up on the spot), 15-year-olds, 30-year-olds, 70-year-olds (all ages). We had good students and poor students, beginners and advanced, devoted students who came for years and fainthearted students who gave up after a few lessons, exciting students and boring students, funny students—you name it, we had it. All of a sudden, we had students in the house five days a week for six hours a day if not more, and they paid, cash, and plenty of it. I found it very exciting—and educational. I couldn't make it to all these lessons, the rats kept me pretty busy. But I came to a lot of them, depending on how much I liked the student. My favorite of all time is named Gina like me, she became my godmother, and did absolutely everything she could for me when I was sick and then dying. I used to sit right there on the desk upstairs (single students) or on the kitchen table (pairs) and put my nose right in the book. It was fun.

Giacomo has so few friends in Venice now, it makes me sad. Gilda has many of the zii I had who live far away—Ulrico, Lello, Wolfango—but I had more. Giacomo has always had a hard life, but since I died he's had so much solitude. When I was alive we had a lot—really a lot—of people in our house. Venice people too, philosophers from the university, my poor Zio Italo who died of cancer a short time after my own death. All sorts of people. We had a big party for my tenth birthday, in 1996. Many of the English students, other Venice friends, over thirty people for my birthday. No, no cats, sometimes I regret that I didn't get to know other cats, I think of Kika and Figlio sometimes, I'm sure we could have become friends. All my life there were no cats in the courtyard—except, at the very end, Birba, Gilda's first great friend, her big sister. I'll tell you about her later. Everyone brought me silly presents, some were real cute, it was a really fun and funny party. Thirty people inside the house, a great time. I loved people. I sat on everybody's lap at the party and they all wished me happy birthday. It's strange how Gilda seemed to love people when she was small, and now she runs away. I don't know why. Maybe because of Giacomo's solitude. In July of 2000 we had another, even bigger party, for Giacomo's fiftieth birthday—really big. Zio Ulrico came from Zurich with Zia Dagmar, Anna and Lisa, Zio Lello came from Sardinia the day before the party with a *big* and delicious piece of lamb we cooked and ate right away. And then the *big* party, in the house *and in the courtyard*, for over fifty people, I've never seen anything like it in all my life. All those people drinking *prosecco*. So much fun! And one year later, the Final Solution, my sickness and then my death, and many new, hard things. There was one other time when fifty people gathered in the courtyard—even more people, no one knows how many. It was five years ago, Veniero's funeral right in the courtyard, Giacomo's great friend, my friend, who lived next door—not in the back but in the courtyard. I know how much Giacomo misses him. And Gianfranco is dead. Without Gilda how would he live? They murdered me, they stole half my life. I am dead. What can I do for Giacomo? He asked me to write this Tail, and I'm doing my very best. The last part of my story is very sad, I know Giacomo will cry a lot, reading it. Why tell it? Because pain is part of *every thing*. This is what I learned in my life. There is such great joy, and such great pain. Not at the same time but—somehow—together. Now, dead, this is the Tail my lifelong companion asked me to tell.

Here I have to begin the last chapter of my story. I survived the chapter in Lili's bar, and things worked out for the best. I had a great life and so much love. Clean living. To say I was a healthy cat is an understatement. Around my fifteenth birthday, in April of 2001, we went to visit our vet, Gigi, for my checkup. Gigi and Giacomo have become real good friends over the years, he takes care of Gilda now. Gigi went to school with our friend Gianfranco, two such wonderful people. So sadly, Gigi and Giacomo went to Gianfranco's funeral together, a little over a year ago. My checkup. Gigi said, 'Ginetta'— he always called me Ginetta—'has the body of a five-year-old cat. She ought to live another fifteen years.' Half my life still to go. And instead, the Second Invasion, and the Final Solution. For me. Wait, I have to tell you Giacomo's favorite rat story. One afternoon that spring, a few weeks after my checkup, I was taking a nap upstairs when Giacomo came over, picked me up, carried me downstairs, opened the front door, and put me down just outside the door. I was still half asleep. Strange behavior, I thought. But I didn't think for long because, immediately, I smelled a rat—literally. Our courtyard isn't extremely big but it's pretty big. It's rectangular, and the diagonal from our front door to the far corner is about thirty feet. And what did I see right there in that corner? Absolutely. A *pantegana*. A big one, bigger than I was. I twitched my nose. For about three seconds I tensed my body like a spring, completely still, and then—zoom! In one double leap I touched down for a nanosecond in the center of the courtyard and then—PEEP! I bet you didn't know. PEEP is the sound a rat makes when an expert action cat like me bites it right in the back of the neck. One quick PEEP and it's dead. Giacomo had seen quite a few rat corpses over the years—far fewer since I started hiding them away in the *palazzo*—but he hadn't had all that many chances to see me in action. I bet he has no idea of how many rats I killed there in the back, all by myself, no one even saw me. But in the courtyard it was different. Far fewer rats but they were special because we had a lot of neighbors living on the courtyard. And they all really appreciated me. Our friend Veniero, Zio Lali, all the women, everybody. 'What would we do without Gina! What a great cat! A genuine old-time Venice cat!' Rats in the courtyard had short lives. But that day was special. 'What a leap, my fifteen-year-old Gina!' Giacomo was so proud of me. He still likes to tell that story, from the last happy time of our life together.

So, the *palazzo* had been empty for several years by then, even the *Pantegana* Suite was practically vacant (my reputation had gotten around). No one was back there at all except me. Once a year or so some Architect or Geometra or other would appear, stroll around, then disappear. After Ada left Giacomo couldn't get in there at all. Some lush and totally wild vegetation had sprung up in one corner. The fig tree was very small but pretty lively. The whole slab of concrete was taking on strange and beautiful colors, whites, grays, and gray-greens, constantly changing over the years. Giacomo said it was like an artwork by Sigmar Polke. But there was also Giacomo's own artwork on the artwork—doubled artwork, he said. Zio Antonin Artaud. His sculpture or, possibly, installation. I don't know if I told you about those ancient carved headstones that marked the rows of vegetables in the garden when it existed? Well, when they cemented over the garden they piled them all up next to our house, near our guest-room window. And left them there. Geometra Nixon had no eye for fine (and valuable) art. (In fact at the time of the Second Invasion they disappeared immediately. An Architect is not dumb like a Geometra. Or, more simply, these Architects were not dumb like Geometra Nixon. As far as art objects are concerned.) So right after the First Invasion ended Giacomo came into the ex-garden for a whole afternoon. He cleaned things up, and then the headstones. Exactly twenty of them. He had an idea. He told me, Gina, watch! It's happening! He put the headstones in a circle—a sort of irregular oval actually—kept moving them all around, re-arranging them, no two were alike, and then, *voilà!* 'Stone Flower' he called it. *Fiore di Pietra.* Something like a daisy. Beautiful. It was there from

1989 until its sudden disappearance in September 2001. He has many great photos of me in and on this artwork.

Around the time of my fifteenth birthday the Architects started coming more often. Too often. They pretended not even to see me. Or Giacomo either, if he came to the window. They even measured a few things with long tape measures. This big empty *palazzo*. We knew that sooner or later something had to happen. Later, please!! Giacomo always said. *Much* later, if possible. But our luck ran out. And everything went much much worse than we could have possibly imagined. We expected something similar to the First Invasion, even if longer. But not this. I'm dead, I've been dead for nine years, but I'm shaking now as I write. September 1st, 2001. The Final Solution. Destroy the world in order to save it—that's what Giacomo kept saying. We weren't just stunned this time, we were devastated. Shock—horror—awe. The First Invasion had been a battle, Giacomo said, but this is the whole Vietnam war. Right here, in a *very* small place. Just for your information—I don't have the heart to go into the details like I did with Geometra Nixon, at least I survived Geometra Nixon—the story is this. A clever Impresario from Bergamo (a city near Milan) (that's why all the time-sharers in the new *palazzo* are *bergamaschi*) found the money to rebuild the *palazzo*. Unfortunately. Which used to be a fine *palazzo* until Geometra Nixon destroyed it completely, so it had to be rebuilt. The money? This time it was honest dealing, it wasn't a scam. He sold the apartments before he rebuilt them. Two apartments of *bergamasco* time-sharers. The others very big, very luxurious, very expensive vacation homes for rich foreigners. Well, good for him, I guess. Who cares about old-time Venetians. The fact is, the Impresario himself was a very nice man. Elegant, dignified, always wore an elegant black hat. He was really very nice to me— petted me, talked to me—and spoke courteously to Giacomo. The problem is that *he was the only nice man in the entire gang.* And it was a big gang— actually, a gang of different gangs. A mob of mobs. There was the Best and Brightest Architect Mob, which refused to talk with Giacomo in person, and their Architect Office, which refused to talk with him on the phone. Don't forget, *Giacomo and I were the only living beings affected by the Second Invasion.* It wasn't a *palazzo* full of people like the first time around, this time it was a *palazzo* empty of people. The whole property is bordered by one canal along the ex-garden, another canal on the far side, a street on the long side, and on this side, us. And who gave a shit about us. They could have set off mini atom bombs back there—which is very nearly what they did—we were the only ones who suffered, Giacomo and I. The other Main Miserable Mob (which had Major Sub-Mobs in its service, especially the Venetian *Palazzo*-Foundations Rebuilding Mob—the worst!) was the Stuff Happens Construction Company Mob. One of the biggest construction companies in all Venice, not some itty-bitty run of the mill company. They refused to talk with Giacomo. *They refused to respect any regulations of any kind.* Just for starters, their workers never wore helmets. That's against the law, workers *must* wear helmets. They put up a huge scaffolding and left it *completely uncovered*—for years, until long after my death—so that all the debris flew off in all directions and some poor worker could be hit by it or could fall off the scaffolding and die. Totally against the law. And they got away with it. For years. Why? They're bastards and they're *big*, Giacomo said. They built an outhouse for their workers—very decent of them. Where? *Right outside our kitchen window*, the smell was horrible. Giacomo complained. Nothing. They got away with it. The workers themselves—the regular ones I mean, not the Sub-Mob workers—were a gang apart. They were all 100% from Macedonia (Macedonia in Macedonia, not Macedonia in Greece). Almost all of them were young. (The only one I liked at all, who was a little bit nice to me the few times he saw me, was the least young.) Their Gung-Ho Fearless Leader (the least young of all, of course) was Jacob the Macedonian, a.k.a. Jacob the Great, though he preferred to be called The Great Jacob. He *did* speak to Giacomo on very rare occasions, when Giacomo's relentless ranting and raving blew his cool, but only to pronounce these immortal words: Get off my back. *I'm just following orders.*

This was the general picture. What actually happened? They put up an enormous scaffolding covering the whole *palazzo*, with two different chutes to throw rubble down. From early September until mid-December they had a really incredible number of workers (many more than just the Macedonian Mob) *to destroy the inside of the building totally.* Totally. Especially that entire forest Geometra Nixon had installed. Speaking of forests—I'm dead, but I cry inside as I say this—practically the first thing they did was take an electric saw and in one minute cut the fig tree right down to the level of the concrete. (Years later—I was dead—they broke up the concrete and pulled out the roots. The roots of the murdered fig interfered with their giant septic tank.) It was small but still healthy and actually had figs and wasn't in their way at all. What kind of people were these people? Giacomo and I loved that fig so much, so did Ada and her family and all the neighbors, it was the oldest member of our entire family, over a hundred years old. Giacomo has plants in pots in the courtyard, we love them, Gilda adores them, today some are 15, 20, even 25 years old. (Many were stolen, by tourists or, probably, traitor neighbors.) The courtyard was bare, without a hint of green, when I came to live here, with Giacomo, but we made it very green. Beautiful. Now the tourists pour in like rats. Cementing up, and then, years later, murdering the fig tree—I couldn't understand this at all. Giacomo kept saying 'the banality of evil' but, I must admit, this was beyond me. It was a horror, that's all I know. A horror. I've been dead for nine years now, but I still have all the memories *from my life that I shared with Giacomo*—it's only because of our connection that I'm still here—along with *all of Giacomo's memories since I died.* I mean, everything he does and thinks, as I said. There are certain tremendous things that we remember *together* because we suffered them *together*, the same suffering, he suffering for me, I suffering for him, and these memories are *doubled*—amplified, they resonate as long as our connection exists, which means as long as Giacomo lives, since I am already dead. One of the most terrible of these memories is those chutes. We didn't expect this. It was like being bombed. From early morning until late afternoon *every thirty seconds there was a huge crash* when they threw old brick, plaster, and all that Nixon wood down the chutes. For the first two weeks Giacomo had to hold me in his arms all day, I was shaking all the time, I was terrified. I felt every crash inside my body, inside my mind. There was no escape. Never mind the dozens of workers, *always screaming* (why?), all the wheelbarrows taking the rubble to the big boats—no, it was the crashing. For two weeks, all day, I couldn't stop shaking. At night, when it was quiet, I couldn't eat. All my adult life I weighed about ten pounds—4.5 kilos exactly. My weight went down to 2.5 kilos. Our vet Gigi gave me some injections. I had lived so many years in peace, so happily (even the First Invasion was next to nothing compared to this, apart from its total surprise), then, in one day, this. Terror. The Big Construction Company wasn't Geometra Nixon, it knew its job, it worked hard, violently, fast. In mid-December, after three and a half months, they took away the chutes. The *palazzo* must have been empty. We were exhausted—really exhausted. In a few months I went from being a healthy young cat to a sick old cat. Giacomo was stunned, confused. He talked about selling our house, or trying to rent another house. He was so tired, he didn't have enough money, he hadn't been able to work. He was worried sick about me, worried to death. You can't believe how worried he was. Gianfranco came to see us, and Gina my godmother. For barely one day, when they took away the chutes, we thought that maybe the worst was over. But, immediately, the next *big* thing started, *the worst thing of all.* The heart, the mind, the core of the Final Solution. THE FOUNDATIONS.

Ten days before Christmas the biggest boat we'd ever seen arrived, with a big crane in it and gigantic machines. They looked like train locomotives. Smaller, but still huge. Three or four of them, I can't remember exactly, I was already so tired. With the crane they lifted them into the *building site* (that's what the ex-garden and ex-geese-courtyard were called now) and lined them up in a row—like a train—stretching from close to the gate on the canal, on under the arch in the wall, to the *palazzo.* The machines filled almost the entire space. What did it all mean? What was happening? At the same time, I remember very well that the weather suddenly turned very cold (way below freezing) and very foggy. The whole space was filled with a whitish dazzle of fog. There were just a few workers—only four or five—but they were extremely busy working on these machines. Very serious looking people. They didn't scream like the others, they barely even talked. This was the Venetian *Palazzo*-Foundations Rebuilding Mob. Giacomo tried to talk to them, they looked the other way. We had no idea what these machines were going to do. Giacomo kept phoning the Architect Office because the Construction Company Office insulted him and refused to talk to him. Finally an Architect came, it was the last day before the Christmas holiday. A pretty long talk. Seems like a pretty decent Architect, Giacomo told me. This Architect explained that all these machines were to force cement deep down underground through holes they drilled in the old foundations, to *solidify* them. Make them more solid. It's true that the old foundations are not bad, but we're building a whole new building on top, it'll be heavier, the *palazzo* is unusually high for a base this size. This foundations-solidifying company is state-of-the-art, avant-garde, best in the world, he said. Yes, sorry, these machines do make some noise, but they'll do the job in just *five days*. Right after the Epiphany. So far so good, Giacomo thought. But then he asked, What about the cement? You'll need a lot of cement for all this. I have very bad bronchitis and my cat is already sick because of all the dust from the chutes. Yes, yes, of course, the cement. *Don't worry about the cement.* This is an avant-garde company, best in the world, and *there are very strict regulations*. I sat inside the kitchen window watching Giacomo. Look! (The Architect was getting carried away with his own enthusiasm. Giacomo said— later—he was like the officer showing off his machine in Kafka's *Penal Colony*.) Look! All the cement goes in here, in the first machine. They have a sort of metal shed that covers the whole machine—they'll install it when they start working, look! it fits right here on top of the machine—with an extremely powerful exhaust fan that will shoot all the cement dust through a pipe off into that corner, on the other side from your house. (In fact, into the empty storage space on the ground floor under Ada's old terrace, quite a good idea.) (Time-sharers from Bergamo live there now.) Yes, yes, don't worry, precise regulations. *Buon Natale!* Merry Christmas! An Architect full of enthusiasm. He vanished into the fog.

We'll never know whether this Architect told us a pack of lies (very possible) or whether he believed what he was saying. But there was a *big lie* somewhere. It's quite possible that if they had used that metal shed and exhaust fan I'd have survived. But they didn't. The second week in January the small group of avant-garde workers returned—dressed in space suits exactly like astronauts on the Moon. A big boat filled with bags of cement was at the gate. Many workers from the boat piled all the bags sky high near the first machine, then they got back on the boat and left. No living beings were in the vicinity except the astronauts, Giacomo, and me. They turned on the machines—they were loud, but the crashing from the chutes had been much much worse—and then *every few seconds a man broke a bag in two and dumped the cement into the machine*. After a few bags the astronaut was almost invisible in a cloud of cement dust. We were stunned. Completely stunned. Cement dust started coming into the house, from everywhere, this is an ancient house, with many cracks and crevices. Giacomo bought a whole lot of tape and taped—double, triple taped—the windows, but it did no good. When they stopped for the day there was *so much* cement dust all over the house, which Giacomo tried to clean up. He could hardly breathe. I started to vomit, and I vomited nearly every day for the last year of my life. They did this for ten days, not five. It was so horrible we don't even really remember it. Early morning and then again around noon the big boat full of bags of cement, the workers from the boat piled them up, the boat left, the machines started up again, the cloud of cement. The astronauts. No words spoken, ever. Silence. Nothing human. No human contact. They finished solidifying the foundations. All the machinery disappeared. The Great Jacob and his Macedonians came back to work again, for about three years. I wasn't here anymore.

I was so sick. Giacomo was so sick. He went to the hospital often to breathe things for his lungs. He had to stay in bed a lot. Gigi our vet—what could he do for me? A cat's lungs are too small for all that cement dust. They were full. He gave me injections, I vomited a little less, then a little less. I was a very strong cat, *and final solution or not I wanted to go on living.* And Giacomo wanted me to go on living, he wanted it so much. He knew I could never be the cat I was before—I was practically half my old size—but, maybe, a healthy cat. Or at least not a real sick cat. I was still fifteen years old, what about the other half of my life? But a terrible shadow had fallen over us. It covered my life until the end, but—this is much worse—it still covers Giacomo's life, and I'm afraid it will cover it until he dies, until both of us come to an end, together. It is really Giacomo's shadow, but I have always tried to share it with him, even though I am not here. He can never forgive himself for not saving my life, somehow. Never. He just cannot do it, he can't forgive himself. This is the terrible thing. I have no words for it. It makes my mind scream. I have a hidden End in writing this Tail—a purpose, a hope. I want to free Giacomo from this Shadow. I want him to forgive himself. He says, My lungs are much better now (over ten year's later, and he still takes medications) (and his health has been very bad for five years, Gilda has been so frightened), but Gina, my cat, I let her die, he says. But it's all wrong. He has a great passion, the Vietnam war, which he hates more than anything else and always will. Millions of people, in their own homes, bombed out of existence, murdered. The land itself murdered. But they resisted, they fought back, and they won! he says. And I didn't do anything to save my Gina's life. Nothing! Why?! But he is unfair to himself, he doesn't tell the story as it really is. The Vietnam people resisted, they stood up to the tyranny that attacked them and—in the End—they won. But millions of them were killed. The whole country was filled with Shadows, with Spirits who didn't know where to die, with Hungry Ghosts. Where is the fig tree? Where is the back garden? We don't know. But I know where I am—I am here, with Giacomo, and he knows it. He knows it perfectly. A connection—this is what matters, not the End and not the Shadow. Vietnam continued to exist because of a connection, after millions of Vietnam people were killed. I am dead—I don't kill rats now, I don't eat jumbo shrimp for my birthday (but Giacomo always has flowers for me, our irises)—but I am here, in our house, with Giacomo and Gilda. Giacomo said, from the first day with the chutes, when he held me shaking in his arms, against his chest, he said we have to go away, we have to leave this house—*our* house—I have to sell it, rent it, I have to save Gina, Gigi just said she has half her life still to live, I have to find someplace for us to go. If he says this now, ten years later, maybe he can fool himself into thinking that it makes sense. But that's not things as it is. It all happened much much too fast. The chutes—in one minute they were here. The cement cloud—in one minute it was here, we were still waiting for the metal shed and exhaust fan. When a B-52 suddenly appeared the people didn't say, Let's move to a new village—it was impossible. They dug holes into the ground, got into them, and hoped for the best. Giacomo has to understand that my death—my agony and death—are part of a much bigger war *that he is fighting*. That he has been fighting all his life, and will fight forever. Even dead I am his ally, his companion in this war. Even when he is dead and we are not here anymore—Giacomo, Gina, Gilda—we hope his written words will keep fighting this war.

Sell the house! rent the house! with bombs dropping on it! Rent another house, save my cat's life—this still torments him. It was a good act, a courageous act for him to bring Gilda into our house (and by *our* I mean also Gilda's of course), one year after my death, his second cat, when he cannot forgive himself for my death, ever. But he did it. And Gilda has done so infinitely much for our connection, and I thank her in my mind every moment. The chutes, the cement—you think Giacomo was not very resourceful, not resourceful at all. He should have picked me up in his arms and carried me away, somewhere. There must be lots of places. I had such a great hunger to go on living. But wherever there is End there must be Shadow. It is easy to *say* do this, do that. And some people don't even *say*, they just *do*. What am I doing now? What am I saying? I'm getting tangled up in my own Tail. In my mind. I'm not a philosopher—not a theoretical, or moral, or practical philosopher. I was a cat with a passion for killing rats and a love for my companion who loved me every instant. WE did what we could—this is what he has to understand. WE. His big big mistake is when he says, I—Giacomo—didn't do everything I could. This is wrong. This was OUR life, OUR house, OUR home, OUR garden, OUR ex-garden. WE did everything we could. But Giacomo is too logical, he thinks it's all about naming and directing shadows. Maybe some day, I hope, when he reads this painful Tail, he'll wake up suddenly and see that *we did what we could.* Not in our dreams, but in our reality. Believe me, being dead is nothing like a dream. I don't even sleep. I'm always awake, watching Giacomo and Gilda dream together. This, too, is our reality. You may think this Tail of mine is very long, after all I'm just a cat. Just a dead cat. But every single animal has a right to tell their Tail. And you may think I blur the line between life and death. It isn't true. The line is sharp as a razor. *I wanted more life.* I am a *dead* cat. I am *here* because of a connection. A connection that gives me not life, or death, or dreams, but a consciousness I share with Giacomo. OUR consciousness, the consciousness of our connection. Of our being together, even in my not being. The consciousness of our love.

That was a long hard winter, the last winter of my life. We both felt very sick, and we were very *angry.* The Big Lie the enthusiastic Architect told us— Giacomo went looking for him, he went to the Office near San Marco, never found him, *no one would talk to Giacomo.* Stuff happens. The City police? Three, four years the big scaffolding was there, *uncovered—big as life*—and the workers never wore helmets. Building stuff was flying off in all directions. What would you like to know about the City police?! We'd like to know *a lot* about the City police. Perhaps they could have made these mobs respect the regulations, and saved my life. And about the City government?! Perhaps they could have put us in a hotel or a room during the time of the (uncovered) chutes and the (totally illegal) cement cloud, and saved my life. But they had other things on their minds, I suppose, much bigger than their regulations, much bigger than their Law. The Stuff Happens Construction Company was (is) the *biggest* in Venice—this is Giacomo's explanation. Might makes right— this is Giacomo's enemy, his war, the war of his life. And of mine.

Meanwhile, the Macedonians were working pretty peacefully. Not so much noise, not so much violence. They had to rebuild the entire *palazzo*—the outer walls piece by piece, brick by brick, for starters, so that kept them very busy. They actually didn't bother us so much, but I *detested* them anyway. I certainly never hated the rats I killed, not at all. I respected them very much. But for me these Macedonian workers were part of the MOB—the criminal mob—that had destroyed my life. Giacomo managed to get along with them, he even managed to speak on occasion with The Great Jacob, to ask him to respect our house. But I detested them all. Because—I have to say this—I already knew I was dying. I didn't know how soon, but I could feel that the inside of my body had been burned away. It could resist, but it couldn't heal. I know that Giacomo had a great dream—a *vision*, that's how he thought of it—that one day, perhaps in two or three years, I would go out through my flap once again into a new garden—a calm, a peaceful garden, with earth again—even if I was a very tired old cat. But I could feel that it was not going to happen. Still, in the spring we were feeling a little better. I didn't vomit every day, and I had plenty of appetite—I was always hungry. Hungry for food and hungry for life. But I wasn't able to eat very much. I did gain back a *little* weight—not all that much. I was like the fig tree had been—smaller, but still strong enough to have a few figs. In April, for my sixteenth birthday Giacomo brought me irises as he always did—our favorite flower, purple has always been our favorite color. And jumbo shrimp, which I ate and enjoyed a lot! I practically never went out into the back. In the late afternoons and evenings and on weekends no one was ever there, but I didn't have the heart for it. It was my *regno* once. Not anymore. The Temple of the Sun stood there gloomy and alone. Giacomo and I decided to concentrate on the plants in the courtyard—which is a very beautiful courtyard, and I'd never fully appreciated it before. Giacomo bought new terracotta pots—small rectangular ones and big round ones—and we got new plants and flowers. It's all for you, Gina, a new and peaceful garden, he said. (Our courtyard neighbors gave us some too.) But my Giacomo had a fantastic idea. He invented a little garden on top of the ancient well-head, with parsley, basil, chives, and tiny plants, lined up in rows in the rectangular pots. And everything was growing! It was fantastic, it really made us happy. It's incredible, but some days I felt too weak to hop up and see it—just imagine! Just one year before Giacomo woke me up to kill that rat, in a single double-leap. So he picked me up and put me right there in the garden. Such a wonderful feeling. So we spent a lot of time together in the courtyard that spring and summer, with all the plants. A great memory for both of us. In my heart I was still an action cat, even if I'd grown pensive in a short time. My favorite part of the courtyard is a spot right next to our house at the end of a little passageway that goes right down to the canal. Gilda loves it but she's a philosopher, and philosophers love to watch water for its own philosophic sake, it's an ancient tradition. But I always loved water too, I think it's a permanent quality of Venetian cats. It's great to see the canal passing by, and hear the little waves. Often I saw fish, and sometimes even a wayward rat swimming by. But, let me tell you the last action story of my life. I warn you, it's a strange one. Believe me, I don't really understand it myself, and it's my own story. Giacomo calls it 'The Rat-Yell' and I know he's always wanted to write one of his *long* stories about it. Or possibly an entire book, the last one in a trilogy, after *Neighbors* and *Travelers*. He's convinced that my connection with *pantegane* merits a book on the scale of *Crime and Punishment*. What funny ideas he's always had!

This is the story. It was around the beginning of that last summer. With the warm weather I was actually feeling quite a bit better—stronger. But—it was contradictory (as Hegel, Giacomo's hero, might say). I felt stronger and weaker at the same time—more alive, and more dead. Well, make of this what you will. That evening we were together in the courtyard, then Giacomo went upstairs to work, I decided to stay out a while to watch the canal. There was a fresh breeze in the courtyard, it was very peaceful. Suddenly I saw a *big rat* swimming by, right in front of me, I reached out, *dug* the claws of one paw right into his back, and *yanked* him right out of the water. Call it reflexes, call it instinct, it just happened, he was *right here, I had him,* I hopped right on his back and *bit* him in the back of the neck, and heard his glorious PEEP of death. This part of the story lasted about three seconds altogether. Frankly, for another three seconds I couldn't believe I'd done it. Me, a cat more dead than alive. What can I say? This moment, and those wonderful moments the first night in our house, when I kept jumping up on the bed and Giacomo kept throwing me off and I understood that he would love me forever and never ever leave me—or me him—these are the moments in which I was *most alive,* my two moments of *total life.* What did I do then, with this rat, a *gift* from the Rat-God or Cat-God, or Cat-Rat-Rat-Cat God (what's in a name), which I knew *perfectly well* was the last rat of my life? I held it firmly between my teeth, went into the house—just inside the front door—and YELLED. Yes, YELL is the word. With the rat between my teeth. It was my last great celebration. Giacomo dashed downstairs—*voilà,* the next contradiction. Perhaps it truly was the contradiction of a contradiction, or actually Hegel's negation-of-the-negation, a *logical* moment. (Giacomo, when he talks about logical moments, is not exactly the screwball you all think he is.) *This was not an exercise in logic,* it was a life-death celebration. A negation-of-the-negation—Giacomo understood this immediately, my beloved Giacomo. I'm still working on it, nine years after my death, and almost ten years after the event. Until then, whenever Giacomo saw me with a rat between my teeth it was because of my desire to give it to *him,* as my *gift,* proof of my devotion and of my love for our life together. But this time *it was a lot more complicated.* This was the end, and shadow. This was MY RAT, and millions of rats, five hundred years of Venetian rats. My life, its death, my death, all together, inseparable. A negation, and a connection. Just as Giacomo and I are inseparable for as long as he lives, even after my death—my negation. I want to try to explain myself. I was not a philosophic cat or a literary cat, but Giacomo is as philosophic and literary as they come.

All my life, but especially in that final period of my life, Giacomo often read me *Heart of Darkness,* and we thought about it a lot together. About the silence and the uproar being two moments of one logic. Giacomo has never believed in progress—I think this negation may be his strongest existential conviction. He believes in Empires, which are born in rottenness (in every sense), live through tyranny, and die in devastation (their own and, especially, of others). And they call it progress! he always says. When you murdered my cat *with your progress,* where were your regulations! where was your law! We had read *Heart of Darkness* so many times that sometimes he'd read me—out loud, slowly, very strongly and clearly—just one page or two. Late that very spring (the last spring of my life) he read me the same page three times—we thought about it for a long time. He called the page End and Shadow. It described a moment of Marlow's journey up the river through the heart of darkness *in search of something even darker* (named Kurtz). Marlow says:

> But still we crawled. Sometimes I would pick out a tree a little way ahead to measure our progress towards Kurtz by, but I lost it invariably before we got abreast. To keep the eyes so long on one thing was too much for human patience.

Giacomo used to *go crazy* when he read this. I think it was exactly the same as my rat-yell. Believe me. Here 'one thing' is the end—he told me—and the journey, the 'crawling,' is the shadow. Wherever there is end there is shadow. 'Measure our progress.' *What progress!?* This is Giacomo's *pantegana*. I was a great cat because I could bite a rat in the back of the neck, and PEEP? What progress?! For Giacomo, for his reading of Conrad, this was the *unspeakable question*. Millions of rats, dead or alive, millions of trees in the heart of darkness. Progress? The state-of-the-art Venetian *Palazzo*-Foundations Rebuilding Mob, regulated *and unregulated—here's progress for you*. Progress towards Kurtz, to embrace him. Democracy, from Athens (where almost everybody was a slave) to the City upon a Hill (where everyone, without exception, is the slave of a *rotten* system). And *we*—my companion, and I, a long-dead cat—ask you, What progress? Beyond Vietnam, Behind Vietnam, the uproar, the silence. The failure of human beings as political animals. What progress? There is no progress unless by progress you mean the journey upriver *to join Kurtz and embrace his final solution.* 'Exterminate all the brutes.' The path to devastation. There is no *end* and no *other* end. Where everything ends. Where rupture founders and shadows end in endless shadow.

The rat-yell! I am *here*, YELLING, just inside the front door, with a stone-dead rat between my teeth, the last rat of my life. Giacomo dashed downstairs, and here I am, with my negation-of-the-negation—YELLING. Did Giacomo expect me to drop the rat at his feet so he could throw it into the canal—the time-honored procedure? With *this yell* I don't think he expected it, and it's sure not what he got. I dashed upstairs and *crawled under the bed with the rat.* What a thing to do! And I did it! Giacomo got his broom and chased me out from under the bed (at least I'd had a chance to catch my breath), and I dashed back downstairs again, yelling, with the rat still between my teeth, right into the guest room and under the sofa-bed. Giacomo pulled the sofa-bed out and came at me with his broom again, yelling GINA! GINA!—we were both yelling now—and I ran back out into the courtyard again, with the rat, YELLING and RUNNING. Giacomo had to chase me around the courtyard. Listen, you know by now that I was a no-bullshit cat and am now a dead no-bullshit cat, and I'm not bullshitting you now. He finally got me in a corner, I stopped yelling and looked at him with the rat between my teeth for a while, then I dropped it. Not in defeat but in victory. Where in the world did I find the energy for all this? How should I know. A mystery. Maybe it was just the energy that comes when you experience, completely, your true nature and the nature of all sentient beings. The energy of life and death, not two and not one. I was just expressing this true nature.

It wasn't such a bad summer. Actually, it was a good summer. No more yelling, even the Macedonians were pretty quiet—not even The Great Jacob yelled much, for once. And they were going on vacation for the entire month of August. One of them told Giacomo about it—all of them off to Macedonia for a month. It's true that I was always hungry and wasn't able to eat very much, but as I recall it now I didn't vomit that often. I slept almost all day, like an old cat. I felt peaceful. The last week in August Giacomo went to Massachusetts to see his mother, sister, brother-in-law, and nieces, he hadn't seen them for a long time. He was only away for six days altogether, I know he would never have left me at all if he wasn't convinced I'd be OK. Zio Andrea, Gina my godmother's brother, and his *fidanzata*, Zia Teresa, came to stay with me, which was great, they had stayed with me before, I loved them. It was a peaceful time. I was sure glad when Giacomo got home. In exactly one year so many terrible things had happened. I still only weighed three kilos. What can I say. We hoped for the best.

But what happened next was unimaginable. Unspeakable. The most horrible moment of all these horrible moments. Equally unexpected, but even more horrible. The Macedonians—The Great Jacob—what people were these people?! These were not Big Mob people, they were little people, working people. Of course, they were part of the Final Solution. But until that day they hadn't done us any harm. After not seeing them for a month, I thought, maybe I can start detesting them a little less. It was just about September 1st (again). A very beautiful day. No workers came, and around noon Giacomo decided to go to the Lido, he wanted to look at the sea. He hadn't gone all summer. He used to dream about taking me with him so I could see it too, especially toward evening when it was very peaceful, but it was too much traveling for me. I was happy seeing the sky. The house was very quiet, I was happy, he left windows open, upstairs and in the guest room too, so I could have a nice breeze. Then, suddenly, all the Macedonians came! Out of nowhere! In the afternoon! They woke me up and I looked at them out of the window. They had small machines I'd never seen before. They turned out to be electric hammers—jackhammers, that's what they're called. All of a sudden there was a TERRIBLE NOISE and our whole house was vibrating and shaking. No! No! They were knocking down the wall—the one between the ex-garden and ex-geese-courtyard, that had been knocked down years before, and then rebuilt, with the arch. The wall actually *attached to our house.* The wall *full of iron or steel,* especially where it was attached to our house. The Macedonians absolutely did not expect iron and steel—it was madness! In the whole world only Geometra Nixon, with his Madman Strategy, could have done anything that mad. It was just a peaceful silly wall, standing there doing nothing. The Macedonians, with two jackhammers, thought they could knock it down in an hour, so a boat could come and take it away. *But without saying one word to Giacomo.* 'You weren't home,' The Great Jacob told Giacomo the next day. With all our windows open, including the one right next to the wall, and the house completely full of dust, but that was the very least of it. *Giacomo screamed so much*—it is the only time I ever heard him scream. What kind of people are you! he screamed. And screamed. He called them murderers. But he was also crying. See why I detested these workers? I didn't trust them. And now Giacomo! His execration was a blazing fire. It still is, to this day. And he had to live with these people for almost three more years. I didn't, I was dead. HOW I HATE THEM.

What happened exactly? It's very simple. When the jackhammers started and the whole house was shaking, I crept slowly down to the guest room. *I thought they were destroying our house this time.* One worker was leaning right on our house and trying to smash the piece of wall attached to it. Attached with steel. It was a big mistake to go so close. I SCREAMED, I screamed at the worker. OK, in the dust and the noise he probably didn't even know I was there. But he certainly knew I was in the house, and with all the windows open. What people are these people? Just following orders. *This time,* after the chutes, and the cement cloud, if they had told Giacomo about the jackhammers—just for that wall, just for one day—he would have taken me away that day, to Zio Neno's, or anywhere. One day, half a day. Instead, I was already half-dead and they murdered me. I went too close to that jackhammer, I was so angry and confused, I was out of my mind. A terrified skinny gray cat screaming in that hell of jackhammering and dust, the worker didn't even know I was there— and didn't care. After barely a minute I felt a terrible pain in my head, then right away it got much worse. My mind was screaming screaming screaming and it just wouldn't stop. Somehow I made it back upstairs, I wanted to get under our bed. Just a few hours later Giacomo got back from the Lido. He found a quiet house, all full of dust, called out to me, went upstairs. He found me half-way under the bed, at first he thought I was dead. He pulled me out so gently, I looked around, happy to see him, I tried to stand up, I was too tired. Giacomo phoned Gigi. He took me to see Gigi right away, it is far, on the other side of the Rialto, near the Venice Hospital in the neighborhood where I was born. (After that, Gigi always came to our house to see me.) Giacomo was crying, it was a long way. *Oh Signore!* Gigi said. *Povera Ginetta!* Half my body was paralyzed. I had had a stroke.

It took me a long time to die. There were new ups and downs, right until the end. My mind was calm after the stroke. Gigi gave me injections, Giacomo took me home and put me on our bed. It was quiet. For the rest of my life the noise outside was far away—except the next day, when Giacomo screamed and screamed at these people. SCREAMED. We were angry and we detested them, forever. But at least, in these last few months of my life, their noise was far away. I had a good silence. Giacomo loved me so much. I felt everyone's love. People came to see me and help me, such wonderful people. Gina my godmother came all the time. Gianfranco came and talked to me. Gigi came. We got to know a new, special person, named Mirka, who lives in the lane that leads into our courtyard. She is a nurse, and she has a black cat named Birba, who was still very young then. When Gilda came Birba was her first great friend, her big sister. Gigi came and talked with Mirka, and then she came every day for weeks to give me an injection, a small one with a very fine needle. She was so gentle. And Birba came with her, every day. She came and walked around our bed and looked up at me, with great respect and sorrow. After my death, all winter long, Birba came every day scratching on our door. Giacomo let her in, she brushed up against him with her back, quickly, affectionately, walked slowly through our entire house, and went back out into the courtyard. A ceremony. There is nothing in the world as good as a good cat. A true cat. Just a cat. A true cat is the same as the Zen master in the story 'The True Path' who says to the dying man, 'If you think you really come and go, that is your delusion. Let me show you the path on which there is no coming and no going.' The true cat is this. Satori.

After I died Giacomo cried for weeks. He didn't want to talk to anybody. He didn't know what to do. It was as though he were looking for me everywhere, in the smallest sound, the slightest movement of the air. For so many years he had never been in our house for one moment without me. He started reading his Zen books and doing Zen meditation (actually, he had been doing it all along.) He had often called me *Shin Ku Myo U*—practically all the Japanese he knew. It means from true emptiness wondrous being. Gianfranco told him, come to Mestre and talk with me about Gina. And he did, they talked many many times, and not only about me. My Zia Ruth sent him a new book that explained how to do a type of Tibetan meditation called *tonglen*. In *tonglen* you breathe in the pain of someone suffering or closed in by death, you take this pain into your heart, and you breathe out relief and openness. You breathe out this relief, and love, for one being, but also for all beings, living and dead, who have had feelings. You breathe in pain, feel it, and breathe out freedom from pain. Giacomo tried to do this when Gianfranco died. For forty days only this, and Buddhist readings. At first he was able to do it, but then it got to be horrible. He breathed in pain, but breathed out even more pain. Not relief, more pain. He was choking on pain. Why? I don't know. Like me, it took our great friend Gianfranco a long time to die, but he was in a hospital, attached to machines, in the night of the world. Giacomo visited him often in the hospital, he was so still, attached to machines. It was impossible to share his consciousness, possible only to see it, and to witness the pain in his soul. But now he talks to Gianfranco again, often, I like to listen to him talk. Gianfranco cannot answer, I cannot answer, but when he talks to us Giacomo takes our pain and gives us liberation from pain. But we want to do it too, for him. When I died Giacomo did *tonglen* for me every afternoon for many hours, from winter right into the beginning of summer. I no longer had any body but I felt every breath he breathed. I felt him breathing in the pain of my dying, breath by breath, taking it so deeply into his heart, his spirit, and his breathing out, again and again, breath by breath, freeing me from my pain. My death, actually, was terrible but also peaceful. But Giacomo needed to find peace, and we found it together. Sort of. It was hard. It's still hard. But we are fighters. This Tail is my fight, my struggle. When I was alive our connection was very strong. When I died Giacomo gave me all his heart, breath by breath, sitting on a cushion on our low hard bed. Breathing in my pain, breathing out relief from pain. He did this. Our connection became an absolute connection. If you can imagine this, you can see how it's possible for me to tell, and to end, this Tail.

Mirka's injections helped me. My back leg was still partly paralyzed, but not half my body like before. I was fighting back, my mind was peaceful. After the stroke my stomach stopped vomiting. Maybe it was just too tired, maybe my body had bigger things to worry about. I was angry. Giacomo was angry. My mind was peaceful. My appetite came back, I was hungry. '*Oh Signore!* She's hungry.' Gigi said. 'That's a good sign.' I couldn't eat much, so Giacomo gave me all my favorite foods. Chicken liver. Lots of fish. Creamy baccalà. Gorgonzola. Because of my leg I couldn't walk around, for weeks I stayed upstairs on our bed, but my leg was improving. It was September, the weather was very beautiful, there was a lovely breeze in the house, and from our bed I looked right out the window and watched the sky. The colors, the clouds, the birds. I'd never felt less alone in my life. All my life I was a peaceful cat, and I killed hundreds of rats. Little by little I managed to walk. Just barely. That leg was very weak and I fell over easily. Giacomo was afraid I'd fall down the stairs. He kept the door closed, and when I asked him he carried me down. Not during the day, except on weekends—I didn't want to see the workers. They were there, but I never looked at them again. In the evening I was able to sit on the kitchen table and have dinner with Giacomo, just as I'd done for almost all my life. I was so happy! In October Zio Ulrico and Zia Dagmar and Anna and Lisa came from Zurich, we celebrated Zia Dagmar's birthday with a ton of jumbo shrimp. But it was also sad. They were sad for me, but they also had sad news to tell Giacomo. Zia Dagmar had leukemia. Giacomo did *tonglen* for her too, and now—ten years and many struggles later—she is doing OK. They all love Gilda, and remember and love me too. Old and true friends are the best thing in the world, a form of the same love that connects us, Giacomo and me, and all of us.

I only went into the courtyard a few times, with Giacomo, to look at the plants and to look at the water, but it was autumn, winter was coming. I was still so hungry for life. On New Year's Eve Giacomo made us a special dinner. Creamy baccalà. FIVE jumbo shrimp just for me! And I ate them all! And after that a tiny dish of ice cream, which we almost never had in our house. It was such a beautiful New Year's Eve. Together.

End and Shadow

Right now it is a stormy, cold evening, the last day of March. This stormy cold reminds me a little of the night I was left in Lili's bar, and of the first night I came to our house. It's time to end my Tail. I'm still not completely sure why I called it End and Shadow, it just came to me out of nowhere. Maybe it means that the end is not everything. *La fine non è tutto.* The hunger ends, the connection no. When my connection with Giacomo ends, at his death, I will fall silent forever. That will be the end of our Tail, and our silence will be its shadow. We will no longer be able to speak to you, but you can speak to us, and we hope you will do it. If anyone reads this Tail, and thinks about it, and wonders how a dead cat could have so much to say, just think to yourself—*It was as though the mist itself had screamed.* Think of the Vietnamese people. Little clouds against big machines. They were nobody, but they kept fighting, they died, and they won the war. *As though the mist itself had screamed.*

About ten days after New Year's I had another stroke. It wasn't like the first one. This one was very hard but almost gentle. It was evening, I was on our bed in our snug warm little house, my head started to hurt, then to hurt more. I started to cry out, little sharp cries. Giacomo is here, he holds me against his body, my head hurts more and more but I'm not frightened. After a while it hurts a little less. I'm lying on my side, then I realize that I can't move at all. Only my head, only my tail. The rest of my body can't move. I hardly feel anything, except Giacomo being here and my body against his. The rest is pretty confused. Giacomo never tells this story, I've never heard him tell it, so I have to rely on my own memories. All I've heard him say is, 'On the last day of her life Gina's beautiful eyes were so bright! Her incredible bright green eyes, still loving life, saying she wants more life.' After this stroke I think I lived another four days. Gigi came the next morning, I remember he cried with Giacomo, Gigi is a very good and a very sensitive man. He gave Giacomo some medicines for me, Giacomo mixed them with my food and I ate them out of his hand—fish, baccalà, gorgonzola. I was hungry. I ate a tiny bit. Then I remember—Gina my godmother is here, with Zia Teresa, Giacomo is crying. I'm eating only a tiny bit. Now Gigi is here, and Mirka, and Birba. Now it's evening, now night, now morning. Now noon, and I eat my baccalà mixed with my medication. But I feel very very tired. Too tired. I don't eat any more. No liver, no fish, no gorgonzola, Giacomo has all my favorite foods, and I can't eat. Yesterday I ate a little. At noon I had that baccalà. Now I can't eat. Terribly tired. Too tired. Now Giacomo is trying to squirt water into my mouth with a syringe, this is all we can do, I can barely swallow but I love the water anyway, like I love Giacomo and he loves me. Then, suddenly, I hear some noise. From the courtyard. It's late afternoon and the Macedonians are going home for the day, screaming a little as usual. I raise my head a little. Giacomo sees me, he sees me listening to the noise, he helps me hold up my head. I am a cat of few words, an action cat. Gilda—my sister—knows *many* words, says many words. But now I must speak. With the last strength I have in my poor body, straight from my mind I pronounce words—real words—of extreme execration. I speak, softly but clearly, my cry of hate. These workers. My murderers. They are not rats, they are people.

A few hours later it is evening. Suddenly it gets hard to breathe. My breathing makes a little noise. Giacomo squirts just a little water into my mouth, it's good. It's the last time, the end. My mind is very peaceful. What a hunger I have had to live. It must be close to midnight. It's late. Suddenly I cannot breathe. What's happening. We are so frightened. Where is my breath! When it finally comes it makes a terrible noise. What can we do. It is late at night. In winter. Giacomo lies down on our bed. On his back. His head is propped up with pillows. He puts me so gently on his chest, my head under his chin, touching his beard. I can feel his heart beating. Very hard. He covers us with blankets. It is warm! Beautiful! He's caressing my head so gently, kissing my eyes, talking to me, *Gina, mia Gina.* My breathing is worse, worse, it's so hard. Just before dawn Giacomo falls asleep. I know he won't sleep long, just a few minutes. Quick. I breathe in the last air of my life, and breathe out for the last time.

31 March 2012

POSTSCRIPT: *for my cats*

two translations I have been working on since the early 1970s

Half of Life (Friedrich Hölderlin)

With yellow pears
and full of wild roses
the land hangs over the lake.
You graceful swans,
and drunk with kisses
dip your heads
into the holy sober water.

Woe is me!
When winter comes
where shall I find flowers
and where the sunshine,
and shadow of the earth?
The walls stand speechless and cold,
vanes rattle in the wind.

244

(Gabriele D'Annunzio, 1935, his last poem)

Here lie my dogs
my useless dogs,
stupid and shameless,
always young, and old,
faithful and faithless
to Idleness their lord,
not to me, nothing man.

They gnaw away underground
in the endless darkness
their bones gnaw at bones
and still they gnaw
these bones emptied of marrow.

Bones I could make
into the flute of Pan!
of seven reeds
—without wax or thread—
the flute of Pan!
If Pan is the All and
if Death is the All.

Every man in the cradle
sucks and slavers over his finger,
every man in the grave
is the dog of his nothingness.

Gilda reflects on blackbirds in the courtyard

quoth the blackbird: 'evermore'

A person who has not had rice cannot have hunger.
A person who gets hungry every day is someone who has had rice.
  Dogen-zenji

I thought the blackbirds in the courtyard would drive me crazy, completely. Instead, they've made me calmer. And they've gotten calmer too. Much calmer. This is the third year they've made their nest in the wisteria, in May. In the leaves of course; the flowers are long gone. The tiny birds were born in early July, last year and the year before. Tiny but healthy. When they fall out of their nest in the wisteria into the courtyard I pet them and protect them. It's June now, the weather is beautiful, my giant sits in the courtyard, with me, and with the blackbirds. The black one with the orange beck, the male (the female is gray) sings—sings PLENTY. And plenty loud. We listen, and read the Zen master Dogen, and the Suzukis. My great passion has always been for birds and butterflies—fast things that fly! I love little lizards but practically never see one. My big sister Gina wiped them out years ago, in the courtyard and in the back garden too. What a killer! An action cat.
  My giant says I'm an incarnation of the Buddha, or is that some kind of joke?

7 September 2018 — Believe it or not, while looking through old notes for my next Tail, 'I Dream of Eudemus,' I just found this paw-written page of Gilda's, here faithfully transcribed. The fragment is absolutely genuine, her paw-prints are inimitable. She must have written it before 'What is it like to be a cat?' or, perhaps, it was the beginning of a new Tail.
The huge and magnificent wisteria a neighbor and I planted in the courtyard in 1986 no longer exists, a madman murdered it a few years ago, may he rot in hell.
Gilda quotes from *Moon in a Dewdrop. Writings of Zen Master Dogen*, North Point Press, 1995.

Tabby
a pensée

Cher ami,

You say I owe you an explanation of why I say that tabbies have the best character. (Do we mean the best of all cats, or of all sentient beings?)

Well, I could simply say that based on my experience of many cats, many of them very wonderful, all the tabbies I've known have had a goodness that is special to them. And many consider the tabby a second-class-citizen cat. A nothing-special cat, a non-species, a no-kind of cat. 'Just a gray tabby.' A rag. But they are a very real kind. You know, in Italian they are called *soriani* because they came on the boats from Syria during the plague. I've never been able to discover whether they brought them on purpose, to kill the rats, or whether they just happened to be on the boats, killing rats, and when a few slipped off into the city they met so many rats they (the cats) went wild with joy. An unrestrained killing spree that saved the city. Apart from Gilda, who never harmed even the tiniest insect or any sentient being, tabbies have always been considered the best rat-killers of any kind of cat. I, personally, have never seen a black cat kill a rat. Gina killed hundreds. I know that the Venetians did not realize for a very long time that it was the rats that carried the plague, it wasn't so obvious. The tabbies taught them. Taught them and saved the Venetians' lives. (Some say it was the fleas on the rats that actually carried the plague, but this is a chicken-and-egg debate that leads absolutely nowhere.) I imagine the people were happy seeing all these rats killed by the cats—and then they noticed that the plague had ceased. Someone made the connection, and since then the Venetians have had a great and special love for the *soriani*. The tabby is the original European cat. In fact on Gina's and Gilda's birth certificates it says '*RAZZA: EUROPEO.*' Period. Yes, the tabbies were the first cats to set paw on European soil. Or stone, in the case of Venice. The others came later. And the tabby arrived with a sense of purpose—I think this helps explain the goodness of her character. (I say 'her' because my tabbies are both females.) A tabby doesn't just do any old thing like many cats, she has a sense of purpose. An idea. And not a bad idea. 'Goodness,' *mon ami*. Many kinds of cats are gentle, affectionate, loving, but a tabby has all that, plus a special tabby goodness.

Did you know that the 'tabby' in English takes her name from a kind of silk taffeta, originally striped and later with a watered finish, in French *tabis*, based on the Arabic *al-Attabiyya*, the Baghdad neighborhood where it was manufactured? I think this is very important. It explains a lot, whatever that lot may be. Silk fabric with a watered pattern—look at a tabby. At the 'pattern' of her fur, which is no-pattern but also most definitely a pattern. Mind you, do not confuse this with Queequeg's infinite tangle of tattoos, 'in his own person a riddle to unfold.' Ahab's harpooner, Ismael's friend—no, his riddle is a personal matter. Free will and the like. Self-portraiting. But the tabby—her fur is ordered chaos. No two tabbies are the same. Chaos is chaos. An abyss, always different. This explains why a tabby is never arrogant or haughty or proud, but does have great self-esteem. The cat, like her fur, expresses pure and simple *catness*. You can't say that about any other kind of cat—black, ginger, gray, white, or blandly or intricately mixed, in spots or in arabesques. It is the chaos labyrinth of the tabby that is the pure expression of catness, of what it is like to be a cat, as Gilda put it. And the tabby's character is equal to her fur. It expresses her complete ease with herself, not in a being-is-nothing way but in a way that accepts and expresses the full complexity of our world. The world persons share with cats. It's like my grandfather: he was special because he was at ease with himself, and he had a wonderful character, strong, and kind. The tabby is at ease with herself. A rare and special character.

This explanation may or may not convince you, but it's the best I can do at the moment.

Appendix

The Failure of Meaning and the Death of God: Ambiguity and 'The Terrible'

for Italo Valent, *alla memoria*

1993: It took me the whole year to write this essay, which is another path leading to—and from—the night of the world. You may find it difficult and obscure at times, but please be patient. It's worth reading. This 'Failure' *is* an inhabitant of my abyss of dreams. More a head than a tail, perhaps. An appendix, I'd say.

The editors of an extremely important and *scholarly* philosophy journal invited me (a nobody!) to write this paper for an issue on 'Philosophy and Tragedy,' but in the end they rejected it. 'Unscholarly.' 'Wild.' Quite a few people did read it, however, and tried, very hard, for years, to get it published. Unsuccessfully. It was too extreme for its own good.

Basically, it is a critique of Jacques Derrida's critique of Hegel.

The text follows the tortuous road from Absolute Meaning (note the capital letters), through its (logical) 'failure' in the dialectic (an original idea of mine), to 'meaning' as Hegel understands it (in my reading of Hegel).

I added a few explanatory comments, in brackets.

I *deeply* apologize for my use of the word 'man.' Deeply. A long hard story. The proper word is *anthropos*.

I. Hegel and the History of Meaning

> Some certain significance lurks in all things, else all things are little worth, and the round world itself but an empty cipher.
> *Moby Dick or, the Whale*, Chap. 99

From Chaos, Meaning. A long story. *To Deinon*.[1] As ambiguous and terrible as 'Man.' Quest for Absolutes, since Time began. For some 'God' that stands firm, always. Eternally bridging the Abyss, linking the meaningless and meaning, commanding: 'there must be meaning.'[2] In the yawning Gap,

---

[1] *To deinon* is 'the terrible' that evokes wonder and awe, 'fear and trembling'; formidable; disquieting. Radically *ambiguous*: attraction and repulsion together (cf. Kierkegaard's *Angst* as 'sympathetic antipathy'), marvelous terror.

[2] J. Derrida, 'From Restricted to General Economy' [hereafter RGE], in *Writing*

something *is there*. Being? Presence? Meaning? 'The system of logic is the realm of shadows.'³ Chaos, shadow of Origin.⁴ Originary separation, separation *as such*, before the separated and of the inseparable. Before Earth and Sky. Before Time. A God before God? *Deinon*—Ambiguity of Origin. Gaia Nyx Ouranus. Earth Night Sky. Mystery of separation and union, laceration and reconciliation. Abstraction—Abyss *of* Meaning—Night of the World. Two Divine Worlds. Ouranus Cronus Zeus. Sky Time Will. 'Clear Spirit'—of Zeus, of Ahab's purifying fire. But, the 'other' world: 'Eldest of Gods, the Earth.'⁵ Erinyes, daughters of Night. Nature and blood. Uncompromising unthinking ordinance. Yes/no. White/black. Puritanism before the letter. Night/day, old and new Gods. Zeus' realm of shadowless light cast against the unfading background of endless shadow. Tragedy. Great Zeus, great in ambiguity. At one with nature, yet dwelling far above it. Human in form, yet absolutely not reducible to man. Absolute Meaning. 'None of this is without Zeus.' Mystery, or a Terrible Machine that makes and guarantees Meaning? Origin—'does not pass over but has passed over' [SL 82-83]. Logos—being *is* nothing. Chaos and Origin—illogical and logical ... ambiguity? Being. Meaning. From Absolute Nature to Absolute Spirit, Homer to Hegel, in the terrible tangle of Time. Logocentrism—logic of a Center or Origin. Being as presence. Science (*epistēmē*). Self-presence of the present.⁶ Hegel's *Science of Logic*: explosion/ implosion, undecidably. 'Plosion'⁷ of the Absolute, of Origin, of God.

With what does Meaning begin? Consider Walter Otto's reading of the origins of Western Meaning.⁸ 'The ancient Greek religion comprehended the things of this world with the most powerful sense of reality possible, and nevertheless—nay, for that very reason—recognized in them the marvelous delineations of the divine.' [HG 10]. Meaning as purely and simply *what is there:* Enter *to Deinon*. The Spirit of Meaning: multiple ambiguity, pressing towards 'omniguity' of sense. *What* is there? 'The interval between man and deity' [HG 3]—'interval,' Shade of the Abyss. Infinite remoteness, infinite

and Difference, trans. A. Bass (Chicago: U. of Chicago Press, 1978), p. 256.
³ Hegel's *Science of Logic* [SL], trans. A. V. Miller (London: George Allen & Unwin, 1969), p. 58.
⁴ Hesiod, *Theogony* [HES], 116 ff. *Prōtista Xaos genet'.*
⁵ Sophocles, *Antigone* 337.
⁶ J. Derrida, *Of Grammatology* [OG], trans. G. C. Spivak (Baltimore and London: Johns Hopkins U. Press, 1976), *passim*.
⁷ The absence of any outside/inside distinction in the 'realm of shadows' points to the undecidability of ex- or implosion, in the resounding clap of originary 'plosion.'
⁸ W. Otto, *The Homeric Gods* [HG], trans. M. Hadas (London: Thames & Hudson, 1954; 1979); *Dionysus: Myth and Cult* [DMC], trans. R. B. Palmer (Bloomington: Indiana University Press, 1965).

nearness: the difference, God—man, unbridgeable. What *is* there? Being as presence: immediacy, indeterminacy, unmediated instability. Meaningless, omniguous, or—ambiguously—both? What is *there? Da.* 'Là cendre.'[9] 'Dasein, being in a certain *place;* but the idea of space is irrelevant here.' [SL 110]. Olympians: 'Deity is the configuration that recurs in all forms, *the meaning* that holds them all together.' [HG 166]. 'Suddenly the deities stood over the realms of life, living manifestations of the *eternal meaning* that pervades each of them.' [HG 162]. Meaning begins, then, in a logocentrism before the letter. In a nostalgia for Origin, a pro-logical, on the way to Logos. In an immediate logic of Origin, a proto-science (*epistēmē*) of being as presence, 'divine' *im-position* (*epi-stēmē*) of self-presence on the present. In the power— the 'will'—of Zeus as an immediate power of Meaning. The splendor of God *is* an eternal brightness 'full of meaning.' Zeus has no need to command 'there must be meaning' because Zeus is always already the living spirit and presence of Meaning. Olympians 'have no history because they *are.*' [HG 235]. Yet they are *in Time.* Cronus was the father both of the Erinyes and of Zeus. In Olympian calm: *to Deinon.* Otto knows and exalts Zeus and his progeny as deities of both being and of having been. Presence is inseparable from absence, yet they never come together in Time, the healer and the destroyer. Wondrous and terrifying—Dionysus, no god of madness but Mad God. The Twice Born, both times in a Time that, even in the face of madness, will not be effaced. *One* God, of life *and* death, of dual essence, 'ecstasy and horror, vitality and destruction, pandemonium and deathly silence, immediate presence that is at the same time absolute remoteness.' 'Oneness' itself.' [DMC 121]. Otto attempts to propose a 'Hegelian' god—'Truth, the Bacchanalian revel'— for whom the hour of birth is the hour of death. But Hegel refers to finite things and to an other conception of 'time.' 'All earthly powers are united in the god: the generating, nourishing, intoxicating rapture; the life-giving inexhaustibility; and the tearing pain, the deathly pallor, the speechless night *of having been.*' [DMC 140]. Otto *trips himself up* on time. The God Who Comes is the God Who Goes, but his coming is not his going, his presenting not his absenting. The Mask of Dionysus is the terrible face of Time, destined to haunt the history of Meaning until … Hegel … and beyond.

1851–52, Herman Melville: both *Moby Dick* and *Pierre* tell of a terrible, ambiguous quest for the Absolute, for an Absolute Meaning.[10] Flight not from but to the Mystery. Doomed from the start. The attempt to decipher

---

[9] J. Derrida, FEU LA CENDRE, 1987. ['La cendre' = the ash. 'Là cendre' = there ash. There where? In the same place as the 'da' in Hegel's Dasein = 'there being.' Nowhere. Everywhere. The idea of space is irrelevant. Please note: the Dasein in this text— translated as 'determinate being'—is Hegel's, and has nothing whatsoever to do with Heidegger's Dasein in *Being and Time.*]

[10] The word 'terrible' literally dominates *Moby Dick*; while in *Pierre or, the Ambiguities,* 'ambiguity' is explicitly referred to in some twenty-five different contexts.

a 'secret script,' 'else all things are little worth.' A chase and an excavation, whose object—Meaning—remains hidden, veiled, mysterious. Or absent? Tragically unattainable. In 1851 Melville wrote Hawthorne: 'Perhaps, after all, there is *no* secret.' *That* is the very secret—Hegel's secret.[11] The 'secret' in his *Logic* is an *open secret*. 'Mystery'—so viciously parodied in *Pierre*—can only be the mystery of self-disclosure, of 'truth without veil' [SL 50], of the untruth of mystery itself. Ambiguity is the might, the power of Hegel's Logic. But there, where being 'is' nothing and the there 'is not' there, the fog of ambiguity is itself the lifting of the fog. Logic, for Hegel, absolutely eschews any private understanding or knowing. It consists, in a sense, in being fully awake. Thinking is awake to its identity with being, and is thus in the wake of the concept.[12] But Hegel's concept, as dialecticity of the real, neither follows nor precedes that saturation of being with thought, of reality with reason, which it 'is,' and is thus a wake for the death of God, the 'plosion' of Meaning. Through [*dia*] logos, dialecticity. A/wake. Moments in the history of Meaning. Heraclitus and the divine Logos: present when we are most awake. Fragment 2: 'Although the logos is common, the many live as though they had a private understanding.' 'Private': *idios*—*idiōtikos*. Precisely the tragic in Melville: 'idiocy' pressed to a terrible extreme—to fatal obsession. Aristotle, too, had a serious problem with sleep—namely, the failure of insomnia. A problem with Time. If time is linked to consciousness, how can time pass when everyone is asleep? [*Physics*, 218b 25]. And what would meaning 'be' without time? A dream? An empty cipher? Even potency and act may be read in terms of sleeping and waking. Aristotle, I suspect, devised *ad hoc* solutions to these enormous problems that smack more of mytho-logos than of logic: passive and active *nous*,[13] first and second *entelechia*. And a dash of common sense: waking must precede sleep. No one is born asleep.

'And the round world itself but an empty cipher.' Parmenides: 'Unshaken heart of well-rounded truth.' Pure being: abstract, the wholly indeterminate. Hegel: being—nothing—becoming. 'Being' is the cipher that indicates

---

[11] I. Valent, 'Il segreto di Hegel,' *Bailamme, rivista di spiritualità e politica*, No. 13, June 1993, p. 157.

[12] *Begriff* is translated throughout as 'concept.' [*Begrifflos* signifies 'devoid of concept,' hence 'ungraspable.']

[13] [There is a long, complicated, and controversial story here. *Nous*—mind, or spirit—in the context of the *De Anima* (On the Soul) is always translated as 'reason.' Aristotle makes a distinction *in the soul* between passive reason that 'becomes all things' and active reason that 'makes all things.' Metaphorically, it is akin to the distinction between sleeping and being awake. Some theologians have seen active *nous* as 'divine reason,' or even as a 'divine spark' that transcends the individual human being. This is controversial, but so is Aristotle's original distinction.]

the immediate, the unconditioned—the meaningless that is always already meaningful. Not the empty but the full cipher: being, the indeterminate that *is* not ('is' nothing) but is 'already' determined. Ambiguous? The lifting of the fog. The 'failure' of Absolute Meaning. Being 'is' nothing: here, being *poses* as the purely indeterminate, and *nothing* poses as what *opposes* the purely indeterminate. Their truth is becoming, the vanishing of vanishing: Dasein. The truth for whoever is awake. Being, as cipher, is always already de-ciphered [*aufgehoben* = superseded], because the cipher says more than the nothing— the shadow—that it is. This is the realm of *shadows*, not of the dream-sodden shades of the Homeric underworld, the dead throng that mocks all logic. Sleep/asleep. Dionysus, the Tragic Mask, awakes to discover the oneness of Hunter and Hunted, the destiny of the Crono-Logos. Then he sleeps once more. And Ahab, the 'grand, ungodly, god-like man'—the obsessed, the 'idiot' who will never awake—fails, to the last, to decipher his own, private cipher. Precisely because it is his own.

Hegel: in the 'realm of shadows'—the *ab-solutum*, the absolutely abstract—meaning is *not* Absolute. Not *ab-solo*, 'from itself alone,'[14] private, 'idiotic.' Not 'ab-solved' from the free play of the concept. The Absolute is what is *not* meaning. What is-and-is-not 'there.' 'Il y a *là* cendre.' [There is *there* ash.] 'Being *is* nothing.' 'Plosion' of Logos. Death of God. Dasein, the absolute originary 'structure' of meaning—absolute logic, logic of the absolute—is itself no Absolute, is not *a* determination, but is determination *as such*: not presence but presenting absence and absenting presence. Living spirit, not dead letter. Gospel truth? 'Everything turns on grasping and expressing the true, not only as *substance*, but equally as *subject*.'[15] The truth of shadow. Substance 'is' subject—but what subject? Man? Philosophy and tragedy. Sphinx, ambiguity, omniguity, *to deinon*. The terrible. *Anthropos*—'man'—the riddle *and* the answer to the riddle. But what man? What being is *human* being? 'Find the slayer!' 'Nothing more terrible [*deinoteron*] than man.'[16] From *Logos* to *Begriff*. But the history of Meaning 'is there.' *Da*. Dialecticity. Onto-theo-logy. Hegel: the plosion, all together, of Being, God and Logos. Not renunciation or loss but a *good* laugh,[17] a/wake, a celebration of the 'failure' of Meaning in which the dialecticity of meaning constitutes itself.

---

[14] W. Desmond, 'Evil and Dialectic,' in *New Perspectives on Hegel's Philosophy of Religion* [NPHPR], ed. D. Kolb (Albany: SUNY Press, 1992), p.172. Desmond refers not to the *Logic* but to the *realphilosophische* category of 'singularity.'

[15] Hegel's *Phenomenology of Spirit* [PS], trans. A. V. Miller (Oxford: Oxford U. Press, 1977), p. 10.

[16] Sophocles, *Antigone* 333. Here *deinoteron* also points to the disquiet of the *meaning* of 'man'—a restless, shifting meaning upon which no *quies* can be imposed.

[17] RGE 256. 'Laughter alone exceeds dialectics and the dialectician. It bursts out only on the basis of an absolute renunciation of meaning....'

II. Pro-Logos: The Mad God

> We obey the gods, whoever the gods may be.
> Euripides, *Orestes*, 418

'Find the slayer!' cries Oedipus, and for us, the spectators, in this cry the tragic, the terrible, is already pronounced and fully present. Nothing can be done. Nothing is *possible* anymore. The actuality [*entelechia*] of the tragic *is* already *there*. Its playing out [*energeia*] is already underway, unswerving. Nothing in heaven or on earth has the power [*dynamis*] to change its course. Oedipus cannot grasp the meaning of his cry. He cries out to the world, when the true object of his cry could only be a mirror—his own image—his shadow—him*self*. The mask of Oedipus is the Mask of Dionysus: unchecked duality, ambiguity, sacrifice, madness, death. The Enigma. The wondrous terror of Meaning.

The Tragic Mask is Ambiguity *as such*. A front with no back, it is there and not there, masking presence and absence, near and far. Dionysus is the god of con*front*ation. His Mask is an af-*front*, it is nothing but surface, it 'has no history.' Myth, the substance—the stuff—of tragedy, is a tapestry without time: this, basically, is what Sophocles upholds, Aeschylus belies, and Euripides explodes. But this all-surface, 'grand, depthless, depth-like' Mask—how can it fail to mask (and thus *un*mask) a 'blackness of darkness.' Mystery and secret. A foreign depth. Between Self and 'living act' stands 'the unreasoning mask.' 'If man will strike'—shrieks Ahab—'strike through the mask! How can the prisoner reach outside except by thrusting through the wall? To me, the white whale is that wall, shoved near to me. Sometimes I think there's naught beyond.'[18] We shall see that the terrible, all-surface Mask of Dionysus masks a double ambiguity: of 'deity' past (Sophocles) and future (Euripides). Aeschylus will set his scene between them, in the present, the 'now' as he would like to see it: as a permanent, problematic mise-en-scène of reconciliation. Double ambiguity, ambiguity of the Double. Looking back, to the ambiguous relation between pre-Olympian and Olympian gods, and the enigma they pronounced: 'man.' And 'looking forward,' to the 'terrible' relation between God and man. Euripides' raving quarry, and shadowy query—'unsolved to the last': What is God? Clear spirit or terrible machine? What if God is unfathomable, inscrutable, 'unreasoning' *Tychē*. Chance. Blind, mindless, 'most terrible [*deinotatos*] and most gentle' *indifference*.[19] Our query to this day. 'Writing in the common sense is the dead letter, the carrier of death,' while 'God's book … is natural, divine and living writing … venerated, equal in dignity to the origin of value' [OG 16,17]. But it is also ciphered. So near to God, to Nature, to his

---

[18] H. Melville, *Moby Dick* [MD + Chapter] (New York: Dell, 1959), Chap. 36.

[19] Euripides, *Bacchae* 861.

Open Book—which is both meaningless and 'full of meaning.' (An open door. But without the key we cannot cross its threshold.) Like 'thinking machines'— *un*deciphering— shall we obey Laws whose meaning we cannot know? If so, then what are we? 'Is Ahab, Ahab? Is it I, God, or who that lifts this arm?' [MD Chap. 132]. 'A poor player/ That struts and frets his hour upon the stage.'[20] The Book of the World, a Mystery. What, if not this, is the Terrible, the Tragic? So near, the secret that *cannot* be secret, unless God is Mad, or Angry with the world. Unsolved. The tattooed savage. 'Queequeg in his own person was a riddle to unfold; a wondrous work in one volume; but whose mysteries not even himself could read, though his own live heart beat against them; and these mysteries were therefore destined in the end to molder away with the living parchment whereon they were inscribed, and so be unsolved to the last.' [MD Chap. 110].

It has been reported that in 420 B.C. when Asclepius was solemnly inducted into Athens, represented by a Holy Snake, for a time the Snake was Sophocles' house-guest. As Wilamowitz observed, one cannot imagine that Aeschylus or Euripides would have cared to entertain a Holy Snake.[21] But Sophocles, drenched in a nostalgia for Origin that Euripides will parody, was poet of the most ancient of tragedies: 'man,' the riddle, twisted between and engulfed by conflicting powers of godhead, now mirrored in the *polis*. Man—*anthropos*—poised between the terrible powers of Non-meaning and Meaning. The only 'Meaning' that survives the Origin is Time, the only Source is a Resource—Cronus, the ciphering, a 'failure' of Meaning that not even mighty Zeus can fathom. In the Tragic Age, while for Sophocles all human acts still 'come from Zeus,' he graphically underscores the futility of action and the ignorance of man. God alone knows—indeed *is*—the Meaning of things, but his Meaning grows shadowy, it is no longer transparently present in a reality where man now seeks his place in the community, the *polis*. Tragedy, here, consists in the ambiguity of a God whose power of abstraction ('mightiest of powers': cf. PS 18) is crumbling. Abstraction the 'absolute power' that separates the inseparable (the Divine that in Hegel becomes 'concept') and guarantees Meaning. Sophocles' God becomes Blind Justice—blinding, not binding. *Tychē*. Oedipus himself.[22] Fortune and Misfortune, blessing and curse. *Pharmakon*—remedy and poison. *Tychē* that in Euripides becomes Madness. The Machine. The Terrible.

Tragedy—there is no escape. Man's 'good intentions' play no part. In Sophocles we witness the clash of old and new forms of *Dikē*—the Earth-

[20] *Macbeth*, Act V, Scene 5.

[21] E. R. Dodds, *The Greeks and the Irrational* [GI] (Berkeley & Los Angeles: University of California Press, 1966), p. 193.

[22] Vernant & Vidal-Naquet, *Myth and Tragedy in Ancient Greece* [MTAG], trans. J. Lloyd (New York: Zone Books, 1988), pp. 125-26.

gods against Zeus—in which 'Justice' itself founders, giving rise to 'ambiguity and reversal,' a confusion of values, 'a rule of ambiguous logic' that demands a new 'human world of meanings.' [MTAG 139; 30]. Oedipus acts, but the real Meaning of his acts is beyond him, ungraspable. [Cf. MTAG 32.] *To Deinon*: both the divine and the human worlds—myth and *polis*—are blurred with a failure of Meaning. Man as agent is tragically placed at the crossroads of action, but neither road is Just, because in this new puzzle of Meaning the missing piece is the Meaning of man. Human and divine discourse (logos) interweave and come into conflict [MTAG 117], so that Oedipus—like Queequeg—cannot read his own 'secret script.' His tragedy mirrors the transition from immediate (divine) to mediated (human) Meaning—the failure *of* Meaning and the failure of Meaning *to constitute itself*. *Pro*-logos, the razor's edge of Silence and Word. Meaning cannot constitute itself in a single word—be it 'God' or 'man'—devoid of text and context. ('God,' notes Hegel, 'is in the beginning only an empty word' [SL 78].) This is the Terrible in Sophocles: 'man,' in the *polis*, is but an *omniguous cipher*: man's being-man is what ties him to all men, *and* precisely what separates him from all men. This, perhaps, is the very origin of the Terrible: the problematicity of Origin itself. The problem is called *koinōnia*, 'communality': How is it possible to compose a community out of 'poor players,' omniguous ciphers?

Faced with this problem, Aeschylus looked to the dawning science of *philosophia*. Evoking 'Zeus, whatever he may be,' the Chorus in the *Agamemnon* (v. 160) goes on to state exactly what, for them, Zeus is. He is the God who 'with truth casts the madness of pain out of the mind' (v. 165-66), the extreme remedy for the painful instability and ambiguity of the world. Zeus is the principle of all things, the identity present in difference, the posited *stability* of Meaning. Zeus, here, no longer coincides with the Zeus of Greek religion (where Meaning as 'what is there' mirrors the instability of becoming), but is essentially the power of *epi-stēmē*, which *stands firm* and 'im-poses' its Truth. But this saving 'grace' [*charis*] or power also comes 'with violence' [*biaiōs*] (v. 182). A 'violence' that reflects the alliance between Zeus and the Erinyes, between the Clear and the *Deinon*. The *Oresteia*, then, traces the course of this coming together in the *polis* of old and new Gods, in which the Terrible 'takes' its rightful place in the eternal, immutable, necessary order of things. Aeschylus' trilogy does indeed mark a key moment in the history of Meaning. It is the opening of the 'pro-logical' as such. The need and demand for a Logos that addresses *man:* for a divine power that relates to the question of *human Meaning*. This will be the philosopher's task. As the center of the world violently shifts from God to man, the way to Logos begins with the illogical, the rational yoked to the irrational— Tragedy. Aeschylus confirms that the ways of Zeus are unknown to man, but that now man knows *what* Zeus is. This attempt to make moral sense of Zeus will be taken up by Plato, and superseded by Aristotle. Euripides, meanwhile, literally 'explodes' it.[23]

In Euripides the 'riddle' shifts from man to the gods—whoever they may be. To label Euripides 'irrationalist' is fraught with ambiguity, because irrational, here, is the *divine* world, Source of ordinance and Meaning, the world that *makes* sense of sense in the immediate presence of deity. A world shattered but still *there*. To call the Euripidean 'hero'—Orestes, Heracles, Pentheus—'irrational' because he 'obeys'—willy-nilly—the powers that *be*, is to demand that he step outside God and the world, into a space that does not (yet) exist. Orestes is not Joseph K., they inhabit different worlds of Meaning. Euripides' deus ex machina is, in truth, god from a Terrible Machine, whose only 'logic' is cruel, indifferent presence. No longer immediate presence of Meaning, but unreasoning mechanical imposition of a Meaning—a God— that for man no longer makes sense, or is patently unjust. The *Orestes* is tragic farce because the gods have become farcical, not man. 'Hail, Apollo,' cries Orestes, 'for your prophetic oracles! True prophet, not false! And yet, when I heard you speak, I thought I heard the whispers of some fiend speaking through your mouth.' (*Orestes*, 1667-69).[24] *This* deus ex machina is not designed to rescue a botched play but a botched God. I consider *Heracles* the most 'terrible' of Greek tragedies. The noblest of heroes, returning to his family after completing his Labors, is struck down by divine Madness, child of Night. But Madness, here, is not mere *Tychē* or unreasoning indifference: the *God* is sent by Hera, driven by 'jealousy of Zeus for a mortal woman's sake' (*Heracles*, 1008-09). The laceration between man and God becomes a seething river of blood. Olympian God—like Ahab's Whale—displays 'unexampled, intelligent malignity' [MD Chap. 41]. Heracles' *questioning* god means precisely that the god *is there*. *This* is tragedy: the divine world shattered, but still there. 'Then Zeus—*whoever Zeus may be*—begot me for Hera's hatred.' 'Who could offer prayers to such a goddess?' (*Heracles*, 1263-64, 1307-08). *This* is terrible: the 'plosion' of godhead. In the *Heracles* we witness the death throes of a world where the power of God to guarantee the Meaning *of* Meaning, to wrest Meaning from Chaos, to determine the determinate, is crumbling. Heracles slaughters *determinate beings*, his wife and sons. It is not ignorance but a madness *not his own* that has separated— abstracted—the determinate from its determinateness and violently stripped the hero of his senses. He will find refuge in Theseus' purely human and 'political' *philia*, the end of the Homeric Gods. The poet puts in question his own tragic poetry: 'If god is truly god, he is perfect, lacking nothing. These are poet's wretched lies.' (*Heracles*, 1345-46). God, not Euripides, is mad.

---

[23] Latin *explodere*: to drive off the stage by clapping.

[24] *The Complete Greek Tragedies*, ed. D. Grene and R. Lattimore (New York: Washington Square Press, 1967). *Orestes* and *Heracles* are translated by William Arrowsmith.

The Bacchae is the culmination and closure of Greek Tragedy—at once parody of Origin and testament of faith. The rationality of the real is shot through with an 'infrastructure' of madness. Meaning is inseparable from the meaningless. Dionysus, *deinos, is* the meaningless, 'full of meaning.' Of Meaning as presence, in Time. The Mad God—like the Machine—mocks the very logic that he *is.* This dying God will breathe his last in the Aristotelian 'God,' thought thinking itself, always awake—the philosopher's God. Aristotle in fact posits a *newly ambiguous* God, both of and not of this world, specifically designed to strip God of any possible ambiguity. To strip Him, then, of that Origin and Meaning which will make a new beginning in the Gospel according to John: 'In the beginning was the Word [*Logos*], and the Word was with [*pros*] God, and the Word was God.' But the 'pro-logue' of this new chapter in the history of Meaning is Aristotle's cosmic God with no 'shadow of turning.'[25] A God that is perhaps, paradoxically, in the ambiguity of active *nous,* more private than public—an idiot's God? Is the God that will guarantee Meaning for nearly two millennia Himself a veiled failure of Meaning underlying and belying the Logos itself? A mere shadow of Truth? '...a walking shadow ... a tale told by an idiot, full of sound and fury, signifying nothing.'[26]

III. Dia-Logos: The Truth of Shadow

> Hegel is *also* the thinker of irreducible difference ... the last philosopher of the book and the first thinker of writing.
> *Of Grammatology*, p. 26

The breakthrough of 'grammatology': by destroying 'the transcendental authority and dominant category of *epistēmē: being,'* 'signified in its brilliance and glory' [OG 92; 286], Nietzsche broached/breached [*entamer*] Meaning as self-presence of the present. Eclipse of Being. Death of God. But Hegel? A question: Is the closure of ontotheology in Hegel's Logic simply the serpent that bites its own tail, or does the circle open, while still remaining—somehow—a circle? [see PS 19]. Nietzsche, a half-century after Hegel, in crying out that God is dead, also explicitly identified His killers. But perhaps Hegel's cry is more original and more originary: 'Find the slayer!' If *this* is what Hegel's *Logic* is all about, it is by no means as 'circular' as it appears. 'In effect I believe that Hegel's text is necessarily fissured; that it is something more and other than the circular closure of its representation.'[27] Hegelian

---

[25] D. Ross, *Aristotle* (London: Methuen & Co., 1923, 1971), p. 183.

[26] *Macbeth*, Act V, Scene 5.

[27] J. Derrida, *Positions*, trans. A. Bass (Chicago: University of Chicago Press, 1981), p. 77.

logos, death of Logos—broaching the abyss [*Abgrund*], 'breaking' the ground [*Grund*]. 'Through' [*dia*] logos, the 'plosion' of logocentrism.

The 'History of Meaning' has proven to be less a 'failure' than a 'transfiguration' of God and Meaning, a transformation beginning with originary immediacy and passing through countless forms of mediation—in search, perhaps, of a new beginning, a new immediacy? An originless Origin, or a new conception of the Originary? The 'Death of God,' for the most part, has not been taken too seriously: God is Dead! Long live God! What *is* important is that there be no permanent laceration in the fabric of a Meaning woven and guaranteed by God—no Gap, no return to the Abyss. God, swallowed by a Night of His own making ('Night gave birth by herself to Death') [HES 211-12], is then promptly vomited up again like Jonah from the whale—'a changed man,' a changed God. For Hegel, God dies many times.[28] And is reborn once? In the *Phenomenology* the death of God as an object of consciousness is posited as a necessary moment of spirit on its way towards absolute knowing, where this 'painful feeling … is the expression of innermost self-knowledge, the return of consciousness into the depths of the night in which I = I.' [PS 476]. Hegel's night of finite spirit, in which the absolute is emptied of all content, is the figure in which all figures vanish, the abyss of bewilderment that is the womb of absolute spirit. In the last paragraph of the *Phenomenology* the plunge into the night of pure self-consciousness is presented as the culmination of the entire experience of consciousness, the *Aufhebung* of Dasein and its transformation into a 'new Dasein,' 'now reborn of the spirit's knowledge'—'a new world and a new shape of spirit.' [PS 492].[29] This *neue Dasein* is the key figure in that violent break with God and the history of Meaning which opens Hegel's *Logic*. Bataille/Derrida have called for a loss, sacrifice, or willful destruction of Meaning, accusing Hegel of never exceeding that circle of absolute knowledge which he himself has drawn. I contest this position and question the notion of a 'transgressive relationship that links the world of meaning to the world of nonmeaning' [RGE 275 *et passim*]. Hegel has no need to link separate worlds of meaning and nonmeaning, because these worlds, in the *Logic*, are *absolutely inseparable*. The 'nonmeaning' triad of being—nothing—becoming 'is' the permanent 'infrastructure' of Dasein as the originary structure of meaning[30]—

---

[28] W. Jaeschke, in 'Philosophical Theology and Philosophy of Religion,' states that 'it is possible to distinguish several—at least five—different meanings of this pronouncement' [God is dead] in Hegel's texts.' See NPHPR, p. 1.

[29] [*Aufhebung*—from the verb *aufheben*, to supersede—is a 'canceling' that preserves what has been canceled, 'lifting' it to a higher level. A surpassing while maintaining. It is the essence of Hegelian self-contradiction and is the heart of his dialectic.]

[30] 'Infrastructure' is an explicit reference to Derrida: see *Of Grammatology*, and R. Gasché, *The Tain of the Mirror: Derrida and the Philosophy of Reflection*

of abstraction as separation of the inseparable. Every true meaning is a figure of Dasein, which is the 'transgressive' par excellence, the unremitting plosion of its own horizon of meaning. The 'ground' [*Grund*]³¹ of 'being' is the abyss [*Abgrund*] where being founders—and, with being, nothing and becoming. This 'foundering' is the failure of Meaning in which dialectical meaning constitutes itself as Dasein—*Grund* of its own *Abgrund*. That which founds its own foundering.

'The system of logic is the realm of shadows, the world of simple essentialities freed from all sensuous concreteness.' [SL 58]. But 'shadow' here is double-edged. Taken out of context, 'simple essentiality' could even refer to Kant's thing-in-itself, when precisely the opposite is the case. Indeed, the *Logic* is in open polemic with Kant—about shadow—about Kant's last-ditch attempt to shore up philosophy against the failure of Meaning. Kant opens his own polemic with Swedenborg by affirming: 'The realm of shadows is the dreamer's paradise.'³² Hegel turns this negative sense of shadow right back against Kant, referring to 'the spectral thing-in-itself left over by the Kantian philosophy, this abstract shadow divorced from all content' [SL 47], only to repropose his own *Reich der Schatten* a few pages later. As 'truth without veil,' *'the exposition of God as he is in his eternal essence before the creation of nature and a finite spirit'* [SL 50, Hegel's italics], the *Logic* turns from sleep to waking, from Being as cipher of God and Meaning to *'pure being,'* 'mere *immediacy* itself,' the self-contradictory *de*-ciphering cipher whose foundering gives rise to Dasein as its ground. Hegel turns from the shadow of truth, expressed in the Preface to the *Phenomenology* in the proposition 'God is being' [PS 38]—*Gott ist das Sein*—to the truth of shadow, the element of the entire *Logic*: *Gott ist Dasein*.³³ Find the slayer? The 'slayer' of God is precisely that separation *of* the inseparable—being and nothing, immediacy and mediation—which produces the 'failure of Meaning' that opens the *Logic*. The slayer is this plosion in which the supremely logical settles accounts with

(Cambridge, MA: Harvard University Press, 1986); on infrastructure in Derrida as *'constitutive* contradiction,' the sense that particularly concerns me here, see R. Gasché, 'Infrastructures and Systematicity,' in *Deconstruction and Philosophy: The Texts of Jacques Derrida*, ed. J. Sallis (Chicago: University of Chicago Press, 1987), pp. 3-20.

³¹ 'Ground/ *Grund'* is not intended here in the precise sense of Hegelian logic (see SL, II, Sec 1, Chap. 3); it is, rather, a deconstruction (a 'plosion') of common philosophical 'ground'—a turning of Meaning against itself that (see below) I consider preeminently Hegelian.

³² I. Kant, first line of *Träume eines Geistersehers erläutert durch Träume der Metaphysik*, Königsberg, bei Johann Jacob Kanter, 1766.

³³ I. Valent, 'Il problema del "Dasein" nella critica kantiana dell'ontoteologia' [PDK], in *Dio e la ragione*, ed. M. Ruggenini (Genoa: Marietti, 1993), p.139.

the absolutely illogical. *Dasein* rises from the ashes of *Sein* as the true cipher of the dialectic. *Da*: *Là* cendre. Meaning, for Hegel, is no longer given or guaranteed by the grace of God, but points to the dis-grace, the fall from grace, of God and Being, and the fatal rigidity of an Absolute that poses as absolute identity and absolute difference. The plosion of Logos in the self-negation of the absolute means more and other than 'taking the negative *seriously*' [RGE 259]. Consider, rather, Hegel's ringing affirmations of the inseparability of immediacy and mediation [SL 68], being and nothing [SL 85]. In *posing* as absolute immediacy, pure being is *opposed* to the truth of shadow in that 'shadowy realm' where being *is* nothing. And in *posing* as absolutely abstract, pure being is not *imposed upon* by nothing. Rather, the separation of being and nothing founders in the 'stable unity' of becoming, which is itself a moment of that foundering which Hegel calls *Aufhebung*, true shadow of Dasein. As the concrete unity of vanishing moments in every dialectical movement, Dasein is 'determinate being,' or 'determinateness as such in the form of being, of *immediacy*' [SL 110]. Dasein is the true face of a new immediacy. Being—nothing—becoming founder—are *aufgehoben*—because they are mere names, meaningless *and* 'full of meaning.' The first triad presents not the narrowest but the broadest horizon of meaning—the meaningful *as such*. Dasein is by no means the emptiest name of the absolute, but is a positing of the absolute's unnamability. The truth of shadow is *dialectical judgment*: the realm of shadows where every figure of Dasein is a meaning, and Dasein is the womb that opens out onto the totality of meaning. Dasein as the 'outcome' of the first triad is the first logical figure: it is the condition of any possible determination or figure, beginning with that determinate *disfiguration* 'being—nothing—becoming' which posits its own total absence of determination. Logic is the condition of the illogical—just as the illogical is the condition of logic. In this sense the *Logic* itself, in the 'form and torment' of its writing, is precisely that 'commentary on its own absence of meaning' which is *called for* by Bataille/Derrida [RGE 261]. The first logical 'advance' is a retreat into the ground, and Dasein as ground is grounded in *Abgrund* or, better, is *grounding Abgrund*, where *Abgrund* is the *Abyss of Origin*—a *new chaos*. This is Hegel's terrible rift in the history of Meaning. Absolute Meaning demands an *Ursprung* [origin, source] from which to spring. But in the 'failure of Meaning' Origin founders, and its crystal plunge is the very *Sprung* or movement of the concept, the 'spasm' of the dialectic—godless meaning, the death of God. Dasein is the originary structure of meaning (logos) in a double sense: meaning as identity of difference, self-contradiction, dialecticity proper; and meaning as the unremitting resolution and reposition of contradiction throughout the *Logic*. But even the *terrible* (being *is* nothing) originary spasm of Dasein is no '*empty*' form of the *Aufhebung*' [RGE 275]: in the *Logic* the illogical appears *as such*—and *as such* is *aufgehoben*. Dasein is a double mask: of the illogical and of the concept. As mask of the illogical, the illogical *is there* in every dialectical movement; and since Dasein is the mask, or structure, of the concept, while the concept is the movement of Dasein, in this dialectical encounter that spans the entire *Logic* the Dasein of the concept shows itself to be the concept of Dasein. [PDK 135].

'No more than any other, the Hegelian text is not made of a piece. While respecting its faultless coherence, one can decompose its strata and show that it *interprets itself.*' [RGE 260]. Does Derrida go far enough? As, precisely, an 'other structure of unity' [OG 86], the *Logic* does not merely interpret itself—no, it *deconstructs* itself, destroying, 'ploding,' transforming the time-honored Meaning of each of its key terms. *Wissenschaft—science—epistēmē.* With what must science begin? With the failure of the *meaning* of science. God—Being—Origin—Logos—Absolute—Thinking—Judgment—Meaning—Time: Hegel turns them all against themselves. The *Logic* is a wake for their mass suicide. They should all be written *sous rature.* The fact that Hegel does not do so—does not 'erase' but *writes* 'being *is* nothing,' the irrational par excellence—shows the *terrible* power of his dialectic. As 'the first thinker of writing,' Hegel has no fear of ambiguity. He posits *and* overcomes it in every figure of Dasein. The free play of the concept (Dasein, mask of freedom *and* necessity) is not ineffable precisely because, while deconstructing the very words it uses, it can in fact *be written.*

Dasein—not presence but presenting absence and absenting presence—and this is shadow. But shadow has *its* own *time*, which is not chronological but purely 'logical.' An *other* time,[34] whose image is neither line nor circle, but the imageless originary structure of Dasein. Cronus, last of the Gods to end his tale: Aristotle's Time, the ciphering of active *nous*, the permanence of Being as presence. Meanwhile, it is important to distinguish the dialectic and the time of the *Logic* from those of the *Phenomenology.* If Cronus—Master of Dionysus, the Tragic Mask—is identified with *logical* becoming, then the entire edifice of the Hegelian logic crumbles in the *failure* of the 'failure of Meaning.' The *Phenomenology* presents a 'servile,' fettered dialectic, essentially limited by the oppositions of consciousness in the realm of finite spirit. And *time* in the *Phenomenology*, like the 'old' Dasein, is clearly something to be *overcome.* Time is 'the concept itself that *is there*,' but spirit only appears in time 'just so long as it has not *grasped* its pure concept, i.e. has not annulled time.' [PS 487]. Which, in the *Logic*, is exactly what occurs in the *zeitlos* 'time' of shadow. The *Logic* is structure as shadow that *is there.* Logical time is another name for the 'infrastructure' of Dasein. Here, infrastructure points

---

[34] Derrida has questioned whether the word 'time' is appropriate in such a context, since 'Time is that which is thought on the basis of Being as presence...' 'An *other* time' is intended to underscore the *difference* between this, and the 'metaphysical' conception of time. See *Margins of Philosophy* (Brighton: The Harvester Press, 1982), pp. 60-63.

to *constitutive* contradiction—to the *illogical* not as contradiction *within* the 'circular closure' of dialectic, but as constitutive *of* the originary structure of meaning. Dasein—double mask, of the first triad as infrastructure, and of the concept—is indeed 'necessarily fissured.' A logical contradiction such as 'being is nothing' points, *ambiguously*, on one hand to dialectical becoming, but on the other to *irreducible difference*—the discrepancy between an explicit statement and how it is stated. The question is not of presence but of difference. The constitutive contradiction of Dasein consists in the irreducible difference it contains between the logical figure and the disfigured, the illogical. The 'infra-structure' of Dasein, moreover, is no underground or subsoil, but the very fiber of the originary structure itself. This 'terrible' relation between structure and infrastructure that irreducibly exceeds dialectic as presence of the present—logocentrism—is the very movement—the spasm—of dialecticity. Dasein, accordingly, is *undecidable* in two irreducible senses that constitute the crowning ambiguity of the *Logic*. On one hand, the moments being/ nothing/becoming indicate the impossibility of meaning—a closed circle, undecidable precisely because *decided once and for all*. But on the other, Dasein is precisely that which *has no Origin*—it is the resource, not the source of the logical. Dasein is determinate being *as such* and never *a* determinate being. It is the determinate that as such is indeterminate and therefore undecidable. 'Irreducible difference': the difference between logical figure and disfiguration *is not reduced* in the entire course of the *Logic*, which is not circular but timelessly, *terribly*, transgressive. Can dialecticity, then, move outside its own horizon, ploding its own privacy—its idiocy? The horizon of the *Logic* is the horizon of Meaning, but its foundation is the foundering of Meaning. Its *Grund*, an *Abgrund*. Its Pyramid, a Pit. Its wake, a celebration of the failure of Meaning.

    And God? Does it make sense to speak of a 'God' in the *Logic*, a rebirth of 'deity' after the plosion of God and Being? Well, if the dialecticity of Hegelian 'logos' is itself a new structure of meaning, then the History of Meaning demands a new God. Onto-Theo-Logy: in Hegel, Logic swallows Being and God, but if a god *is there* nonetheless it can only be *the concept*. And originary *structure*—what, after all, 'is' structure? Another 'poet's wretched lie'? The Terrible all over again? But to 'deconstruct' structure means to deconstruct de-con-*struction* itself. Have we a ghost in the machine? Or rather, a *Geist* yes, but is there a machine? Hegel 'ploded' Absolute Meaning. But can 'plosion' be 'ploded,' or is the truth of plosion some secret undecidability—ex- or im- plosion? An open question: 'plosion' in *The Bacchae*. Does Euripides *ex*plode the Mad God, clapping him off the stage, or *im*plode him into the very marrow of 'Being'? Perhaps not failure, but *sacrifice* of Meaning. The Machine: is Hegel its most powerful adversary or its greatest—unwitting?—proponent? In turning from Hegel to Melville, recalling Marx's cry (from Aeschylus) 'I hate all the Gods!' (1844), the landscape is still littered with Euripidean *personae*, prey to some god 'from a machine,' a *terrible* God, a God from the Abyss of Origin. An ancient playwright's vision of a broken world? But the fact remains that *the machine is now*. A Mad God, *there* on the horizon and ready to dawn, enveloping mankind and Meaning in its foreign darkness.

IV. Epi-Logos: An Angry God

> Or is it, that as in essence whiteness is not so much a color as the visible absence of color, and at the same time the concrete of all colors; is it for these reasons that there is such a dumb blankness, full of meaning, in a wide landscape of snows—a colorless, all-color of atheism from which we shrink.
> *Moby Dick*, Chap. 42

The absolute *must* be there, *needs* to be there—is *there*, and absolutely *is not* there. Hegel and Melville. Dasein and presence. Melville's tragedy. Quest for an Absolute where—alas—same *is* same and different *is* different. Pure 'cant.' Melville just 'Kant (can't)'[35] get around it. Most startling in *Pierre* are the explicit, scathing references to *'Kant, can't, cant.'* Pierre is not the Hegelian but the Kantian Idealist, condemned by his own Thought— Pure Reason—to inhabit the 'divine unidentifiableness' of the world and God. And Ahab! 'Oh! how immaterial are all materials! What things real are there, but imponderable thoughts?' [MD Chap. 127]. Pierre and Ahab, dominated, devastated by their *own* omens, their *own* secrets—insisting to the last on the presence, the infinity of 'Truth without veil' and the untruth of omen and secret. Monstrous. The Abyss. How much has this to do with the ungraspable—*begrifflos*—thing-in-itself? Truth as subject, not substance. The problem of Meaning restricted to the element of Thought (= Being) alone. 'If no advance is made beyond the abstract negative aspect of dialectic [i.e. Kant's expositions] ... reason is incapable of knowing the infinite.' [SL 56]. *Bad* infinity—Herman Melville. The ultimate ambiguity and undecidability of *Moby Dick* is due, in part, to this abstract negative dialectic, exemplified by the contrast between Ishmael's and Ahab's understanding of the Whale, 'unsolved to the last.' Meanwhile, the sardonic narrator in *Pierre*—'I write precisely as I please' [P 280]—speaks only to mock and to parody. Ahab: 'something in this slippery world that can hold' [MD Chap. 108]. Hegel: what 'holds' is the slippery itself, the infrastructure of Dasein. *Truth*. 'I tear all veils,' proclaims Pierre early on, before foundering in 'this night, which wraps my soul.' [P 91]. 'With the soul of an Atheist, he wrote down the godliest things ... And every thing else he disguised under the so conveniently adjustable drapery of all stretchable Philosophy. For the more

---

[35] H. Melville, *Pierre* [P] (New York: Meridian Classic, 1988), p. 303.

and the more he wrote, and the deeper and deeper he dived, Pierre saw the everlasting elusiveness of Truth; the universal lurking insincerity of even the greatest and purest written thoughts.' [P 380].

Melville, like Hawthorne, was a devout pessimist in an optimistic age. The Puritan loosens his noose. Emerson transforms God Himself into 'the divine,' which Thoreau promptly discovers at Walden Pond and Whitman celebrates in every leaf of grass. And all this—somehow, roughly—in Kant's name. Transcendentalism. Romanticism in a Puritan setting. The divine spark (Aristotle's active *nous?*) in man and nature. The real, material world expresses deity as a series of signs, Ahab's 'linked analogies,' his ambiguous return to the immediacy of Meaning. Melville stares with horror at the 'infrastructure' of it all, its foreign depth, the terrible cleavage that *is there.* The Eternal Puritan—an Angry God. In *Moby Dick*, tragedy; in *Pierre*, farce. *Eternal* separation: soul/body, good/evil, saved/damned, light/dark, white/black. Fixed oppositions that create Absolute Meaning. *Begrifflos: God* as the *abstract* negativity of an Absolute that *cannot be grasped.* Undecidable: hell on earth. A/wake for the sleeping spirit. Xenophon: 'It is in sleep that the soul best shows its divine nature.' [GI 135]. Plato: body as prison of the soul. Subject, not substance. 'Oh God! that man should be a thing for immortal souls to sieve through!' [MD Chap. 125]. And the *Parsee*, Ahab's waking shadow—the fire that never sleeps. Ishmael, the Pacific: 'mixed shades and shadows, drowned dreams, somnambulisms, reveries; all that we call lives and souls, lie dreaming, dreaming, still.' [MD Chap. 111]. Hegel, *Philosophy of Religion*: 'The anguish of knowing evil is registered in terms of a series of historical gradations of inwardization, starting with the Parsee religion which keeps the cleavage external.'[36] Chasm, Chaos. External—the Abyss—the Whale. Melville's riddle: if God exists, He must be the source of good *and* evil, and above all of Meaning and Value. And if he does *not* exist—*cant.* 1741, Jonathan Edwards, 'Sinners in the Hands of an Angry God.' Terrible Vengeance and Wrath of the *Infinite God.* Derrida, Theologism, the major obstacle to grammatology—a secret script 'formed by the Lord God's own finger.' [OG 76]. *Pierre*, terrible parody: 'The Finger of God? But it is not merely the Finger, it is the whole outspread Hand of God; for doth not Scripture intimate, that He holdeth all of us in the hollow of His hand?—a Hollow, truly!' [P 168]. Pierre—Gospel Truth. The *Tragic Mask* in Hegel's logic is the 'cant'—Kant's 'can't.' For Hegel, as I see it, the tragic consists in the failure to grasp Dasein's infrastructure and undecidability; in the separation of illogical and logic; in the isolation of identity from difference, being from nothing, vanishing from vanishing, laceration from reconciliation. *Abstract* negativity—Pentheus dismembered. And the tragic in Melville? The shadow of truth, which in Hegel 'does not pass over but has passed over' into the truth of shadow, is *fingered* and fixed in the 'blackness of darkness.' There is

[36] W. Desmond, 'Evil and Dialectic' in NPHPR, p. 167.

no escape. Melville *fixes* the dialecticity of 'being-there,' *pins it down*, looks it in the eye and, unblinking, accepts the consequences: 'Silence is the only Voice of our God.' 'These drowning men do drown.' [P 237; 343]. 1856, Hawthorne: 'Melville informed me that he had "pretty much made up his mind to be annihilated." ...He can neither believe, nor be comfortable in his unbelief.' *Bad* infinity. Terrible: the *ill*-logical. Melville's sickness unto death.

Cleavage—an Angry God. The failure 'to bring thoughts together.' Hegel: 'I am the struggle between the extremes of finitude and infinity. I am not one of the fighters locked in battle, but both, and I am the struggle itself. *I am fire and water...*'[37] Ishmael: 'This fire-ship ... on the great shroud of the sea.' Ahab, the Persian—'Clear spirit of clear fire'—would parch the sea, turn it into ash, to isolate and reveal a beached, solitary whale, terrible creation of his own obsession, the Absolute he cannot live with or live without. *The Whale*, no more *there* than *not* there—everywhere, and nowhere. *Là* cendre. Melville against the background of Hegel's *Logic*. In Dasein, the logical, Hegel sees the illogical, the infrastructure. In *Moby Dick*, and in *Pierre*, I see two *bad* readings—of the first triad, and of Dasein. Not illogical but *ill*-logical—unfounded foundering, the foundering of foundering, the failure of the failure of Meaning. 'The clear spirit of clear fire' *is* 'the blackness of darkness'—the truth of shadow shrouded by the shadow of truth. In Melville the riddle *and* the answer to the riddle is *God*—who *is not there*. God, for Melville, is not *dead* but *missing*—that missing piece in the puzzle of Meaning which for Ahab is Moby Dick. Absolute Evil, without which there can be no Absolute Good. But difference founders, doubly. Ahab and Ishmael. For Ahab being and nothing, pure white and pure black, are the same, absolutely—not vanishing moments but the obliteration of difference. His monomaniacal chase is for a God of Absolute Meaning where white is white and black is black. But by isolating Dasein from its infrastructure Ahab creates the exact opposite of what he seeks. God turns out to be an Infinite Empty Ciphering, where white slips into black and black into white, forever. Find the slayer! Dasein is the slayer of God as Absolute Meaning, but Ahab creates a monster—Absolutely Slippery Being, *ill-logical*, resembling that instability of 'sense-certainty' (now it's here—no, now it's there; no, now it's gone) which opens the *Phenomenology*. But in the 'realm of shadows' there is absolutely no escape. The Whale is Ahab's private cipher, meaningless Meaning, the dead march that mocks all logic. Indifference. No difference between predator and prey. Ahab is poised on the edge of that abyss where *Grund* is *Abgrund*, that abyss where Hegel's logic *demands the failure of Meaning*. But he will not take the plunge. With all his might, Ahab insists on grasping the 'unmistakable' Whale as absolute cleavage, the 'unexampled intelligent malignity' of an Angry God. But absolute cleavage

---

[37] *Lectures on the Philosophy of Religion*, Introduction, in *Hegel On Art, Religion, Philosophy* (New York: Harper Torchbooks, 1970), p.187 (trans. modified).

is no cleavage. Here, Good and Evil, neither separate nor inseparable, are the same. Imposing Evil, for 'crazy Ahab'—'demonic, madness maddened'—is all the Good there is. Ahab is *lost*. His terrible Fire illuminates the night, but cannot transform it into day. The failure of Meaning fails and Ahab founders, literally sucked down into the 'vortex' where no meaning *is there*. Ishmael alone escapes to tell the tale. The shadow of truth. While for Ahab there is one Captain—'Fate's lieutenant'—and one God, for Ishmael Moby Dick is not an Angry God but the simple 'unsourced' fluidity of divine mindless power—'ubiquitous' and 'immortal' ('ubiquity in time'). The Whale is effaced, 'has no face,' just a brow 'pleated with riddles' of Deity [MD Chap. 79]. The breaching of the Whale—for Ahab his 'act of defiance'—is, for Ishmael, 'the grand god revealing himself.' 'Meaning,' *whatever it may be*, is the divine that takes *all* forms. Ishmael is the one who sees in 'the whiteness of the whale' the *indefiniteness* of the divine, its rightful, terrible mystery. 'Hideous whiteness'—'this crowning attribute of the terrible'—by 'its indefiniteness shadows forth the heartless voids and immensities of the universe.' [MD Chap. 42]. In that 'dumb blankness, full of meaning' can we perhaps glean an *abstract* shadow—a sign—of the infrastructure of Dasein, of *foundering*—of that unnamable undecidability 'presupposed' by the *Phenomenology* in which Hegelian meaning constitutes itself? Dasein, slayer of the Name of God, that gives God a *bad* name. The 'atheism from which we shrink' is, precisely, meaning without God. Hegel's 'god'—the concept— is, precisely, determinate indeterminateness, ordered chaos. Meaning. The 'terrible' in both Hegel and Melville is the confusion of man and god, so that the meaning of man *is* the meaning of god. Hegel, accordingly, claims to know *both*—and Melville, *neither*. This is the essence of the Tragic: the Enigma has always been 'man'—*là* cendre, cinders, whatever is left of the fire—since the only meaning that *is there* is the meaning of man.

Pierre: the *Ambiguities*, as *ill*-logical. Dasein—a logic whose infrastructure is the *illogical*. Not *a* determination but determination *as such*. The broadest horizon of meaning. In a *bad* reading, the *presence* of determination as such—'ambiguity requires the logic of presence' [OG 71]—is taken as *any determination whatsoever*. The first, originary opening of meaning as such, misread as full openness of the totality of meanings. Chaos mistaken for Truth. The originary structure of meaning reduced to presence of the vanishing of vanishing. Infrastructure stripped of structure. Dasein, *determiner* of the indeterminate, abandoned to the undecidability of indeterminate determination. Omniguity. Ambiguity all around. 'Dark night of the soul.' Pierre, as godlike positer of Meaning, posits him*self* at the center of a raving omniguity of relations: mother as sister—father as saint *and* sinner—'sister' (and *here* the center will 'plode') as wife—fiancée as cousin. Ambiguity piled upon ambiguity. No escape—everything escapes him. Small wonder, then, that Pierre needs a *Begriff*— something to *grasp*—

something *deeper* than this whirling vortex of his own making. Something that sustains the omniguous superficiality of *his* world. Pierre *needs a secret,* something 'in-itself,' a deeper Meaning, a deep, deep Origin that can make sense of his *own* nonsense. An excavation, for something that *is not there.* Melville's narrator is pitiless. In place of Origin, we are given a terrible parody of Origin. 'Nothing but surface stratified on surface. To its axis, the world being nothing but superinduced superficies. By vast pains we mine into the pyramid; by horrible gropings we come to the central room; with joy we espy the sarcophagus; but we lift the lid—and no body is there!— appallingly vacant as vast is the soul of a man.' [P 323]. And indeed Pierre, with all his 'crew,' like Ahab, 'breathing his defiance,' founders and is sucked down into his own abyss. 'Are they all 'sleep?' 'The riddle of that face.' *Images.* Crushed between two ambiguous, ambiguously smiling portraits—of his father as a young man, and of *'a stranger's head, by an unknown hand'* [P 391] in which his 'sister' thinks she recognizes 'their' father—Pierre awakes to the ambiguity *of* Ambiguity, to the ultimate undecidability and irreducible ambiguity of his world. His ambiguous, self-proclaimed 'sister' could be just anyone at all—'wife or sister, saint or fiend!' The Center *cannot* hold. Pierre awakes, only to meet the 'untimely, timely end—ambiguous still' [P 402].

Jena, 1805–06, *Nacht der Aufbewahrung:* Night of Preservation.[38] *To deinon:* terrible portrait of originless origin, of source as resource that *precedes meaning and name, and is always there.* Not the night of 'I = I'—of self-consciousness, but a foreign pre/pro-dialectical world of images 'preserved in the spirit's night.' *Before* meaning, nameless terror. *Melville* inhabits and depicts this wild, relentless tempest of dream-images run amok, of images that well up from the abysmal depths of consciousness (the *un*conscious) but never exist *for* consciousness. Images that are present as absence and absent as presence [*die nicht als gegenwärtige sind*] but, unlike Dasein, are never grasped *as such.* And *this,* says Hegel, is 'man' [*Mensch, anthropos,* human being!], the enigma: 'this night, this empty nothing.' 'What exists here is night, the interior of nature—*pure self.* In phantasmagoric representations it presses in from all sides; suddenly a bloody head darts out—there another white form, and just as suddenly they vanish. We see this night when we look a human being in the eye—entering a night that becomes *terrible* [*furchtbar*]. From this eye, *the night of the world* reaches out to us.' If *logic* is a mirroring of self in other and other in self, the *tain* (a foil) of the mirror is that *energeia* which makes the mirror *reflect,* while also unmasking the mirror *as* mirror, and the image as *mirror*-image. In the structure and infrastructure of Dasein we have seen the *Abgrund*—the abyss—mirrored in Dasein as its ground— and 'other'? Yes, but an *other* 'other,' an other not of dialectical closure but of fissure. A different, originary, other. In the night of the world—the 'in-

---

[38] Hegel, 'Naturphilosophie und Philosophie des Geistes' in *Jenaer System-entwürfe III* (Hamburg: Felix Meiner Verlag, 1987), p. 172.

itself' of spirit—'pure self' as other *is not reflected* by the mirror of the eye. It is *absorbed*, is *nothing*, is *not there*. Man, 'this empty nothing,' is a stain on the mirror. A terrible shadow, a tainting of the tain—a presence, absent, that foils self/reflection and, as foil to the concept, gives us the Tragic Mask. 'Is Ahab, Ahab?' 'The greater idiot ever scolds the lesser ... Who art thou, boy? I see not my reflection in the vacant pupils of thy eyes.' [MD Chap. 125]. Hegel: from chaos, meaning. *To deinon: en ainigmati,* darkly. Melville's personae—like Oedipus—with no mirror in which to see them*selves*, are left to 'wander' [L. *ambigere*] in the night of the world.

V. Postscript: Wake of the Dead Letter

Distant, waltzing melodies, as of ambiguous fairies dancing on the heath.
            Pierre or, the Ambiguities, p. 79

1853: *Bartleby the Scrivener*: doubled écriture. Undecidable: Self-portrait or portrait of a dying God? 'Wonderful mildness.' 'The silent man.' The Terrible.

Being There: 'I would prefer not to.' The Tombs. The yard. 'The heart of the eternal pyramids.' 'Walls of amazing thickness.' 'Dead-wall reveries.'

A quiet land of masks and shadows. *All* we learn about Melville's scrivener—about his *is* and his *has been*—is that he 'would prefer not to' ... be there; he refuses to be anywhere else; and, in the P.S., that he used to work 'in the Dead Letter Office at Washington, from which he had been suddenly removed by a change in the administration.'

Sous rature? An empty cipher? *There* nevertheless? 'Il y a là cendre.'

'For the letter killeth, but the spirit giveth life.' [II. Corinthians 3,6].

Wake. Wake. A/wake. Poor Bartleby. 'He's asleep, ain't he?' 'With kings and counselors,' murmured I.

'Find the slayer!' cries Oedipus, the parricide. A cry of shadow, terrible and perfectly ambiguous. Meaningless and 'full of meaning.' We can do nothing but look on.

PART THREE

VIII. I Dream of Eudemus

a tail of the night of the world

for Gianfranco, *sempre con noi*

O night, mother of mercy, blessed night, who gives to human anguish the lovely gift of sleep, rise, rise from your abyss —
Euripides, *Orestes* vv. 173-178

— it was written I should be loyal to the nightmare of my choice.
Joseph Conrad, *Heart of Darkness*

Each one of us is this night, this pure nothing, which in its simplicity contains everything, an infinite wealth of many representations and images, none of which stands before us, or which are not as present. What exists here is night, the interior of nature—*pure self*. In phantasmagoric representations it presses in from all sides; suddenly a bloody head darts out—there another white form, and just as suddenly they vanish. We see this night when we look a human being in the eye—entering a night that becomes *terrible*. What is it? What is reaching out from this eye? I see it! *It's the night of the world.*
Hegel, *Jena Philosophy of Spirit* (my free translation)

[I advise the reader to skim through the 'sources and references' at the end before beginning to chase this Tail.]

facts: an uncertain reality

Eudemus of Cyprus is a rare case of someone who owes his place in history to a dream, and not to a dream about him but to a dream he had. I, of course, modestly, who have no place in history, often dream of Eudemus' dream. And, often, of Eudemus himself. In a world dominated by 'just plain facts' (whatever they are), I dream of Eudemus, famous for a dream. Which is not a fact but, in a manner of speaking, 'a shadow's shadow.' Wait! You say you've never heard of Eudemus, so how famous can he be. OK, 'famous' is an exaggeration. But I do dream of him often. Of him and of his dream.

Now, what are the facts?

First fact: Eudemus of Cyprus was—presumably!—born in Cyprus. When? Who knows, but, possibly, somewhere around 384 BC, the year Aristotle was born, and *that's* a fact. Just as it's a fact that Eudemus and

Aristotle were schoolmates at Plato's Academy (but I'm coming to that), so they *might* have been about the same age, or possibly not (it's not a fact). We also know that he was *banished* from Cyprus. Why? Not a clue. Why is anyone 'banished'? For spitting in the subway? No, 'banished'—sent into *exile*—takes something more. Some *political* reason, in my opinion. Perhaps he was riled up about the Vietnam War and told everyone on Cyprus they were fighting on the wrong side. This is plausible! But highly anachronistic. How about the Peloponnesian War? A good guess, but—if, in fact, he was born about the same time as Aristotle, or even a decade or two earlier—it was already over. In 404 BC. Riled up about some other war? Absolutely possible. Likely, in fact.

Second fact: After being *banished* from Cyprus Eudemus went—straight or circuitously—to Athens, where, a political exile, he enrolled in Plato's Academy. Where—no less!—he and Aristotle became best friends. Dear, close, and inseparable *philoi* (the plural of *philos*). This is an unshakable fact. In fact, right after Eudemus' death, in battle, in Sicily, in 354 or 353 (another fact, which I shall come to in a moment), Aristotle wrote one of his earliest works, a (lost) dialogue: *Eudemus* or *On the Soul*, which was a *consolatio mortis* for his dear friend and former schoolmate. So Eudemus is also famous for this. Which, admittedly, is not one of Aristotle's most famous works, but Aristotle is *very* famous, so even his least famous (lost) dialogue is, relatively, famous.

Third fact: After leaving Athens we find Eudemus, in 359 or 358, in Thessaly, desperately ill. At death's door, so to speak. When did he leave Athens? This is hard to say, we don't even know when he got to Athens. A better question: Why in the world did he leave Athens? Again, we haven't got a clue. Did he leave gracefully or take a powder? Who knows. I *suspect* he may have gotten riled up politically *again*, but I may well be entirely wrong. Perhaps he got riled up *philosophically*, those Platonists were a zealous bunch, with their Big Ideas about the Theory of Ideas et cetera. About the *soul*, for example. Maybe he didn't buy it, who knows. Or, perhaps, he left Athens out of unadulterated wanderlust. It's possible. A ramble. We have no facts. The fact we do have—our third fact—is that we find him, desperately ill, in Thessaly, *where he had his famous dream*. In 359 or 358. What in the world was he doing in Thessaly? Not a clue. After all, Thessaly is one of the most beautiful regions in Greece. Sun and fun! Green valleys, blue waters, shining streams, lush hills, Mount Olympus, what more could you want. Though I can imagine Eudemus saying, No place is a good place to get a sickness unto death. Despair! And he's laughing! I'm dreaming. Yes, even in Eudemus' day Thessaly was renowned for its luxury, high living, and great food. In fact 'roistering in Thessaly' was already proverbial, as Plato notes in his *Crito*—scornfully! But, Plato was Plato, not a fun-lover. He had strange Ideas.

Eudemus! What are you doing in Pherae, the capital of Thessaly, around 358 BC? There's deep shit in Thessaly. A river of shit. A plague of deep-shit Tyrants. A wide, wide river. Jason of Pherae, with major imperial ambitions, assassinated in 370, followed by his brother Polydorus for just one year until his brother (possibly, I'll get back to this) Alexander of Pherae poisoned him. (Most people back then spent their spare time studying poisons.) Alexander takes tyranny seriously, he pulls no punches: aggressions, massacres, raidings, plunderings, besiegings, assassinations. In a word: carnage. And Eudemus saunters off to Pherae! And falls deathly sick. (Of what? Not a clue. Plague? I doubt it.) And *has his famous dream.* The most famous report of this dream is in Cicero—famous himself—who reports it as if it were Aristotle in person reporting it. But there are other sources. In any event:

> Eudemus of Cyprus, on a journey through Thessaly, in its cele-
> brated capital, Pherae, under the cruel sway of the tyrant Alexander,
> fell desperately ill. The doctors had given him up for dead. In this
> terrible state Eudemus had a dream. He beheld a young man of
> extreme beauty, who delivered three prophesies: Eudemus would
> soon recover, the tyrant would fall, and after five years Eudemus
> would return home.

Lo and behold, Eudemus did recover, immediately. Alexander of Pherae was soon killed by his wife's three brothers, his body thrown into the streets for the populace to piss on and the dogs to mangle. As for Eudemus' returning home after five years—

Fourth fact: This brings us to our fourth Eudemusian fact. Five years later here he is, at the gates of Siracusa, fighting. (No, Siracusa was famous for walls, Thebes was the one with gates.) Not fighting with a *philos* over philosophy, no, fighting a battle. In the heat of battle. In Eudemus' time, in Greece, in Sicily, or wherever, there was a battle every day of the week, and several on Sundays to honor the gods. Now, how in the world did Eudemus of Cyprus end up in Siracusa, five years after his *coming home* dream? One hell of a good question! Who knows. It's a fact, period. Here he is, *remembering his dream*, and saying to himself, What's happening? I'm a Cypriot, not a Sicilian. And, with that, he was killed. Fell in battle. The end. No, actually this is the beginning, not the end.

Fifth fact: Cicero writes that Aristotle relates that, back in the Academy, when, mindful of the dream, towards the end of the fifth year they had high hopes Eudemus would return to Cyprus from Sicily, they heard he'd been slain in a battle near Siracusa. *At this point* the Platonists in Athens— and, possibly, the Platonists in Siracusa too, Plato had friends in Siracusa, he'd been there three times, in 387, 367, and 361—cooked up an *eminently Platonistic* interpretation of Eudemus' dream, namely: *The soul returns to its true home when death releases it from the prison of the body.* This was the moral they drew, and Aristotle heartily endorsed it in his early (lost) dialogue *Eudemus* or *On the Soul.* That the Platonists, including Aristotle, interpreted

Eudemus' dream in this way is *a fact*, our very last Eudemusian fact. It is also the reason why, in certain circles, the dream is famous to this day.

I dream I'm a historian

At this point, if I were a 'mere recording organism' I would stop right here. I've recorded the dream, and that's a fact. But we don't just record facts, we dream dreams. I hear Gianfranco laughing! Write stories, Giacomo, write another story! Dream on! Wait—*I hear Eudemus laughing too*. Along with Gianfranco. A tiny chorus of laughter, radiating and glowing. I told you, I often *dream* of Eudemus' dream, *and*, often, of Eudemus himself. I'm dreaming him now. I'm dreaming him, I'm going to *keep on dreaming him*, and nothing and no one can stop me! I dream of Eudemus in Thessaly, what in the world is he up to. A soldier of no fortune, and with a name to come? A common everyday mercenary in a world overrun with mercenaries, obsessed with mercenaries, plagued by mercenaries? Mercenaries and slaves, that's the world! Did you know that Athens, the cradle of democracy, in the 6th and 5th centuries BC had the largest slave population in the ancient world—some 80,000 'souls' (if they had souls). The Athenians had an average of three or four slaves per household. It reminds me of present-day Venetians with their dogs, three or four per household—here in Venice, the cradle of European cathood! *Soriani* like my Gina and my Gilda saved the city from the plague and over the past thirty years have become an endangered species, while dogs shit merrily away in the streets and you're lucky if they don't bite you. A general census of Attica in 317 BC reports: 21,000 (democratic) citizens, 10,000 (slightly democratic) metics (i.e. foreign residents, a.k.a. legal immigrants), and 400,000 slaves. I rest my case. Plato, by the way—an average middle-class Athenian—owned five slaves at the time of his death; he reports that rich Athenians had fifty slaves each, easily. Greece, Sicily, wherever, a world of soldiers and slaves resting on a foundering foundation of mercenaries. Mercenary versus mercenary, that's what's happening. Is this the sickness that plagues Eudemus? That nearly killed him in Pherae, where he had his dream? I don't buy it. I can't believe it. It's not what I'm dreaming, of Eudemus. I dream his world, of chaos and carnage. Wait! I see it now. Siracusa—I've been there, lots of times. Selling earrings. Working on the art magazine. The Ear of Dionysius has eavesdropped on my joys and my sorrows. Wolfango, my friend, my brother! Look! 353 BC, Siracusa! Eudemus in the heat of battle. Wait! Let's set the scene. Back up to 415, the 'Athenian Expedition.' Back, back, further back, ye gods, *I'm dreaming the entire Peloponnesian War*. And what a war it was! Twenty-seven long years, 431 to 404. Ups and backs, lefts and rights, on seas and on lands, the Aegean, the Ionian, Attica, Sparta, the Peloponnesus, Athens, Corinth, Thebes, Macedonia, Ionia, Thrace, Sicily, the more the merrier. All over the place. Thucydides, in long tangled sentences difficult to translate, wrote its history in painstaking and dramatic detail. He was also marvelously imaginative, inventing all sorts of speeches that no one ever actually delivered, but could quite plausibly have delivered. For starters he invented Pericles' Funeral Oration, then the realpolitik Melian Dialogue (I'm coming to that), the speeches of generals on all sides, and lots more. Now, the title of his book is, precisely, 'The History of the War Fought Between Athens and Sparta by Thucydides the Athenian'—even the title is long. (Thucydides himself started out as an Athenian commander—a *strategos*—but was *banished* after losing a battle with Spartans in Thrace—they were fighting over silver mines—so he happily set out on his new—far more successful—career as a historian.) But the war has gone down in history as the *Peloponnesian War*, giving everyone who hasn't read Thucydides' *long* book the impression that the whole war was fought in the Peloponnesus, which is totally untrue. Fake news! It was the Athenians who called it the Peloponnesian War—the ancient Athenians, followed, fervently, by Athens-loving modern historians ('cradle of democracy' et cetera). Spartans, all the Peloponnesians, and many other ancient Greeks—and, most definitely, the Siracusans—had every reason in the world to call it the Athenian War (or, for symmetry's sake, the Attic War—Attic as in Attica, the region around Athens, no reference to attics). Remember the Vietnam War? OK, it's true it was fought in Vietnam, but the Vietnamese call it the American War, and with extremely good reason. It's the peace-loving Americans who call it the Vietnam War, bravely waged to save the world from commie gooks.

Now, how did it all begin? (The Athens-Sparta war I mean, never mind Vietnam.) OK, I'm backing up even more—back to the *Athenian Empire*. But—let's be fair—before that, we have the *Persian Empire*. The Greco-Persian Wars, from 499 to 448, known in Greece, more simply, as the Persian War. (And what did the Persians call them/it?) Persia, a great Empire! Darius the Great, followed by Xerxes I, attempted to subjugate Ancient Greece, and they came reasonably close to succeeding. A great war, between 'barbarians' and Greeks, though Thucydides isn't wrong when he calls the so-called Peloponnesian War 'the greatest and most terrible war' (so far, of course), since, as he notes, the Persian War was a relatively 'speedy' war, with just a few battles. But they were great! Memorable. Theatrical. Famous. Who hasn't heard of Marathon! The lethal power of the Greek hoplites, armored men who locked shields to form phalanxes. In 490 BC an Athenian army of 10,000 hoplites resisted and then *routed* 25,000 Persians, whom everyone thought were invincible. Bless you, Philippides (some say Pheidippides, take your pick), running all that way to Athens without stopping to yell 'we have won' before collapsing and dying. Mythic! Ten years later Xerxes returned to Greece with a staggeringly large army of, possibly, 250,000 men. But, amazingly, the army itself staggered. This second invasion is famous for the battle of Thermopylae, one of the great last stands in recorded history. Unlike General Custer, King Leonidas and his 300

Spartans enjoyed a *magnificent* and *glorious* end. Their sacrifice opened the way
to ultimate victory, especially when the Athenian navy got into the act. Those
tricky Athenians were genuine philosophers—*philoi sophia*, lovers of trickiness.
(*Sophia*, a long story: from cleverness to cunning, to what we call 'wisdom.')
Admirable admirals, they craftily lured the Persian ships into the Straits of
Salamis, seriously reduced their room to maneuver, and spectacularly whipped
their asses. The following year, back on land, the hoplites got back into the act,
and it was curtains for the Persians. They lost the Battle of Plataea and headed
home. The last thirty years of these wars spelled glory for the Athenians. They
kicked the Persians out of their garrisons in Macedonia and Thrace, and later
freed the Ionian cities from Persian rule. They were living it up! No more little
squabbles between city-states but big wars big time. Did you know that in the
old days, before the so-called Classical Age (from 480—the Persians—until
323, the death of Alexander the Great), warfare in Greece mostly consisted of
minor but vicious skirmishes between city-states (known as *poleis*, the plural
of *polis*). (*Poleis* with nothing better to do? Frankly, I don't know why people
had to fight all the time. Perhaps because, in their spare time, when they
weren't studying poisons they were busy reading the *Iliad*?) These skirmishes
were, in fact, usually small one-sided attacks rather than skirmishes—attacks
on the enemy's crops and harvest. Call it the bad neighbor policy. One city
would rush off to disrupt a harvest, then rush back home to harvest their own
harvest. Don't you find this shabby! Cheap shots, cheap thrills. OK, they also
did things that were less cheap, such as ravaging the countryside by uprooting
trees, burning houses and crops, and killing everyone they met outside the city
walls. It was thanks to the Persians that warfare got less shabby.

Athens! Watch out for the Athenians. Ambitions. Democrats. Big
Ideas. (Plato was an Athenian. Unlike Aristotle the Stagirite, from Stagira, in
Macedonia, and Eudemus of Cyprus, from Cyprus, presumably.) Imperialists!
You see, during the two Persian invasions—Darius, then Xerxes—the Greek
city-states all pitched in to combat the barbarians. The Hellenic League.
Athenians and Spartans together, and everyone else. Greeks. Allies. Victors.
But then, as I just said, the Athenians got Big Ideas. Philosophers. They wanted
to keep on fighting. They had their hoplites, they had their magnificent fleet,
why stop now! The Persians were on the run. Asia Minor, northern Greece, all
there for the taking. Later, they even took a (pot) shot at Egypt. The Spartans,
and their Peloponnesian friends, were not enthusiastic about all this fighting.
The Athenians started yelling 'Ionia for the Ionians!' The Spartans got fed up
and went home. So, in 478 the Athenians formed a new League, a Big League,
with hundreds of *poleis*, supposedly their *allies* but actually under their thumb.
This League was called the Delian League since its *treasury* was on the island
of Delos. Athens managed to transform most of its allies into tribute-paying
subjects or reduced them to colonies. (Or to slaves, or killed them.) There was
so much money heaped up on Delos that, in 454, Pericles, the great democrat,

moved the treasury to Athens, effectively establishing what historians (real historians, not dream-historians) call the Athenian Empire. Meanwhile, with good reason, the Peloponnesians were getting restless, so they revived their old League, called, quite logically, the Peloponnesian League, led by Sparta. This League supported oligarchies and opposed tyrannies and democracies, but, in fact, it was more 'democratic' than the 'cradle of democracy' Delian League. In any event, by 458 the two Leagues were already at each others throats. Battles all over the place, with sporadic outbreaks of peace. The Athenian fleet had become a holy terror. The Spartans, pissed off, threatened to invade Athens. Imperialist Athens was busy gobbling up tribute from its erstwhile so-called allies—Aegean islands in particular. Naxos was the first to rebel, then Thasos, they paid for it dearly, Naxos was forced to tear down its walls! Thanks to all this loot—pardón, tribute—Athens was in the throes of a cultural renaissance, with outstanding urban renewal. They built the Parthenon! Spartans at the gates? What, we worry! We'll build the Long Walls! Between our fleet and our walls no one can touch our marbles. (Many years ago I had a Dutch friend here in Venice who once used the old Dutch expression 'to fall between the wall and the ship.' With reference to how he lost his fiancée. I can still remember what this expression means, but it would take too long to explain it.) The famous Long Walls of Athens, 4 miles long, an impregnable corridor connecting the city with its ports at Piraeus and Phalerum. Siege-proof, thanks to its constant link to the sea. With the building of these walls Athens happily became an inland island. An Empire. Ye gods there's nothing like a wall! The Long Walls of Athens stood stalwartly until, alas for them, the Athenians lost the Peloponnesian War and the Spartans tore them down. Empire, how fleeting. But you can't beat a Wall, it's always a Big Idea. Practically, perhaps, a Platonic Idea. Trump! Trump! Have you been reading Plato! Your 'big, beautiful wall' across the US/Mexican border, 2,000 miles long. Bless you, Trump, truly a Big Idea. And now you have an Idea that's even Bigger, to help the Spaniards fend off those goddam nigger Bedouin rapists. Wow! A True Beauty of a Wall right across the scenic Sahara desert. The Sahara border—you say—can't be bigger than our border with Mexico. But, say the Spaniards, it's over 3,000 miles long, and we don't even have a border in the Sahara. Trump is unfazed and unfazeable. Details, *mon vieux!* We need to take walls seriously. A Wall is a Big Idea! Look, the Chinese have a truly *GREAT WALL*, and we've hardly got shit. There are too many gaps in our walls. *We must close the wall gap with China!* An abyss! We must not allow a mineshaft gap! A doomsday gap! I'm raving! It's Doctor Strangelove. George C. Scott! This American carnage stops right here and stops right now!

   Good. A blast. So much for Trump. After this preamble it's time for the *Peloponnesian War*. Gianfranco! You're laughing again! Enjoy your meal! *Buon appetito!* Thucydides is truly a world-class historian, for this *History* of his he's gone down in history in his own right. These great speeches he invents. Pericles, his Funeral Oration, rocking the cradle of democracy. And, ye gods, we have no gods in Thucydides! Homer! and, more recently, Herodotus, were chock-full of gods, but Thucydides goes cold turkey. The real theme of his book is Athenian imperialism. As he says right off the bat, the primary cause of the war is 'the growth in power of Athens, and the alarm this inspired in Sparta.' Realpolitik combined with insane imperial aggression. The culturally degenerate effects of war on humanity itself. The atrocities committed by Greeks against Greeks. In Sicily, the Athenians losing their marbles, figuratively if not literally. (It was the Brits who looted the marbles.) Thucydides' 'greatest and most terrible war.' His *History*, in a word, of *carnage*. A great read. The Spartans and their allies— the Peloponnesian League, which supports oligarchies and opposes tyrannies and democracies—claim to wage war against Athens in order to save Greece from Athens' tyrannical ambitions; or, we might say, 'democratically tyrannical' ambitions. Most Greeks side with Sparta at the beginning, believing they are fighting a war of liberation. (Che lives!) At the end, who knows what they think. Pericles—poor man, he died of the plague barely a year after his Funeral Oration—goes so far (sez Thucydides) as to speak of the Athenians' *moral superiority*, based on their superior generosity to others without calculation of profit or loss, and on the sheer *grandeur* of their ambition. They seek an unlimited Empire despite the great dangers and terrible misfortunes involved. This ambition is a sign of their noble superiority. Of their exceptionalism. (A City on a Hill. An Acropolis!) But, in Thucydides, the Spartans make great speeches too. Everyone makes great speeches. Though, in the end—and at the beginning, and in the middle—it's the Athenians who leave us with a bad taste in our mouths.

So, as we know, the war begins in 431. Basically, the Spartans can't take it anymore. Too much Athenian ambition, even if they call it *grandeur*. Et *voilà*, the Walls. (Trump!) Pericles, the wall-strategy. After the Persians left, the Spartans *strenuously objected* to the building of the Long Walls, in word and deed—they defeated an Athenian army at Tanagra (near Thebes) to prevent their construction, but they got built anyway. Now, with the *fait accompli* (Why does this part of the *History* move me to French? Did the French ever have an Empire?), everyone is focused on the Walls. Pericles' whole strategy is his wall-strategy. He knows that the Spartans want to invade the land surrounding Athens. He knows they will attempt to draw Athens into a land battle by ravaging their crops, like in the old days. (The Spartans are traditionalists.) So he commands the Athenians to remain behind the walls ('big, beautiful walls') and rely on their navy to win the war for them. After all, nothing prevents them from sauntering on down to the Piraeus, as Socrates does, to chat with friends about the Republic. Caves. Ideas. Shadows on walls. Meanwhile, the campaigns of the first few years are basically the same old thing: the Spartans send a land army to ravage Attica, hoping to draw the Athenians out; the Athenians stay behind their walls and send a fleet to sail around the Peloponnesus, sacking cities and burning crops. In this way, the Athenians do avoid a land defeat. On the other hand, they lose a hell of a lot of their own crops and deplete (slightly) the treasury (of the Delian League! or is that some kind of joke, as Bob Dylan put it), sapped (somewhat) by naval expeditions and the expense of imported grain. What's more, to make matters *considerably* worse, a plague ravages the city in 430 and 429 BC, just when everyone is huddled together inside the walls. Highly unsanitary. Bad luck. Dropping like flies. Pericles, one of the first to go. Between one and two thirds of the Athenian population dies. What a plague! Even foreign mercenaries refuse to come to Athens. The Spartans abandon their invasion. Still, there are battles here and there. Thucydides, still a *strategos*, loses one in Thrace, as we saw, and is banished. The Athenian fleet, less plague ridden, continues its raids on the Peloponnesus. Things heat up. Towns are captured. 422 BC, Fearless Leaders are killed at the Battle of Amphipolis—Brasidas the Spartan, Cleon the Athenian, one tangle of shadows. A truce. 421, the Peace of Nicias, also know as the Fifty-Year Peace. It lasts about a year and a half. 418, the Battle of Mantinea, the largest land battle of the war, a complete victory for Sparta! For Athens, the pits. The mineshaft gap. Now what? The admirable admirals? *How about invading Sicily!* A Big Idea. We'll call it the Sicilian Expedition, even if, quite rightly, the Siracusans, presumably, will call it, for the sake of alliteration, the Athenian Aggression, or the Athenian Invasion, or, simply, the Athenian War. We'll send a *massive armada* and make a *major comeback*, say the Athenians. Let's roll! Let's went! Don't grudge me the story.

Wait! Not so fast. I'm still dreaming I'm a historian, but Thucydides is a real, not a dream-historian. At this point in his *History*, at a minute to midnight, *just before* the Sicilian Expedition, the *heart* of his *History*, he gives us its *soul*, the pages for which he, himself, will go down in history. The Melian Dialogue. Political science. A masterpiece. What's happening? The islands don't want to pay tribute to Athens. To Athens! The cradle of democracy! Shame on them. First it was Naxos, back in 471. Lost its walls, its fleet, its shirt. Then Thasos, 465. Same deal, after two years of siege. Later, in 428, the city of Mytilene revolted, and the whole island of Lesbos with it. Revolting! The Athenians were furious, they sent 1,000 hoplites and *walled the city out of this world.* (The technical term for this maneuver, believe it or not, is *investment.*) The surrender of the Mytileaneans was followed by a heated debate in Athens, dramatically reported by Thucydides with lots of invented speeches. One faction advocated executing all the men in Mytilene and enslaving the women and children, while the moderate faction suggested that only the ringleaders be executed. The Assembly wavered. In the end only 1,000 ringleaders were executed, though some say it's fake news and the true figure was only 30. So be it. Naturally Athens tore down walls and confiscated ships, and lots of tribute was paid. For the record, after the debacle in Siracusa Lesbos was one of the first islands to begin intriguing against the Athenians. Wait! *I'm dreaming the siege of Melos!* A world historical siege, as Hegel might have put it. A brilliant debate! What's the story? First, the facts. I'll get to the Dialogue in a minute. The Melians have chosen to remain neutral in the Peloponnesian War. 416, the war going south for the Athenians. They need some major investments—*tributes* I mean, not walls—to finance their next desperate aggression. Cash for the imperial coffers. Melos has never paid tribute to Athens before, and they refuse to pay now. So, let's invade. Athens sends some 3,400 men and 38 ships to conquer the small prosperous volcanic Cycladic island of Melos, now known as Milos. (Famous for the Venus de Milo, with her missing arms, but at that time she hadn't been sculpted yet.) After setting up camp the Athenians send emissaries demanding that Melos join the Delian League (that *is* some kind of joke) and pay tribute to Athens *or face annihilation.* The Melians reject the ultimatum. The Athenians, with their siege mentality, lay siege to the city. The Melians fight back, but can't break the siege. Too bad for them! The Melians surrender. The Athenians, without debate, execute all the adult men and sell the women and children into slavery. Euripides, who's seen it all, *di tutti i colori,* 57 Varieties, is deeply shocked and immediately, with one hand, writes *The Trojan Women,* while waving goodbye to the massive armada bound for Siracusa with the other. Forward! Into the slave's life! writes Euripides, godless, and full of gods. Immortal. Want poetry? Ask Ezra Pound. Want tragedy? Ask Euripides. After the massacre the Athenians settle 500 of their own colonists on the island. In 405, close to the *very end* of the Peloponnesian War, the Spartan general Lysander expels the Athenian settlers from Melos and restores whoever's left of the original Melians. A fact. A new Spartan ally. Pure political realism, Spartan style? Could be. Real or dreamed, history is a story. *His* story. Whose? and I don't mean *his* or *hers.* An uncertain reality. An abyss of dreams. As Gilda says: a Tail. Is a Tail. History? The chasing of a tail, or, Tail. A decision.

Thinking. Imagining. An idea just pops into my head. Fine. No problem. The problem is that then I start to chase it. Like a cat chasing her tail. OK. But, then, this idea I'm chasing leads me to another idea. And I chase it. From one idea, another. Another. Another again. Free association. How free? What association.

The abyss comes later. No! it's already here. It's always been here. 'It's the abyss that keeps us all alive, only the abyss,' says my adored Thomas Bernhard. What might it mean if Thucydides' Melian Dialogue were the center of our political universe? Who knows. The Melian Dialogue—perhaps—is Grand Narrative at its best. Perhaps Lyotard himself couldn't do better. But, *better than what?* Better than what? (Pardon the compulsive repetition.) Is this what it's all about? Trumping Trump? Why the hell not. How hard can it be. Very hard. Not hard.

Dialogue! Melian Dialogue. Let's went. What's happening. 'Sicily for the Sicilians!' But who in the world are they. Just a minute—Melos. Thucydides. Dialogue. It's snappy. The Athenians are in a hurry. For starters, their basic premise: Cough up the tribute or we'll wipe you out. The Melians try to slow things down. The Athenians: If you're not prepared to *look the facts in the face* and try to figure out how to save your country, this Dialogue stops right here and stops right now. Plain speaking. Facts are facts. No fake news. The Melians try to wriggle around. Ye gods, what ever happened to fair play and fair dealing. Liberty and justice for all. The Athenians shoot them in the face with this realpolitik whopper: The strong do what they can and the weak suffer what they must. (Did Kissinger say these things publicly, or only in private? I don't remember.) We don't want any trouble in bringing you into our Empire. We want you to be spared for your own good and for our own good. The Melians inquire, pre-Hegelianly: How could it be just as good for us to be slaves as for you to be masters? A straight answer: You, by giving in, would save your lives; we, by not annihilating you, would refill our coffers. The Melians argue that they are a neutral city and not an enemy, so Athens has no need to conquer them. The Athenians' riposte: If we accept the neutrality and independence of Melos we'll look weak. Our subjects (call them slaves if you like) will think we left Melos alone because we're not strong enough to conquer it. (Just add a few dominoes and *WELCOME TO VIETNAM.*) The Dialogue goes on and on. The Melians argue it would be shameful and cowardly to submit without a fight. The Athenians counter that there's no shame in submitting when you don't have a snowball's chance in hell. But these feisty Melians insist that they still have a slim chance and they'll regret not trying their luck. The Athenians laugh in their faces. Then the Melians say that the gods will help them because justice is on their side. You're dreaming, say the Athenians. This is realpolitik! It's the natural order of things for the strong to dominate the weak. The Melians play their last card: The Spartans are coming! They'll help us. Bullshit, say the Athenians, the Spartans have better things to do. Your lack of realism is shocking. — The Melians are well and truly trumped. Their last words are solemn and dignified: Our decision stands. We are not prepared to give up in a moment the liberty our city has enjoyed for 700 years. We invite you to allow us to be friends of yours and enemies to neither side. — The End. Investment. Check your portfolios. The Athenians build a wall completely around the city of Melos. The Siege. Starvation is a normal goal of sieges and the ancient Greeks had plenty of experience with them, but this siege is extreme. The expression 'Melian hunger' comes to be a byword for extreme starvation. The Melians surrender. The Athenians execute all the adult men and sell the women and children into slavery. Euripides writes *The Trojan Women.* The Athenians set sail for Sicily. Banners jangle in the breeze.

415 BC. Into the slave's life. The 'Sicilian Expedition' is the heart of the *History*. It's easy to say 'imperial overstretch.' This is high drama. Greek Tragedy. The last straw. Mad arrogance. Bad tactics. Mediocre generals. The trumping of Empire.

Athens has been taking pot shots at Sicily for quite some time. The island is dominated by the powerful city of Siracusa (no relation, as I said earlier, to Syracuse, New York). Siracusa is almost as big as Athens, but with a magnificent, truly scenic harbor and a fertile hinterland—comparing it with dusty Attica makes the chickens laugh, as we say in Italian. The Athenians have been trying to worm their way into Sicilian politics by pretending to be the protector of the smaller cities, 'threatened' (they say) by the might of Siracusa. The Big Idea, of course, is to stretch their Empire. Make the world safe for democracy. But the Sicilians prove tough nuts to crack. They have the gall to scream 'Sicily for the Sicilians!'—the ancient equivalent of 'Yankee Go Home!' And, even closer to home, 'Venice for the Venetians,' which really makes the chickens laugh. But in Sicily they stop laughing, and in 425 the Athenians go home. For a while. Meanwhile, it's true that the Sicilians are pretty busy fighting among themselves. Leontinians, Segestans, Selinusians—everyone's worried the Siracusans might gobble up the whole island. A valid concern, possibly. Back in Athens, the city is divided between a 'peace party' and a 'war party.' Back in Sicily, in 416 the Segestans attack the Selinusians and ask the Athenians for help, claiming they can fund the cost of sending a fleet and offering 60 talents of uncoined silver up front (a hefty sum, I believe). So, back in Athens, after a long, lively, and very complicated debate that I won't go into, the 'war party' wins the day, promising 'peace in our time' in Sicily. Words are cheap. In this case, the consequences will cost an arm and a leg, not to mention the rest of the political body.

Let's cut to the chase. Instead of a reasonably-sized imperial adventure the Athenians decide to go whole hog. A massive armada! Over 100 ships and 5,000 hoplites is absolutely no joke. Plus some allies, for a grand total of: 134 triremes, 5,100 hoplites, 480 archers, 700 slingers, 120 other light troops, 30 cavalry, along with 130 other supply ships and all the crews of the triremes and other non-combatants (cooks possibly? ambulance drivers?). All this to help the (60-talented) hick town of Segesta (which you've almost certainly never heard of, though I've been there, it's quite picturesque), if you buy that I'll sell you another one! No, the whole armada heads straight for Siracusa and attacks immediately. Quite a skirmish. They push back the Siracusan left wing causing the other wings to fly, but the Siracusan cavalry comes to the rescue. It's late in the year now, time for the winter break. The Siracusans build new forts and a wall extending the territory of the city. In the spring of 414 even more troops arrive from Athens, along with 300 talents of silver, which, I'm told, is a *huge* sum. In the summer the Athenians attack the Epipolae, the cliff above Siracusa, killing half the defenders. What's next? *Both sides begin building walls.* A war of walls. Thucydides describes this marvelously, he's a real wall expert. *I dream dream dream of this war of walls.* This *Mad* magazine 'Walls versus Walls.' What, me worry? Fortifications, sieges, counter-sieges, blockades, counter-blockades, attacks, counter-attacks, and if you happen to win one put up a trophy. I wish you could see this map I have here of walls and counter-walls. Cross walls. Ditches. The Athenian circumvallation, known as 'the Circle,' is designed to blockade Siracusa from the rest of the island, while the Siracusans build a number of counter-walls from the city to their various forts. The Athenians destroy part of the first counter-wall so the Siracusans immediately build a new one, this time with a ditch. The Athenians attack and capture the new counter-wall but are driven off by the Siracusan counter-attack. Now the Siracusans destroy 1,000 feet of the Athenian wall but can't square the Circle. The Athenians now manage to extend their wall to the sea, completely blockading the city by land, while their fleet enters the Great Harbor to blockade them by sea.

What's next? The Spartan general Gylippus arrives to help the Siracusans, with his 700 marines, 1,000 hoplites, 100 cavalry, and 1,000 Sicilian allies. First thing, they build another counter-wall on the Epipolae. Look! Gylippus is building it with stones the Athenians had put down in a line for their own wall. Thucydides is going to town, he has a real flair for describing this walls versus walls. Now the Siracusans complete their counter-wall, making the Athenian wall useless! Things look bad for the Athenians, they're losing the war of walls. Their general, Nicias, is worn out and would like to call it a day. He sends messengers to Athens with a letter: 'The enemy has built a single wall and carried it past the end of our fortifications, which means there's no way we can blockade the city without major reinforcements. The fact is, we the besiegers have become the besieged.' Nicias wants to return home. (Like Eudemus? Forget it, he's not dreaming.) Athens sends two new generals, Demosthenes (no, not the orator, the one with pebbles in his mouth) and Eurymedon, along with 73 ships, 5,000 hoplites, a great force of javelin-throwers, slingers, archers, and ye gods know what else. Siege engines. What happens? Demosthenes attacks the counter-wall on the Epipolae—a disaster! Many Athenians fall off the cliff to their deaths. A night battle on unknown terrain (a cliff, no less!), the Athenians are far from home, they can't tell friend from foe, they're attacking one another in the dark, Athenian versus Athenian in hand-to-hand combat! A dark day for Empire. The night of the world. Time to call it a day. Now, it looks like the Athenians really are sailing home, but, what happens? A lunar eclipse! Ye gods, says Nicias, who is highly superstitious, I'd better ask the priests what to do. The priests tell him to wait for 27 days. Good news for the Siracusans, who immediately attack 86 Athenian ships in the harbor with 76 ships of their own and defeat them! General Eurymedon is killed, and he just got there. Deep shit in the Great Harbor. Now the Siracusans begin to blockade the entrance to the port

completely, trapping the Athenians inside. Welcome to the O.K. Corral. The
Titanic sails at noon. The Athenians abandon their upper walls and build
a small walled enclosure for their sick and injured. Their last pathetic little
wall. Everyone else takes to the ships. Before the battle Gylippus, *the Spartan*,
delivers a fiery speech—invented, cosmopolitically, by Thucydides—to the
Siracusans: 'Let us go into battle with anger in our hearts. These Athenians
are not only enemies but the most deadly enemies of all, since it was to
enslave *our* [sic!] country that they came here.' Each side has about 100
ships, but the Athenian ships are extremely cramped and have no room
to maneuver. Collisions are frequent, the Siracusans are ramming them.
Athenian *sophia*, on the run. Headed south. (Where?) Furious battle. It's a
rout! Great shouting and cheering! The whole Athenian fleet, either sunk or
smashed on the shore. Panic! The imperialists running for their lives, into
the hinterland, their wounded crawling behind them, their dead unburied.
The Siracusans hot on their heels. Volleys of javelins, cavalry charges on
their flanks, a rain of missiles. Enslavers on the brink of being enslaved,
notes Thucydides. Nicias' troops panic, they can't find drinking water, it's
September, it's hot in Sicily, ye gods they're trampling each other to death!
From Melian hunger to Sicilian thirst in two short (long) years. A massacre.
The few prisoners left alive are held (famously) in sunbaked stone quarries,
believe me it's no picnic. Demosthenes and Nicias are executed, against the
will of Gylippus, who wants to take them back to Sparta, as trophies.

Back in Athens the news is trickling in and it isn't fake. Ye gods! Lost
the whole fleet! 10,000 hoplites, 30,000 oarsmen. All those talents! The
cradle of democracy. Peace in our time. And the Peloponnesian War goes
on, anticlimactically, for ten tired years. In 411 the Athenian democracy is
overthrown in favor of an oligarchy, and Persia joins the war on the Spartan
side. Poor Athenians, they left their heart in Siracusa. In 404 the war is over.
Sparta tears down the Long Walls. The next Empire will be Spartan, and
short-lived.

at Plato's Academy

So much for the so-called Peloponnesian War. War! War! Never out of style.
Make war not love. Grab 'em by the pussy. Unflagging watchword. Wait! *I'm
dreaming. I dream of Eudemus in Athens, peripatating down the loggia of the
Academy with his friend Aristotle.* Eudy and Aris, you dig. Schoolmates, *philoi*,
pals. Talking, talking, strolling through the olive grove. Physics and metaphysics.
Arguing dialectically. *Philosophizing*, bless their hearts. Plato's Academy!
Founded in 387, in a grove of trees sacred to the goddess Athena, but the
school is named after a legendary Athenian hero named Akademos. It's outside
Athens proper, to the north, near Colonus, the Athenian suburb where

Oedipus had his Sophoclean transfiguration, or transmogrification, or whatever in the world happened to him, in the end. Stuff happens. To be precise, I read somewhere that it's exactly 6 stadia outside the city walls. How far is that? A subject of heated debate! As long as six stadiums—football, baseball, cricket, what was their sport? Track and field. Wrestling. How long is an ancient Greek stadium? The consensus, in some quarters, is that a stadium was some 200 yards, making 6 stadia some 1,200 yards, but others say the Academy is about a mile outside the city. Ye gods, a mile outside the city walls! Isn't that dangerous? Then again, the Spartans have recently torn down the Long Walls and, I suppose, the city walls too. In any event, Aris and Eudy are dialectizing. Bearded friends. Everyone had a beard back then, it was like a permanent 1968, when kids grew beards radically chicly for a couple of semesters, then shaved them off. I still have mine, it just turned 50. Meanwhile—you *have* heard of Athena, Goddess of *Wisdom and War*. Stupendous combination. Tricky. Democratic. Philosophical. Either the city of Athens was named after her or she was named after the city of Athens, a moot point at this point. Born from the head of Zeus. Owls, olive trees, and snakes. Patronne of the Athens Acropolis *and* of the Spartan Acropolis. A true democrat. (Melville, for that matter, wrote that 'Death is this Democrat.') Parthénos, a virgin—#Me Too. No fake news. Soul on Ice, you dig. Let's went, we're long gone. Eudy and Aris, I can hear them dialectizing. *I'm dreaming.* What are they drinking? Ouzo, no. Santorini wine! Could be. Schoolmates like to drink, and I don't mean Coca-Cola, or mojitos either. We're not in Cuba, libre or not. This is Plato's Academy. Raki, not rum. I've been wondering, would you say they're about the same age? *A good question.* It's hard to tell. What do we know about them? What just plain facts do we have? Well, Aristotle was born in Stagira, a Macedonian village, in 384. He was well-connected, his father was personal physician to King Amyntas of Macedonia, known at the time as Macedon, a nice job, alas both his parents died, somehow, when he was 13. When he was 17 he was admitted to Plato's Academy, where he studied and philosophized for 20 years, from 367 until Plato's death in 347. We know lots of things about Aristotle. After the Academy he went back to Macedonia, to Pella, the capital, as head of King Philip's Royal Academy, where his star pupil was, famously, Alexander the Great. Alexander, encouraged by Aristotle who, himself, had absolutely no love for barbarians, became, as we know, a Great Invader, repeatedly invading *all over the place*, until he died in Babylonia at the age of 32. Alas, he drank some bad Babylonian wine, presumably *poisoned*. (Back then *everyone* was studying poisons, as I mentioned.) Meanwhile, in 335 Aristotle went back to Athens and founded his own school, the Lyceum, where he wrote most of his books. On papyrus scrolls, by the way. Unlike the Academy, the Lyceum is *right in the center* of Athens, between the fine neighborhoods of Kolonaki and Pangrati, near the Hilton Hotel. Located in a temple dedicated to Apollo Lyceus—Apollo the

An Abyss of Dreams

Wolf-God—the school is nested in a wonderful peaceful park filled with olive and pomegranate trees and fragrant plants—rosemary, lavender, oregano, and thyme. Alas, Aristotle had to leave town again, in a hurry, after Alexander's death in 323. Suddenly, Macedonians were *personae* dangerously *non gratae*. So he settled in Chalcis, on the island of Euboea, not far from the village of Marmari where, more recently, I wrote 'Marmari Nights,' but, alas, he died almost immediately, at the age of 62. While we're at it, we know a lot about Plato too, even if his date of birth, somewhere between 429 and 423, is—like the length of a stadium—heatedly debated. (Not that it really matters.) There are a lot of facts but also a lot of myths about him. He came from one of the wealthiest and most politically active families in Athens and grew up—we note—straight through the Peloponnesian War, with its extremely unhappy ending for the Athenians, in 404. What's more, these Athenians, famously (thanks to Plato's dialogues), put his teacher, Socrates, to death, on trumped up charges, in 399. But I want to say this about Plato. Many people, absolutely ignorantly, think of him as a pure academic—after all, he founded the original Academy. His entire work has remained intact for some 2,400 years, an academic's dream. His 'Philosopher King' was pure academia, you think, like all his Big Ideas. Fake news, my friends. Myth. He was, in fact, an *action* academic, something like JFK's 'best and brightest' who top-managed the Vietnam War, or—in spades—our friend Henry Kissinger, may *we* rest in peace. But Plato was *even more action*, he *actually* risked his neck, repeatedly. Where? *In Siracusa!* You thought we were done with Siracusa, after the 'Athenian Expedition'? Hell no. Eudemus—I dream of him!—was, as we already know, killed there, in battle, in 354 or '53, and that is a fact, one of our few Eudemusian facts (we only have 5 of them). And here's another fact for you, a series of facts, and, believe you me, we'll get back to these facts, this *series* of facts: Plato went—traveled, *sailed*, it was a long, hard, perilous trip—to Siracusa three times. In 387 (he was around 40), in 367 (around 60), and again in 361 (when he died, around 347, he was 80—or, possibly, 75). Plato was a great traveler and Siracusa a great city, ruled by a great tyrant, Dionysius I, truly a Tyrant's Tyrant—Platonically speaking, an Ideal Tyrant. A Big Idea. The Tyrant and the Philosopher did *not* hit it off and Plato had to run for his life! Hightail it back to Greece. But not before making 'the most enthusiastic convert I've ever had,' as he puts it in his Seventh Letter—Dion, the tyrant's brother-in-law, just twenty years old and a born Platonist. A dreamer of Philosopher Kings, who turned out to be a *bona fide* tyrant like everyone else. Siracusa! From tyrant to tyrant. Dionysius I, until he was poisoned. Then Dionysius II, until he was exiled. Then Dion himself, exiled to Athens, who returned, tyrannically, and was then choked, and then stabbed, by mercenaries in the pay of an *Athenian Platonist* (ha ha!), who has gone down in history as Callippus *of Siracusa*. A tyrant of the first, and last, water. Then Dionysius II again, who returned from exile but then got exiled again, he was part commuter

part tyrant. Ye gods, it all got worse and worse! Not a single Philosopher King
in sight. *D'un tyran l'autre*, as Céline would have loved to have put it if only
he'd studied Ancient Siracusan History. A wild and terrible series of tyrants. An
Age of Tyrannical Chaos. Mercenaries and slaves. A Eudemusian Age. I dream.
And what do we know about Eudemus of Cyprus? I gave you the 5 facts right
off the bat. He's from, presumably, Cyprus; *banished*, he somehow ends up in
Plato's Academy, where his *philos* is Aristotle; in 359 or '58, desperately ill, he
has a dream in Thessaly; 5 years later, 354 or '53, he's killed in battle in Siracusa;
then, the Platonists go to town over his 'returning home' dream and Aristotle
writes *Eudemus* or *On the Soul*. Tough love but that's all we have. Apart from
my dreams, of course! But—shadows' shadows. Who knows? *When* is he at the
Academy, with Aris? And, I wonder, are they the same age, or not? When?
Now, a fact: the Academy itself, with its ivy-leagued walls or, more factually, its
olive groves. Plato inherits the property at the age of thirty. (But *when* was he
30? In the fatal year, for Socrates, 399? Or a few years later?) It's a fine grove for
brainstorming with friends. He makes it formally Academic sometime after
387, after surviving his first trip to Siracusa, by the skin of his teeth. Dionysius
I, a true tyrant. Kill hard, die hard. But—you wonder—why doesn't Plato just
stay home in his grove and write dialogues? He gives the reason himself in his
famous Seventh Letter, which, if possibly spurious, is, I think, quite plausible.
And useful. He addresses the letter to Dion's bewildered followers in Siracusa,
presumably self-styled Platonists, right after Dion has been choked and then
stabbed to death with a short Spartan sword by Callippus' mercenaries and
before the Siracusans revolt against Callippus and exile him from the city.
Believe me, we'll get back to this. Callippus manages to hold the fort,
tyrannically, for some 13 months, before running for his life. After Siracusa
this *Athenian Platonist* [!], Callippus *of Siracusa*, tries to conquer Messina but
his mercenaries are defeated, so he crosses the Strait and actually conquers
Rhegium (now Reggio Calabria) where, sad to say, his own mercenaries stab
him to death with the same sword that killed Dion. Is this what Plato means,
in the *Republic*, by justice? No, it isn't. Poetic justice. No. — In any event, the
year is, approximately, 353, approximately the very year Eudemus is killed, in
a battle, near Siracusa. Fact, not dream. — Meanwhile, in that very year Plato
writes his Seventh Letter. (And Aristotle, his *consolatio mortis: Eudemus* or *On
the Soul*.) He tells us that in his youth he fully expected to embark on a political
career, but that the exceedingly sorry state of Athenian politics dissuaded him.
The Thirty Tyrants who ruled Athens in 404 and 403 made the previous—
corrupt—government 'look like an age of gold,' he says, graphically, but then
their successors put Socrates to death! No, Plato says, this Realpolitik is not for
me, I have Big Ideas, and one of my Biggest is the Philosopher King, it's the
only way to stop this carnage, he thinks. But, speaking of *action* academics,
there's one passage in the Letter that, for what it's worth, I've known by heart
for 50 years. Since 1968. Plato, in 353, is reminiscing. He's telling Dion's

bewildered followers why he accepted Dion's urgent invitation to return to Siracusa in 367. Dion's nephew Dionysius II has just taken over from his poisoned father and Dion has the Wild Idea that Plato can turn him into a Philosopher King. Why oh why doesn't Plato tell him, straight out, that Philosopher Kings don't grow on trees. — I hear Gianfranco laughing again! But Eudemus is crying. Carnage. It's the Eudemusian Age. — Plato accepts Dion's invitation. Ask not what your Republic can do for you, ask what you can do for your Republic. Famous last words. Dionysius the Elder, Dionysius the Younger, it's all deep shit, with deeper and stinkier shit to come. Rivers of shit. Veritable Mississippis, as Mark Twain might have put it. Chokings, stabbings, exiles, also *of the mind*. Chaos, Big Time. Dig this, bro, it's Plato, in 353, thinking back on his second visit to Siracusa, in 367: 'In the end what weighed with me was the consideration that, if ever an attempt was to be made to put into practice my convictions about law and government, now was the time; *if I could persuade even one man fully to adopt my views I should have attained my whole object.*' My italics. I truly see what he's driving at here. Norman Morrison, his sacrifice, his self-immolation under McNamara's windows. The empty shield. 'Encouraged by these thoughts I set out from home. My motives were not what some supposed; what chiefly influenced me was fear of losing my self-respect and turning out in my own eyes a creature of mere words reluctant to embark upon any action.' No, this is not Norman Morrison, his hope that 'individual lives have been changed by this.' But it is worthy of respect. In this story of mine, which is, *in fact*, a frontal, or retro frontal, attack on Platonism. On its soul, its coming home. *Viva Gianfranco!* Viva Artaud. I dream of Eudemus, *sempre con noi*. Plato concludes his reminiscence: 'These were the motives that led me to abandon my normal pursuits, which are far from discreditable, and live under a despotism that seemed inconsistent with my convictions and my character.' A good letter for bad times. Let the good times roll! When? When. Or whenever.

The Eudemusian Age. But how old is Eudemus! Here he is at the Academy, with Aristotle, bearded brothers—are they about the same age, or is Aristotle a little older, or much older, or is Eudemus a little older, or much older? I've dreamt of them, peripatating, so many times, but I just can't tell. It's a strange dream. Let's take a different tack. A second sailing. What year is it? Dyed-in-the-wool facts: Aristotle came to the Academy when he was 17, in 367, and Eudemus, after leaving the Academy, had his dream in Thessaly in, say, 358. When Aristotle was, *in fact*, 26. This narrows things down, somewhat. Let's say Eudemus left the Academy—but why? why did he leave?—and went, immediately, straight, non-stop, like a marathon man, to Pherae, the capital of Thessaly, where, immediately, he fell sick and had his dream, which I often dream. In this case we could say he left Athens in 358, Pherae is not that far from Athens, it's not like Siracusa. Now—if you follow me—he and Aris *could* have been classmates and friends since 367, for 9 years! If they're exactly the same age. On the one hand, I don't think anyone under 17 was admitted to the Academy; on the other, it would mean that Eudemus was under 17 when he got himself banished from Cyprus and then sailed, abysally, all the way to Athens. A 16-year-old doing something so Politically Big that he gets himself banished! This, frankly, is not plausible. I think he had to be at least 20, at the very least, which means he *could* have entered the Academy in 364, when Aristotle was 20, so they could have been classmates and friends for 6 years. If they were the same age. But who says they were the same age! And for how long were they classmates and friends? We have no idea! Maybe they were friends for a month, a lot can happen in a month, maybe Eudemus got to Athens in 358, when he was 20—6 years younger than Aristotle—stayed for a month, then left for Thessaly, dreamed, and then died in Siracusa when he was 25. This, alas, is possible! A veritable *enfant prodige*. But I don't believe it, it's not what I dream. And Aristotle wrote his famous (lost) dialogue *Eudemus* or *On the Soul* for someone he only knew for a month? Possible, but, I doubt it. A different tack entirely: Who's to say Eudemus isn't 20 years older than Aristotle. This is definitely less implausible than the 6-years-younger hypothesis. People can be extremely close friends even with a 20-year age difference. But—in 364 Aris is 20 and Eudy is 40? Classmates for 6 years. The same age or a 20-year difference? Eudy dreams at 26 and dies at 31, or, possibly, dreams at 46 and dies at 51. Who knows? Facts. *YE GODS WHAT DOES IT MATTER.* What matters is this Age of Tyrannical Chaos. This carnage that just *will not stop*. This Eudemusian Age.

Wait! *I'm dreaming. I dream of Eudemus in Athens, peripatating down the loggia of the Academy with his friend Aristotle.* Not only are Aris and Eudy peripatating and dialectizing in the grove, it seems to me they are actually *arguing.* What's happening? Hold on, I have my portable Ear of Dionysius right here. Let's eavesdrop.

A— Hey Eudy, my dear philos, I've been wondering just how old you actually are. You've got this ageless air about you. Agewise, a certain *je ne sais quoi.*

E— Good question bro. Agewise? Beats me. I've been rambling for as long as I can remember. The wine-dark sea. Big islands. Small islands. The birds slash away at time. Rambling. How far, how long. How in the world did I end up in this Academy, this grove? The Old Man. Philosophy. *Philia. Sophia.* We two, you and me, philos to philos, bro to bro. Dream, reality, or in-between. Or both. Or neither. Who knows? Who's on first? Two is one. One is two. Not two, not one. Or one is one. Or two, two! Or who's counting? Never mind. Let's went.

A— You're a troubled soul, Eudy. You love to laugh, wildly, like cats love the sun. But there's a dark patina covering your existence. Night. The abyss of night. The night of the world.

E— Bro! Let me be a full moon in your eyes. Light! Light! The bright eye of night.

A— Night, says Hesiod, gave birth to hateful Doom and black Fate and Death, and to Sleep and the tribe of Dreams. He doesn't say anything about being loyal to the nightmare of our choice.

E— Though he does say that in the beginning there was Chaos, the Gap, the Abyss, and then, from Chaos, wide-bosomed Earth, the sure foundation, and Erebus, and black Night. And Night gave birth to Aether and to Day, and Earth gave birth to starry Heaven.

A— Starry heaven. At the end of Plato's new book the souls of the dead shoot like stars, heading for their new lives.

E— The Old Man has Big Ideas, Aris. Really Big. About Soul. About a separate World of Forms, inhabited by non-sensible 'Ideal' substances with no matter whatsoever.

A— Dude, you piss me off with these catchy lines you drop. Point blank, you shoot me with 'what's the good of the Idea of the Good, it's too good to be true.' We're talking about the Theory of Forms and, out of the blue, you spout 'matter matters.' Wise up, my philos. This is explosive stuff.

E— Shit, bro, stuff happens. We can catch a lot of fish with lines like these.

A— We can also catch holy hell from the Old Man. You can't say it squares with his Big Ideas.

E— I'm hip, dude. But if we don't want to be squares ourselves we'd better do some thinking of our own. Plato's big on dialogues but he writes all the parts.

A— But the Theory of Forms is his Biggest Idea of all, it's too big to fail. Tread lightly, bro, at the Academy the ears have walls. The power elite. Say what you want, but the gate is strait.

E— Well pardon my trampling but I think the Theory's full of holes. Mr. Plato tear down this wall! In a nutshell you're saying that only the world of ideal Forms really exists and this world we live in is a joyless hollow. A realm of shadows. Look! This house doesn't exist, we only see it at all because it participates in the Form of House. Imitates it. Mimics it. Is possessed by it, like a colony possessed by an empire. The Form of Beauty is real, but a beautiful object—a thing of beauty—is a sham. A shadow on the wall of a Cave, as he puts it, poetically. But, as he often says, poets tell many lies.

A— He also says an old man can sooner run than learn, which, possibly, is neither here nor there. He also lectured about being given weapons by a friend when he was of sound mind, but then he went mad and reclaimed them. Possibly a reference to the doomsday gap, or the mineshaft gap. Or both. Or neither. Maybe he's obsessed with permanence, Eudy. Forms are timeless and unchanging, physical things are changing all the time. Forms are perfect, objects are never what we think they are. Maybe he's seen too many walls torn down, so he invented a world where Wall stands Eternal.

E— But he calls this ideal Wall the *real wall*, you dig. It's one thing to excogitate 'another world,' but then he says it's the only true world. I mean, a flower falls, even though we love it. Walls really do get torn down, and often. And painfully. The Long Walls of Athens. Long gone. Old postcards.

A— Slow down, Eudy, I don't think you're giving the Old Man his due. Here we are hanging out in this grove, philosophizing, and he just got back from his third trip to Siracusa. He's been in political shit up to his neck. A river of shit. It's true that he believes this ideal world is the only real world, but what exactly does he mean? Take this new book of his, the *Republic*, a blockbuster, which he calls 'On Justice.' Remember when he said that this ideal City, with its Philosopher King, doesn't exist anywhere in this world—we could see he wasn't happy about it. At all! But, Eudy—its Form exists. In a separate world, a non-physical world—a world without matter, an immaterial world. But it's a world *we can know*—that's his point. A world we can know better than we know this world of fleeting shadows, this blind tyrant-to-tyrant world. He sees another world, a truer world—

E— But it doesn't exist! It's a dream world.

A— Hold your horses, Eudy. It's not a world he's just pulled put of a hat, like the proverbial rabbit. Visions exist, and are very real. And very powerful. Remember what he said, 'a City laid up in heaven as a Form for him who wills to see, and seeing, to found a City in himself. Whether it exists anywhere or ever will exist *is no matter*. His conduct will be an expression of the laws of that City alone, and of no other.' Frankly, Eudy, I think it takes balls to say a thing like this.

E— *Touché*. As long as it doesn't make you resign yourself to *real* tyrannical cities. A new Republic or a new Apology? Democracy or Empire? Or both? Or neither? Let's start over. Matter matters. Form and matter. What's the story? *Philia. Sophia.* Philosophy. The problem of universals. Ideals. A real problem. Big Ideas, big problems. You dig.

A— Hell yes, bro, I dig, but you're the one digging down down down into the mineshaft, the gap, the abyss, the pits, or whatever we want to call it. Chaos. What do you expect to find, or not find, or find and not-find, at the bottom? A sure foundation? The Venus de Milo? The Mona Lisa?

I'M DREAMING, YOU DIG.

E— Fuck the Louvre, bro. They call me Eudemus of Cyprus and I don't even know where Cyprus is. Where in the world is Cyprus, land of my birth, presumably! What's in a name! I'm looking for Herman Melville.

A— You're a little early, dude.

E— Hell no! It's never too early for Moby Dick. Everywhere! Immortal! Ubiquitous in space and in time. That great white motherfucker never sleeps. He's worse than a bat, or a mosquito. Sleep. Dream? But who sleeps? Ergo, who dreams!

A— Bro! spare me this other kettle of fish, it's hard enough just being awake. Sleep, dream. Why dream? What's the good of it.

E— A damn good question, actually. I wish I knew. But weren't we talking about that Big Idea, the Theory of Forms. The Form of the Good or, as some say, the Idea of the Good. But what's the good of it!

A— Why do you say it's too good to be true?

E— Wise up, bro, he makes one Big Idea the 'cause' of all the others, one Form the basis for understanding all other Forms. The Idea of the Good is what allows us to understand everything else, like the sun that allows us to see what we see. But *what* do we see, if the Form of the Good doesn't apply to the physical world! Experience—the message of the senses—doesn't say shit about 'true' being, sez he. There's no Goodness in things only things in Goodness! [An explosion of Eudemusian laughter.] *The ears have walls*, now that was a good one! Form is emptiness and emptiness is form, that's easy. Form is form and emptiness is emptiness is the strait gate.

A— What in the world are you talking about, dude.

E— Nothing special, just an old saying. Be cool.

A— I think you're raving slightly.

E— Quoth it, nevermore. Raven black. Listen up. I have two basic quarrels with the Old Man. I mean his separate world of Forms and his immortal souls shooting like stars. Methinks he's jiving us. Form, soul, no matter, no body. Nobody! What does nobody matter! An Idea too big to fail, but it doesn't hold water. It's full of holes.

A— Shit, Eudy, you make the hairs of my beard stand on end.

E— Take the walls out of your ears, Aris, and listen up. One last stab at the Theory of Forms. Look! A physical object. This finger. A sham! A dream! It doesn't exist. What really exists is the Form—Fingerness. Phenomena are its momentary portrayals. Shadow fingers, bro! Form is in another world but it 'causes'—he sez—plural representations of itself in objects in this world. Form is real, unreal objects imitate—mimic—it. Fingerness is timeless and unchanging while fingers are changing all the time. The Form is perfect, objects are cheap imitation. Ye gods they're not even real! They don't exist!

A— Shadows on the wall of the Cave. The puppet theater of this world. Mime, mimic, imitate the Form. But, Eudy, he also puts it in another way, when he says that particular instances, which are not identical to the Form, *participate* in it. The Form is distinct—and universal—and the particulars partake, take part, in it. Or of it. Or, possibly, take it apart. Participation is tricky.

E— Tricky, my philos! You bet your ass it's tricky. Forms are the puppeteers, but who are the puppeteers' puppeteers? Particular objects—which, for that matter, don't really exist—participate in the Forms. A Big Big Idea! How in the world do they do it? Participation! What in the world does it mean! I think it's got more problems than a snowball in hell. Participate in a debate. Participate in a school play. Participate in an anti-war demonstration. I know what this means. But participate in a Form, I mean, who's he kidding.

A— I have to admit it, we're in shithole country. He digs himself one hell of a hole. If many objects participate in one distinct Form it means that the Form somehow shares itself out to all of them. For him the Form's distinctness means it exists as an independent being—exists somewhere, or nowhere, or both, or neither. But if it exists independently how can something, which doesn't exist, participate in it? Or, even worse, if the Universal and the particulars all exist and are the 'same' since the particulars participate in the Universal then the Form is not one but many, which is exactly what he doesn't want to say. If they are only 'like' each other then they participate in one Form that is the same and others that are different. So if we say that the Form and a particular are 'alike' then there must be another, or third Form that, participated in, *makes* them 'alike.' It makes my head spin like a plugged nickel. I can't tell whether I'm stumped or trumped.

E— It's the Third Man, bro! An argument that punches a shithole in the participation wall worse than a horde of illegal immigrants.

A— A great film, dude! With Joseph Cotten and Orson Welles. Shot in Vienna.

E— Knock it off, my man. We're having a serious argument here, even if we're dreamed.

A— The stuff that dreams are made of, as they say at the end of *The Maltese Falcon*. Humphrey Bogart. Peter Lorre. San Francisco.

E— Yes, great films, even if we're before their time. Third Man argument, Third Bird argument, let's be cynical and take the Third Dog argument.

A— No such film, so much the better. Let's argue!

E— Participation. If a dog is a dog because it participates in the Form of dog, then a third Form would be required to explain how dog and the Form of dog are both dog, and so on, ad infinitum. If you ponder this, Aris, you'll see, as you said, that it spells deep shit.

A— Dog eats dog, eats dog, eats dog, so to speak. Indigestion. No dogness in the dog only the dog in dogness, but who's wagging the tail?

E— It's the same deal with the guardians in the *Republic*, remember? The guardians will have to be watched over at every stage of life to be sure that they hold fast to their doctrine, which means that the guardians require guardians, and so do the guardians' guardians and the guardians' guardians' guardians and—you get the idea, and it's not a Good one. In the end you'll have a city of guardians and no one left to guard them, or it.

A— A strange city and strange guardians, Eudy.

E— This is where participation gets you, pal. An unholy clambake. And he wriggles right out of it! A genuine *coup de théâtre*. A Big Idea called Recollection. He says we already know the Forms because we were in the world of Forms before our births. Participation, imitation, or what have you only recalls these Forms to memory.

A— An elegant solution, bro.

E— Hold on, there's more to it. Who/what recollects? Who else—what else—but the immortal soul! This is what it all boils down to. When the shit hits the fan never mind mind or no-mind, never mind the body, it's the soul! Forget Billie Holiday, forget body and soul—

A— 'But if you will listen to me, and believe that the soul is immortal and able to endure all evil and all good, we shall always hold to the upper road, and in every way follow justice and wisdom.' Remember? The last page of the *Republic*. 'Then the souls went to sleep, and it was midnight; there was thunder and an earthquake, and at once they were carried up along different ways to their birth, shooting like stars.'

E— It's myth, bro, but it sure solves the problem. Plato's faith and the faith of the true Platonist. The Old Man truly believes that long before our bodies ever existed our souls existed and inhabited Heaven, where they became directly acquainted with the Forms themselves—a Big Idea if ever there was one. We may have a little trouble recollecting them clearly, but with strenuous philosophical effort we can do it. Somewhat. What's more, just as our souls existed before birth, it's obvious that they exist after death.

A— Shooting like stars into new bodies, new lives.

E— New lives of shadow, bro. This realm of walking shadows. Only the World of Forms is real. A bleak picture. All the world's a cave and the soul, poor player, strutting and fretting, is trapped in it. A prisoner. And the body—even worse. The body is its prison. Life is a sickness and the only cure is death, the liberation of soul from body. Going home. It gives me the shivers.

A— Remember, in the *Phaedo*—the one he calls *On the Soul*—when he says that the soul attains virtue only when it is purified from the body. Strong stuff.

E— Shivers. The Old Man. 'He who has got rid, as far as he can, of eyes and ears and, so to speak, the whole body, these distractions that keep the soul

from acquiring truth and knowledge—who, if not he, can possibly attain to
the knowledge of true being.' Of a reality that, he thinks, is *certain*. It's myth,
bro. Or delusion. It scares me.

A— I know. You think there must be some other way. When we were
drinking raki the other night you went on and on about Socrates' dream.

E— I love that story, bro, that dream. I dream it often myself. For me it's
important. He puts it at the beginning of the *Phaedo* but for me it's The End,
as Jim Morrison put it. (Pardon me, I'm dreamed.) When the music's over.
You can't burn out if you're not on fire. Socrates' recurring dream: Enough
dialoguing! Practice and cultivate the arts! Make and cultivate music! Write
poetry! Socrates, write me five stories! [Who said that?] Just a dream. A
shadow's shadow. Life goes on. Is tomorrow another day? Or the same, my
philos, always the same. Where do I come from? Where am I going?

A— Someone is dreaming you, I can feel it. Not very philosophical of me,
but I can feel it. Why dream, who's dreaming, who knows.

E— I embrace you, my true brother. We are so long gone. What's left? Your
gigantic corpus. My dream in Pherae. Plato. Platonists. A tangle of shadows.
Past, future, and no present. Carnage. Loyalty. The nightmare of our choice.

A— The hemlock. 'A cock to Asclepius,' Socrates' last words. Death the cure
for life. Giving thanks to the god of healing. Soul released from this prison
of life. 'It is only my body you are burying,' he says.

E— It's a kind of hunger, Aris, a terrible hunger. It's not a hatred of life or
hunger for death, it's a hunger for—what? What is Plato so hungry for, this
is the real question. The big one. He says it's for knowledge of true being,
but what does it mean.

A— He also says that we can attain this knowledge only when we're dead.
We are convinced—he says—that if we are ever to have pure knowledge of
anything we must get rid of the body and contemplate things by themselves
with the soul by itself.

E— On the same page he says that wars and revolutions and battles are due
simply and solely to the body and its desires. Why this war on the body?
Is this what he learned from reading Thucydides? Is this the message of his
three trips to Siracusa? But his hunger, so much hunger, I don't get it. For
another world. For Form without matter. It's a hunger that splits the world
in two—but why? These endless dualities! — Soul/body, mind/matter,

intellect/sense, reason/emotion, reality/appearance, unity/plurality, perfection/imperfection, immortality/mortality, permanence/change, eternity/time, heaven/earth, waking/sleeping—

A— Eudy, slow down! My mind's flipping like a plugged nickel.

E— I thought it was *spinning* like a plugged nickel.

A— That was the Third Man, or Third Dog, or whatever. Hey Eudy, remember that other dream Socrates had, the one in the *Crito*, three days before he drank the hemlock? With the gloriously beautiful woman dressed in white robes who takes that line of Achilles' in the Iliad—'And if the great Earthshaker gives a breeze the third day out I'll make it home to Phthia'—and twists it around a little. Crito says it's a tricky dream that makes no sense, but Socrates says it's perfectly clear.

E— Sure! The 'going home to the pleasant land of Phthia' dream. Crito is confused because Socrates has never been anywhere farther than the Piraeus so how can he make it home to Phthia, which is Achilles' home town. In Thessaly, with its green valleys, blue waters, shining streams, and lush hills. It's the same old 'hunger for true being' story, I suppose.

A— Attained after death. You're right, Eudy, these Platonists are famished worse than the Melians. But—there's something really special about them. You know, that *je ne sais quoi* they have. Fanatics, but sincere. Convinced! I think there's something gentle about those shadows in the Cave. Something that grabs me.

E— Myth, my philos, that's what grabs you. I've been thinking—Aris, I think the Old Man needs new ideas. Not Big Ideas, just—ideas. Not king-sized, no, normal-sized. And spare me the quip about old dogs and new tricks, we've had our fill of dogs.

A— Hell yes, that Third Dog was a pit bull. New ideas. What do you have in mind?

E— *MATTER MATTERS*, that's what I have in mind.

A— Holy shit, where have I heard this before.

E— Brace yourself, bro, it's a whopper. A Muhammad Ali, possibly.

A— Get on with it, don't grudge me the story.

E— Instead of a World of Forms absolutely separate from matter, let's consider a world in which form is embedded—enmeshed—in layers of matter and matter is molded into more and more complex forms. Instead of Another World where matter doesn't matter, let's look at *this* world of *informed matter*. At real concrete things that are born, and die, and change, and move. At a world—*this* world—whose form and meaning is to be found not apart from but embedded in its matter.

A— You're kicking Plato in the balls, my friend. Keep your voice down. And your head.

E— OK, let's whisper. But, as you said, here in this grove it's not the walls that have ears but the other way around. Anyway, I'll take my chances. And I beg to differ, I love Plato, he's a genius and a great teacher. Not much sense of humor, but nobody's perfect. I just want to suggest some new ideas. I mean, Form 'causing' participation in Form, it's far out, bro, you dig. I don't buy it. Dangerous merchandise. Without *matter*—if you don't take matter *seriously*—things fall apart, the center cannot hold, as some great poet will say some day. Mere anarchy, loosed upon the world.

A— Ye gods, Eudy, we don't want that!

E— Stick with me, bro, I've got a few points to make. New normal-sized ideas. For example, every substance in the universe is individual. Dig it, the universal—what Plato calls Form—though perfectly real and objective has no *separate* existence. Matter and form are separate but inseparable, like a wax object and its shape. Matter—which matters!—is a term that exists only in relation to form. It's the materials of a thing as opposed to the structure that holds the thing together. Aris, it's easy as pie. A piece of cake. Physical objects are composites of form and matter. The matter of an object is the stuff that makes it up, while the form is the shape the stuff takes. A simple example: the matter in a bronze shield is the bronze itself, and the form is the round shape. The form is primary because it gives the thing its distinctive nature. Informed matter. For the roundness of the shield you don't need souls after death carousing with Forms in another world. It's the shape the stuff takes.

A— I know, stuff happens. The shield is empty. But *how* does it happen?

E— I'm coming to that—the causes. But you shot me for shooting you with 'matter matters,' give me a minute please, bro. We're dreamed, we have the whole history of philosophy here.

A— Shoot, Eudy, shoot, I'm wearing my bulletproof vest.

E— Bro, philosophically speaking I may need a full metal jacket. Plato is a tough nut to crack. These Platonists, all wrapped up in their Big Ideas.

A— Philos, are we talking about bullets or nutcrackers?

E— Never mind the Nutcracker Suite, or the Great Gate of Kiev either. But a slingshot won't do the job. Listen up. New ideas.

A— No ghetto blasters please!

E— Easy, bro. Keep your boomboxes to yourself. Your mineshaft gaps. Your doomsday gaps. I am trying to invent the future. New ideas, goddamit. How does a house happen? By imitating a Houseness in Heaven? Participating in it? What's the 'cause' of this house right here, this concrete individual house? Well, I think it has four 'causes' and you need all four together to produce the effect.

A— To build the house.

E— Dig it, bro, we're doing philosophy now. A house. You need material— stone, or wood. You need a plan of the structure of what a house is. You need someone to work on the house—a builder. And you need to keep your eye on the ball. I mean, if you decide to play football with a round piece of wood, with no idea of the rules, without players, and without trying to score goals, you won't have much of a game. Sure, stuff will happen, but it won't make any sense. Now, four causes—material, formal, efficient, final—but— remember!—they all go together. Each one is equally necessary. Philosophy, bro. OK, instead of causes we might just call them explanatory principles. Conditions that are necessary to account for the existence of a thing *if they all work together*. No Chinese menu allowed. If you just take the stone and the goal of building a house and forget about the plan and the builder no house will happen. If you have 22 players and play by the rules but don't have a ball and posts linked by a crossbar you're fucked, my philos.

A— A far cry from participating in the Form of Footballness.

E— A new approach, Aris. But I have a much bigger quarrel with the Theory of Forms. No separate world of universals can explain this world of change. Form indicates a 'such,' never a 'this'—a characteristic, not a concrete thing. Which is why Forms—mimicry, imitation, participation—can never explain the reality of generation—of stuff *happening*—but only stick us with a static realm where nothing moves.

A— This is a big problem, Eudy. We see everything moving around, coming to be, passing away, and Plato doesn't seem to have any Big Idea about it. Recollection doesn't do the trick.

E— Watch out, bro, here comes a real big one. Matter, form, informed matter—let's say that matter is *potentiality* and form is *actuality*. And you can't have one without the other.

A— Like love and marriage. Soup and a sandwich.

E— More or less, my philos. Now, let's say that motion is the actualization of something that exists potentially. In the motion of building a potential house, with all four causes working together an actual house happens. It's not tricky at all. Actuality is related to potentiality like a man who is building to a man who knows how to build. It's like waking to sleeping; like someone actually seeing to someone who has sight but has his eyes closed; like what is shaped out of matter to its matter. In a word, we're talking about the potentiality in a single thing of passing from one state into another. And even though they are inseparable, actuality is prior to potentiality: we don't see in order to have sight, we have sight in order to see.

A— Holy shit Eudy, how in the world did you cook all this up.

E— I don't sleep much. I sit out here in the grove all night and look up at the abyss. The eye of night. It makes me philosophize. I don't see Plato's separate World of Forms, his Big Ideas. His immortal souls shooting like stars. I get new ideas. Here's a little Moby Dick for you—an On the Soul. Prisoner of the body, he says. Until liberated by death. No. I disagree. Soul is what makes a living thing alive. Soul and body are not two substances, but inseparable elements in one single substance. Like form and matter you can call soul and body separable only in the sense that they can be distinguished by the philosophic eye. Explanatory principles. Necessary conditions. Just as a wax object consists of wax with a certain shape, so a living organism consists of a body with the property of life, which is its soul.

A— With all this philosophy in your head I bet you have something to say about the gods. Some idea of some sort.

E— Sure, some sort of basic notion, not too big. For starters, don't you think there are too many gods floating around, all over the place.

A— Quite right, and in too many shapes and forms. Why human forms at all? Remember what Xenophanes said about people of different races making their gods look just like them, and that if animals had gods—

E— Cat-shaped gods, dog-shaped gods. Fish- and fly-shaped gods. Xenophanes was a real killer. Got himself kicked out of Ionia and moved to Sicily. Great food in Sicily, they say. Eggplant. A good guy.

A— And why so many gods, couldn't just one do the trick.

E— Well, I have a good idea for god. It follows quite logically from what we said about form and matter, informed matter, potentiality and actuality. Dig this, bro.

A— I'm ready, Eudy. With you, god knows, anything goes.

E— OK, a dash of theology never killed anyone, possibly. Perfectly logical. Let's went. All sentient beings are mortal. We all die. The earth we stand on will die. The only things that don't die are change and time. If time came into being or ceased to be it would mean there was a time before time was and a time after time has ceased, and for me personally, and philosophically, this makes no sense. It's the same deal with change. Change isn't identical with time but they are inseparable. By definition. The only continuous change is change of place, and the only continuous change of place is circular motion. Ergo, there must be an eternal circular motion.

A— Have you seen it yourself, Eudy, during you sleepless nights?

E— Hell no bro, I'm giving you pure logic and you ask what I have for breakfast. Bear with me a minute. To produce eternal motion there must be eternal substance *capable of causing motion*, exactly what Plato's Forms cannot do. *Et voilà*, potentiality and actuality. The essence of this eternal substance must be activity, not power. Unadulterated actuality. Otherwise it would be possible to not exercise it and change would not be eternal *necessarily*. Ergo such substance will be immaterial, since it must be eternal. You dig.

A— Frankly, Eudy, it's you digging … drifting, swirling, falling …

E— until I become a plain white bird …

A— high, nearly still, in a dream …

E— Stay with me, my one and only philos. *Hypocrite lecteur! Mon semblable!*

A— Where, where, and wherever you are headed, strange image, strange prisoner.

E— Look! There is something that moves with unceasing circular motion—
the starry heavens. There must be something that moves it. But what moves
and is moved is tainted. There's a stain on the mirror. There *must* be something
that moves without being moved. Something with no shadow of turning.
Our real experience tells us so. And this unmoved mover must be the eternal,
substantial, purely actual being whose existence we have *logically* demonstrated.

How can anything cause motion without being moved? Without mutual
contact of mover and moved? God! you say. I say high and alone and blind.
Ye gods *I AM DREAMED*. Dreamed and dreamer. Dig *this*: the unmoved
mover must cause movement in a non-physical way, *by being an object of
desire. This*, my Aris, is a big one. Not a Big One, just a big one. Melville.
Not a Melian hunger but a *bon appétit*. A *big bon*. A bon-bon. A Moby Dick.
Mon frère! Something so human, even if an outsized whale.

Where am I headed? How old am I? I *am* from Cyprus—presumably,
who knows. Why did I end up in Athens? OK, it's the center of the world,
the cradle of democracy, and of philosophy, Seville hasn't been invented yet.
Arabs! *Mes frères!* Later, much later, when you and I are ancient dust. You still
speak, your corpus. I am dust that speaks, silently. No fortune, and no name
to come.

Wide, wide river. An object of desire.

God has no practical interest in the world. Any such interest could only
detract from his perfection.

Who/what am I, agewise. No idea. Young! But, I feel a little tired. Where
I may be headed is no concern of yours. I'm
high and alone and blind
above the sea you had left behind.

WE'RE DREAMED, YOU DIG.

A— Quite frankly, Eudy, I think you're completely out of your mind.

I WAKE UP. Aris and Eudy peripatating and dialectizing in the Academy
have vanished. Look! A fact. Thessaly. Our third Eudemusian fact. Green
valleys, blue waters, shining streams, lush hills. Tyrants.

who's roistering in Thessaly?

Eudemus, what are you doing in Thessaly? Let's recap our Eudemusian
facts. You were born, presumably, in Cyprus, since they call you Eudemus of
Cyprus. (But what about Callippus *of Siracusa*, that goddam *Athenian!*) You
were *banished* from Cyprus—why? and how old were you?—and made your
way to Athens, where you enrolled in Plato's Academy. I have just dreamed,

at length, of you and Aristotle, your philos, peripatating and dialectizing in the grove. And now—suddenly!—you're in Thessaly, deathly sick, dreaming your dream, and that's a fact. Why dream? Who knows. But this third Eudemusian fact—I hardly know what to say. It's beyond words. One day you're in Athens, in the grove, and the next you're in Thessaly—in Pherae of all places—deathly sick, and dreaming.

Well, let's calm down and try to think this through. Reasonably, if possible. This uncertain reality. This fact. Look! Something we know. We know you're in Pherae (for how long? let's say, not too long) in 359 or 358. How do we know it? We know it because everyone *actually knows* that you are killed in battle, near Siracusa, in 354 or 353, exactly *five years after your dream in Pherae*, ergo, you must have been in Pherae five years earlier, ergo in 359 or 358. Deduction! Logic. Unshakable. Now, when do you leave Athens? Just for the hell of it let's give ourselves a break and say not too long before 359 or 358, or even *in* 359 or 358. This is not a fact, it's a case of mental laziness and a desire not to pile problems on problems, uncertainties on uncertainties. Unless it's absolutely necessary. It's not that far from Athens to Thessaly, you can walk it in a week or two. I did it myself years ago—OK, a mixture, a little hitch-hiking and a lot of walking. It's true, I made several stops—Thebes for example—but not long stops, just to look around. You too, Eudy, may make some stops, longer stops possibly—*but goddamit let's say you got there pretty fast*. Let's just say it. Just this once let's take it easy, just a little. What is, or isn't, an electron? What if reality is a probability wave. What if the only rule is chaos, so what! Stuff happens. Calm down. Take it easy. If possible. The sky above, the earth below. If your nose runs and your feet smell you're built upside-down, so what. Let's roll. Why dream? What the hell.

Until the shit hits. Eudy, *when did you get to Athens? How long were you in the grove?* We haven't got a goddam clue! Ye gods we've been through this before. Bogged down in numbers, dates, lower mathematics. *Real low.* What does it matter? Well, alas, leaving a place—Plato's Academy no less!—after you've been there, say, for a month, is quite different from leaving it after you've been there twenty years. Alas in your case, Eudy, both cases are possible. We don't have the ghost of a fact. Not a clue. I dreamed a dialogue, peripatating and dialectizing, but I can't dream dates. Shit, I can't even dream time. It's not in the cards. Alas all we have are facts, and very few of them. We know that Aristotle got to Athens in 367, when he was 17, a fact, and was *around* 26 when—we think, and therefore we are—you left, however old you may have been. Gracefully or taking a powder. But Aristotle's age is essentially and fundamentally unrelated to any Eudemusian fact in this vale of tears. Low low mathematics. You and Aris might be the same age. Eudy, you can't be younger, you'd have been too young to get yourself banished from Cyprus, even if you did spit in the subway. You *could* be twenty years older, born—in Cyprus, we presume—in the last year of the Peloponnesian War, five years before Socrates drank the hemlock. Twenty years older than Aris! That would make you his philos and *big* brother. No! not Orwellian. Who knows? The butterfly effect. Irrelevant. What counts is that you are philoi, peripatating and dialectizing pals, for a day, a week, a year, or maybe 6, or possibly 9 years. What's the problem now? The problem *now* is that we need to know *why you leave.* We've successfully begged the question of *when*, exactly, you leave, good for us! But if we want to have any idea at all of what in the world you're doing in Thessaly, where you have your famous dream, we need to have some idea of why you *go* to Thessaly—to Pherae, to be precise. Some idea of how in the world you end up in Thessaly. And, as I see it, there's a connection between why you *go* to Thessaly and why you *leave* Athens. This, I admit, is not a fact, but there is some logic here, and logic is not to be sneered at. We want to know what you're doing in Thessaly, and I say we need to know *why you left Athens. Who knows!* A violent anti-Cypriot uprising? Forget it, in Athens they don't give a shit about Cyprus. (At the time! 1974 is another matter.) It's true, Aristotle later left Athens twice—in 348, and again in 322, just before he died in Chalcis—because of anti-Macedonian sentiment, but ye gods the Macedonians were gobbling up half the world, what does Cyprus have to do with it! Calm down. Eudy, why do you leave? Earlier, I suggested three possibilities. Unadulterated wanderlust—this is outrageously credible. Whether you're 20 or 40—wanderlust. You say to yourself, suddenly, enough bullshitting (the elite call it brainstorming) in the grove. Enough inventing the future of philosophy. I need to wander around. To ramble. Let's went! as Pancho, the Cisco Kid's sidekick, used to say.

Plausible? Perhaps. Wandering off to roister in Thessaly. Why not a nice cruise! How about the Peloponnesus? Who knows? Two other possibilities. Politics again? Riled up (again). Banished (again). Spitting in the subway? Molotov cocktails? Could be! I need to think about it. Or is there some subtle philosophical issue? Are you riled up philosophically? Or—perhaps—do you get the *Academics* riled up philosophically? The Platonists! The Old Man himself! If this Tail were a democracy I think I'd vote for this one, considering that long dialogue I dreamed, Eudy and Aris in the grove. But—*I dreamed it, you dig.* Reality may, definitely, be uncertain, but a dream is a dream. Certainly. A dream, in some sense, is not a fact, and that's a fact. Why dream? is another question, but a dream is a dream. Unshakably. Not a question. No question. Freud, ye gods, it's ages since I've mentioned Freud! His *short* dream book, *On Dreams.* The one with the spinach. Great stuff! What else do I remember? Let's see. The '*manifest* content of the dream' is the dream itself. The '*latent* content of the dream' is the meaning of the dream as discovered—twenty years later, possibly—through psychoanalysis. Our favorite example of analysis is, unquestionably, Freud's explanation of the spinach in the 'table d'hôte' dream: From the beautiful eyes of one of his children who recently refused to eat his spinach to his remembering that as a child he himself detested spinach to his mother's telling him he ought to be glad to have spinach to his being reminded of the duties of parents to their children to two verses of poetry by Goethe. Yes, the work of psychoanalysis is long hard work. But what I'm really thinking of is the 'dream work,' namely 'the process that transforms the latent into the manifest content of dreams.' In other words, the process *by which the dreamer* transforms the dream thoughts into the dream contents. During the dream. A tricky and complicated job, says Freud, involving condensation, displacement, and a 'final bit of interpretative revision.' He, if you recall, prefers short dreams with long meanings, while I tend to prefer long dreams with short meanings. The dream work can transform very simple thoughts into very complicated dreams or, possibly, very complicated thoughts into very simple dreams. Why in the world did I bring all this up? An excellent question! Two reasons. First reason: What's going on in my dream of Eudy and Aris in the grove? Stuff is happening, but what is it? What's the dream doing? Is it working? Does it work? Did I dream something so complicated that no one can make heads or tails of it, or so simple that it makes the chickens laugh? Or both? Or neither? In any event let us not forget that there are absolutely no *facts* in the dialogue I dreamed. Nothing but dream thoughts and the dream contents that I, the dreamer, transform them into. No facts! OK, my sharper readers may, possibly, have noted that the things Eudy says in the dialogue are, roughly, things Aristotle—the real, not the dream-Aristotle—will write, on papyrus scrolls, some twenty years later, when he gets back from Macedonia and founds his own school, the Lyceum. Eudy's 'new ideas': informed matter, four causes, potentiality and actuality, unmoved movers. Isn't it strange that, in the dream, the dream-Aristotle is more distraught than edified by his friend's ideas—wait! We do have one fact here: Aris and Eudy really are friends. In fact. In dyed-in-the-wool historical fact. Real friends, not dream friends. But everything said in the dialogue is dream work. Nothing tells us whether Eudemus gets himself or the Platonists or Plato himself riled up. Does he get *riled up himself,* philosophically, and quit the Academy? Does he say things like *MATTER MATTERS* publically, to the Platonists, with the walls in their ears, or privately, where the walls have ears, and, either way, get himself kicked out? Eudy riled up, or Plato and the Platonists pissed off, or both, or neither—who knows. A dream dialogue can't tell us. Too bad! At least we'd know why he leaves Athens. But we still wouldn't know why in the world he ends up in Pherae, of all places, ruled by, arguably, the most gruesome of tyrants in an age when tyranny was *de rigueur.* The Eudemusian Age.

Second reason for bringing all this up: I had a dream last night and I haven't got the foggiest notion of what it means. Or why I had it. Not a clue. What's happening? A ton of extremely bizarre manifest content and not a drop of latent content that I can see. Help! No, no spinach, but it was hysterically funny. I woke up laughing so hard I was crying. So I might as well tell it to you. In my opinion dreams like this don't grow on trees. [Gianfranco is laughing! Eudy is laughing!] I hope I can remember it, it's very tricky.

I am a talk-show host 1960s style. The guests are a human girl and her companion, referred to as 'of extraterrestrial origin,' or as an 'out-of-this-worlder.' Just a nice insignificant couple. But the 'man' has a strange way of speaking, of answering the simple questions. The girl says: he has a totally different grammar. What? Yes, for example: the word 'girl' is not just girl, it is a slightly different word for 'girl' at 8 am, at noon, at 4 pm, at 8 pm, at midnight, et cetera — it's not the same 'girl' at these different times of day, so for him it's not the same word. No kidding! Yes, listen. And the companion said 'girl' in a slightly different way for the different hours of the day! Remarkable beautiful words, just a little different from one another. Very funny! (Very musical, like the *acqua alta* sirens we have here in Venice, 1 to 4 tones depending on the tidal forecast, an eerie musical scale.) Then they went on to other words, other examples — 3 or 4, I can't remember now — eat, talk, walk, I think 'girl' was the last on the list, it was really funny, he said something like 'chee' 'chay' 'choy' 'chu' et cetera meaning 'girl' at different times of the day or night, like, 'chee, time to get up,' 'chay, time for lunch,' 'choy, it's teatime,' 'chu, time for bed.'

Well, that's the dream. I wish I knew what to make of it. No unmoved mover here. No 'Eudemus will return home.' Just hard dream work.

After this entertaining aside let's get back to Eudemus. Eudy! *Why* are you leaving Athens? Let's start with this, again, and then, possibly, try to figure out *why you're going to Pherae*, of all places. There might be a connection. Anyway, let's take a shot at it. Now—if not *philosophically* are you, perhaps, *politically* riled up? Or, is some one, or some many, *pissed off* at you, *politically?* Obviously, it's hard to say. We don't have the ghost of a fact, but—wait! We have the Eudemusian Age. Let's see what's going on in Athens, politically. Some local carnage, perhaps, that you just can't stomach.

First, let me say this about Athens, because I have a lot of friends in Athens—no, not in ancient Athens—and Athenians are pretty touchy. (As are Greeks in general—just call the ex-republic of ex-Yugoslavia 'Macedonia'!) 'Cradle of democracy': in fact Athenian democracy was established in 508 BC and went on, with a few brief interruptions (the Thirty Tyrants didn't last long), for 180 years. At its peak you couldn't beat Athens for its tragedians, its philosophers, its Acropolis. (The Acropolis is still there.) Democracy: it's also true, as I mentioned, that slaves outnumbered citizens (of various standing) by over ten to one. It's also true that Athenian civil society was, if possible, even more militarized than present-day Israel! (To say nothing of the mercenaries.) It's also true that, when it had the chance, Athens flexed its muscles *imperialistically*, in a way that, fortunately, Israel can only dream of. Meanwhile, while I was dreaming I was a historian we lived through the

Persian War, the Athenian Empire with its very bad joke called the Delian League, and that *pièce de résistance* popularly and particularly unpopularly known as the Peloponnesian War, with its own *pièce de résistance* known (in Athens!) as the Sicilian Expedition. But, let's take a closer look at post-Peloponnesian-War Athens. From the cradle of democracy to its grave? No, that would be unfair. Was the Spartan Empire short-lived? You bet! War war war every day and twice on Sundays? No doubt about that. Let's see. Things are pretty complicated. You've never heard of the Corinthian War, 395–387? Well, not every war has, or merits, a Thucydides. But *imperialism*—you've definitely heard of that. Spartan 'expansionism' all over the place. Everybody's worried—Thebes, Athens, Corinth, Argos, even the Persians take their side, worried about Sparta. Everyone's shouting 'Sparta Go Home!' Dream on! War. Fought on land near Corinth (hence the name) and at sea in the Aegean. On land, a stalemate. At sea—behold! the Persian fleet whips the Spartans' ass. Mops them up. And the admirable Athenian admirals? Have no fear, they are busy recapturing old Delian League islands. In fact they recapture so many that the Persians decide to switch sides and back the Spartans. Without the Persians the allies are forced to sue for peace. The upshot: the Spartan hegemony is dented but intact, Athens is making a comeback, and the Persians are finally able to interfere at will in Greek politics. No question, the real winner is Persia, which—wait! Ye gods, I just discovered that by the year 380 the Persians capture both Egypt and Cyprus. *CYPRUS!* Holy shit, how old is Eudemus in 380? Here we go again. Aris was born in 384, but what if big brother Eudy is twenty years older. Around 380, a fine young man, throwing Molotov cocktails at Persians in Paphos. Getting himself banished by the imperialist barbarian Persians. Frankly, I didn't dream this, I haven't dreamed it, I'm not dreaming it now, and I don't intend to dream it in the future. Why not? I don't know, I just—don't. Dream it. It may be true, it may be a *fact*, a *possible* fact, but—let me put it this way. Let's say that *in fact* a UFO landed here in the back garden an hour ago, very quietly, sat there for ten minutes, then took off and disappeared. Absolutely no one noticed. Not even my cats. It's December and it's 11 at night. What sort of fact is this? Would *you* call it a fact? Would I? Shall we change the subject! *I dream of Eudemus*, this is a fact. In *fact* I often dream of his dream. Right now I'm trying to imagine *why he's leaving Athens* and, especially, *why in the world he's going to Pherae*, of all places. I've already dreamed that whole dialogue in the grove. I don't know, I just feel that, at this point, the *possible* fact that when he was around 20 he was throwing Molotov cocktails at Persians in Paphos—I don't know, I just feel like it's none of my business. I didn't dream it.

Ye gods let's not get bogged down in this Molotov cocktails in Paphos business. The Corinthian War is over, what's next? It's the Eudemusian Age. Ready or not, here's the Second Athenian League! The Delian League—remember? some kind of joke—wasn't bad enough, the Athenians want to do an encore. Defend the Aegean city-states against the gook creep Spartans, imperialists! The Thebans, too, are worried about the Spartans, so they join the League too. But watch out, Thebes is a loose cannon, Athens is playing with fire, and in the Aegean the natives have good reason to be restless (again). But we'll get back to them later. These Leagues are not built to last. Meanwhile, Thebes decides it needs a League of its own, a local League in Boeotia, the Boeotian League, spitting in the face of the Spartan Empire. Let's roll! War! The Battle of Leuctra, 371, near Leuctra, a village near Thebes. The Thebans have a super-general, Epaminondas, he totally outclasses the Spartans and sends them packing. I told you their Empire would be short-lived. So who's the Boss now? Who knows. Let's keep fighting! The Spartans are on the ropes, the Thebans are on a roll. A rumble in the jungle. The Battle of Mantinea, 362. At stake, hegemony over Greece. The Thebans, led by their world-class general, backed by the Arcadians and the Boeotian League, versus Sparta, backed by the Eleans, the Mantineans—and the Athenians, formerly worried about Sparta, now worried about Thebes. The venue: near the town of Mantinea, in the Peloponnesus, near Argos (and not all that far from Sparta). The Thebans look forward to a shindig, a marshmallow roast, and in fact they whip the Spartans again. Alas, however, Epaminondas is mortally wounded. Without him Thebes goes to pieces, a collective nervous breakdown. Sparta, meanwhile, is broken down militarily. Both sides shot down. The upshot of all this: The Macedonians are coming! Philip, son of Aristotle's father's friend, King Amyntas, and father of Alexander the Great. A fine new Empire. Fine, and fairly short-lived. SPQR: The Senate and People of Rome, but that's another story. It's Athens we care about! Aris and Eudy at the Academy, until Eudy *leaves* the Academy. *When?* and, especially, *why?* (And *how* does he end up in Pherae, of all places, in 359 or 358?) What's up in Athens? Deep shit with the Second Athenian League, that's what's up. These goddam islanders, with their perverse sense of justice. Chios, Rhodes, Cos, plus Byzantion—all great vacation spots—get tired of being ripped off by Athens and break away from the League. This, obviously, means war. 357, the Athenian fleet sets sail, commanded by the admirable admirals Chares and Chabrias. (Eudemus has just had his dream in Pherae.) This little-known war, known, for some reason, as the Social War, a.k.a. the War of the Allies, was, actually, a wild little war. A confusing head-spinner of a war. Why, for example, is it called the Social War? Socialists? Marxists *ante litteram?* In any event, off to a flying start, during midsummer of 357 Chabrias and his fleet attack Chios, the fleet is defeated and the admiral is killed. Chares takes over and proceeds to lose quite a few ships here and there in the Aegean. In 356 his fleet loses big time at the Battle of Embata. At this point King Philip the Macedonian smells blood—gold, silver, and much-needed timber—and leaps into the Aegean himself, having a field day. Chares is low on money, Athens is losing another League—and now

Persia gets into the act! Hitting Athens when she's down, the Persians ask her to leave Asia Minor, threatening war. Athens has had it. Goodbye Asia Minor. Goodbye League. The Athenian 'peace party' wins the day. Make love not war, for once. The money left in the war chest is to be used for public entertainment. Circuses, not bread. Is that why they call it the Social War?

I call it the Eudemusian Age. Wars wars wars—and tyrants? We certainly haven't seen any Philosopher Kings, but we haven't actually seen many *bona fide* tyrants either. Where are they? Sicily has tyrants galore! But Greece? It just struck me, a bolt from the blue. Pherae! Green valleys, blue waters. At this very moment Pherae is the tyrant capital of Greece. Shining streams, lush hills, and *tyrants*. Right here in Thessaly, roistering away. Eating, drinking, being merry, aggressing, massacring, raiding, plundering, besieging, assassinating. Jason of Pherae is the trailblazer. He succeeds Lycophron I of Pherae, *possibly* his father (get ready for a *lot* of confusion, no one really knows what's going on in Pherae, it's like Albania under Hoxha) as tyrant of Pherae and in the 370s is appointed *tagus* (despot) of Thessaly. Jason has big ideas—no, not Platonic Big Ideas, just good healthy despotic imperialist big ideas. In a word, he wants to be Alexander the Great, who hasn't quite been born yet. Not only would he like his own Empire in northern and eastern Greece, he'd invade Persia if he could! Jason is a great believer in mercenaries. He's said to have said that citizen armies are full of old men and young boys, while mercenaries are just right. The real McCoy. 24 carat, or carrot, or whatever. Fit as fiddles. 'Mercenaries can't be beat'—he says—'and I treat mine right. If they do a good job for me aggressing and assassinating, let the good times roll, let them roister, they deserve it.' Many present-day football coaches agree with him, some don't, some are undecided. It looks like I'm dreaming I'm a historian again. In any event, 'roistering in Thessaly' is proverbial, I didn't make it up, Plato says it himself in the *Crito*. Alas, as a rule tyrants come to a bad end, and Jason is no exception. He was assassinated in 370 by a group of unidentified young men, *probably* on the orders of his brother Polydorus. Now—hold on to your hats, this is confusing, even for a dream-historian. After ruling for one year Polydorus is poisoned—that's a fact. Who poisoned him? Well, various real historians have various real ideas, though the reality itself is uncertain. Diodorus Siculus says it was Alexander, another *brother*. But Xenophon says it was his brother Polyphron, who, in his turn, was murdered by his *nephew*, Alexander, Jason's *son*, in 369. (Do we have two Alexanders here or just one?) Plutarch notes that Alexander (which one?) worshipped the spear with which he murdered Polyphron as if it were a god. Brother, nephew, uncle, son, never mind, it's all in the family.

Now—we note that *this* Alexander, of Pherae, be he Jason's brother or son, or neither, or whatever, is the *real* tyrant Eudemus *dreams*, in Pherae, in 359 or 358, and that's a fact, part of the third Eudemusian fact. As tyrants go Alexander is exemplary. He manages to tyrannize all and sundry for a dozen glorious years, from 369 to 358, approximately. Total dedication. He truly takes tyranny seriously. Right off the bat the states of Thessaly, which managed to stomach Jason, refuse to submit to Alexander because—they say—of his 'profligacy and cruelty.' They ask Macedonia for help, but the Macedonian help is half-hearted so they ask the Thebans, who, foolishly, send an unarmed 'negotiator' named Pelopidas. Unarmed? Alexander throws him straight into prison. In 368 the Thebans send a large army into Thessaly to rescue their negotiator but Alexander, aided by Athenian auxiliaries (Athens is still worried about Thebes), wipes out almost the whole Theban army. Thebes sends another army led by the super-general Epaminondas, so Alexander unhappily agrees to an (uneasy) truce (a true tyrant knows no truce), but Epaminondas is rough and tough and Alexander is forced to confine himself to Pherae and quiet down (somewhat). But when the super-general is killed at Mantinea in 362 Alexander goes wild. Athens awakens from her Theban nightmare and finds this wild man at her gates. Alexander starts off with piratical raids on Tinos and other cities of the Cyclades, plundering them and making slaves of the inhabitants. *Athenian style,* I bet the islanders are saying. (But I'm a dream-historian.) (Where's the Second Athenian League to protect them? Now *that's* some kind of joke.) Then he besieges Peparethus (present-day Skopelos) and even lands troops in Attica itself, seizing the port of Panormus, just east of extremely scenic Cape Sounion. The Athenian admiral Leosthenes admirably breaks the siege of Peparethus but Alexander breaks through the admiral's blockade in Panormus and—loyal to the nightmare of his choice—seizes some Attic triremes and *plunders the Piraeus.* And this is no kind of joke. Or is it?

After these exploits Alexander returns to Pherae to resume his roistering. But not for long. By now the whole world has it in for him. He's made a name for himself, he's earned his PhD in Tyranny, but enough is enough. Plutarch paints a vivid picture of his murder, possibly in 358, perhaps around 357. (We can see why the date of Eudemus' dream is disputed, everything in Pherae is disputed.) (The exact motive for the murder is so ludicrously disputed that I won't even mention it.) Plutarch was a first-rate historian, he sets the scene magnificently. Alexander's palace in Pherae. Guards watch throughout the night, everywhere except in his bedroom, which is at the top of a ladder with a ferocious dog chained to the bedroom door. Thebe (I presume she has nothing to do with Thebes?), Alexander's *wife* and *cousin,* or, possibly, *half-sister,* as the *daughter* of Jason of Pherae (all one big dysfunctional family), conceals her three brothers in the house during the day, has the dog removed (how? poisoned?) when Alexander goes to bed, covers the steps of the ladder with wool to muffle the murderous footsteps, and leads her little brothers up to the bedroom. She has taken away Alexander's sword, but her brothers lose their nerve anyway. A tyrant is a tyrant. She threatens to wake him! *Finally,* somehow or other, the little brothers murder him. As I believe I mentioned earlier, his body is then thrown into the streets for the joyful populace to piss on and the dogs to mangle. And *let us not forget* that this murder fulfills the second prophesy in Eudemus' dream.

Eudemus, *Why are you leaving Athens? Why Thessaly? What in the world are you doing in Pherae*, of all places? Wanderlust. Philosophical disputes at the Academy. Riled up politically, again. Shining streams and lush hills, and you fall desperately ill, and have your dream, for which you are famous, and which I often dream, and I often dream of you, Eudemus! I'm dreaming you now, I'm going to keep on dreaming you, and nothing and no one can stop me. *What are you doing in Pherae?* Ye gods a clue! A bolt from the blue. The tyranny capital of Greece. Alexander, of Pherae, in Thessaly, wild man, *bona fide* tyrant. Stealing a couple of Athenian triremes and plundering the Piraeus while you and Aris are peripatating and dialecticizing in the grove. Informed matter, four causes, potentiality and actuality, unmoved movers. Plato's three trips to Sicily. Not a Philosopher King in sight, only chokings and stabbings. Carnage. His Seventh Letter, an old man now, he writes—in 353, the year you die, Eudemus—about his first trip to Siracusa, in 387, he was around 40: 'If ever an attempt was to be made to put into practice my convictions about law and government, now was the time; if I could persuade even one man fully to adopt my views I should have attained my whole object.' His views on Justice. The Philosopher King. The Republic. *I dream he didn't persuade you, Eudemus.* In fact, in the end he didn't persuade Aristotle either, his star pupil. Why Pherae, Eudy? I have an idea now, a theory, or call it a dream. I see you! The eye of night. Sitting in the grove all night looking up at the abyss. You don't see Philosopher Kings, in Heaven or on earth. What do you see, in your mind, in the grove? You see carnage. Inane endless war. You see the epitome of carnage. It's name is tyranny. Wars in the defense of tyranny. Matter matters. You want to see tyranny for yourself. You're heading for Pherae.

a Tail of two Platonists

Two Platonists? Tyrants! Dion of Siracusa, Siracusan, and Callippus of Siracusa, a.k.a. Kallippos the Academic, unadulterated Athenian and that's a fact. But let me not get ahead of myself. Tyrants have long tails and long tails deserve long Tails. If you asked the tyrannical mafia *capo dei capi* Toto Riina, known as *ù curtu* [shorty], a.k.a. *La Belva* [The Beast], Beast! How long is your tail? he'd have said (the poor man died recently): What fucking tail, I have no tail, but my Tail is endless! Men of honor tell many lies. All tyrants have tails. *D'un tyran l'autre.*

True tyrants chase their tails like cats. They never get anywhere because they're already there. They say 'stuff happens' and that's that. That's all she wrote. But I mean *certain* cats and *true* tyrants. For some cats chasing their tails is an exercise in logic. The cat-equivalent of my reading Hegel's Logic, his 'decision to consider thinking as such.' Likewise, formally speaking, Tyranny, in *ancient* Greece (not the Greece of the Colonels, which I saw for myself) is one of several forms of government, or constitution. Plato, in the *Republic*, admits that, alas, the Ideal State exists only in Heaven, not on earth. In light of this sad fact he lists four forms of degenerate states, on a scale from the least to the most degenerate. The least degenerate is Timocracy, based on love of honor. The next-to-least is Oligarchy, government of the few (Sparta's favorite), a.k.a. Plutocracy (now popular in Russia), based on love of money. What's next? 'Democracy, I suppose, should come next,' Plato says. Democracy doesn't square with his fundamental principle of *justice*, that men born with different capacities should do only the work for which they are fitted. He calls democracy 'an agreeable form of anarchy' in which everyone is free to do what they like. (His critique is harsher and more subtle, but let's not get bogged down.) But what's worst? Tyranny! No question about it. For genuine degeneracy you can't beat Tyranny, sez Plato. Tyrants! Despots! The direct reverse of Philosopher Kings. The triumph of injustice. The negation of liberty. The pits. So says Plato, and Plato has *a very long tail*.

He also tends to exaggerate. To go overboard, when he's not being *thrown* overboard, like on his first trip to Siracusa. He managed to get Dionysius so riled up that this Tyrant's Tyrant, this *Ideal Platonic Tyrant* wanted to take him for a long walk on a short pier. Rub him out. 'Neutralize' him. Luckily for Plato the Tyrant settled for selling him into slavery, which, in itself, wasn't so great, but, in the end, a Sicilian friend bought him his freedom back for 20 minas. (That's the equivalent of about 20 pounds of silver, if I've calculated correctly. Another fact: freedom isn't free. Or cheap either.) Poor Plato hightailed it back to Greece with his tail between his legs. Lived to philosophize another day. I've sidetracked myself. My point was this: in ancient Greece, and Sicily, not all tyrants were oppressive, unjust, and cruel—i.e. tyrannical in the modern sense. They weren't Philosopher Kings either, but then again, who is? Plato and Aristotle were the first to give tyranny a *real bad name*, slamming tyrants as lawless monsters who revel in extreme and cruel rampages against their own people and others. But, for a couple of centuries before their time, the tyrants were often the good guys, with tyranny a way station between radical oligarchy and budding democracy, 'where evil comes up softly like a flower,' as Baudelaire put it. (I was kidding before, of course the French had an Empire, how else could they be so democratic today?) 'Tyrant' was more or less synonymous with 'king.' Take Sophocles' Oedipus for example: Oedipus Tyrannos, for the Latins Oedipus Rex, for us Oedipus the King. He wasn't so bad, despite his complex. But for both Plato and Aristotle a king is a good monarch and a tyrant a bad one. They didn't care, it seems, that early Greek tyranny grew out of the struggle of the under classes against the aristocracy or against priest-kings. Popular coups generally installed tyrants, who often became quite popular rulers. Peisistratos became the first tyrant in Athens in 546 and he wasn't a bad guy at all, though his tyrant-son fucked up and got himself 'tyrannicided.' There's a pattern here: tyrannical families tended to 'degenerate' (as Plato liked to say). From good to bad to worse. Take Gelo, Hiero, and Thrasybulus of Gela, in Sicily, tyrannizing in turn, from 484 to 465. Three tyrant brothers, at first tyrants just of Gela, then of Gela and, more ambitiously, also of Siracusa. Gelo benevolent and popular; then Hiero, famous for having invented the *secret police* (I saw it for myself in Athens in 1970: jeeps rolling through the streets, day and night); then Thrasybulus— the son of a bitch didn't last a year. Democracy budded. For a while. Sixty years later Siracusa became the Tyrant capital of the world. Dionysius Elder and Younger, then our two Platonists, and the shit got deeper. Wide, wide river, as the Fugs put it. Crossing this river of shit. As we shall see. Clearly. Later. If, possibly, it's true that Eudemus wanted to see tyranny for himself, in Siracusa he saw the *crème de la crème*. Not that Pherae was Disneyland. The Siracusans, the Pheraens, gave tyranny a bad name, and that's a fact. These tyrants came after, or before, or after *and* before, the 'soft' definition of a tyrant as an 'illegitimate' ruler (whatever that means!), a.k.a. a 'usurper.' Who may, possibly, be a nice guy, basically. But what is it exactly that usurpers usurp? Sovereignty, such as it is? And what do you call them when their sovereignty (such as it is) is itself usurped? Usurped usurpers? Tyrannized tyrants? Who are we kidding. 'Where Law ends Tyranny begins,' said John Locke. But what Law? Whose? Tyrants! No right to rule. But what if the people preferred them to 'legitimate' kings or to the aristocracy or the priests. What if *a lot* of people figured that timocrats, plutocrats, *and democrats*, all living in *stately mansions*, were ripping them off, and thought they could get a better deal from a tyrant. What about it! Are they all in need of lobotomies? Tyrant! OK, let's not get bogged down in words, words are cheap. I was speaking of Eudemus—I *dream* of Eudemus but I also *speak* of Eudemus. I have to tell you that Cicero, in his account of Eudemus' dream, notes, *en passant*, that Aristotle says that Eudemus was 'on his way to Macedonia' when he stopped in Pherae to have his dream. This may or may not be true, I do not consider it a Eudemusian fact. Can we trust Cicero on this? Can we trust Aristotle on this? How about a grain of salt. But I wanted to talk about Macedonia anyway. (I should say 'Macedon' but I'm crazy about the word 'Macedonia.' It's so fruity.) Was Philip a tyrant? Was Alexander the Great a tyrant? I, personally, do not know of real (not dream-) historians referring to them as tyrants. Eudemus! Did you mosey on up to Macedonia after recovering from your dream to see tyranny for yourself? Were you disappointed? *If*, in fact, you moseyed on up there. It's not a fact that you *in fact* did. Reality is uncertain. Even—or especially—historical reality.

Philip II of Macedon, born in 382, was two years younger and considerably less philosophical than his fellow-Macedon Aristotle. He was 'king' (*basileus*) of the Kingdom of Macedon from 359 until his assassination—stabbed by one of his bodyguards—in 336, when the baton was passed to his son, Alexander the Great (*Aléxandros ho Mégas*). Alexander was born in 356, in Pella, a couple of years after Eudemus' dream in Pherae, and died in Babylonia in 323 under highly uncertain circumstances, probably involving a particularly exotic poison. So—were they tyrants? If they aren't tyrants, who is? you may ask, especially if you've seen *Blade Runner*, director's cut. Words are cheap. Why not call them *imperialists!* Expansion! New frontiers! Time for a new empire, a big one! Not a new idea, or a Big Idea in Plato's sense. Hankerings to conquer the world, what's wrong with that. No law against it. Where in the world would we be without imperialists. Past, present, and future, the history of the world is a history of empires. There's no 'take it or leave it,' it's a goddam fact. To condemn someone for being an imperialist is like condemning the sky for being blue. How shall we define imperialism? How about this: Subjecting other cities/countries/peoples to your own rule for *your* own good (and profit, and peace of mind), normally under the purely fictitious pretense that it's for *their* own good (of some unspecified sort). Ye gods what's wrong with that! It's the white man's burden. Our Christian duty. What's more, just think: Without imperialism we wouldn't have *wars*, and *we certainly cannot live without wars*. No way! Without *wars* our geese are cooked. We're *fucked*, you dig. Teddy Roosevelt once said, 'I should welcome almost any war, for I think this country needs one.' Hear, hear! Tell it like it is! Expand! If you don't expand you're dead. It's quite true, in the United States empire does not exist, they are merely fighting to protect and defend freedom, democracy, and justice *all over the world*. In their hearts, they've *already expanded*. Now it's 'love thy neighbor' time, time to be loyal to the nightmare of your choice, as Conrad put it. Eudemus, *mon semblable,* did Philip disappoint you? You say he's not the tyrant you want to see for yourself? Alexander of Pherae was much better, *he* made you dream. Or perhaps you weren't disappointed in the least. War war war, you're in the world capital of war. These Macedonians would go all the way to the moon to fight a war. Perhaps you didn't find the tyrant of your choice, but you found carnage galore. Tyrant? What's a tyrant? You saw, for yourself, *what tyranny is*. It's what everyone's fighting for! It's what all this war war war is all about: *the defense of tyranny.* Wars in the defense of tyranny. For your own good. For our own good. For everybody's own good. What's bad? Nobody even understands what tyranny is but they're all fighting wars to defend it. Holy shit, Eudy, they're knocking down our towers, why! We're just doing our best to defend our tyranny.

Philip, though imperialistically overshadowed by his son, and, possibly, not exactly a tyrant, was a first-rate imperialist in his own right. Tip-top. No, he didn't keep a ferocious dog chained to his bedroom door or sell Plato into slavery, or dissolve his enemies in acid like later-day mafia tyrants, but his expansionist vision was unflagging. He never stopped fighting wars, and that's what counts: *never stop fighting wars*. Day and night. Night and day. Body and soul. Soul and body. Here, there, wherever you can. He became king in 359 (Eudemus' dream was in 359 or 358) and *right off the bat* attacked the Paionians and the Thracians who had invaded eastern Macedonia and then crushed 3,000 Athenian hoplites on the coast. In 358, the Illyrians: with his phalanx infantry and famous spear, the sarissa—twenty feet long!—some 7,000 Illyrians bit the dust. 357, war with the Athenians again, over the gold mines of Mount Pangaion: he defeated them twice, taking Amphipolis and Potidaea. Gold mines, *good as gold*—the stuff of empires. 356, he conquered the town of Crenides and changed its name to Philippi. (Both father and son loved to name cities after themselves.) In 355-354 he besieged Methone, capturing the city but his right eye was wounded by an arrow and he lost it. (His son Alexander had eyes of different colors, one blue and one brown.) All this just to rev up his war machine, which was about to go into high gear: *et voilà*, the so-called Third Sacred War, 356-346. A long tricky war, with more battles than the mites on a mangy dog. The *casus belli?* Delphi, with its Oracle, is in Phocis (the region between Thebes and Thessaly), the Phocians were supposed to take loving care of it, and what did they do? They *cultivated* the sacred plain—*plowed it up*. The horror! The Amphictyonic League, dominated by Thebes, slapped them with a heavy fine, and did they pay it? Hell no, they *plundered* the treasury of the Temple of Apollo and hired mercenaries—a *big army of mercenaries*. These tricky Phocians. The Thebans attacked them, all hell broke loose, win, lose, hire more mercenaries, enough campaigns for a dozen Richard Nixons. Then our Philip got into the act, big time. He attacked Pherae, banished the last tyrant, got himself appointed *tagus* of Thessaly, and even married Jason's niece. (Jason, if you recall, was the brother, or father, or neither, of Eudemus' tyrant, Alexander of Pherae.) After that he *took good care* of the sacrilegious Phocians. The Battle of Crocus Field was—say the 'real' historians—the bloodiest in ancient Greek history: 6,000 Phocian troops killed, their leader either hanged or crucified, 3,000 taken prisoner and then *drowned*, as ritual demanded for temple-robbers. (The alternative to drowning was *pushing them over a cliff*, but they happened to be in a field.) Philip, Defender of the Faith! What faith? Greek faith! After a couple dozen more campaigns—*we cannot live without wars*—he'd taken over the whole country. In 337 he created his own Big League, the League of Corinth, and was finally ready for his Pan-Hellenic invasion of Persia, which had been his Big Idea all along. Just think, until Crocus Field the Greeks had considered the Macedonians barbarians. Foreigners. Illegals! And look at them now. Philip leading the crusade against the Persians, those 'goddam barbarians' as Aristotle, the Stagirite, put it. And then what? He got himself assassinated. At Aegae, his very own ancient capital, at the lavish wedding of his daughter Cleopatra of

Macedon. The story is a spicy one, to be taken with a grain of salt. Philip had at least seven wives—Olimpias, mother of Alexander and of Cleopatra, and his last wife, Cleopatra Eurydice, to name but a few. (Watch out, Cleopatra was a popular name in antiquity, never mind Egypt and Elizabeth Taylor.) But, as the story goes, he also had a lover, a fellow named Pausanias of Orestis, whom Philip dumped for a new, younger lover, also named Pausanias. (Incredible coincidence, or perhaps, at the time, Pausanias was an incredibly common name.) To mollify the first Pausanias somewhat Philip named him one of his seven bodyguards, quite an honor. Alas Pausanias wasn't sufficiently mollified and assassinated him. Poor Philip, all set to invade Persia. Oh well, live hard, die hard. Was he a tyrant? I'd say it's a question of semantics.

As for Alexander the Great, Eudemus was already dead. He never dreamed of his exploits so they don't concern us. After all, what can you say about a man, tutored by Aristotle, king at 20 and dead before he turned 33, who rode roughshod over half the world. Traipsing from Asia Minor to The Levant, Syria, Egypt, Assyria, Babylonia, Persia, Afghanistan, Pakistan, and on into India. Permanently like Achilles. He untied the Gordian knot by slicing right through it with his sword. From India he went back to Babylonia where, it seems, he was poisoned, exotically. Historians—and botanists!—are still arguing about this. Some say he just drank too much bad Babylonian wine. What's more, his big belly ache took twelve days to kill him. What sort of poison acts so slowly? Luckily, in 2003 a New Zealand poison expert named Leo Schep appears to have found the answer. He says it was a plant called white hellebore (in Latin *Veratrum album*), which was in fact known in antiquity, when, as I mentioned, most people spent their spare time studying poisons. Especially, it seems, in Thessaly, Sicily, and Macedonia. But never mind all this, you want to know about the two Platonists. Let me assure you that Tails like this don't grow on trees. [Gianfranco! Eudemus! Are you laughing or crying?] Platonists! Pulling my leg! It's time to pull your tails.

Let me begin at the beginning: Siracusa, Tyrant capital of the world. Dionysius the Elder, Plato's friend, so to speak. After all, he didn't kill him, just sold him into slavery. Why is he riled up? What is Plato doing there anyway? Where, as we know, he meets young Dion, the Tyrant's brother-in-law and chief diplomat, 'the most enthusiastic convert I've ever had,' as he puts it, enthusiastically. As usual, exaggerating. Now, let's speak more soberly of this Dionysius, avoiding, if possible, exclamations and exaggerations. I hope you will have a chance, some day—if you haven't already—to get to Siracusa and see the Ear of Dionysius, tapered at the top like a teardrop. For me it beats the Taj Mahal. (Which, alas, I've never seen.) If nothing else, it's a beautiful ear—actually a limestone cave dug, in antiquity, to store water, you dig. It's right next to the ancient Greek Theater, where they stage great Greek tragedies to this day, and I *have* seen a few, years ago. The name,

Orecchio di Dionisio, was coined in 1608 by the great, and *maudit*, painter Caravaggio after he saw it for himself. According to one legend (possibly created by Caravaggio himself, never trust these artists), Dionysius used the Ear as a prison for political dissidents. Thanks to the perfect acoustics he used to eavesdrop on their plans and plots. In the hard-core legend he carved the Ear to amplify the screams of prisoners being tortured. What would Eudemus say? What would Gianfranco say? I myself went to Siracusa many times, to sell earrings but, later, for the art magazine and *especially* to see my friend Wolfango, my brother! *mon semblable!* and I entered the Ear whenever I could. It gave me a sense of serenity. Of a world without conflict. Would Dionysius sell me into slavery, at best, for this? What is Plato doing there? Dig this. Dionysius—cruel, suspicious, vindictive, a true Tyrant's Tyrant, the pits, like Alexander of Pherae—is also a poet and tragedian, of sorts, and a patron of the arts. He likes having literary figures visit him—historians, poets, philosophers—but he also likes to mistreat them. Tyrannically! In 387 Dion, his right-hand man, convinces him to invite the great Plato, who is a great traveler and accepts the invitation. Young Dion is wild about Plato, and pours all the Platonism he can muster into the Tyrant's ear. (By 'ear' here I don't mean the teardrop limestone cave.) Philosopher Kings! Plato is not wild about Siracusan society, devoted, he says, to *unadulterated roistering—* 'feasting and drinking and the pursuit of love,' as he puts it in his Seventh Letter. No, not Platonic. Not exactly Plato's Idea of the Great Society, in a pinch he prefers LBJ's. No, the Tyrant and the Philosopher don't hit it off. Dionysius is offended when Plato speaks out—undiplomatically—against tyrannical leaders and orders his assassination, but, as we saw, settles for selling him into slavery. But all of Dionysius' guests have their problems. There's a famous story about Philoxenus of Cythera, a dithyrambic poet and exponent of the 'new music.' Dionysius has him arrested and sent to the quarries for voicing a less than enthusiastic opinion on one of the Tyrant's poems. Friends get Philoxenus released the next day (for guests in Siracusa it's *very* important to have friends) and, alas, the dithyramber is confronted with another Tyrannical poetry reading. Dionysius reads his own work and the audience applauds. When he asks Philoxenus how he liked it, the poet turns to the guards and says 'take me back to the quarries.' But let's start over. Unlike Alexander of Pherae, who was basically a murderous clown, Dionysius is a first rate tyrant. He's a genuine imperialist, unlike the slimy horde of Siracusan tyrants to come. Born in 432, he saw the 'Sicilian Expedition' for himself. He fought in the war against Carthage that began in 409 and was elected supreme military commander in 406, but he's hell-bent on tyranny. Siracusa has been a democratic republic since 465, enough is enough. Behold the tyrannical mind! He stages a false attack on his own life and gets the city to grant him 600 mercenaries to guard his person. In the end he covers his ass with a thousand trusted 'guards' (not to be

An Abyss of Dreams

confused with the 'guardians' in Plato's *Republic*) and, *voilà*, he's tyrant. Mercenaries and tyrants go hand in hand, like soup and a sandwich. Apart from his artistic pastimes Dionysius loves to fight wars. He fights a long one with Carthage, captures Rhegium and sells the inhabitants into slavery, and then—besieging, plundering, and pillaging—goes straight across Italy to the Adriatic, founding the cities of Ancona, Adria, and Issa. In the end, we can't say he gives tyranny a bad name. Just think, he builds 17 miles of walls around Siracusa, 5 feet wide, with 14 towers and ditches 30 feet deep. He transforms Siracusa into the most powerful city of the Western Greek world, commanding an empire not to be sneezed at. Alas, like all tyrants he comes to a bad end. In 367, after almost 40 years of heartfelt tyranny. According to some sources he was poisoned by his physicians at the instigation of his son and successor, Dionysius the Younger. According to others, after winning a prize for his tragedy 'The Ransom of Hector' at the Lenaia festival in Athens he was so elated that he drank himself to death.

Dionysius the Younger is thirty years old when he becomes tyrant. Compared to his Elder he cuts a comic figure. If it's true he had his father poisoned I'd say he shot himself in the foot. He's inept. He never gets the hang of being a tyrant. He only stays afloat at all thanks to Dion, his uncle, one of our 'two Platonists.' Dion is the son of the Siracusan statesman Hipparinus, who served with Dionysius I in the army. Dion's sister Aristomache married Dionysius I, who also married Doris of Locris at the same time—an unorthodox version of a double wedding—with Doris the mother of Dionysius II. In any event, this makes Dion the Elder's brother-in-law and the Younger's uncle. What's more—what a tangle—one of Aristomache's daughters married Dionysius II and another married Dion, her uncle, which—if I've got this straight—makes Dion the brother-in-law of both the Elder and the Younger. Relatives aside, what counts here is that Dion—*young* Dion, twenty years younger than the Elder—is the Elder's most trusted advisor, his chief diplomat, his Kissinger Junior. (Yes! I'm thinking of 'Young Frankenstein,' Italian translation 'Frankenstein Junior.') The Elder is so happy with Dion's diplomacy that he gives him the keys to the Siracusan treasury, demanding only that he be informed daily of Young Dion's withdrawals. Dion happily makes himself the wealthiest men in Siracusa, and nonetheless has the gall to criticize the Elder, occasionally. A tough cookie, this Dion. But what matters here is his meeting Plato in 387 and Plato's calling him his 'most enthusiastic convert.' So Dion—*of* and *in* Siracusa—*is a Platonist*, converted when he's 20. What in the world does this mean, practically, if not logically, speaking? Or, if we prefer, logically, if not practically? Or how about—socially? Or antisocially? Historically? Ahistorically? Conventionally? Anticonventionally? Significantly? Insignificantly? Does it matter? Possibly yes. Or not. *I dream of Eudemus*, the rest is dross. Facts! Uncertain reality, or a certain irreality. What's up. What's down. What's neither *and* both. Dion, a Platonist. (Just wait until we get to Callippus!) What are we talking about. Hard to say. I wish I knew. Hunger. A Tail. The night of the world. Forgive this brief rant. I was talking about Dionysius the Younger and I don't have much to say about him. In 367, tyrant, he's thirty years old, inept, inexperienced, he puts himself entirely in Dion's Platonist hands. Dion thoroughly disapproves of the new tyrant's dissolute and debauched lifestyle and convinces him to invite Plato back to Siracusa. Dion tells Plato he has a Big Idea: Let's transform *this* Dionysius into a Philosopher King! Call it a long shot, call it a dream, it's definitely one hell of a farce. For Dion, if we wish to exaggerate, we could even say 'from farce to tragedy': his nephew/brother-in-law the Tyrant *banishes* him almost immediately, in 366. Dion goes to Athens. Plato is left in Siracusa to fend for himself, getting nowhere: the Younger is no more Platonist than the Elder. Not a Platonist bone in their bodies, or souls. Plato returns to Athens. Dion is in Athens. Callippus *of Siracusa* (*sic*) is in Athens, since he's Athenian. Everyone's in the grove. Aristotle arrives in 367. Eudemus, as we know, is probably there, or about to be there, or has, possibly, been there for up to twenty years. Back in Siracusa Dionysius is in deep shit. Without Dion he's barely able to tie his shoes. The populace is riled up: smart tyranny is one thing, but stupid tyranny quite another. This tyrant is a screwball. To defend the good name of tyranny he does try to be as cruel as possible. In 357, as we'll see in a moment, Dion finally slaps together a small army and returns to Siracusa. The populace is delighted, they've had more than enough of Dionysius, who happens to be tyrannizing in Calabria at the time. Exile! It's Dion's turn to tyrannize. (Platonistically?) So Dionysius goes on tyrannizing the poor Calabrians, with great cruelty, until he returns to Siracusa in 346, retaking power only because, after a decade of extreme carnage, the city is in the throes of absolute anarchy and chaos. Welcome to the pits of the Eudemusian Age. (Eudemus himself 'went home,' *so to speak*, back in 354.) After a couple of years Dionysius manages to crawl out of the abyss and make his way to Corinth, where he dies miserably a year later. All things considered, his main claim to fame may be the famous 'Sword of Damocles' anecdote. (Alexander the Great has his Gordian knot, which he cuts short, absurdly, but he also conquers half the world.) If the story is true it could mean that the Younger isn't a complete idiot after all. Let's see—Cicero tells us that Damocles, an obsequious courtier in Dionysius' entourage, one day exclaims to the Tyrant: How lucky you are, with all your power, authority, and magnificence! In response, Dionysius offers to change places with Damocles for one day. Taste my great fortune for yourself, he says, generously, and Damocles sits right down on the throne. But Dionysius, who has made many enemies during his reign, hangs a huge sword right above the throne, held at the pommel by a single hair of horse's tail. This, Dionysius tells Damocles, is what it's like to be a tyrant. Great power and great peril. A fine Tail.

I dream of you, Eudemus, I dream of your dream, I know your five Eudemusian facts by heart. Speak to me, Eudemus! You are dead, you cannot speak. But you can be dreamed. And I can speak to you. I see you, sitting in the grove all night looking up at the abyss. Is it true that you left the Academy because you wanted to see tyranny for yourself? You can't tell me, all I have are your facts, such as they are. An uncertain reality. All I can do is chase my Tail. Let's see tyranny for ourselves. A Tail of two Platonists—this is the Tail you want me to tell. Your dream, Eudemus! Your hunger.

Dion, a tough cookie. Already a wealthy patrician by birth, thanks to Dionysius the Elder he gobbles up huge chunks of Siracusa. Filthy rich. Platonist. But his plan to transform the Younger Tyrant into a Philosopher King backfires, badly. Blows up in his face. The Tyrant's entourage gangs up on him, so he and his friends hatch a plot to overthrow him. No dice. He's outplotted. Forced into exile. Banished. He's heading for Athens, his tail between his legs, soon to be followed by Plato, with *his* tail between his legs, leaving Dionysius to tyrannize Siracusa in peace for a decade, from 367 to 357. In Athens Dion lives it up. High society. He's still receiving enormous revenues from his estates back in Siracusa. He's living in the stately mansion of the patrician Athenian Callippus *of Siracusa* (*will someone please tell me why he's called Callippus of Siracusa*), a.k.a. Kallippos the Academic, a fellow Platonist whom he met during the Eleusinian Mysteries. They hang out together in the grove, brainstorming, a.k.a. studying Platonic philosophy. Dion buys himself a big house in the country, to rest his weary mind on weekends. He travels throughout Greece, making friends. Filthy rich patrician Sicilian Platonist. He's treated as a celebrity. Everything's fine, until 361 when that screwball Dionysius decides to seize all his properties in Siracusa and cut off his revenue. Dionysius convinces Plato to come back to Siracusa for a friendly little chat about their friend Dion, the most enthusiastic convert he's ever had. This is Plato's third (and last!) visit, and, believe me, he's pushing his luck. Elder or Younger, Plato infuriates them, they do *not* hit it off. Ye gods this Plato, for a Big Philosopher he's a slow learner. His defense of Dion turns into a shouting match and Dionysius throws him in jail, where he sits until a friend manages to spring him. (A guest in Siracusa? If you don't have a friend you're toast.) The Tyrant is totally riled up, he sells Dion's entire estate and pockets the money. Back in Athens, Dion gets the news that he's been royally fucked. Does he take it lying down? Not our Dion. *Dionisio delendo est!* Dionysius must be destroyed! It takes him a few years, but by 357 he manages to convince some 800 'friends'—a.k.a. mercenaries—from all over Greek to help him liberate Siracusa from Tyranny. They all get together on the lovely Ionian island of Zakynthos. (The Venetians will call it The Flower of the Levant.) Callippus is with him, they brainstorm for a while. Together our two Platonists will finally make Siracusa Platonistic! The fleet sets sail for Sicily. Dionysius knows he's coming, half the world knows he's coming, subtlety and secrecy are not Dion's strong suits. Ergo, he sails straight across the open sea, thirteen days, makes it to the south coast of Sicily, is hit by a storm, the fleet nearly smashed to pieces against the rocks off the coast of Africa. (Dion was not an admirable admiral.) His Carthaginian friends give him a hand, he makes it back to Sicily, somewhere west of Agrigento, a long way from Siracusa. Let's went! On his long march his band of Platonist mercenaries is joined by 5,000 revolted Sicilians who all have it in for Dionysius for a great variety of reasons. Welcome to Siracusa. Dion attacks at dawn, Dionysius is away tyrannizing the Calabrians, the Siracusans go wild with joy and kill the Tyrant's supporters. *Et voilà*, easy as pie, Dion strolls into town, wearing brilliant armor, a garland crowning his head, and proclaims the Tyrant deposed. Dionysius comes back a week later, I must say he puts up a pretty good fight, but Dion's well-trained foreign mercenaries are too much for him. The Tyrant and his remaining men hole up in the citadel and Dion *is elected* to lead Siracusa. Democratically! The people speak. But Dion is tyrannical to the marrow of his bones—haughty, devious, double-dealing, to say nothing of cruel, suspicious, and vindictive. After all, he was the Elder's right-hand man, and now he lets the Younger slip out of the citadel and hightail it out of town. A Platonist. A genuine Platonistic Tyrant. He and Callippus. Both of them. Democracy? 'An agreeable form of anarchy.' (But 'for genuine degeneracy you can't beat Tyranny,' the Old Man says.) Dig this— Dion takes a stand against the democratic reforms the people just elected him for! Land redistribution, new commanders, expulsion of foreign officers, a.k.a. mercenaries. The people *revolt*. They won't eat this shit. Dion, with his 3,000 highly unpopular foreign mercenaries, decamps to Leontini (now Lentini), about 20 miles to the north, where he's well received. His mercenaries are so popular that the Leontinians make them honorary citizens. In Leontini the Sicilian Congress holds a meeting, denouncing Siracusa (for being democratic!), but the Siracusans say: Enough tyranny! *Basta*. At this point, back in Siracusa, with Dion out of town the populace decides to lay siege to the citadel where Dionysius' son, Apollocrates, and *his* mercenaries are holed up. It looks like their geese are cooked, but at the last minute reinforcements arrive, led by a Neapolitan named Nypsius, who sails his fleet into the Great Harbor. The Siracusan fleet wins a sea battle! Like in the good old days, when they sank the 'Sicilian Expedition.' The populace goes wild with joy and spends the whole night drinking. The next day, with all the Siracusans asleep and/or hung-over, Nypsius and his troops come out of the citadel and pillage the city. The populace sends an embassy to Leontini asking Dion for help. Dion says 'Let's went!' Before he can get there Nypsius orders his men to burn the city! A slaughter. Dion arrives the next day, cheered by the populace. Nypsius and his Neapolitans are hiding behind the destroyed palisade of the acropolis, but the Siracusans attack, Nypsius and his men retreat back into the citadel, no dice, his soldiers are captured, Nypsius escapes. Dionysius' son, Apollocrates, dead tired of the long siege (who knows where his tyrannical father is), surrenders the citadel to Dion, the Great Platonist Liberator. First as tragedy, then as farce, forget it, this is all pure farce. Not even Euripides would stick a finger into this pie. The Siracusan assembly, Plutarch says, 'supplicate Dion as a god with prayers.' Dion's opponents take to the hills. Alas, the Siracusans start shouting again about redistributing land and restoring democracy. But Dion considers democracy no better than tyranny. Worse, in fact. A Philosopher King? No, just a tad too much to ask for, even for Dion. His idea is a Platonistic state ruled exclusively by aristocrats. He has the populist leader Heracleides assassinated. The populace is not happy. Watch out. *Le coup de théâtre.* Enter Callippus, our second Platonist. Ye gods what a Tail this is. Antonin Artaud was absolutely right, reality is superior to all history, to all fable, to all divinity, to all surreality. Reality, such as it is. Uncertain. But Callippus must be real because nobody could possibly invent him. Dig it. Dionysius, in exile in Calabria, offers him a bribe to kill Dion, his friend, his house-guest, his fellow Platonist, his comrade-in-arms in the struggle against the Tyrant. What does Callippus do? He takes it! *Bien sûr!* (But why all this French, what's wrong with me?) A piece of cake! Most of Dion's closest friends have been killed by Dionysius the Younger, and Callippus is the best friend he has left. Ye gods with friends like this! Callippus uses the money with which Dionysius bribes him to bribe some of Dion's troops to defect to him. Then he wins Dion's trust by betraying some of the bribed soldiers to Dion, who then enlists Callippus as a *secret agent* (Conrad is getting a real kick out of this) to discover further plotters. What's more, whenever someone tells Dion that Callippus is plotting against him, Dion, quite logically, thinks that Callippus is acting in his role as spy. It's a barrel of monkeys! At this point Dion's only son falls from a window and dies. Dion's wife and sister discover Callippus' plot, but Dion is paralyzed by grief for his son's death and fails to take action. His wife and sister insist that Callippus is plotting against him, Callippus *of Siracusa* denies it, I'm loyal to Dion, he says, and I'll prove my loyalty. The wife and sister insist that he take the Great Oath, in a ceremony in Persephone's temple, and he takes it. He immediately decides to kill Dion during the feast of Persephone, goddess of vegetation, queen of the underworld. Dion is celebrating at home with his friends. Callippus' assassins are friends from Zakynthos, Flower of the Levant. His mercenaries. They choke Dion and then stab him with a short Spartan sword. Exit Dion, Platonist, the most enthusiastic convert he's ever had. Callippus, unadulterated Athenian, Tyrant of Siracusa. He sends a message to Athens bragging of his deeds, but his hold on the city is tenuous. Friends of Dion revolt, but are crushed. The year is 354/353, the year Eudemus dies. Falls in battle, Cicero says, citing Aristotle, at the gates, so to speak, of Siracusa. The natives are restless. Extremely restless. Callippus of Siracusa is Tyrant of Siracusa for only 13 months. The revolted Siracusans revolt. No, the revolting Platonist isn't killed, he's too quick. Hightails it out of town. Lives to tyrannize another day? Not really. He heads north and tries to conquer Messina, but his army is defeated. With his remaining mercenaries he wanders around Sicily, getting nowhere. So he crosses the Strait and manages to conquer Rhegium, old stomping ground of both the Elder and the Younger Dionysius. In Rhegium being tyrannized is *de rigueur*. What does Callippus do now? Platonist. Tyrant. He mistreats his own mercenaries, and his comrades Leptines II and Polyperchon stab him to death with the same short Spartan sword that killed Dion.

So ends this Tail of two Platonists. But the tyranny launched by Dionysius the Elder back in 405 has a very long and extremely gruesome tail. Dion has unleashed a decade of absolute anarchy, chaos, and extreme carnage, strangely placated, slightly, when Dionysius the Younger returns for a couple of years. This decade is the abyss of the Eudemusian Age, which is itself an abyss without top or bottom, beginning or end. Wars, empires, tyrannies—you can see it all for yourself, right now, as Eudemus does. In Pherae. In Siracusa. Right here, where you are. Siracusa, the city that outwalled and sank the Athenian Empire, a roiling shithole. In ten easy lessons, from a City on a Hill to an Abyss of a City. The pits. Ho Chi Minh to Pol Pot. Eudemus! I'm dreaming of you. Wars in the defense of tyranny. You see them for yourself.

travelers, or, snow in a church

> ouvrez-moi cette porte où je frappe en pleurant
> la vie est variable aussi bien que l'Euripe

I first read Guillaume Apollinaire's somewhat Symbolist avant la lettre Surrealist poem *Le voyageur* in 1973, and for decades—until quite recently —I confused *Euripe* with *Euripide*. (French is a tricky language, as we are discovering.) Ye gods, confused the Euripus Strait—a narrow channel separating the Greek island of Euboea from the mainland—with Euripides. But—may I say?—with good reason. A rock and a hard place. *C'est la vie.* Both the Strait and the Tragedian are, as the Poet puts it, *variable.* Extreme decided flux. Read Euripides' *Orestes*, or his *Heracles Mainómenos!* Unpredictable violent change. Lightning in a clear blue sky. Chaos, anarchy, carnage. Butterflies bursting into flame. We obey the gods, whoever the gods may be. My door, your door, our door. Let's knock. *Estremo rossocenere.* A calm sea. A wild whirlpool! *Je frappe.* Open this door! Tear down this wall! Oceans of tears. A tear in the fabric. Ramble, rumble, stagger. Travelers. *En pleurant.* Exiles feed on empty dreams of hope, notes Aeschylus. Why dream? *La vie est variable.* Being is nothing. *La donna è mobile.* An abyss. Eudemus, *mon semblable!* There you are, I dream you. A traveler. You've left Athens. Why? Headed for Pherae. It's not far. This must be the place. To see tyranny. For yourself.

324   An Abyss of Dreams

Dream on! Apollinaire, what a character. Pretty wild. An original in an original age. He was born in Rome in 1880 with a long Polish name, Wilhelm Albert Włodzimierz Apolinary Kostrowicki—even his name was pretty wild. We're lucky he tamed it. His mother was a Polish noblewoman, his father was 'unknown' (so to speak). He moved to Paris around 1900 and made lots of friends—Picasso, Braque, Rousseau, Chagall, Cocteau, Satie, Breton, Duchamp, Jacob, the more the merrier. Montparnasse, Montmartre, Café de la Rotonde, Au Lapin Agile. Apollinaire—poet, playwright, short story writer, novelist, art critic. Dabbled in anarchism. Defended Dreyfus. He was arrested in 1911 on suspicion of aiding and abetting the theft of the Mona Lisa, but it was actually an Italian house painter, Vincenzo Peruggia, who stole it all by himself. (Peruggia was caught two years later trying to sell it in Florence.) A bad shrapnel wound to the temple in World War I. He died in 1918, in Paris, of Spanish flu. The man was a trailblazer and a prophet. He coined the term Cubism in 1911, Orphism in 1912, and Surrealism in 1917, three years before Surrealism even existed. Avant la lettre. But he, himself, was Surreal, and the Beat Generation owes him an arm and a leg. (I'm sure that if he had been in London instead of Paris he'd have coined the term Vorticism before Ezra Pound did, he was a natural-born coiner.) My favorite poem of his, *Le voyageur*, is from his 1913 collection *Alcools*, it's chock-full of amazing, visionary, and often incomprehensible verses. *Un oiseau langoureux et toujours irrité/ et le bruit éternel d'un fleuve large et sombre.* The poem begins and ends with his reference to *l'Euripe*, which, in my humble opinion, is eminently obscure. *Aussi bien que l'Euripe*, what in the world is he talking about. The Euripus Strait, not exactly world-famous. But I've been there myself. Quite recently. And Aristotle died there. It's not a fact but I'm absolutely certain that Eudemus took a good close look at it on his way to Pherae. Eudemus! I dream of you, often, looking up at the abyss and down at the Euripus Strait. Meditating on its incessantly reversing flow. Enchanted by its insane vortexes.

Euripe, here we are now. Where? We're about 60 miles north of Athens in the city of Chalcis, the main city on the long, narrow island of Euboea, 110 miles long and varying in width from 31 to less than 4 miles. (The modern Greeks call it Evia, but let's not confuse it with Évian, the mineral water, yet another French word.) We met Chalcis before, when Aristotle had to hightail it out of Athens in the year 322 because of anti-Macedonian sentiment. Ye gods they actually accused him of impiety, those unapologetic cradlers-of-democracy, just like they'd done with Socrates back in 399. Aristotle said, quite rightly, 'I will not allow the Athenians to sin twice against philosophy,' and decamped to the estate he'd inherited from his mother (who died when he was 13) in Chalcis. Why did he prefer Chalcis to the estate he inherited from his father (who also died when he was 13) in Macedonia, in Stagira? Who knows. Maybe he didn't feel up to the trip, Chalcis was a lot closer. In fact he was worn out and died soon after making it to Chalcis, at the age of 62. But there's also a myth about his going to Chalcis, which nobody actually believes. (It's also said that Aristotle said 'the older and more solitary I become, the more I have come to love myth.') Or, let's say, there's a frivolous popular tradition that he went to Chalcis expressly to solve the problem of the crazy tidal currents in the Strait and when he failed, abjectly, to solve it, he flung himself into the Euripus and drowned. The stuff of myth. Strait is the gate, and narrow is the way, which leadest unto life. So to speak. And the gateless gate? Is it even narrower? Or, perhaps, it's wide as a lost horizon. So many problems. So many questions.

Meanwhile, between a rock and a hard place, what, exactly, is the problem with this Strait? Why, for example, did Guillaume Apollinaire write *la vie est variable aussi bien que l'Euripe?* Did he ever see this *Euripe* for himself? (Not to be confused with *Euripide*, whom he definitely never saw.) I very seriously doubt it. Extremely seriously. He was born in Rome, lived in Paris, was wounded in the temple by shrapnel, in World War I, somewhere, but definitely not in Chalcis, died in Paris, and was buried in the Père Lachaise Cemetery. What does the Strait of Euripus have to do with it? Maybe he read about it in his own poem. Hell yes, poets tell many lies. But the problem with the Strait of Euripus has nothing to do with Apollinaire, goddammit, it's the Strait itself, the Gate, the Walls, whatever, but not the poet, and not the philosopher either. No! It's a problem of hydrodynamics, and of chaos theory. Nonlinearity. Sensitive dependence on initial conditions. Twisted changeability. Butterflies. Science! Mathematics! Imagination! I dream of you, Eudemus, *mon frère.* The ears have walls. Gate is the Strait. Heaven help us, we rich innocent creatures. Here's the story. The Euripus Strait is 5 miles long and varies from just 130 feet to 1 mile in width. But what everyone's interested in are the extremely strong, and *variable*, tidal currents, which often reach velocities of 12 knots and—and this is the point!—reverse direction seven or more times a day. A real head-spinner. A problem. Bad as a crazed monkey in a tight barrel. What's more, when the flow is about to reverse the Strait forms vortexes. I saw them for myself. Recently. Terrible whirlpools. Call me Ishmael. The Pequod is out of sight! Look! Queequeg's coffin! Try sailing up it or down it, it's the nightmare of your choice. You can't sail against the tide, it's much too strong, so you go with the flow, and then—vortexes. And then, suddenly, it reverses completely. Euripus! Whose side are you on. (Or is that some kind of joke.) It's what Guy Debord might well have called 'The Strait of the Spectacle.' A puzzle, a mystery, it puts on one hell of a show. Modern Strait scholars—scientists—are still wracking their brains and, I must say, have come up with numerous—more, or less, credible—explanations. Like it or not, the exact mechanics and timing of the flow are still not fully understood. In a nutshell, the problem stems from the very long length of the entire Euboean channel. (Euboea itself is some 110 miles long, as I said.) The albeit small fluctuations down the channel from the north end and up the channel from the south end (if, in fact, we consider north 'up' and south 'down') are separated by several hours, so when they meet at the narrowest point—the Euripus—anything goes. It's chaos. Up is up and down is down but the whole caboodle is in a constant state of flux. As undecipherable as Queequeg's tattoos or Moby Dick's brow, 'pleated with riddles.' Unpredictable. Uncertain. But, in my opinion, by *variable* Apollinaire doesn't just mean constant change, he also means *violent* change. *Euripidean* change. Sudden reversal. The stuff of tyrants and madmen. Surreality. Tragedy. Farce. 'The languorous bird always irritated. The eternal noise of a wide and sombre river.' *Violently 'variable.'* Lyssa, spirit of frenzy. A deus ex machina mad as a hatter. Heracles' *undoing,* to put it mildly. *Mainómenos.* Sudden outrageous fury. Bloody murderous. Even if, as poets know, the most violent, and *variable,* form of violence is *mental.* Intellectual. Spiritual. Slow, relentless, endless. Vice versa, violent deaths are *quick.* Shot through the heart, decapitated, electrocuted. The sudden way. Then again, torture is, unquestionably, violent but, by definition, it's not quick. Waterboarding takes time. Some may consider the endless baffling *variable* of the Euripus a form of torture, but not Eudemus! Hell no. For him, I dream, this *Euripe,* this *variable,* is a perfect example of the *wondering* that is the source of all philosophy. Eudemus! I dream of you. *Variable?* You're wondering about it now.

All this reminds me of a dream I had last night. Wondering about Eudemus wondering about the Strait Gate. Believe me, *wonder* is a mighty power. A Strait. A vortex. A rock and a hard place, I can't get it out of my head, it's the stuff of the dream. By the way—you'd never heard of the Strait of Euripus but how about the Strait of Messina? Yes! And how about 'between Scylla and Charybdis,' the original proverbial 'between a rock and a hard place.' They're in Homer's *Odyssey,* two rock-monsters that are 'a bow-shot apart' and Ulysses has to steer his ship between them. There's no way of coming through unscathed, all he can do is guess where the shit is less deep. The nightmare of his choice. My point: for thousands of years everyone has assumed they're in the Strait of Messina but—just imagine!—recently, someone said that Homer was actually talking about the Strait of Euripus. A violent historiographic reversal. What's the reasoning? Well, for Homer Chalcis is a whole lot closer to home than Messina, no doubt about that. But, hard evidence? First, Homer says the rock-monsters are 'a bow-shot apart.' Second, it seems that by rock-monsters Homer means rocky coasts, and, in any case, there are no such 'rocks' in the Strait of Messina. Now, let's try to shoot an arrow from Sicily to Calabria, coast to coast—say, from Messina to Villa San Giovanni, where the ferries go. (In the fervent hope they'll never actually try to bridge it.) Ye gods, the old college try. Well, to say 'it's a long shot' would be ludicrous. But the Euripus Strait is only 130 feet at its narrowest, they've been building bridges there since 411 BC, any old archer could navigate that. Third, Homer says that Charybdis, the whirlpool rock-monster, disgorges the flood thrice each day and swallows it another thrice, and there are no such tides in the Strait of Messina but there sure as hell are in the Euripus, in spades. Fourth, a little more historiographically, Homer says that Ulysses, after somehow making it through the Strait, comes to an island with numerous sheep and cattle. But, in antiquity, Sicily was famous for its wheat, a genuine breadbasket, while Euboea was famously full of sheep and cattle. There's even more, but I'll stop here. Dig this dream, bro. It's not as entertaining as the 'out-of-this-worlder' dream, but, a dream is a dream (is a dream), as Gertrude Stein (another friend of Apollinaire's) might well have said.

Unfortunately, it seems, I am traveling. By train. Attempting to travel. All things considered I should stay home, permanently, cat or not. [My cat died recently.] But, this is a dream, and I'm traveling. Why? Who knows. Going where? Not a clue. The scene could be a very small station somewhere outside Milan. Hinterland. Not even a station really, more like an oversized bus stop. A few dozen people of all sorts, a few with small suitcases, some children, no dogs fortunately, a couple of benches. No platform, there are two tracks right in front of us, one in each direction, but in the direction of what? No signs. Where are we going, or attempting to go? Where, or its opposite. A rock, or a hard place? The tracks are in miserable condition—no, not rusted, but there's grass growing here and there, between the rails. To get to the track on the far side you'd have to walk over the track on the near side. We're waiting forever. Hours hours and hours, no sign of a train, in either direction. Nobody saying much, the little said is said softly. Waiting. I just stand here. Dead tired. For ever. A long time. What's that? Something's coming, we see something on the track on the far side, far down the track. It's coming. Yes, it's actually coming. Here it comes. Here it is. Could you call it a train? The whole thing is only one carriage and a small one, rounded in the front, dirty-brownish, barely bigger than a large automobile. I cross the track and mosey on over—it's so full of people it's unbelievable! Packed. The entire space is completely totally full. I slip my way in—no idea how—and actually sit down. Immediately the tiny train (I'll call it a train) begins to chug its way down the track. My fellow passengers seem joyful—they want to celebrate. They say, Let's make some coffee. *Un bel caffè!* I'm wondering where we might be going. Where are we headed for? The *bel caffè* is ready, a celebrating young woman has a tray full of small quite attractive cups. The coffee really is beautiful. In each little cup, a dark brown color like the eyes of a Santorini donkey, shining and shimmering, with a lovely froth on top. Tiny bubbles like Christmas decorations. I haven't had coffee in forty years, I think I'm allergic to it. I take a cup. I wake up.

What in the world does this have to do with Eudemus. Well, who knows. Possibly nothing. Or, it may have everything to do with Eudemus—I mean, the Eudemus I dream of. The *dreamed* Eudemus I dream. Doktor Freud, any comments? Well, I, myself, have something to say. I raise my hands and spread out all my fingers, as Joseph K. put it. I say, if the 'out-of-this-worlder' dream was short on *latent* content and long on *manifest* content, this one is the 'direct reverse' (as Melville liked to say). *Manifestly* speaking this is a pretty dull dream, practically nothing happens, a 'shadow' of my usual action-and-image-packed dreams. But *latently* there's an abyss of meaning here. A pit, a shaft, a mine, a veritable *Schacht* as Hegel puts it, in his Anthropology, referring to the abundance of images and content deposited in the pit of the 'soul,' by which he means, basically, the unconscious mind. Stay tuned, we'll get back to this. Meanwhile, Old Eel, I'll give you *latent!* Eudemus is a traveler. Apollinaire wrote *The Traveler.* I've been dreaming, and thinking, of them. I, myself, have been getting nowhere. Waiting for a train, going east, going west, going up, going down. Going nowhere. But, let's get to the good stuff, the *really latent* latent. The depths, the obscure, the abyss—the *spinach*, as the good Doktor put it, in his unforgettable 'table d'hôte' dream.

Ready or not—grass growing here and there on the tracks. Between the rails. Swear! said the Ghost. Old mole! (It's Hamlet's father.) Hitch-hiking through Yugoslavia in the early '70s, to and from *Greece.* (Is this a *Greek* dream?) The main road, the Yugoslavian National Highway, *main* stretch, *a two-laner*, between Zagreb and Belgrade, and so few cars that *I saw grass growing out of cracks in the road.* Unforgettable. Profound. Latent. 'A dumb blankness, full of meaning, in a wide landscape of snows,' as Melville noted.

Two tracks right in front of us. I hate trains. Only one carriage and a small one, rounded in the front, dirty-brownish. Here I am. Back in the '70s again. In my 'little camel'—she's pretending to be a minivan, a Renault 4 *fourgonnette* (French again), a wild but gentle animal. Wagnerian. Courageous. Passionate. We're hoping to make it through the (old, and perilous) San Gottardo Pass, in winter, like Hannibal with his elephants, 'in a wide landscape of snows.' Little old camel. Improbable, but possible. We chugged. We made it. Chasing images.

Un bel caffè! Wait—this is so meaningful, so *latent*, it turns Freud's *spinach* into a grain of sand. A chase! An idea just pops into my head. *Un bel caffè!* This, in the dream, makes me dream *doubly*—even triply, if I dream of Eudy, having coffee with Aris in the grove. Eudy and Aris, drinking out of those tiny cups. *Un bel caffè!* This is Greeks, twice over. Here. There. *Caffè, kafé.* Here's my *philos* Stavros Tornes. In this very house, in Venice, in 1977. *Il bel caffè!* His very voice. Here, now. The most extraordinary *anthropos* I've ever known. *Ouvrez-moi cette porte!* An exile, a traveler, a true artist. An artist of art, of life. Of image, of reality. *Uncertain.* Certainly. A man, like Eudemus, who saw things for himself. A filmmaker. *Cineaste.* Stavros told me, 'I am convinced that with my passion for life, the intensity of my joy, my living every moment *right down to the dregs*, I can overcome real biological death.' When we made *un bel caffè* downstairs in the kitchen, for Stavros it was beyond ecstasy. He literally went out of this world. *Il bel caffè! Il bel caffè!* When he returned to the world he was prepared to leave it again at any moment. A line of verse— ecstasy, he was gone. Ritsos. Kavafis! 'You tell yourself: I'll be gone/ To some other land, some other sea.' A few years later he made it back to Greece, which he'd left in 1949 when he was 17, and made a series of incredible, beautiful, and unique films, which I love *extremely*. Greek national television broadcast one in 1988, the day he died. Biological death. Why?

The latent content of the dream. Greeks. Let's have another cup. *Otan pineis stin taverna*—this time, in the taverna, in 1973, in Athens, Plaka, Odos Panos 6, the Street of Pan. It will wend its way up all the way to the Acropolis. Meta-memoir, it's all meta-memoir. Long after. Long before. A taverna. Rows of tables outside, *in the street*, on both sides. Athens, the old days. Another special *philos*, the taverner, named Poulakis, 'little bird.' *Jamais irrité*. Never. From Crete. A poet. A free spirit. He also ran a small brothel upstairs, above the taverna. I slept in the spare room, tiny as the cot I slept on, my door opening out onto a huge magnificent terrace, looking up to the Acropolis. *Ouvrez-moi cette porte!* Athens. Tiny train. Beautiful coffee, shining and shimmering. Odos Panos 6. Lazy mid-afternoon, nobody around. Suddenly Poulakis says, 'Watch out, Iakove, the old Turk fortune teller is coming [like the little train in the dream]. If she likes your face she'll tell you your fortune.' A *real* old Turkish woman. Shriveled. She likes my face. Poulakis shouts into the taverna, 'bring a *kafé tourko.'* I drink it. *Un bel caffè*. She turns the cup upside down. Black sand. Coffee grounds. She studies them *forever*. [Hours hours and hours, no sign of a train, in either direction.] *Finally* she looks at me and pronounces her sentence: 'No love until you're an old man.' (It's more graphic in the original Greek.) 'But I'm just a kid!' I say. I raise my hands and spread out all my fingers. 'The grounds don't lie,' she says. Maybe this is why I've never liked coffee. Or trains. Freud! Old Eel. Was that enough *latent* content for you. What! You say I'm missing a quote from Goethe. Fair enough, here's a dab of Hölderlin:

> *Die Mauern stehn/ Sprachlos und kalt, in Winde/ Klirren die Fahnen.*
> The walls stand speechless and cold,/ vanes rattle in the wind.

Not bad. It gains a fresh meaning in this connection.

L'Euripe, a Strait. I chase it. What association? How free? Change of fortune. Sudden. Violent. Tragic reversal. Farce. Exiles. Travelers. Dreams. An abyss. *Variable*. Let it rip. Euripides. Your violently *variable* vision of the world. Of this *uncertain reality* we call world. Temporarily like a donkey. Permanently

Eudemusian. *La donna è mobile.* Absolute anarchy, chaos, and extreme
carnage. See it for yourself. Dreamed, dreaming. Euripides *tells it like it is.*
And isn't. You dig. Certainly uncertainly. Reality, surreality. Melian hunger.
In real life? Like a cat chasing her tail. *The Trojan Women.* Banners jangle in
the breeze. Unpredictable violent change. Euripides, *mon semblable! Mon
frère!* What a life. Where do we come from? Where are we going? Down to
the stars. Up to the very dregs. A white day. A clear black night. Studded
with stars. Being is nothing. I dream of Rip and Eudy together, sitting out
there all night, looking up at the abyss. The Eudemusian Age. Gate is the
Strait. Euripides was born in 480 on the island of Salamis, a large island
not literally a stone's throw (or bow-shot) from Piraeus. But the Straits of
Salamis are pretty damn Strait. Just over a mile, a strong swimmer could
swim them easily. Lord Byron, for example. Some say that in Venice he swam
to the Giudecca and back every morning. Be that as it may—remember the
Battle of Salamis? A *major* setback for the Persian Empire. The admirable
Athenian admirals craftily lured the Persian ships into the Straits of Salamis,
seriously reduced their room to maneuver, and spectacularly whipped
their asses. Mopped the Straits with them. In 480, the year Euripides was
born. What's more, tragedianly speaking, Aeschylus fought in the battle,
personally, and Sophocles was just old enough to celebrate the victory in a
boys' chorus. Socrates was born about ten years later. Rip and Soc. For their
fellow Athenians, the volatile tragedian and the shifty sophist were nothing
but gurus of a decadent intellectualism. Egghead creeps. The comic poets—
Aristophanes in particular—lampooned them both, constantly. An oracle
told little Rip's father, Mnesarchus (a tricky name), a retailer, that his son
was fated to win 'crowns of victory,' so the boy was trained for a (short?)
career in athletics, which did not materialize. No, the boy's fate was the tragic
stage. Where, scandalously, he won only five victories in his long career. The
last (for *The Bacchae*) coming after his death. In any event, his oracle was,
possibly, no more (or less) credible than my old Turk fortune teller—who,
alas, and who knows, was a straighter shooter, oracularly speaking. Shriveled.
I'm an old man right now. Meanwhile, Euripides had two disastrous
marriages, both his wives were unfaithful. (Perhaps they preferred Tarzans
to eggheads.) He became a recluse, making his home in a cave on Salamis.
It's said that he put together quite a library in the cave, and engaged in daily
communion with the sea and sky. Too bad Eudemus was born too late to
join him. Just like *Euripe* and *Euripide* I think Rip and Eudy would have
made a great pair. I dream. Aris was a real pal, a boon companion, but, I
dream, he didn't have the sense of humor Rip and Eudy did. This is not a
fact, it's just something I dream. (It's a little-known fact that Hegel, in fact,
had a great sense of humor. He told jokes at the drop of a hat.) Then again,
their conversations in the grove may have been decisive for the long, and
short, history of philosophy. Rip made his own tragic history. A decadent

intellectualism? I think Euripides was light-years ahead of his time. Quite possibly, tragically ahead of *our* time. Euripides got old, and dead tired of the deep shit in Athens. The love you take is equal to the love you make, sang the Beatles. But it's not the same deal with shit, figured old man Euripides. So he 'retired' to the rustic court of King Archelaus in Macedonia. He died there in 406, about 74 years old. How did he die? We don't actually know. The Macedonian winters were long and hard. Euripides was an islander, not a Macedonian like Aristotle. (Who, for that matter, chose to die in temperate Chalcis.) Allow me one myth more: He died after being attacked by King Archelaus' Molossian hounds, and his cenotaph near Piraeus was struck by lightning. In any event, his death, his life, was nothing to sneeze at.

Euripe/Euripide. Violent reversals. Tragedies. *Heracles Mainómenos*, a.k.a *Furens*. A fury. Absolute anarchy, chaos, extreme carnage. A tragedy. Rage and frenzy in a clear blue sky. Butterflies bursting into flame. Zeus, an unjust god. *A tyrant!* Impossible, says Heracles, I don't believe it. Poets tell many lies. A god cannot be a tyrant. (And vice versa, I presume.) God is perfect, says he. Is that so. How about Lyssa, Madness personified. The sudden way. Being is nothing. Rage. Frenzy. Perfectly Mad. Lyssa, daughter of Night, sprung from the blood of Uranus when he was castrated by Cronus. Deep shit. Unvarnished. Pie in the sky? Dream on. Heracles, home from his labors, happy as a lark. Home sweet home. Thebes of the Seven Gates. Hearth, home, wife, kids. Adios bow and arrows, it's slippers time. Guess what! Strait is the gateless gate. Welcome to *l'Euripe*. What's going on. What's up. What's down. The City has been usurped. Lycus, motherfucker. Tyrant. Slime personified. A usurper. A plain speaker. His 'reasoning': Heracles is in Hades, he won't be back. But his sons, these little devils, when they grow up they'll slit my motherfucking throat. Revenge. Quick! Off with their heads. Burn them alive. Exterminate all the brutes. *I am the power here.* Says he. The sudden way. Nick of time. Heracles returns from the Dead. Oh happy day! Just this minute his wife was saying: 'Help us! Come, even as a ghost, even as a dream, just come!' *Et voilà,* here he is, 'unless some dream comes walking in the light,' she says. Ye miserable gods! says Heracles. Lycus! Usurper. Unspeakable slime. In the blinking of an eye, he's wasted. Slaughtered. Neutralized. Disaster is reversed! sing the Chorus. Adios usurper. Motherfucker. Tyrant. Justice flows back! Heracles! Your happy hearth and home, your family, your slippers. So ends the play? Like hell. This is the Euripus, as seen, for himself, by Euripides. The reversal is reversed! A crash of thunder. Lyssa! Madness! Gorgon-faced and holding a goad, in a black chariot on the roof of the palace. 'And, behold, there came a great wind from the wilderness.' This—beyond a shadow's shadow of a doubt—is the deepest shit in any extant or non-extant Greek tragedy. This is as deep as it gets. The pits. The abyss. Heracles! Your labors. Your family, purring at your feet. Madness! Lyssa, Daughter of Night! What Justice! Heracles is mad. *Mainómenos.* A frenzy. 'Suddenly he changed.' He draws his bow. *His arrows bring down his three sons, and his wife.* Unbelievable, not even Lycus, scumbag that he was, planned to kill the wife. Swirl, Euripus, whirl. 'And I only am escaped alone to tell thee.' The chase. Call me Ishmael. What's the point? Zeus, whoever Zeus may be, says Heracles, a survivor. The Tragic. *Variable.* A traveler. *Le bruit éternel d'un fleuve large et sombre.* A languorous bird always irritated. A moth. A flame. A moth-eaten flame.

Luckily—you say—in his old age Euripides must have mellowed. I mean, during his last years in Athens before 'retiring' to Macedonia. Where, possibly, he was attacked by Molossian hounds. Must have mellowed. He'd seen, and written, enough violent reversals, and reversed reversals, for one lifetime— you say. By the time of his 'retirement' in 406 he'd lived through the entire inglorious Peloponnesian War (so-called), almost to the last dismal dregs. He'd been infuriated by Melian hunger and the Sicilian Expedition (so-called), which he condemned in his *Trojan Women.* 'Forward! Into the slave's life.' In 408 he wrote *Orestes,* his last play in Athens. Mellowed? Ye miserable gods, his engine is revved up more than ever. This parting potshot at any semblance of political sanity. It seems that almost everyone hated the play at the time, and ever since. First as farce, then as farce. (In Macedonia he wrote *The Bacchae* and *Iphigenia in Aulis,* a spoof on human sacrifice, and triumphed at the Great Dionysia in Athens in 405. Shortly after his death.) Mellowed? Swirl, Euripus, whirl. This is where *Euripe* and *Euripide* fuse. A single flame. A gateless gate. I dream of Eudemus! Wild is the whirl, and deep is the pool, which leadest unto life. Euripides' *Orestes,* tragedy, comedy, farce—all and/or none of the above. Gate is the Strait to the Eudemusian Age. Whatever the play is and/or isn't it is definitely a masterpiece of *avant-garde* political art. A brilliant mélange of Bruegel the Elder and Jackson Pollock. A vivid painting of an Athens that has lost any last claim to *decency.* Never mind *credibility.* What's going on? Well, it's Euripides' version/vision of a slice of the House of Atreus myth. The slice Aeschylus made famous in his *Oresteia.* Unlike Aristotle, who, as we know, said 'the older and more solitary I become, the more I have come to love myth,' for Euripides myth is what he reads in the daily newspaper. Fake news, to be taken with a ton of salt, and stomped on. In Euripides' play the characters are the usual suspects: Agamemnon (but he's already dead, killed by his wife and her lover) and his wife Clytemnestra (also dead, her son Orestes killed her, and her lover, for killing his father), Agamemnon's brother Menelaus (still alive) and his wife Helen *of Troy* (very much alive, and kicking). Here we go again, it's just like Callippus *of Siracusa,* an unadulterated *Athenian.* Helen *of Troy,* but she's from *Sparta!* Though her parents were Zeus, in the form of a swan, and Leda, wife of the *Spartan* king Tyndareus. Mixed blood but not *Trojan,* horse or otherwise. Alas poor Helen, 'tis pity she's a whore. She launched, and sank, a thousand ships. The characters—who else? We have Tyndareus (alive), father of Helen (alive) and Clytemnestra (dead). Then—all alive—we have Hermione (a young girl), daughter of Menelaus and Helen, Orestes and his sister Electra (mourning becomes her), and, last but not least, Pylades, Orestes' faithful pseudophilosophical *philos*. The action, a howling tangle— wait! I need to say one thing, otherwise the play will make even less sense than the practically no sense it makes. Whereas Aeschylus relates the myth more or less as it actually mythically happened, Euripides turns it upside down. (And, possibly, inside out.) The whole point of the *Oresteia* is that Orestes' killing his mother *gives rise* to the institution of civil justice—in short, the courts. But in Euripides the court system already exists, just as it did in contemporary Athens. Which lays Orestes wide open to the charge of killing his mother (possibly justly) *when he should have hailed her into court*. Deep shit. His only defense, then, is that 'Apollo made me do it.' But, as things turn out, Apollo is not the calm Olympian of 'myth' but a rough and tumble political boss. More gangster than god. What's more, these courts Orestes *should have hailed his murderous mother into* alarmingly resemble Joseph K.'s courts in the attics. Deep shit *bis*. *Large et sombre*. Languorous bird. Highly irritated.

Action! Wide, wide river. *Un bruit éternel*. Orestes, six days after killing his mother, tormented by the Furies, is finally getting some sleep. His sister Electra is watching over him, mourning everyone she can think of—father, mother, her sister Iphigenia, long since humanly sacrificed by her father, at Aulis, for the sake of a favorable wind for the Greek ships headed for Troy. This is when the Chorus of women of Argos sing these marvelous lines I love so much: 'O night, mother of mercy, blessed night, who gives to human anguish the lovely gift of sleep, rise, rise from your abyss.' Dream on, bro! Unfortunately Orestes wakes up, driven wild by demons. He blames Apollo for ordering the matricide, pronouncing, in his own defense, the immortal line: 'We obey the gods—whoever the gods may be.' Meanwhile, the Argive courts—such as they are—have decided to nail Orestes' hide to the wall. (Of a cave, possibly.) Menelaus shows up, just back from Troy, with Helen. Uncle Menelaus, he'll save the day! Dream on. Euripides paints him as an asshole, à la Hieronymus Bosch. Banter: Orestes tries to convince him. *Reason* with him: 'Listen, Uncle Men, I was wrong to kill my mother. But when my father mustered an army to attack Troy he did a wrong, but he did that wrong *for you*, to right the wrong your whoring Helen did. Ergo, wrong for wrong, you owe me that wrong now.' It's the courts in the attics, bro! Ye gods what reasoning. Gate is the Strait. Orestes' goose has gone from cooked to deep fried. Enter Pylades, his *philos*. Just in time. The natives are restless. They want more blood, on whomever's hands happen along. Justice! We have courts goddamit! Pylades has a neat idea: Fight back! Don't just sit here waiting to die. Let's went! A friend in need. Orestes goes to face the mob—pardón, the meeting, the courts. A proper trial. The sentence. Death. By stoning? Like a dog, à la Joseph K.? No, by the suicide of their choice— Orestes, and Electra too. But, now the good part. Pylades goes into high gear, the lad has Big Ideas. Even when he's lying down he doesn't take things

lying down. Swirl, Euripus, whirl. *Le oiseau est irrité.* Pylades has decided to
die with his *philos,* absolutely, but, a Big Idea: since we have to die, let's try
to make that asshole Menelaus suffer too. How? *Let's murder Helen!* That will
kick him in the balls. Yer a true *philos,* sez Orestes, *Death to Helen! Viva la
morte!* Maybe the mob will give us a prize. Wait! Now Electra has a Big Idea
of her own: let's take Hermione hostage. Why the hell not. She reasons: Once
Helen is dead Menelaus will be hot as a hornet. When he comes after us, dear
bro, just set your sword at Hermione's throat and he'll cool off fast. Let us
pray! Orestes invokes his father's ghost, but Pylades goes whole hog: 'Zeus!
[no less!], great power of Justice! help us now! help us to victory!' — Ye men
of Athens! Right about now you're muttering, in chorus, old man Euripides
has really lost his mind. He'd better go back to the cave. — Banners jangle
in the breeze. The dear, close, and inseparable *philoi* (and I don't mean Eudy
and Aris, in the grove) enter the palace. *Tout de suite* Helen is screaming
bloody murder. Meanwhile, Hermione returns from her wreathing of, and
pouring libations on, Aunt Clytemnestra's grave, Electra pounces on her
with a tale of woe, Hermione enters the palace, Electra sounds the alarm,
Orestes sets his sword at her throat. Electra enters the palace. Things are
looking good. Helen is on her last legs. *Kill the whore!* What! Suddenly, the
lady vanishes! Flies through the roof. Now what. What would Aeschylus and
Sophocles say about all this. Princes of Tragedy, who shall wear the Crown?
What's next? Menelaus returns, who knows where in hell he's been. The
palace. Wife dead (?), daughter with Orestes' sword at her throat. *Break
down that door! Ouvrez-moi cette porte où je frappe en pleurant!* The *philoi*
appear on the roof, Hermione between them, Orestes holding a sword at
her throat. Electra's there too, with blazing torches. Orestes and his Uncle
Men exchange outrageous insults. Deep shit? Wide, wide river? Hell no,
that's not the play. *Un bruit éternel?* I dream of Eudemus. The Eudemusian
Age. *Gianfranco is laughing. Eudemus is laughing.* Suddenly *Apollo,* the true
culprit (?), appears *ex machina.* (What *macchina?* as the Italians put it. A
Fiat? A Ferrari? A Ford cabriolet? Or are we In the Penal Colony?) Apollo in
person, with Helen right behind him. So ends the play. With machines like
this, who needs enemies. The Great God, Master of Delphi and its Oracle,
speaks: Menelaus, be cool. Helen is here with me. She lives, and in the Great
Sky she sits enthroned forever, a star for sailors. (Possibly not exactly what
Uncle Men had in mind years ago when he set out for Troy.) But, sez Apollo,
cheer up. You'll marry soon again, to yet another whore, 'tis pity. As for you,
Orestes, drop your sword, Hermione will be your loving wife. And gaily give
Electra in marriage to Pylades, your bro, you dig. What the hell more do you
guys want. Go and honor Peace, loveliest of goddesses.

That's it. That's all she wrote. A mad but also sad play. The machine. A terrible
vision. *Euripe/Euripide,* I rest my case. For me, it's the greatest of all Greek

tragedies, but, what do I know. We live in the Eudemusian Age. Gate is the Strait. I didn't suddenly dream I was a drama critic. No, but I was compelled to chase this Tail. *Gianfranco is laughing. Eudemus is laughing.* It's a sad story. There is nothing more terrible than snow in a church.

Which reminds me of a scene in Andrei Tarkovsky's incomparable *Andrei Rublev.* Tarkovsky and my *philos* Stavros Tornes were born in the same year, 1932, and died a year and a half apart, in 1986 and '88. They are inseparable in my mind, and heart. 15th-century Russia, Andrei Rublev the revolutionary painter of icons. The city of Vladimir, Andrei has worked for years, filling the Vladimir cathedral with his paintings. 1408, the Tatars raid the city. They burn it, murder the men, rape and murder the women. In the film you can see it for yourself. They force their way into the barricaded church, where the majority of the populace has taken refuge. The Tatars show no mercy, they massacre the people and burn all of Andrei's paintings. They have destroyed the roof of the church. Corpses cover the floor. Andrei has survived. After the storm he converses with the ghost of Theophanes the Greek, his dead master. Why this carnage? It begins to snow. Andrei muses: There is nothing more terrible than snow in a church. The white leaves falling. Drifting, swirling, falling. Snow in an old man's eyes. Carnage. Survivors. Silence. I become a plain white bird. A grassy island in the river. Horses frolic under the driving rain. Eudemus! *Euripe/Euripide,* your vortex, *ouvrez-moi.*

I see it for myself

I know why I'm leaving Athens but I don't know why I left Cyprus. This is terribly strange. Inexplicable. Spooky. I don't really know how old I am. Why not? Am I really from Cyprus? I'm not sure. They call me Eudemus of Cyprus. Here at the Academy. In the grove. That's all I know. Why don't I remember anything about Cyprus? What I did there. What happened to me. Why I left. I was in love with a girl and she died suddenly. Why? I had a question I couldn't answer. I left. If I was actually ever there. Figments. Dream fragments. In flashes. I remember a long sea voyage. Sort of remember. Homer. The wine-dark sea. Deep blue. Rippled. The sky a lighter blue. Sleek. Silky. The sea is full. The sky is empty. Pure. Absolutely empty. Sea and sky. Always. Sea roars. Sky purrs. Islands sometimes. White islands. Green islands. Birds! Birds! They slash away at time. Many birds. White birds. The empty sky.

I am dreamed. I'm certain of this. I know it. How? I don't know. Who dreams of me? I have no idea. I know I am not exactly here. Not exactly real. How do I know this? A feeling? No. Not a feeling. I know it. For sure. It's a certainty. My only certainty. Waking. Sleeping. Dreaming. Ebb. Flow. Always. In flashes.

An Abyss of Dreams

I don't know anything with certainty. About anything before the grove. What I did before I got to the Academy. What happened to me. Why don't I know anything about it? When I began to be dreamed I was in the grove. This explains it. I'm in the grove. And I am dreamed. I know that wherever I go I will be dreamed. Forever. To the last moment. Until the very end.

In the grove they call me Eudemus of Cyprus. I'm in the grove. Therefore I am a Platonist. That's what being in the grove means. I know this. Do I yearn to 'go home' to Cyprus? If I'm actually from Cyprus. My life there was unspeakable. If I'm actually from Cyprus. I can't speak of it. Won't speak of it. Have never spoken of whatever I did in Cyprus. Of whatever they did to me in Cyprus. Banished me. They say. In the grove. They say. I don't. I know I wasn't dreamed. In Cyprus. That's all I know.

I'm leaving the grove. Leaving Aris. Leaving the Academy. Leaving Athens. I have almost no belongings. My legs are strong. My sandals are sturdy. I will see it for myself.

Why am I leaving the grove. Because I'm dreamed? Because I'm a traveler. In the empty sky. My mind is a flashing. I may be here. Or not. Or in-between. Here. Not exactly. The flashing is all I know. Certainly. The only certain reality.

I'm dreamed. I also dream. There's nothing strange about this. On the contrary. If I didn't dream I couldn't know I'm dreamed. I know I dream. I know. I know I know. I am conscious. I'm dreamed. So I don't sleep much. I don't sleep long. I don't sleep deep. I'm dreamed. I'm a traveler. On the surface of sleep. My consciousness spreads out. Like a lily pad. It takes little dips. From time to time. Little dips. My sleep. Dips drenched in dreams. I dream because I'm dreamed. I know this. I'm certain.

I'm leaving the grove. Because I need to see it for myself. What? What's actually happening. Outside the grove. Outside the walls. Actually the grove is outside the walls. Not far outside. But I mean outside all the walls. Every single wall. That exists. That doesn't exist. Walls. The grove has walls. Of its own. There's a whole lot going on. Plato is a great teacher. Great. He sees the walls. And what's beyond the walls. And teaches it. He sees the City that exists. And the City that doesn't exist. He's been to both. He's a traveler. He's taught me a lot. I am grateful. I think he has his blind spots. Some of his ideas worry me. Dismay me. Alarm me. Especially his idea of the soul. He says our souls exist before birth. And exist after death. Soul and body are separate. Soul is imprisoned in body. It hungers for liberation. When we die the soul is released. From the prison of this life. It returns to its true home. Where? Who knows. Outside all the walls. What walls? What outside? Plato says 'beyond.' Beyond what? What beyond? Coming home to what's beyond. This is not what I mean by 'outside all the walls.' I need to see it for myself. What? What I mean. See what I actually mean. I need to find out. To see it. I'm leaving the grove.

I'm dreamed. I remember everything that happened. In the grove. Perfectly. Before the grove, imperfectly. Or not at all. Because I wasn't dreamed. Before the grove. I spent years listening to Plato. Discussing what he said. With Aris. I love the grove. It's a great place to be. It's not out of this world. It's not a prison. Quite often Aris and I go down to the Piraeus. Like Socrates used to do. We take a good look. At where the Long Walls used to be. The Spartans tore them down. Quite rightly. Not so long ago. When Athens lost the Peloponnesian War. Forever. One war at a time. Twenty-seven years of idiocy. Carnage. From war to war. In Piraeus we drink raki. In a taverna. We also drink raki in the grove. Raki is raki. A taverna is a taverna. The grove is the grove.

Thirst is thirst. Hunger is hunger. Travelers. I also remember everything that happened. Outside the grove. Since I've been in the grove. Dreamed. Quite recently something big happened. I didn't see it for myself. In the Piraeus. It's one reason why I'm leaving the grove. For me, it's important. To my mind. The Tyrant of Pherae, in Thessaly. Attacked and plundered the Piraeus. Alexander of Pherae. Quite recently. We heard about it in the grove. We spoke about it in the grove. We didn't see it. For ourselves. I didn't see it. For myself. All these wars. Everyone attacking everyone. Everyone being attacked. By everyone. Walls. Long walls. Short walls. Invisible walls. No walls. The sea. The sky. Full. Empty. In flashes.

In the grove we study philosophy. We study the Theory of Ideas. We study theory itself. The idea of theory. The reality of theory. My idea is this. Theory is uncertain. Reality is uncertain. Only uncertainty is certain. I think. Plato heartily disagrees. I keep my idea to myself. I see it for myself. I discuss it with Aris. We don't see it together. I see it. In and for myself. I discuss it. Not with Plato himself. He's too Big.

In the Academy we don't just study pure ideas. Or Ideas. We have to study what happens. Plato says. And what happened. It's called history. Political history. Present history. Past history. There may be theory behind it. There may be no theory behind it. At all. Maybe it happens. Maybe it just happens. A fine distinction. A split hair. I think Plato has staked his human existence. On this hair. His three trips to Siracusa. For example. Trips and Tyrants. Important. For him. For us. For me. He saw it for himself. This has made him a great teacher.

I am dreamed. I know. Recently something happened. Alexander of Pherae. Plundered the Piraeus. This Alexander is a piece of shit. They say. In the grove. A terrible Tyrant. Vicious. Shameful. To call him a mad dog would be an insult. To mad dogs. They say. Frankly I don't doubt it. In the least. Tyranny is the worst form of government. They also say. I don't doubt it. Attica is dry and pretty dusty. Thessaly is lush and green. Thessaly is its Tyrant. Alexander of Pherae. This is what it means to be a Tyrant. What does it mean to be a Tyrant? Inside the walls. Outside the walls. Actually existing walls. Or imagined walls. Imagined? Who imagines them. The people inside them. Naturally. Alexander can sit in Pherae. In the taverna. Drink all the raki he wants. But a Tyrant has other ideas. Big ideas. Little ideas. Let's invade the Cyclades. Plunder the islands. Make the people slaves. Islands are islands. White. A few are green. Athens is Athens. They lost the Peloponnesian War. A while back. Recently they got the Thebans off their backs. Because at Mantinea the Theban general was killed. Athenians are Athenians. Losers are losers. Democrats. Anarchists. No Philosopher Kings. Cape Sounion. Scenic sunsets. Alexander attacks. Then he attacks the Piraeus itself. Plunders it. Goes home to Pherae. Alexander. A Tyrant. What happens. What does it mean. I don't see it for myself.

I have two fellow Platonists. Who left the grove recently. I saw them for myself. In the grove. Leaving the grove. Good fellows. Bad fellows. I'm dreamed. I don't pass judgment. I have a lot to learn. From them. I know it. It's not just some feeling. Learn something. From them. They're older. More experienced. Saw more things. Dion. From Siracusa. Banished from Siracusa. By Dionysius the Younger. Son of Dionysius the Elder. Tyrants. Dion met Plato in Siracusa. Many years ago. The most enthusiastic convert he's ever had. Plato calls him. He came to Athens. When he was banished. To the grove. He's been here a while. Like Aris. Like me. He's about 50 now. Dion's friend is named Callippus. He's incomprehensible. Puzzling. Opaque. He's also in the grove. Fellow Platonists. Callippus is very rich. Patrician. Upper crust. Big house in Athens. Dion always had lots of money coming in. From his estates. In Siracusa. He built a big house in the country outside Athens. Partying. Roistering. High living. Then Dionysius cut off his income. Quite recently. Dion was furious. Out of his mind. I saw this for myself. Tyranny! he screamed. Loud. Plato went back to Siracusa. To plead Dion's cause. No dice. Dion and Callippus left the grove. Together. They met with Plato at Olympia. In the Peloponnese. At a Festival. Plato on his way back to Athens. From Siracusa. Dion absolutely furious. Plato told us. Screaming Tyranny! Tyranny! all the time. It seems he wants to raise an army. Revenge. Return to Siracusa. He and Callippus. Together. Kill the Tyrant. Dion wants to be the Philosopher King. Of Siracusa. So they say. It seems.

I'm leaving the grove. To see it for myself. I have almost no belongings. My legs are strong. My sandals are sturdy. Traveling. I head for the town of Marathon. Due north. Then east. The grove is just north of Athens. Here's the road. It's not far to Marathon. Barely 25 miles. Here I am. The town is in a plain. Not far from the sea. There are fields full of fennel. On all sides. The word 'marathon' means a place full of fennels. The place is famous for its battle. During the first Persian invasion of Greece. The Persian King Darius I. Darius the Great. King of Kings. Can I call him a Tyrant? Or just a King? What's the difference? Why did he have to invade Greece? Isn't that Tyrannical? Is he a King just because his territory is large? If it were smaller he'd be a Tyrant? Is that the difference? I mosey around Marathon for a couple of days. Thinking about this. The battle was amazing. The Athenian army of 10,000 men routed 25,000 Persians. A small army routed a big army. Does this make the Athenians good? The Persians bad? Democrats routing Tyrants? Democracy. An agreeable form of anarchy. Plato says. Or does size have nothing to do with it. Good or bad. I'm not sure. I need to think about it.

I'm leaving Marathon. Headed due north. Then north-west. A place I heard about in the grove. I want to see it for myself. It's not far at all. About 20 miles. The South Euboean Gulf. I skirt the coast. Here's the port-town of Oropos. I head inland. Into the hills. For just a few miles. I see something remarkable. In a small ravine. Between two hills. A stream. A sacred spring. A Temple. A Sanctuary. Dedicated to Amphiaraus. The Amphiareion of Oropos. Dedicated only about 50 years ago. During the Peloponnesian War. Amphiaraus is the Argive attacker at the Sixth Gate. In Aeschylus' tragedy. *Seven Against Thebes*. A prophet. He's against this war. Against all wars. Intricate images. On the shields. Of all the other attackers. And defenders. His shield is empty. No image at all. Amphiaraus is against all forms of Tyranny. The Tyranny of images. All the attackers are killed. In the play. In another version the prophet does not die. He rides off in his chariot. Headed due east. The Thebans hot on his heels. Zeus loves his prophets. He throws his thunderbolt. The earth opens up. It swallows Amphiaraus. Right here. Where I am now. Why am I right here? I'm dreamed. The Amphiareion is an Oracle of dreams. A dream Sanctuary. People come here for healing. The plague that killed Pericles. Inside the Long Walls. Dreaming Athenians. The Sanctuary was full. Ritual dreaming. First, purify yourself. Then, sacrifice something to the Oracle. Amphiaraus. A ram is traditional. Spread out its skin. Lie down on it. Wait for the revelation of a dream. I like this place. I stay quite a few days. I see it for myself.

I go back to Oropos. I head straight up the coast. The Gulf of Euboea. Euboea is a very long narrow island. The open sea. On the far side. The Aegean. On the near side. Mainland Greece. The Straits of Euboea. Between mainland and island. The latitude of Athens. To the south. Almost to Thessaly. To the north.

I'm going to Chalcis. Just 20 miles north. A big town. On the island. Halfway between north and south. I enjoy this beautiful walk. The Gulf gleams. Bright. Not wine-dark. Almost the color of the sky. No birds. Here's Chalcis. Amazing. Thrilling. Stirring. The Euripus Strait. I've heard so much about it. Aris is bewitched. I see it for myself. It's magical. Dreamed! Unreal. Real. Absolutely certainly uncertain. No place for Plato. The island and the mainland meet. Like a hummingbird and a flower. An easy bow-shot apart. Right here. I see them touch and not-touch. The water goes wild. Goes crazy. Loses its mind. The flow from the far north. The flow from the far south. Meet. Do not meet. Converse! It's a wild conversation. What does it mean? Or not. Meaningless. Full of meaning. Land and water. Form and matter. Potentiality and actuality. In the grove I was dreamed. Wide awake. Matter matters. It's the water. It sees it for itself. No facts. Only ideas. Right in the middle. Between possibility and reality. The idea of an event. The actual event. Between them. Actual as real-unreal. Mind no-mind. Land is land. Form is form. But matter is mad. It matters. This is why I'm traveling. To see it for myself. The Euripus Strait. No poet could invent this. The Euboeans decided to become mainlanders. About 50 years ago. They built an itty-bitty bridge. A dike, actually. A short one. Long as a hummingbird. Facing the flood from the north. The flood from the south. Just look at this bridge. I see it for myself. They left gaps in the dike. To allow the tides to flow through. One gap is wide enough for a single ship. All this made the crazy current even crazier. Sane/insane. Who's counting. No-bridge/new-bridge. The flow reverses. The vortexes. Bridge/no-bridge. Never mind. The reversals. Always. Is it Democracy? An agreeable form of anarchy. Every drop. One-drop one-vote. Or Tyranny? Who's the Tyrant. What does it mean. Or, is the water always prepared. For taking some kind of form. In its activity. Does it have some rules. Or theory. Or truth. If it does, are these rules knowable? Unknowable? Does it matter. I just look. I don't think. I empty my mind. It happens. Direct, pure experience. To empty water from a cup does not mean to drink it up. Whatever reality there is is virtual. Simple and complex uncertainty. I see it for myself. The Strait itself is the only certainty. There is no Philosopher King.

I head for Thebes. It's not far. About 20 miles. The treks come later. Thessaly. Macedon. Greece is not big. Distance is distance. Near is near. Farther is farther. Far is far. I see it for myself. Thebes today. Thebes in antiquity. Thebes recently. Plenty of wars. Tragedies. Antiquity. Myth. Cadmus. Oedipus. Dionysus. Heracles. Cadmus founded the city. Built its Acropolis. The Cadmeia. Named after him. Here it is. Fine piece of work. Inspiring. Inspiring what? Inspiring the ancient Thebans. To take over the whole region. Hegemony. They built Walls all around the Acropolis. Thebes. One of the first fortified cities. In Greece. Well fortified. Big thick stone Walls. Cyclopean. A great job. In the Walls they built Seven Gates. This made them famous. Thebes of the Seven

Gates. Everyone talks about these Gates. But they make no sense without the Walls. Gate-less Walls are imaginable. Somehow. But Wall-less Gates. No. Impossible. Gates in the middle of nowhere. I'm dreamed. Order in the Gates! Why seven? Who knows? Thick walls. Big boulders on natural rock. Bricks to top them off. Fortified. Inspiring. Inspiring Democracy? Inspiring Tyranny? Thebes. Never met a war you didn't like. You have always been inspired. Ambitious. Like everybody else. Athens. Sparta. Pherae. You name it. Power. Territory. Spoils. Wars. Battles. Skirmishes. Walls. Gates. I spend several days walking round and round. From Gate to Gate. Each Gate is a pair of Gates. Actually. Open. Close. A pair. We should say the First Gates. The Second Gates. Et cetera. Round and round. Elektrai Gates. Homoloides Gates. Proitides Gates. Borraiai Gates. Neistai Gates. Hypsistai Gates. Onkaiai Gates. Round and round. See it for myself. Thebes gives food for thought. A feast. For the mind. Political mind. Thebes. An Oligarchy. For Plato the least degenerate form of government. After Timocracy. Thebes! Never miss a war. Stick your Oligarchic nose in every business. In every pie. Your Oligarchic finger. Walls. Gates. Thebes! Whose side are you on. You hate Athens. Why? Democratic. Expansionist. Imperialist. Second Persian invasion. Xerxes. King of Kings. Son of Darius the Great. King of Kings. Tyrants? Or just Kings? Thebes. Thermopylae. You send a risible crew. 400 men. To fight the Persians. A Great Wave. With the Athenians and Spartans. Unenthusiastically. After the defeat you change sides. Immediately. Zealously. At Plataea you fight for Xerxes. Against the Greeks. Unrisibly. And lose. Again. Thebes of the Seven Gates. Peloponnesian War. You're firm allies of Sparta. The winning side. You secretly side with Athens. Right after the war. You fight against Sparta. You win some. You lose some. You declare yourself a democracy! You have the best general of them all. Epaminondas. A formidably trained army. Drilled. Democratically trained. Drilled. Democratically. Round and round. From Gate to Gate. I go. Elektrai Gates. The main Gates. The road to Athens. On each side. A large circular tower. The reciprocal suicide of Eteocles and Polyneices. Here. Thinking. Whose side? Forms of government. Just names? Or worse. I see it for myself. Thebes! With a general like this. Ten years ago you defeat Sparta at Leuctra. Decisively. All over Greece they hail you. Champions of the oppressed! New Democrats. You swarm through the Peloponnese. Cripple Sparta. Definitively. You're the Boss. The Big Democrat. The Tyrant. A Theban Empire! Of Seven Gates! Not quite. Forget it. Athens teams up with Sparta. Thebes and Athens? Occasional alliance. Reciprocal hatred. At Mantinea, three years ago. Big battle. Your big general. Against Spartans, Athenians, Eleans, Mantineans. You hold your own. Epaminondas is mortally wounded. In the heat of battle. Death, ye gods! Good night sweet prince. The end of an Empire that never began. On your knees. Thebes. Sparta. Athens. Look! A new Tyrant. The Macedonians are coming.

Round and round. I'm dreamed. I don't dream I'm a historian. It's these Gates. I see them for myself. I remember. I studied history in the grove. History. Past and present. Eteocles and Polyneices. Elektrai Gates. Homoloides Gates. Proitides Gates. Borraiai Gates. Neistai Gates. Hypsistai Gates. Onkaiai Gates. Alexander of Pherae. Have no fear. A genuine *bona fide* dyed-in-the-wool Tyrant. Of the first water. They say so in the grove. They're right. Plunders the Piraeus. Thebes. Watch out. You cuddle him. Some years back. All Thessaly is scared to death of Alexander of Pherae. Thebes! You tell all Thessaly: Have no fear. We'll take care of it. You send your Theban envoy. To Pherae. Pelopidas. Your great negotiator. Epaminondas' boon companion. Unarmed. Into the lion's mouth. Alexander throws him into prison. Immediately. So you send a whole army. To rescue him. No dice. Alexander wipes you out. He goes wild. Raises hell all over the place. You Thebans calm him down. Somewhat. You're making a comeback. At Mantinea Epaminondas is killed! Alexander goes wilder. Athens fears Thebes no longer. Alexander fears Athens no longer. A scenic Sounion sunset. A raki in the Piraeus.

I'm leaving Thebes. It's time. Heading north. A short trek. My sandals are sturdy. It's not raining. A couple of days. I take my time. Due north. Past a big lake. Lake Hylica. Straight on up to the coast. North Euboean Gulf. Good long walk. Right along the coast. In flashes. Almost to the end of the Gulf. I'm dreamed. Thermopylae. 'The Hot Gates.' Sulfur springs. The entrance to Hades. Mythical. Narrow coastal pass. I see it. For myself. Xerxes. Second Persian invasion. A revenge match. Ten years after Marathon. Gigantic Persian army and navy. Cyclopean. Xerxes gets serious. Enough bullshit. King of Kings. It's time to conquer all of Greece. The Greeks decide to head him off. At the pass. Narrow. Between the mountain and the Malian Gulf. Only way through. South to North. North to South. Here it is. I look long and hard. Meditate. For several days. These Kings of Kings. Not Philosophers. Not Democrats. Tyrants? What is it that they want? Conquest. Empire. What does it mean? A Big Idea. A whim. A dream. But the blood! The last drop of blood! I'm dreamed. Everyone dreams. Fight on! Greeks from many cities. Led by Leonidas of Sparta. 7,000 men. Against the Great Wave of Persians. Invincible. The Persian fleet. Themistocles of Athens. Let's head them off in the Straits of Artemisium. At the same time. Between the northern tip of Euboea and the southern tip of Magnesia. Southern Thessaly. That's the idea. More Platonic than real. In flashes. The Cave. Shadows on the wall. Leonidas. Down in history. A snowball in hell. Your Greeks are outnumbered. Overwhelmingly. You're outflanked. The game's up. You send the others home. You make your last stand. 300 Spartans. To the last drop of Spartan blood. You're famous! The stuff of lyric poetry. What was the use. Exactly. Simonides the poet writes, 'Here obedient to the laws of Sparta you lie.' I wonder about these laws. Shadows? I think they're carved. In stone. Forever. And ever. Meanwhile, the

King of Kings and All His Men. Go completely wild. Everything goes south.
They run roughshod through Boeotia. Razing everything in sight. Athens next.
The whole city decamps to the island of Salamis. Xerxes torches the whole city.
Smashes the statues. Destroys the temples. Razes the Acropolis! It will have to
be rebuilt. From scratch. A new Parthenon. Pericles will rebuild it. Years later.
Xerxes. The reason for this carnage? The unreason? Life goes on. I'm dreamed.
I'm overexciting. Wondering about all this. These wonders. Of destruction.
This carnage.

The fleet! What ever happened to the fleet. Themistocles. Artemision. The
Persians run into a spate of bad luck. Luckily. Off the coast of Magnesia. A gale.
Sinks a third of their ships. Their overwhelming number of ships. They send
a bunch more into the Straits of Artemision. Another storm! Shipwrecked.
This levels the playing field. Somewhat. Finally the two sides fight. For one
day. Equal losses. Then, news of the Thermopylae endgame. A two-pronged
defense is useless. Without one of the prongs. The Greeks withdraw to Salamis.
Where the whole population of Athens is holed up. Fight another day. Maybe
I really am starting to dream I'm a historian. Going through all these things
twice. I learned all this in the grove. I was dreamed by then. I know this. With
certainty. Certainly. Or? Or the only certainty is uncertainty. An uncertain
reality. But real. Reality. Uncertain. Certainly. A little history is a dangerous
thing. So is a little reality. Not free. You have to pay. Themistocles is less famous
than Leonidas. He's a smart cookie. Xerxes is feeling invincible. On land. On
sea. The fleet. In the narrows of the Straits of Salamis. Themistocles lures
them in. They get tangled up. The Greeks wipe them out. They sink. Man
the lifeboats. It's curtains for the King of Kings. What tragedy. Speaking of
curtains. Aeschylus fought at the Battle of Salamis. Young Sophocles celebrated
the victory. Euripides was born. On Salamis. Where he lived. Later he lived
there in a cave. Born just before the Battle itself. Just after the Battle itself.
During the Battle itself. In any event. Xerxes goes home. What the hell, he
quips. The destruction was mutual. His invincible soldiery soldiers on. For a
while. The invincible Persian army. The Greeks defeat them. At Plataea. They
defeat the fleet at Mycale. Curtains. For Persian Tyranny. In Greece. What does
it all mean? What curtains. What Tyranny. What do I see for myself.

I'm heading farther north. I need to see it for myself. I need to see it better.
More clearly. Less hysterically. I'm dreamed. Dazzled. Slightly. Calm. Collected.
Clear. Certainly uncertain. For myself. Figments. In flashes. Thermopylae got
me by the balls. Past history. Old stories. What will become of me? In Pherae.
Present history. Tyranny Now. My sandals are sturdy. My soul? Such as it is.
Free. No prison. Just let me walk awhile. This is beautiful country. I'm already
in the city of Lamia. Northernmost North Euboean Gulf. Innermost inlet.
Two-faced Lamia. Daughter of Poseidon. You look South and North at once.

I follow the coast. I'm going east. Along the north coast of the Malian Gulf. In the shadow of Mount Othrys. Along the north side of the Straits of Artemision. Then north. Along the west coast of the Pagasean Gulf. So beautiful. I'm dreamed. I need to sleep. A path. An intuition. I head inland. Fields. A field. An empty space. I need to sleep. Sunset. Field dusk. The sea somewhere to the east. The sun behind my back. Nightfall. It's completely dark. Suddenly! Black. Completely. Not a glimmer. Not a star. Black. I close my eyes. Strange. It's a little less black. I open them again. Blacker! I look around. In all directions I see only complete blackness. I see it. I see the blackness. For myself. I lie down on the soft earth. In the blackness. Earth. The sky does not exist. Earth blackness. I'm asleep. Instantly. I'm dreaming! I'm dreamed and dreaming. I dream black earth. So black. Deep deep black. Fields of black earth. Stretching endlessly. In all directions. Gentle furrows. A sense of richness. Of wellbeing. Harvested. Invisible endless harvests. Empty black fields. Ridge and furrow. Black earth. I dream it all night long. Dawn. I wake up. Suddenly. I'm going further north. To Thessaly.

I'm heading due north. I'm in Thessaly. I follow the west coast of the Pagasean Gulf. All the way to the top. Where the coast bends east. Mount Pelion is just to the north. The mythical land of the Centaurs. Chiron, the tutor of ancient heroes. Jason. Achilles. Theseus. Heracles. I head inland. Due west. Just a few miles. I come to Pherae. Capital of Thessaly. Alexander's city. The Tyrant! Kill Kill Kill. Blood, gore, guts, and veins. Eat dead, burnt bodies! Cruelty. Brutality. Barbarity. Ferocious. Fiendish. Vile. War! Blood! Kill! His city. I see it for myself.

The horror! Pherae. I didn't expect this. Twisting little streets. Full of garbage. Colorless ugly houses. Snarling dogs. All over the place. Pheraens. Slaughtering. Massacring. Ravaging. All over Greece. Home in Pherae. They don't give a damn. Next stop? Who knows. Filth. Grime. Goo. Alleys. Walls! Walls everywhere. But what do they wall? Wall in. Wall out. Just stand there. Dumb blankness. No. I see writings on the walls. Alexander's Tyrannical tweets. *PHERAE FIRST. MAKE PHERAE GREAT AGAIN. FUCK EVERYONE.* Hardly anybody on the streets. Where is everybody? I mostly see armed guards. All dressed alike. Carrying clubs. Maces. Axes. Swords. Knives. Daggers. Spears. What do they think they're guarding. What? Who? Each other, maybe. Look! A taverna. A sad café. No ballad. A bunch of men. Old. Young. In-between. Drinking wine. Drinking raki. Just sitting there. Not speaking. I see one missing an arm. One a leg. A hand. An ear. A nose. An eye. Veterans. Of wars. In the defense of Tyranny. Pheraen warriors fight like madmen. They say. Monsters. Fiends. Like Alexander. Their Tyrant. Fearless. Wild. Crazy. Raids. Skirmishes. Battles. All the other Greeks are big on phalanxes. Orderly rows of hoplites. Disciplined. Keep your ranks. Attack in unison. Ritually. Orderly. Not the Pheraens. Wild.

Anything-goes individualists. Like their Tyrant. Fuck phalanxes. Jackasses. Rows and rows of men. Holding spears. Thrusting. Pheraens don't like throwing spears either. Throw it. It's gone. Your enemy picks it up. Throws it back at you. We're not here to play games. On the battlefield. Say the Pheraens. Hand to hand combat. Sword fights. Eye-gouging wrestling matches. Like in Homer. They say. Spears! Shove them up their asses. Atrocities galore. Blood, gore, guts, and veins. The Spartans have some sort of blow-torches. Flame-throwers. Poison gas. Good stuff! Say the Pheraens. We're working on it. Eat dead, burnt bodies! We spend our spare time studying poisons. An ancient tradition. *MAKE PHERAE GREAT AGAIN.* Hell grant soon we hear again the swords clash! But—these men look numb. Like living dead. What's happening. Too many battlefields? Too much blood? There's no wine like the blood's crimson! Numb. Mute. Life. Death. Certain uncertainty. War. Blood. A lifetime. A deathtime. What happens. In their heads. Their souls. What soul? Imprisoned in their bodies? Or is soul what makes a living thing alive. I muse. Wounded souls. Living dead. Home now. For now. The Tyrant, too, is home. Unpredictable. Ferocious. Brutal. Here. At home. What happens. After the battle. The war within. From the battlefield to the soul. The women! Where are the women. All invisible. Where's the populace! The normal people. Huddling in corners. Crouching in alleyways. Roving invisibly. In fear. Stricken by a terrible trauma. Everyone. Together. Warriors and warred. Bringing the war home. Is there a doctor in the house? In the Tyrant's house. Wounded souls. Drink their blood like wine. Terror. Trauma. Tyranny. A certain reality. A certainty. War. Blood. War. Blood. Gore, guts, and veins. *Otan pineis stin taverna.* Just sitting there. Slaughtered. Massacred. Ravaged. Where's the Tyrant? What's he drinking? Look! His palace. I see it for myself. The ugliest palace I've ever seen. By far. A nightmare. Guards everywhere. Inside, Alexander is guarded. By a dog as ferocious as he is. They say. Plato says that the soul is immortal and able to endure all evil and all good. Look! A new tweet. *EXTERMINATE ALL THE BRUTES.* What brutes, Alexander? Yours? Mine? Whose? Why? To rob them of their treasure? What treasure? What brutes? Elephants? Dogs? Cats? Your ivory, Alexander! Your blood diamonds! I'm dreamed. Your darkness. The nightmare of your choice. Perhaps this is the essence of Tyranny. You don't even know what brutes to exterminate. You don't know why you exterminate. All the brutes. You had your fun in the Piraeus, Alexander. Plundering. I was in the grove. I didn't see it for myself. Plato says, we shall always hold to the upper road, and in every way follow justice and wisdom. Eat dead, burnt bodies! Suddenly I have a terrible headache. Terrible! Shivering. Shaking. My head is burning. Fire! My brain's on fire!

Where am I? In Pherae. Somewhere. On a bed. In a room. Who's that? A doctor? My head is screaming. It's about to explode. At the gate of hell! I fall asleep. I dream. I'm dreamed. I dream. I see a handsome young man. A prophet. He speaks to me. Softly. He says, Eudemus, you will get better very soon. Then he says, Eudemus, Alexander, this cruel Tyrant, will die very soon. Then he says, Eudemus, in five years you will return to your home. I wake up. Dazed. Dazzled. Very tired. But a day later I feel fine. A prophetic dream. I hear a lot of noise in the streets. Confusion. Commotion. People shouting. I feel a little tired, but fine. I go out to see what's going on. The streets are full of people! Shouting. Shouting meaningless shouts. What's going on. I ask someone. He shouts in my face, The Tyrant is dead! Fuck the Tyrant! Alexander. I see it for myself. His body thrown into the street. In front of his ugly palace. The people are pissing on it. The dogs are mangling it. The dogs of his nothingness. Gnawing at his bones. Emptied of marrow.

Eudemus, in five years you will return home. The prophet said. His third prophecy. What to make of it. I'm dreamed. Someone is dreaming of me. Of me and of my dream. Who? Who knows. I only know that someone dreamed of me. In the grove. I know that someone dreams of me. And of my dream. Right here. Right now. That's all I know. Going home in five years. Perhaps to Phthia. Like Socrates. Who dreamed a gloriously beautiful woman. Dressed in white. Who told him that in three days he'd be going home. To the pleasant land of Phthia. Which is a stone's throw from here. From Pherae. But it's Achilles' home. Not mine. Or Socrates'. We're not Achilles. Not in mind. Or matter. Not permanently. Or temporarily. Going home to Phthia. In the grove they called me Eudemus of Cyprus. In the grove I began to be dreamed. I don't know why I left Cyprus. All I know is that I wasn't dreamed in Cyprus. What did I do in Cyprus? What did they do to me in Cyprus? I have no idea. If I saw it for myself why don't I remember it. Cyprus, my home. Eudemus of Cyprus. I don't know. I don't know anything about anything before the grove. Does Cyprus actually exist? Just because people say so. What if they're wrong. Do I actually exist? Just because people say so. They might be wrong. All I know with certainty is that I'm dreamed. And that I had a dream. A dream also dreamed. With three prophecies. The first two were fulfilled immediately. But the going home. Where. Why. How. I wasn't dreamed in Cyprus. That's all I know. About Cyprus. The going home prophecy needs a prophecy. Of its own. Prophesying the prophecy. Interpreting the dream. Going home. The hunger to go home. Do I hunger to go home? Where. What home. Who. What hunger. Home means hunger. I don't dream of home. I'm dreamed. Not at home. Dreamed in the grove. Is the grove my home. No. Do I hunger for the grove. No. I want to see it for myself. Outside the grove. I'm dreamed everywhere. I, Eudemus. My dream. Dreamed everywhere. Do I hunger for everywhere. No. I just want to see it for myself. In flashes I think I exist. I think I exist in flashes. It's all absolutely certainly absolutely uncertain. What 'it' did I want to see in Pherae? For myself. Did I see it? Before Alexander was killed. Pissed on. Mangled. Do I see it now? The Tyrant's bones. Emptied of marrow. What have I seen? Writings on walls. Armed guards. Wounded souls. People living in fear. That's not it. No, actually, it is it. But I still want to see it for myself.

I'm heading north. Far north. All the way north. To Macedon. To north Macedon. A trek. Thessaly is big. Then Macedon. Very big. My sturdy sandals. Winter will come. See it. For myself. I look around. I'm inland. No sea. Countryside. I've never seen anything like it. Stunning. So green. Magnificent. Trees. Tall poplars. Green firs. Forests. Rocky crags and cliffs. Shimmering. I'm on the path to Larissa. A big town. On the Pineios River. I take my time. A few days. Walking. See it for myself. Pherae. The Tyrant. The dream. Larissa. A beautiful city. Some legends say Peleus was born here. And his son, 'swift-footed' Achilles. Others say they were from Phthia. Farther south. I can see Mount Ossa. To the northeast. White. A fine film of snow. I head farther north. Along the river. Taking my time. A couple of days. I come to an amazing place. The Vale of Tempe. A gorge cut by the Pineios. On its way from Larissa to the sea. The Aegean. A figment. Ossa is right here to the east. In flashes. The great peaks of Mount Olympus. To the north. In the distance. I'm dreamed. Stunning. Tempe. Celebrated by the poets. A favorite haunt of Apollo and the Muses. On the border between Thessaly and Macedon. A gorge. Myth. The trident of Poseidon cut through the rocks. The Greeks intended to face the Persians at the Tempe Pass. During the second invasion. But thought better of it. For better. Or worse. The massacre was at Thermopylae. Tempe is a superbly peaceful place. I spend a couple of days here. But I need to see it for myself. It. Why the world is not a peaceful place. Why all these wars. This carnage. This Tyranny. I'm following the Pineios again. Northeast. To the sea. Where the Aegean turns into the great Thermaic Gulf. The heart of Macedon. Embracing the Gulf. The coast takes me due north. I'm heading far north. To Pella. The new capital. Of Macedon. King Archelaus built it. A few years ago. In the marshlands of Lake Loudiake. I already know Macedon. Like the palm of my hand. From years of conversation with Aris. My *philos*. Like the palm of his Macedonian hand. He knows where his home is. I'm in the great shadow of Olympus. The gods called it home. Zeus. Their King. The light! The permanent snows. I stand here on the shore. I put my foot into the sea. I turn around. A plain. Perfectly flat. I walk. A couple of miles. A small town. Foothill. The land is rising. A taverna. I have an omelet. I have tomatoes. Olives. Goat cheese. Wine. From this town the land rises. Quickly! To the peak of Mount Olympus. Straight up. Two days march. To the peak. They say. But I have promises to keep. Olympus is the home of the old gods. Time to see the home of the new Tyrant. For myself.

Pella. A fine long walk. Straight up the coast. To the northern tip of the
gulf. And beyond. Through the towns of southern Macedon. Dion. Pydna.
Methoni. Then inland. And north. To Pella. This is Macedon. A big, rugged
land. Not a city-state. A tribal kingdom. Of warriors. Courage. Daring.
Fearless. The Greeks have emptied themselves out. They say. Athens. Sparta.
Thebes. Dregs. Emptied. Imperially. Ambitiously. Tyrannically? Macedon is
full. A brand-new King. Philip II of Macedon. They say he wants to be the
new Cyrus. Not just King but King of Kings. Cyrus the Great and Darius the
Great. Put together. Great Greatness. Empire. Conquest. Greece. Persia. The
world. Such as it is. War. Blood. War. Blood. There's no wine like the blood's
crimson! Hell grant soon we hear again the swords clash! This is the it I want to
see for myself. A fresh Empire. Fresh Blood. Fresh Tyranny. Fresh as wild mint.
Fresh as this fair breeze from the Gulf. Fresh towns along the coast. Dion.
Pydna. Methoni is the last town on the Gulf still controlled by Athens. Philip
will take care of it soon. Fresh breeze. Long walk. North. A decision. Keep
going north to Pella. Or take a rugged hike inland. To see the old capital. Aigai.
For myself. Aigai. The national hearth of the Macedonian race. All the Kings
are buried there. Past and future. A sacred city. But Archelaus wanted a fresher
capital. Fresh ambitions. Pella. North of the Gulf. Inland. More secure. A fresh
new Empire. A true great capital. Archelaus had interesting ideas. My *philos*
Aris told me about him. A dab of history. But don't dream I'm a historian.
Going through all these things twice. King Archelaus laid the foundations of
Macedon's military power. He was also a man of culture. He invited Euripides
to his new palace in Pella. Euripides among others. Never mind the others.
Euripides, straight from his cave on Salamis. He liked Pella. It seems. He wrote
his *Bacchae* and *Iphigenia in Aulis* there. Triumphed at the Great Dionysia
in Athens. Shortly after his death. In Pella. He also wrote his Macedonian
Quartet. In Pella. *Alcmene. Temenus. Temenidai. Archelaus.* Honoring this *arche
laus*. Leader of the people. (A far cry from Alexander of Pherae. If I may be
so bold.) But good king Archelaus came to a bad end. A crying shame. What
justice? He was killed in the same year Socrates drank the hemlock. During a
hunt. By one of his royal pages. The page had three accomplices. One of them
once insulted Euripides. Commented on his bad breath. To his face. Bad taste.
Right in front of Archelaus. This outraged the King. He invited the Tragedian
to flog the future accomplice. The accomplice never forgave him. A hunt. Exit
the King. In the grove Aris also reminded me that his long-dead father was
personal physician to King Amyntas III. Who came to the throne after ten
years of abject confusion in Macedon. Following the ludicrous assassination of
Archelaus. In the history of the world this may be of little importance. But for
Aris it's important. Amyntas' favorite son was Philip. Who wants to be King of
Kings. Cyrus the Great and Darius the Great. Put together. I, however, myself,
leave Aigai to the past and future and continue north. Figments. Recalling
these dabs of history. I'm dreamed. I want to see Pella for myself. In flashes. I

want to see how things stand. For myself. And where they're going. For myself. And others. So many wounded souls. A doctor in the house. Dream on. Let us dream on.

Philip has been King for less than a year. For the moment just plain King. Not yet King of Kings. He's only 23. He had an eventful youth. When he was 14. He was taken hostage in Thebes. Somehow or other. For several years. But he made the most of it. He learned all about military science from Epaminondas. The great Theban general. It will serve him well. He wants to conquer the world. Pella is the place to be. Here and now. I'm already at the tip of the Thermaic Gulf. Heading northwest. Two days walk. I'm in Pella. Direct reverse of Pherae. Clean. Orderly. Military-looking. Groups of men training. Drilling. Everywhere I look. Rows of hoplites shoulder-to-shoulder. Not with the usual Greek spears. No. Look! Philip! Your great invention. A heavy pike 20 feet long. The sarissa. Impregnable walls of pikes. Visionary. A morale-builder. Plus your fabulous Macedonian cavalry. You're well on your way. From rugged tribal kingdom to world power. Attack everyone! One at a time. Conquer cities and rename them after yourself. Hope your future son will do the same. One day. Does all this make you a Tyrant? Like Alexander of Pherae! Time will tell. Or won't tell. What a Tyrant really is. Who's a Tyrant. Who isn't. Time will tell. Or won't.

In Pella everyone's heard about my dream. In Pherae. The three prophecies. How in the world did everyone hear about it? I wish I knew. I'm dreamed. Nobody knows this. I spend the winter in Pella. Snow. Hard frost. Macedon. I see it for myself. Spring. Summer. I have news from the grove. Dion, and the incomprehensible Callippus. They've raised an army. Bought an army, to be exact. Mercenaries. Sun and fun on the green island of Zakynthos. In the Ionian Sea. Off the northwest coast of the Peloponnese. Training? Drilling? I doubt it. Seriously. Dion is not Philip of Macedon. By a long shot. Roistering? That's more like it. In any event. They're preparing. To set sail for Siracusa. Kill the Tyrant! says Dion. Long live the Philosopher King! This is it. I'm dreamed. I have to see it for myself.

soul doctor

Welcome to Zakynthos! says Dion, Platonist and statesman. Welcome to Zakynthos! says Callippus, incomprehensible and opaque. Good fellows, bad fellows. Who knows? Welcome, Eudemus of Cyprus!! chime in 800 motley mercenaries. Raring to go. Men of much fortune, and with a bad name to come. Nice to see you, I say. I'm dreamed. I dreamed. But this is not a dream. It's a certain reality. Highly uncertain. Such as it is. I see it for myself. They're all shouting. Whack the Tyrant! Long live the Philosopher King! In unison. A rave. Raving and dreaming are not the same. I've been all over Macedon. Every nook and cranny. They're very busy. Training, drilling. Fighting, invading. War! Never stop. I never heard anyone in Macedon shout 'Long live the Philosopher King!' Or 'Long live the King!' for that matter. But right now I'm in Plato country. Dion doesn't drill his troops, they wouldn't stand for it. He just rants at them. Platonistically. Listen.

The high tide of Tyranny in Greece may have diminished, but in Sicily they're surfing the waves. Plato, our Leader, speaks often of his 'second sailing.' It's a metaphor. When the winds fail, the sailor turns to oars. He no longer relies on any help outside himself. This is Plato's 'second sailing.' It means never stop struggling for answers to the Big Questions. Life, death, the immortality of the soul. The World of Forms. The Theory of Ideas. When all looks lost we get our second wind. Socrates was ready to make a fresh start on the very last day of his life. The Great City of Siracusa is in the grip of a terrible Tyrant. He has powerful forces at his command. We stand alone in this Good Fight. We are few, they are many. But we have Ideas and they don't. Their Ship of State is battered by Great Waves, but we shall set it right. We have the True Vision of an Even Keel. Justice! Philosophy! Peace! Together we set out on this second sailing. Set our oars up, that we swing mid fellows!

Wow! This sure woke me up. 'Plato, our leader'—who's he kidding. This is a gang of mercenaries. Your family dog cares as much about Plato as they do. 'A terrible Tyrant'—Dionysius the Younger, Dion's nephew-cum-brother-in-law and former protégé. I'm dreamed, but I could never dream a rant like this. On this beautiful green island. *What* is coming up softly, like a flower? Macedon to Zakynthos. Traveling. A long march is not a stroll. Empire. Emptiness. Winter snow in the mountains. In flashes. Swirling. Falling hard. Drifting to Zakynthos. Spring flowers. Tyrants. Mercenaries. I'm dreamed. Platonists. Philosopher Kings. I see it for myself.

Dion can spin a yarn, no question about that. When he was the Elder Tyrant's chief diplomat he sweet-talked birds right out of the trees. So they say, and I believe it. Methinks, such men are dangerous. Who's he pitching his patent medicine to now? To his 'forces'? Don't forget to pay them, Dion, or they'll throw you overboard. Fast. To me and to Callippus, fellow Platonists? I can hear Callippus, the Athenian, saying, opaquely, 'it's Greek to me.' This speech— what's the point? It's perfectly pointless—is that the point? Philip of Macedon has sarissas twenty feet long, that's his point. What is Dion really doing with his 800 motley mercenaries? I have a much bigger question. I raise my hands and spread out all my fingers. What am I doing! Here. With Dion. Going home. To Siracusa. Is that dream in Pherae getting to me? The third prophecy, the 'going home.' See 'it' for myself—is the 'it' losing its clear outline? Which, in fact, was never all that clear. Alexander of Pherae plundering the Piraeus. Lit a fire. Which drove me out of the grove. Is that 'it'? A question I can't answer. Not a good or bad question. Good like a good cause. Bad like a bad cold. A question I can't answer. Period. I'm dreamed. Is this the price? For being dreamed. For my dream.

Dion's second sailing. In his youth, as Dionysius the Elder's right-hand man, he was surfing the waves himself. Got filthy rich. He literally had the key to the Siracusan Treasury. The Elder was a truly terrible Tyrant, a veritable Tyrant's Tyrant, says Plato, himself, so it must be true. Dion was the Tyrant's trusted advisor and chief diplomat. Carthage was the big problem. The goddam Africans were swarming all over Sicily, interfering with the Elder's own swarming. Dionysius the Younger managed to have his father, the Elder, poisoned, and took over as the 'terrible' (says Dion) Tyrant he is today. Dion, meanwhile, took over as the Younger's right-hand man. As Dion, himself, told me, in the grove, the Younger was barely able to tie his shoes without Dion. This 'terrible' Tyrant. Dion had the Big Idea of transforming him into a Philosopher King. With Plato's help. Dion and Plato ganged up, philosophically, on the 'terrible' Tyrant. Who, unphilosophically, put his foot down, stomping on his right-hand man and banishing him from Siracusa. This was Dion's first sailing. All the way to Athens. When he told me about this, in the grove, it occurred to me that his Big Idea was overwhelmingly absurd. Still, we can't blame him. The old college try. After all, Plato calls Dion the most enthusiastic convert he's ever had. Alchemists have been trying to transform base metals into gold for thousands of years. Still, Dion does tend to overdo it. He peddles the Philosopher King as a miracle cure for all ills. Here, in Zakynthos, he's got his medicine show on the road. Is there a doctor in the house! For Plato a Philosopher King possesses a love of knowledge, intelligence, reliability, and a willingness to live a simple life. Any candidates? Only true Philosophers have access to the Ideas, says Plato. In particular, to the Idea of the Good. A ruler with no access to the Idea of the Good is a snake-oil salesman, Plato says. In his recent book, the *Republic*, which I read in the grove, he says that the Ship of State needs a Captain. A True Captain, he says, needs to pay attention to the seasons, the heavens, the stars, the winds, and everything proper to the craft, if he is truly to sail a Ship of State. This, as Dion, himself, puts it, is a metaphor. He must be willing to live a simple life, Plato says, far less metaphorically. Dion! Callippus! Here I wait so patiently. There's nothing wrong with sailing by the seat of your pants, but, a simple life? Hold your horses. Dion! As the Elder's right-hand-man you poured the Siracusan treasury into your own pockets, and then bought up half the city. The choicest estates. All this, out of your desire to live a simple life! Or is that no kind of joke. Back in the grove, Aris and I and our fellow Platonists lived in the grove. Itself. Simply. You lived in Callippus' royal palace in town and bought a stately mansion in the country. Long live the simple life. And you, Callippus the Opaque! I've seen you. Philosophizing in the grove, but you had your dinners catered by a swank eatery in Kolonaki. Living 'simply' on bread and cheese here on Zakynthos. Slumming. My ass. Your refined palate. I bet you have every 5-star taverna on the island hanging on your every hankering. Gourmet. Today they call you Callippus the Academic. Tomorrow, I bet, Callippus of Siracusa. The Siracusan cooking is out of this world. The stuff of truly famished Platonists. It will sink your ship in the end. Possibly, your ship and mine. We Platonists are somehow connected. I'm dreamed. You eat. We all have a sea voyage ahead of us. Eat up! At sea nobody cooks. Biscuits. Jerky. We hope for a fair wind. And a True Captain.

We're setting sail. Wish us luck. It won't be an easy trip. The Tyrant knows we're coming. No need of spies, Dion's rants have been heard round the world. Written on all the walls. Platonically speaking. Ideal walls. Of caves. Of cities. In the middle of fields. Walls with gates and gateless walls. Dammit all, everybody knows we're coming. Dion, this is not smart. There's a time-honored route from here to Siracusa. Slow and steady, sticking close to the coasts. Up the Ionian, across the strait, then straight down along the coast of Italy. But the Tyrant has his whole fleet waiting for us along the Italian coast and everybody knows it. Birds know it, bees know it, even educated fleas know it. Dion, himself, knows it. So what do we do? No problem! sez our True Captain. We'll sail straight across the open sea. Thirteen days. Not an island in sight. Not a bird. Not the shadow of a bird. But this Dion has a charmed life, damn his eyes. We make it to Pachynus. The extreme south-east point of Sicily. Siracusa a hop and a skip to the north. Dion almost home. Callippus in ecstasy. He's shouting. They have the best tomatoes in the world here in Pachynus! He's half out of his mind. With some beautiful eggplant and great local cheese we can cook up an immortal dish! What is Dion hungry for? Home? Pachynusian tomatoes? Guess again. Captain, our Captain. He's less fathomable than the unfathomable Callippus. Our Ship of State sails farther west. Why! What sort of Big Idea is this? What sort of fellows are these? One's crazy and the other's out of his mind. What am I doing here! I'm dreamed, but that's no excuse. We're sailing west, along the southern coast of Sicily. Straight into a gigantic storm that sweeps us right out to sea. Ye gods the coast of Africa, we're smashing against the rocks—we luck out. The Carthaginians are glad to see us. Dion's old friends. They give Callippus some tomatoes. We all have couscous. Rest up. The Tyrant must take us for goners. Long gone. The Cunning of Reason, says Dion. He may have a point after all. Or this snake-charmer may, simply, be charmed. We head back to Sicily.

Western Sicily. Carthaginian Sicily. Our Great Helmsman has a Big Idea. Just 800 (overly well-paid) mercenaries. Motley. Measly. A puny crew. The Tyrant has formidable forces. We need more men. The Carthaginians give him enough supplies for a proper army. We barnstorm through southern Sicily. A veritable Platonist roadshow. Agrigento, Gela, Camarina, into the Siracusan hinterland. Dion raves. We round up quite a crowd. Some 5000 revolted Sicilians delighted to revolt against the Tyrant. Who, meanwhile, having given us up for lost, has sailed off to tyrannize Calabria, as usual. Does Dion know what he's doing or is it all blind luck? Either way, I'm wondering what sort of Platonist he is. What sort of Philosopher King he'd make. Siracusa here we come. The Tyranny capital of the world. I see it for myself. Tyranny Sicilian style. They say it makes Alexander's plundering look like child's play. Though, as I saw for myself, Pherae is no playground. Kill Kill Kill. Eat dead, burnt bodies! Wounded souls. A sad café. We attack at dawn. Lo and behold, the people welcome us with open arms. After all this Tyranny they are thoroughly revolted. Dion has friends in Siracusa. The Siracusans themselves slaughter the Tyrant's supporters. The revolted revolt. Dion, in shining armor, a garland on his head, leads us into the City. Platonism triumphs!

If only it were true. Now it's my turn to be revolted. I wish I were back in the grove. What am I doing here. I wanted to see it for myself. Instead I'm in the thick of it, myself, and I'll never get out. Going home to the pleasant land of Phthia. In flashes. Laugh or cry. Or both together. Dion in shining armor. A madhouse. At the edge of chaos. It hit me all at once. For some reason I'm thinking about Plato's Idea of the soul. A Big Idea. Recollection. We know the Forms because our immortal souls were in the World of Forms before our births. The soul does not forget. But we forget, because the soul is corrupted by its connection with the body. True philosophers devote their lives to destroying this connection. True Platonistic philosophers. This is what I was taught in the grove. Walls. Writing on walls. Soul imprisoned in body. *Hungering* for liberation. When we die the soul is released, at last, and returns to its true home. Outside the walls. Beyond. The third prophecy in my dream. My returning home. Looking now at Dion in shining armor I wonder, *with horror*, what if this is it. What if I have returned home. Soul, released from the prison of this world. My destiny of death. Plato says, the soul is immortal and able to endure all evil and all good. He says nothing of wounded souls. Like I saw in Pherae, at the taverna. In every corner of Macedon I saw souls hungering for wounds. Of my own free will I decided to follow Dion to Siracusa. Why in this sorry world did I decide such a thing? I laugh I cry. Do I buy Plato's Big Idea of Recollection? Not on your life. Not even if he sells it for half a red cent. I'm not a good Platonist. I'm not Dion the Platonist in shining armor either. Forgive me, my fellows, but I don't buy any of it. Dion, the Philosopher King. Did I sail the wide open sea for thirteen days, absurdly, to sell the Sicilians this. This snake-oil. The Immortal Soul, before birth, contemplating the World of Forms—this is Plato's hunger, not mine. Soul is what makes a living thing alive. This is my simple vision. We live, and soul makes us live. Life is a property of living things, just as knowledge and health are. Soul relates to body as form relates to matter, and matter matters! There is no 'connection' that needs to be destroyed. Matter can be potential, or actual. Exactly like mind. This is my faith. Mind can be potential or actual, passive or active, asleep or awake. But sleeping mind has such enormous power! We call it dreaming. Dreams can be prophetic. But difficult to interpret. 'Returning home.' What if you don't know where home is. What if—far worse—you don't know *what* home is. What if, then, you become famous for a prophetic dream. Not because you soon recovered, and the tyrant fell, but because of your 'coming home.' All over Greece, all over Macedon, they're talking about this dream, why why why? Now it's about to infect Sicily. Like the plague that ravaged Athens. So happily protected by its Long Walls. Brand new. Its death trap. I'm dreamed, I know this. With certainty. I dreamed. I know this, with certainty. But that's all the certainty I have. Everything else is uncertain. Dion here in shining armor is an eminently uncertain reality. To say the least. My seeing it for myself has, itself, become, now, here, in the dead center of Siracusa, an uncertain reality. What is certainty worth? Possibly, absolutely nothing. Especially if it doesn't exist. The problem is that I exist. Uncertainly. Certainly. *Hunger* goddamit, this is the problem. We're not even real. Not exactly real. I know it. A certain reality. An uncertain reality. We're all hungry. But, may I ask—*hungry for what?* May I ask! I raise my hands and spread out all my fingers. Again. Dion. Plato. Eudemus. Hungry for what? Somewhere in my bones. Not yet emptied of marrow. But it will come. Hungry. For a good laugh. For what exists. But nothing exists! Dion, Philosopher King of Siracusa. Your home. Do you exist? Plato! Your World of Ideas. Of souls Recollecting. Do you exist? I vote no. On both counts. A referendum. *Huis Clos*. No Exit. An Exit. Exit the King. Exit Plato. What about me. Do I exist. I vote not exactly. In a manner of speaking. In flashes. I'm kidding. What exists? Laughter and tears. Dreamers. Dreamed-ers. Hunger? I vote yes! I'm hungry. For what? To see it for myself. For my writing on the wall. What else? Let's vote. What am I doing here. Another referendum. Am I really here. Not exactly. What are we all hungry for. Let's vote. Democratic. Deficit. Surplus. Who's counting. What does democracy have to do it. An agreeable form of anarchy, as Plato put it, graphically. Personally, I really don't know what I'm talking about. What writing on the wall. I only know that I'm dreamed. Certainly, for what it's worth. I dreamed, in Pherae. I remember it well. Alexander of Pherae *made* me dream. So I dreamed. So what! Why are they talking about it halfway round the world? *HUNGRY FOR WHAT?* This is what I'd write on my wall. Platonically. Or not. I sit in the grove all night and look up at the abyss. I see the muddy bottom. The savory dregs. The writing on the wall.

Dion in shining armor. I see it for myself. Right now. This very moment. No take it or leave it. Here it is. Here I am. Why? Shall we take another vote. I vote no. I vote for no more votes. It's the abyss that keeps us all alive, only the abyss. We live, and something *makes* us live. Called soul. Just a name. Coming home. To Siracusa. Dion of Siracusa. Callippus the Opaque. Some day they'll call him Callippus of Siracusa. I bet. Overwhelmingly absurd. Eudemus of Cyprus. Any less absurd? Any less overwhelming? Coming home. To the pleasant land of Phthia. Roistering in Thessaly. Dion has friends in Siracusa. Friends. Platonists. Or not. Who's counting. Everyone's shouting. Always so much shouting going on! The populace. No war for a whole week and they fall into a perilous lethargy. Blood, gore, guts, and veins. Shining armor! Have no fear. All hands on deck. Where's the Tyrant. *Deposed*, Dion proclaims. We'll see. The writing's on the wall. Let the good times roll. A week later, and here he is now, the 'terrible' Tyrant, Dionysius the Younger. Protected by his loyal fleet. Has he learned to tie his shoes by himself? Who knows. He slips into the Old City of Siracusa, called Ortigia. Like a spider into its web. An impregnable fortress, and picturesque to boot. The world-famous Fountain of Arethusa, an infinitely ancient spring, gushing, full of papyrus. Never mind. It's time for war. Ever since the Elder started picking fights *with everyone in sight* there hasn't been a glimmer of peace in this town. Carnage. Kill Kill Kill. It never stops. There are more mercenaries here than the grains of sand in the hourglass of this world. The populace is already exhausted. *The souls are wounded.* And what's on everybody's mind? Blood, gore, guts, and veins. That's all anybody's thinking about. I see it for myself. *And this time I'm in the thick of it.* Thick as a brick. The Tyrant's in the citadel. A neat idea. He invites Dion over for a chat. Dion, after all, is his uncle-cum-brother-in-law. Family ties. Let's work things out. Dion, Callippus, and I mosey on over to Ortigia, to the palace. Not at all ugly like Alexander's in Pherae. The Tyrant throws us into prison. Immediately. Have no fear. The next day Dion's mercenaries and, it seems, the entire populace, storm the citadel. Ferocious fighting. Hand to hand. Eye-gouging. I, Eudemus of Cyprus! I burst out laughing! *Laughing*. Hard. A real good laugh. This sums it up. Between laughing and crying laughing wins out. Eudemus of Cyprus, laughing in Siracusa. Fighting. Kill Kill Kill. We nail their asses to the walls of the citadel. A triumph. The populace is delighted. They *elect* Dion Leader of Siracusa. An agreeable form of anarchy. How agreeable? What anarchy? High anarchy. Dion has just been elected and *he takes a stand against elections.* Cerebral faggoty bullshit, he calls them. Degenerate. UnPlatonistic. We're off to a flying start. Things are looking just great. Callippus is devouring these little round tomatoes—best in the world! he says—baked with eggplant and cheese. *I'm laughing.* What's next. The populace wants democracy. Dion says *d'un tyran l'autre*. No, actually he says Philosopher King. Plato. He's dreaming. Uncertainly. The populace says, you're bullshitting us. Big time. *I'm laughing.* The Siracusans *depose* Dion. Un-elect him. Refuse to pay the mercenaries. Ye gods they refuse to pay the mercenaries! The geese are cooked. We decamp. Dion, Callippus, I, Eudemus of Cyprus, and 3,000 hungry mercenaries. We head north just a few miles to the pleasant town of Leontini. Dion has friends in Leontini. The Leontinians give us the key to the city. Why?! What have we ever done for (or to) them. Dion, of course, would prefer the key to the treasury. Damn your greedy paws, Dion, you can't have everything. I wonder—*why* do the Leontinians give us the key to the city? I have a theory. They look stressed out of their minds. They don't know if we're coming or going. They don't know if *they're* coming or going. Too many wars. Too much Kill Kill Kill. Soul is what makes a living thing alive. These people are alive but they've forgotten what *makes* them live. They only pretend to live. They go through the motions. These are wounded souls. This is no laughing matter.

Meanwhile back in Siracusa the populace insists. For some incomprehensible reason they're convinced that democracy is better than tyranny. A stubborn illusion. Here in Leontini Dion is furious. He keeps shouting Philosopher King! The stressed out Leontinians are jumping out of their skins. They're at the end of their tethers. They're looking for trees to climb. We all wait for news from Siracusa. The Tyrant has escaped but his son and *his* mercenaries are still holed up in Ortigia. What news? The populace lays siege, they're about to attack. Suddenly a Neapolitan named Nypsius sails his fleet into the Great Harbor. A friend of the Tyrant's. The Siracusans kick his Neapolitan ass. A great victory. They go wild. Get dead drunk. The whole populace is asleep. Nypsius gets his ass together and *burns the city*. Lo and behold, here comes a Siracusan, out of breath, to report all this. Begging Dion to save the city. Dion, bless his soul, doesn't hesitate. We're off to save Siracusa. And we do. Hand to hand. Eye-gouging. Dion the Savior. A charmed life. His tyrannical enemies flee the city. Dion is Boss. Philosopher King! he shouts. Again. Democracy! the people shout. Again. It all goes on and on. Round and round. Intrigues. Assassinations. Speeches. These warfarers. *Suddenly I see it for myself.* They've all lost their minds. This is madness. A *bad* case of post-traumatic stress. A serious disorder. *Wounded souls.* Is there a doctor in the house! *I'm laughing.* Like mad. *Laughing laughing laughing.* No, not until I cry. A pure laughing laugh. Suddenly I know why I'm here. Who I am. No, not exactly. Uncertainly, certainly. This uncertain reality. *Needs a doctor.* Here I am. Eudemus of Cyprus. Soul doctor. Coming home.

Hegel's anthropology

Eudemus, *mon frère*, let me give you a little rest. You need it. Soul doctor. You've found your calling. *You're laughing.* The first *psyche iatros* in the history of the world. The dawn of psychiatry. *Gianfranco is laughing! He's back!* In Siracusa. Tyranny. Carnage. Platonists. Eudemus! You're coming to the end of your Tail. Coming home. Soon. Not quite yet. Right now, it's time for Hegel. Ye gods, a Tail is not a Tail without Hegel. And for once I'm not going to tell the one about 'being is nothing.' The one with all those great lines, like '*Being, pure being*—without further determination.' And then 'Being, the indeterminate immediate is in fact *nothing*, and neither more nor less than nothing.' The first lines of his *Science of Logic*, after the Prefaces and the Introduction. No! Not that one this time, we've already been through that in *Why Dream? Eudemus is laughing. Gianfranco is laughing.* This time I'm telling a different Tail. A Tail of the night of the world. Actually, a tail, not a Tail. It's the night of the world chasing its tail. Like Gilda, my second cat. This chase is what Hegel calls his 'anthropology.' I'm sure it was inspired by his cat. *Now Hegel is laughing!* Meta-memoir. You think he must be terribly serious. Fake news! In the long history of this vale of tears nobody has ever enjoyed a good laugh more than Hegel.

Now, let's be serious. Scholarly speaking, Hegel's 'Anthropology' refers to a sub-section of Part Three of his *Encyclopaedia of the Philosophical Sciences*, namely the *Philosophy of Spirit*. For the record, Part One is the *Logic*, known as the *Lesser Logic* to distinguish it from the one I quote all the time, the *Science of Logic;* and Part Two is the *Philosophy of Nature*. Meanwhile, the *Philosophy of Spirit*, whose tail I shall be pulling, is divided into three Sections: Subjective Spirit, Objective Spirit, Absolute Spirit. However, only the first of the three Sections concerns us. This Section is divided into three Sub-Sections, all of which concern us, more or less. The first Sub-Section is—*voilà*—'Anthropology. Soul,' divided into three parts: Natural Soul, Feeling Soul, Actual Soul. The second Sub-Section is 'Phenomenology. Consciousness,' divided into Consciousness Proper, Self-Consciousness, Reason. The third is 'Psychology. Spirit,' divided into Theoretical Spirit, Practical Spirit, Free Spirit. There's a lot of meat on the fire here, as the Italians put it. An entire steer. A whole herd of cattle. Have no fear, I won't go whole hog. No, I'll hold my horses. But—soul, body, mind, spirit, Hegel tackles them all, as only he can. Subjects that, as we know, are very much on Eudemus' mind. As an alumnus of the grove. And now, as the first soul doctor in history.

Let me say this: when I say 'anthropology' I don't just refer to the 'Anthropology' Sub-Section but to all three Sub-Sections together. I can get away with this because, in fact, I'm not a scholar, and neither is Eudemus, or Gianfranco, for that matter. *They're laughing again.* (Anyway, a scholar would never use a word like 'scholarlyly.') What's more, I also refer—in spades—to a quite early work of Hegel's known as the *Jena Philosophy of Spirit*, one of a series of writings known as the *Jenaer Realphilosophie*, written, in Jena, in 1805/06, years before he wrote the *Encyclopaedia*. It is here that Hegel speaks of 'the night of the world' on, possibly, the most daring and vivid of the many thousands of pages he wrote in his books. I quote from this page at the very beginning of 'I Dream of Eudemus'—a Tail which is, itself, a tail to this quote. Which I am chasing, and may actually catch. To a certain, or definitely uncertain, extent. Before too long.

What's more, I call 'Hegels anthropology' everything Hegel wrote that I consider anthropological, in Hegel's sense. What sense? Let's say, an abyssal sense. Related to the abyss. The *logos* of *anthropos* is a logic of the abyss. Meanwhile, abyss aside, in my unscholarly opinion there are two words that are the key to Hegel's philosophy. One is *Begriff*, mistranslated as 'notion,' correctly translated as 'concept.' The other is *Geist*, mistranslated as 'mind,' correctly translated as 'spirit.' *Geist* is an *anthropologically*-charged word. The *Geisterreich*, the realm of spirits, is not a mental world. No. *Geister* are ghosts, phantoms, spirits of the night. The *Geisterreich* is, like it or not, the world we live in. Till death do us part. It's the abyss that keeps us alive. It's the Eudemusian Age. Kill Kill Kill. But there may, possibly, be a soul doctor. In the house. On, or off, the wall. This is the tail I'm chasing. No, actually, I'm chasing *all* the tails. The ten-thousand tails. This is the magic of my cat. When she chases *her* tail she chases *all* the tails. And Tails.

Let me show you, in a nutshell, what I mean by Hegel's anthropology. In his own words. Not in a book but in a *psychotherapeutic* letter he wrote, in 1810, to his friend Windischmann, who is troubled by a tome he's trying to write on the subject of magic. Soul doctors. In antiquity, Eudemus. In modernity, Hegel. I, myself, as we shall see, call their technique 'abyss therapy.'

> Consider yourself convinced that the frame of mind you depict to me is partly due to this present work of yours, to this descent into dark regions where nothing is revealed as fixed, definite, and certain; where glimmerings of light flash everywhere but, flanked by abysses, are rather darkened in their brightness and led astray by the environment, casting false reflections far more than illumination. Each onset of a new path breaks off again and ends in the indeterminate, losing itself, wresting us away from our purpose and direction. From my own experience I know this mood of soul, or rather of reason, which arises when it has finally made its way with interest and hunches into a chaos of phenomena but, though inwardly certain of the goal, has not yet worked its way through them to clarity and to a detailed account of the whole. For a few years I suffered from this hypochondria to the point of exhaustion. Everybody probably has such a turning point in his life, the nocturnal point of the contraction of his essence in which he is forced through a narrow passage by which his confidence in himself and everyday life grows in strength and assurance—unless he has rendered himself incapable of being fulfilled by everyday life, in which case he is confirmed in an inner, nobler existence. Continue

onward with confidence. It is science that has led you into this labyrinth of the soul, and science alone is capable of leading you out again and healing you.

This is the 'science' Gianfranco practiced on me, successfully, when I was in trouble, 'to the point of exhaustion.' Not to heal, but to make the suffering bearable. Write five stories! he insisted. (This is the last of them, so many years later, dedicated to him. Written in, and with, his spirit.) Radiate and glow! I think Hegel's 'incapable of being fulfilled by everyday life' is the same as Artaud's 'not satisfied to remain mere recording organisms.' Later on, I, myself, practiced this abyss therapy on Gianfranco, unsuccessfully, when he was in trouble. I didn't do it well enough. It doesn't always work. Sometimes the night of the world blots us out completely. *But this terrible night is also the source of our health and creativity.* Eudemus, Hegel—this is their great discovery. From chaos, order. From carnage, illumination. Looking up at the abyss. The free play of the concept, says Hegel. Eudemus says, I see it for myself. 'No one shows a child the sky.' To empty water from a cup does not mean to drink it up. Satori is direct, pure experience of what is right here.

Eudemus, as we know, is dreamed. What he's actually up to now is far from clear. On the battlefields of Siracusa. Practicing a therapy he's invented himself. The soul doctor in action. In his last action. His 'coming home.' From and to the abyss. *What* is he up to? Let Hegel be our guide! Let's hop and skip through his anthropology and see what happens.

'Anthropology. Soul.' The soul—says Hegel—is not a separate immaterial entity. Ye gods, a stab at the heart of Platonism! 'Wherever there is nature the soul is its universal immaterialism, its simple ideal life. Soul is the *substance* or absolute basis of all the particularizing and individualizing of spirit.' But, Hegel says, 'soul is only the *sleep* of spirit—the passive *nous* of Aristotle, which is potentially all things.' Now he sums up the three forms of soul. At first, in its immediacy, soul is the *natural* soul, which only *is*. Then, it is a soul that *feels*. Individualized, the *feeling* soul enters into correlation with its immediate being, and, in the modes of that being, retains an abstract independence. Finally, as *actual* soul, its immediate being—its corporeity, or bodily nature—is molded into it.

The *natural* soul is where we find the distinction between sleeping and waking. Sleep is the state in which the soul is immersed in its differenceless unity, while waking is the state in which it has entered into opposition to this simple unity. This, we note, means that sleep *comes before* waking. Logically speaking. The fact that the states of sleep and waking are inherent in spirit, which, in its truth, is pure activity, stems from the fact that *spirit is also soul*—which, for Hegel, is something like saying that *the sky is also the abyss*. Spirit, as soul, lowers itself to the status of natural, immediate, passive being.

But, to sleep! *perchance to dream?* Absolutely! First, Hegel takes dead aim at the 'inadequate' distinction between sleeping and waking that claims, 'vaguely,' that *we only think when we're awake.* Fake news, says Hegel. We think *plenty* when we sleep. A thinking that we call *dreaming.* Hegel notes that we may be extremely bored while awake but have a lively interest in what we dream. Then again, he 'criticizes' our dreaming because it's all 'picture-thinking' that neglects the conceptual. Dreaming is neither 'intelligent' nor 'reasonable.' But he doesn't deny its charm and power. Mere picture-thinking wrests things out of their context and isolates them, which is why in dreams everything drifts apart and crisscrosses *in the wildest disorder.* But ye gods this is his anthropology! In the natural soul everything gushes right up from our abyss, as if from the Fountain of Arethusa in Ortigia. For Hegel to denigrate dreaming would be like spitting on his mother. (Or his cat.)

Next, the *feeling* soul, where Hegel refers to the abyss explicitly. He uses two different words. *Abgrund* is the *mot juste,* truly a *bon mot,* especially when he contrasts *Grund* (ground, foundation) with *Abgrund* (no-ground, abyss). A contrast that has inspired such translations as 'the ground falls to the ground' and my own personal 'foundering foundation.' But Hegel, anthropologically, likes the word *Schacht,* which means shaft, pit, mine. (We've seen this in that Strangelove riff on the mineshaft gap.) Anyway, dig this great quote:

> Every individual is an infinite treasury of sensations, ideas, acquired lore, thoughts; yet the ego is completely indivisible—a featureless mine [shaft, pit, abyss] in which everything is preserved without existing. It is only when *I* call to mind *an* idea that I bring it out of that interior to existence before consciousness.

Meanwhile, Hegel is still thinking about *dreaming,* which is a hot topic in both the natural and feeling souls. He notes that

> in the dreaming state the human soul is filled not merely with single, isolated feelings but, more than is usually the case in the distractions of the waking soul, it attains to a profound and powerful feeling of its *entire individual* nature, of the *total compass* of its past, present, and future; and just because in this state the individual totality of the soul is felt, dreaming must be included in our consideration of the self-feeling soul.

Next, he compares dreaming to the state of the child in the womb and, right after that, he discusses sleepwalking. But what really interests him is insanity—madness—which he calls '*a dreaming while awake.*' 'Between health and insanity the difference is like that between waking and dreaming, except that in insanity the dream falls within the limits of being awake.' He gives us a full-fledged treatise on the forms of insanity, from the least to the most degenerate (reminding me of Plato's from Timocracy to Oligarchy to Democracy to Tyranny): idiocy, the distracted mind, the rambling mind, folly, world-weariness, melancholia, mania, frenzy. But he concludes, believe it or not, with a whole series of abyss-therapy case studies.

Take—he says—the case of the Englishman who believed he had a hay-cart with four horses in his stomach. He was freed from his delusion by a [soul] doctor who, having assured the lunatic that he could feel the cart and horses and so gained his confidence, persuaded him that he possessed a remedy for reducing the size of the things supposedly in his stomach. Finally, he gave the man an emetic and made him vomit out of the window, just as, with the doctor's connivance, a hay-cart was passing by outside, which the man believed he had vomited. Psychotherapeutic. A clear case of looking up at the abyss.

Now, let's hop and skip. From 'Anthropology' proper to 'Phenomenology. Consciousness.' But we've already had our fill of consciousness in *Why Dream?* with its famous question 'What is consciousness?' The *the* question. Full to the brim. So we're skipping straight to 'Psychology.' But, you say, psychology is not anthropology. I object! For a soul doctor psychology is anthropology *par excellence*. And vice versa: anthropology is psychology *par excellence*. Be that as it may, we're about to get to what really interests us. The abyss. The unconscious. The night of the world. As I said, Hegel divides his Psychology into Theoretical Spirit, Practical Spirit, and Free Spirit. Luckily, we can forget about the last two. Meanwhile, he cuts Theoretical Spirit into quite a series of juicy slices: 1) Intuition; 2) Representation, itself sliced into Recollection, Imagination, Memory; 3) Thinking. All these terms are as Greek as the Acropolis, but, watch out: this is Aristotle's Greek, not Plato's. 'Recollection,' for example, has nothing to do with Plato's Big Idea, just as Hegel's 'soul' is not a separate immaterial entity. He says, explicitly, that it's in community with the body, not imprisoned by it. Hegel may call soul the sleep of spirit and equate Theoretical Spirit with Intelligence, but far be it from him to cast aspersions on the soul. It's not a question of Plato, love him or leave him. Soul is lots of things for Hegel without being immortal. Shooting like a star. Soaring through the universe Recollecting the World of Forms. After all, as Eudemus says, soul is what makes a living thing alive. Abyssal, yes. But soul has an abyssal intelligence all its own. Soul has a 'supernatural extra brilliant intelligent kindness,' as Allen Ginsberg *Howls*. Hegel chimes right in.

But let's cut to the chase. We have 'intuition,' which merely transforms internality into externality. But then we have 'representation,' which is recollected or inwardized intuition. Representations are mental images or ideas, and I do *not* mean Platonic Ideas. And now, 'recollection (inwardization), which consists in *the involuntary calling up of a content that is already ours.*'

At this stage we have a content that is not only intuitively perceived in its immediacy but is at the same time recollected, inwardized, posited as *mine*. As thus determined the content is what we call *image*.

But never mind imagination and memory. For our (anthropological) purposes recollection is quite enough.

Intelligence, as it at first recollects the intuition, places the content of feeling in its own inwardness—in a space and time of its own. In this way the content is an *image* or picture liberated from its original immediacy and abstract singleness among other things and received into the universality of the ego. The image loses the full complement of features proper to intuition and is arbitrary or contingent, *isolated from the external place, time, and immediate context in which the intuition stood.*

In this passage, 'in a space and time of its own,' Hegel gives us his inkling of an *uncertain reality*. His sketch of Eudemus.

I know I am not exactly here. Not exactly real. How do I know this? A feeling? No. Not a feeling. I know it. For sure. It's a certainty. My only certainty. Waking. Sleeping. Dreaming. Ebb. Flow. Always. In flashes.

In flashes, the abyss. The *image*—Hegel says—'*is of itself transient.*' Uncertain. Why? The ego internalizes its presented content by gathering up and separating the external image or impression and then making it part of its internal structure, but since the impression is only transient it quickly vanishes from consciousness.

Intelligence is not only the consciousness and actual existence recollected within it. *The image no longer exists, but is preserved unconsciously.* To grasp intelligence as this *nightlike abyss* within which a world of infinitely many images and presentations are preserved without being in consciousness is, from the one point of view, the universal postulate that bids us treat the concept as concrete, in the way we treat the germ as affirmatively containing, in virtual possibility, all the qualities that come into existence in the subsequent development of the tree. [...] From the other point of view intelligence is to be conceived as this *unconscious abyss*, i.e., as the *existent* universal in which the different has not yet been realized in its separations. Precisely this potentiality *is the first form of universality offered in mental representation.*

This is Section 453 of the *Philosophy of Spirit* and it's the last section we shall read together. 'Imagination' and 'memory' will have to fend for themselves, along with Practical Spirit and Free Spirit. What, exactly, Hegel is saying here has been heatedly debated ever since he wrote it. Is he actually anticipating Freud? Could be. Uncertainly. Certainly not exactly. Meanwhile, in his 'Addition' (better known as *Zusatz*) to this Section Hegel really bends over backwards to tell us what he means.

> The image is mine, it belongs to me; but, to begin with, it has no further homogeneity with me, for it *is not thought*, it is still not raised to the form of *reason*. Between the image and myself there is a relationship that is not truly free, which still stems from the standpoint of intuition and according to which I am only the inner side, and the image is for me something external. Therefore, to begin with, *I do not yet have full control of the images slumbering within the abyss, I am not yet able to recall them at will.* We have no idea of the infinite hosts of images of the past that slumber within us. Now and then they do awaken by chance, but we cannot call them to mind. Thus the images are *ours* only in a *formal* manner.

Welcome to the heart of Hegel's anthropology. As I see it. As Eudemus sees it. For himself. Slumbering, for the moment. Later, smoldering. Hegel, here, says *'not yet,'* but there's more to it than *'not yet.'* A lot more. The unconscious, the *un*-rational *par excellence*—this nightlike abyss, or nocturnal shaft, or sunless pit, or what have you—*is what makes rational self-conscious thinking possible.* The unconscious *Abgrund* is the ultimate *Grund* from which consciousness emerges—the 'pure determinate negativity' that is present *throughout* the development of spirit. The 'negative totality,' which is Hegel's way of saying that *it's all connected.* Ye gods this is no trifling matter. At all. Reason—*relation*—is, so to speak, Hegel's Philosopher King. His Big Idea. The concept, the free play of the concept, the conceptual. *Connection*, and *contradiction*. This is 'it' for Hegel. This is what he sees for himself. Determinate negativity. Thinking as such. The ground that falls to the ground. Call it a mountain high as the sky, with its feet planted absolutely unfirmly in the abyss. The bottomless. Absolute murk. And *planted* truly. Eudemus might say, a mountain high as the abyss. Conceptual thinking, rationality, the *highest*—but, as I keep saying (quoting Thomas Bernhard), it's the abyss that keeps 'it' all alive. Only the abyss. Hegel! You can't beat him. With a stick or anything else. He has the wildest ideas anyone's ever had. Wilder than Gianfranco's ponytail. Here, he says *I do not yet have full control of the images slumbering within the abyss.* But he's pulling our legs. Tickling us. *Laughing!* Not yet full control. But we might wake up tomorrow, or next week, and suddenly have it. Satori! I'm kidding. It's the abyss that keeps us all alive, *not vice versa.* Or—wait, that's not entirely right.

Let me put it this way. When *we* water a plant *we* are keeping the *plant* alive, but it's also true that the *plant* is keeping *us* alive. The abyss itself would die, vanish, melt away if we didn't keep '*it*' alive. How do we keep '*it*' alive? Hegel tells us how, on that page he wrote in Jena, where he calls the abyss 'the night of the world.' *By actually entering this terrible night we keep the abyss alive,* and the abyss returns the favor, keeping us alive. But—give me a moment, I'm coming to this. It's not quite that simple. No free lunch. 'Entering this night' has a price. *Salato,* the Italians say. Salted. Pricey.

Let's back up. 'Anthropology': the soul has not yet achieved consciousness but is still shrouded by the unconscious. But 'still shrouded by the unconscious' is a little like saying that water gushing up from a spring is still shrouded by the spring. Fake news. The spring keeps the water alive *and* the water keeps the spring alive. What matters is the gushing. But I want to get back to that business about psychology is anthropology *par excellence* and vice versa. John Sallis, a good philosopher I used to know personally, wrote some sharp pages on the subject. (Gina, our first cat, adored him. She sat on his lap all the time he was here.) First, he notes that, in the *Philosophy of Spirit,* 'certain forms of imagination are displaced from psychology to anthropology, to a phase where, as a result of the element of corporeality that still remains undetached from spirituality, the subject is susceptible to disease.' By 'disease' he means 'madness.' He notes that 'in madness it is as though one made the futile attempt to remain outside a whole whose very nature is to have no outside.' But I particularly note this '*still* remains undetached,' which, I must say, is precisely what Sallis goes on to note and go to town on. Because, we wonder, when in the [night of the] world will corporeality actually *be detached* from spirituality! This is a *the* question, or possibly even *the* the question, in Hegel's anthropology, i.e., his *logos* of *anthropos.* A logic of the abyss. Let me, for once, put it bluntly. For Plato, here, on one side of the wall [of the Cave], we have pure immaterial immortal soul, and on the other side we have, alas, this prison, 'this unfortunate body.' (Pardon my paraphrase of J. William Fulbright's witty reference to the Vietnam war as 'this unfortunate war.') But Hegel— like Billie Holiday—claims that body and soul are in community. Like love and marriage, more or less. *Voilà* the writing on the wall! Have no fear, John Sallis has read it. First, he says: 'In its inception imagination takes over the stock of images issuing forth from the nocturnal pit, bringing them forth voluntarily without the aid even of those corresponding intuitions that were still required for recollection. Here it is a matter of "dissolving the nocturnal gloom enveloping its wealth of images and banishing it by means of the bright clarity of presence" (§ 455 *Zusatz*).' But then he poses the *the* question. 'The question is whether the nocturnal pit can be so thoroughly illuminated by the light of presence or whether even after the advent of reproductive imagination there do not remain withdrawn in its dark depths slumbering images that are not at the call of spirit. And does the nocturnal pit perhaps cast its shadow over the entire course of the imagination? Do even those images brought forth from the pit by reproductive imagination not bring along something of its darkness?' Sallis goes on eloquently to make a more intricate point, but my blunter point stops here. Is it a question of body over mind? Ye gods this would kick the shit out of Plato! Let's tone it down. Softer question. Is the darkness delible or indelible? Now—sez Eudemus—if the darkness is *indelible*, let's turn the disease into the cure. Abyss *therapy*. Suffer! Dream! Forget about forgetting! Blood, gore, guts, and veins. *The battlefield is not going away.* Fight on. Dream and be dreamed. Why dream? Why not? Or, perhaps, because body and soul, body and spirit, anthropology and psychology, *are inseparable*. 'Separated and inseparable,' Hegel says, in his *Science of Logic*. (Which I'm not quoting, this time.) *Contradiction is the question.* Abstraction. Separation of the inseparable. Abyss. Contradiction. The night of the world. The day of the spirit. *Here* we can say night is day. Being is nothing. *But also*: nothing is being. Day is night. This is *Hegel's anthropology*. 'You can get anything you want at Alice's Restaurant.' It's the abyss, goddamit! Prison, the house of freedom. For *post-and/or pre-traumatic stress* we need a *therapy of freedom*. Close the asylums, the goddam world is one! Siracusans! Leontinians! Sicilians, Greeks, Macedonians, Persians, the more the merrier! Your grandparents live by Kill Kill Kill, your parents live by Kill Kill KIll, you live by Kill Kill Kill. But, possibly, your generation will be the one that says *what the fuck is all this kill kill kill*. I don't feel well. I'm stressed out of my mind. Totally disordered. Am I coming, going, in-between, neither, both. *Help!* I could use a good doctor. A soul doctor! I could use one. Freedom! Our infinite pain, our true path, our destination. Our destiny of death.

   Il nostro destino di morte. This has been a long Tail, and tail, this 'I Dream of Eudemus.' I've been working on it on and off over the past nine years, since Gianfranco died, on November 29th, 2010. Working constantly for the past nine months. Excuse me, I've already said this: 'The day of his funeral, in Mestre, there was flooding in Venice and a shroud of bitter freezing fog. What an ugly day! I'd never been to the Mestre cemetery and it looked like the ugliest place on earth. I watched them lowering the coffin and covering it with the ugliest slimiest clay I've ever seen.' And this is Gianfranco! I don't get it! I cried for weeks. Sure, I wish Artaud could have met him. But—my friend! Welcome to the abyss. No, it just cannot be that simple. *Or that painful.* Gianfranco, you kept telling me, *NAME YOU PAIN.* The writing on the wall. Do not let your suffering become infinite. A bad infinity. Psychology is anthropology, or anthropology is psychology, or vice versa, or *vice versa* vice versa. Are we coming or going, came or gone. In our beds with our lovers, if we have beds, and/or lovers. In our lands with our homes, if we have lands, and/or homes. Goddamit this is not a Chinese menu. Take not you pick—tooth, body, or soul. A toothpick, perhaps. A soul pick? Forget it. Forget about forgetting. This is abyss therapy. 'I returned to the cemetery one year later. I couldn't believe it was the same place I had been to one year earlier. The sun slanting through the tall cypresses, the silence.'

The dead cannot speak to us but we can speak to them, and we *must* do it. When John Sallis was my house-guest ages ago he wrote me a few lines from Hegel's *Aesthetics*, on a tiny scrap of paper: 'Yet whoever claims that nothing exists that carries in itself a contradiction in the form of an identity of opposites is at the same time requiring that nothing living shall exist. For the power of life, and still more the might of the spirit, consists precisely in positing contradiction in itself, enduring it, and overcoming it.' Contradiction, the missing piece in the puzzle of Hegel's anthropology. I've known, personally, quite a few good philosophers—mostly Italians, since I live in Italy. But Giulio Severino was special. In a complex way he was, for me, Gianfranco's Double. Again, a great mane of white hair. Not wild like Gianfranco's, no disheveled ponytail, but, a great mane. We met at his seminar here in Venice, conversed intensely, exchanged letters, I looked forward to seeing him again. Then he died, suddenly. This is a Tail of Eudemus, his dream, my dream of him and of his dream, these tails, but, before getting back to Eudemus, himself, and to Gianfranco, himself, I need to say a few words about Giulio Severino's *philosophical experience* of the night of the world. Wait—maybe I'd better repeat that graphic quote from the *Jena Philosophy of Spirit*. After all these Tyrants and Platonists I bet you can barely recall it.

Each one of us is this night, this pure nothing, which in its simplicity contains everything, an infinite wealth of many representations and images, none of which stands before us, or which are not as present. What exists here is night, the interior of nature—*pure self*. In phantasmagoric representations it presses in from all sides; suddenly a bloody head darts out—there another white form, and just as suddenly they vanish. We see this night when we look a human being in the eye—entering a night that becomes *terrible*. What is it? What is reaching out from this eye? I see it! *It's the night of the world.*

Spirit springs from the abyss and returns to it. Spirit brings life and destroys it. 'Our destiny of death.' Suddenly I have so much to say! When I met Giulio at his seminar I asked him, in particular, what Hegel really meant by the word *furchtbar*. Giulio translated it, in Italian, as *terribile*—a translation I fully endorse: a night that becomes *terrible*. Sure, words are cheap. Take you pick. The nightmare of your choice. Terrible - terrifying - frightening - chilling - hair-raising - blood-curdling - appalling - disconcerting - harrowing - gruesome - nightmarish - monstrous - dreadful (à la Kierkegaard) - traumatic (à la soul doctor). Scary - spooky - creepy - hairy. The more the merrier. OK, I let off some steam. Sue me. Why the hell not. But the *word* is not the point. The word *killeth.* The question is what Hegel *means.* When he says that 'spirit sinks into itself and arises from its abyss.' No one had a clearer and deeper vision of this than Giulio Severino. A veritable abyss expert. He wrote me, privately:

I believe that the 'terrible' of which Hegel speaks does not refer to the night we see and that we enter when we look a man in the eye, but to what *occurs* in this night and to what we see in the idea that glitters there. Whoever looks into a man's eyes—this, perhaps, is what Hegel means—sees in them the infinite pain that smolders in his unconscious, not only for the death of God, i.e., for the coming to light of His absence from the world, but also for the destiny of death of man himself. In the *Encyclopaedia,* after saying that 'the *essence* of spirit is … *freedom,* the absolute negativity of the concept as identity with itself,' Hegel goes on to say that spirit '*can* abstract from everything external, and even from its own externality, from its existence: it can bear the negation of its individual immediacy, *infinite pain*; that is, it can keep itself affirmative in this negativity and be identical for itself.' (§ 382). This passage makes it easier to understand in what sense, for Hegel, man and his thinking have to do with the abyss.

'What *occurs* in this night': the image of the abyss (the mineshaft, the pit) refers not only to the cavity, the hollow, but also to *the substance it contains.* In the *Jenaer Realphilosophie* Hegel describes the first phase of the journey of spirit, the passage from intuition to imagination to memory. At a certain point in the text he writes—in the margin, literally—'night of preservation.' In this night everything that has ever entered an individual's consciousness is preserved, *but without being present in consciousness.* Psychology is anthropology *and vice versa.* Not a spirit of contradiction but the contradiction of spirit. Giulio Severino writes:

The night of preservation makes its appearance at the beginning of the dialectical process, within the bright forms of the intelligence, as that which precedes and conditions the emergence of consciousness and of the I. In speaking of this night Hegel dwells on the nocturnal side of the life of spirit, on the vast sphere of its unconscious psychic life.

It is as if the thin crust on which the dialectical process rests were to crack and give way, allowing us to glimpse, in the void underlying the succession of moments, an unsuspected realm of dark forms and powers.

An individual is a whole world of representations buried in the night of the I. But they *dart out* again. Return. Unsummoned. Uncontrolled. Anarchically. Tyrannically. Chaotically. The *terrible* is that there is nothing 'beyond' the abyss, no psychology that 'goes beyond' anthropology *once and for all*. Beyond the walls. What walls? Beyond what? What beyond? Asks Eudemus. He sees it for himself. Coming home to what's beyond. But *what* is beyond? *After* memoir. But nothing *beyond*. In a passage of the *Lesser Logic* (§ 24 *Zusatz*) Hegel writes: 'The I is this void, this emptiness, this vacuum, the receptacle for anything and everything, for which everything is and which preserves everything in itself.' What 'I' is this! *What* self! says the Zen master. Hui-neng, the Sixth Patriarch, said, famously: 'If everything is empty, where shall the dust settle?' This is Hegel's anthropology. The logic of the abyss. Of chaos. Of leaving the grove.

The abyss is not a mystical foundation or obscure substrate. It is not a part of the soul, but is a fundamental *moment* in the living totality Hegel calls spirit. A *logical moment*, as he puts it in his *Logic*. The *terrible* is a basic, permanent, and timeless *moment* of human experience. Hegel's 'abyssal ground' is a two-faced mask: on one face, inexhaustible depth; on the other, the lack—the absence—of ground. We are far from Freud here, as Giulio Severino notes. In Freud, in Jung, the unconscious is part of a deterministic conception of the psyche—a conception that is completely extraneous to Hegel's idea of spirit. Hegel attempts to understand the determinations of the unconscious and spirit's gradual, dialectical gushing out of these determinations. For Freud the unconscious is a part—a slice— of the soul. For Hegel the unconscious abyss is a fundamental moment in the formation of spirit. More precisely, this abyss is *the ground that does not ground*. We cannot *look into* the abyss precisely because the abyss is our very own *foundering foundation*. Our 'self' that *is not there*. Our 'I' of night.

Eudemus, *cher ami*, you're back! You're a soul doctor now. Sitting under the starry sky of Siracusa, looking up at the abyss. Abyss to abyss. *D'un abîme l'autre.* I dream of you, looking up, pondering your dream. Your coming home. Your destination. Let's give Giulio Severino the last word, for a Hegelian moment. He has something important to tell us. His eloquence. His penetration. His great mane of white hair, like Gianfranco's but tamer. Eudy! I know you don't speak German, though your French is surprisingly good.

> The 'night of preservation' is a realm of shadows that contains within itself, potentially and unconsciously, all the experiences and all the moments of spirit. Spirit unfolds from this night, positing itself and nature in their reciprocal difference and in the distinctions proper to each. The night of preservation is a sphere within the I and its world. It 'reaches out' to each one of us as the interior of our self and of a nature devoid of self. It is the dark world that we see and we enter and that becomes *terrible* when we look someone in the eye,

because it is *time itself*, which each of us is in ourself—time, in and for itself, that is proper to spirit.

Like the id of Nietzsche and of Freud, the human self is, for Hegel, the still unconscious subject of spirit. In Hegel this subject, before falling into time, is the condition of the ideal development and of any possible realization of spirit. Thus, the metaphor of the night, in referring to the human unconscious, is the sign of our temporality as well as our eternity, our infinity and our finitude, our greatness and our destiny of death.

abyss therapy

A battlefield. My life. Why? Because of my dream? Because I'm dreamed? Who knows. The reality is uncertain. The why is infinitely less certain. This is the only certainty. Coming home? It's about time. Nearly five years. Since my dream. In Pherae. The horror! Colorless ugly houses. Snarling dogs. Full of garbage. A rabid tyrant. My dream. My destination. In the thick of it. This five-years-coming-home. A destiny? Of what? Of coming home. Uncertainly. Where? What home? What's home? What's destiny? What destiny? What's a dream? *Why dream?* Many questions. Answers? The more the merrier.

What's Dion up to? What gives in Siracusa? Justice! Philosophy! Peace! This Good Fight. An Even Keel. Buy it and I'll sell you ten more. Snake-oil. Pure grain. Dion is Boss. Right now. At the moment. The natives are restless. To say the least. Philosopher King. Kill Kill Kill Kill. What else is new. Let me take a look around. I see it for myself. Unfortunately. The populace! The people. Wounded souls. Dion! Savior! He comes and goes. He's back. Again. The populace is riled up. Already. Again. We got back from our jaunt to Leontini. The Siracusan Assembly supplicated him as a god. With prayers. The great and shining hero. The savior. Dion! Give us peace and love! Most of his opponents hightailed it out of town. Heracleides decided to tough it out. Populist. Tough love. A veritable man of the people. Dion's pal in the old days. When they plotted together to overthrow Dionysius. The Younger. This time we did overthrow him. After our terrible sea voyage. After our barnstorming. The Younger Tyrant. Overthrown. More or less. Dion, *elected*, took his stand *against* elections. The populace was revolted. Heracleides formed his own political party. The Assembly appointed him Admiral. An Even Keel. Admirable. Dion, naturally, took umbrage. He always wants it all. Heracleides won a naval battle. Defended the city. Defeated the Tyrant's fleet. Dion was irritated. Naturally. Heracleides made big speeches. Demanding democratic reforms. I heard them for myself. A True Populist. Big populist proposals. Land redistribution. Fuck foreign mercenaries. Local commanders. Dion was royally pissed off. Platonist.

Philosopher King! The populace was all with Heracleides. So we took off for
Leontini. Recent history. Old story. But now we're back. Mercenaries and all.
And me. Too. In the thick of it. Peace and love. Lots of luck. This carnage
stops right here and stops right now! Who in the world said such a thing? Who
knows? Words are cheap. I see people tearing out their hair. Men, women,
children. Jumping up and down. Stressed out of their minds. Looking for trees
to climb. Worrying about the permanent war economy. Who needs it! Well,
Dion does. Platonist. Democracy is worse than tyranny. Sez he. Reversing
Plato's scale of degeneracy. Tyranny. The pits. Democracy. Agreeable form of
anarchy. Dion wants a permanent war Aristocracy. He calls it a Platonist state.
A Bad Idea he didn't pick up in the grove. The people are riled and wooly. They
want to tear down the Tyrant's citadel. Ortigia for the Ortigians! Forget it, says
Dion. It'll come in handy. Dion wants *it all*. His problem isn't the people. It's
Heracleides. Man of the people. He refuses to join the Aristocratic Senate.
He's riled up. The citadel. The mercenaries. He stands on a crate and makes
speeches. It's true. He's been hatching a plot. Dion tells me, Eudy, enough is
enough. Me! Tells *me*. What do I have to do with it? I'm dreamed. What in
the world am I doing here? Callippus is off somewhere eating Pachynusian
tomatoes. Heracleides. True Populist. Dion decides to neutralize him. Rub him
out. Sends his mercenaries. Secretly. Adios. Dion leads the funeral procession.
Himself. Natives extremely restless. Heracleides assassinated. Stabbed. The
populace is looking for someone to Kill Kill Kill. Riled up is not the word. A
metallic stink. Yes! We have no spaghetti. The water has boiled out. Burned the
bottom of the pot. Ash-red. Livid.

What's next? I go into action. Myself. I invent my own battlefield. Soul doctor.
The nightmare of my choice. I tighten my sandals. Roll up my sleeves. My own
battlefield. Right here. Right now. At the edge of chaos. At the ash-red border
of the night of the world. The abyss! *Mes semblables,— mes frères!* The grove.
The lessons of the grove. What's the good of the Idea of the Good. Matter
matters. It's the abyss that keeps us all alive, only the abyss. Men, women,
children, cats, dogs, birds, they all need help. Everyone's in deep shit. Cats
growl. Birds fall out of the sky. Stressed. Distressed. Post-traumatic? But it's
all one continuous trauma. Not temporary. A permanent trauma. A battle
without beginning. Or end. Or middle. Chaotic. A field of lost horizons. No
limits. No borders. A dream? A destiny? At dusk. Looking at the swifts and
the swallows. I've seen the Euripus Strait. Calm. Furious. Wild. At dusk. At
dawn. All day. All night. All the time. What trauma? I see it for myself. The
constant invasive presence of death. Of killing and dying. Our destiny of
death. *Post*-trauma? Sure. *Pre*-trauma? You bet your motherfucking ass. Take
your pick. Post-. Pre-. A referendum. Again. To live with. To die with. The
traumas we've already been through. Are they less terrible than the traumas to
come? Now. Tomorrow. These goddam traumas. Yesterday. Now. Tomorrow.

First soul doctor in the history of the world. I ask myself, which is worst? In my medical opinion. I vote *pre*-trauma. A shot in the dark. The abyss is outside of time. But we are *in time*. We *are* time. Unfortunately. Among other things. A vote? Which is worst? I hear a great Greek chorus droning. Screaming. Fuck Chinese menus! Group A. Group B. Post-. Pre-. The trauma is *all the time*. *Pre. Now. Post.* Goddamit and fuck you all. The writing's on the wall. I'm dreamed. I dreamed. Nearly five years ago. What wall? What's a wall? What ears have walls? *Why* did someone say: This carnage stops right here and stops right now! Ye gods know who said it. *Why* did he say it! I've never even thought of such a thing. In my entire Eudemusian existence. Why should it. Stop. Start. Be in time. What in the world does pre-traumatic stress mean? Wait! I think I know. *I'm laughing. Gianfranco is laughing.* Why? We think we're so smart? We think everyone else is a mere recording organism? Hell no, that's not it. We laugh because we sit under the starry sky and look up at the abyss. And see it. Take the time. To see it. It keeps us all alive. Shit, you say. I'd rather worry about a trauma I already had than one I actually will have. Why! I laugh. Fuck the old one. The big trouble is the new one. The next. And never mind the one *right now*. Unfair! You shout. Well, fuck you. Fairness has absolutely nothing to do with it. Zero. You're off base. Go directly to jail. Do not pass go. Guess what. Populace! You need my therapy. If you want to survive, barely, in the miserable least. Permanent carnage. This is the Eudemusian Age. But you're lucky. I'm available. At your service. Abyss therapy. The abyss never sleeps. Never dreams! *We* dream. Why? *Why dream?* A miniscule question. The big one is: Why Kill Kill KIll? Just because you can get anything you want at Alice's restaurant? No dice. This does not compute. I'm dreamed. Answer not valid.

Let's talk medicine. No! Not snake-oil and medicine shows. The direct reverse. Not 'fact' medicine. Facts are rare as roaming dinosaurs. Certainly. A lot less certain. Terrible lizards. Uncertain medicines. Hell or high water. Soul medicines. Psychotherapeutic pharmaceutics. It's the abyss! Wish us luck. Ready or not. *Otan pineis stin taverna.* Who's drinking in the taverna. It looks a lot like Pherae. Just sitting there. Missing. Arms. Legs. Hands. Ears. Noses. Eyes. Missing. A sad café. Ravaged by tyranny. Blood, gore, guts, and veins. Degenerate forms of government. What Plato calls 'Justice.' Tyrant's Tyrants. Listen up, *mes frères.* Never mind *healing.* Forget it. Name your pain. Let's make the suffering bearable. Write stories! Five stories each. Chase your Tails! It will give you a mental ease. Possibly, a big release. You say: Shit! They gouged out my eye. Cut off my ear. Sliced off my arm. Butchered my leg. Soul doctor! How about it. What shall I say. How about: Cheer up! It'll grow back. Not on your life. And/or death. I don't say that at all. This is *abyss* therapy. We sit here together. At the tristesse taverna. Under the clear starry Siracusan sky. We look up at the abyss. We say: The limbs are long gone. *Fuck the phantoms.* The phantom eye that pretends to see. The phantom ear that pretends to hear. The phantom limb that pretends to feel. Fuck them all! This is the Eudemusian Age, goddamit. Anarchy. Chaos. Carnage. Civil war. Permanent. Endless. *Mes amis,* look up at the abyss. Closely. Closely! Keep looking. You'll find what you think you're missing. Namely *nothing.* You have what you have. You have what you don't have. You are what you aren't and you aren't what you are. Certainly absolutely uncertainly. And vice versa. The nightmare of your choice. Be loyal!

Believe it or not I'm getting good results with this therapy. Half the city is busy writing stories. The people are less worried about old traumas and more worried about new ones. A healthy sign. Some of them are telling jokes. Listen. They're shouting *kill for peace.* Refreshing political irony. An inkling of political theater. Many have stopped pulling out their hair. I saw some women laughing. I heard a cat purr. What's next? How about *the labor theory.* Let's give it a try. It's abyssal. Wholesome. A tonic for wounded souls. Not *moral* therapy. No. *Morale* therapy. A new therapy. How about reinforcing rationality, a sense of hope, connections to the outside world. Through labor. No, fuck that. Let's boost *morale* through labor. Creativity. A sense of freedom. Wait. What labor? This populace. Men. Women. Children. Cats. Dogs. Birds. The only labor they know is the labor of war. Patiently fighting for one tyrant against another. For another against the one. The second against the first. The first against the second. Battle. Killing. *Being killed.* Pulling out hair. Pushing up daisies. This world. All one goddam battlefield. Stress. Distress. Tyrant to tyrant. *D'un tyran l'autre.* The thick of it. I'm in it. Myself. Eudemus of Cyprus. I'm dreamed. I dreamed. In Pherae. The doctors gave me up for dead. In five years I'll return home. I dreamed. This uncertain reality. This populace. Every day a brush with death. What brush? Perhaps we should take up painting. Labor. The theory. The sad café. Labor. Work. The stressed are forced out of their diseased interiority and impelled towards the real world. Of killing and dying! My idea is a little different. People must work. In order to be fully free. We need a therapy of freedom. Through labor. What labor? Some more Kill Kill Die Die? More of the same? Let's try something different. Take a stab at it. You never know. Here's my idea. *Teaching.* When they're not writing stories everyone will be teaching everyone else. Teaching what? *Never mind teaching what.* Everyone chooses five subjects. Any five at all. Physics. Philosophy. Back-scratching. Arm-wrestling. Jumping-up-and-down. For example. Then they take turns teaching their subjects to everyone else. Men to men. Men to women. To children. To cats. Women to men. To women. Children to dogs. To women. To other children. *A whole lot of teaching going on.* Never mind learning! This has nothing to do with learning. The idea is to show this distressed populace *a new chaos. Which they produce themselves.* Freely. Creatively. Chaotically. After all this Kill-Kill-Kill chaos foisted on them. All the time. This is an extremely powerful therapy. Dynamic. Absolutely abyssal. The theory of labor. Applied through freedom therapy. The height of the abyss. Amazing. You need to see it for yourself.

Everyone's writing stories and teaching everyone. A beautiful chaos. Hopefully. But the distress is deep. The pain. The horror. Meanwhile, this stressed populace has one big problem. As I see it. For myself. Apart, of course, from the endless trauma. The battle fatigue. For battle fatigue they might as well take a little nap. The battle is an abyss. It never sleeps. It's not going anywhere. Not going away. Absolutely no end. In sight. Or out. Of sight. Forget it. The Eudemusian Age. My Age. No, an even bigger problem. *The people suffer from hope.* They're always looking for some solid ground. Under their feet. A strong foundation. They can count on. A silver lining. In the storm. *But it doesn't exist.* Death has no silver lining. The waters of Euripus are never still. The storm is a perfect storm. Everything is always changing. In *this* town. In *this* Age. Change can only mean *for the worse.* The Tyranny, goddamit. And you want a Promised Land. Just around the corner. This, *mes amis,* is the deep-shit problem. Hope. At the very bottom. *Under it all.* Solid ground. But it doesn't exist. This is why I have become a soul doctor. Nearly five years after my dream. Why I am practicing abyss therapy. The search for a strong foundation. Which doesn't exist. This is the greatest sickness of all. The ultimate abyss. Under the bottom. Of the bottomless. The populace! I can't pretend to be a True Populist. I dreamed and I'm dreamed. But I can tell you this. The foundation you dream of is sheer foundering. The ground *always* falls to the ground. Not sometimes. Not from time to time. Every time. *All* the time. Your 'ship coming in' is permanently sinking. Your solid ground is an abyssal ground. Write stories! Let everyone teach everyone! It's good abyss therapy. But what therapy for the abyssal ground? *For the hurtful hope that the ground is solid.* A long hard therapy. Longer than I am. Longer than this world. *This* world? There is no other. This is it. I see it for myself. The gushing of the spring. Its death. Its life. Inseparably. A solid ground? Dance on uncertainty! Like a cat chasing her tail. Pure love is permanently fleeting. Terrible as time. Terrible as the night of the world. Going home? To the abyss. Where spirit wells. Source. Not origin. Gushing. Always. Source. The foundering fountain. Soul. The might of spirit.

'I was standing and the earth was not there. I have risen, a spirit passing through.' A doctor. In the house. On the field. Let's put it this way. *Name your suffering.* The problem of hope is a problem of control. Of the desperate desire to control. In a world abyssally out of control. Mastery. Of the world? Of *our* world. What mastery! On this bottomless battlefield we can't even say: I decide to brush my teeth. A being-is-nothing decision. Being *absolutely* nothing. Control? The only masters are the masters of war. Tyrants. We dream of a solid ground. Of control. Let's be blunt. *Not mastering our struggles.* Abyss

therapy begins right here. Right now. *By not mastering.* By giving up any idea
of mastery. Illusion. Control. Self-control. Other-control. Forget it. The abyss
of soul. No power over it. No possession. But the night is studded with stars.
We look up at the abyss. The battle! You want control? Let your spirit roam the
battlefield. Like a sheep or cow. Control it by giving up all control. A novice
soul doctor. Let me say this. Abyss therapy is hard therapy. But it *can* work. A
little. A little more than not at all. The not at all of mystic herbs or mushrooms.
Noxious mind-bending chemicals. Shrunken heads. Abyss therapy can work
a little more than this traumatic *less.* Or more than a little more. No laughing
matter. *Gianfranco is crying. Drugs drugs drugs. Pills. Slimy scumbags. Even if,
once in a while, they keep you more or less alive. Pills! They only kill you from time
to time.* I know. Abyss therapy is hard. I see it for myself. Soul doctoring is hard.
Being soul-doctored is hard. What's soft? Keep an eye on your sheep. Don't tie
them to a rock or let them ramble off some cliff. Just keep an eye on them.
Artistic disorder! That's what we need. Abyss therapy. Populace! Next therapy.
Let's put dots on paper *any old way.* Be mischievous. Don't think. Just do it.
If you try to arrange them out of order you'll probably end up with a portrait
of your mother. Forget order and no-order. Just do it. Put dots on paper. On
papyrus. On a slab of limestone from the Tyrant's quarry. Dots. Just do it.
The *freedom* of water gushing *in* the fountain. The *necessity* of water gushing
in the fountain. Exactly the same. Completely different. Gushing is gushing.
Contradiction. The might of spirit. Being is nothing. Gushing *in.* Somewhere
to gush. Gushing up without gushing down? The stuff of magicians. Medicine
shows. Artistic disorder. That's what we need. Just put the dots on the page.
Don't hope for the best. If you *just do it* maybe it won't look like a portrait of
your cat. It's quite possible. Put dots. Leave them alone. Leave *yourself* alone.
What self! See it for yourself. Out to pasture? Control your cow. Give her
lots of room. Wide open spaces. A wild east. Wild west. Whatever. Roam
around. Good milk. Don't *ignore* her. Hell no. Keep an eye on her. Just barely.
Freely. Necessarily. A delicate web. I call this *taking care of her.* The swifts. The
swallows. At dusk. The meadow is the meadow. The abyss is the abyss. Dawn.
What dawns? Who knows. Control? Let them wander around. Don't ignore.
Don't beware. Care. Just do it. Soul doctor. I'm dreamed. I dreamed. It's all
beyond me. Nothing's beyond me. Eudemus of Cyprus. Beyond me? No, no
beyond. The meadow is the abyss? Certainly. Uncertainly! Am I actually from
Cyprus? Have I ever been to Cyprus? Why did I leave Cyprus? If I was ever
there. And I left. What's a name. What's in a name. What's a dream? *Why
dream?* I know I was in the grove. For years. Possibly. I know I dreamed. I
know I'm dreamed. I'm in Siracusa. Certainly. Not that I know it. It's just a
fact. I dreamed. In Pherae. Coming home in five years. Nearly five years ago.
Another fact. But I don't know facts. I know what I am. Am not. Am what
I'm not. Not what I am. This uncertain reality. Facts are facts. I am I. What I!
'Eudemus of Cyprus.' A name. A soul doctor. What's going on. Abyss therapy.

Let's be blunt. Fine points are long gone. *D'un tyran l'autre.* Abyss therapy. Keep things under control by letting them get out of control. Planning your life. Planning your battle. Means drawing a clear outline. Then filling it in. Spontaneously. Like water from a spring. Filling. Emptying. Wildly. Freely. Necessarily. Same deal for planning your death. What can we do about this goddam *uncertainty.* The people ask. Well, *la vie est variable.* Never forget it. Change. The only certainty. Uncertainly. The only thing you can count on. Never expect anything. Whatever exists is unexpected. Tyranny! *Voilà* your certainty. *Count* on it. One. Two. Three. Uncertainly. Wait for things you're certain will never come. Uncertainly. To avoid disappointment. Abysally. Write five stories. Teach everyone. Put dots. Write poetry! Be drunken! The writing on the walls. Plastered! Chasing images. Roaring drunk. The plastered walls. The grove. The ears have walls. What walls? What ears? What plaster?

I play my last card. I don't play cards. Soul doctors don't play cards. No card tricks. They contradict themselves. Constantly. Contradiction is hard. Free. Necessary. The might of spirit. Grin and bear it. Never stop laughing. What can I do? For this populace. For myself. For myself, zero. Ground zero. The ground falls to the ground. The foundering foundation. No way up. Or down. For that matter. Everyone wondering about my dream. In Pherae. At the sad café. The Siracusan cats. Wondering about my dream. I dreamed it. This I cannot deny. Going home. Five years. Nearly up. Eudemus of Cyprus. *EU* means good. *EU-DEMOS*, the good of the people. Including cats. I love them. And birds. Little and big. So wonderful! I don't care for dogs. I love children. Especially little children. Playing. Like cats. My name means good-peopled. Good of the people. The *demos.* For example: Euthymus means of good cheer. Good-spirited. *Thymos.* Eudaimon means fortunate. Of good destiny. *Daimon.* A big word. But *thymos* is big too. *Demos.* If *demos* isn't big, what is. *Tyrannos,* I suppose. Big. Unfortunately. This unfortunate war. Beginningless. Endless. Middleless. Eat dead, burnt bodies! Who's counting. Good of the people. Call me Eudemus. In my certainly abyssal uncertainty. Good. Soul doctor is my happy destiny. Heading for the end. My last card. What is it? *DREAMS.* Of course. The writing on the wall. Dream on! A rare case of someone who owes his place in history to a dream. Not to a dream about him. To a dream he had. They say. They, who dream of me. Owe my place. The Platonists say. My *philos* Aris will say. Here. There. The night sky in Siracusa. Heavier. More dense. In the grove. Airy. Lighter. Ethereal. I am here. Where uncertainly I am. For the moment. For a moment. Of Cyprus. Dreamed. I dreamed. Abyss therapy. What's a dream? Who knows? I know! I raise my hands and spread out all my fingers. A dream is a *conversation.* I, too, have conversed. Awake. With Platonists. In the grove. With Aris. In the grove. With these two slimy Platonists, Dion and Callippus. In the grove. Way out of the grove. With the Siracusan populace. I converse and doctor. At the same time. Have I conversed ever since my birth? In Cyprus. Uncertainly. On the sea. The birds. The islands. On my way to the grove. Did I converse? I don't recall. Why not? I definitely conversed. In the grove. With Platonists. Plenty. Aris! With Dion too. Callippus too. So busy. Always eating. Always thin as a rail. Such men are dangerous. Methinks. The pulp. Abyss therapy. A dream is a conversation. *Voilà* the keystone. Such as it is. I do what I can. Can't. Don't want to. Want to. They don't want. They want. They can. They can't. Just do it. Or? Soul doctors don't grow on trees. *Gianfranco is laughing.* The trees are laughing. The children. The cats. Laughing. A profession? Soul doctor. Time will tell. The first in the history of the world. The others will fend for themselves. Now. The pulp. The populace! The people dream. The nightmares of their choice? Not on your life. Or death. They take as good as they get. Just take it. No choice. Stuck. With it. Nightmares. Pre- and post-traumatic stress. They cut off your ear? *Dream on.* Now they cut off your nose! This carnage stops right here and stops right now! Who said so! Who knows? The gist. The grist to your mills. *A dream is a conversation.* The heart of abyss therapy. Conversation. It can't be beat. Say, you're alone. On a raft. On the open sea. You meet a *semblable.* On another raft. A fellow human being. What do you do? Converse, goddamit! Don't just sit there. You're completely alone. At a tristesse taverna. Drinking. A *semblable* sits down. Now what? Converse! With a dream it's the same deal. But better. You're sleeping. Between battles. After the battle. Before the battle. During the battle. Now what? Ye gods a dream! What is it? It's a conversation! An *ideal* conversation. No less. No, not Platonic Ideal. No. Look up at the abyss. This is the abyss conversing with you. Your very own abyss. In your very own bed. On a bench. In a ditch on the battlefield. Wherever the hell you are. An ideal conversation. Go for it! Be happy! But, you say, they're cutting off my leg. In the dream. The horror! *Do not worry.* Converse. Just converse. Are all conversations pleasant? I never said so. On that raft. On the open sea. *Ye gods it's not a semblable.* It's the Creature from the Black Lagoon. *Do not worry.* Converse. A *dream* conversation. An *ideal* conversation. You can break it off. Draw it out. Start it up again. You wake up. Sooner or later. Fall asleep again. Wake up again. Asleep. Awake. Rejoice! You're not alone. You have your abyss. Full of wild ideas. To the rafters. Abyssal ideas. Your very own. An infinite treasury. But they scare me shitless. Sometimes. You say. *Do not worry.* Sunny days. Cloudy days. Rainy days. The more the merrier. *Dream* storms. Do they drench? But *why* the Creature from the Black Lagoon? You say. On the raft. Why not Aphrodite? In a bikini. Dream on, *mon frère.* Your abyss is an *infinite treasury.* There is no wind that always blows a storm. What! *Why dream?* You ask. What a question. Why converse?! Why talk with anybody ever? Why make sounds? Signs. Noises. Sighs. Screams. Groans. *Why not just be completely silent!* Who's listening anyway. Talk to your wife. Your children. Your revolted friends. Are they really listening? They're all dreaming god knows what. I'll talk to myself! You say. At least I listen. To myself. I'll talk to my cat. She always listens. If she's not too busy. No No No No. This is *abyss therapy.* Therapy by, in, for your abyss. *Conversation, mon semblable.* We need a *con*versation partner. *Make the suffering bearable.* Write stories. Teach everyone. Let your cow roam. *And dream.* You do it anyway. Like it or not. Ye gods you ask *Why Dream?* The nightmare of your choice. *Be loyal!* You have an abyss. I have an abyss. We all have an abyss. Rejoice! A dream is a conversation with your abyss. *The abyss always listens.* It has no deaf ear. The perfect partner for your conversations. The abyss. The true conversationalist. *Name your pain.* The abyss will help you. Never lose faith in your abyss. The abyss will never lose faith in you. Absolutely. Never. Soul doctor. My calling. Not a true populist. A miserable soldier. Soul doctor. Coming home. I'm getting the hang of it. This last card is an ace. In spades. Listen. A true conversation is like a mirroring. A double mirroring. My words to your mirror. Your words to mine. Sound. Wait! A stain on the mirror. Mine or yours. Or both. *Troubled* conversation. Noise. Bad dreams. Look! The mirror is *all one stain.* The con-versation breaks off. There is no *versing-with.* The poetry of the abyss. Broken. Silenced.

like a drum-tap at the edge of the universe
a single drop of water in a secluded mountain pool
so faint, so distant is the voice of the world
so enormous the silence, like a cry of shadow

Courage, mon semblable! My *very* last card. I say: the abyss is the perfect mirror. A bright mirror. Without stain. Clear as a shimmering mountain pool. When your dreams rise from your abyss just watch them and be happy. If nothing else, they're a sign that you're still alive. *Converse with your abyss of dreams.* It's listening. It always answers. The true conversationalist. It keeps us all alive. I know. You're distressed. A wounded soul. You're in deep shit. Dig it, bro. It's the Eudemusian Age. It's the world that's in deep shit. Be happy to be in it. *There is no other world.* You're stressed out of your mind. *Well so is the world.* Name your pain. Dream. We're never alone. I, myself, am never alone. Doubly. I dream. I'm dreamed.

Estremo rossocenere. Extreme ash-red. At the ash-red border of the night of the world. The local reality. Uncertainly all too certainly. The usual mercenaries. Dion has had Heracleides stabbed. Dion leads the funeral procession. Himself. What's next. What more do you want. Paradise on earth? Place your bets. Hold a referendum. Peace and love? The populace is fed up to the gills. So what! Jumping out of their skins. Who cares! Stressed totally out of their minds. Soul-doctored or not. The age of cruel miracles has long since drawn to a close. What else is new. Callippus. Callippus is not new. What's he up to. It's very simple. Mind-bogglingly simply complicated. Callippus must be real. Nobody could possibly invent him. Dionysius the Younger. I had the pleasure of his company. When he invited Dion, Callippus, and me over to his palace. In Ortigia. Threw us straight into his dungeon. But we have friends in Siracusa. Now the Younger Tyrant is back in Calabria. Enjoying his exile. Feeding on empty dreams of hope. As exiles do. A dilemma. Does Calabrian cooking beat Siracusan cooking? Hard to decide. We'll call it a split-decision. Skip the referendum. Plato got nowhere with Siracusan Tyrants. Younger, Elder, what have you. My soul-doctoring might have helped the Younger. Definitely not the Elder. A Tyrant's Tyrant. He would have sent me off to the lime quarries. *Tout de suite.* To converse with the quarried poets. No, perhaps the Younger. Dreaming, putting dots, writing stories, everybody teaching everybody. Maybe somebody would have taught him how to tie his shoes. Meanwhile, the Younger 'tries' to bribe Callippus. To get him to neutralize Dion. 'Tries.' Easy as pie. Like asking a bird to sing. A bee to sting. A flea to bite. What are friends for. So to speak. Callippus knows he can't spend *all* his time devouring his new dish. Pachynusian tomatoes, eggplant, local cheese. Baked in a hot oven. It's amazing. He let me taste it for myself. Now he's taking some time off to assassinate his great pal Dion. Why the hell not. Easy as baked tomatoes. The Younger has already neutralized most of Dion's closest friends. Callippus is the best friend he has left. Dion! Savior! Saint! Platonist! With a friend like Callippus you *have it all*. Callippus, bribed, bribes Dion's mercenaries. Cash! Then he betrays the bribed mercenaries to Dion. Dion enlists Callippus as a secret agent. To spy on possible plotters. Smart move. Everyone tells Dion that Callippus is plotting *against* him. Dion says hell no. He's plotting *for* me. Goddamit where do I fit in. In all this shit. I know. This is the Eudemusian Age. But what am I supposed to do? I. Myself. What self. Eudemus of Cyprus. In the thick of it. Of what. Reality is uncertain. But the uncertainties here are certain as all hell. Dion trusts Callippus. As if he were his brother. His mother. His dog. Trust. A serious mistake. I, myself, saw it coming. My fellow Platonists. To each his own Big Idea. Dion, Philosopher King. Some kind of joke. But what kind? Callippus. Whose fellow Platonist? Faithful friend. My ass. Dion trusts Callippus. But Callippus gilds the lily. Gild? Absolutely nobody trusts him. Except for Dion. So he wants the lily solid gold. Dion's wife, Arete. Her name means 'virtue.' His sister, Aristomache. Whose name means 'fighting best.' Believe it or not. The good fight. They don't trust Callippus. Not the six inches they could throw him. Dion's only son falls out of a window. Dies. I know. All this is hard to believe. Dion is distressed. To say the least. Stressed out of his mind. Jumping out of his skin. A wounded soul. Dion! For one fleeting moment. Something in common with the populace. *Extremely* fleeting. Loyalty? To the nightmare of your choice. His wife and sister don't trust Callippus. To say the least. They demand a loyalty oath. Loyalty to Dion. Philosopher King of Siracusa. Sure thing, sez Callippus. He takes the Great Oath. In Persephone's temple. He breaks his vow. Right after the Oath. Remember Zakynthos? The lush green

island from which we set sail. A flower. Full of mercenaries. Siracusa. Full of
Zakynthinian assassins. Pick a card. Any card. A couple pay Dion a visit. A
house call. Soul doctors. Body doctors. What have you. They choke Dion and
then stab him with a short Spartan sword. Exit Dion, Platonist. The most
enthusiastic convert Plato ever had.

My fellow Platonists. What now. Suddenly. Callippus is Tyrant of Siracusa.
Once known as Kallippos the Academic. Unadulterated Athenian. Suddenly,
for all time, Callippus of Siracusa. Ye gods *what* is this shit. Beyond belief.
Deep deep shit. A river of shit. I, myself, Eudemus of Cyprus. If I've ever even
been to Cyprus. I don't swear by it. No Great Oath. I'm an islander. Yes! I think
so. A certainly uncertain fact. A certain feeling I have. The grove. Fact. Feeling.
My travels. My second sailing. To Sicily. If I'm not in Sicily now where am I.
What in the world is a fact. Certainly! Uncertainly. A soul doctor. A dreamer.
A slave. What now. I'm hardly anybody. Callippus! You cut a sorry figure.
Any figure at all. Better than no figure at all? Goddamit. I decide to brush my
teeth. An honest-to-goodness being-is-nothing decision. But you, Callippus,
what do you decide? To take your stand. To defend your absurdity. You're the
Tyrant. Now. You, and your loyal mercenaries. *And after you it will be even
worse.* Fuck you all. This is the Eudemusian Age. I dreamed. In Pherae. Very
nearly five years ago. Very very nearly. Coming home. A faint feeble plaintive
voice. My voice? Eudemus! Good-peopled! It's the populace! I see them for
myself. They're all writing stories. Putting dots. Teaching. Dreaming. *Good
for them.* Goddamit. Wounded souls. Soul doctor. I spoke my piece. Of the
puzzle. A lot of people are tearing out their hair less. Jumping fewer inches up
and down. But what's new. What's changed. What's better. I did what I could.
In the thick of it. Dream on. I'm dreamed. I'm happy to be dreamed. I'm not
alone. Yes! The abyss! But. Someone's dreaming me. It's good. Not the Idea of
the Good. Just simply good. For nothing. If you like. Being is nothing. *Logos.
Anthropos.* Human logic is a logic of the abyss. What's next. The battlefield.
Again. Platonists. Again. Old friends of Dion's. A fistful of mangy dogs. The
most enthusiastic converts this Nightmare has ever had. Philosopher Kings!
Where am I. In the thick of it. I see it for myself. I wanted to see something
else. For myself. But. I take as good as I get. This destiny. This is what I see
for myself. Misery. A tiny troupe of feisty Platonists. Ready to resist. Revolted.
Revolting. Again. What am I'm supposed to do? I lend my name to an entire
Age. Blood, gore, guts, and veins. I am its slave. Figments. In flashes. This is
the way. Forward! Into the slave's life.

This revolt of the revolted Platonists is not revolting. In dire straits we do
what we can. Certainly. What we can't. Revolt. I am a single drop of water.
A secluded mountain pool. I speak to you. Why? Somebody dreamed me.
Otherwise, nothing. Silence. I am a soul doctor. The first in history. Being first

is no virtue. What counts are the followers. Did anyone follow? Gianfranco followed. I had ideas. Not so Big. Just ideas. And a practice. A therapy of freedom. A therapy of the abyss. Just think. Friends of Dion revolting against Callippus. The new Tyrant. Me with them. What more. What next.

The birds slash away at time. Eudemus of Cyprus. Going home. To the black earth of Sicily. To decomposition, peace, and torment. To an abyss of dreams. Traveling forever. Twisted by stillness and winds. Lost among islands.

sacrifice and the slave's life

What does it mean to be a slave? All necessity, no freedom? In his Logic Hegel shows us that the zero degree of necessity is the zero degree of freedom. No necessity, no freedom. A contradiction? Hegel's is a *logic* of contradiction. Being is nothing. So it begins. No distinction. Pitch black. A shot in the dark. Self-contradiction. Being there. Just barely. Existing. Naked. With nothing. Open the roof to the rains! Do you call this freedom? Perhaps Callippus does. Not Eudemus. He knows. He's seen it for himself. Tyranny. Absolute freedom? Yes. And no. The tyrant thinks he's absolutely free. To tyrannize. But what about the tyrannized? The populace. The *demos*. The bad-peopled. They *know* they're slaves. Absolutely. If they're still alive. Quite an accomplishment. They won't be for long. Neither will the tyrant, as a rule. Callippus didn't last long. Longer than Dion's last friends who revolted against him. But not much longer. Longer than Eudemus. But Eudemus is dreamed.

Being is nothing, says Hegel. Then, he says: being is not nothing. Distinction. They are not two and not one. They are separated and inseparable. Bare determinate being is not nothing. Just barely. Not a phantom. Even if the emperor has no clothes he's still the emperor. In a naked sense. Not a phantom emperor. A naked emperor. That's his problem. This time I'm talking about slavery. The slave's life. We say 'slave' and we think, quite rightly, 'not free.' Not free from what? Not free from necessity! Exactly Hegel's point. Being is nothing means freedom is necessity. The very beginning of freedom—the edge of freedom—is the very beginning of necessity. Necessarily. Freely. Certainly uncertainly. If you think that 'being is nothing' means all freedom and no necessity you've lost your mind. Sez Hegel. You've let your sheep ramble off a cliff. You've lost control. I like to talk about being-is-nothing decisions. My favorite example is 'I decide to brush my teeth.' A decision. Barely. At the edge. Not to be confused with a no-mind 'just do it.' Teeth-brushing is, definitely, a decision. Rational. At the edge rationality. I *decide* to brush my teeth. What a gloriously free decision! You say. I say, free? *Where's the necessity?* Being is nothing. Brush, floss, let them rot, the world won't come to an end. Or you either. Chairman Mao never brushed his. You brushed yours yesterday. Skip today. Brush them tomorrow. Life goes on. But, you decide. To brush them right here and right now. Callippus *decides* to make eggplant parmigiana. Invent it. Discover it. Good for him. With Pachynusian tomatoes. The supremely good. Fuck Parma, he says. They can dream of tomatoes like this in Parma. The *crème de la crème* of tomatoes. Not to mention this Sicilian eggplant. Cheese? OK, you can't beat Parma for cheese. Another split-decision. Then again, did Parma exist at the time? In any event, is this a being-is-nothing decision? Was inventing the wheel a being-is-nothing decision? Was discovering America a being-is-nothing decision? As decisions go, deciding to make eggplant parmigiana is not the same as deciding to brush your teeth. A Pachynusian tomato is not a being-is-nothing. In this eggplant decision I detect a pinch of necessity. A smidgen. Possibly a small dollop. A serious matter. A decision is a *serious* matter. (*Eudemus is laughing. Gianfranco is laughing.*) A lot may hang on it. Or from it. Callippus. Now Tyrant of Siracusa. Whatever he will *decide to decide* in the future is his own miserably goddam business. So much the worse for him. Tyrant. Tyrannize. Declare Chinese the language of Siracusa. From midnight tonight. A being-is-nothing decision. You could call it 'arbitrary' but arbitrary has nothing to do with it. Free will. Pre-determination. Was dropping the bomb on Hiroshima an arbitrary decision? A being-is-nothing decision? Hell no. At Hiroshima on August 6th, 1945, we are not at the beginning of the Logic. We're close to the end. A Final Solution. An end. A new beginning. Last chapter of the Logic, 'The Absolute Idea.' The free play and self-realization of the concept. The long *logical journey* that proceeds *in the necessity of the concept* from being is nothing to the *supremely free*. It's complicated. The concept has spoken its *whole piece* and become the supremely free. Which it has been all along. *Necessarily.* It's all about *the relation*, sez Hegel. Never mind being, never mind nothing, just think their *relation*. If you like, call it a journey from the zero degree of freedom to the supremely free. But this does not make it a journey from absolute necessity to no necessity at all. Not on your life.

Shall I stop rambling? Make my point? My cow is falling off a cliff. The slave's life. What does it mean to be a slave? This is my point. Sacrifice. At the *very end* of the Logic Hegel says that the *supremely free* makes the *supreme sacrifice* of freely releasing itself *into nature*. Bidding adieu to the system of logic. To the realm of shadows. Giving up *thinking as such* and moving into *the world*. Why such a big move? It has *absolutely* nothing to do with Plato's Cave. It seems that, in the end, supreme freedom can only express its freedom by freely sacrificing itself. By leaving logic behind? That's how it looks. But is it possible? The zero degree of necessity is the zero degree of freedom. *Logically speaking*. But I'm asking what it means to be a slave. *Is this a logical question?* Logic is the realm of pure thinking. My point. My question. Is this. *Is there such a thing as a logic of practice?* A logic of the world. Not of shadows but of solid things. If we say that logic is practice where in the world are we? What does it mean to be a slave? All necessity, no freedom? Logically or practically? *Same deal? Or not?* A question like this makes me want to dive into the abyss. Where are my soul doctors! Gianfranco, dead these long years. I saw him dying. For myself. Miserable. Famished. Eudemus dying with his tiny troupe of feisty Platonists. Miserably? Or laughing? Who knows. He's seen it for himself. The Eudemusian Age. But at least Eudemus is *dreamed*. Fighting. Fighting what? Let's put dots, write stories, teach arm-wrestling. Dream. Converse with the abyss. Dive into the abyss. But never forget. This is not the journey. We're not going anywhere. We're not coming home. *We are the abyss.* Our soul. Our spirit that takes a dive. The might of spirit. Dive away! Dream on! We're right here. Right now. The abyss. Keeps us all alive. Nothing but the abyss.

How can a tyrant be absolutely free if the people are absolutely slaves? A ruler is no ruler without the ruled. This is the message of the abyss. That keeps us all alive. Look at them! At the sad café. In Pherae. In Siracusa. Tyrant! Can you call this ruling. Tyrant! You need somebody to rule. And you don't even know it. A city is not a prison. Not a slave plantation. You never noticed. The tyrannized and the ruled are not the same. Look! They're drinking in the taverna. Just sitting there. Not even speaking. Sighing from time to time. From the leaves of their hearts. And you think you rule them. But they're not even there. Just barely existing. Naked. With nothing. You're goddam lucky if some dreamer comes along and gets them to write stories, teach everybody, put dots. Dream. Now maybe you can actually rule them. Just a little. A smidgen. The bare minimum. The difference between being and nothing. Which are the same. And not the same. Spoken. My piece. Of the puzzle.

— Tyrant! What's on your mind? Speak. Your riposte. Give us an easy piece.
— You say, the people are hungry. Why? Hungry for what? For putting dots on papyrus and jumping up and down? You say I don't rule them. I say, who gives a shit? They're goddam unruly. What do I care? What, me worry? Let them read *Mad* magazine. *L'état, c'est moi*, goddamit. Hungry? Let them eat cake. Tomatoes. Eggplant. Cheese. Let them sit in the tristesse taverna and sigh from the leaves of their heart. I have them *under control*. Under my thumb. I have my mercenaries, goddamit it! What about them. I rule them and they control these unruly sheep and cows.
— Your mercenaries! You don't rule them you *pay* them. Different kettles of fish. You control them and they control your populace. You're right. No True Populist will bring you down. If the revolted revolt they won't get far. But if the mercenaries get riled up, it's curtains all around. The tyrannized are slaves but the mercenaries are free. Sacrifice is out. Disneyland is in. Fun City. The

permanent war economy. The military-industrial complex. Guns and butter. Kill Kill Kill Kill. It's the Eudemusian Age.

Hypocrite lecteur! If you recall, Callippus of Siracusa, in the end, was Tyrant of Siracusa for about thirteen months. The revolted did manage to revolt. Eventually. Atrociously. Successfully. Atrocity! Excelsior! No. Not Dion's feisty Platonists. Poor Eudemus. No. The laborers. Farmers. Builders. Long live the next tyrant. *D'un tyran l'autre.* For the record, the next ten years were the most atrociously tyrannical in Sicilian history. An exemplary Atrocity Exhibition. The height of the Eudemusian Age. In Sicily. Post-Eudemus. Himself. After his 'homecoming.' This height, of course, was an anthill compared to the Great Atrocities the world has seen since then. Look out the window. The sun never sets. Meanwhile, after Siracusa, Callippus went off to Rhegium to tyrannize the Calabrians. Everyone tyrannized the Calabrians. They were more tyrannized than anyone. For some reason. While he was at it Callippus decided to tyrannize his own mercenaries. His very last decision. Logically, practically, the last thing he decided to decide. They stabbed him to death with the same sword that killed Dion.

Would Euripides have dedicated a tragedy to Callippus? Platonist! Perhaps he's a better subject for the Roman playwrights. More a Caligula than a Heracles. Not tragic enough for Euripides. But tragicomic? *Orestes* is tragic but there are lots of laughs. *Iphigenia in Aulis* is extremely tragic and absolutely hysterical at the same time. One of Euripides' very last plays. It won first prize at the Great Dionysia in Athens, along with his *Bacchae.* In 405, shortly after his death, in Macedonia. Iphigenia, pure, innocent. Sacrificed. She dies with dignity, willingly, 'for the good of all Greeks.' Heroically. Meanwhile Euripides makes the great Homeric heroes—Agamemnon, Menelaus, Achilles—into modern politicians. Ambitious. Double-dealing. Corrupt. The Athenian equivalent of Tammany Hall. A world of slaves, mercenaries, and, alas, politicians. The cradle of democracy. But why am I thinking about Euripides again? For once, a straight answer. Because I'm thinking about *sacrifice* and *slaves.* 'The slave's life'—the last words of *The Trojan Women.* Of course, I *always* think about Euripides. I even confused him with the Euripus Strait. He's one of my heroes. How can I not think about someone who writes lines like: 'That mortal is a fool who, prospering, thinks his life has any strong foundation: since our fortune's course of action is the reeling way a madman takes, and no one person is ever happy all the time.' But, right now, *sacrifice* and *slaves* are on my mind. *Human* sacrifice. This is not some kind of joke. Blood, gore, guts, and veins. Never mind Alice's Restaurant. These ancient Greeks play for keeps. The Greek fleet, in Aulis, is ready to set sail for Troy. Agamemnon, killing time, accidentally kills a deer in a grove sacred to Artemis. Artemis kills the winds. They can't set sail. The seer Calchas reveals that to appease the goddess Agamemnon has to sacrifice his eldest daughter, Iphigenia. Nowadays 'sacrifice' is not such a big word. Economists use it all the time. Along with 'austerity' and the like. Back in Homer's day it meant cutting the sacrificial victim's throat so violently that she or he is decapitated. There has to be plenty of blood to satisfy the goddess or god. No, it's no joke. It's history. Past and present. In Greece archeologists have found evidence of human sacrifice from the 10th to the 7th century BC. Homeric Greece. In Crete, in a cemetery in the foothills of Mount Ida, they found the skeleton of a man whose arms were bound behind him and his throat cut so violently that he was decapitated. ISIS has performed plenty of rites like this. Recently. The Athenians at the Great Dionysia knew exactly what Euripides meant by 'sacrifice.'

We have another major 'sacrifice' in *The Trojan Women*. A tragedy in the tragedy. One of many actually. If flinging Astyanax, the young son of Hector and Andromache, from the battlements of Troy isn't tragic, what is? In this tragedy each and every Trojan woman is a tragedy in her own right. Hecuba, Andromache, every last one. Euripides wrote this tragedy in 415 BC, poised between Melian carnage—siege, hunger, slaughter, slavery—and the debacle of the Sicilian Expedition. But my subject right now is sacrifice. I'm thinking of Polyxena, the youngest daughter of King Priam of Troy and his queen, Hecuba. Human sacrifice. Again. At the end of the Trojan War. Can this really be the end! Achilles has been killed, shot in the heel. Troy has lost the war. Its men are dead or dispersed. Its women are wailing, with good reason. Especially Hecuba, the queen. The King is dead, most of her sons and daughters have been killed. Her favorite grandson, little Astyanax— what a gruesome end! And now poor Polyxena. Double trouble. The Greek fleet has no wind for its sails. Again! Why, this time? It's Achilles' ghost! He's come back. To demand the *sacrifice* of Polyxena to appease the wind god. A veritable *revenge sacrifice*. The heel that shot him was one of her brothers. Achilles, even dead, will not stand for it. (I've said many times, it's better to be temporarily like Achilles than permanently like Achilles.) She is to be 'sacrificed' by Achilles' son, Neoptolemus, at the foot of his father's grave. Sacrificed. Her blood a fountain dousing the great man's tomb. A red shower of death to please the dead. In *The Trojan Women* Euripides pulls no punches. Andromache: 'They cut [her] throat to pleasure dead Achilles' corpse, above his grave.' Hecuba: 'Poor child [...] *sacrificed to a dead man*.' Flung from the battlements. Sacrificed above the grave. *Kindertotenlieder*. Andromache: 'Our life transformed, as the aristocrat becomes the serf.' Hecuba: 'Such is the terror of necessity.' Andromache became Neoptolemus' concubine. Back home in Thessaly, they had three children. Polyxena had said she preferred to die as a sacrifice to Achilles than to live as a slave.

Eudemus! I miss you already. Your tiny troupe of feisty Platonists. Fighting. Dying. 'Coming home'? Sez who. To the pleasant land of Phthia? Sacrifice and slavery. I'm in a black mood now. Can this really be the end? A black mood. Like the Euripidean black cloud that comes out of nowhere and, in an instant, covers the clear bright sky. Completely. Like Hegel's bloody head that darts out, and just as suddenly vanishes. In the night of the world. I know that the Eudemusian Age will never end. But I was just wondering: Did it ever begin? Did it begin with Eudemus, himself, with his dream in Pherae? Does it go back to the night of beginningless time? Or does it begin right here and right now, in the abyss? In the abyss that keeps us all alive. What does it mean to be a slave? Perhaps it means as many things as there are slaves. But *human sacrifice*—what does it mean? This 'dumb blankness, full of meaning, in a wide landscape of snows.' Is it Nietzsche's version of the abyss, which looks back at us when we look into it? Homer and his heroes. The *Iliad*. The origins of 'Western civilization.' So-called. Personally, I call it the Eudemusian Age, because I Dream of Eudemus. Myths. Heroes. Cradles of democracy. Platonists. Eudemus sees Tyranny. For himself. I see, for myself, this scene in Book XXIII of the *Iliad*. A great scene! Dramatic. Heroic. Moving. Achilles' love for Patroclus, his dead companion. Great poetry. Tragic poetry. The Greek warriors following Patroclus' lifeless body on its last journey, to the great funeral mound. They have cut off locks of their hair and thrown them on the corpse till they covered it like a garment. Achilles walks behind, supporting the head, sorrowing for his comrade. Building the pyre. It is time for the funeral. In 'Western history' this must go down as the 'mother' of all sacrifices. Human sacrifice. I give you Robert Fitzgerald's translation, 1974, I'm old-fashioned, or out of fashion, it's the only translation I have. I'm loyal to the nightmare of my choice.

> They added timber and enlarged the pyre to a hundred feet a side. On top of it with heavy hearts they laid the dead man down. Sheep and shambling cattle, then, in droves they sacrificed and dressed before the pyre. Taking fat from all, splendid Achilles sheathed the body head to foot. He piled flayed carcasses around it. Amphorae of honey and unguent he arranged in order, tilted against the bier. He slung the bodies of four fine horses on the pyre, and groaned. Nine hunting dogs he fed at the lord's table; upon the pyre he cut the throats of two, *but as for the noble sons of Troy, all twelve he put to the sword,* as he willed their evil hour. Then in the midst he thrust the pitiless might of fire to feed upon them all, and cried upon his dead companion: 'Peace be with you even in the dark where Death commands, Patróklos.'

Make no mistake. This is a nightmare. Of somebody's choice. Achilles concludes his 'oration' with an exaltation. A *Kindertotenlied*, of sorts. The fire will devour twelve noble sons of Troy—children!—together with you, Patroclus, *mon frère*. But wild dogs, not flames, will feed on Hector, Priam's son. We may reflect, if we like, on the manner in which the twelve Trojan children were 'sacrificed.' Never mind the sheep, cattle, fine horses, and faithful dogs. Emptied of marrow. Like it or not, this is the source of our civilization. If we like, we can see it for ourselves. Right here. Right now.

the night of the world

What can we say about the Eudemusian Age? We don't even know exactly when it is. We can't say, it's like Nixon's term. From 1969 to 1974. Even Attila the Hun had a term. From 434 to 453. But Eudemus, thanks to his dream, and to my dreaming his dream, and him, lends his name to an entire Age that has no term. Past, future, what can we say? Eudemus saw tyranny for himself. In Pherae. In Siracusa. But the past was no picnic. Just think of Achilles' bloodbath for Patroclus, 'peace be with you.' Even in the dark where Death commands. *The horror.* Then again, the future will be worse. Things Eudemus didn't see for himself. Things we have only heard of. Things that actually happened that we can only imagine. Tatars and Huns, barbarian hordes, sweeping across the steppes to fuck your mother. Sultans, Khans, Presidents, and Prime Ministers. Massacres. Ears for beers. Terrifying illegal immigrants. Rapists. Unimaginable weapons. Fire from the sky. Trench warfare. Mustard gas. Fire bombing. Atom bombs! What would Achilles have to say about Hiroshima? Stuff happens. Final Solutions. All's fair. Eudemus, *mon semblable!* Soul doctor. You lend your name to all this. This Eudemusian Age.

November, 2010. It's cold and very windy. Blustery. Bitter freezing fog. There has been a lot of flooding in the city. *Acqua alta.* Sirens. But, this month, there have also been bright sunny days. Right now I'm in Campo San Giovanni e Paolo. The square is dominated by this big statue of the condottiero Bartolomeo Colleoni on his horse. When Colleoni died in 1475 he left a lot of money to the Republic of Venice, on the condition that they set up a big statue. No funeral pyre. No human sacrifice. Just the statue.

I'm going to the Venice hospital. The *Ospedale Civile.* Next to the big church. San Giovanni e Paolo. I've been going twice a week for about two months. To visit my friend Gianfranco, who is in a coma. Difficult visits. Today is special because Eudemus is coming with me! He wants to see Gianfranco for himself. Soul doctor to soul doctor. Gianfranco in a coma. Eudemus dreamed. A doubly uncertain reality. We go up to the Reparto Rianimazione. The Intensive Care Unit. It is quite an adventure. A long corridor. It's like entering a prison. Or a United States Consulate or Embassy. A formidable-looking door. We ring a bell. An electronic voice. We have to give our names and the person we are visiting. The first time I came I had to register. Fill out papers. Eudemus is welcome because he's with me. And because he's dreamed. What's more, he is a soul doctor. I'm not a doctor of any kind. The door opens electronically. We go in. Another long empty corridor. I tell Eudemus again, *no laughing*. I know how he loves to laugh. I know how Gianfranco loves to laugh. But he's in a coma. So he's not laughing. I tell Eudemus, again: Please! In the Reparto Rianimazione there is *no laughing*. I hope I can trust him on this. We go down the corridor to the very end. We don't see anyone. On the left there's an open door. The dressing room. We go in. We still don't see a living soul. Not one single *anima viva*. Here, in Rianimazione. There's no undressing in the dressing room. Only dressing. So to speak. All the dressing is with brand new, totally sterile material. Disposable. Never to be used again. In fact when we leave the Reparto Rianimazione we take it all off and place—not throw— it carefully in a trash bin. (I'm sure this bin has a more sophisticated name. Which I don't happen to know. Ask a doctor.) We put special covers on our shoes. Other covers on our heads. Others on our mouths. Special gloves. We put on a big complicated apron (so to speak) that covers everything else. All disposable! We are entering a sterile environment. We're ready to enter. Now we see someone! Two or three Rianimazione doctors. Not soul doctors, like Gianfranco and Eudemus. You could call them 're-souling' doctors. Not for dead souls, à la Gogol. But for souls on the border between life and death. 'Abyss souls' could be an appropriate term. Some come back to life. Most, unfortunately, do not. It's not Dante's 'give up all hope.' But pretty close. It's not Purgatorio! Purgatorio is for 'believing' souls. *Credenti*. Believers. The Christian faithful. Gianfranco, Eudemus, and I are not Christian faithful. We are *loyal*, not *faithful*. Loyal to our friends. Loyal to all our *semblables*. Loyal to the abyss that keeps us all alive, only the abyss. Eudemus and I are ready to venture into the Reparto.

How Gianfranco ended up here is a Long Tail. Which I do not need to chase. And shall not tell. I know the Tail but won't tell it here. It's private. Believe it or not, there are still a few things in this Age that are private. Eudemus himself is not public. He's dreamed. Which is another matter. I will only say that Gianfranco had a congenital heart defect. It spelled big trouble for him his entire life. In the end it killed him. Along with the fact that *he never quit smoking*. For more than a week or two. There's definitely an element of suicide here. *Which I do not understand*. A fact I hate. He had two major heart operations, big ones. Even after the second he kept on working—and smoking!—for a few years. Then he had to stop. Working. Retire. Early. A true soul doctor like him would never retire voluntarily. But why did he keep smoking? Let me be 'charitable' and call it a profound philosophical question. He'd moved from Venice to Mestre, the mainland, to a huge and hugely cluttered apartment.

Books, objects, I loved that apartment, it was such a chaos! For a decade or so
I went to see him, every week or two. We talked, *laughed,* and soul-doctored
each other. Who did the better soul-doctoring? Hard to say. A split-decision. I
can only say, as I said earlier, that later on, when he was in big trouble, I tried
to practice *his* abyss therapy on him. Unsuccessfully. I didn't do it well enough.
It isn't always successful. Or, Gianfranco had come to a point where, for him,
there was no more therapy. After all the therapy he'd given everyone else. All
his life. As far and as long as he could. The therapy for him broke down.
Sometimes the night of the world blots us out completely.

As I saw it for myself, his breakdown took the form of *sheer hunger.* Pure.
Nothing but hunger. Hunger for nothing? No. But who knows for what.
For the unnamable, certainly. It was a hunger at a life's end. A soul hunger.
Incorrigible as I am, I hit you again with Mister Kurtz. *Heart of Darkness.* I *know*
you'd prefer *Bartleby, the Scrivener.* Gianfranco would have preferred him. 'The
heart of the eternal pyramids.' 'With kings and counselors, murmured I.' But
Bartleby, much as we love him, is out of town. He's not in Venice right now.
He's down on Wall Street. Occupying it, perhaps. Not home. Not coming
home. Kurtz is right here right now. In the Reparto Rianimazione I saw him
for myself. I see him now. For myself. Coming home, goddam him. Conrad,
that goddam genius. Gianfranco! For me, every day you're coming home.
With Eudemus. *Unconscious?* In a coma. We went to see you together. We
see you for ourselves. We see you in your Rianimazione bed. Naked. Covered
by—pardon the expression—a shroud. You've 'grown down' to half your size.
Your great white mane of unruly hair, beard, ponytail, all shaved away. Naked.
Your naked head and face. But your body. Like a fish. A slim sardine. In your
shroud. If the bed didn't raise your head you'd be practically invisible. Just
tubes, going in and coming out of you. Everywhere it's humanly possible. Your
breath, your blood, your urine, your feces. The drip drip of your 'food.' What
else is there. Rianimazione. No. No tube for your soul.

Painful as it is I want to sketch my remembrance of the last year of your life.
Your hunger. For what? For nothing. For what has no name. Every July we
spent my birthdays together. For many years. You came from Mestre. Heat,
hell, and high water—no, no high water in July. You played with Gilda.
Laughed. What funny faces she made! We had fish in Campo San Giacomo.
Just the two of us. The last July of your life you told me, Why not have a real
party! Invite some friends! The beginnings, or ends, of hunger. My dear friend,
you were *so hungry.* Not for fish, which you barely touched. Hungry for—
more. No, not 'more light,' like Goethe. More. Period. More of 'it,' whatever
'it' is. Hungry to go on. Thin, weak, tired. Hungry. I remember you now, years
later. A lifetime later. The end of your life. You came from Mestre. In the heat.
To Campo San Giacomo. I had invited a few friends, after our years of *tête à*

tête. You wanted to see new faces. New souls. You were hungry for everything. (Except food.) I remember your hands fluttering like a Japanese fan. Flapping quickly and lightly. With the exquisite delicacy of a Venus flytrap. Your trap snapping shut to capture any insect or spider that came along. Voracious. Like Kurtz? 'I saw him open his mouth wide—it gave him a weirdly voracious aspect, as though he had wanted to swallow all the air, all the earth, all the men before him.' It's true, Gianfranco, you were *voracious.* But for what? What. For life that now meant, simply, bare survival? Going on. A lobster clawing at whatever's in the flow. For Kurtz *voracious* means wanting to devour *everything.* You were snapping—at what? At the last sparkles, glitters, glimmers of what we call living. Of what *you* had called living. Soul-doctoring. All day. Every day. Long long days. Six days a week. At the *public* mental health center. Palazzo Boldù. Absolutely free. Helping people, like me, in soul-trouble. *Lots* of them. Conversing with them. Giving them the smallest amount of psychiatric drugs you could. The minimum. Slimy pills. Sundays. You got up before dawn. Long hours on the train. To an addiction rehabilitation community, near Trento. Home after midnight. Sundays. Your 'day off.' For years. For decades. Was this the life you so desperately hungered for? In Campo San Giacomo. Where you barely touched your fish. Weirdly voracious. Mister Kurtz—'There was nothing either above him or below him, and I knew it. He had kicked himself loose of the earth.' *Gianfranco, you're laughing.* Loose of the earth, and then what. *You laugh.* No mere recording organism. Plato's Cave! My friend, my brother. Kurtz. *The horror.* And you console him! Soul hunger? Kurtz wanted *IT ALL.* Like Dion. Tyrannically. My dear horrible Kurtz. You want *IT ALL.* Your river. Your ivory. 'My Intended, my station, my career, my ideas.' *IT ALL.* You even want to *know* everything. Like Aristotle in Dante's Limbo, 'master of those who know.' *Mastery.* That's what you want. Kurtz. You even want to choose your own nightmares. To *master* them. No, Kurtz, yours is not soul hunger. Dion—not soul hunger. Soul doctors could do nothing for you. Alas, soul doctors can do nothing to cure *the hunger for mastery.* Soul doctors converse with dreams. Converse with conversations with the abyss. 'Ah! but it was something to have at least a choice of nightmares.' Yes. It's quite something. Gianfranco! Here you are now. In the Reparto Rianimazione. They don't even give you this choice. In your coma. Do you dream? How you loved it when I told you my dreams! A raging flood. Like leaves twisting in the wind. My wild abyss of dreams.

Gianfranco. I've been coming to see you twice a week for about two months. Dressed like a man on the moon. All this disposable stuff. And you naked under your shroud. Small and thin as a sardine. After a few weeks I got used to your naked head and face. There are four beds in the Reparto. Though I'd call them units rather than beds. Units in the Unit. Tubes. Machinery on all sides. Pumping in and out. One other 'unit' was already occupied the first time I came. By a man. So sometimes there were other moon-suited visitors. He died a few weeks ago. Now there's a woman in another 'unit.' The Reparto always feels very big and very empty. The silence. Apart from the machines. The breathing machine makes a little noise. You always had a breathing-tube in your mouth. Then, one day, they took it out. You're breathing without a tube! A good sign. I suppose. I'm not sure. I'm allowed to stay for thirty minutes. I hold your hand in both my moon-gloved hands. The whole time. I speak to you. Through my surgical moon-mask. The whole time. About anything I can think of. Anything that pops into my head. The first time I came I filled out forms. À la Kafka. 'Friend.' Not 'family.' 'Family' can come any time they want and stay as long as they like. In fact your sister, brother-in-law, niece, always come in the mornings. I always come in the afternoons. So I never see them. After filling out the forms I was allowed to speak with a doctor. He said: 'Talk to him. It's impossible to tell whether he understands anything you're saying. But he can tell that someone's talking to him.' 'Can I touch him? Hold his hand?' 'Absolutely. Touch him all you like. He can feel it. He can tell.' So, I'm not sure he recognizes me at all. But I talk away. Let me say this. The first few weeks his eyes were open. I suppose this was good. A good sign. Of what? Frankly, I didn't like anything I saw in his eyes. Eyes like dark dimly glowing embers. Far away. Expressionless. Or did they express? Darkness. Sorrow. Regret. I don't know. I only know that they did not see me. Or did they? I can't imagine that they did. He seemed to be looking out into absolute distance. Or, possibly, *in* into absolute distance. Nothing but distance. Nothing. A terrible looking. If he was looking at all. It was very difficult to get used to these eyes. Then I came one day and his eyes were closed. Every time I come now his eyes are closed. One time I asked the doctor, 'Does he ever open them? When I'm not here.' 'No, since the day he closed them he's never opened them again.'

Here I am with Eudemus. In our moon suits. Eudemus is not laughing. He is shocked. Suffering. To see Gianfranco this way. He stands very still as I take Gianfranco's hand. I tell Gianfranco, Eudemus has come with me today! To visit you. He is the first soul doctor in the history of the world. In Pherae, in Siracusa. He saw Tyranny for himself. He saw people in big soul-trouble. Men at a sad café. Silent. Sighing from the leaves of their hearts. Missing arms, legs, hands, ears, noses, eyes. Wars. All the time. Just like today. Women, children, cats, dogs. Stressed out of their minds. Jumping up and down. Remember! Just like at Palazzo Boldù. That girl who jumped up and down all the time. Thanks to you she never jumped out the window. Remember! You helped her. You helped everybody. Eudemus did too. He discovered, or invented, abyss therapy. Played it by ear. To help people in soul-trouble. Just like you did. He got them to write five stories. He got everybody to teach everybody. He got them to put dots on paper, chaotically. He conversed with their dreams. He played it all by ear. Just like you. Your ears have no walls. Unfortunately he died in battle. In Siracusa. Along with a tiny troupe of feisty Platonists. Fighting against a bad Platonist tyrant. Defending the bad name of a dead Platonist tyrant. He's famous for a dream. Five years before his death he dreamt that five years later he would return home.

I see that Eudemus is crying. Quietly. Gently. Crying for a question he can't answer. I, myself, cry. Often. Hard. For Gianfranco. For Wolfango. For my cats, Gina and Gilda. But I never imagined Eudemus crying. For my soulful friend, whose soul is about to leave him. No! Not his soul. His *life*. Soul, says Eudemus, is what makes a living thing alive. Soul and body are separate and inseparable. Not two and not one. A community. We die. The people who love us mourn our passing. Miss us. Cry. Softly. Hard. Often. From time to time. It is our destiny of death. It is what Eudemus has always seen for himself.

Suddenly Gianfranco opens his eyes. We have never seen anything like it. And never will again. It is as if the abyss itself has screamed. There are absolutely no words for what we see in these eyes. No words. Absolutely none. It is *terrible*. What is reaching out to us from these eyes? We see it! *It is the night of the world.*

Gianfranco's dream

[late May, 2014; the dream is in Italian]

The dead of night. I'm in bed with Gilda. The phone rings. It's Gianfranco.

— I want to give you my phone number. So you can call me any time you want. Ready? Write this down. 1235 813 213455 89144233 —

— Whoa! Gianfranco! A pretty long number.

— Wait, I'm not finished. Keep writing. 3776109 871597 2584418 —

— The end, Gianfranco. The end! This looks like a bad infinity.

— The end is the end. Night screams at the seagulls. The dead have long numbers. This one is Fibonacci and Mao having a *big hug*.

Grande è la confusione sotto il cielo. Perciò la situazione è favorevole. Ricordati! Dai nomi ai tuoi dolori. Che la sofferenza non sia tutto un cielo sopra di te.

Everything under heaven is utter chaos. Things couldn't be better. *Name your pain. Name your suffering.* Don't let it all be one great sky. Hanging over you. With its weight of sorrow.
Death! What's the point?

— The dead have long phone numbers —

His laugh *EXPLODES*. Filling the room. This mansard. To the rafters. A blizzard! A wild blizzard of laughter. An infinite blizzard of snow. The tiny dream gymnasts. Supreme effort. Beyond all effort. Striving beyond striving. No idea of gain. The zendo. Love as terrible as time. Watching the slow leaves falling. Bright! Swirl! Like snow in an old man's eyes.

Now I see him, his wild white mane of hair, beard, ponytail. All one. All longer, thicker, fuller, whiter than ever. Without end. This huge whiteness. Filling space to the rafters. *His laugh!*

—Look! *Sono il tuo uccello bianco e solo.* Your plain white bird. High. In a dream.

Whose dream, my friend! Is this you dreaming me? Me dreaming you? Gilda dreaming a camel? Or just one big hug of a dream.

In any event, since then we have been able to talk once again. Sometimes. Many times. Short times. Snippets. No, not on the phone.

And from time to time Wolfango talks to me too. Suddenly. Just a few words. Or, more likely, he gestures. His hand hurling emptiness. A white bird reaching heaven. My friends! My brothers! The eyes of night. *Sempre con noi.* My cats will love you forever.

the ends of hunger

> Eudemus of Cyprus, on a journey through Thessaly, in its celebrated capital, Pherae, under the cruel sway of the tyrant Alexander, fell desperately ill. The doctors had given him up for dead. In this terrible state Eudemus had a dream. He beheld a young man of extreme beauty, who delivered three prophesies: Eudemus would soon recover, the tyrant would fall, and after five years Eudemus would return home.

Eudemus! When I began chasing your Tail you were just a handful of bare facts. Now we have become dear friends. True *semblables*. We've come a long way together. Make no mistake. You 'are dreamed' because I dream of you. But you also exist on your own. You have your own Eudemusian facts. *Historical facts,* such as they are. You have your *uncertain reality.* What's more, let us not forget that you are *famous* for your dream. All on your own. Not because I dream you. Just five facts. A short sketch but with a long tail.

First fact: You were born in Cyprus, presumably. Second fact: Banished from Cyrus, you traveled to Athens. To Plato's Academy. Where your *philos* was Aristotle. Who later became famous as 'master of those who know.' Third fact: You left Athens and traveled to Thessaly, to Pherae. Where you had your famous dream. Fourth fact: Five years later you were killed in battle in Siracusa. Fifth fact: The Platonists. In Sicily, if any of them were still alive. Which is doubtful. But especially in Athens, where they were very much alive. In the grove. The Platonists interpreted the 'returning home' in your dream as your immortal soul returning to its true home. Because your death has released it from the prison of your body. It's time to say a few words about this fifth Eudemusian fact. This interpretation of your dream. This Platonistic hunger.

We've seen how hungry Gianfranco was, at the end of his life. Yet he wasn't hungry by nature. Kurtz, of course, was voracious all the time. Melville, in *Billy Budd,* speaks of Claggart's *Natural Depravity,* pinning the term on Plato. So with Kurtz we could speak of *Natural Voraciousness.* But I'm thinking of Plato himself. I imagine Socrates, his master, as a calm sort of guy. An Even Keel. A true conversationalist. Good company. Certainly not voracious. Sure, he had some big ideas that Eudemus and I don't agree with. About the immortality of the soul. Imprisoned in the body. Death the cure for life. But, fair enough. He's quite calm about it. I bet he didn't even put capital letters on his ideas. It's Plato who is never calm. Socrates says, a cock to Asclepius. The hemlock? Cheers! It's Plato, himself, who says: 'He who has got rid, as far as he can, of eyes and ears and, so to speak, the whole body, these distractions that keep the Soul from acquiring Truth and Knowledge—who, if not he, can possibly attain to the Knowledge of True Being.' True Being. *A certain reality.* In my opinion, the man is *famished.* Permanently. By nature. *Natural Hunger,* that's Plato. A *Hunger* that infected the Platonists first and then half the world. And then the other half. Forever. A world that is famished for Knowledge of True Being. *For certainty.* A certainty that is not of this world. A *Platonistic World* of certainty. Another World. But Plato looks for it under every rug. Why in the world did he go to Siracusa *three times!* Looking for Philosopher Kings under the rugs. Famished. By nature. For life? For death? I'd say, for something that is neither life nor death. For Immortality? Plato! What's up!

You're a Platonist. Yourself. The Soul is already Immortal and you're famished for Immortality! It doesn't make any sense. What's the good of the Idea of the Good, says Eudemus. Matter matters! Plato! Famished for Philosopher Kings, when there are Tyrants on every corner. Famished for an Ideal City. But everyone's a slave, a mercenary, or a tyrant. Everything's blood, gore, guts, and veins. Famished for Immortality. But what is Immortality? What does it mean? I think I know what Plato thinks. Immortality? It's just like the Ideal City. Whether it exists anywhere or ever will exist *is no matter*. A City laid up in heaven as a Form for him who wills to see, and seeing, to found a City in himself. A *City*, OK. But *Immortality* is another matter. Plato! You have pangs of *Natural Hunger*. Contagious hunger. *Terribly* contagious. You're a raver by nature. Philosophically speaking. You don't shout. You rave softly. But you make your point. Down with the abyss! Death to our destiny of death!

Plato is persuasive. Immortality of the Soul. Back in the grove everybody bought it. Except Eudemus. I dream. In his dream dialogue with Aris, his *philos*, Aristotle still buys it. But Eudy sows seeds of doubt. Eudemus, of course, has already seen for himself all the main arguments that Aristotle will endorse many years later. When he has his own grove. Endorse! I'm chased by my own imaginary dialogue! Who knows what Eudy was really doing in the grove. Whatever he was saying, if anything, is not a Eudemusian fact. It's a perfectly uncertain reality. But I *dream* of Eudemus. A dream is spirit's conversing with the abyss. Says Hegel. Soul, the sleep of spirit. And contradiction, the might of spirit. Eudy, my friend! I see you, in the grove, under the starry sky, with Aris, looking up at the abyss. I hear you, discovering, inventing. Fresh ideas without capital letters. 'Matter matters.' Form and matter. Potentiality and actuality. The four causes. The unmoved mover. Soul (*psyche*) as what makes a living thing alive. 'Endorsing' Aristotle's mature philosophy. *Ante litteram*. In this case the letter giveth life. Aristotle was, by nature, a marine biologist. It took him many years to come into his own as a philosopher. For Dante he was 'master of those who know.' But then *Platonism caught fire*. Like Patroclus' funeral pyre. 'As if shot from a recent volcanic eruption of the volcano Popocatépetl.' Practically nobody knows it, but since the Renaissance—in Modernity, in Post-Modernity—'we live and breathe and have our being' *in Platonism*.

Eudemus regrets all this. He saw Plato for himself. He saw Platonists for himself. In spades. Dion. Callippus. And friends. And enemies. All Platonists. Aristotelians hadn't been invented, or discovered, yet. Except for Eudemus. Himself. Possibly. A figment. Greatly dreamed. Barely existing. In flashes. Speaking of flashes, I'm not here to praise Aristotle. No panegyrics. But I'm not here to bury him either. My NYU professor Dave Leahy, my great friend, formulated a distinction between Platonic and Aristotelian philosophy *so succinct and so complex* that in fifty years I haven't quite fathomed it. But I'm still trying. Even without Dave himself to help me anymore. Dave, Gianfranco, Wolfango, my great old friends are dead. *My great laughing friends.* Now both my cats are dead. Gina! No great laugher but so much love. *Our connection.* Gilda! *You laughed so much and made us laugh.* The incarnation of Buddha in the world. A year ago you 'went on.' You rejoined the crystal river from which you came. So painfully. Suffering Buddha. You caressed the tiniest insects and the motes in the air. And me. You were the body and the mind of Buddha. I know that some sentient being has taken your place. Perhaps a fly. Or a tiger. Satori. There is no body and no mind!

Dave Leahy's distinction. Plato says: '*I am the one.* One man makes many women pregnant.' Aristotle says: '*I am the many.* I give birth to the one.' That's it. The distinction. Let me put it just a little less succinctly. *Plato:* Form. Idea. World of Forms. World of Ideas. Participate! 'I am the one.' *Aristotle:* Concrete individuals. Matter matters. The world given to us in experience is of concrete individual things acting and reacting to each other. Contemplating them we become aware of characters common to many individuals. These characters are as *real* as the individuals themselves. There is no separate world of universals. We cannot explain this world of change by the operation of Ideas that are out of this world. As Plato does. Whatever we know we know of *this world.* There is no other. This world of change. This uncertain *reality.* No separate World of Forms. This world of form and matter. Potentiality and actuality. 'I am the many.' This is Aristotle. His theory that conceives being (*ousia*) as a compound of matter and form is known as hylomorphism. We could also say: a community of matter and mind. He applies the theory to living things. He defines a soul as that which makes a living thing alive. A soul is related to its body as form is to matter. A living organism consists of a body with the property of life, which is its soul. All this depends on his distinction between potentiality and actuality. Reality is not stony but fluid. Not certain but uncertain. What's more, potentiality exists *for the sake of* actuality. We don't see in order to have sight, we have sight in order to see. Matter exists *for the sake of* receiving its form. In stronger terms: matter strives for form. Even stronger, and quite possibly too strong: matter *hungers* for form. This *unconscious teleology of nature* is the most problematic aspect of Aristotle's philosophy. Arguably, it is also the most fruitful. In a certain regard, it is the seed of Hegel's dialectic. Let us not underestimate the *uncertainty* of hylomorphic reality. Eudemus doesn't, that's for sure. It's the beating heart of the Eudemusian Age. Which means *carnage* that does *not* stop right here and stop right now! As somebody suggested. But it also means *careful disorder*: 'There are some enterprises in which a careful disorderliness is the true method,' as Melville wrote, in his infinite genius. Eudemus is his heir. *They* know the difference between fact and reality. This very difference that is the *physical and theoretical* basis of modern physics. Physical *and* theoretical. Pure Aristotle, Eudy's *philos*. In flashes. Let me quote a few lines from an 'old' book (1958) on the 'new' physics. By Werner Heisenberg, the creator of quantum mechanics, author of the Heisenberg uncertainty principle (1927). Ilya Prigogine, 'chaos theorist,' would endorse this:

> In experiments about atomic events we have to do with things and facts, with phenomena that are just as real as any phenomena in daily life. But the atoms or the elementary particles themselves are not as real; they form a world of potentialities or possibilities rather than one of things or facts. [...]
> Probability in mathematics or in statistical mechanics means a statement about our degree of knowledge of the actual situation. In throwing dice we do not know the fine details of the motion of our hands that determine the fall of the dice and therefore we say that the probability for throwing one special number is just one in six. The probability wave of Bohr, Kramers, Slater, however, meant more than that; it meant a tendency for something. It was a quantitative version of the old concept of 'potentia' in Aristotelian philosophy. It introduced something standing in the middle between the idea of an event and the actual event, a strange kind of physical reality just in the middle between possibility and reality.

This advent of probability marks the end of certainty. My dream of Eudemus. In flashes. Our five 'facts' are islands on a sea without shores. The birds slash away at time. I'm coming to my point now. My last point, which is, precisely, my first. Our fifth, and last, Eudemusian fact. The interpretation of the dream. We've just been speaking of the 'mature' Aristotle. The Aristotelian Aristotle. The 'master of those who know.' When Eudemus 'fell in battle' in Siracusa his *philos* wrote a dialogue entitled *Eudemus* or *On the Soul*. It is a *consolatio mortis* for his dead friend. Written around 353 BC. Aristotle was 31 and had been in the grove for 14 years. Eudemus, of course, left a little more than five years earlier. Five years, plus the time it took him to make his way to Pherae. Where he dreamed he would 'return home' in five years. Homeless, and returning home! A fine turn of phrase. As we know, five years later he 'fell in battle' in Siracusa. Most everyone on earth at the time, if they happened to know of Eudemus' dream, would have said: 'Too bad! The third prophesy wasn't fulfilled. He died. He didn't return home. To Cyprus, or to wherever in the world he came from. He'll never become famous for *this* dream!' Most everyone *except the Platonists*, of course. They *went to town* on this dream. They made it into a *famous* dream that some people still dream of today. A *truly prophetic* dream. After five years Eudemus *returned home*. His fame, and the fame of his dream, owes a great deal to Aristotle himself, of course. He was

Plato's star pupil at the time, which, in itself, was no small claim to fame. To say nothing of his becoming 'master of those who know' later on. Even though this early work of his, *Eudemus* or *On the Soul,* has been lost, scholars have worked hard piecing the sense together. Any text of Aristotle's is big scholarly business. The composition is *pure Platonism.* Plato himself couldn't have said it better. The argument is quite similar to the *Phaedo,* which is also known as *On the Soul.* Though, it seems, Aristotle is even more adamant. Hungrier, perhaps? I wish I knew why. We do know that, in his *Eudemus,* Aristotle attacks *any and every* position that is opposed to—or may threaten—the doctrine of the immortality of the soul. 'Adamant' may be an understatement. Eudemus was killed five years after the prophesy in the dream. You see! It is true prophesy. He came home. At the Academy it was something to be celebrated. It *was* celebrated. True Platonism vindicated! Aristotle himself recorded the event. In one of his earliest works.

The fifth Eudemusian fact. The interpretation of the dream. Actually the least surprising of the facts. Eudemus! Born and banished. Came to the Academy. Left the Academy. Had a possibly prophetic dream. Facts that add up to quite a story. But the fact that the *Platonists* interpreted the third prophesy in your dream *perfectly Platonistically*—there's no surprise here. Eudemus! Rejoice. It made you famous. In some circles. Your dream has become *good publicity* for Platonism. What's the problem?

Well, I have two problems. The second concerns *Plato's terrible hunger.* We've seen Melian hunger. Gianfranco's hunger. Kurtz's hunger. Understandable hungers. But I can't get a grip on Plato's. His hunger for Knowledge of True Being. It's slimy. It slips away. I'll get back to it in just a moment.

My first problem is uncertain. Possibly imaginary. A problem of uncertainty. Eudemus and I have become friends. I helped him find his voice and he's had a lot to say. He's told his Tail. I've chased the tail of my dream of him and of his dream. He saw things for himself. He's told us what he saw. For himself. For me he's very real. A real friend. A brother. A true *semblable.* He came with me to the *Ospedale Civile.* Together we saw Gianfranco open his eyes. That terrible day. The night of the world. Yet, as you can imagine, his reality is *singularly* uncertain. I invented it. Everything. Except for the five Eudemusian facts. But my Eudemus is an elementary particle. The physicists say—and I understand them—that elementary particles are not facts. They form a world of potentialities or possibilities. But what about the Eudemusian Age? I think it's far more than a mere possibility. I think it's certainly an uncertain *reality.* You can interpret it as you like, but *it is actual.* The fact that the Eudemus I invented is rigorously *Aristotelian* is considerably less actual. It's sheer possibility. To its very marrow. Why did I do it? It's quite simple. I don't like the way the Platonists took possession of his dream. Occupied it. Imprisoned it. The dream belongs to Eudemus, not to them. It's free. We know Eudemus spent time in the grove. We know he and Aristotle were close friends. But we don't know if he bought the doctrine. It's possible. But it's possible he didn't. It's possible he was really the person I imagine in the dialogue. It's possible his friend Aris knew he didn't buy the doctrine. It's possible that in his *consolatio mortis* Aristotle *used* his friend and their friendship to further his own Platonistic ends. To create a famous Platonist hero. It's possible that years later he regretted it. When—and this is a fact—he came to believe that a soul is that which makes a living thing alive. That the soul is not separated from but in community with the body. That it doesn't 'return home' when your friend falls in battle. Fighting a bad Platonist tyrant to defend the bad name of a dead Platonist tyrant. — By the way, the circumstances of Eudemus' death may well be a bull's-eye historical fact. I have researched my Tail with great passion. The history is not invented. — I think my friend Eudemus may not be getting a fair shake. Existentially, so to speak. I feel really bad for him. You may think this is crazy. But, he and I have become friends. What's more, I think it is typical of the Platonists to *impose* Big Ideas. On anyone they can. 'Returning home.' Not even the *unconscious abyss* is anybody's home. The night of the world is *what we are*, not what we go home to. It is the uncertain reality of our self and of our world. In flashes. A bloody head darts out! Our human existence. More figment than fact. True Being? Plato takes no prisoners. His ears have walls.

My second problem is terribly complex. Elementary physical hunger is simple. Melian hunger is an extreme case. But straightforward. Intellectual hunger is more nuanced. Complicated. But Plato's *existential* hunger may be unfathomable. Hegel doesn't tackle it in his Anthropology, but it might be a special form of conversation with the abyss. The abyss that keeps us all alive. Only the abyss. Not origin but source. An absolute disorder that is our only resource. A gushing not in the past or future but right now. Right here. An uncertainty, a disorder, that is not our sickness but our health. *Existential* hunger. Hunger for Knowledge of True Being. All I can say, for sure, is that this is not Aristotle, or Hegel either. It's the bottom line of Plato's hunger for division. For dichotomy. Body versus soul. Matter versus mind. Mortality versus immortality. This world versus the other world. Eudemus and I say: Separated we perish. Together we see it for ourselves. Dichotomies. How about tyranny? Tyranny versus—what? Tyranny has no opposite. Unless you believe in Philosopher Kings. Or unicorns.

The divine versus the human is the most terrible of all dichotomies. *Divine* hunger. Gods versus the world. Greek gods. I'm speaking Greek now. I want to end with a Tail Eudemus told me recently. A tail of the night of the world. In the Eudemusian Age, says Eudemus, *the gods want the end of hunger. Of their* hunger. The end of their separation from the human world. They're tired of it. *To what end* is this separation, they're saying. What's the good of it. It just makes us *hungry*. Extremely hungry. Divinely hungry. We look down from Olympus, we peer out of our sacred groves, and all we see are saints, poets, and seafarers in the hands of hungry gods. In the old days it was different. Homeric heroes. Permanently like Achilles. All those sacrifices! What pyres! The smoke got in our eyes but we were happy. We took part in the wars. Took sides. Fought with one another. At least it made some sense. Sacrifices! We didn't ask for them, they just did it. It was only human. We gods never make sacrifices. To be gods means *to be sacrificed to*. We never went hungry. But these days, with all these tyrants, mercenaries, and slaves almost nobody makes sacrifices anymore. What a world! When people aren't saying Kill Kill Kill they're saying God God God. But the sacrifices! They've made us into *hungry gods*. Famished. We're starving. Can this really be the end! The problem is this *goddam separation*. The world is full of *human* food but we can't eat it because we're separated. Plato calls it *Natural Separation*. Separation by nature, he says. Nothing can be done about it. We gods think you need new philosophers. Tough love. Fewer facts! More uncertainty! What else does it mean to be a god. We're hungry for human sacrifice because we have no choice. We see so much destruction. Carnage without end. This hunger! This Eudemusian Age! Destruction! And they say it's our fault. It's not true! We are gods, not destroyers.

The ends of hunger. Eudemus tells me, in this Eudemusian Age if somebody should actually happen to burn something as a sacrifice an amazing thing happens. Terrible, yet beautiful to behold. This is the end of his Tail, as told by old gods:

We starving gods. Our separation. In the old days people were always burning cattle, horses, dogs. The occasional human. They knew we were hungry. For sacrifice. Now we're starving. And practically ignored. The sacrifices have become as rare as the tears of a cat. Look! The sparkle, the glitter, the bright smoke! A sacrifice! Succulent. Savory. Quick! Our hunger for what joins us with the world is so great that we turn ourselves into flies! We, the gods. Flies! We flit down from heaven to frolic in the smoke. Mingling. Savoring. Glimmering smoke. Glittering god-flies.

Eudemus sees it for himself. Coming home.

5 July 2019

400

An Abyss of Dreams

sources and references

There are few direct and exact quotes in the text. All my sources for Thucydides, Plato, Aristotle, and Euripides are books I purchased when I was a student in the New York University Classics Department, Washington Square, 1968-72. I still have them and practically all the lines I refer to I know by heart, and modify at will. In the case of *The Peloponnesian War*—which I reread in its entirety quite recently, with great pleasure—I modify the original translation completely. But I greatly love all these translations, which have been my companions for some fifty years.

Let me list them:
Thucydides, *The Peloponnesian War*, translated by Rex Warner, Penguin Classics, 1954 (1968).
Plato, *The Last Days of Socrates* (for *Crito* and *Phaedo*), translated by Hugh Tredennick, Penguin Classics, 1954 (1969).
Plato, *Phaedrus & Letters VII and VIII* (for the *Seventh Letter*), translated by Walter Hamilton, Penguin Classics, 1973 (1983—I bought this one later).
Plato's Republic, translated by A. D. Lindsay, Everyman's Library, 1935 (1969). (The one I know by heart.)
The Republic of Plato, translated by F. M. Cornford, Oxford University Press, 1941 (1970).
Aristotle, David Ross, Methuen, 1923 (1968).
Euripides, *The Complete Greek Tragedies,* edited by David Grene and Richmond Lattimore, first edition University of Chicago Press, 1956–58, my editions are Washington Square Press, 1968. I have all the volumes, Aeschylus and Sophocles included. My sources here are:
—*Heracles*, in Volume II, translated by William Arrowsmith.
—*The Trojan Women*, in Volume III, translated by Richmond Lattimore.
—*Orestes*, in Volume IV, translated by William Arrowsmith.

Now, in order of appearance:

For starters, my references to 'carnage' and 'American carnage.' Allow me to quote this in full, even great lines like these may be forgotten in time. It's from Donald Trump's [first?] Inaugural Address.

A nation exists to serve its citizens. Americans want great schools for their children, safe neighborhoods for their families, and good jobs for themselves. These are just and reasonable demands of righteous people and a righteous public.
   But for too many of our citizens, a different reality exists: mothers and children trapped in poverty in our inner cities; rusted out factories scattered like tombstones across the landscape of our nation; an education system flush

with cash, but which leaves our young and beautiful students deprived of all knowledge; and the crime and gangs and the drugs that have stolen too many lives and robbed our country of so much unrealized potential.
This American carnage stops right here and stops right now.

D'un tyran l'autre: I play on the title of Céline's book *D'un château l'autre*, translated in English as *Castle to Castle*.

I do quote, directly, the first two lines of Lawrence Durrell's marvelous and very free translation of Kavafis' great poem 'The City,' published at the end of *Justine*, 1957, the first volume of *The Alexandria Quartet*, Faber and Faber, 1968:
You tell yourself: I'll be gone/ To some other land, some other sea.

I mention, in Greek, the first line—*Otan pineis stin taverna*—of a famous Rebetiko song by Vassilis Tsitsanis, songwriter and bouzouki player. Let me translate the first four lines:
When you drink in the taverna/ You sit there and don't speak/ From time to time you sigh/ From the leaves of your heart.

'The destruction was mutual.' Jimmy Carter's judgment on the Vietnam war.

I have two 'deconstructed' lines from Shunryu Suzuki: 'always prepared ... for taking some kind of form' and 'to empty water from a cup.'
from *Zen Mind, Beginner's Mind*, Weatherhill, 1970, p. 117:
something which is always prepared for taking some particular form, and it has some rules, or theory, or truth in its activity. This is called Buddha nature, or Buddha himself.
from *not always so*, HarperCollins, 2002, p. 36:
'to empty' water from a cup does not mean to drink it up. 'To empty' means to have direct, pure experience.

'Kill Kill Kill. Blood, gore, guts, and veins. Eat dead, burnt bodies!' is straight out of Arlo Guthrie's LP record album *Alice's Restaurant*, 1967. Monologue with ragtime guitar backing. The refrain: 'You can get anything you want at Alice's Restaurant.'
'They don't give a damn. Next stop?' is a fragment of a Country Joe McDonald lyric ('Next stop, Vietnam!').

I also quote two lines from Ezra Pound's 'Sestina: Altaforte,' in *Personae*, New Directions, 1926 (1971):
Hell grant soon we hear again the swords clash!
There's no wine like the blood's crimson!

My many references to Conrad's *Heart of Darkness* are considerably indirect, apart from *EXTERMINATE ALL THE BRUTES*.

'Men of much fortune, and with a bad name to come' plays on a line from Ezra Pound's *Canto I*. The speaker is Elpenor, in Pound's rendition of the *Odyssey*. 'Set our oars up, that we swing mid fellows!' are, almost exactly, Elpenor's last words.

'When the winds fail, the sailor turns to oars' is from *Socrates' Second Sailing*, by my NYU professor Seth Benardete, Chicago: University of Chicago Press, 1989, p. 2.

'I raise my hands and spread out all my fingers' refers to the last page of Kafka's *The Trial*.

For Hegel's letter to Windischmann, May 27, 1810, see *Hegel: The Letters*, translated by Clark Butler and Christiane Seiler, Bloomington: Indiana University Press, 1984, p. 561.

'Write five stories!' For the record, the five stories for Gianfranco are: Parroty; Neighbors (started twice, far from finished); Marmari Nights (an elementary particle); The Empty Shield (which turned into a whole book); and I Dream of Eudemus.

On 'Hegel's Anthropology' in general, see:
Jon Mills, *The Unconscious Abyss. Hegel's Anticipation of Psychoanalysis*, Albany: SUNY Press, 2002.
Daniel Berthold-Bond, *Hegel's Theory of Madness*, Albany: SUNY Press, 1995.
On the quotes from *Hegel's Philosophy of Spirit*—it's rather complicated. I don't have a copy of the more recent, unquestionably superior M. J. Petry translation, which Mills quotes, and I read his quotes. So I have to make do with: *Hegel's Philosophy of Mind*, translated by William Wallace in 1894! The Additions (*Zusätze*), however, were translated by A. V. Miller around 1969. The edition is Oxford: Oxford University Press, 1971. I completely 'modify' (paraphrase) some of the quotes, others I mostly modify, a few (Miller's) I modify just a wee bit less. I can honestly say that the translated Hegel in the text is overwhelming better than in the published translation. I was a translator for thirty years. The slave's life. In my analysis of the text I quote from § 389, § 390, § 398 *Zusatz*, § 403, § 405 *Zusatz*, § 408, § 408 *Zusatz*, § 451 *Zusatz*, § 452, § 453, and § 453 *Zusatz*.

'the *highest*—but, as I keep saying (quoting Thomas Bernhard), it's the abyss....' This brings me full circle, to the epigraph at the beginning of *An Abyss of Dreams*, which is an epigram in Bernhard's book *In der Höhe*, grievously mistranslated as *On the Mountain* (London: Quartet, 1991) by Sophie Wilkins. I absolutely don't see a *Berg* in this title. *Höhe* has to do with height, the heights (possible titles: *On the Heights,* or *On High*). On high as opposed to in the depths. *Highest* as opposed to *lowest.* The abyss. That keeps us all alive.

for 'John Sallis, a good philosopher I used to know personally' see his *Spacings— of Reason and Imagination,* Chicago: University of Chicago Press, 1987, pp. 152-157.

'we need a *therapy of freedom':* A reference to the great Italian psychiatrist Franco Basaglia (1924-1980), whose famous law, the *Legge Basaglia* (1978), closed the insane asylums in Italy. His credo: *la libertà è terapeutica.*

on Giulio Severino: after his death I proposed a stunning collection of his writings to a U.S. publisher—my translation, financed by Giulio's two children—but the publisher, *extremely obtusely,* turned it down. A shame! Truly a great loss for readers who don't read Italian.

'Giulio Severino writes'/'the last word for the moment': I give my own (free) translation from the last pages of his incredibly intense essay *Il tempo in Hegel* [Time in Hegel], published in *Il tempo in questione,* edited by my friend Luigi Ruggiu, Milan: Edizioni Angelo Guerini e Associati, 1997, pp. 256-264. I apologize for the sexism, he really does say 'man.' I eliminated a lot of 'men,' but did leave a few.

'We are far from Freud here, as Severino notes.': see his *Inconscio e malattia mentale in Hegel,* Genoa: il melangolo, 1983, pp. 72-74.

'The night of preservation [...] *reaches out* to each one of us': more literally, *hangs out towards.* This is a wild young Hegel. I've changed his metaphor. A therapy of freedom.

'Yes! We have no spaghetti.': the actual song is 'Yes! We have no bananas,' composed for a Broadway show in 1922 and first sung by Eddie Cantor.

'*mon semblable,—mon frère!':* for the record, it's Charles Baudelaire, *Fleurs du mal,* 'Au Lecteur.' The whole line: *Hypocrite lecteur! mon semblable,—mon frère!*

'It will give you a mental ease': a reference to The Fugs' anti-war political-theater song 'Kill for Peace,' 1966.

'I was standing and the earth was not there. I have risen, a spirit passing through.' From the liner notes on an album by the absolutely extraordinary jazz saxophonist Albert Ayler. Actually, Eudemus is composed either by/of the music, and spirit, of John Coltrane, or by/of Bach's Well-Tempered Clavier. In the background, Thelonious Monk. I write by music.

'Artistic disorder!': By all means see my favorite page in *Zen Mind, Beginner's Mind*, p. 32, in the chapter titled 'Control.' Full of dots, sheep, and cows. A large, spacious meadow. Suzuki-roshi.

'The age of cruel miracles has long since drawn to a close.': I reverse the last line of *Solaris*, both the book by Stanislaw Lem and the film by Andrei Tarkovsky.

'This is the way. Forward! Into the slave's life.': see the last lines of Euripides' *The Trojan Women*.

'the Great Atrocities': an oblique but cogent reference to J. G. Ballard's *The Atrocity Exhibition*.

'That mortal is a fool': this is a direct quote from the William Arrowsmith translation of *The Trojan Women*, lines 1203-1206.

Kindertotenlieder: 'Songs on the Death of Children,' a song cycle (1904) for voice and orchestra by Gustav Mahler. The words of the songs are poems by Friedrich Rückert.

'dumb blankness, full of meaning,': see *Moby Dick*, Chapter 42, 'The Whiteness of the Whale.' '—a colorless, all-color of atheism from which we shrink.'

'I give you Robert Fitzgerald's translation': *The Iliad*, Garden City, N.J.: Anchor Books, 1974, pp. 540-541. The translation is divided in verses, which I have made continuous.

'As if shot from a recent volcanic eruption of the volcano Popocatépetl.': Antonin Artaud, the last line of 'Van Gogh. The Man Suicided by Society.'

'we live and breathe and have our being': Acts of the Apostles, 17:28.

'Dave Leahy's distinction': this is very painful for me. The distinction was our ongoing conversation, which began in the late 1960s and continued for nearly half a century. He died in 2014 and is greatly greatly missed.

'a careful disorderliness': *Moby Dick,* the first line of Chapter 82, 'The Honor and Glory of Whaling.' He also wrote, in Chapter 32, 'Cetology' (whale logic): 'The classification of the constituents of a chaos, nothing less is here essayed.'

'a few lines from an 'old' book': One of my NYU books, which I still have, Werner Heisenberg, *Physics and Philosophy, The Revolution in Modern Science*, New York: Harper Torchbooks, 1962, p. 186 and p. 41. For 'newer' books on uncertain reality see: Bernard D'Espagnat, *Reality and the Physicist*, 1990; original title *Une incertaine réalité*, 1985. But why do they mutilate these titles, they kill the point. By all means also see: Ilya Prigogine, *The End of Certainty. Time, Chaos, and the New Laws of Nature*, New York: The Free Press, 1997. At least The Free Press did not feel free to massacre the original title, *La fin des certitudes*.

'saints, poets, and seafarers in the hands of hungry gods': Now this is a wild one, luckily I'm at the end of my line. I combine Jonathan Edwards' 'Sinners in the Hands of an Angry God' with the description of Italians as *santi, poeti e navigatori*. For the record, and speaking of tyrants, the description is from a 1935 speech by Benito Mussolini.

'We are gods, not destroyers.': I play on the last line of Ezra Pound's last Canto, in *Drafts and Fragments of Cantos CX-CXVII*, New York: New Directions, 1942 (1968), p. 32: 'To be men not destroyers.'

VIII

Gilda's Riposte: On the chasing of my tail

a coda

'Two is one.'
—Thelonious Monk

Gina wonders why in the world I chase my tail. Giacomo is kidding when he says it's my Science of Logic, but he may have a point. The Logic is an action book. Action theory. Thinking as such. Direct experience of what is happening right here right now. Satori. I think. I make up my mind. No-mind. I chase my tail. Gina is an action cat. All practice, no theory. Rat theory? Who knows? She likes to kid me. Big sisters are big kidders. She wrote a long Tail. Her meta-memoir. She never chases her tail. I often chase mine. I do it more now than when I was little. I also meditate a lot now. Zen. With Giacomo. Or on my own. With or without a cushion. I meditate because my mind is full of wild monkeys. Jumping around. Like crazy. It's because I think *about* things now. Why? I wish I knew. Many years ago, when I wrote my short Tail, my gentle rant, I never thought *about* things. Now I do. Things change. Why? Because life is a dream? Because life is *not* a dream? Why dream? Because it's the abyss that keeps us all alive. Is that an answer? Since I wrote 'What is it like to be a cat?' I've started to ramble. So I meditate. Ramble. Meditate. Giacomo! My partner. Since I wrote my Tail he's rambled through a thousand pages. I opened all his gates! Two *long* Tails. We write together. Zillions of ideas. No, we don't make things up. We write what we see. In pure thought? Furry or not. No. Thinking *about*. See what I mean. It all started with that short Tail. I started thinking *about* things. Thinking them into existence. Never mind *out* of existence. What's this? An idea! Where in the world did it come from? Who knows? I chase it. From one idea, another. Another. Another again. Like a chain. The Tail gets long. Then real long. Then it's many Tails. Didn't I just say we write what we see. We don't think things into existence. Am I contradicting myself? *Yes!* Nothing exists that doesn't carry in itself a contradiction. Said Hegel. An identity of opposites. It's the might of the spirit. It's tail-chasing. No, not on the wall over the canal. Not anymore. The spirit's willing but the fur is weak. Not on the wall of the Cave either. But everywhere else. In the courtyard, on the old red bricks. In the back garden, on the grass. In the house. Upstairs. On the rugs. In the sunny patches! It's more dramatic. Gina wonders why in the world I do it. I owe her an explanation. A new Tail of my own. A coda. 'On the chasing of my tail.' Short, but tricky. Tail-chasing. *Una parola*, as we say in Italy. A word. Easier done than said.

Let's start over. I think this Tail needs a preamble. Gina wonders why in the world I chase my tail. Giacomo may have a theory. He watches me very closely. Logical knowledge is rooted in perceptual knowledge. Chairman Mao says that theory begins with practice and must return to practice. Two is one, says Thelonious Monk. We love him and his music so much! My sister deserves an answer, but I'm not good at answers. Cats are not big answerers. They said Monk wasn't a big answerer either. Fake news! One day everyone kept asking him to explain the difference between classical music and jazz. Monk! Answer! Answer! So he said, 'Two is one.' That was that. It stopped the whole room. That's my kind of answer. We have the same birthday, October 10th. Monk is over a hundred now, even if he's dead. I'm still a reasonably young cat. OK, I'm not *real* young, like when I was younger. Like when I wrote my first Tail. But I'm not an old cat either. No, age no longer exists. They stole half of Gina's life, but I don't have half of life, or a third, or two thirds, or a fourth. No, life is all one. Like atoms and the void. And the swerve, the *clinamen*. It's just life just death. Just day night, night day. Sun-Faced Buddha who lives ten thousand years. Moon-Faced Buddha who lives one day and one night. The stars in the abyss. The abyss in the stars. We've been reading the atomists again lately. Democritus, Epicurus, Lucretius. Michel Serres tells us about them, in his book, *The Birth of Physics.* I guess this has nothing to do with anything, but you never know. It just popped into my head. Gina loved Lacan, I like the atomists. Plain speakers. I like that one where they say, cross the same river twice, forget it! You can't even sit twice on the same bank. It's change, the Roshi says. Transiency. Flashings into the vast phenomenal world. I know about this without thinking about it. I decided to write a preamble but look! It's a ramble. Maybe this is what it's *like* to be a cat. We dream so much, Giacomo and I. But we're also dreamed. I dream him, he dreams me. *Ergo,* we're dreamed. Logic. Action. Not two, and not one, our Roshi says. Mind, body. Mind, no-mind. No-mind? Maybe this is what it *is* to be a cat. Pure joy. Big mind. No-mind. Wait! Be. Have. Do. No-mind is not something you have, it's something you do. Change. Learning! For ten years now Giacomo almost never goes out of the house. Not for more than an hour. Or two. Big bad health! I take care of him. He takes care of me. Pure love. This is *way* beyond thinking about. I'm scattering all over the field. *All* over. Yes, my first Tail was a tight Tail. This is more like a loose cannon. A total tail-chasing. I follow whatever pops. Giacomo says: *Brava, Gilda!* This is it! The whole point. A chain. Free association. How free? What association? Mind, no-mind. No-mind is not something you have, it's something you do. I'm repeating myself. It runs in our family. I *fail* to see the difference between my partner and me. Call us Ismael. We're chasing. We'll never stop. Ever. You don't *have* no-mind, you *just do it.* And I don't mean basketball sneakers. No logo! To empty water from a cup does not mean to drink it up. I am a cat. A tail is a tail. Two is one. Not two, not one. Logic is healthy! To empty a bowl of water does not mean to drink it up.

Drinking is drinking. Emptying is emptying. To fill the bowl, first empty it. When you do this, *everything is filling.* Mind is no-mind. Two is one, as our dear friend Monk says. Not two, not one, our friend, Suzuki-roshi, says. A cat. A tail. I'm a lot older than I was when I asked what it's like to be a cat. Now I think *about* things. Alas? Progress. Regression? Freedom is necessity. Necessity is freedom. A cat philosophizes. Alas. Why alas? A good question. We want a bare minimum of an idea of why we are here. What in the world we're doing here. What is it like to be a cat? Why do I ramble now? I was once a furry form of pure thought. My partner and I—we dream more than ever. Unfortunately? Good question. Why dream? The beginning, an abyss. The end, an abyss. The middle—who in the world knows? Fortunately, we also meditate more than ever. Cushion, no cushion. Zen. Together. On our cushions. No cushions. Every moment. Lives. Dies. Forever. Now. When?

Paper tigers. Real tigers. Without contradiction nothing makes sense. A dead land of silence and shadow. The might of the spirit. Chairman Mao! We've been reading him. Plenty! His Red Book. His Tail, 'On Contradiction.' Mao knows what it's like to chase a tail. It's not a dinner party. Not painting a picture. Not doing embroidery. A chase! Ask Ahab. Ask the Whale. Call me Ismael. We learned from our Chinese neighbors in the courtyard that 'mao' means 'cat' in Chinese. In fact they call me mao. Actually *mao*-cat is not pronounced *exactly* the same way as *Mao*-chairman. Our neighbor—he's very smart—tries to teach us. He says, listen: mao mao mao. Then, listen again: Mao Mao Mao. The 'a' is *just a little different.* He says. My partner and I listen very carefully. We prick our ears all the way up. We hear the tiny tiny difference, but we could never say it ourselves. It's like Lucretius' clinamen, the swerve of the atom. Atoms fall straight down in the void and then—who knows why, who knows when— they make a *tiny* swerve. The smallest possible. So small you could almost call it theoretical, but it's the direct reverse. It's the most practical thing in the world. Without the swerve absolutely nothing would ever *happen.* Absolutely nothing! It's like a single drop of water in a secluded mountain pool. Swerved! The world is born. Nothing was happening, and now the mountain's full of cats, birds, giants. All because of this tiny swerve. It's like Monk's music. What an imagination these atomists have! But wasn't I talking about Mao? What a rambler I've become. If my partner doesn't help me I'll ramble right off into the wilderness. Don't worry, Gilda! he says. You'll turn it into paradise. Such joy, writing Tails together. But we chase tails on our own. This is what I have to explain to Gina. It's like killing rats. No one can do it for you. Like meditation. Put a hundred monks in a zendo, sitting all together. But each one meditates on his own. Minds are many, but no-mind is just one.

One, many. This reminds me of the sad fact that Venice has gone to the dogs. Totally. A *cat city,* gone to the dogs. Nowadays, in this city, if you don't have a dog you're *out of it.* A lost soul. We cats have become outsiders. Freaks. Giacomo is angry all the time. Dog shit all over the streets. Very big very scary dogs. Usually black. Or brown. Little dogs, barking their heads off. Have you ever heard a cat bark! he says. Or a dog purr. They talk about Rottweilers as if they were kittens. Vicious. Servile. Little old ladies ecstatic about pit bulls. Cute! they say. Giacomo says, philosophically, all dogs are one dog, but one cat is all cats. He says, there's more difference between individual cats than between most individual persons. But dogs! All dogs are the same goddam dog. He gets riled up. But there's food for thought here. What *is* it like to be a cat? Chasing tails. A few days ago a young black African *drowned himself* in the Grand Canal right in front of the train station. A big crowd (mostly tourists) watched them fish him out. Suicided. They 'neutralized' all the stray cats in the city some thirty years ago. Entire cat communities. Rounded them up and took them to a remote island in the lagoon. Then the dogs took over. Young immigrants, says Giacomo, are the new strays.

But wasn't I talking about Mao Tse-tung! Now known as Mao Zedong. Who said 'chasing a tail is not a dinner party.' OK, he actually said 'revolution is not a dinner party,' but show me a cat without poetic license and I'll show you a dog. We cats are poets. And we purr. What's more, what is tail-chasing if not continuous revolution! I'll get back to this. Mao also said: 'Everything under heaven is utter chaos. Things couldn't be better.' I told you, it's the abyss that keep us all alive. Mao even said—this is one of our favorites—'It is often not a matter of first learning and then doing, but of doing and then learning, for doing is itself learning.' Meanwhile, we've been reading his Tails 'On Practice' and 'On Contradiction.' Great stuff. Contradiction! The might of the spirit. Tyger Tyger. Paper. Real. Mao said: 'Just as there is not a single thing in the world without a dual nature (this is the law of the unity of opposites), so imperialism and all reactionaries have a dual nature—they are real tigers and paper tigers at the same time.' A thought after my own heart. 'Real tigers that devour people by the millions and tens of millions. Look! Living tigers, iron tigers, real tigers. And paper tigers! Dead tigers. Bean-curd tigers.' Two is one. It's Monk's dance! U.S. imperialism has the atom bomb, said Mao. A real tiger. A paper tiger! Mao! Cat logic. Mao-cat, Mao-Mao. The clinamen. Revolution. Tail-chasing. Not a dinner party. Not doing embroidery. Contradiction.

I cut to the chase. Swoosh! The sudden way. Gina pokes fun at me because I chase my tail. A lot. On the refrigerator. Around the computer. Everywhere. A dash of good-natured fun between sisters. She never chased her tail even once, she says. Would have sooner hopped on a boat to the moon. Why do I do it? Is Ahab Ahab? *The chase.* 'Oh! Ahab, not too late is it, even now, the third day, to desist. See! Moby Dick seeks thee not. It is thou, thou, that madly seeks him!' Why oh why? *There is no why.* My riposte? No why. Only the how. The how it happens. How! Easier done than said. As I said.

Here I am. Sitting on a rug. In a patch of sunlight. Behind me, my shadow on the light-purple wall. Meditation posture. A straight line—ears, eyes, nose, mouth, chest, forelegs, paws. Perfectly straight. Relaxed. Perfectly stable. Eyes half-closed. Paws planted firmly but gently on the rug. I could sit like this *forever*. Buddha nature. No beginning. No end. *What's this?* My tail is resting on my paws. Gently. Precisely. Delicately. Deliberately? *What's happening?* It moves. Just a little. A tiny bit. Does it happen by itself? Or do I make it happen? *I don't know.* I only know what happens next. Suddenly. I see it! What is it? A tail. What tail? MY tail? I'm not sure. It *moves*. A tiny tiny bit. Wow! My eyes are open now. I look down. I look at it. Is it really *mine?* I guess so. Must be. But—what's happening? Is it really *moving?* Yes! Now what? Is it really *mine?* Is it *me* or *not me?* I'm not sure. A tail. Since it's curled around me from the right I poke it with my left paw. A tiny little poke. Yes! Look! It *really* moves. Something's going on. I poke it again. Softly. This time it *really really* moves. I poke. It moves. What's next? Poke. Move. I poke it to *stop* it, but now it's *moving* more than ever! Is Ahab Ahab? Call me Ishmael. One little poke leads to another. The tail moves more than ever. MY tail? It doesn't *seem* to be my tail. It *seems* to be moving on its own. Poke poke poke—it's running away! When you ask me how I'm doing, is that some kind of joke? I've got a situation here. The tail—and it *must* be *my* tail—is moving. More than ever. No problem? The problem is that now I start to *chase* it. What else can I do? What choice do I have? The chase is on. Poke move poke move. *In a minute I'm spinning around.* Spinning around *myself. What self! What cat! What tail!* A revolution—says Mao—is not a dinner party. Not painting a picture. Not doing embroidery. What is it? It's a chasing of a tail. Of my tail. One cat. One tail. A chase. Monk's dance! Two is one. No beginning. No end.

Why? How? Straight, No Chaser? What's happening? Do I *make* it happen, or does it *just happen?* Two is one. Not a dinner party. Just like Ahab with Moby Dick? Well, maybe not *exactly* like Ahab with Moby Dick. Like what? I owe Gina an explanation. A bona fide riposte. What can I say? I'm just a cat. When I stroll around the house, courtyard, or back garden, my tail points straight up at the sky. But a chase, as Mao said, is a long march. It's not a stroll. Sometimes I ask Giacomo, *why* do I do it? Why do I chase my tail? He shrugs his shoulders. How should I know, he says, I'm not a cat. Is that some kind of joke? But—he adds—I'm very happy you don't do it anymore on the wall over the canal. *That* was hard to take. Luckily, my partner and I love to read the atomists. Lucretius. Michel Serres. Great tail-chasers. Original thinkers. Just what I need! Original thinking. The clinamen! Lots of people—ancient, modern, and post-modern—think this tiny swerve *is* some kind of joke. But my partner and I love it, and take it seriously. Atoms and the void. It depends on how you look at it. Cold infinite spaces. Eternal silence. Terrifying. Everything eternally isolated form everything else. Immutable. A river flowing so smoothly it doesn't flow at all. Unchanging. You can't cross it even once. This is what Mao called metaphysical, the opposite of dialectical. For atoms to be dialectical there has to be *just a little* deviation from the straight line. A *tiny* whirlpool in the river. Then something happens. Everything happens! Lucretius writes so beautifully, a real poet: 'When the atoms are traveling straight down through empty space by their own weight, at quite indeterminate times and places they swerve just a tiny bit from their course, just so much that you can call it a change of direction. *If it were not for this swerve, everything would fall downwards like rain-drops through an abyss of space.* No collision would take place and no impact of atom on atom would be created. Nature would never have created anything.' Listen—a *perfectly* undisturbed flow is called laminar. Michel Serres explains that a laminar flow is merely ideal and theoretical. In practice, turbulence has *already* happened. A miniscule spiral. Vortex. Eddy. Whirlpool. A *perfectly* smooth flow is *self-contradictory*. That's one side of the story. On the other side, a flow *flows*. Always. As Lucretius said, 'the atoms have no rest in their course through the depth of space.' No rest! Absolute restlessness. Why?! What's the story? Where does the clinamen come from? Why does turbulence happen? Michel Serres, our friend, takes a shot at it. He says: 'The clinamen is, first, the infinitesimal turbulence, but it's also the passage from theory to practice. What's more, without it we understand nothing of what goes on. It's a matter of experience.' Satori! A Zen explanation. I don't mean to be catty, but maybe Gina should have read Serres instead of wasting her time on Lacan. But—what about tail-chasing? What ever happened to my riposte? Why do I *do* it? *Why the chase?* A matter of experience? Is that an answer? How about: only in theory do we *not* chase our tails. In practice it's *a fact*. A fact? What fact? What's a fact? An uncertain reality, *that's* a fact. Let's take a shot at it. Action! Serres says that death is like an atom without a clinamen. I chase my tail because a tail is a chase. *This* is what it's like to be a cat. Here it is. My tail is resting on my paws. Gently. Precisely. Delicately. Deliberately? Guess what! It's *already* moving. *The atoms have no rest.* The chase is on. Already! My tail—do I, 'myself,' make it move? Who are we kidding! *It makes me move.* An imperceptible infinitesimal spiral. A caress. Revolution! A caress creates a world.

Look! Chairman Mao is back. Luckily. He'll help us, one last time. 'On Contradiction.' There is internal contradiction in every single thing. *Therefore, it moves.* Itself. Said Mao. Listen, he sounds just like Hegel: 'There is nothing that does not contain contradiction; without contradiction nothing would exist.' 'Life consists precisely and primarily in this—that a being is at each moment itself and yet something else.' The chase—does it just happen or do I make it happen? My riposte: two is one. Let's put it this way. Here I am. A cat. Here it is. A tail. Two things eternally isolated from one another and immutable. 'The eternal silence of these infinite spaces terrifies me.' Now *this* is some kind of joke! *But*—call me Ismael—my tail and I *are also opposites*. There is a difference between a cat and a tail. A long Tail! Mao said: 'In every single thing there is a movement of opposites *from beginning to end.* Each and every difference already contains contradiction and *difference itself is contradiction.'* Wait! Contradiction is one thing, but *self-*contradiction is not quite the same. Contradictory can also mean *one-sided.* Mao said: 'To be one-sided means seeing the part but not the whole, the trees but not the forest.' 'To be one-sided and superficial is at the same time to be subjective. All objective things are actually interconnected and are governed by inner laws.' Inner laws of tail-chasing? It's not as crazy as it sounds. Subjective. Objective. Cat—Tail. Subject—Object. Tail—Cat. Subject—Object. Subject—Subject. Object!—Object! Two is one. Mao—mao. Chairman—cat. The *chase.* A Tail. Let's call cats the forest and tails the trees. Or vice versa. Somehow, they are separate. But you can bet your life that they're inseparable. *The tail-chasing is their separating. Inseparably.* But who done it? Who's the culprit? Have we gotten nowhere? Wait! Not *just* difference. Not *just* contradiction. *Self-*contradiction. An *identity* of opposites. But this is *thinking itself.* Not thinking *about* but thinking as such. The *identity* of the tail and the cat. *In their opposition.* Two is one, *struggling.* Not striving but struggling. No idea of gain. It's Monk's music! The abyss that keeps us all alive. A dream struggle. An abyss of dreams. I don't see the tail, I think the tail. Or is it the tail that thinks me? Theory practice, practice theory. Things thinking, thinking things. Here, the cat; here, the tail. Here, the tail; here, the cat. What *happens?* Thinking happens. Thinking separates cat and tail, tail and cat, and *thinking thinks them together.* This thinking that thinks them together is known as *on the chasing of my tail.* I see the tail I am, and the cat I am, *together. In thought.* Separated and inseparable. Michel Serres also said: 'For something to exist rather than nothing there must be a fluctuation in this uniform flow, there must be a deviation from equilibrium.' This deviation—turbulence—is commonly called *thinking.* What! Do cats think?! Enough of these jokes. I, Gilda, have progressed (possibly) from a furry form of pure thought to the wuthering depths of pure thinking. I have rambled, *considerably.* But there are lots of ramblers more scatterbrained than I am. And most of them do not happen to be cats.

I was afraid of getting in over my head with this riposte. But, in the end, it's worked out pretty well. A long march is not a stroll. Mao once said, 'Some comrades do not like to think much about difficulties. But there are no straight roads in the world. The prospects are bright, but the road has twists and turns.' Now it's time to get back to my everyday cat life. Tail-chasing happens quite often, but I have many other cat things going on. Look! My partner just brought me a snack. Exquisitely half-boiled chicken breast, cut into tiny pieces. On my special little red and white dish. Do you think I devour it immediately? No way! There's cat business here. First I sniff at it a few times. Then I look up at Giacomo for a while, just a little forlornly. As if thinking of our mortality. I lick my lips for a split second. I can't resist. *Then* I devour it, and make him so happy! *This* is what it's like to be a cat. It's the abyss that keeps us all alive, only the abyss. We dream, we're dreamed. A cat is always an adventure. Such joy! Just doing everyday cat things. It's easy because Giacomo loves me so much, and I love him so much. I'm so glad he named me after a fly! We like to be lively. Today, for example, was sheet-changing day. With me around even just making our bed can be quite a tangle, but you should see him trying to change the sheets! The prospects are bright. Every time he unfurls a sheet—bottom, top—I leap into the fray. A *wild* tangle. Mao calls this 'unconditional and absolute struggle.' I even try to wriggle my way into an empty pillowcase. How we laugh! This is life. Changing sheets. Chasing tails. Writing Tails, together. We're so happy! Our house. The courtyard. The back garden. Sun. Rain. Day. Night. Such joy! Sleeping. Waking. Every moment. Adventure. I go to bed pretty early, round midnight. I curl up on the blanket, so happy. When he finally comes to bed I stretch out on his chest with my head resting on his beard, I hug him, just like when I was a kitten, I purr and purr. And he says *paradiso*. It's pure love. I don't think of him as a giant anymore, size no longer exists. When we meditate together, side by side, we are just two meditating. Not two and not one, the Roshi says. Our friend Monk says two is one. Giacomo says *paradiso*. I just purr.

September 2019

There came a great wind from the wilderness./ I only am escaped alone to tell thee.

Gilda's death came quickly, with unimaginable suffering. A clear blue sky, a terrible lymphoma. Two months of her pain—and cheerful sorrow. Suffering Buddha, she purred during chemotherapy. This was Gilda. She liked to be a cat. Then, my endless sorrow. I have done my best to tell her last Tail. Gilda and I worked on it for years. Together. Tail-chasing. Mao. Michel Serres. Now I've done it on my own. *Gilda! How I miss you!* Now, and forever. This Abyss of Dreams we were writing together was not supposed to end this way.

Postscript

At the age of 70, two years after Gilda's rejoining the river of life-death, I invited a kitten to join me again, here in this house. A Siamese, like in the oldest days, before the Invasions. Her name is Satori, sudden awakening. In fact she awakens in every moment, wildly, chaotically. I don't think she'll ever be a great cat-writer like Gina and Gilda, but, who knows. Maybe someday she'll write *The Sisters Karamazov*. Anyway, she's Gilda's satori, and we all love her.

last references

'Two is one': Robin D. G. Kelley, *Thelonious Monk. The Life and Times of an American Original*, New York: Free Press, 2009, p. xix.
'Monks dance!': he was known to dance during his concerts, see him for yourself: https://www.youtube.com/watch?v=XjJYeCYOhA&index=27&list=RDYunra2 Fhwpo
'Straight, No Chaser' is a composition of Monk's. As is 'Round Midnight.' Gilda and Monk are soul mates.

Mao Zedong, 'On Practice' and 'On Contradiction,' in *Collected Writings of Chairman Mao*, Volume 3, El Paso: El Paso Norte Press, 2009.
'Paper tigers' are in the Red Book, *Quotations from Chairman Mao-Tse-Tung*, 1966, Chapter VI. 'No straight roads' are in Chapter XXI.

'When the atoms are traveling straight down': see Lucretius, *The Nature of the Universe* [De rerum natura], translated by R. E. Latham, Penguin Classics, 1951 (1966), p. 66.
'the atoms have no rest': p. 63. It's Book II, 'Movements and Shapes of Atoms.'

On the clinamen and lots more, see Michel Serres, *The Birth of Physics*, Manchester: Clinamen Press, 2000, in particular pp. 6-7, 82-83, 184, 148.

'The eternal silence of these infinite spaces terrifies me.': Pascal, *Pensée 206*. Epigraph to Thomas Bernhard's novel *Gargoyles*.

a great wind from the wilderness: Job, 1:19.

Acknowledgements

Antonin Artaud, excerpts from *The Theater and its Double*, translated by Mary Caroline Richards. Copyright © 1958 by Mary Caroline Richards. Used by permission of Grove/Atlantic, Inc. Any third-party use of this material, outside of this publication, is prohibited.

Antonin Artaud, excerpt from 'Here Lies,' translated by F. Teri Wehn and Jack Hirschman, excerpts from 'Van Gogh: The Man Suicided by Society,' translated by Mary Beach and Lawrence Ferlinghetti, and excerpts from 'I hate and renounce as a coward,' translated by David Rattray, in *Artaud Anthology, Second Edition*, edited by Jack Hirschman. Copyright © 1965 by Jack Hirschman. Reprinted with the permission of The Permissions Company, LLC, on behalf of City Lights Books, citylights.org.

Patrick Barkham, excerpts from 'Jeremy Deller: "I'm more interested in ideas than money,"' from *Guardian Weekly* (17 February 2012). Copyright © 2012 by Guardian News & Media Ltd.

Sigmund Freud, excerpts from *On Dreams* translated by James Strachey. Copyright 1952 by W. W. Norton & Company, Inc., renewed © 1980 by Alix S. Strachey. Used by permission of The Institute of Psychoanalysis, London and W. W. Norton & Company, Inc.

Sigmund Freud, excerpts from *Beyond the Pleasure Principle*, translated by James Strachey. Copyright © 1961 by James Strachey. Used by permission of The Institute of Psychoanalysis, London and Liveright Publishing Corporation.

Ezra Pound, excerpts from Canto I, Canto LXXXI, Canto CXIII, and Canto CXV from *The Cantos of Ezra Pound*. Copyright 1934, 1948, © 1962, 1969 by Ezra Pound. Reprinted by permission of New Directions Publishing Corp. and Faber and Faber, Ltd.

Tsang Nyön Heruka, excerpt ['The nature of mind cannot be thought…'] from *The Life of Marpa the Translator*, translated by the Nalanda Translation Committee under the direction of Chögyam Trungpa. Copyright © 1995 by Chögyam Trungpa. Reprinted with the permission of The Permissions Company, LLC on behalf of Shambhala Publications, Inc., Boulder, Colorado, www.shambhala.com.

Lightning Source UK Ltd.
Milton Keynes UK
UKHW011531220922
409271UK00001B/6

9 781848 618466